The Palgrave Handbook of National Security

Michael Clarke · Adam Henschke ·
Matthew Sussex · Tim Legrand
Editors

The Palgrave Handbook of National Security

palgrave
macmillan

Editors
Michael Clarke
Centre for Defence Research
Australian Defence College
Canberra, ACT, Australia

Australia-China Relations Institute
University of Technology Sydney
Ultimo, NSW, Australia

Matthew Sussex
Centre for Defence Research
Australian Defence College
Canberra, ACT, Australia

Griffith Asia Institute
Griffith University
Brisbane, Australia

Adam Henschke
Department of Philosophy
University of Twente
Enschede, The Netherlands

Tim Legrand
Department of Politics and
International Relations
University of Adelaide
Adelaide, SA, Australia

ISBN 978-3-030-53493-6   ISBN 978-3-030-53494-3   (eBook)
https://doi.org/10.1007/978-3-030-53494-3

© The Editor(s) (if applicable) and The Author(s), under exclusive license to Springer Nature Switzerland AG 2022

This work is subject to copyright. All rights are solely and exclusively licensed by the Publisher, whether the whole or part of the material is concerned, specifically the rights of translation, reprinting, reuse of illustrations, recitation, broadcasting, reproduction on microfilms or in any other physical way, and transmission or information storage and retrieval, electronic adaptation, computer software, or by similar or dissimilar methodology now known or hereafter developed. The use of general descriptive names, registered names, trademarks, service marks, etc. in this publication does not imply, even in the absence of a specific statement, that such names are exempt from the relevant protective laws and regulations and therefore free for general use.

The publisher, the authors and the editors are safe to assume that the advice and information in this book are believed to be true and accurate at the date of publication. Neither the publisher nor the authors or the editors give a warranty, expressed or implied, with respect to the material contained herein or for any errors or omissions that may have been made. The publisher remains neutral with regard to jurisdictional claims in published maps and institutional affiliations.

Cover image: © tzido

This Palgrave Macmillan imprint is published by the registered company Springer Nature Switzerland AG
The registered company address is: Gewerbestrasse 11, 6330 Cham, Switzerland

CONTENTS

1 National Security: Theories, Actors, Issues 1
Michael Clarke, Adam Henschke, Tim Legrand,
and Matthew Sussex

Part I Theories

**2 Understanding National Security: The Promises
and Pitfalls of International Relations Theory** 23
Matthew Sussex

**3 National Security and Public Policy: Exceptionalism
Versus Accountability** 53
Tim Legrand

**4 Ethics and National Security: A Case for Reasons
in Decision-Making** 73
Adam Henschke

Part II Actors

**5 Nothing to Fear but Fear Itself: The National Security
Policy of the United States** 95
Christopher J. Fettweis

**6 Chinese National Security: New Agendas and Emerging
Challenges** 117
Jingdong Yuan

7 Russia's National Security Posture 139
Matthew Sussex

vi CONTENTS

8 **Between Aspiration and Reality: Evolution of Japanese National Security Policy** 169
Yuki Tatsumi

9 **India's National Security Challenges and the State Response** 187
Harsh V. Pant and Akshay Ranade

10 **Turkey: The Security Policy of a 'Lonely' State** 219
Bill Park

11 **Securing Iran in the Internet age** 241
Dara Conduit

12 **Brazil: In Search of a Security Space** 261
Vinícius G. Rodrigues Vieira

Part III Issues

13 **Nuclear Weapons and National Security: From the Cold War to the "Second Nuclear Age" and Beyond** 287
Matthew Sussex and Michael Clarke

14 **Maritime Security: Problems and Prospects for National Security Policymakers** 329
Carolin Liss

15 **Intelligence and National Security: The National Security Problematique** 351
Paul Burke

16 **Machine Learning, Mass Surveillance, and National Security: Data, Efficacy, and Meaningful Human Control** 371
Scott Robbins

17 **Information as an Evolving National Security Concern** 389
Adam Henschke

Index 409

Notes on Contributors

Paul Burke is an Intelligence and Counter-Terrorism Professional with 30 years of strategic experience in managing the Intelligence and Security domain primarily within UK government. Holding a Doctorate in Policing, Security & Community Safety, and an M.A. in Intelligence Studies, he previously worked as UK National Intelligence Adviser on Counter-Terrorism, within Iraq's Ministry of Interior in Baghdad (2004–2006), and as UK National Intelligence Mentor on Counter-Narcotics in Kabul (2007–2009). He is currently a Senior Researcher at the Counterterrorism Ethics at Delft University, The Netherlands.

Michael Clarke is Senior Fellow at the Centre for Defence Research, Australian Defence College, Visiting Fellow at the Australia-China Relations Institute, University of Technology Sydney, Australia. His research is focused on Chinese governance of the Xinjiang Uyghur Autonomous Region (China), Chinese foreign and security policy, nuclear proliferation and non-proliferation and American grand strategy. His research has been published in leading journals such as *International Affairs, Journal of Contemporary China, Asian Security, Global Policy, Orbis, Journal of Strategic Studies, Diplomacy & Statecraft, Nonproliferation Review*, and *Terrorism and Political Violence* among others. He is also the author of *Amercian Grand Strategy and National Security: The Dilemmas of Primacy and Decline from the Founders to Trump* (Palgrave 2021), *Xinjiang and China's Rise in Central Asia— A History* (Routledge, 2011) and (with Andrew O'Neil and Stephan Fruhling) *Australian Nuclear Policy: Reconciling Strategic, Economic and Normative Interests* (Routledge, 2015), and is the editor (with Anna Hayes) of *Inside Xinjiang: Analysing Space, Place and Power in China's Muslim North-West* (Routledge, 2016), editor of *Terrorism and Counter-Terrorism in China: Domestic and Foreign Policy Dimensions* (Oxford University Press, 2018) and

viii   NOTES ON CONTRIBUTORS

editor (with Matthew Sussex and Nick Bisley) of *The Belt and Road Initiative and the Future of Regional Order in the Indo-Pacific* (Lexington Books, 2020).

Dara Conduit is an Alfred Deakin Postdoctoral Research Fellow in Political Science at the Alfred Deakin Institute for Citizenship and Globalisation, Deakin University, Australia, and a Non-Resident Scholar at the Middle East Institute in Washington D.C., USA. Dara's research interests centre around authoritarianism, with a regional focus on the Middle East, especially Syria. Her research focusses on questions related to contentious politics inside authoritarian regimes, including the relationships between governments and their opponents, and each party's tactical (especially online) innovation. Dara's book *The Muslim Brotherhood in Syria* (2019) received the inaugural Oceania Book Prize in International Studies in 2020 and was ranked by *International Affairs* in 2020 as one of the "Top 10 books" written by women and reviewed by the journal in the previous 12 months. Dara's other academic work has been widely published in journals, including *Democratization, Political Geography, Studies in Conflict and Terrorism* and *The Middle East Journal*.

Christopher J. Fettweis is Associate Professor in the Department of Political Science, Tulane University, USA. He specialises in American grand strategy and foreign policy. He has published widely on these subjects in a range of leading journals including *Security Studies, Survival, Political Science Quarterly, Contemporary Security Policy* and *Orbis*. He is also the author of *Psychology of a Superpower: Security and Dominance in U.S. Foreign Policy* (2018), *The Pathologies of Power: Fear, Honor, Glory and Hubris in U.S. Foreign Policy* (2013), *Dangerous Times? The International Politics of Great Power Peace* (2010) and *Losing Hurts Twice as Bad: The Four Stages to Moving Beyond Iraq* (2008).

Adam Henschke is Associate Professor in the Department of Philosophy, University of Twente, The Netherlands. He is an applied ethicist, working on areas that cross over between ethics, technology and security. His research concerns ethical and philosophical analyses of information technology and its uses, military ethics and on relations between ethics and national security. He has published on surveillance, emerging military technologies and intelligence and cyberspace. He is also interested in moral psychology, experimental philosophy and their relations to decision-making and policy development. He is the author of *Ethics in an Age of Surveillance: Personal Information and Virtual Identities* (2017) and editor (with Fritz Allhoff and Bradley Jay Strawser) of *Binary Bullets: The Ethics of Cyberwarfare* (2016).

Tim Legrand is Associate Professor in the Department of Politics and International Relations, School of Social Sciences, University of Adelaide, Australia. His research is concerned with national and international dimensions of global security decision-making, particularly in transnational networks and institutions. His work traverses a range of security themes, principally in global blacklisting and sanctions, cyber security and critical infrastructure, terrorism, political violence and political exclusion. This research is oriented around a cross-pollination of public administration (law, sociology and public policy) literatures and International Relations (critical security studies, global governance) perspectives to navigate the complex terrain of security in domestic and international spaces. He has published on these subjects in *Terrorism and Political Violence, Security Dialogue, British Politics, Political Studies* and *Review of International Studies*. He is also the author of *The Architecture of Policy Transfer Ideas, Institutions and Networks in Transnational Policy-making* (2021) and (with Lee Jarvis) *Banning Them, Securing Us? Terrorism, Parliament and the Ritual of Proscription* (2020).

Carolin Liss is Assistant Professor in the Department of International Affairs at Vesalius College, Belgium, where she specialises in maritime security—particularly piracy and the privatisation of security—and South-East Asian politics. She has published on these issues in *SAIS Review of International Affairs, Contemporary Southeast Asia, Australian Journal of International Affairs* and *Review of International Political Economy*. She is also the author of *Oceans of Crime: Maritime Piracy and Transnational Security in Southeast Asia and Bangladesh* (2011) and editor (with Ted Biggs) of *Piracy in Southeast Asia: Trends, Hot Spots and Responses* (2017).

Harsh V. Pant is Professor of International Relations at King's College London, UK, and Director, Studies and Head of the Strategic Studies Programme at Observer Research Foundation, New Delhi, India. He has been a Visiting Professor at the Indian Institute of Management, Bangalore; a Visiting Fellow at the Center for the Advanced Study of India, University of Pennsylvania, USA; a Visiting Scholar at the Center for International Peace and Security Studies, McGill University, USA; a Visiting Professor at O.P. Jindal Global University, Sonipat, India; a Visiting Professor at Banaras Hindu University, Varanasi, India; and an Emerging Leaders Fellow at the Australia-India Institute, University of Melbourne, Australia. His current research is focused on Asian security issues. His most recent books include *New Directions in India's Foreign Policy: Theory and Praxis* (2018), *India's Nuclear Policy* (2018), *The US Pivot and Indian Foreign Policy* (2015), *Handbook of Indian Defence Policy* (2015) and *India's Afghan Muddle* (2013).

Bill Park is Senior Lecturer in the Defence Studies Department at King's College London, UK, where he specialises in the politics and security of the Middle East with a particular focus on Kurdish issues, Iraq and Turkey. He has published widely on these topics in a range of leading journals including *International Affairs, Ethnopolitics, Middle Eastern Studies, Turkish Studies* and *Mediterranean Politics*. He is also the author of *Modern Turkey: People, State and Foreign Policy in a Globalized World* (2011) and editor (with Wyn Rees) of *Rethinking Security in Post-Cold War Europe* (1998).

Akshay Ranade is Assistant Professor in International Relations at MIT School of Government, Pune, India, where his areas of specialisation include International Relations and India's foreign and security policy. He completed an M-Phil from Centre for International Politics, Organization and Disarmament (CIPOD), School of International Studies (JNU), New Delhi, India. As a part of M-Phil Dissertation, he worked on the topic "United Nations Global Counter-Terrorism Strategy and Non-Proliferation of Weapons of Mass Destruction: A Study of the Role of 1540 Committee". He has previously worked with Observer Research Foundation (ORF), New Delhi, under its Strategic Studies Program. He has presented papers at various national and international conferences including at University of Cambridge, UK; Dublin City University, Ireland; and JNU, New Delhi, India, among others.

Scott Robbins is a Post-Doctoral Research Fellow at Bonn University, Germany. Scott recently completed his Ph.D. in the Ethics of Artificial Intelligence at the Technical University of Delft, The Netherlands (title: *Machine Learning & Counter-Terrorism: Ethics, Efficacy, and Meaningful Human Control*). He has a B.Sc. in Computer Science from California State University, Chico, USA, and an M.Sc. in Ethics of Technology from the University of Twente, The Netherlands. He is a founding member of the Foundation for Responsible Robotics and a member of the 4TU Centre for Ethics and Technology. He has published his research in *Surveillance & Society*, *Science and Engineering Ethics*, and *AI & Society*.

Matthew Sussex is Senior Fellow, Centre for Defence Research, Australian Defence College and Adjunct Associate Professor at the Griffith Asia Institute, Griffith University, Australia. His research specialisations are centred around security studies with a particular focus on Russia and Eurasia, and incorporates Australian foreign and security policy and great power competition in Asia and Europe. His recently completed solo and collaborative book projects include *Conflict in the Former USSR (2012); Violence and the State* (2015); *Power, Politics and Confrontation in Eurasia* (2015); *Russia, Eurasia and the New Geopolitics of Energy* (2015) and is the lead editor (2017) of a special issue of the *Australian Journal of International Affairs* on the topic of national security.

Yuki Tatsumi is a Senior Fellow and Co-Director of the East Asia Program and Director of the Japan Program at the Stimson Center, Washington D.C., USA. Before joining Stimson, Tatsumi worked as a Research Associate at the Center for Strategic and International Studies (CSIS) and as the special assistant for political affairs at the Embassy of Japan in Washington. Tatsumi's most recent publications include *Balancing Between Nuclear Deterrence and Disarmament: Views from the Next Generation* (2018) and *Lost in Translation? U.S. Defense Innovation and Northeast Asia* (2017).

Vinícius G. Rodrigues Vieira (D.Phil. in International Relations, Nuffield College, University of Oxford, UK, 2014; M.A. in Latin American Studies,

University of California, Berkeley, USA, 2010) is a Postdoctoral Tenure-Track Researcher at the Institute of International Relations of the University of São Paulo (IRI-USP), Brazil. He was a Fellow (Non-Resident) of the Summer Program in Social Science of the Institute for Advanced Studies of Princeton (2015–2017), a Fung Global Fellow at Princeton University, USA (2018), and has held visiting positions at Yale University, USA (2012) and Vanderbilt University, USA (2004). His research focuses on the intersection between material and ideational factors in International Political Economy (IPE) and he is the secretary of the International Political Science Association's (IPSA) research committee on that subfield. His work has been published in *International Studies Quarterly*, *International Negotiation*, *Brazilian Political Science Review*, and *Journal of International Relations and Development*.

Jingdong Yuan is Associate Professor at the University of Sydney, Australia, where he specialises in Asia-Pacific security, Chinese defence and foreign policy, and global and regional arms control and non-proliferation issues. A graduate of the Xi'an Foreign Language University, People's Republic of China (1982), he received his Ph.D. in Political Science from Queen's University, Ireland, in 1995, and has had research and teaching appointments at Queen's University, Ireland, York University, UK; the University of Toronto, Canada; and the University of British Columbia, Canada, where he was a recipient of the prestigious Iaazk Killam Postdoctoral Research Fellowship. He is the co-author of China and India: Cooperation or Conflict? (2003) and editor (with James Reilly) of *Australia and China at 40* (2012), and articles have appeared in Asian Survey, Contemporary Security Studies, Nonproliferation Review, and Washington Quarterly, among others.

LIST OF FIGURES

Fig. 15.1 UK 6-stage intelligence cycle (National Policing Improvement
Agency, 2008, p. 11) 353
Fig. 15.2 Intelligence sources and methods overview 356

CHAPTER 1

National Security: Theories, Actors, Issues

Michael Clarke, Adam Henschke, Tim Legrand, and Matthew Sussex

It would be an exaggeration to claim that the symbol of national security is nothing but a stimulus to semantic confusion, though closer analysis will show that if used without specifications it leaves room for more confusion than sound political counsel or scientific usage can afford.[1]

M. Clarke (✉) · M. Sussex
Centre for Defence Research, Australian Defence College, Canberra, ACT, Australia
e-mail: Michael.clarke@uts.edu.au; Michael.clarke@anu.edu.au

M. Sussex
e-mail: matthew.sussex@anu.edu.au

M. Clarke
Australia-China Relations Institute, University of Technology Sydney, Ultimo, NSW, Australia

Strategic and Defence Studies Centre, Australian National University, Canberra, ACT, Australia

A. Henschke
Department of Philosophy, University of Twente, Enschede, The Netherlands
e-mail: a.henschke@utwente.nl

T. Legrand
Department of Politics and International Relations, University of Adelaide, Adelaide, SA, Australia
e-mail: tim.legrand@adelaide.edu.au

M. Sussex
Griffith Asia Institute, Griffith University, Brisbane, Australia

© The Author(s), under exclusive license to Springer Nature Switzerland AG 2022
M. Clarke et al. (eds.), *The Palgrave Handbook of National Security*,
https://doi.org/10.1007/978-3-030-53494-3_1

It is often assumed that the term 'national security' implies a particular set of underlying judgements about the ways in which political communities might go about guarding against potential harms and protecting their interests. To the extent that the nation-state remains the prevailing referent object of security under such a formulation, characterisations like this are broadly correct. But it is also then often assumed that national security implies a particular type of security concept, not to mention practice. It has become commonplace, for instance, to refer to a 'traditional' national security paradigm, as though the state is somehow irrelevant or incapable of adapting to change.[2] Though there is a dominant orthodoxy in the study of national security, our view is that it is a caricature to depict national security as an old-fashioned or narrow field of study.[3] Wolfers shows us that national security, being symbolically and politically laden, can *impoverish* rather than enriching debate, if analysed uncritically. We therefore believe that it is fundamentally erroneous to dismiss it as the exclusive domain of *realpolitik* and outmoded conceptions of the 'national interest' in contemporary international society. Rather, we see national security as the epicentre of contemporary socio-political questions of the state's role in promulgating and protecting national values. We therefore agree with T.V Paul and Norman Ripsman's observation that states remain the basic security actors in international relations, and this means that deepening our knowledge of national security in contemporary circumstances is vital.[4] Yet, we qualify this position by acknowledging that state far from the *sole* agent of security in a rapidly disaggregating security environment. This is especially so since state capacities in identifying, categorising and responding to harm have become stretched by globalisation, advancements in technology and the rise of a host of threats, from transnational criminal and terrorist actors to natural disasters and disease outbreaks.

It would be wrong, of course, to suggest that national security has been absent from the literature on security studies. There has been much contemporary scholarship on national security policy in democratic nations, centred especially on the transatlantic space.[5] In addition, a large body of work exists on the national security posture of Asian nations, particularly Japan[6] China[7] and Australia as well. Often this has been done using a specific theoretical lens, or from a particular paradigmatic perspective. Regional Security Complex theorists (Wirth, 2015), neoclassical realists (Saltzman, 2015) and liberal scholars (Ikenberry, 2008) have all participated in this, with much worthwhile scholarship produced as a result. But we consider it remarkable that there has been relatively less scholarly attention paid to examining the concepts, sources, methods and types of national security policy in comparative context. This is surprising for a number of reasons. First, the threat matrix for virtually all the major powers has changed markedly alongside the securitisation of numerous challenges that are transnational, environmental and effectively intermestic in nature. Comparing how different actors conceive of these challenges and prioritise resources to meet them is an important undertaking that is missing from both theoretical and applied scholarship in the mainstream literature on security studies. A stream of critical security studies, on the other hand, has forged an alternate perspective on the articulation of power through the state's security apparatus and its agents. Second, while functional and ideational similarities on the basis of regime type offer useful scope for comparative analysis, it is surely equally important to identify the similarities and differences that exist across diverse approaches to domestic political organisation.

Uniting the contributions to this volume is a common perspective on contemporary national security. While the types of participation in security activities are changing, the main purposes of actors making such a contribution remain largely consistent with one general proposition: that although security policy-making now features more actors, their agendas tend to be instrumentalised through conventional rubrics about the national interest. At the same time, normative values are intersecting with material considerations; non-traditional threats are meeting old ones; and new actors are challenging established elites in ways that often seem mystifying. Making sense out of the complex milieu of national security theories, actors and issues policy is therefore a main objective of this volume.

Borrowing from Richard Rosencrance and Arthur Stein, we can conceptualise national security policy as not simply consisting of a means-end causal chain of how a state attempts to attain security but also as a form of public policy that "reflects a nation's mechanisms for arriving at social choices" through "the commitment, extraction and mobilization of societal resources".[8] Crucially, the manner by which such decisions to commit, extract and mobilise societal resources are arrived at is often the product of a complex interplay between not only external stimuli but also domestic political and institutional preferences, economic orientations, strategic culture[9] and "ruling domestic ideas".[10] One of the doyens of Cold War history, Melvyn Leffler, suggested the adoption of a "national security approach" to bridge what he viewed as the long-standing divide between largely realist international relations scholars, who suggest that a state's behaviour responds (or should) mainly to changes in the international distribution of power, and diplomatic historians, who emphasise the importance of domestic political, economic and social forces in shaping how a state's policy-makers respond to the external environment.[11] Such an approach that focused on the "the dynamic interaction" of these two sources of national security policy behaviour (i.e. system-level dynamics and unit-level variables) offered the best way to bridge this divide. A "national security approach" Leffler argued not only "acknowledges that power plays a key role in the behavior of nations and the functioning of the international system" but:

> ...that a nation's power depends on its political stability, social cohesion, and economic productivity as well as the number of its troops, tanks, planes, ships, missiles, and nuclear warheads. It recognizes that an overarching synthesis must integrate political economy, military policy, and defense strategy. It assumes that

fears of foreign threats are a consequence of both real dangers in the external environment and ideological precepts, cultural symbols, and mistaken images.[12]

It is arguably this synthesis between key domains of foreign and domestic policy that lies at the heart of theory and practice of national security policy. In order to adequately grapple with the breadth and scope of this synthesis, this *Handbook* examines a number of questions around themes that overlap, but are also within discrete analytical categories: major theoretical contributions, major actors and major issue areas.

Part I: Theories examines how national security has been conceptualised and formulated within the disciplines of international relations, public policy and ethics. The contributions in this part of the volume will be explicitly concerned with providing answers to two key questions: (i) What are the major attributes of the theorising of national security in each discipline, and (ii) how have these paradigmatic characteristics affected, for better or ill, our understandings of the concept and its utility? Here we seek to discover how useful various theoretical perspectives from political science, public policy and ethics might be in helping us understand variances in national security concepts and practices. In other words, does current scholarship adequately account for national security, and what—if anything—does the academic study of national security offer to policy practitioners?

Matthew Sussex examines the promises and pitfalls of international relations theory for the study of national security. He begins by noting that although "national security" is a concept that is used with great familiarity by both scholars/analysts and government professionals, there remains a great deal of variance in understanding what the term refers to, and how to operationalise it amongst and between these two groups. Amongst scholars, both the concepts of the "nation" and "security" themselves are highly contested, spawning an expansive literature focused on an array of central questions such as: What does it mean to have security? What specifically is being secured? How do issues make it onto national security agendas, and how are they prioritised? Who are (or should be) the key decision-makers, and how do their individual and institutional preferences shape outcomes, for good or otherwise? How do conventional notions of security differ from alternative (and arguably equally legitimate) ways to understand it? What emphasis should we give ideas about security with different primary emphases—from national security to global, human, environmental, societal and other formulations?

Sussex notes that although such concerns often appear irrelevant to the day-to-day management of national security of government professionals, theories of international relations have in fact the virtue of acting as roadmaps, providing a conceptual lens through which the complex challenges and opportunities associated with national security might be prioritised and navigated. He argues that the conceptual overlay that international relations theory provides can be helpful in illuminating the assumptions we make about security in practice, to explain international interaction, to help prioritise main threats and tasks that require resourcing, and to offer some degree of clarity to an increasingly multifaceted field of policy-making. The chapter demonstrates this in three major parts. First, it identifies the landscape in which national security policy-making takes place, where conventional cleavages between policy arenas—like foreign policy and domestic policy—are increasingly breaking down due to factors relating to globalisation. Second, the chapter moves to specific theories and the ways that they explain, prescribe and even try to predict outcomes. In doing so, it focuses on three main approaches to international relations: realism, liberalism and constructivism. Third, the chapter applies these theoretical approaches to three national security problems in order to demonstrate how their core assumptions can produce radically different interpretations and solutions. The chapter then concludes with some potential lessons for national security policy planners about how theory might be usefully employed.

Tim Legrand explores national security through the lens of contemporary public policy. The chapter sets out the historic and emerging imperatives of security and society to gauge the extent to which national security decision-makers are meeting or diverging from the core precepts of policy-making in liberal democracy. The chapter begins by tracing the evolution of contemporary public policy norms, drawing attention to primacy of input and output legitimacy: the public's recognition that policy decisions are made transparently, based on evidence and public input, and serve fairly the public interest. Though these qualities are unevenly distributed in public policy processes across liberal democracies, there is wide consensus amongst scholars that at the heart of modern government there is an imperative to demonstrably and transparently serve the public interest. Scholars emphasise the need to maintain visible scrutiny of government decision-making and maintain the accountability of elected officials for the outcomes of those decisions. In addition, it widely accepted that evidence and evaluation have a key role to play in ensuring that policies are effective and efficient.

The chapter situates 'national security' decision-making within the broader schema of government's role in serving the public interest. Here, Legrand finds that national security policy is faced with several 'methodology' challenges in acquiring the right evidence or undertaking robust evaluation to inform its policy development. Nonetheless, Legrand argues, national security officials have largely ignored these norms and instead have increasingly positioned national security policy as either exceptional or ascendant in democratic decision-making. Legrand outlines how this has occurred in three distinctive overlapping evasions of public policy norms. First, critical scholars have shown how national security has become exceptionalised, removed from the realm of political contest by a claim for necessity and emergency. Second, the 'exceptionalised' reflex has led to an erosion of policy policy's demand for scrutiny and accountability, with national security being held as 'above politics', subject to bipartisan agreement, but not susceptible to public visibility of its functioning. Third, being made exceptional and deprived of scrutiny and accountability, national security has become exempt from the basic need to (demonstrate) effectiveness and/or efficiency by using evidence or evaluation. Finally, the chapter considers, against the backdrop of these exemptions from policy-making norms, how security decisions are not only becoming increasingly ascendant, but is also the prime lens through which non-security social challenges are viewed—in respect of climate change, education, social policy and more—further expanding the remit of national security officials and their powers. The chapter concludes by reflecting on the illiberal implications for liberal democracy and advocating the need for a return to the primacy of liberal democratic norms in policy-making irrespective of its portfolio.

Adam Henschke concludes Part I by providing an examination of the challenges that arise in relation to ethics and national security, framed around issues of decision-making. The core problem that this chapter seeks to understand is what *ought* people do when national security is at stake. As such, he offers an account of ethics and national security as the justificatory reasons that are given to protect and preserve a state and its people. The chapter is not an effort to answer any specific question about ethics and national security; rather, it maps spaces in which questions of ethics and national security occur, and what ethical considerations mean for national security decision-making.

Henschke establishes the central problem by first presenting how ethics relate to national security, and then, second, outlining some sceptical challenges to this assertion. The chapter argues how, despite ethical issues of national security being an open question, this does not mean that 'anything goes'. It shows that one of the real challenges of discussing ethics and national security is that this is a dynamic space, and what may seem impermissible in one situation may become permissible if the situation changes. The problem here is that one's answer about what is right to do can, and indeed should, change as the situation changes, but any changes must be supported by good reasons. The chapter finishes by offering a general set of steps to help integrate ethics into national security decision-making.

Part II: Actors shifts the focus of the volume from these disciplinary concerns to consideration of how core actors in international affairs have conceptualised and practised national security over time. In this part of the volume, there will be contributions focused on exemplary cases including major powers such as the United States, Russia, China, Japan, India and rising regional powers such as Turkey, Iran and Brazil. This part of the volume will provide definitive analyses of the evolution and practice of national security policy by each actor with a particular emphasis on two core questions: (i) What factors have been central in shaping how each actor conceptualises and implements national security, and (ii) how has this impacted upon their ability to achieve their national security objectives? These analyses will in turn reflect on Wolfers' framing of the 'referents' of national security.

There are two key findings that unite the contributions in this part of the volume. The first concerns the clear resonance of the "national security approach" identified by Leffler. Here, each of the contributors highlights

1 NATIONAL SECURITY: THEORIES, ACTORS, ISSUES

the significant impact of not only external stimuli but their interaction with domestic politics, ideology and strategic culture in shaping how each actor examined conceptualises and implements national security. The second finding concerns the globalisation of the "national security state".[13] This concept, first popularised with reference to the privileging and politicisation of "national security" in the United States during the Cold War, refers to three distinct but overlapping meanings. First, the term has often been deployed to describe the evolution of the so-called "real-state" of the Cold War era in which primacy was afforded to the protection of borders, physical assets and core values through military means.[14] Second, it has referred explicitly to the institutionalised provision of security and prioritisation of it over other functions of the state. The most obvious example of this, of course, was the 1947 National Security Act in the United States that established a unified Department of Defense, and associated national security bureaucracy and intelligence agencies.[15] There have also been other studies that have examined the role such institutionalised provision and prioritisation of security in state formation in the developing world.[16] Third, the term has also come to refer to the collection of institutions, structures and processes within an individual state responsible for the conduct of foreign policy. Each of these three meanings is explored by the chapters in this part of the *Handbook*.

Christopher Fettweis' examination of the national security policy of the United States examines the evolution of American strategic culture, seeking to explain the national security policy choices Washington makes today. It explains the influence of geography on the development of its approach to security and the pathological obsession with complete safety that dominates its thinking. *The world is a dangerous place*, he suggests Americans are often told by their leaders, which is true only to those without historical context or memory. This is paradoxical as while no country is ever completely safe or free from danger the United States today is as close to that ideal as it has ever been. It faces no existential threats, yet worries obsessively. Iran, North Korea, ISIS, electro-magnetic pulses, Vladimir Putin, Chinese bankers, Mexican migrants and a variety of other minor irritants have risen to the level of apocalyptic threats in the American marketplace of ideas. If there is one consistent element in the narrative of US national security policy, Fettweis argues, it is *fear*.

This pathology, he suggests, is a product of the United States' geographical insularity, political culture and preeminent power position since the end of the Second World War. Fettweis shows that geographical insularity and the country's political culture—which has tended to eschew concentration of political and military power—historically predisposed Washington to the pursuit of national security strategies of restraint, whereby it defined threats, interests and opportunities narrowly, and maintained appropriately small militaries with which to address them. Since the Second World War, however, the bases of national security strategies of restraint have been altered by the rapid expansion of American power and interests which has, in turn, resulted in concomitant expansion in the country's perceptions of possible security threats. This, Fettweis notes, has seen the identification by successive US administrations since the end of the Cold War of a consistent set of possible security threats to the country's national security from traditional (great-power peers), non-traditional (terrorism and rogue/failed states), technological (nuclear, cyber, AI) to imagined (unknown unknown) threats. This, he concludes, has fundamentally undermined the United States' capacity to attain its expansive national security objectives.

The national security policy of the People's Republic of China (PRC) is examined by Jingdong Yuan. He provides an analysis that argues that while continuing to emphasise traditional national security concerns such as sovereignty and territorial integrity, Beijing under President Xi Jinping has reconceptualised national security, adopting a more comprehensive understanding and definition of what constitutes national security, and undertaken to restructure a policy-making process to address emerging security challenges. This is demonstrated through a discussion of the manner in which the new national security concept adopted in 2015 encompasses both external and domestic security threats, and expands security issues to include military, economic and non-traditional, ranging from energy security to maritime piracy. Given the multiple sources of potential and real threats to national security interests, the restructured (and ongoing) policy-making process is aimed to anticipate and understand national security issues in strategic terms while at the same time coordinate and execute responses to threats in a more efficient and timely manner.

In this manner, the examination of China's national security policy highlights the impact of changing domestic and external environments on Beijing's conceptualisation and pursuit of national security. Domestically, as Yuan notes, China, as a one-party authoritarian state controlling a vast territory and population, remains concerned with regime security and legitimacy. Externally, the chapter demonstrates that while the country no longer faces the threat of foreign invasions, it is confronted with rising territorial disputes and growing instability in its periphery. Meanwhile, as China has become ever more integrated into the global economy, its demands for raw materials and energy, and its interest in safeguarding commerce are placing greater emphasis on the non-military aspects of national security. Additionally, China's national security is also inextricably linked to great-power relations in the region and the evolution of the existing security architectures in the Indo-Pacific. In sum, Beijing perceives that the post-Cold War international and regional security environments have become more complicated even as they are largely seen as conducive to China's continued economic development. These factors have been pivotal in stimulating the development of new institutional structures—such as the National Security Commission in 2015—to assist the Party-state to assess national security threats and implement effective strategies to manage them. The chapter concludes by noting that China's national security concept and practice remain unique in that the emphasis continues to be placed on domestic as well as external security, and the holistic way whereby the CCP seeks to understand and address various challenges.

Of all the major powers in contemporary international politics, Matthew Sussex suggests, Russia's national security policy has appeared the most unstable, traversing a trajectory from an initial pro-Western orientation after the Soviet collapse to a strategy of multipolarism where cooperation with the West has been conditional on national interests coinciding. More recently, its national security posture has often been that of a bellicose and muscular "spoiler" defined by a willingness to use military force, offensive cyber weapons and information warfare, hybrid capabilities, espionage and sabotage. The chapter addresses two key questions here: Why has Russian national security policy followed this path, and what have been the major factors that have driven Russia's turn towards its current posture? To answer these questions, this chapter explores the sources of Russian national security policy, its main rationales, and the constraints and limitations on Russian choices in future. In doing so, it makes an argument that some readers may find surprising or confronting: that even though its methods have become much more assertive over time, there has actually been remarkable consistency in Russian national interests since the Soviet collapse.

The chapter concludes that while Russia will probably continue to utilise the various instruments at its disposal in attempts to disrupt and fragment Western nations—which includes meddling in its elections, Machiavellian diplomacy and using the economic, technological and military forces at its disposal— it is important to note that Russian assertiveness stems in many ways from a fear of future weakness. Having concluded that a rising China will over- take the United States as the world's most influential actor, Russia faces a new set of security dilemmas on its vulnerable southern flank, in its relatively undeveloped Far East and in the potential for being sidelined as the PRC's economic juggernaut moves on. As a result, fears of entrapment or irrelevance will be powerful drivers of Russian policy in the years to come. This means that we should not consider Russia's current national security stance to be fixed, unchanging or irrevocable. Indeed, Russia has long favoured a pivot state role between Europe and Asia, to maintain its great-power status as well as insu- lating it from major global power blocs. Of course, much of this will depend on external forces that Russia cannot control, and it equally relies on domestic political stability. This is by no means assured. But at the very least it suggests analysts should be cautious in making convenient assumptions about Russian behaviour, either in terms of how it will react to international events, or how it attempts to shape them itself.

Yuki Tatsumi then provides an examination of Japan's national security policy. She begins with the observation that throughout post-Second World War history, Japan has struggled to reconcile two contradictory elements when it comes to its national security policy. First, Japan's experience of the complete defeat in the Second World War which ended in its unconditional surrender, followed by the Allied occupation until it regained its sovereignty in 1951 and adoption of its Constitution which declared that Japan would not possess "land, sea, and air forces, as well as other war potential", has had a profound effect on its national psyche. Second, in parallel with this, Japan quickly emerged as a major front in the Cold War rivalry between the United States and then the Soviet Union in East Asia, shaping its national security posture for decades. For the bulk of the Cold War period, Tatsumi notes Japan's national security policy was anchored in three fundamental principles: reliance on the United States as its ultimate security guarantor via the US-Japan alliance, exclusively defence-oriented posture for the Japanese Self-Defence Forces (JSDF) and minimisation of the role of the JSDF in its national efforts to promote and protect its national interests. Furthermore, Japan also imposed additional restrictions on its national security policy. These restrictions included: Three Non-Nuclear Principles (no possession, no production or no introduction of nuclear weapons onto Japanese soil); Three Principles of Arms Exports (effectively a total ban of the exports of defence equipment from Japan) and limiting the use of space only to peaceful purposes (such as weather monitoring and communications).

Since the end of the Cold War, each of these pillars of Japan's national security policy has been challenged. Tatsumi argues that beginning with the First Gulf War in 1991, it became apparent that Japan's economic might alone would not in and of itself increase the country's influence in international affairs. In the following decades, rising tension in East China Sea and South China Sea, and successive crises on the Korean Peninsula courtesy of North Korea's nuclear ambitions have encouraged Japan to revise its stance of minimising the role played by Japanese Self-Defense Force in its national security policy. Finally, the perceived decline of the United States, coupled with the inclination towards unilateralism and nationalism of the Trump administration, means that Tokyo finds itself less and less certain about the sustainability of United States' staying power as a dominant player in its region, let alone the guarantor of Tokyo's own security. The chapter demonstrates that these factors have in fact played a major role in stimulating the Abe administration's efforts to recalibrate and reform the country's existing national security institutions and overcome the constraints imposed by the 1951 Constitution. Despite the Abe administration's efforts here, the chapter concludes that the persisting normative constraints embodied in the Constitution will likely continue to frustrate the efforts to reform Japan's national security policy.

India, unlike other major democracies, Harsh V. Pant and Akshay Ranade note, does not have a formally declared national security policy or strategy. They argue that this has been the result of a largely "reactionary" approach to national security that attempted to address security threats sporadically as and when they arose and an enduring preference for "non-alignment". Thus, Pant and Ranade detail the manner in which post-independence India charted for itself a path free of great-power rivalries by not getting associated with any power-blocks as this was deemed to be the best way of ensuring freedom of action and defence of India's national interests. In the post-Cold War period, in contrast, New Delhi's national security policy has been indelibly shaped by the structural change in the international system (i.e. the opportunities and constraints of American unipolarity) and a major domestic political transition away from the Nehruvian political and economic model towards a broadly neoliberal one since the early 1990s.

The combined effects of these changes, Pant and Ranade argue, have been to moderate India's traditional "non-alignment" posture in practice, although not rhetoric, via its deepening engagement and cooperation with the United States and to stimulate greater levels of political and economic engagement with East and Southeast Asia under the Look East policy. Nonetheless, they note, one of the major impediments in articulating an agreed national security strategy in this period has been a lack of political consensus in not only understanding the nature of security threats, but also ways of addressing them. This lack of consensus has occasioned ad hoc responses to security challenges, driven prominently by the nature and instincts of the top political leadership. They illustrate this via an examination of New Delhi's approach to key external and internal national security challenges in the form of Indo-Pakistan and Sino-Indian relations on the one hand and left-wing extremism and insurgency in the Northeast. Pant and Ranade conclude that India's response to its strategic environment has been a function of the nature of its political leadership, their ideological preferences and the contemporary issues that needed to be tackled. There has not been a single, coherent, comprehensive assessment of India's strategic environment and its responses consequently have been episodic and ad hoc.

Like many other states, Turkey's national security policy, William Park notes, is rooted in a range of factors ranging from geopolitical position, historical experience, domestic political system and culture, and level of economic development. Yet he argues that not many countries have quite so complex a security context as Turkey. This stems largely from its geopolitical location. It is simultaneously a European and in particular Balkan, Middle Eastern, Caucasian, Mediterranean, Black Sea, Eurasian and Turkic country. Developments in its multiple neighbourhoods can offer opportunities, threats or both simultaneously. Furthermore, the ways in which Turkey's neighbourhoods shape the country's national security agenda have often depended on larger regional and global dynamics over which Turkey has little control. Since its inception, the national security policy of the republic has been obliged to adapt to British and French colonial presence, the emergence of the Soviet Union, decolonisation, the creation of the state of Israel, the Iranian revolution, the Cold War and its demise, the invasion of Iraq, the 'war on terror' and the 'Arab Spring'. Today much of Turkey's neighbourhood, and the Middle East especially, remains unstable and unpredictable. The quantity, complexity and dynamic nature of the security issues that are thrown up by the sheer march of events across its various borders are almost impossible to encapsulate and can give a manic quality to Turkish endeavours to cope with them.

Turkey, he suggests, is as much an echo chamber of this tumult as an actor within it.

Park details how Turkey's national security policy for much of the time since the establishment of the Republic in 1923 has been framed by a number of foundational pathologies that make it a "lonely" state. First, the dismemberment of the Ottoman Empire and the Treaty of Sevres drawn up by British and French officials in 1920 foresaw an independent Armenian state, held out the prospect of a Kurdish state, envisaged the enlargement of Greece to include parts of Anatolia, suggested the establishment of foreign protectorates over parts of Anatolia and allowed for the imposition of other financial and military restrictions on Turkey. While Kemal Ataturk's victory over Greece ensured it was never imposed, it nevertheless created in Turkey a lasting conviction that even its closest allies were bent on its dismemberment. This worldview, Park notes, has been integral to the development of a "national security regime" ethos propagated via the educational system, the media and by leading politicians and bureaucrats, for whom its precepts are a constant refrain. Second, Ankara has long been viewed as an "outsider" within its many regional neighbourhoods. In the Middle East, for instance, Turkey is often still seen as a former coloniser due the Ottoman legacy and, while partially incorporated into Europe due to its geopolitical position on the Soviet Union's southern flank during the Cold War, its Europeanness is far from accepted. In short, Park argues, Turkey has a foot in many camps but is not truly integral to any of them. It is an odd fit in all the regions it abuts. This "loneliness" suggests that, over time, the best Turkey can hope for are functioning transactional bilateral and multilateral relationships. A deeper "belonging" to any of the political and cultural constellations and states that it neighbours will likely remain elusive.

Dara Conduit examines the national security policy of the Islamic Republic of Iran (IRI). She begins by noting that the IRI has been consumed by national security concerns since its establishment in 1979, including its invasion by Saddam Hussein's Iraq in 1980, its isolation by the international community and domestic contestation over the future shape of the Republic. While Iran has a large population, a diverse (although severely mismanaged) economy and strong regular and irregular armed forces, Conduit argues that the central engine of Iranian national security policy is in fact a deep and abiding sense of insecurity and vulnerability encompassing both domestic and external domains.

The chapter thus examines Iran through the lens of regime security, first looking at the founding moments of the Islamic Republic to identify key drivers of regime insecurity, before turning to an overview of the key features of Iranian regime security over the past four decades. Conduit notes the manner in which such perceived vulnerability has driven policies by the regime—including the harsh repression of domestic opponents, efforts to export its model of revolution, the cultivation of proxy non-state actors across the region and the pursuit of nuclear technology—that have heightened rather than ameliorated Tehran's domestic security and regional security dilemmas, prompting counter-measures by neighbours and foes including Saddam Hussein-era Iraq, Saudi Arabia, Israel and the United States, and feeding the cycles of regional insecurity that have characterised the international relations of the Middle East for decades.

The chapter then provides an examination of the ways in which recent technological innovation has fomented significant changes in regime security in Iran. The spread of the internet—and social media in particular—was initially viewed as a panacea for the country's opposition, with observers breathlessly (and prematurely) proclaiming a 'Twitter Revolution' in the weeks after the disputed 2009 presidential election. But with time the Internet has proven a valuable tool through which the country's intelligence apparatus has also been able to counter its internal and external Others. Hence, the chapter concludes that while many of Iran's founding regime security challenges remain unresolved, the twenty-first century has provided it with new mechanisms to counter perceived threats.

Vinícius Rodrigues Vieira notes that Brazil has conceptualised national security over time as a function of systemic and domestic constraints that have regulated the country's ambitions in its region. Yet, Vieira argues, the very concept of "region" for Brazilian policy-makers has evolved significantly across time in response to both systemic and domestic change. It may seem obvious nowadays that South America—comprising all states in the Western Hemisphere south of Panama—is the "natural" security space for Brazil. However, Vieira details that it was not until the late 1970s that Brasilia started to pursue more in-depth relations with neighbouring states other than those in the so-called Southern Cone, which comprises Argentina, Paraguay, Uruguay and Chile—the latter with no border with Brazil. As the region where a power is located serves as a frame for acting in the world, Brazilian security policy therefore shifted as its conception of its region evolved, including even the South Atlantic and, hence, South-West Africa.

The notion of "region", then, Vieira argues, can be considered a meta-concept for Brazilian national security as it has shaped how Brasilia has framed threats, interests and objectives over time. He illustrates this by tracking the historical development of Brazilian national security policy from independence in 1822 to the contemporary period. From independence in 1822 until the Military Dictatorship (1964–1985), the focus of Brazilian security concerns was related to actors with interests in the Southern Cone. As industrialisation advanced, so did Brazil's material capabilities, prompting Brazil to pursue stronger ties with the Andean countries in South America's Pacific Coast as well as to look across the Atlantic to recover ties with post-colonial Africa. As re-democratisation was consolidated in the 1980s, however, national security then became a public policy like any other, being subject to the demands from domestic civil society, on the one hand, and challenged by transnational actors, like cross-border crime syndicates, on the other.

Vieira notes that across this time Brazil had to rely on either competition or consent with its major Southern Cone challenger—Argentina. Without collaboration between Brasilia and Buenos Aires, no regional intergovernmental organisation (IGO) comprising most states in the landmass below Panamá (where Central America ends) would be possible. However, Venezuela's rising profile in the 2000 as a petrostate with revisionist ambitions at the international level acted to bring together for the first time the two main groups of countries into which South America has been traditionally divided: the Southern Cone and the Andean Region—closer to the Pacific and the Caribbean, an arc formed from Bolivia to Venezuela. Also located in South America, Guiana and Suriname had never been integrated into the region due to their non-Iberian heritage and late independence from European powers (United Kingdom and The Netherlands, respectively).

The chapter suggests that a convergence of systemic and domestic factors constrained the institutionalisation of Brazilian leadership in the region as the recently-dead Union of South American Nations (UNASUR) and its South American Defense Council became ineffective due to diverging interests with key states in the region, particularly Argentina, Chile, Colombia and Venezuela. Such a divergence, in turn, has stemmed from what Vieira terms a "silent competition" between China and the United States for influence over the Western Hemisphere from the 2000s onwards. This competition resembles the quest for influence in Latin America between Britain and the United States during the *Belle Epoque* and has led Brazil to take Washington's side before flexing its muscles to pursue autonomy. Brazil therefore faces a "reverse spiral" consisting of the de-escalation of military strength as the country does not have its leadership recognised by both neighbours and great powers and has its sovereignty de facto complicated by illegal non-state actors. Yet, Brasilia remains focused on South America and the South Atlantic as the means of preserving sovereignty and autonomy in a world that appears to be moving towards bipolarity. The chapter concludes with a consideration of whether the election of Jair Bolsonaro, a retired army captain, as president in 2018 represents a new turning point in Brazil's security policies insofar as he supports re-alignment with the United States after pursuing for more than half-century autonomy in foreign policy and, hence, in security affairs.

Part 3: Issues then provides in-depth analysis of how individual security issues have been incorporated into prevailing scholarly and policy paradigms on national security. We take as our starting point the assumption that national security cannot be completely divorced from 'traditional' interpretations, in which policy is shaped by agencies, ministries and other institutions tasked with the protection of national interests from exogenous threats. Here, then, some contributions will focus on 'traditional' security issues such as nuclear proliferation, intelligence and terrorism/insurgency. Simultaneously, however, it is also clear that since the end of the Cold War the issues broadly defined as 'national security issues' have significantly broadened to encompass a range of 'non-traditional' and emerging areas. Thus, other contributions will, for example, provide examination of such issues as cyber-security, counter-terrorism and biosecurity.

In their chapter on nuclear weapons, Matthew Sussex and Michael Clarke assess how a more complex and multipolar twenty-first-century security environment will impact on how we understand nuclear politics. They trace the evolution of nuclear strategy from the Cold War to the present, mapping out how the role of nuclear weapons changed from being a central feature of Cold War stability, to now being a central concern in new global and regional security environments. To demonstrate this, Sussex and Clarke also examine the nuclear doctrines of the three major nuclear weapons states: the United States, Russia and the PRC. Each of these provides useful examples of how changing patterns of order are creating new pressures and incentives around nuclear weapons. For the United States, the challenge has been to articulate a clear and consistent strategy in which deterrence still plays a role and is not undermined by its own actions—especially since Washington has also prioritised missile defence systems and other capabilities to disrupt the nuclear capabilities of other nations. For Russia, conversely, nuclear weapons have become a much more crucial aspect of Moscow's strategy for protecting its sovereignty, in addition to power projection. Under Vladimir Putin, Russia has adopted a posture of nuclear brinkmanship, developing a suite of first strike weapons and a new nuclear doctrine based on achieving escalation dominance in a conventional or nuclear conflict with a peer competitor. The PRC, meanwhile, has chosen to allow nuclear weapons to play a relatively minor role in its security posture. But with the expansion of its zones of interest prompted by the ambitious Belt and Road Initiative, coupled to its ongoing military modernisation efforts and more muscular US attempts to blunt its rise, nuclear weapons are becoming more prominent in Beijing's strategic calculations. Finally, the chapter surveys some potential future flashpoints to show how nuclear weapons are reflecting new power dynamics. Noting that whereas Cold War bipolarity facilitated deterrence through relatively clear and consistent nuclear dyads, future security environments are likely to be far more fluid, taking in nuclear 'trilemmas', more complex multipolar nuclear politics and a blurring of the lines between conventional and nuclear deterrence.

Carolin Liss' chapter demonstrates that maritime security is an integral part of national security considerations, not only for coastal states but for all states engaged in international trade. She notes that amongst maritime security threats, what are considered relevant to national security changed over time, as did the role and practices of naval forces. The chapter examines the link between national and maritime security over time in three major parts. The first part provides an historical overview, which situates maritime security in the context of national security. It discusses the relationship between the emergence of nation states, control of water areas by states, the monopoly of violence at sea, maritime trade and national security. Liss pays particular attention to how the distinctions between the political and economic, the national and international, and the private and public emerged and changed in the maritime sphere, shaping national maritime interests. By tracing how interests in the maritime sphere changed over time, the historical overview explains how the current understanding of maritime security and its relationship with national security emerged.

The second part offers an overview of maritime security issues that are today of concern for national security, with a special focus on the 'rise' of non-traditional maritime security threats. The third part then discusses how navies and other government agencies have adapted their operations to face these challenges, considering the special nature of the maritime sphere and the need to address problems in cooperation with other states. It further examines how, and why, new actors such as Private Military and Security Companies are today engaged in addressing maritime security threats and how they work alongside state agencies. It demonstrates that non-state actors again play a role in addressing maritime security threats that are of national security concern—even if their motivations are not necessarily in line with national interest. The chapter concludes by noting how maritime security is today an integral part of national security and state agencies are adapting their operations to the changing security environment. However, the chapter suggests that current developments indicate that we may witness, at least to some extent, a return to a system in which the private and political and the national and international begin to become blurred again in the maritime security domain.

Raffaello Pantucci then turns our attention to the examination of one of the quintessential national security issues of the contemporary era: counter-terrorism. He begins by noting the parallel development of terrorism and state responses to it over time. The chapter tracks this history through four distinct phases in modern counter-terrorism: first, the pre- and immediately post-9/11 period; second, the Al Qaeda dominant period (from 2003 to 2010); third, the lone actor period (2007–2018); and finally, the diffuse period (2013–2018). There is overlap between these four stages as the broad practice of counter-terrorism and countering violent extremism as well as the threat picture is not clearly absolute in its nature, leading to a certain bleeding over between phases. This historical approach, Pantucci argues, allows us to see that while the classical counter-terrorism approach practised in a pre- and immediately post-9/11 period was defined by aggressive campaigns to track down, kill or disrupt terrorists and their networks, one of the major lessons to emerge from Europe in particular in the post-9/11 period was that the threat picture was one that emanated from within Western societies as well as outside. This significantly shaped a subsequent response which focused on trying to prevent terrorists groups before they moved into action—the operating assumption being that unless this was successfully done, it would be impossible to kill your way out of the problem (especially when it came from within the societies in question).

Pantucci argues here that while it remains unclear as to what policy frameworks are actually effective in the countering violent extremism space, the capabilities of states to disrupt networks and groups have become more effective. Likely in part in response, terrorist groups have sought to steer their adherents in a new direction of isolated cells and a strategy of lone actor terrorism. This has created a new challenge to counter-terrorists who both struggle to identify and disrupt such disparate networks, as well as develop strategies to prevent people being drawn towards such ideologies. A final wrinkle to this narrative is the growing sense of pervasive struggle that also accompanies this lone actor methodology which creates a counter-reaction in societies and has been in part a generator of a growing ideological response on the opposite end of the scale.

Paul Burke's chapter then looks at intelligence as an aspect of national security. While intelligence has always played a role in effective national security, with the attention given to the role that intelligence plays in policy in the US and UK decisions to invade Iraq, and the revelations by Edward Snowden about global and domestic surveillance programs, intelligence has increasingly become an area of public interest and concern. In order to understand what intelligence does, Burke's chapter provides an overview of the intelligence cycle. This, he argues, gives a more detailed understanding of the different steps that are involved in effective intelligence, giving us an opportunity to better appraise the role that intelligence plays in national security.

On Burke's account, the intelligence cycle has six main steps: direction, collection, collation, evaluation, analysis and dissemination. He then summarises different types of intelligence, depending on the means used to gather the information: SIGINT, from signals or communications, HUMINT, from human sources and OSINT, an emerging field of intelligence gathered from open source or publicly available information. The chapter then looks at what roles organisational structure, intelligence gaps and failures, and the politicisation of intelligence play in the greater national security context. The overall proposition of Burke's paper is that by giving clarity on the intelligence cycle and its larger context, we are in a better position to understand the role that intelligence plays in ongoing national security discussions.

Following from the previous chapter on intelligence, an emerging domain of national security policy and practice—the role of machine learning in mass surveillance—is examined in detail by Simon Robbins. Robbins begins by noting that Machine Learning (ML) is being proposed as a tool to enhance national security by enabling mass surveillance in a variety of ways—some of which are being implemented by state institutions. He argues that this should cause great concern as the use of ML in this already problematic context will likely exacerbate existing ethical and social issues as well as create a few of its own.

The chapter highlights the many issues confronting the use of ML in the context of national security and mass surveillance, with a focus on the ethical challenges posed by ML. This attention to ethics serves two purposes. First, given this fast-moving field, an ethical focus allows for broader recognition of the issues arising from ML—even though particular aspects of the technology will continue to change, many of these ethical issues will remain constant. Second, these issues are chosen because they are important—not only are these likely to be ongoing issues for national security, they warrant concern and attention. The first set of issues stems from the data used to train ML algorithms—the sources, the methods and the labelling. The second set of issues concerns the efficacy of ML, without which it would be unethical to use. Finally, due to the opacity of the features causing a particular ML decision, there are social issues surrounding human accountability and responsibility when something goes wrong. That is, how do we ensure that humans are in meaningful control over ML algorithms that could result in ethically salient consequences? Navigating all of these issues will be difficult; however, knowing that they exist is the first step towards ensuring that ML is implemented for mass surveillance in a way consistent with liberal democratic values.

Part III concludes with Adam Henschke's exploration of information as a domain of national security concern and threat. The chapter is primarily concerned with the issues that arise when malicious actors, agents or groups exploit information to further their ends in ways that pose a threat or challenge to national security. The specific focus for this chapter is the way that information is evolving as a national security concern. That is, that a range of information technologies are changing the role that information plays in our lives, and as part of this, the evolution of the uses of technologies mean that our understanding information as a national security concern also needs to evolve. Henschke demonstrates this evolution by reference to three recent challenges to national security: the rise of international terrorism, the return of foreign influence operations and what we can call the 'oligopolisation of epistemic power'.

The basic argument of this chapter is that while information has long been an aspect of national security, the rise of information technologies and their integration into our personal and professional lives is playing an increasingly important role in national security. The recent evolution of terrorism and violent extremism was enabled in part by social media, foreign information operations have been used to disrupt domestic political processes in surprising ways, and the rise of 'surveillance capitalism' has resulted in the diminution of states as the primary epistemic actors in the national security space. These forces, Henschke suggests, mean that information is an evolving and increasingly important national security concern.

NOTES

1. Wolfers, A. (1952). 'National Security' as an Ambiguous Symbol. *Political Science Quarterly*, 67 (4), 481–502.
2. Sil, R., & Katzenstein, P. (2010). Analytic Eclecticism in the Study of World Politics: Reconfiguring Problems and Mechanisms Across Research Traditions. *Perspectives on Politics*, 8 (2), 411–431.
3. Newman, E. (2010). Critical Human Security Studies. *Review of International Studies*, 36 (1), 77–94.
4. Paul, T. V., & Ripsman, N. (2010). *Globalization and the National Security State*. Oxford: Oxford University Press.

5. See for example: Dannreuther, R., & Peterson, J. (Eds.). (2006). *Security Strategy and Transatlantic Relations*. Abingdon: Routledge; and Webber, M., Sperling, J. & Smith, M. (2013). *NATO's Post-Cold War Trajectory: Decline or Regeneration*. New York: Palgrave Macmillan.
6. See for example: Hughes, C. W. (2004). Japan's Re-emergence as a Normal Military Power. *Adelphi Papers* (pp. 368–369). Oxford: Oxford University Press; Lind, J. (2016). Japan's Security Evolution. *CATO Institute Policy Analysis*, 788 (February), http://www.cato.org/publications/policy-analysis/japans-security-evolution; and Oros, A. (2008). *Normalising Japan: Politics, Identity and the Evolution of Security Practice*. Palo Alto, CA: Stanford University Press.
7. Christensen, T. J. (2011). The Advantages of an Assertive China. *Foreign Affairs* (March–April), https://www.foreignaffairs.org/articles/east-asia/2011-02-21/advantages-assertive-china; and Ji, Y. (2015). China's National Security Commission: Theory, Evolution and Operations. *Journal of Contemporary China*, 25 (98), 178–196.
8. Rosencrance, R., & Stein, A. (1993). Introduction. In Rosencrance, R., & Stein, A. (Eds.), *The Domestic Bases of Grand Strategy* (p. 13.). Ithaca, NJ: Cornell University Press.
9. See, for example: Ball, D. (1993). Strategic Culture in the Asia-Pacific Region. *Security Studies*, 3 (1): 44–74; Johnston, A. I. (1995). Thinking About Strategic Culture. *International Security*, 19 (4), 32–64; Gray, C. S. (1999). Strategic Culture as Context: The First Generation of Theory Strikes Back. *Review of International Studies*, 25 (1), 49–69; Lantis, J. S. (2002). Strategic Culture and National Security Policy. *International Studies Review*, 4 (3), 87–113; Meyer, C. O. (2005). Convergence Towards a European Strategic Culture? A Constructivist Framework for Explaining Changing Norms. *European Journal of International Relations*, 11 (4), 523–549; Glenn, J. (2009). Realism Versus Strategic Culture: Competition and Collaboration? *International Studies Review*, 11 (3), 523–551; and Bloomfield, Alan. (2012). Time to Move On: Reconceptualizing the Strategic Culture Debate. *Contemporary Security Policy*, 33 (3), 437–461.
10. The role of "ruling domestic ideas" regarding military strategy in pre-1914 Wilhelmine, Germany, for instance, has been highlighted by Stephen Van Evera as a contributing factor to the outbreak of the First World War. See: Van Evera, S. (1984). The Cult of the Offensive and the Origins of the First World War. *International Security*, 9 (1), 58–107.
11. Leffler, M. (1990). National Security. *Journal of American History*, 77 (1), 143–144.
12. Ibid.,143.
13. See: Ripsman, N., & Paul, T. V. (2005). Globalization and the National Security State: A Framework for Analysis. *International Studies Review*, 7 (2), 199–227; and Ripsman, N., & Paul, T. V. (2010). *Globalization and the National Security State*. New York: Oxford University Press.
14. See, for example: Deudney, D. (1995). Nuclear Weapons and the Waning of the Real-State. *Daedalus*, 124 (2), 209–231; and Paul, T. V. (2005). The National Security State and Global Terrorism: Why the State Is Not Prepared for the New Kind of War. In Aydinli, E., & Rosenau, J. (Eds.), *Globalization, Security, and the Nation State: Paradigms in Transition* (pp. 49–64). New York: SUNY Press.

15. See Zegart, A. (2000). *Flawed by Design: The Evolution of the CIA, JCS, and NSC*. Stanford: Stanford University Press.
16. See, for example: Ayoob, M. (1995). *The Third World Security Predicament: State Making, Regional Conflict and the International System*. Boulder, CO: Lynne Rienner.

Part I

Theories

CHAPTER 2

Understanding National Security: The Promises and Pitfalls of International Relations Theory

Matthew Sussex

'National security' is a term most analysts and government professionals working across an array of different policy arenas would be familiar with. But like others in the international relations lexicon, on closer inspection there is a great deal of variance in understanding what the term refers to, and how to operationalise it. Unfortunately applying established theories of international politics to national security problems can sometimes confuse instead of clarify. In the scholarly literature, the very idea of what constitutes a nation in the first place is contested. So too are definitions of security, as well as its referent objects. What does it mean to have security? What specifically is being secured? How do issues make it onto national security agendas, and how are they prioritised? Who are (or should be) the key decision-makers, and how do their individual and institutional preferences shape outcomes, for good or otherwise? How do conventional notions of security differ from alternative (and arguably equally legitimate) ways to understand it? And what emphasis should we place on ideas about security with difference primary referents—from national security to global, human, environmental, social and other formulations?

For some national security policy professionals navigating this landscape may seem counterproductive to the work that they do. They have a point: in many respects abstract theories of international relations have little relevance to

M. Sussex (✉)
Centre for Defence Research, Australian Defence College, Canberra, ACT, Australia
e-mail: matthew.sussex@anu.edu.au

Griffith Asia Institute, Griffith University, Brisbane, Australia

© The Author(s), under exclusive license to Springer Nature Switzerland AG 2022
M. Clarke et al. (eds.), *The Palgrave Handbook of National Security*, https://doi.org/10.1007/978-3-030-53494-3_2

23

the practical day-to-day operations of protecting a nation from threats. And it is also true that the international relations scholar—even one working on security issues—and the national security practitioner occupy different worlds with different priorities. The international relations scholar is interested in problems primarily as an intellectual exercise. As long as their research is rigorous they are free to envision large-scale solutions to security challenges, often with little regard for praxis.[1] The practitioner, on the other hand, is differently constrained by the need to follow established practices, navigate complex webs of interpersonal and institutional preferences and above all produce policy recommendations (often in granular detail) in a way that precludes high-level strategic thinking.

Yet practitioners can potentially learn much from theories of international relations. Just as the work of the practitioner cuts across a number of different policy arenas the study of international relations is also broadly multidisciplinary, taking in political science, economics, law, history and a host of other areas of knowledge and insight. Theories also have the virtue of acting as roadmaps, providing a conceptual lens through which the complex challenges and opportunities associated with national security might be prioritised and navigated. This is not to say that national security in practice is synonymous with national security in theory—far from it, in fact. But the conceptual overlay that international relations theory provides can be helpful in illuminating the assumptions we make about security in practice, to explain international interaction, to help prioritise main threats and tasks that require resourcing and to offer some degree of clarity to an increasingly multifaceted field of policymaking.

Accordingly this chapter surveys how some of the main international relations theories can assist in understanding national security problems. It is by no means intended to be comprehensive, since such an undertaking would take a book in its own right. First it identifies the landscape in which national security policymaking takes place, where conventional cleavages between policy arenas—like foreign policy and domestic policy—are increasingly breaking down due to factors relating to globalisation. Second, the chapter moves to specific theories and the ways that they explain, prescribe and even try to predict outcomes. In doing so it focuses on three main approaches to international relations: realism, liberalism and constructivism. Third, the chapter applies these theoretical approaches to three national security problems in order to demonstrate how their core assumptions can produce radically different interpretations and solutions. The chapter concludes with some potential lessons for national security policy planners about how theory might be usefully employed.

The National Security Landscape: Changing Definitions, Themes and Processes

The first hurdle anyone seeking to study national security will encounter is clarifying precisely what 'security' actually means. Definitions are important because they affect the scope of agendas, imply what is to be prioritised and set out the 'menu for choice'[2] in terms of the types of issues that matter to national security practitioners. Here we can choose to define security very broadly: simply as 'freedom from harm', for instance. We might also suggest that it is freedom from fear, or freedom from want.[3] Broad definitions can be an advantage in the national security space because they encapsulate virtually all the potential threats and challenges that actors might face. But this can also be a hindrance, since it adds numerous issues that need to be addressed within the context of national security policy, while providing little clarity as to what should be the priority areas for focus. Of course, the problem is reversed when adopting a narrow definition of security. If, for example, we define security as has been conventionally done in the past—strictly as ensuring the safety of states against threats from other states[4]—then we rule out a whole host of other challenges that nations face from non-state actors such as terrorists, environmental challenges, economic dislocation and poverty, and natural disasters and many others. Each of these poses real risks to the integrity of states as well as the lives of the people who live within them, and demand policy responses.

Globalisation and the acceleration of the technological revolution is exacerbating these trends rather than ameliorating them. This means that distinctions between foreign and security policy as instruments to deal with the external environment, and domestic policies that attend to governance within the state, are less meaningful. Here, both analysts and scholars used to distinguish between *Aussenpolitik* (foreign relations) and *Innenpolitik* (domestic policy including law enforcement).[5] And yet such distinctions are often functionally unhelpful in a modern and globalised world. They simply cannot account, for instance, for a terrorist in the Philippines sponsored by radical charities in the United States using cyber tools to cause loss of life by remotely hacking an electricity grid in Tehran.

Statehood, Securitisation and National Security

But just as the national security environment can seem hopelessly complex, the nature of national security offers some clarity over a second fundamental criterion for a good working definition: what security is referring to. Because national security it is tied to protecting the nation—specifically the nation-state—the main actor in defining national security is fairly clear-cut. States have international legal personality, they have physical borders, are centres for economic activity, and have a *sovereign* centralised authority that makes policy and controls the means of organised violence (the capacity to make laws and fight wars with other states).[6] Naturally, there are disagreements about what constitutes a nation-state in the first place. Debates are common about whether 'the state' refers to a superstructure of institutions, elites and leaders; or as a more corporate and fluid actor that comprises its culture, traditions and citizens as markers for how it behaves.[7]

This is why some international relations theorists reject the idea that we should look inside a state to see how its culture and history might inform its behaviour, because in doing so we are studying uniqueness rather than commonalities from which we might make generalisations and predictive models. We also run the risk of producing a theory of foreign policy rather than one that can reliably identify the structural conditions that shape how nation-states interact with one another.[8] Conversely, just because we might seek to limit a definition of national security to the state as the referent object of national security does not mean that the only responses it makes are against direct threats to its physical sovereignty. Indeed, it might well incorporate elements of human security into its official policy doctrine, seeking to promote the safety of people regardless of national boundaries (and often because of them, in the case of persecuted peoples).[9] Knowing something about the historical and cultural drivers behind its policy in this context is therefore arguably vital.

Because the types of issues states must deal with as potential threats are so sweeping, a chief danger is that national security becomes a de facto dumping ground for anything that might harm or threaten a state's institutions, integrity or its citizens. Elites, lobbyists and interest groups within societies can be adept at agitating for a particular issue to be *securitised*: in other words, to be placed on the security agenda.[10] Doing so may often come from altruistic motivations, like the example of doctors' groups seeking to develop cures for infectious diseases that can spread rapidly across state borders. But security is inevitably also prone to politicisation, in which an issue is advanced as a security threat due to ideological, socio-economic or even xenophobic attitudes. Campaigns to restrict refugee intakes from areas of the world beset by poverty, social dislocation, ethnic difference or civil violence on the grounds that letting large numbers of such people inside a state will rob existing citizens of jobs, drain the welfare purse, and result in urban ghettos of displaced people who will not assimilate and turn to violence or crime is a classic example of this.

But with either example above, whether altruistic or ideologised, successfully placing an issue on a nation's security agenda has real and pragmatic outcomes for those championing it: national security issues are high governmental priorities; they receive more funding and are frequently subject to less scrutiny than other policy matters because of their perceived importance. For policymakers working in a national security environment, and responsible for giving clear and objective advice, the fact that politicians and leaders may also be champions of such policies—for votes, for prestige or for influence—makes domestic power structures an important factor in how national security issues are selected and pursued.

National Interests

Determining the broad parameters for national security also requires a conception of the *national interest*. Here it is axiomatic that the primary aim of a state is not to collapse or be subsumed into another state. At the highest level of analysis, then, states can be regarded as having only one interest: national survival, or the preservation of sovereignty.[11] But this is of limited use to policymakers who are routinely called on to develop ways to address various different risks under the rubric of national interests. Hence national survival can be broken down to encapsulate other more specific interests of a state that often include the physical security of its territory and citizens, the prosperity of its people and the preservation of national values, culture and way of life. In this way, preserving a state's mode of political organisation (whether democratic, authoritarian or hybrid models) is tied to its understanding of history, and the domestic consensus—which is sometimes broad-based and on other occasions more of an elite consensus—about its core interests that need safeguarding.[12]

This means that a nation's *values* can also influence its conception of the national interest when it comes to promoting norms abroad. Many liberal democracies, for instance, see themselves as norm entrepreneurs, promoting human rights, global governance, cooperation in institutions and adherence to international law.[13] But other states can see these as mechanisms of control and ways to justify more pragmatic interests. There is plenty of scholarship, for example, on cultural relativism and human rights, raising the question of whether the Western notion of Kantian universalism prioritises the rights of the individual at the expense of alternative views that stress the importance of the collective.[14] By the same token, the historical preference of the United States for democracy promotion and participation by all states in an open liberal trading order can be viewed as a means of enshrining its own preferences in a form of 'lite imperialism', controlling the institutions of global governance as well as projecting US interests and power abroad—sometimes using force—to maintain its hegemonic position.[15] The same can be said of military-security alliances such as NATO, which can be interpreted as a vehicle to promote peace and collective security amongst members, or alternatively as a way to shut others out of the European security order, containing them and treating non-members effectively as threats.[16]

Sovereignty and International Law

The way we choose to understand national interests also has a bearing on how we see the nature and purpose of international cooperation, as well as the role and significance of international law. For some commentators international law is an important cornerstone of international stability, and complying with it encourages habits of trust and cooperation in institutions, trade agreements and security accords.[17] And since most states obey most principles of international law most of the time, the rules and principles developed within the architecture of global governance—from the United Nations Security Council to the World Trade Organisation—both helps to encourage compliance with legal norms, and acts as a brake on states that might seek to pursue self-aggrandisement or engender zero-sum games in their dealings with others.

Critics of that view, on the other hand, counter that international law is customary with no means of enforcing it other than the preferences of powerful states, and that international regimes often marginalise others.[18] A good example here is the Non-Proliferation Treaty, which non-members such as India and Pakistan contend enshrines a privileged club of legitimate nuclear weapons states (conveniently, those that had them when the treaty was being developed). At the same time it de-legitimises as law-breakers those who subsequently sought to develop nuclear weapons in order to safeguard their national security from existential harms.[19]

Devising national interests as a framework to implement national security policy is also contextual, depending on time and place. This means that assumptions about the way international structures work, as well as their purpose and meaning, are rarely fixed and unchanging. The concept of state sovereignty enshrined in Article 2 of the UN Charter is a good example of this. Not only has there been a tendency since the end of the Cold War to see sovereignty as contingent on good behaviour, but the period also witnessed a surge of interventions in the affairs of states on humanitarian grounds—in Rwanda, Somalia, former Yugoslavia, Libya and others. For some, this is a welcome development, and an indication of international laws and norms evolving to act as a further brake on states that seek to persecute parts of their own citizenry.[20] For others it is a risky endeavour that diminishes international law and prompts vigilantism.[21] Still others see it as 'organised hypocrisy', whereby states readily interfere in the affairs of others, but seek to vigorously thwart attempts to compromise their own sovereignty.[22]

Power, Influence and International Order

Just as the structures of global affairs frequently change, so too does our understanding of what constitutes a nation's ability to shape the environment around it to suit its own preferences. As a central concept in national security planning, an appreciation of *power* is critical, but what contributes towards it is a thornier question. The historian E.H. Carr identified three main domains of power: military, economic and cultural.[23] For him the most influential of all would be cultural power, but for the obvious problem that unless it was accompanied by the wherewithal (military and economic power), cultural power was not particularly useful. Others like Hans Morgengthau, writing in the late 1940s, sought to identify the elements of national power. For Morgenthau, having a large military and economy certainly contributed to national power. But so too did an abundance of national resources, population, geographic size, population, national morale and the quality of a state's government as well as its foreign policy.[24]

There are problems with this approach, since it blends quantitative and qualitative themes. Having a large military means nothing unless it has modern equipment and good doctrine. Without these a large army is merely cannon fodder for an adversary. National resources can indeed boost a nation's influence and make it rich—the oil states of the Middle East are a good example—but equally they can be targets for others that seek to possess them (as Kuwait discovered in 1991). A large land area can be valuable, especially if accompanied by favourable terrain or what John Mearsheimer called the 'stopping power of water'.[25] And yet if populations are spread thinly around a large landmass it can be a recipe for strategic weakness, just as having a large population and very little land for them to live in. By the same token, good national morale is unlikely to be of much value if the state is weak militarily, or is economically dislocated.

Applying measures of power to assess a nation's capacity to coerce or compel others is therefore much more of an art than a science. This is made more difficult when using other formulations, like Joseph Nye's division of national capabilities into 'hard' and 'soft' power[26] (or even 'smart' and 'sharp' power[27]) because it is never clear which type of power fits in which category, or which one takes priority in specific priority areas of national security policy. Indeed, Nye's view that power is about getting others to 'want what you want' as much as it is getting them to 'do what you want'[28] implies an outwardly focused socialisation process to national security policy that has manifestly not succeeded in socialising a rising PRC within a liberal rules-based order. And just as we might also agree with Hedley Bull's view that great powers are 'front rank' military powers, have large economies and therefore rights and responsibilities in the maintenance of international order,[29] this relegates nations like Japan to second tier status. But the obverse of this—that power can be found more in terms of cultural referenda, through status, prestige and legitimacy—often runs the risk of downplaying the importance of military capabilities as fundamental to a nation's ability to act independently, as well as being able to shape regional security agendas as well as norms and laws within them.

Complicating this even further is the fact that power is by no means a static variable. It is a historical fact that major powers rise and fall, and we currently seem to be on the cusp of such a reconfiguration. Whereas much has been made of the liberal order that maintained peace and stability in areas and at a time where liberal democracy was at its strongest, there is no guarantee that the norms and laws inherent to democracy will be any stickier (as force multipliers for states seeking to maximise their power and influence) than other leading worldviews at different times in history. Indeed, the malaise that has swept liberal democracies in the aftermath of the Global Financial Crisis has both internal and external dimensions that are of fundamental concern to policy planners in Western democratic states.[30] A spreading downturn in public trust in democracy's core institutions, a return to trade protectionism, the rise of new nationalisms and scepticism about the institutions of liberal order have been accompanied the rise of the PRC and its own efforts to substitute the Western security order with a China-centric one.

The fact that Beijing favours a much more statist emphasis on sovereignty and non-interference changes the security calculus for many national security policy planners, who must consider how to respond to a potential sea-change in world order as the centre of global economic power pivots from the West to the East. Should they balance against China? Or bandwagon with it? Form alliances of like-minded states? Or hedge their bets until it is clear how the competition between the United States and the PRC will play out? Bearing in mind that national security policymaking is not just about serving interests but also signalling intentions, the ways in which responses to challenges like large-scale renovations to international order are perceived—both by domestic as well as international constituencies—is also an important consideration. For instance, the way China seeks to promote its agenda through the Belt and Road Initiative (BRI) as a peaceful rise based on mutual respect is an important way to mobilise international support and quell fears that Beijing will seek to impose a rigid form of hegemony over continental Eurasia.[31] Equally, how a nation such as Australia responds to these changing power dynamics—either by strengthening its security alliance with the United States or by encouraging closer ties to the PRC—will be read by its allies and regional nations as an important marker of its intentions.

Making National Security Policy in an Age of Globalisation and Shifting Power: Balancing Risk and Resilience

National security policymakers must therefore balance a host of often-competing threats and opportunities. Some are conventional, relating to the external environment, like the proliferation of nuclear weapons. Others are strictly domestic, such as the potential for civil disobedience in authoritarian nations. But increasingly they tend to cross state boundaries, or at least are influenced by transnational forces. This is true of transnational terrorism as well as foreign interference through the use of disinformation campaigns and the manipulation of public opinion by hostile powers. It is also true of threats like environmental degradation and global warming, which have no respect for political boundaries. The increased prevalence of drought, flooding and rising sea levels are all factors that demand national security responses given that they threaten the livelihoods of many citizens of nation-states worldwide. In some cases, like the low-lying islands of the South Pacific, which face being inundated as a result of global warming, they are truly matters of national survival.[32]

Managing such a complex threat environment has led many states to seek new ways to assess their national security priorities through the prism of risk and resilience.[33] As a means of measuring hazards and taking pre-emptive action to ensure that state institutions are able to survive all but the most catastrophic national security challenges, such an approach has merit. It has the potential to engender greater institutional coordination, earlier threat-detection and the diversion of assets to meet difference risk categories that often overlap. As a means to shift away from reactive policy planning and embrace more nimble and adaptive policy behaviour, building multifaceted resilient capacity into a nation's critical infrastructure can help inoculate states against future threats, and provide a means of triage as risks gain in severity and immediacy.

Such an approach can be found, for instance in national action plans to guard against pandemic diseases, against devastating natural disasters and crises from an array of different economic, social and environmental contingencies.[34] But critically, resilience frameworks are fundamentally dependent on two vital factors: resourcing and accuracy. A nation like Zimbabwe, for instance, has vastly different capabilities in meeting national security challenges to Germany, and no amount of strategic foresight can overcome a lack of national capacity. By the same token, risk modelling is highly contingent on diagnosing the problem correctly. If this is inaccurate based on overestimation of capabilities or under-prioritisation of risk (as frequently occurs in national security planning), then a state can suffer as a result.[35]

THEORIES OF INTERNATIONAL RELATIONS AND NATIONAL SECURITY CHOICES

What specifically do the major international relations theories offer the national security policy planner? Each of them has its strengths and weaknesses, but they are all potentially instructive in a number of ways. Focusing on the leading approaches of realism, liberalism and constructivism, the chapter now turns to investigate how international relations scholarship can inform contemporary national security practitioners. Space constraints present a more fulsome evaluation of some of the other useful tools offered by international relations theory. These include the Regional Security Complex Theory (RSCT) associated with the Copenhagen School[36]; the insights of global security theorists from the Welsh School[37]; and the English School's emphasis on international society[38]; as well as other contributions from critical security studies and critical geopolitics.[39] However, the main approaches to international relations provide plenty of conceptual fodder that can be covered in some detail.

Realist Approaches

Of all the theories of international relations, realism remains highly relevant to the study and practice of national security. This is primarily due to the fact that realism is a paradigm that focuses on how states behave, what their key interests are and how they respond to threats. Although it is often miscast as a cynical approach to international relations, the attempts by realists to offer policy prescriptions in as objective and value-free a manner as possible provides policy planners with a largely unvarnished view of international interaction in which the international landscape is one of constant competition, and where the use of force cannot be ruled out. And whereas realism's predictive capacity has often fared poorly—it did not predict the end of the Cold War, for instance[40]—it nonetheless remains the premier approach to understanding the use of material power and raw national interests in international relations.

The core assumptions of realism would be relatively familiar to national security practitioners. To begin with, realists tend to view international politics as inherently competitive. But how assertive states are depends on what strand of realism one subscribes to. For neorealists, who emphasise the importance of structural dynamics in international politics, the lack of an overarching body to systematically enforce the principles of international law (in the same way that domestic laws are enforced) means that international relations is best conceived of as being in a state of constant anarchy.[41] Because states seek primarily to survive, the best means of doing so is through the accrual of power at the expense of others. This means that conflicts of interest—including war, as 'politics by other means'—are inevitable.[42] But for neorealists anarchy also has a conditioning effect: states react to anarchy through the prism of fear, making them naturally defensive and hesitant to cooperate, but also war-averse.[43] In contrast, offensive realists see anarchy as less of a constraint on behaviour and more of an inducement.[44] This means states as raw rational utility maximisers, and will not hesitate to try and outdo others—including when ostensibly cooperating—if the opportunity presents itself.

In addition to a structural argument, this is also based on realist readings of human nature. For realists, history shows there is no guarantee that self-interest and greed can be eliminated from the human condition.[45] And of all people's failings, none is more prevalent than the desire to dominate others in some way. Therefore, the possibility of eradicating the drive to power is utopian and unrealistic. Under these conditions international politics is best viewed as a power struggle, and makes the promotion of the national interest the primary obligation of states.[46] The anarchical international system necessitates the maintenance of military capabilities which are sufficient to deter attack from others, because although alliances may help states safeguard their security, the continuing loyalty of allies cannot be relied upon.[47] This creates a *security dilemma* whereby self-help becomes the principle guiding how states behave.[48] Indeed, for realists the national duty of self-protection cannot be entrusted to international organisations or law because they are regularly based on moral principles that are interpreted subjectively and may therefore be enforced selectively. But if all states act in their self-interest, stability will result from a natural balance of power. This leads to another important point of commonality between realists: that they view ideology in national security policy as rhetorical messaging to justify policy to domestic and international audiences (at best), or as fundamentally bad policy that harms the rational pursuit of the national interest (at worst).[49]

The way power is distributed leads realists to infer that the type of international system will also dictate the way states within it interact. In bipolar systems, as witnessed during the Cold War, for instance, the presence of two opposing poles of power makes choices fairly simple: a bifurcated world leads to blocs of alliances that are also inherently stable.[50] Even nuclear weapons, managed through deterrence, contribute to the stability of bipolar systems, because they make the risk of war so catastrophic that each side refrains from policies that might prompt overt hostilities to break out. In managing their competition they also use proxy conflicts to avoid fighting themselves, and generally respect each other's spheres of influence.[51] In contrast, multipolar systems are much more fluid, characterised by numerous great powers competing for influence. Under those conditions alliances are temporary and the risk of wars increase as major powers seek to outdo one another. Without clear rules about where one great power's sphere of influence ends and another's begins, multipolar environments are dangerous, both for major powers as well as smaller ones.[52]

In addition to valuable lessons about security dilemmas, the behaviour of great powers and the nature of the international system, realism can also be useful in helping national security policy planners understand the behaviour of smaller states. For realists, those states that are not great powers have essentially four options when dealing with major powers: they can *balance*[53] against them by forming counter-coalitions; they can *bandwagon*[54] with one of them; they can try to *hide* (which is rarely successful); or they can *hedge*[55] by seeking to position themselves in between major powers. This helps to explain how middle and smaller powers behave during times of crisis, and why nations with important strategic assets like natural resources, energy supplies or geographic position can exert disproportionate influence over larger states.

The fact that realism is so multifaceted, covering most international aspects of interest to national security professionals, means that it can be confusing to navigate. In fact, realists often make arguments that are diametrically opposed to those made by other scholars from within the same paradigm. For instance, realists do not agree on whether balance of power systems is more stable than hierarchical ones[56]; whether states are defensive or aggressive; whether balance of power or balance of threat is the main reason states form alliances[57]; whether states can be global hegemons or just regional ones[58]; or whether cooperation in regimes is more or less common when vital national interests are at stake.[59]

Realists also differ over the extent to which examining a state's domestic traditions influences its behaviour. For neorealists there is no point in crossing levels of analysis to unlock the 'black box' of the state because mixing unit-level analysis with system-level analysis leads to unreliable conclusions. But for neoclassical realists, who accept much of the neorealist canon about states' motivations, interests and power, the way that domestic elites perceive threats is vital for how their foreign and security policy is shaped and articulated.[60] That they tend to do so due to internal discourses and entrenched patterns of behaviour that come from each nation's history and experience with national security lends important context to understanding why states sometimes behave counter-intuitively. As a result, neoclassical realists emphasise that understanding what leads states to make national security choices—which comes from both within and outside the state—is just as important as the structural conditions that permit or constrain their behaviour.[61]

Liberal Approaches

Like realism, liberal approaches to understand international relations and the types of challenges facing national security policy planners tend to be multi-faceted. The liberal project in international relations is primarily geared around mitigating the negative effects of international anarchy, with varying degrees of emphasis as to whether laws, institutions or political systems are most effective.[62] At one end of the spectrum one can find neoliberal institutionalists, who tend to agree with realism's core assumptions about the anarchical nature of world politics, and the tendency of states to seek power over others.[63] But they do differ on the role played by institutions in encouraging good habits amongst states, and the gradual development of increasingly robust forms of global governance to constrain their behaviour.

For Daniel Deudney and John Ikenberry, participating in institutions is appealing to states. This is because they have a 'cobinding' effect that builds trust amongst participants, reduces transaction costs and ultimately leads to mutually beneficial cooperation that can spill over into other areas.[64] And whereas realists view cooperation under anarchy as being scarce and driven by competition—because states are positional and hierarchical, seeking relative gains over others[65]—liberals counter that states are atomistic, and do not care whether others gain more. Hence they are more likely to embrace cooperation on the basis of absolute gains (that everyone gains something by taking part) than by trying to deliberately out-compete one another. For neoliberals, this helps explain the motivations of states in seeking to form free trade agreements, participate in collective security agreements and even reduce their sovereign control over their affairs by engaging in grand supranational visions such as integration in the European Union.

A second leg of the liberal tripod concerns the role of capitalism and trade in mitigating the effects of international anarchy. Echoing Immanuel Kant's 'Spirit of Commerce' in his essay on perpetual peace,[66] the interdependence produced by peaceful economic competition is one of the main factors liberals stress in bringing about peaceful regional and world orders. Put simply, the position here is that trade makes peace. When nations engage in frequent cross-border trade, not only does it encourage cooperation in other arenas, it leads their economies to become intertwined. This makes conflict less likely, because states will see the risks of losing that trade as fundamentally more significant than any gains that could be made from fighting. Moreover, liberal theory stresses that domestic constituencies that rely on cross-border trade are likely to agitate powerfully for policymakers to find peaceful solutions to disagreements.[67] Of course, this presupposes that trade is balanced, which it rarely is. It also ignores the fact that what appears to be interdependence can in reality mask vulnerable overdependence: if a state relies on its energy supplies too heavily on one of its trading partners, that exposes it to the potential for significant pressure to be applied. The over-reliance of states like Germany on Russian gas, for instance, has enabled Moscow to exert considerable leverage in watering down sanctions regimes against its conduct in Ukraine because it has the capacity to threaten the interruption of a third of Germany's gas supply.

The third source of liberal international order—and probably the most contentious in the twenty-first century—stresses that the type of political system a state possesses will help determine how pacific it will be. Here the 'democratic peace' thesis stresses that democracies will likely avoid confrontation with one another because they have similar respect for domestic and international law, a similar preference for trade and interdependence, and shared political understandings about the importance of a rules-based international order.[68] Following the collapse of the Cold War, Francis Fukuyama's 'End of History' thesis gained significant prominence for its argument that history—as a contest of ideas—had been decided, and that liberal democracy was the victor.[69] As the former Soviet states turned towards pluralist forms of government, a widely-held view was that universal democratisation, and hence a much more peaceful world order, was imminent. Western nations embraced 'peace dividends', cutting back on defence expenditure, and enhanced cooperation in the United Nations was seen as a forerunner to global governance, and the behaviour of the United States prompted enthusiasm for humanitarian intervention to improve the lot of persecuted peoples, and to warn repressive regimes that sovereignty was not a cloak that would permit genocide and abuse.

But events such as the September 11, 2001 attacks on the World Trade Centre and the Pentagon demonstrated that history was far from over, and the initial enthusiasm around the Arab Spring revolts soon dissipated when it became evident that authoritarian regimes had won out over democratic ones. A spate of failed interventions from former Yugoslavia to Libya demonstrated that unless the international community was prepared to state-build after intervening, the results could be more chaos and dislocation.[70] They also raised questions about the extent to which liberal values should be exported by force, in line with the more radical Wilsonian internationalism of the neoconservative Bush Jnr administration.[71] Meanwhile, the rise of China and Russia's return to authoritarianism suggested that the liberal socialisation project had failed to create new democracies amongst leading hubs of global power. The economic malaise of the Global Financial Crisis, the downturn of support for the EU and the rise of statist right-wing parties across the West raised the spectre that the liberal order was far from immutable. And this deepened even further after the election of an exceptionalist US President in Donald Trump, who promptly began unravelling America's leading role in the economic, institutional and even security aspects of the liberal order.

As a result, liberalism ended the second decade of the twenty-first century in a much weaker position than it had ended the last decade of the previous century. The notion of a post-liberal order, the rise of protectionism and trade wars, and a lack of confidence in international institutions all combined to make liberal approaches to national security potentially less attractive than in the past. And while many states in the West have continued to stress the importance of defending and promoting liberal values as the source of liberalism's utility in maintaining peace and stability, the recent return of great power politics and statism to international affairs makes the future of liberal predictions about the future of world order far less certain than before.

Constructivist Approaches

Constructivist approaches to international relations are relatively recent, rising to prominence primarily as a critique of realism's lack of predictive power during the collapse of the USSR and the end of the Cold War. Rather than focusing on international anarchy, material power and rational national interests as the dominant condition, variable and means of state behaviour, respectively, constructivists argue in favour of a different conception of international interaction that is fundamentally the product of socialisation. Drawing inspiration from the postmodern turn in the humanities and the sciences, constructivist argue that the stuff of international relations—interests, power and anarchy—are fundamentally normative. For Alexander Wendt, whose *Social Theory of International Politics* was the first large-scale articulation of a constructivist research paradigm,[72] it is identity and ideas that are the keys to understanding international behaviour. Anarchy, Wendt argued, was not a constant phenomenon, or even close to universally understood. Instead it was what states made of it, which left room for different interpretations of how the games of international relations was played out, for different constructions of regional and world order, and for states to adopt different foreign and security policies, shaped by a variety of external, transnational and internal stimuli.[73]

Because constructivists view national interests as the product of a state's identity, they argue that interests and identity are mutually constituted.[74] A state's national security policy is therefore the product of its socialisation experience, of important domestic historical and cultural totems, and its political and strategic culture. Within the complex world of international interaction different discourses on world order, security and foreign policy intersect to produce often very different interpretations of what is important in the formulation of national security agendas. Shaped by their identity and ideas, states can adopt numerous forms of security policy that might be militaristic, Hobbesian, liberal, post-Westphalian or many others.[75] Theirs views on international law and human rights might be universalist or cosmopolitan.[76] The issues that are securitised in their policies are the product of discursive practice, becoming speech acts that are then incorporated into policy.

The breadth and scale of constructivism makes it potentially of use in explaining a variety of security phenomena, including those issues that are typically described as falling into 'grey area' or 'non-traditional' domains. The reflexive approach of constructivists means they do not view the state as fixed, or factors such as anarchy as iron laws of international relations. Instead constructivists focus on the role of multiple agents in international politics, from international institutions to participants in civil wars, refugees and individuals themselves.[77] To make sense of this, constructivists also highlight the role of norms in governing behaviour, which actors with a given identity tend to associate themselves with,[78] and which can be subject to change as different societies alter their views of what kind of behaviour is acceptable. Norms can be constitutive, creating new actors, or prescriptive. They can also be regulatory, guiding and conditioning behaviour based on what is deemed legitimate or illegitimate within a given group of actors. Norms diffuse transnationally, teaching states how to behave based on how international organisations structure their preferences.[79] Once a tipping point on how norms are observed is reached, they then cascade throughout international society, engendering wider compliance.[80]

From this perspective, European integration can be understood as an iterative process linked to identity that gained momentum as actors across Europe realised that cooperation was better than centuries of bloodshed. But constructivists also seek to explain 'traditional' security issues as products of socialisation. Nuclear non-use, for instance, is a leading example for constructivists of the power of norms, where the empirical fact that states have not used nuclear weapons since 1945 demonstrates that it is not acceptable or legitimate to do so.[81] Similar arguments can be made here around evolving norms on issues like the proscription of terrorist groups; the de-legitimisation of sexual violence and the trafficking of people; and the creation of norms in favour of robust action on human rights and climate change.[82]

Viewed in this way, constructivism provides national security practitioners with a variety of tools to understand how different actors behave, chart processes of change and predict which identities and norms are likely to become dominant in future. It can help shed light on the evolution of nationalistic discourses within a particular society to show how identities change over time; explain why some states are more war-prone than others; and highlight the reasons why people turn to violence through processes of radicalisation. By the same token it can identify normative arguments that appeal to particular cultures over others, and prescribe ways to ameliorate conflict through learning and discourse.

This said, constructivism has also been the target of significant criticism from established theories of international relations. Its emphasis on identity and ideas can produce research based on highly subjective judgements, and completely contradictory claims about which norms are changing (and how) can be made with the same data. It is also the case that constructivism can lend itself more readily to cartoonish depictions of state's foreign and security policies based on stereotypes about national character, myths and motivations. And by treating agents and structures as mutually constituted it raises the question of how far up and how far down ideas and identities go in determining which norms become dominant, and why others do not. Liberals argue here that constructivists create a self-fulfilling prophecy: that one can find norms, ideas and identity wherever one looks, but it is far harder to prove conclusively that they shape behaviour and interaction. Realists in particular charge that what states claim to be norms are often just more pragmatic interests being instrumentalised—in other words, masquerading as 'good behaviour'.[83] They also note that ideas tend to change when power and structural forces compel them to (that actors adopt new identities based on how much material capacity they have at their disposal). In the landmark example of the end of the Cold War, for instance, the ideas and identity of Gorbachev's USSR altered with the realisation that the Soviet Union was bankrupt—in other words its power had declined—and was forced to seek an exit from costly bipolar confrontation.[84]

FROM THEORY TO PRACTICE: CASE STUDIES ON MAJOR NATIONAL SECURITY ISSUES

Having outlined the general worldviews of each major conceptual approach, the question arises: in what specific ways do various theories of international relations explain major issues on states' national security agendas? Below the chapter evaluates three case studies that have been pressing security concerns, and are likely to continue to require states to respond. Although there are many potential candidates for review the chapter deliberately selects a security problem where the agents are non-state actors; a security challenge of global importance that crosses state boundaries; and a more traditional national security issue based on structural change in the international system. What should be particularly instructive here is that realism, constructivism and liberalism each offer very different interpretations of the root causes of these issues, as well as what policymakers might do to address them.

The Global War on Terror

After the events of 9/11, a plethora of explanations were offered for the rise of transnational terrorism. In particular, Samuel Huntington's 'Clash of Civilisations' thesis returned to prominence after having earlier been dismissed in the mid-1990s.[85] Huntington postulated that conflict was increasingly about faith and family, and blood and belief—and that the broadest level at which people identify was within civilisations. Civilisations were bound to clash, he argued, when they were based on fundamentally incompatible principles, and the chief candidate here was for a looming conflict between Islamic civilisation and the Judeo-Christian civilisation of the West. And although many commentators rejected Huntington's thesis as being too broad, a self-fulfilling prophecy, or even xenophobic,[86] it continued to have an impact on the way international relations theorists responded to the subsequent War on Terror, if only to highlight how more mainstream approaches differed from it.

Here liberal explanations saw 9/11 in terms of root causes that were linked to economics, and the US response as a test of liberal hegemony. A lack of economic opportunity in the Middle East, it was claimed, had created a generation of people who resented the power and wealth of the West, and fundamentally rejected it.[87] For liberals the turn to radical religion was an understandable response from those who felt marginalised and hopeless, especially considering that they had often received poor treatment at the hands of illiberal local elites. For other liberals focused on what to do about the root causes of transnational terrorism, the key was to foster opportunity and development in these fractured societies. But others took this further, arguing that it was the moral duty of the United States as the unipolar actor, in concert with the West, to spread democracy to regimes that fostered radicalism and persecuted their people, using force if necessary. This became a cornerstone of US policy under the neoconservative Bush administration, supported by others such as Tony Blair, in justifying attempts to make the world 'safe for democracy'.

Realists, on the other hand, were almost unanimous in their condemnation of both the liberal diagnosis and the response to it by US neoconservatives.[88] They pointed out that since the threat of terrorism was not sufficient to threaten the survival of the United States, it was a second-order threat that would be made worse by a global war on terror. In lumping together all grievances concerning Muslims as part of a global struggle—many of which had highly local origins and little to do with religion—realists argued that the Bush administration was magnifying the risk of new attacks.[89] They also observed that economics seemed to have little to do with the 9/11 attacks, which were carried out by well-educated members of the elite and middle class, especially in Saudi Arabia. And they fundamentally disagreed with the promotion of democracy by force, seeing it as a national security overreaction driven by ideology and popular passions rather than the national interest. Instead, they argued that the war on terror was in fact becoming a war against threats to American interests, since many of the justifications used by the Bush administration for its actions—like the invasion of Iraq, for instance—were based on flimsy pretexts about state support for terrorism.[90] The upshot, realists argued, was that the war on terror would upset local power balances in the Middle East, alienate those hostile to the West even further and become little more than an attempt by the United States to maintain its hegemonic position.[91]

Constructivist readings of the war on terror were fundamentally different from both realist and liberal interpretations, although they tended to pick up on similar themes. Stressing the importance of radicalised identities, constructivists saw the emergence of radical Islam as a fundamental rejection of Western values, and of US hegemony. Reflecting on how narratives gained traction in

Islamic societies, a number of studies traced the rise of Wahhabism and the strongly anti-American writings of Sayeed Qutb as influential in creating a view of a hegemonic and decadent West.[92] Examining how discursive practice emerged from these origins, constructivists also sought to demonstrate how Al Qaeda's loose cell-based structure could be adapted to local conditions while still being consistent with the notion of a broader struggle to restore traditional conservative Islamic values. Others took the war on terror as an example of so-called new wars that—in contrast to wars of the past—were based on radical identities, new economics, new modes of conflict and new actors.[93] Yet while constructivists added much to the richness of explanations for the war on terror, their prescriptions were less persuasive. Critics responded that there was little new in terms of why terrorists sought to fight, and that constructivist solutions (which consisted of fostering understanding between peoples as well as global cosmopolitan international law) were both unworkable and impossible to operationalise in a world still dominated by states that pursued more pragmatic interests.[94]

What is instructive about this case is that each view provides some useful clarity to both causes and solutions, each is also missing important detail. For example, while many realist critiques of the war on terror might seem persuasive, realism itself does not account for the threat of transnational terrorism in the first place. As a theory of international interaction where the sole (or at least dominant) actor is the state, realists struggle to locate terrorism within a national security paradigm that ensures the state protects its citizens from harm. And while constructivist explanations for the causes of 9/11 are often helpful, their prescriptions seem to overplay the strength of cosmopolitan norms in promoting peace and stability. Finally, laying aside the appropriateness of spreading democracy by force, liberals are correct to point to economic factors as a leading cause of conflict. However, the follow-on effects of civil war and social dislocation in Iraq, for instance, suggest that the international community has been less than successful in state building.[95]

Climate Change

The prospect of global warming, the melting of polar ice-caps and rising sea levels is increasingly receiving attention from national security policymakers, acknowledging that the science on climate change is more or less settled. What is less clear is how (or indeed whether) states will be able to respond to this global problem. Because realism is a theory of how states behave in the international system, realists have tended to focus on how states will respond to its effects, and tend to offer a fairly gloomy prognosis. To begin with they identify climate change as a potential cause of future conflict.[96] Shifts in rainfall patterns that accompany climate change will affect food production and the livelihoods of many, as well as access to reliable supplies of freshwater. This could prompt economic disruption and the movement of people into less affected areas, while rising sea levels will result in large numbers of climate change refugees. Some states will respond with harder border protection measures, while those who admit too many refugees risk weakness and internal conflict. Others will judge that securing food and water outweighs the costs of violence, raising the prospect of water wars and food wars.[97] And for realists, global attempts to arrest the pace of climate change are likely to be stymied by states that seek to cheat on international obligations; use their participation as a vehicle for virtue-signalling or to berate others; or simply opt out of climate action altogether.[98]

Liberal approaches to climate change see it as a key test for global governance in overcoming the temptation of states to cheat on their commitments. Stressing the importance of the global climate change regime in helping to reshape patterns of international behaviour, they see climate action through epistemic communities as contributing to a vital global good.[99] The increasing tendency for states to codify their responses to climate change into international law and regulatory mechanisms via the IPCC, building on the Kyoto Protocol and the Montreal Protocol, is proof positive for liberals that international cooperation can ameliorate the negative effects of an anarchical international system. So too is the adoption of emissions mitigation targets, cap-and-trade systems and the creation of a market for carbon, underscoring the liberal argument that positive habits of cooperation can result from collective action on global problems. Liberals also worry that efforts to combat climate change can negatively affect economic development. But this also plays into realist arguments about cheating, in which small states that are large emitters (such as Singapore) benefit from categorising themselves as developing states, and therefore receive extra emission credits. Moreover, without the large-scale cooperation of major powers such as the United States, it remains to be seen whether this will be effective in reducing the overall effects of climate change.

For constructivists, responses to climate change are indicative at the top level of how norms are adopted as a result of the development of widespread communities of understanding.[100] Although the process of norm uptake and diffusion has been patchy, many constructivists nonetheless remain optimistic about the prospects for concerted global action since responding to climate change is increasingly becoming securitised, although—like realists—they also warn about the potential for progress to be hijacked. In particular, constructivists have sought to explain why states take the positions they do in international climate negotiations as part of their attempts to investigate how agents and structures behave. They have noted that domestic populations can be swayed against accepting the reality of climate change when it is linked through discourse to political affiliation and tribalism rather than science.[101] In the United States, for instance, it can be argued that climate change has become politicised in the same way as gun control and abortion, reinforcing identities that seek to push back against assumptions about 'big government' and higher taxation to pay for climate mitigation.[102] At the same time, the presence of sceptics about climate change in the decision-making apparatus of states creates a feedback loop of incentives, whereby both leaders and followers have interests in reinforcing a hostile view.

Like the example of the war on terror, responses by leading theories of international relations to the threat of climate change offer both clarity and confusion. Realism's emphasis on competing interests, cheating and the prospects for conflict should serve as a useful reminder to national security policymakers that no matter how damaging a long-range concern climate change may be, it is frequently filtered through the prism of state interests and associated with power. Since states are the main respondents in climate change mitigation, their intentions and choices are therefore vital. This holds for constructivist and liberal interpretations too. While there is definitely solid evidence that combatting climate change is progressively becoming integrated into states' security agendas, the normative suasion (in the case of constructivist views) and the legal-regulatory effectiveness (in the case of liberal ones) of climate change mitigation remains an open question.

Shifts in Global Order: The Rise of China and the Relative Decline of the United States

As would be expected for a theory of power and interests, the shifting regional and global order is a strong aspect of realist scholarship. Some of this focuses on US security policy choices, chiefly concerning whether Washington should maintain its deep engagement in the Asia-Pacific (and elsewhere), adopt an offshore balancing role or pivot to a more isolationist posture.[103] Other contributions have addressed questions of geopolitical and geo-economic order under conditions of US retrenchment, and the implications of China's rise for the hedge-and-balance postures of many US regional allies.[104] The implications of the Trump presidency—for US power, and for America's alliance networks—has similarly been a topic embraced by realist scholarship. On China itself, realists debate whether the PRC has the wherewithal to construct a viable post-liberal order through its ambitious Belt and Road Initiative; what a Sino-centric order might look like; what role smaller powers might play in mediating great power competition; and whether we are about to witness a new form of bipolarity, multipolarity or even non-polarity.[105]

Liberals have also sought to tackle the theme of changing order, although their prescriptions tend to revolve around the need for economic interdependence in the Sino-US relationship to act as a brake on conflict, as well as the importance of binding a potentially revisionist China within the existing liberal rules-based order.[106] In security affairs, liberals have sought to champion nascent attempts to form coalitions of like-minded states (especially amongst liberal democracies) in competition with the PRC.[107] This is not just to perform power-balancing functions, but also to embed regulatory and legal codes of conduct in maritime Asia, to guard against the potential for Chinese dominance of connectivity and digital technologies through rules and safeguards to combat the theft and manipulation of data, and by strengthening international law as it pertains to cyberspace.[108] Particularly within democratic nations, as well as with an eye to protecting weaker actors that may be tempted by Chinese investment, liberals have warned of the dangers of 'debt-trap diplomacy', as well as the need to secure critical infrastructure and inoculate societies against threats of foreign interference.[109] The failure of the liberal project to socialise China has been a sore point for many liberals here, who have responded by pivoting to examine how liberal states can strengthen themselves, as well as assessing the extent of centralised control wielded by the CCP over Chinese politics, society and economics.

Although the fragmentation of the West and the rise of new nationalist identities has been a central feature of constructivist scholarship on changing order, increasing attention has been paid by constructivists to the nature of Chinese identity in international society. A number of studies in this respect examine China's troubled history with the West, and specifically its desire to build a strong China in the aftermath of the Hundred Year Humiliation.[110] Combining Confucianism with Maoist ideology, and more recently the era of 'Xi Xinping thought', constructivists have south to trace China's shifts in identity to accommodate statism, managed capitalism and increasing nationalism in its complex internal discourses on its place in the world.[111] Others, like Alistair Ian Johnston, have examined Chinese responses to notions of socially constructed orders in international relations, assessing its strategic culture and challenging the notion that it is a revisionist power.[112] And still other constructivist contributions have examined how Chinese ideational preferences shape the behaviour of its trade partners, as well as international institutions. Constructivists have also applauded the emergence of Chinese interpretations of international relations, noting that the Western-centric nature of the discipline had led to an overemphasis on Eurocentric norms, practices and institutions.[113] Like realists, constructivists have challenged the idea of a 'liberal' rules-based order, asking how liberal it really is—and whether it can even be said to exist.

Like the two previous examples above, the issue of changing global and regional order reveals profound differences as well as commonalities in liberal, realist and constructivist worldviews. But international order is a fast-changing phenomenon, and many of the current attempts to chart its trajectory and likely outcomes will fare poorly with the benefit of hindsight. Yet this also serves to highlight one of the challenges involved in applying international relations scholarship to current-day national security policy practice: whether it is realist, liberal or constructivist assessments of a particular contemporary issue that might appear more persuasive, it is often the case that the course of events later leads to fundamentally different conclusions in the future.

CONCLUSIONS

International relations theory can be both useful and problematic for the practice of national security. On the one hand it provides security policy professionals with competing ways to understand long-term patterns of inter-action, threats, the rise and fall of major powers, the role of non-state actors, and how states and international societies reconstruct themselves over time. But on the other hand it highlights the risks involved in allowing theory to become the driver of policy responses. For instance, the tendency amongst national security planners to refer to a state as pursuing a 'realist' or a 'lib-eral' security policy may be convenient, but is also a potential pitfall. It would be rare indeed that the totality of a state's decision-making apparatus becomes so captured by one theoretical approach that it can be said to drive its behaviour. Investing theory with agency in this way is therefore something that many international relations theorists would be uncomfortable with. Indeed, national security policies are the products of many departments and many hands, some influential and others much less so, and this often varies consider-ably over time. It may well be that some states seem to act in a manner more reminiscent of *realpolitik* than others, just as it might equally be the case that other states appear far more rules-bound. Explaining whether this is a product of structures, agents, internal discourses, interests or identities is certainly a job for international relations theory, but should not be relied upon by national security policy professionals as ironclad indicators of behaviour.

Second, because theory is a form of shorthand or worldview built on assumptions, it therefore describes ideal types rather than messy reality. Even the most ardent realist, for instance, would acknowledge that social and cultural phenomena have an impact on how actors behave in international rela-tions, just as many constructivists will worry that power and interest models can sometimes explain national security risks and challenges more neatly than identity and norms. But mixing and melding assumptions in the real world has far more dramatic consequences than in academic study. Whereas a student is likely to get marked down for claiming that realism explains the UN better but liberalism is better at explaining the EU, basing national security on cherry-picked aspects of international relations theory risks misdiagnosing problems, being inconsistent with application of findings, and ultimately selecting a harmful policy prescription.

Third, it should be noted that international relations theory has a poor track record when it comes to prediction. This is something the discipline continues to struggle with, and should also sound a note of caution to national security policy planners about being too reliant on the expectations of a partic-ular paradigm. And, as detailed in this chapter, the breadth and scope of each of the major theoretical approaches to international relations means that one can often find diametrically opposed findings within the one tradition of scholarship.

Even with these caveats, though, the study of international relations offers much to the national security policy practitioner. It provides multiple tools for unpacking pressing current security problems, as well as learning from past ones. Regardless of whether it embraces a positivist (realism and liberalism) or reflexivist (constructivism) ontology, each combines rich empirical detail with well-demonstrated observations about opportunities and threats in the international security landscape. And in a globalised era where risks and dangers to national security can often seem overwhelming, international relations theorists and national security policy makers have a common purpose: to better understand the increasingly complex nature of world affairs, and successfully navigate a path through it.

NOTES

1. Bruce Jentleson. 2002. 'The Need for Praxis: Bringing Policy Relevance Back In', *International Security*, 26 (4), pp. 169–183.
2. Bruce Russett, Harvey Starr and David Kinsella. 2010. *World Politics: The Menu for Choice*, Wadsworth: Cengage.
3. Barry Buzan. 1991. *People, States and Fear*, London: Harvester Wheatsheaf, p. 36.
4. Melvyn Leffler. 1990. 'National Security', *Journal of American History*, 77 (1), pp. 143–152 (p. 143).
5. Fareed Zakaria, 1992. 'Realism and Domestic Politics', *International Security* 17 (1), pp. 177–198. See also Jack Snyder, 1991. *Myths of Empire: Domestic Politics and International Ambition*, New York: Cornell University Press.
6. On sovereignty and legitimate violence, see Charley Tilly. 1975. *The Formation of National States in Western Europe*, Princeton: Princeton University Press; Max Weber, 1948. 'Politics as a Vocation' in Hans H. Gerth and Charles W. Mills (eds. & transl) *From Max Weber: Essays in Sociology* (New York City, NY, USA: Oxford University Press), 77–128; and Philipp Lottholz and Nicolas Lemay-Hébert. 2016. 'Re-reading Weber, Re-conceptualizing State-Building: From Neo-Weberian to Post-Weberian Approaches to State, Legitimacy and State-Building', *Cambridge Review of International Affairs*, 29 (4), pp. 1467–1485.
7. George Lawson, 2016. 'The Rise of Modern International Order', in John Baylis and Steve Smith (eds.), *The Globalization of World Politics*, Oxford: Oxford University Press.
8. Kenneth Waltz, 1996. 'International Relations Is Not Foreign Policy', *Security Studies* 6 (1), pp. 54–57.
9. See, for instance, Tim Dunne and Nicholas Wheeler, 2004. 'We the Peoples: Contending Discourses of Security in Human Rights Theory and Practice', *International Relations*, 18 (1), pp. 9–23.
10. On securitisation, see Barry Buzan, Ole Wæver, and Jaap de Wilde. 1998. *Security: A New Framework for Analysis*, Boulder: Lynne Reiner; and Ole Waever, 1995. 'Securitization and Desecuritization', in Ronnie D. Lipschutz (ed.) *On Security*, NY: Columbia University Press, pp. 46–86.
11. Kenneth Waltz, 1979. *Theory of International Politics*. New York: McGraw-Hill, p. 91.
12. On this point, see, for instance, Hal Brands, 1999. 'The Idea of the National Interest', *Diplomacy and Statecraft*, 23 (2), pp. 239–261.
13. David Chandler, 2013. 'Promoting Democratic Norms? Social Constructivism and the "Subjective" Limits to Liberalism', *Democratization*, 20 (2), pp. 215–239.

14. See, for example, Jack Donnelly, 1984. 'Cultural Relativism and Human Rights', *Human Rights Quarterly*, 6 (4), pp. 400–419; Michael Goodhart, 2002. 'Origins and Universality in the Human Rights Debates: Cultural Essentialism and the Challenge of Globalization', *Human Rights Quarterly*, 25 (4), pp. 935–961; Anthony J. Langlois, 2001. *The Politics of Justice and Human Rights: Southeast Asia and Universalist Theory*, Cambridge: Cambridge University Press; and Peter Baehr, 2016. *Human Rights: University in Practice*, Houndmills, Basingstoke: Palgrave, pp. 9–19.
15. On this, see Anatol Lieven, 2012. *America Right or Wrong: An Anatomy of American Nationalism.* London: Oxford University Press; and William Walker, 2009. *National Security and Core Values in American History.* New York: Cambridge University Press.
16. For instance, Christopher Layne, 2000. 'US Hegemony and the Perpetuation of NATO', *Journal of Strategic Studies*, 23 (3), pp. 59–91.
17. Anne-Marie Slaughter, Andrew S. Tulumello and Stepan Wood, 1998. 'International Law and International Relations Theory: A New Generation of Interdisciplinary Scholarship', *The American Journal of International Law*, 92 (3), pp. 367–397.
18. Stephen Krasner, 2000. 'International Law and International Relations: Together, Apart, Together?', *Chicago Journal of International Law* 1 (1), pp. 93–100.
19. Michael Wesley, 2005. 'It's Time to Scrap the NPT', *Australian Journal of International Affairs*, 59 (3), pp. 283–299.
20. For example Alex J. Bellamy, 2008. 'The Responsibility to Protect and the Problem of Military Intervention', *International Affairs*, 84 (4), pp. 615–639.
21. Nicholas J. Wheeler, 2000. 'Humanitarian Vigilantes or Legal Entrepreneurs: Enforcing Human Rights in International Society', *Critical Review of International Social and Political Philosophy*, 3 (1), pp. 139–162.
22. Stephen Krasner, 1999. *Sovereignty: Organized Hypocrisy*, Baltimore: Johns Hopkins University Press.
23. For an excellent summary of Carr's views on power, see John Mearsheimer, 2005. 'E.H. Carr Versus Idealism: The Battle Rages On', *International Relations*, 19 (2), pp. 139–152. The classical realist Hans Morgenthau saw also culture as a significant vehicle for expansionist state policies. As he put it, cultural imperialism was 'the most subtle and, if it were ever to succeed by itself alone, the most successful of imperialistic policies'. Thus, Morgenthau stated, the imposition of culture and ideology on a vanquished nation would cement its position 'on more stable grounds than any military conqueror or economic master. See Hans J. Morgenthau, 1993. *Politics Among Nations: The Struggle for Power and Peace* (Brief Edition), New York: McGraw Hill, p. 72.
24. See the chapter on the elements of national power in Hans Morgenthau, 1977. *Politics Among Nations: The Struggle for Peace and Power*, 5th ed. New York: Alfred A. Knopf.
25. See chapter 4 of John Mearsheimer, 2001. *The Tragedy of Great Power Politics*, New York: W.W. Norton.
26. Joseph Nye, 1990. *Bound to Lead: The Changing Nature of American Power*, London: Basic Books. See also chapter 4 on wielding soft power in Joseph

Nye, 2004. *Soft Power: The Means to Success in World Politics*, New York: Public Affairs. For a more critical view, see Eric Li, 2018. 'The Rise and Fall of Soft Power', *Foreign Policy*, August 20. https://foreignpolicy.com/2018/08/20/the-rise-and-fall-of-soft-power/.

27. On smart power see Joseph Nye, 2009. 'Get Smart: Combining Hard and Soft Power', *Foreign Affairs*, July/August. https://www.foreignaffairs.com/articles/2009-07-01/get-smart. For 'sharp' power, see Christopher Walker, 2018. 'What Is Sharp Power?', *Journal of Democracy*, 29 (3), pp. 9–23.

28. Nye, 1990. *Bound to Lead*, p. 52.

29. Hedley Bull, 1977. *The Anarchical Society*, New York: Columbia University Press, p. 64.

30. See the extensive debates on the end of the liberal order: for instance, John Ikenberry, 2018. 'The End of Liberal International Order?', *International Affairs*, 94 (1) (January), pp. 7–23; Thomas Wright, 2018. 'The Return to Great Power Rivalry Was Inevitable', *The Atlantic*, September 12. https://www.theatlantic.com/international/archive/2018/09/liberal-international-order-free-world-trump-authoritarianism/569881/; Stephen Walt, 2018. 'Why I Didn't Sign Up to Defend the International Order', *Foreign Policy*, August 1. https://foreignpolicy.com/2018/08/01/why-i-didnt-sign-up-to-defend-the-international-order/; and Patrick Porter, 'A World Imagined: Nostalgia and Liberal Order', *CATO Institute Policy Analysis*, no. 843. https://www.cato.org/publications/policy-analysis/world-imagined-nostalgia-liberal-order.

31. For instance, Zheng Bijian, 2005. 'China's "Peaceful Rise" to Great-Power Status', *Foreign Affairs*, 84: 18; Weifeng Zhou and Mario Esteban, 2018. 'Beyond Balancing: China's Approach Towards the Belt and Road Initiative', *Journal of Contemporary China*, 27 (112), pp. 487–501; and William A. Callahan, 2016. 'China's "Asia Dream": The Belt and Road Initiative and the New Regional Order', *Asian Journal of Comparative Politics*, 15 (1), pp. 1–18.

32. Justin T. Locke, 2009. 'Climate Change-Induced Migration in the Pacific Region', *The Geographical Journal*, 175 (3), pp. 171–180.

33. David Chandler, 2009. 'Resilience', chapter 40 in Miryam Dunn Cavelty and Thierry Balzacq, eds. *Routledge Handbook of Security Studies*; London: Routledge.

34. Christian Fjäder, 2014. 'The Nation-State, National Security and Resilience in the Age of Globalisation', *Resilience*, 2 (2), pp. 114–129.

35. David Blagden, 2018. 'The Flawed Promise of National Security Risk Assessment: Nine Lessons from the British APPROACH', *Intelligence and National Security*, 33 (5), pp. 716–736.

36. On RSCT see Barry Buzan and Ole Waever, 2003. *Regions and Powers: The Structure of International Society*, Cambridge: Cambridge University Press.

37. The leading work from the Welsh school of world security is Ken Booth, 2007. *Theory of World Security*, Cambridge: Cambridge University Press.

38. On the English School, see, for example, Andrew Linklater and Hidemi Suganami, 2009. *The English School of International Relations: A Contemporary Reassessment*, Cambridge: Cambridge University Press; Richard Little, 2000. 'The English School's Contribution to the Study of International Relations', *European Journal of International Relations*, 6 (3), pp. 395–422.

Interestingly, one of the first times the English School was mentioned was in a call for it to be disbanded. See Roy Jones, 1981. 'The English School: A Case for Closure', *Review of International Studies*, 7 (1), pp. 1–13.

39. See, for example, Christopher Browning and Matt McDonald, 2013. 'The Future of Critical Security Studies: Ethics and the Politics of Security', *European Journal of International Relations*, 19 (2), pp. 235–255.

40. This said, no other major approach to international relations predicted it either—but it is a telling criticism of neorealism that a theory based on explaining systems of international relations offered no early insight about when the system was about to change. See, for instance, Richard Ned Lebow and Thomas Risse-Kappan (eds), *International Relations Theory and the End of the Cold War*. New York: Columbia University Press.

41. See Kenneth Waltz, 1994. 'Realist Thought and Neorealist Theory', in Charles Kegley (ed), *Controversies in International Relations Theory: Realism and the Neoliberal Challenge*, London, Basingstoke: Palgrave, pp. 67–82; Silviya Lechner, 2017. 'Why Anarchy Still Matters for International Relations: On Theory and Things', *Journal of International Political Theory*, 13 (3), pp. 341–359.

42. This was the term coined by Clausewitz and used frequently to describe armed conflict. Carl von Clausewitz, 1982. *On War*, London: Penguin Classics.

43. Jeffrey W. Taliaferro, 2006. 'Security Seeking Under Anarchy: Defensive Realism Revisited', *International Security*, 25 (3), pp. 128–261.

44. Glenn Snyder, 2002. 'Mearsheimer's World: Offensive Realism and the Struggle for Security', *International Security*, 27 (1), pp. 149–173.

45. Chris Brown, 2009. 'Structural Realism, Classical Realism and Human Nature', *International Relations*, 23 (2), pp. 257–270.

46. Owen Harries and Michael Lind, 1993. 'Realism and Its Rivals', *National Interest*, December. https://nationalinterest.org/article/realism-and-its-rivals-952.

47. Glenn Snyder, 1990. 'Alliance Theory: A Neorealist First Cut', *Journal of International Affairs*, 44 (1), pp. 103–123.

48. Robert Jervis, 1978. 'Cooperation Under the Security Dilemma', *World Politics*, 30 (2), pp. 167–214.

49. Morgenthau, *Politics Among Nations,* pp. 567–568.

50. John Lewis Gaddis, 1986. 'The Long Peace: Elements of Stability in the Postwar International System', *International Security*, 10 (4), pp. 99–142.

51. Ibid.

52. Jack Levy, 1998. 'The Causes of War and the Conditions of Peace', *Annual Review of Political Science*, 1, pp. 139–165.

53. Here it is important to distinguish between balancing (as a foreign policy strategy) versus balance of power (as a condition in which power is balanced).

54. Schweller, 1994. 'Bandwagoning for Profit: Bringing the Revisionist State Back In', *International Security*, 19 (1), pp. 73–107; and Robert Jervis and Jack Snyder, eds., *Dominoes and Bandwagons: Strategic Beliefs and Great Power Competition in the Eurasian Rimland* (New York: Oxford University Press, 1991).

55. Kei Koga, 2018. 'The Concept of "Hedging" Revisited: The Case of Japan's Foreign Policy Strategy in East Asia's Power Shift', *International Studies Review*, 20 (4), pp. 633–660.

56. See David Kang, 2004. 'Hierarchy, Balancing, and Empirical Puzzles in Asian International Relations', *International Security*, 28:3, pp. 165–180; and David Kang, 2003. 'Getting Asia Wrong: The Need for New Analytical Frameworks', *International Security*, 27 (4), pp. 57–85.

57. On balance of threat see Stephen Walt, 1985. 'Alliance Formation and the Balance of World Power', *International Security*, 9 (4), pp. 3–43.

58. John Mearsheimer, for instance, argues that great powers can only be regional hegemons, not global ones. See Mearsheimer, 2001. *The Tragedy of Great Powers*, p. 33.

59. For instance, Robert Jervis, 1982. 'Security Regimes', *International Organization*, 36 (2), pp. 357–378.

60. For more on neoclassical realism as a theory of foreign policy, see William Wohlforth, 1993. *The Elusive Balance: Power and Perception During the Cold War*, Ithaca: Cornell University Press; Gideon Rose, 1998. 'Neoclassical Realism and Theories of Foreign Policy,' *World Politics*, 51 (1), pp. 144–172; and Steven Lobell, Norris Ripsman and Jennifer Taliaferro (eds) 2009. *Neoclassical Realism, the State and Foreign Policy*, Cambridge: Cambridge University Press.

61. On this, see, for example, Jennifer Sterling-Folker, 1997. 'Realist Environment, Liberal Process and Domestic-Level Variables,' *International Studies Quarterly*, 41 (1), pp. 1–25.

62. For an excellent summary that is still relevant today, see Michael Doyle, 1986. 'Liberalism and World Politics', *American Political Science Review*, 80 (4), pp. 1151–1169.

63. This has led them to be unkindly branded as realists 'by any other name'. See John Mearsheimer, 1995. 'A Realist REPLY', *International Security*, 20 (1), pp. 82–93.

64. Daniel Deudney and John Ikenberry, 1999. 'The Nature and Sources of Liberal International Order', *Review of International Studies*, 25 (2), pp. 179–196.

65. Joseph Grieco, 1996. 'Anarchy and the Limits of Cooperation: A Realist Critique of the Newest Liberal Institutionalism", in Charles Kegley (ed.), *Controversies in International Relations Theory*, pp. 151–171.

66. John Oneal, Frances Oneal, Zeev Maoz, and Bruce Russett, 1996. 'The Liberal Peace: Interdependence, Democracy, and International Conflict, 1950–85'. *Journal of Peace Research*, 33 (1), pp. 11–28.

67. Ibid.

68. See, for instance, Michael C. Wiliams, 2001. 'The Discipline of the Democratic Peace: Kant, Liberalism and the Social Construction of Security Communities', *European Journal of International Relations*, 7 (4), pp. 525–553; Steve Chan, 1984. 'Mirror, Mirror on the Wall...: Are the Freer Countries More Pacific?', *Journal of Conflict Resolution*, 28 (4), pp. 617–648; and Bruce Russet, 1994. *Grasping the Democratic Peace*, Princeton: Princeton University Press.

69. Frances Fukuyama, 2006. *The End of History and the Last Man*, New York: Free Press.

70. Alan Kuperman, 2008. 'The Moral Hazard of Humanitarian Intervention: Lessons from the Balkans', *International Studies Quarterly*, 52 (1), pp. 49–80.

71. Brian Schmidt and Michael C. Williams, 2008. 'The Bush Doctrine and the Iraq War: Neoconservatives Versus Realists', *Security Studies*, 17 (2), pp. 191–220.
72. Alexander Wendt, 1999. *Social Theory of International Politics*, Cambridge: Cambridge University Press.
73. Alexander Wendt, 1992. 'Anarchy Is What States Make of It: The Social Construction of Power Politics', *International Organization*, 46 (2), pp. 391–425.
74. Alexander Wendt, 1994. 'Collective Identity Formation and the International State', *American Political Science Review*, 88 (2), pp. 384–396.
75. Christian Kreuder-Sonnen and Bernhard Zangl, 2015. 'Which Post-Westphalia? International Organizations Between Constitutionalism and Authoritarianism', *European Journal of International Relations*, 21 (3), pp. 568–594.
76. Craig Calhoun, 2003. 'Belonging in the Cosmopolitan Imaginary', *Ethnicities*, 3 (4), pp. 531–553.
77. Mary Kaldor, 2013. 'In Defence of New Wars', *Stability: International Journal of Security and Development*, 2 (1), pp. 1–14.
78. A landmark work in this respect is Peter J. Katzenstein (ed.), 1996. *The Culture of National Security*, New York: Columbia University Press.
79. Martha Finnemore and Kathryn Sikkink, 1998. 'International Norm Dynamics and Political Change', *International Organization*, 52 (4), pp. 887–917.
80. Ibid.
81. See, for instance, T. V. Paul, 2010. 'Taboo or Tradition? The Non-Use of Nuclear Weapons in World Politics', *Review of International Studies*, 36 (4), pp. 853–863.
82. Peter Haas, 2004. 'When Does Power Listen to Truth? A Constructivist Approach to the Policy Process', *Journal of European Public Policy*, 11 (4), pp. 569–592.
83. John Mearsheimer, 1995. 'A Realist Reply', p. 88.
84. Stephen Brooks and William Wohlforth, 2001. 'Power, Globalisation and the End of the Cold War: Re-evaluating a Landmarks Test Case for Ideas', *International Security*, 25 (3), pp. 5–53.
85. See Samuel Huntington, 1996. *The Clash of Civilisations and the Remaking of World Order*, New York: Simon & Schuster; and also his earlier 1993 article 'The Clash of Civilisations?', *Foreign Affairs*, 72 (3), pp. 23–49.
86. After Huntington's article was published, the subsequent edition of *Foreign Affairs* saw a number of responses. Robert Bartly, amongst others, argued that the greatest potential for conflict was within rather than between civilisations. This point was reinforced by Jeanne Kirkpatrick, who argued that the primary targets for fundamentalist Muslims were their own governments. Fouad Ajami saw Huntington's work as a dangerous rallying call to the right wing in the West, and Albert Weekes noted that Huntington had reignited the debate between 'microcosmic' and 'macrocosmic' forces in international relations, but rejected the idea of a 'civilization' controlling world politics. Only Kishore Mahbubani was relatively complimentary towards Huntington, suggesting that the West had become blind to internal institutional weaknesses. See Robert Bartly, 'The Case for Optimism'; Jeanne Kirkpatrick, 'The

Modernizing Imperative'; Fouad Ajami, 'The Summoning'; Albert Weeks, 'Do Civilizations Hold?'; and Kishore Mahbubani, 'The Dangers of Decadence', all in *Foreign Affairs*, 72 (4), 1993. Later critics focused on the issue of 'Globalization as Westernization'. See, for instance, John Ikenberry et al., 1997. 'The West: Precious Not Unique', *Foreign Affairs*, 76 (2), pp. 162–165.

87. This is a contentious argument; see, for instance, Michael Freeman, 2008. 'Democracy, Al Qaeda, and the Causes of Terrorism: A Strategic Analysis of U.S. Policy', *Studies in Conflict & Terrorism*, 31 (1), pp. 40–59; and James Fearon and David Laitin, 2003.'Ethnicity, Insurgency, and Civil War,' *American Political Science Review*, 97 (1), pp. 75–90.

88. See Schmidt and Williams, 2008. 'The Bush Doctrine and the Iraq War', pp. 191–220.

89. Daniel Deudney and John Ikenberry, 2017. 'Realism, Liberalism and the Iraq War', *Survival*, 59 (4), pp. 7–26.

90. For example Trevor Thrall and Eric Goepner, 2017. 'Step Back: Lessons for US Policy from the Failed War on Terror', *CATO Institute Policy Analysis*, 814.

91. A particularly influential study here is Robert Pape, 2005. *Dying to Win: The Strategic Logic of Suicide Terrorism*, New York: Random House.

92. Marc Lynch, 2006. 'Al-Qaeda's Constructivist Turn'. Terrorism, Homeland Security, Strategy, Praeger Security International, June.

93. For instance Mary Kaldor, 1999. *New Wars: Organised Violence in a Global Era*, Princeton: Princeton University Press.

94. Edward Henderson and J.D. Singer, 2002. '"New Wars" and the Rumours of New Wars?', *International Interaction*, 28 (1), pp. 165–190.

95. On this, see, for example, Roland Paris, 2014. 'The "Responsibility to Protect" and the Structural Problems of Preventive Humanitarian Intervention', *International Peacekeeping*, 21 (5), pp. 569–603.

96. A good example here is Michael T. Klare, 2001. *Resource Wars: The New Landscape of Global Conflict*, New York: Henry Holt.

97. For instance: Helga Haftendorn, 2000. 'Water and International Conflict', *Third World Quarterly*, 21 (1), pp. 51–68; and Marc Cohen and Per Pinstrup Andersen, 1999. 'Food Security and Conflict', *Social Research*, 66 (1), pp. 375–416.

98. For an excellent assessment, see Frank Grundig, 2006. 'Patterns of International Cooperation and the Explanatory Power of Relative Gains: An Analysis of Cooperation on Global Climate Change, Ozone Depletion, and International Trade', *International Studies Quarterly*, 50 (4), pp. 781–801.

99. See, for example, Arild Underdal, 2017. 'Climate Change and International Relations After Kyoto', *Annual Review of Political Science*, 20 (1), pp. 169–188.

100. See, for instance, Mary E. Pettenger, 2016. *The Social Construction of Climate Change: Power, Knowledge, Norms, Discourse*, London: Routledge.

101. Pierre Jacques et al., 2008. 'The Organisation of Denial: Conservative Think Tanks and Environmental Skepticism', *Environmental Politics*, 17 (3), pp. 349–385.

102. Ibid.

103. This debate is covered in Stephen Brooks and William Wohlforth, 2013. 'Don't Come Home, America: The Case Against Retrenchment', *International* Security, 37 (3), pp. 7–51.
104. Paul McDonald and Joseph M. Parent, 2011. 'Graceful Decline: The Surprising Success of Great Power Retrenchment', *International Security*, 35 (4), pp. 7–44. See also Kyle Haynes, William Thompson, Paul MacDonald and Joseph M. Parent, 2012. 'Decline and Retrenchment—Peril or Promise?', *International Security*, 36 (4), pp. 189–203.
105. On nonpolarity see Richard Haas, 2008. 'The Age of Nonpolarity', *Foreign Affairs*, May/June.
106. A variety of views on this are put forward in Greg Raymond, Hitoshi Nasu, See Seng Tan and Rob McLaughlin, 2018. *Prospects for the Global Rules-Based Order*, Canberra: Australian National University Press.
107. Aaron L. Friedberg, 2018. 'Competing with China', *Survival*, 60 (3), pp. 7–64.
108. A leading example of this is the Tallinn Manual on international law and cyber security. See Michael Schmitt, 2018. *Tallinn Manual 2.0 on the International Law Applicable to Cyber Operations*, Cambridge: Cambridge University Press.
109. Mark Green, 2019. 'China's Debt Diplomacy: How Belt and Road Threatens Countries' Ability to Achieve Self-Reliance', *Foreign Policy*, April 25. https://foreignpolicy.com/2019/04/25/chinas-debt-diplomacy/.
110. William A. Callahan, 2006. 'History, Identity, and Security: Producing and Consuming Nationalism in China', *Critical Asian Studies*, 38 (2), pp. 179–208.
111. See Feng Zhang, 2019. 'The Xi Jinping Doctrine of China's International Relations', *Asia Policy*, 14 (3), pp. 20–33; and Camilla Sorensen, 2015. 'The Significance of Xi Jinping's "Chinese Dream" for Chinese Foreign Policy', *Journal of Chinese International Relations*, 3 (1), pp. 53–73.
112. Alastair Ian Johnston, 2019. 'China in a World Of Orders: Rethinking Compliance and Challenge in Beijing's International Relations', *International Security*, 44 (2), pp. 9–60.
113. See, for instance, Amitav Acharya and Barry Buzan, 2007. 'Why Is There No Non-Western IR Theory: An Introduction,' *International Relations of the Asia–Pacific* (Special Issue), October.

CHAPTER 3

National Security and Public Policy: Exceptionalism Versus Accountability

Tim Legrand

National security policyis a form of public policy, though many might be forgiven for thinking otherwise. This is because the last twenty years have seen contortions by states across the world over the extent to which national security policies might be allowed to collapse or sidestep long-held principles of public policy under the pretext of protecting liberal democracy. This chapter addresses the public policy dimensions of national security and seeks to explain how national security policy has supplanted 'normal' modes of public policy, carving out its imperatives as either exceptional or ascendant in democratic decision-making. In doing so, I first explore the brief history of the public policy-national security relationship, then turn to policy-making trends in Western models of government. My core claim is that while national security is a crucial element of the broader gamut of public policy initiatives undertaken by liberal democracies, it has steadily encroached on, set aside or transgressed core public policy principles, especially in the arena of legitimacy.

Public policy as a discipline is a broad church of approaches that various overlaps with political science, public administration, sociology, geography, criminology and others, and I do not propose to unpack them here, much less relate them all to national security. Yet, it is important to situate this chapter amidst the congregation if not the choir. In keeping with other colleagues in this volume, my approach is of political science: My overarching focus is on the

---

T. Legrand (✉)
Department of Politics and International Relations, University of Adelaide, Adelaide, SA, Australia
e-mail: tim.legrand@adelaide.edu.au

© The Author(s), under exclusive license to Springer Nature
Switzerland AG 2022
M. Clarke et al. (eds.), *The Palgrave Handbook of National Security*,
https://doi.org/10.1007/978-3-030-53494-3_3

processes by which national security strategy articulates through formal political decisions: in this case, *policy decisions*. Here, we must narrow even further. Contemporary public policy[1] can refer to: Those scholars who seek to unpack the process by which decisions are made and, sometimes, to therefore offer insights for its improvement (for example, Harold Lasswell); or those who seek better explanatory accounts of contemporary policy-making processes; scholars who see analysis of and intervention in policy-making as fundamentally incompatible. In this chapter, I elaborate on the policy as a mode of intervention, the implementation of the will of the government: 'the resources available to the public sector to produce change in the economy and society.'[2] And so my focus is on the instruments of (national security) policy, how they are used and how they relate to prevailing norms in any given society.

What Is Public Policy?

Public policy refers to the spectrum of capabilities and resources that lie in the hands of government—of any ideological persuasion—to deploy in pursuit of its agenda. Goodin et al. put this plainly: 'Ruling is an assertion of the will, an attempt to exercise control, to shape the world. Public policies are instruments of this assertive ambition [...]'.[3] Hence, for Michael Howlett and M. Ramesh '[p]ublic policy is, at its most simple, a choice made by a government to undertake some course of action,'[4] or as Thomas Dye's glib observation goes, it is 'anything a government chooses to do or not do.'[5] Depending on the ideological disposition of the state, however, public policy can take on any number of different forms: in short, public policy is an extension of the state's ideological superstructure.

Understood thus, public policy—as a matter of rule—is as old as political community itself: the provision of communal goods in exchange for security. Certainly, we might invoke Machiavelli's *The Prince* as one of the earliest texts on security and public policy, in which he advises the would-be prince to keep a contented population to maintain a stable state: 'It is necessary for a prince to have the people friendly, otherwise he has no security in adversity.'[6] We might invoke Hobbes observation that an insecure life, without the state, is 'nasty, brutish and short.' Hobbes, as one of the enlightenment thinkers, such as Locke and Rousseau, sought to establish the precepts of how people cohered as a political community in which their freedoms were safeguarded, and the conditions of that relationship—the social contract—cohere between the state and its citizens: the conditions of contemporary liberal democracy.

Before we turn to how public policy is operationalized in national security, let us dispel the notion that public policy—as a practice—is inherently a moral 'good.' We might aim (and hope) for public policy practices to be intrinsically 'good,' but the reality is that public policy is an instrument of those in power, for better or worse. Western democracies, in the name of security, have implemented policies of grotesque excess. The horrors of colonialism led to many, but few worse than King Leopold II's hands-for-rubber quotas in the Congo, or the British use of concentration camps during the Mau Mau Uprising in Kenya. Liberal democracies have been comfortable for centuries with policies criminalizing homosexuality or queerness, sustaining racism, entrenching sexism and trapping communities in poverty. For those so affected by the colonial or domestic liberal democracy, it was the *state itself* that was their greatest source of insecurity, a point we might keep in mind when considering the excesses of authoritarian regimes. Of course, authoritarian countries have been at their very worst where the machinery of government administered its policies of oppression efficiently: The Holocaust was administered as a matter of policy by a compliant and complicit German state bureaucracy,[7] while the rigid bureaucratic application of Soviet Union's forced collectivism saw millions starve to death under forced redistribution of food.

A Brief History of Public Policy

The horrors of state-sanctioned genocide witnessed during the World War II stimulated the appetite for 'policy sciences' to be forged as not only a field of study, but of practice too. It was founded in post-war U.S., with a view to applying a science-like approach to enhance policies' effectiveness. Its progenitor, Harold D. Lasswell, anticipated a 'policy science of democracy' as a corrective to or safeguard against the 'garrison-police state' such as those responsible for Europe's devastation. In such states, he argued: 'The specialist on violence rises in power as other skill groups subside, such as the specialists on civil administration, party and pressure-group administration, and specialists on propaganda or persuasion'.[8] Public policy, he hoped, would emerge as a technocratic approach to resolving social dilemmas in a manner holding to liberal democratic norms and without the resort to violence. Writing in 1950 as the Cold War was setting in as the chief global security dynamic, Lasswell further related the underpinning principles of democracy to national security, arguing that 'all measures proposed in the name of security' should be measured against their impact on the 'goals, values and institutions of America':

> The principle of civilian supremacy is a characteristic of democratic government, and has obvious and immediate relevance to the defense crisis. Freedom of information is an essential feature of that public enlightenment which is valued in its own right, and is also an essential means to sound public opinion. The civil liberties of the individual are means of safeguarding the equality of respect which is a basic value in a free society.[9]

In his contemporaneous note of that era, when public policy as a scholarly discipline was in its infancy, Gabriel Almond observed:

> It has been suggested that the issues of national security policy differ from other

issues of public policy in three respects—the highly technical character of the issues, the element of secrecy, and the gravity of the stakes and the risks involved.[10]

An analytical note penned by a CIA analyst in 1954 wrestled with the conundrum of developing policies to protect against Communist Party influence, arguing: 'It is difficult to devise laws and administrative orders that strike at the [Communist] Party and yet do not interfere with the activities of non-Communist opposition groups.'[11] The analyst's puzzle presaged the ongoing paradox of liberal democracy, as Jeff Huysmens was to later note: 'The paradox arises when security knowledge and technology that is meant to protect liberal democracy against violence seriously risks to undermine it.'[12] The paradox was not to fall away with the thawing of the Cold War and yet for a short moment in the 1990s, as the demise of the Soviet Union became apparent, policy planners dared to think of a world in which *economic* security would become the dominant paradigm of security policy, calling attention to: 'the usefulness of economic instruments as substitutes for or complements to military or political means of achieving U.S. national-security and foreign-policy objectives.'[13]

Additionally, one ongoing legacy of national security strategy in the Cold War has been a particular mode of public policy thinking. The dynamics of the nuclear arms race had led to the emergence of a new mode of decision-making: game theory. This approach sought to establish quantitatively the optimal choice in any given win-lose scenario involving humans, in this case the exchange of nuclear warheads, was premised on a rational choice model of decision-making. This new style of decision-making, which emerged from the RAND Corporation, was vaunted as a means to not only determine the most efficient decision in any given scenario, but also predict how rational actors would behave if their preferences were known. Using mathematical models—and philosophically premised on a belief in the rational, utility-maximizing human—game theory was held up as the holy grail of social science (indeed, the positivist *science* of the social) which could enhance policy-makers capacity to understand cause and effect and, given the right incentives, design public interventions that would achieve the intended policy outcomes. This new application later took on the label Public Choice Theory and was heralded as the ultimate technocratic tool to explain, predict and control social behavior.[14]

Public Policy in Liberal Democracies

At its heart, the evolution of policy sciences is problem-oriented, holding that social problems could be solved by a rigorous application of scientific analytical techniques and the design of causal, prescriptive actions, or as John Dryzek puts it, 'to identify cause and effect relationships that can be manipulated by public policy under central and coordinated control.'[15] As alternative visions of policy-making have emerged, not least because of messy reality, today the rationalist, causal model of policy-making remains ascendant under the rubric of evidence-based policy-making (EBPM). Early proponents of EBPM acclaim the value of 'well-founded' and 'objective' research[16] and argue that rationality—understood as a utilitarian appraisal of policy problems and application of causal logics to achieve optimal socio-economic outcomes—should trump the value-laden dogma of ideological politics. This was held so by reforming Prime Ministers, and most prominently the UK's New Labour administration in the late 1990s, which asserted 'we will be guided not by dogma but by an open-minded approach to understanding what works and why.'[17] Likewise, as the former Australian Prime Minister Kevin Rudd noted:

> A third element of the Government's agenda for the public service is to ensure a robust, evidence-based policy making process. Policy design and policy evaluation should be driven by analysis of all the available options, and not by ideology [...] Policy innovation and evidence-based policy making is at the heart of being a reformist government.

Achieving this with an EBPM approach is not only a matter of problem-solving, but of solving public goals efficiently with slim public resources: 'the ability to marshal the necessary resources to make intelligent collective choices about and set strategic directions for the allocation of scarce resources to public ends.'[18] Yet temptation of the technocratic approach is to frame all social problems as solely technical and value-neutral. John Dryzek suggests the approach 'implicitly assumes an omniscient and benevolent decision maker untroubled by politics.'[19] For later EBPM scholars,[20] what are construed as policy problems to be addressed, what sort of evidence is used, how, when and by whom remains inherently political?[21] Hence policy, in their view, remains an extension and instrument of political interests of all ideological stripes.

In liberal democracies, decision-makers are accountable to the public whose preferences are expressed through political processes. Government derives decision-making authority from free and fair elections, and in doing so receive a popular imprimatur to implement their policy agendas. It follows that policies are should accord with citizens' well-being (or at least do not unfairly discriminate in their design or application). Where public policies are understood to accord with public interests, they are endorsed as *legitimate*, which for Fritz Scharpf is 'a socially sanctioned obligation to comply with government policies even if these violate the actor's own interests or normative preferences, and even if official sanctions could be avoided at low cost.'[22] Yet, liberal democracies do not come with a handbook on how to attain legitimacy. Beyond elections, which are a precondition of liberal democracy, there is no universally mandated approach to identifying public priorities, and states have arrived at their own idiosyncratic accommodations of how the citizens' rights are accorded and protected. Debates on the precise mixture of liberal democracy's qualities are legion, but as Patrick Dunleavy suggests, 'At a minimum, agreement has been reached that rights of free expression, organization and elections of officials should always be included.'[23] In liberal democracies, public policy must accord to prevailing values, not least the rule of law, but also the protection of human rights and minority rights, to secure legitimate outcomes:

> Successful attainment of political *legitimacy* for a policy involves the extent to which *both* the social outcomes of policy interventions *and* the manner in which they are achieved are seen as appropriate by relevant stakeholders and accountability forums in view of the systemic values in which they are embedded.[24]

This entails both the process-oriented and outcome qualities of policy instruments are required separately and jointly to achieve democratic legitimacy. As Fritz Scharpf[25] termed it, *input legitimacy* is decision-making that acquires the consent of the affected public through participatory processes, and *output legitimacy* is the accountability of decision-makers and the relative performance of the policies in meeting the public interest. In practice, this has meant that decision-making process is transparent, involves elected officials that can be held to account, and that the public are allowed input to the decision-making process. These are minimum expectations, which is why Good et al. argue: 'every democratic polity worth the name has some mechanisms for obtaining public input into the policy-making process.'[26]

To attain output legitimacy, policy instruments themselves should be evidence-based, which means that in practice they should be effective in meeting their stipulated aims, efficient in how they use resources to meet those aims, equitable in the distribution of their benefits, and not serve private or marginal interests. Understanding the relationship between public policy and legitimacy matters because the national security decisions made by those in power should reflect the interests of the public and not unfairly target or exclude minorities. And it also matters because legitimacy is central to achieving goals: 'In order to penetrate and reshape societies, governments must have the legitimacy and efficiency to acquire information and mobilize consent, while simultaneously resisting capture by private interests.'[27]

National Security and Public Policy in Liberal Democracy

National security agendas across the world have, in the past twenty years, been dominated by the so-called war on terror. From the mid-1990s, Al Qaeda's attacks across the world inverted the traditional modes of security policy: The 'opposition between two power blocs has been replaced by a more complex and unpredictable set of relationships', as the UK's National Security Strategy claims. Security institutions that had operated on the basis of a known and knowable state antagonist with tacitly agreed rules to the game were confronted by a new class of non-state threat that seemingly accepted no political answer offered by the West, and seemed to defy the capacity of public policy agents to provide the sorts of effective approaches demanded by a technocratic model. At the time, UK Prime Minister Tony Blair said of Al Qaeda: 'Neither is it true that they have no demands. They do. It is just that no sane person would negotiate on them.'[28]

International terrorism is not the only threat stipulated by Western states in their national security outlooks.[29] The range of orthodox threats remain part of their risk assessment. This includes transnational crime, weapons of mass destruction, conflicts within and between failed states, the outbreak of conventional warfare between advanced militaries and pandemics. In addition, a range of qualitatively 'new' threats are becoming recognized and taken into the 'security' portfolio, including climate change, poverty, water, energy and food security and technology failures in critical infrastructure.

Methodological Challenges of National Security Evaluation

For Arnold Wolfers, security is 'the absence of threats to acquired values', and this is the ostensible goal of national security policy. Yet, measuring progress toward that aim presents us with clearest differentiation of national security from public policy approaches. Managing the orthodox and unorthodox sources of threat set out above has been an ongoing challenge since they are issues that are not always easily amenable to intervention. Because the overarching policy approach adopted by national security officials has been of prevention and/or deterrence (both of which are successful by the *absence* of the phenomenon at hand), national security policy-making therefore has a methodological problem of measurement of security policy success.

First, measuring the deterrence of threats that are high-impact but relativity rare, such as nuclear war, demand ongoing vigilance often with little clear payoff or visible progress to measure policy success against. That this is so does not, of course, lessen the importance of the necessity to deter, as explained by a RAND analysis of deterrence in counterterrorism:

> Deterrence is also a major factor in the cost-effectiveness of many security programs. For instance, even if a radiation-detection system at ports never actually encounters weapon material, if it deters would-be attackers from trying to smuggle such material into the country, it could easily be cost-effective even if associated program costs are very high.

Second, demonstrating effectiveness of the *preventive* approach is problematic where robust longitudinal data is not available. For example, terrorist events happen only infrequently in Western states (compared to other forms of violent crime). In addition, determining the causal effect of one policy is remarkably difficult amidst the general complexity of the social world, but compounded by the range of other counter-terrorism initiatives in operation at the same time. Indeed, laws and powers exist in a state of competition, whereby the success of one initiative can interact with and potentially diminish the success of other initiatives. By way of illustration, a low percentage of prosecutions for terrorism offences might indicate that counterterrorism laws are relatively ineffective. But that measure of success is almost certainly complicated by the 'upstream' initiatives of security agencies in disrupting or deradicalizing would-be terrorists: The effectiveness of one element of counterterrorism almost always interacts with others, and so deriving a single measure of success is highly problematic.

These methodological challenges operate as *a priori* impediments to casting national security in the same light as non-security policy. Against this backdrop, national security policy has manifold challenges in meeting the core injunctions of public policy in liberal democracies. Yet, rather than work to resolve these issues, states have retreated further from those injunctions. In the remainder of this chapter, I explore in three dimensions how national security legislators have largely exceptionalized, expanded and exempted national security policy from the core imperatives of policy-making. They signal not only the immediate past, but perhaps a dim future for public policy.

Exceptionalized Policy-Making in Liberal Democracies

A growing view of national security politics attends to the process by which national security threats are made 'exceptional' from the normal view of politics and policy. A range of critical scholars,[30] prominently Carl Schmitt[31] and Georgio Agamben,[32] have traced the narratives and strategies employed by states to create a 'state of exception' in which national security questions beyond the reach of the public and legislature and become immune to liberal democracy's usual checks and balances. This is the premise of the work— most prominently by Buzan et al.— on securitization, which depicts national security policy as having a unique power to co-opt, dominate and trump democratic safeguards. In this vein of reasoning, security is deemed 'a practice of authorization to manage and create insecurity, to affirm an ontology of inclusions and exclusions, of inside and outside.' The result is a 'vision of divisions between the legitimate and the illegitimate, the normal and the exceptional, the political and non-political.'[33] In the framing of Buzan et al., the process of 'securitization' involves a grammar of security in which public officials depict 'a plot that includes existential threat, point of no return, and a possible way out.'[34] Doing so 'thereby generates endorsement of emergency measures beyond rules that would otherwise bind.'[35] Such impulses of exceptionalism, as I suggest above, have always been at the heart of national security decisions. Yet, these impulses were brought into stark relief by September 11th, 2001 and the global onset of Islamist violent extremism. Huysmens draws attention to the range of security issues 'exceptionalised' in this era:

> A rise in political exceptionalism is at the heart of the political contest of issues such as the status of the prisoners in Camp Delta in Guantanamo Bay,

the increase in policing powers, the impact of the fight against terrorism on fundamental freedoms, the difficulty to express dissenting voices in the US, the legality of pre-emptive warfare, and the legitimacy of the war on Iraq.

In the era of 'the global war on terrorism,' differences between national security issues and non-security issues have deepened substantially. The emergency of international terrorism, declared globally by UN Resolution 1373, precipitated a wave of anti-terrorism legislating across the world: *all* states to a greater or lesser degree were required to amend or install anti-terrorism laws to comply with the Resolution.[36] Despite the UN Secretary-General Kofi Annan's 2002 warning that 'we must not allow the struggle against terrorism to become a pretext for the suppression of legitimate opposition or dissent,'[37] the UN Human Rights Council has recognized that many state states have used anti-terrorism powers as a cynical legal pretext to 'to repress human rights defenders,' impose 'excessive restrictions on the right to freedom of expression', legitimize 'torture and ill-treatment' and apply a 'chilling effect on minorities, activists, [and] political opposition.'[38] Though these are largely illiberal democracies and authoritarian states concerned in the worst excesses of national security abuses, Jeff Huysmens notes the risk for liberal states:

> In such a situation security policy can intensely sustain the justification and institutionalization of exceptional policies and emergency measures that hollow out central characteristics of liberal democratic government.[39]

As an example, we might turn to the practice of proscription: An exercise of sovereign fiat that reaches back to the earliest days of statehood in Rome and pre-modern European history, and today retains a central place in the security apparatus of liberal, illiberal and authoritarian governments alike.[40] In this context, Jenny Hocking has argued that powers to designate and criminalize terrorist organizations without judicial process represents the antithesis of democratic values:

> Proscription is the end product of a fear of democracy itself, a desire to limit the realm of legitimate political debate, to exclude political voices and to structure politics in a manner which is, by its very design, anti-democratic.

In summary, the consequence of the exceptionalization of national security policies is at best a temporary but necessary suspicion of liberal democracy in protection of its own values. At worst it can legitimate violent and illiberal practices and undermine the core values of liberal democracy. On either view, the principles of public policy are stifled, with legitimacy the first victim of national security decision-making.

Scrutiny, Accountability and Exceptionalism

The conditions of exceptionalism have contributed to a second departure from public policy legitimacy norms: National security decisions are largely shielded from the normal processes of scrutiny, transparency and accountability.[41] John Uhr observes that 'governments have few if any expectations that Parliament has a part to play in national security policy and practice,'[42] and Andrew Neal similarly finds the executive-dominated decision-making represents 'an analytical blind spot regarding security politics and an incomplete picture of the workings of security.'[43] Speaking in Parliament, a UK legislator, Lord McNally, declaimed the veiling of national security decision-making from Parliament:

> I am not content to allow Ministers simply to pat us on the head, give us a knowing look to the effect that they are in receipt of secret information which, if only we could see it, would make our toes curl and, therefore, we should nod through every piece of new legislation that they want.[44]

Notwithstanding these objections, what has emerged in the course of day-to-day politics across many Western democracies is a consensus that security policy is a bipartisan matter. The display of unity is intended to sidestep the cut-and-thrust theatrics of legislatures, speed up the decision-making process (especially where emergency measures are invoked) and provide stable leadership to the public on a matter of gravity. In the midst of debates on measures to combat radicalization, the (then) Australian opposition leader, Bill Shorten, called for 'responsible bipartisanship' with the government, stating 'national security is a matter which goes above the day-to-day politics.'[45] Parliamentary security committees operate in the same manner. The UK's Home Affairs Committee reports that it 'operates in a bipartisan fashion,' mirroring Australia's Parliamentary Joint Committee on Intelligence and Security which lists as a main function building bipartisan support for national security legislation. Yet, the ensuing erosion of debate on security decision-making has not gone unchallenged. As Andrew Carr argues, 'the history of the twentieth century is inexplicable unless we shift from thinking of democratic debate as being an impediment to national security, to recognising it as a necessity.'

By way of example, returning to the example of proscription above, UK's legislators in opposition have frequently made explicit overtures to bipartisan decision-making, offering little if any scrutiny of government claims for the necessity of banning of an organization. In a 2005 debate, for instance, MP Dominic Grieve offered support for a government proscription order, stating: 'We have to accept that a great deal of this must be taken on trust [...] and we must therefore accept the government's word that the security services have told them that they pose a danger.'[46] Baroness Smith of Basildon echoed that sentiment in 2014, announcing, 'we base our judgment in support of proscription orders on the assurances of Ministers.'[47] Later still, in 2015, MP Keith Vaz made explicit the implicit policy: 'as far as I can remember, no order of this kind has ever been opposed, because we trust and accept the good faith of the Minister when he tells the House that dreadful organisations are seeking to propagate terrorism, which is indeed true.'[48] In this example, output legitimacy of a key security policy is left wanting. In sidestepping their role as scrutineers of government policy, members of legislatures in opposition remove the opportunity for the public to not only observe scrutiny in action, but also abdicate their responsibility to hold government to account, both of which are central to the qualities of output legitimacy in public policy.

Exempting National Security from Public Policy Imperatives

The exceptionalization of national security policy from the normal bounds of public policy can be observed in the practices of policy-making too; and specifically in the imperatives that all policy should be derived from evidence and informed by evaluation. The question of effectiveness continues to hang over all national security initiatives that encounter this issue of demonstrating whether or not they work as designed. It remains unclear whether governments have investigated measures of effectiveness, but a 2014 report of the Privacy and Civil Liberties Oversight Board found that '[US] government has failed to respond responsibly to the urgent plea to "develop a comprehensive methodology for assessing the efficacy and relative value of counterterrorism programs"'.[49] This ambiguity weighs heavily over the need for public policies to demonstrate efficacy:

> Many of these interventions (and more) have become part of our daily lives and discourse, but we have no idea whether or not they fulfill the promise of reducing terrorism, terrorism-related risk or harm as there is no research to support these interventions. Indeed, some of these interventions may also have collateral and unintended effects of reducing civil rights or our quality of life.[50]

Notwithstanding the methodological challenges in evaluating national security policy, political figures have not shied away from claiming success for their programs. Typically, where efficacy cannot be shown, instead the counterfactual measures of 'attacks averted' or 'lives saved' are used. For example, the Prime Minister of Australia, Tony Abbott, claimed in 2015: 'Since [September 2014], there have been two attacks in Australia, and security and law enforcement agencies have disrupted a further six attacks.'[51] In 2014, the CIA Director John. Brennan claimed this as justification for abuses committed by U.S. intelligence agencies: 'Our review indicates that interrogations of detainees on whom [enhanced interrogation techniques] were used did produce intelligence that helped thwart attack plans, capture terrorists, and save lives.'[52]

Of course, there is no doubt of the economic impact of terrorist attacks. In their analysis of post-9/11 security programs implemented by the US government, John Mueller and Mark Stewart[53] estimated that the 9/11 attacks in which almost 3,000 people were killed resulted in up to US$200b in losses. The 2013 Boston bombing in which 3 were killed and 264 people injured also resulted in US$500m in losses. The 2005 London bombings in which 52 were killed 52 more than 700 people injured incurred around $3–5 billion in losses. Yet, at what point are the costs of security initiatives economically viable, and to what degree are these cost–benefit analyses undertaken? They conclude that: 'For the most part, we have concluded that the costs of such programs as presently carried out generally outweigh their benefits.'[54]

Why do governments seem reluctant to evaluate, at least publicly, their security policies and initiatives? While internal audits and monitoring are sometimes in place, as with the Independent National Security Legislation Monitor in Australia or the UK's Independent Reviewer of Terrorism, only very rarely do their unredacted assessments see the light of day. As suggested earlier, at one level, there is a need to maintain state secrecy to facilitate operational effectiveness. Few governments would be candid in revealing where their defensive policies fall short. On another level, security agencies are unlikely to be enthusiastic in permitting external audits of their effectiveness. But perhaps the most compelling explanation is that security is known by its practitioners to be inherently inefficient, and that evaluating its efficiency in conferring a public benefit—diminishing an already negligible threat in some cases—may prompt public outcry and a questioning of funding levels.[55]

The Expanding Remit of National Security Policy

The last two decades have seen national security policy expand in remit while maintaining its exceptional status. With the demise in the 1990s of the Soviet Union as a 'unifying threat' to western democracies, today's security environment is marked by a rise in 'non–traditional' as well as 'transnationalised' and decentered threats. Protagonists include cyber–attackers, foreign interference in democratic processes, criminal organizations and, especially, terrorist organizations. But it also includes those of the natural world. COVID-19 and climate change suggest a future in which the accidental by-products of human progress number amongst the greatest existential risks. These are accompanied by security 'narratives' which contend these are of qualitatively different nature, scope and capability compared to 'old' state–centric threats. As noted above, the rise of these new threats has bankrupted the state-centric balance of power. According to Philip Cerny, these contribute to a 'new security dilemma'[56] in which the sources of today's threat are not easily discernible. At the same time, across Western democracies, there are growing arguments that policy issues that are not traditionally understood to be related to national security have a role to play in nevertheless diminishing security risks.

For securitization scholars, security operates as a 'master narrative' of the state's organization of politics and the polity.[57] For critical scholars, 'security' has been imbued with a political and discursive force: is not merely a status, but it is an act[58] which constrains the capacity of non-government actors to dispute the nature or outcomes of that security. And so a whole swathe of issues are viewed through the lens of national security, including (im)migration[59]; education policy[60]; climate change and the environment[61]; religion[62]; and health.[63] The UK's National Security Strategy makes this point, for example:

> Over recent decades, our view of national security has broadened to include threats to individual citizens and to our way of life, as well as to the integrity and interests of the state. That is why this strategy deals with transnational crime, pandemics and flooding – not part of the traditional idea of national security, but clearly challenges that can affect large numbers of our citizens, and which demand some of the same responses as more traditional security threats, including terrorism.[64]

This broadening is not necessarily a new direction: indeed, national security imperatives have rarely dissuaded governments from encroaching on social or education policy. For example, the British government in the eighteenth century faced down the threat of a rebellion from Scottish clans under the 'Jacobite' banner of James II. To secure against future uprisings, British parliamentarians approved the Act Of Proscription that, amongst other measures, introduced new education measures in an attempt to secure loyalty to the British crown: The law called for school teachers to signal 'their good affection to his Majesty's person and government' and 'as often as prayers shall be said in such school, to pray, or cause to be prayed for, in express words his Majesty, his heirs and successors, by name, and for all the royal family.' That strategy, while archaic is not an anachronism: the UK's contemporary counterterrorism 'Prevent' strategy, stipulates:

> Schools should be safe spaces in which children and young people can understand and discuss sensitive topics, including terrorism and the extremist ideas that are part of terrorist ideology, and learn how to challenge these ideas. The Prevent duty is not intended to limit discussion of these issues. Schools should, however, be mindful of their existing duties to forbid political indoctrination and secure a balanced presentation of political issues.[65]

The expansion of national security imperatives into such domains, while not new, does not augur well for the reversal of such trends. Indeed, the UK government has recently doubled-down on this approach, introducing its new security policy framework: 'Fusion doctrine,' which co-opts the full range of socio-economic levers available to the government:

> A wide range of government departments contribute to making the UK a harder target for those who wish to do us harm and the social reform departments help

NATIONAL SECURITY AND THE SHADOW OF ILLIBERALISM

As a coda to this chapter, I return to the warning made in the opening paragraphs that public policy is not inherently 'good,' but an extension of the ideology of those in control. It follows that better policy may not lead to better government, but it does hold the corollary that public policies act as weathervanes for prevailing ideological beliefs within governments, whether explicit or implicit. If this is true, on the examples outlined above, we might fear that the risks of excessive and exceptionalized 'emergency' national security powers become normalized and that liberal democracies slide gradually into illiberalism. That illiberalism casts such a large shadow is not much of a dramatic suggestion for two reasons. First, Marlies Glasius warns that the abandonment of accountability is not one to be taken lightly: 'We should refocus our understanding of authoritarianism from failure to hold elections to *sabotaging accountability*.'[67] The deliberate and ongoing erosion or sidestepping of accountability in security decisions, not only in the general exceptionalizing of security but also demonstrated in the UK's deployment of proscription powers, is warning enough that accountability as a central quality to the output legitimacy of public policy is in peril. Second, we label systems as illiberal democracies, Patrick Dunleavy suggests, 'where minority freedoms are persistently denied not because they infringe upon the freedom of others but because of majority 'tyranny'.[68] In many instances over the past twenty years, such intrusions on minority rights have become habitual across Western democracies. The 2019 US travel ban on selected Muslim-majority countries is a case in point; but we might equally point to the UK's stop-and-search powers given to police forces.

The risk is that targeting of minority communities leads to the creation of 'suspect communities.' As Christina Pantazis and Simon Pemberton have shown, measures combating terrorism have been disproportionately applied against Muslim communities, with the result that those communities become victims of institutional behavior that regards them a priori as potential terrorists.[69] A typical example is the UK's use of suspicionless stop-and-search as a forms of preventative policing. Section 44 of the *Terrorism Act 2000* permitted a senior police officer to designate in secret—and without any judicial or parliamentary oversight—any area in which police officers were permitted to stop-and search-individuals without any prior cause. The designations lasted 28 days, and for many continued for years on a rolling basis. During the Iraq War, for example, designated areas included vast areas, including the whole of Greater London as well as whole counties, being subject to rolling renewals since the *Terrorism Act 2000* after 2001. The resulting implementation of stop-and-search led to black and ethnic minorities being disproportionately targeted by police. The European Court of Human Rights (ECHR) subsequently ruled the policy unlawful, finding 'statistical and other evidence showing the extent to which police officers resorted to the powers of stop-and-search under Section 44 of the Act and found that there was a clear risk of arbitrariness in granting such broad discretion to the police officer.'[70]

Liberal democracies are in the minority of governments around the world. In 2018, Freedom House estimated 1.6 billion people around the world faced criminal or civil sanctions for their political views, who face a choice between silent acquiescence, unlawful resistance or to seek asylum overseas. In authoritarian countries, national security is synonymous with the regime's interests, and the apparatus of the public administration *is* the apparatus of regime-maintenance. John Keane catalogues the public engagement initiatives practiced by despotic regimes, from the Orban government, Tajikistan, UAE, Brunei, and Singapore, whom he labels 'the headmasters of the wizarding school' in the world of despotism.[71] For authoritarian regimes, security decisions are made in the interests of the regime, even where ostensibly they engage the public:

> These experiments in public engagement show that the new despotisms are structured by a silent contract between the ruling authorities and their subject populations: the rulers will deliver what their subjects need in exchange for their quiet loyalty.[72]

In this context, in addition to the range of external threats to the state, authoritarian state policies treat their public as a threat. Alvarez et al. find that the dominant political cultures of Latin America's military regimes were 'organized around the administration of exclusion' at its most brutal:

> Exacerbated authoritarianism transformed political exclusion into political elimination through state repression and systemic violence. Bureaucratic and technocratic decision making procedures provided an additional rationale for further contracting the definition of politics and its participants.[73]

We may also cast our eyes to the lessons of the Holocaust, in which the Nazis were able to frame the Jewish people, and others deemed undesirable by the state, as threats to national security and therefore subject to the lawful arbitrary violence of state agents. Similar constructions of minorities as national security threats, absent safeguards, allowed similar atrocities to occur—amongst others—in Cambodia, Rwanda, Bosnia, and most recently Myanmar.

Conclusions

In liberal democracies, national security policy is often the destructive elephant in the room. Notwithstanding the paradox of protecting liberal democratic norms by breaching them, the imperatives of national security—certainly in the current era—have often paid scant regard to norms of policy-making in a liberal democracy. The qualities of input and output legitimacy, though we cannot expect these to be unrestrained in security spaces, have nonetheless been neglected, with few expectations that legislators, much less the public, have a part to play in the determination of those policies or in holding to account those charged with their administration. Above, we have explored the exceptionalizing tendencies at play, in which security policy-makers write their own excuse-note relieving themselves of their obligations to the public in respect of scrutiny and accountability, and efficiency and effectiveness. What is more, this is an expansive and expanding realm which has encroached and is co-opting non-security portfolios as national security matters. It is this final dynamic which is worthy of extended reflection beyond this chapter, for as we have seen in this chapter, the security lens is one that is frequently shrouded in respect of its effectiveness and efficacy. In 2011, the Independent National Security Legislation Monitor, having regard for the full suite of Australia's national security policies made this frank observation:

> Ultimately, it will not be the CT Laws that deter and prevent terrorism, if that outcome is realistic at all, but much broader and deeper elements and dynamics of Australian and international society that include as just one formal part the counter-terrorism laws.[74]

The suggestion here is that the cart is before the horse: that national security imperatives can be better achieved—and perhaps can only be achieved—not through its instinctive reach for hardened security measures in harsh criminal sanctions or more muscular policing, but in attending to the long-term societal dynamics from which such security challenges emerge. What is more, rather than maintaining the privileged position of national security policy in decision-making, genuine progress toward this objective can only be achieved by applying authentic principles of public policy in a liberal democracy.

NOTES

1. I recommend the interested reader to obtain a copy of Peters, B. Guy, and Philippe Zittoun. (2016). *Contemporary Approaches to Public Policy. Theories, Controversies and Perspectives*. UK: Palgrave Macmillan.
2. Ibid.
3. Goodin, R.E., Rein, M., and Moran, M. (2006). The Public and Its Policies. In *The Oxford Handbook of Public Policy*. London: Oxford University Press, 3.
4. Howlett, M., and Ramesh, M. (2003). *Studying Public Policy: Policy Cycles and Policy Subsystems*. London: Oxford University Press, 3.
5. Dye, Thomas R. (1972). *Understanding Public Policy*. Englewood Cliffs, NJ: Prentice-Hall, 2.
6. Dye, Thomas R. (1972). *Understanding Public Policy*, 46.
7. Dietrich, D.J. (1981). Holocaust as Public Policy: The Third Reich. *Human Relations, 34*(6), 445–462.

8. Lasswell, H.D. (1950). *National Security and Individual Freedom*. New York, NY: McGraw-Hill, 47.
9. Ibid., 57–58.
10. Almond, G.A. (1956). Public Opinion and National Security Policy. *Public Opinion Quarterly*, 20(2), 371–378.
11. Central Intelligence Agency (1957). Legal vs. Illegal Status. Some Considerations Relevant to Banning a Communist Party. Senior Research Staff on International Communism. No.300. 4 January.
12. Huysmans, J. (2004). Minding Exceptions: The Politics of Insecurity and Liberal Democracy. *Contemporary Political Theory*, 3(3), 322.
13. Neu, C.R. (1994). *The Economic Dimensions of National Security*. Washington, DC: RAND corporation, vi.
14. See McCumber, John. (2016). *The Philosophy Scare: The Politics of Reason in the Early Cold War*. Chicago: University of Chicago Press, 72–77.
15. Dryzek, John S. (2009). Policy Analysis as Critique. In *The Oxford Handbook of Public Policy*. Ney York: Oxford University Press, 190–203 (190).
16. Solesbury, William. (2002). The Ascendancy of Evidence. *Planning Theory & Practice*, 3(10), 90–96.
17. Blunkett, D. (2002). Speech Delivered at the Economic and Social Research Council, 2 February.
18. Painter, M., and Pierre, J. (2005). *Challenges to State Policy Capacity*. Houndsmills: Palgrave, 2.
19. Dryzek, John S. (2009). Policy Analysis as Critique.
20. Pawson, R. (2002). Evidence-Based Policy: In Search of a Method. *Evaluation*, 8(2), 157–181; Sanderson, I. (2000). Evaluation in Complex Policy Systems. *Evaluation*, 6(4), 433.
21. Head, B. (2010). Reconsidering Evidence-Based Policy: Key Issues and Challenges. *Policy and Society*, 29(2), 77.
22. Scharpf, F. (2003). Problem-Solving Effectiveness and Democratic Accountability in the EU. Working Paper 03/1, Max Planck Institute for the Study of Societies, February.
23. Dunleavy, P. (1987). *Theories of the State: The Politics of Liberal Democracy*. London: Macmillan International Higher Education, 5.
24. Luetjens, J., Mintrom, M., and t'Hart, P. (2019). *Successful Public Policy: Lessons from Australia and New Zealand*. Canberra: ANU Press, 5.
25. Scharpf, F. (1999). *Governing in Europe. Effective and Democratic?* Oxford: Oxford University Press.
26. Goodin, R.E, Rein, M., and Moran, M. (2006). The Public and Its Policies. In *The Oxford Handbook of Public Policy*. London: Oxford University Press, 10.
27. Kleiman, Mark A.R., and Steven M. Teles. (2006). Market and Non-market Failures. In *The Oxford Handbook of Public Policy*, 638.
28. Blair, Tony. (2005). Speech To Labour Party On Terror. *BBC News*.
29. For example, *The National Security Strategy of the United States of America*.
30. For examples, see: Aradau, C., and van Munster, R. (2009). Exceptionalism and the ' War On Terror': Criminology Meets International Relations, *British Journal of Criminology*, 49(5), 686–701; Lister, M. (2019). Explaining Counter Terrorism in the UK: Normal Politics, Securitised Politics or Performativity of the Neo-Liberal State? *Critical Studies on Terrorism*, 12(3), 416–439; Jarvis, L., and Legrand, T. (2017). 'I Am Somewhat Puzzled': Questions,

Audiences and Securitization in the Proscription of Terrorist Organizations. *Security Dialogue*, *48*(2), 149–167.

31. Schmitt, C. (1985). *Political Theology: Four Chapters on the Concept of Sovereignty*. Translated by George Schwab. Cambridge, MA, London: MIT Press.

32. Agamben, G. (2004). *State of Exception*, translated by Kevin Attell. Chicago: Chicago University Press.

33. Charbonneau, B. (2008). *France and the New Imperialism: Security Policy in Sub-Saharan Africa*. London: Ashgate Publishing, 7.

34. Buzan, B., Waever, O., and de Wilde, J. (1998). *Security: A New Framework for Analysis*. London: Lynne Rienner, 33.

35. Buzan, B., Waever, O., and de Wilde, J. (1998). *Security: A New Framework for Analysis*, 5.

36. Stiles, K.W. (2006). The Power of Procedure and the Procedures of the Powerful. *Journal of Peace Research*, *43*(1), 37–54 (47–48).

37. Annan, K. (2002). 'Secretary-General to Commission On Human Rights': goo.gl/REheiD.

38. United Nations. (2016). *Report of the Special Rapporteur on the Rights to Freedom of Peaceful Assembly and of Association*: goo.gl/hXDGhi, 8–9.

39. Huysmans, Jeff. (2004). Minding Exceptions: The Politics of Insecurity and Liberal Democracy. *Contemporary Political Theory*, *3*(3), 321–341 (324).

40. See Jarvis, L., and Legrand, T. (2020). *Banning Them, Securing Us?: Terrorism, Parliament and the Ritual of Proscription*. Manchester University Press.

41. Mueller, J., and Stewart, M.G. (2011). *Terror, Security, and Money: Balancing the Risks, Benefits, and Costs of Homeland Security*. Oxford: Oxford University Press.

42. Uhr, J. (2004). Terra Infirma? Parliament's Uncertain Role in the War on Terror. *University of New South Wales Law Journal*, *27*(2), 339–344.

43. Neal, A. (2012). Events Dear Boy, Events: Terrorism and Security from the Perspective of Politics. *Critical Studies on Terrorism*, *5*(1), 107–120 (108).

44. House of Lords Debates. (2001). 27 March: Column 152.

45. Australian Broadcasting Corporation. (2014). Government Stresses National Safety as Parliament Resumes. *Insiders*, 31 August.

46. Grieve, D. (2005). Hansard HC, 13 October: Column 473.

47. Smith, Baroness. (2014). Hansard HL, 19 June: Column 1013.

48. Vaz, K. (2015). Hansard HC, 21 January: Column 331.

49. PCLOB. (2014). Report on the Telephone Records Program Conducted under Section 215 of the US Patriot Act and on the Operations of the Foreign Intelligence Surveillance Court. Privacy and Civil Liberties Oversight Board, Washington, DC. January 23. Cited in Stewart, M.G., and Mueller, J. (2017). *Are We Safe Enough?: Measuring and Assessing Aviation Security*. Elsevier.

50. Lum, Cynthia, Kennedy, Leslie, and Sherley, Alison. (2006). Are Counter-Terrorism Strategies Effective? The Results of the Campbell Systematic Review on Counter-Terrorism Evaluation Research. *Fletcher Forum of World Affairs*, 2, 489–516.

51. Abbott, T. (2015). Australia's Counter-Terrorism Strategy. *Media Release*, 24648, 23 July.

52. Central Intelligence Agency. (2014). Statement from Director Brennan on the SSCI Study on the Former Detention and Interrogation Program. Press Release, 9 December.

53. Mueller, J., and Stewart, M.G. (2011). *Terror, Security, and Money: Balancing the Risks, Benefits, and Costs of Homeland Security*. Oxford: Oxford University Press.
54. Stewart, M.G., and Mueller, J. (2017). *Are We Safe Enough?: Measuring and Assessing Aviation Security*. Elsevier, 204.
55. For example, see Bronitt, S.H., Legrand, T., and Stewart, M. (2015). Evidence of the Impact of Counter-Terrorism Legislation. In Lennon, G., and Walker, C. (eds.), *Routledge Handbook of Law and Terrorism*. Abingdon, Oxon: Routledge, 297–312.
56. Cerny, P.G. (1998). Neomedievalism, Civil War and the New Security Dilemma: Globalisation as Durable Disorder. *Civil Wars, 1*(1), 36–64.
57. Buzan, B., Waever, O., and de Wilde, J. (1998), *Security: A New Framework for Analysis*.
58. Ibid., 14.
59. Ceyhan, A., & Tsoukala, A. (2002). The Securitization of Migration in Western Societies: Ambivalent Discourses and Policies. *Alternatives, 27*, 21–39.
60. Gearon, Liam. (2013). The Counter Terrorist Classroom: Religion, Education, and Security. *Religious Education*, 108.
61. Trombetta, M.J. (2011). Rethinking the Securitization of the Environment: Old Beliefs, New Insights. In Balzacq, T. (ed.), *Securitization Theory: How Security Problems Emerge and Dissolve*. New York: Routledge, 135–149.
62. Vuori, J.A. (2011). Religion Bites: Falungong, Securitization/Desecuritization in the People's Republic of China. In Balzacq, T. (ed.), *Securitization Theory: How Security Problems Emerge and Dissolve*. New York: Routledge, 186–211.
63. Sjöstedt, Roxanna. (2008). Exploring the Construction of Threats: The Securitization of HIV/AIDS in Russia. *Security Dialogue, 39*, 7–29.
64. UK Government. (2010). A Strong Britain in an Age of Uncertainty: The National Security Strategy. HM Government. https://assets.publishing.service. gov.uk/government/uploads/system/uploads/attachment_data/file/61936/ national-security-strategy.pdf.
65. UK Government. (2011). *Prevent* Duty Guidance for England and Wales. HM Government. https://www.rbkc.gov.uk/pdf/Prevent_Duty_Guidance_ England_Wales.pdf.
66. UK Government. (2018). The National Security Capability Review (NSCR). HM Government, March. https://assets.publishing.service.gov. uk/government/uploads/system/uploads/attachment_data/file/705347/6. 4391_CO_National-Security-Review_web.pdf.
67. Glasius, M. (2018). What Authoritarianism Is … and Is Not: A Practice Perspective. *International Affairs, 94*(3), 515–533.
68. Dunleavy, P. (1987). *Theories of the State: The Politics of Liberal Democracy*. London: Macmillan International Higher Education, 6.
69. Pantazis, C., & Pemberton, S. (2009). From the 'Old' to the 'New' Suspect Community Examining the Impacts of Recent UK Counter-Terrorist Legislation. *British Journal of Criminology, 49*, 646–666.
70. European Court of Human Rights. (2010). Chamber Judgment *Gillan and Quinton v the United Kingdom*, 12th January.
71. Keane, J. (2020). *The New Despotism*. Harvard: Harvard University Press, 95.
72. Ibid., 96.
73. Alvarez, S.E. (2018). *Cultures of Politics/Politics of Cultures: Revisioning Latin American Social Movements*. Abingdon: Routledge, 10.

74. Independent National Security Legislation Monitor (INSLM). (2011). Annual Report. December, 13. https://www.inslm.gov.au/reviews-reports/annual-reports/independent-national-security-legislation-monitor-annual-report-2011.

CHAPTER 4

Ethics and National Security: A Case for Reasons in Decision-Making

Adam Henschke

INTRODUCTION

This chapter offers an introduction to the challenges that arise in relation to ethics and national security, framed around issues of decision-making. I offer an account of ethics and national security that as *the justificatory reasons that are given to protect and preserve a state and its people*. The chapter is not an effort to answer any specific questions about ethics and national security; it will not give any guidance about the morally right thing to do in a given national security context. Instead, the chapter seeks to map spaces in which questions of ethics and national security occur, and what ethics means for national security decision-making.

The chapter proceeds as follows. It sets up the problem in two ways—first presenting how ethics relate to national security, and then outlining some sceptical challenges to this assertion. The chapter then shows how I am framing the concepts of ethics, national security and liberal democracies.[1] The chapter next explains how, despite ethical issues of national security being an open question, that it does not mean 'anything goes'. It shows that one of the real challenges of discussing ethics and national security is that this is a dynamic space, and what may seem impermissible in one situation may become permissible if the situation changes. The problem here is that one's answer about what is right to do can, and indeed should, change as the situation changes, but any changes must be supported by good reasons. The chapter finishes by

A. Henschke (✉)
Department of Philosophy, University of Twente, Enschede, The Netherlands
e-mail: a.henschke@utwente.nl

© The Author(s), under exclusive license to Springer Nature Switzerland AG 2022
M. Clarke et al. (eds.), *The Palgrave Handbook of National Security*,
https://doi.org/10.1007/978-3-030-53494-3_4

73

offering a general set of steps to help integrate ethics into national security decision-making. As said, the chapter does not seek to offer answers to what one ought to do with relation to national security issues, but is an attempt to help clarify the complexities around answering such questions.

THE PROBLEM: ETHICS AND NATIONAL SECURITY

The core problem that this chapter seeks to understand is what ought people do when national security is at stake. This problem is, in part, an ethical issue. By that I mean my interest is not 'what have people done in such situations?', nor 'what might people do in such situations?', nor even 'what does the law tell us what people should do?' The first formulation is a descriptive question, the province of areas like history and political science. The second formulation is more speculative, the province of social science or psychology. The third formulation is legal and is concerned with how formalised or conventional legal norms guide or prescribe practice and policy. While these are all interesting areas, some covered elsewhere in this book, they are not my primary interest. Instead, my interest is what ought people, particularly decision-makers do in the given situation? In particular, my interest is in the reasons that underpin or justify why we might say they ought to do this, or ought not to that.

For some, setting up the problem as an ethical issue is perhaps a folly. This can be explained by two variants of a sceptical challenge. I have posed the problem as 'what ought people do, when national security is at stake'? For some, they may simply see this as a foolish question—where issues of national security are concerned, there are no ethical questions. Considering that decisions around war as one of the key issues in national security, as Michael Walzer writes in *Just and Unjust Wars*, such discussions are hardly new:

> For as long as men and women have talked about war, they have talked about it in terms of right and wrong. And for almost as long, some among them have derided such talk, called it a charade, insisted that war lies beyond (or beneath) moral judgment. War is a world apart, where life itself is at stake, where human nature is reduced to its elemental forms, where self interest and necessity prevail. Here, men and women do what they must to save themselves and their communities, and morality and law have no place. *Inter arma silent leges*: in time of war the law is silent.[2]

Or as Tony Coates writes, "The very notion that morality may be applicable to such a destructive enterprise as war will strike some as bizarre, even perhaps scandalous. The contrary assumption that war lies beyond any moral pale is not only a common one, but one that, particularly in the light of twentieth-century experience, often seems irresistible".[3] Decisions around war are tightly linked to national security, and in such contexts, so some thinking goes, ethics do not apply. This scepticism has traction in theoretical arguments and public statements:

> The realist tradition in international relations has argued that self-interested states constitute the principle agents of international affairs, and attempts to oppose this on universal grounds would be either futile or dangerous: futile because policies motivated by ethical universalism would break on the rock of statist realism; dangerous because, in a Hobbesian world of interstate competition, ethical universalism would leave the relatively decent states vulnerable to the aggression of the most ruthless.[4]

We also see this scepticism publicly expressed by decision-makers. For instance, when faced with how to respond to the concerns about terrorism, many governments around the world have seen fit to pass laws and policies that abrogate individual liberties in order to protect and maintain national security. Daniel Andrews, a relatively left-leaning progressive state leader in Australia stated that "[n]otional considerations of civil liberties do not trump the very real threat, the very real threat of terror in our country today".[5] This is despite the fact that Australia faces very little actual existential threat from terrorism. The point is that, due in part to the competitive and anarchical context in which national security decisions are made, national security is often treated like some special realm or set of decisions where ethics need not apply. Whether it was ancient Rome, or non-authoritarian present-day Australia, ethical concerns take a back seat when national security is in play.

A parallel sceptical challenge arises from those who, rather than seeing national security as a province free of ethics, doubt that political leaders or people engaged in national security *actually care* about ethics or make their decisions based on ethical reasoning. This becomes particularly important when considering public statements by national security leaders or representatives, who seek to justify their actions by reference to ethics. The sceptic here sees such statements as either window dressing or rhetoric, deployed to convince people that what is happening is correct, when the leaders simply do not care about or believe what they are saying. "[T]he realist regards the utopian or moralist as at best a dangerous if well-intentioned fool, at worst as a self-indulgent hypocrite, more concerned with the preservation of spurious moral purity than with the avoidance of conflict or the alleviation of human distress".[6]

My response to both of these sceptical challenges is that there are indeed ethics in national security decision-making. This may be in relation to the content of specific decisions or actions, or it may be at a higher level, where we look to see why a particular decision was made, or how a particular policy was formulated. I am not saying that every decision about national security is the ethically correct decision, nor that those engaged in such decision-making are necessarily ethical or acting in line with publicly stated reasons for action. History is littered with examples, where national security decisions are devoid of ethical consideration, and those making such decisions warrant significant criticism. To take one example, the decision by UK Prime Minister Tony Blair to join the US invasion Iraq in 2003 was justified in part by the ethical reason of preventing human rights violations in Iraq.

> We must face the consequences of the actions we advocate. For me, that means all the dangers of war. But for others, opposed to this course, it means – let us be clear – that the Iraqi people, whose only true hope of liberation lies in the removal of Saddam, for them, the darkness will close back over them again; and he will be free to take his revenge on those he must know wish him gone.[7]

History has shown that these concerns played a limited role in the decision, that such statements were in part rhetorical devices than wholesale motivations for action.[8] Rather, my point is that there is ethical content to those decisions, and that such decisions are the province of ethical enquiry, analysis and criticism. In what follows, I offer a set of tools that can help with such enquiry, analysis and criticism.

ON ETHICS, NATIONAL SECURITY AND LIBERAL DEMOCRACIES

The three core concepts for chapter are ethics, national security and liberal democracies. Simply stated, for this chapter, I take ethics to be the extended discussion of what we judge one ought to do, underpinned by justificatory reasons. I take national security to be about the survival or persistence of the nation. In addition, I take liberal democracies to be representative democracies that take certain values to be important in how their societies are structured, their laws written and enacted, and how citizen-government relations develop and persist.

Ethics

As I am presenting it here, ethics is the disciplined exploration of reasons for why we pass judgments of praise or blame on some decision, action, behaviour or person. I mark ethics out as different from morality, in that morality can be understood as the passing of judgments of praise or blame, whereas ethics as a discipline is interested in the reasons *justifying or seeking to justify* those judgments.[9] For instance, consider you came across a group of people setting fire to a cat for fun.[10] I would assume that most of us judge that setting fire to cats for fun is wrong, is impermissible, is blameworthy etc. That is, we pass moral judgment on setting fire to cats for fun. Ethics, as a discipline, however, would seek to offer reasons as to *why* this is wrong.

Following Michael Smith, not just any reasons will do—ethics is interested in *justificatory* reasons.[11] If the people burning the cat asked why they should stop, common ethical reasons would be that the cat is the subject of a life and so is deserving of particular forms of respect, that unnecessary suffering ought to be avoided or prevented or that as none of the people burning the cat would like to be burnt alive for fun, they ought not do that to the cat. These reasons track roughly to the ideas of: rights or basic recognition respect; utilitarianism; and justice, respectively. The sceptic might respond that these are mere assertions, that there may be no such thing as moral truth, and even if there were, we have no way of knowing when we have found the moral truth. What I say here is that these are legitimate concerns of moral epistemology.[12] However, in terms of moral *authority*, we typically do hold particular justificatory reasons to be authoritative. Jonathan Haidt's work in moral psychology and moral anthropology, for instance, proposes a moral pluralism built on "(at least) six psychological systems that comprise the universal foundations of the world's many moral matrices".[13] These are care/harm, liberty/oppression, fairness/cheating, loyalty/betrayal, authority/subversion and sanctity/degradation.[14] He adds authority and group membership and the sanctity of objects and practices to the more standardly investigated values of rights, suffering and justice as the foundational reasons for particular judgements. Moreover, Haidt argues that some combination of these six moral systems can be found around the world, in all cultures and communities. The point here is that though questions of moral epistemology are open questions, we largely do take certain reasons to be *authoritative*, they do function as justifications for particular judgments.

The relation to national security is this: if we take ethics to be in part a statement about what one ought to do, or a judgment about what is impermissible, permitted or obligatory, we find such statements and judgments in discourse around national security. Moreover, if pressed on why a certain action is impermissible, why a government policy is permissible or why a nation's decisions are obligatory, we will find some set of justificatory reasons underpinning those actions, policies or decisions. This idea also finds expression in what the core function of ethical norms is—They "make us *accountable* to one another… [W]e are in a position to hold one another to account and to demand and expect things of each other".[15] This approach to reasons as public accountability has obvious applications to the relations between a state and its citizens, particularly for liberal democratic nations, where public accountability is a key feature (see below). Further, the idea that our publicly stated reasons mean we can demand and expect things of each other has significance in the international sphere, where nations can be held accountable for their decisions and actions by reference to their publicly stated reasons for those decisions and actions. However, in order to get a fuller understanding of how such reasons operate, we need to also understand what the nation is, what security is and why they are important.

Nations and States[16]

As Andrew Vincent notes in his *Theories of The State*, "[w]hen dealing with the State, we must be aware that it is the most problematic concept in politics. Anyone who has studied it in any depth will have become aware of this fact". Part of this problem is that the nation is both real and imagined. There is a "problem of its ambivalence – its certainty and yet its elusiveness. It has a tendency to slip in and out of many practices and concepts with alarming ease". While it is a creation, a social construction that does not exist in the same way that a person or a table exists, the nation is also a reality. "We begin and end our lives within its confines. Thus as well as being a complex concept, it is also an everyday reality that we cannot ignore".[17]

While it is admittedly elusive, there are certain elements, which are common in how a state is conceptualised. In one of the landmark treatments of the state, Max Weber identifies law, people and territory as being common to states.

> [A] compulsory political association with continuous organization will be called a "state" if and in so far as its administrative staff successfully upholds a claim to the monopoly of the *legitimate* use of physical force in the enforcement of its order... The primary formal characteristics of the modern state are as follows: it possesses an administrative and legal order subject to change by legislation, to which the organized corporate activity of the administrative staff, which is also regulated by legislation, is oriented. This system of order claims binding authority... over all action taking place in the area of its jurisdiction. It is thus a compulsory association with a territorial base.[18]

Andrew Vincent repeats this view: "[E]very State in fact has a territory, legal system, judiciary, monopoly of force and so on... [further] a State exists in a geographically identifiable territory over which it holds jurisdiction. Within this territory there exists a population, many of whom will be classified as citizens – namely that they have specific rights and immunities within that territory".[19] So, while recognising that the nation is a construction, we can also find commonalities; a range of bureaucratic apparatus including, but not limited to legal institutions, a people or groups of people to whom those bureaucratic apparatus apply and typically, some geographic territory or physical space and the legitimate use of force. Of course, there are going to be examples where these elements are found but do not constitute a nation, or where states lack or have variation on the elements. However, we do find common elements, which indicate what reference to the nation might mean.

In terms of the legitimacy or authority of the state, at least for modern liberal democratic states, the state is considered to gain its legitimacy from the support and endorsement of its citizens.[20] One common way of explaining this is by reference to a hypothetical social contract that people enter into with the state. This idea finds its roots in Thomas Hobbes' thinking. "As he had already made clear in explaining the political covenant, he assumes that we can never be expected to submit to sovereign power unless we believe that the outcome will be a more peaceful and settled way of life than we could hope to lead in the state of nature".[21] Put simply, it is in people's self-interest to collectivise certain aspects of their life, as there are particular goods that are either only achieved or secured collectively, or are better achieved collectively.

One particular feature of a nation is that, though it exists because its people and citizens created it and granted it legitimacy, it extends beyond the life of any of its people. "While sovereigns come and go, and while the unity of the multitude continually alters as its members are born and die, the person of the state endures, incurring obligations and enforcing rights far beyond the lifetime of any of its subjects".[22] Nations typically exist before and persist beyond that of their constituent parts. This endurance creates a permanence, a sense of past, present and future, as well as obligations that the nation's citizens may incur because of being born into the given nation. Such persistence of the nation may also generate duties in citizens to the persistence of the nation. As Quentin Skinner notes, quoting Emer de Vattel, "Sovereigns come and go, but the person of the state endures, which is why its interests must be given the highest priority".[23] As with the idea of the social contract, this is of course a highly contested notion, but it does speak to some of the ethical issues in national security—what rights or goods must individuals give up to be part of the nation, and what obligations does citizenship generate for individuals?

Security

This leads us to the notions of security. One idea here is that the state's primary purpose is the security of its people. "According to the fictional theory, the conduct of government is morally acceptable if and only if it serves to promote the safety and welfare of the person of the state, and in consequence the common good or public interests of the people as a whole...*Let the Safety of the People be the supreme Law*".[24] On Weber's account, one defining feature of the state is that it, and it alone, has can legitimately use particular forms of force. This "monopoly of force is tied to specific ends, namely the maintenance of internal order and external defence".[25] Here, the defining feature and justifying purpose of the state are to provide security. This idea finds expression in the assertion that the state's first duty is the security of its citizens.[26] That said, liberal democracies see limits on what the state can do here. "The original impulse of the liberal tradition, found in Locke and Kant, is the idea of the moral sovereignty of each individual. It implies limitations on the ways in which the state can legitimately restrict the liberty of individuals even though it must be granted a monopoly of force in order to serve their collective interests and preserve the peace among them".[27]

Another way of understanding security is in the discourses that arose in the period following World War II and into the Cold War period. Here, the idea of security, specifically national security was strongly associated with national defence and the military. "[L]ike most other traditionalist work in this area, the theory has focussed primarily on the state as the key unit and on the political and military sectors".[28] Again, "[s]ecurity, in the Cold War had come a long way from its carefree origins and its primary usage in reference to the person. Now it belonged primarily to the state; people, like the armed forces, were its instruments, and also, potentially, its enemies... the politics of national interest, in the conditions of the time, attached it literally to the state".[29] Thus, security became subsumed under the idea of national security, where state and military actions were its defining features.

Following this, people began rethinking of security as something beyond the realm of the military and other traditional security institutions. This "narrow, state-centred and military-focussed definition of security served the needs of a discipline confident in its ability to map the international order objectively and to apply the methods of natural sciences to the relations between states". However, for others, such a narrow focus was problematic, as they saw security as including a number of areas beyond the state and the military. "This dissatisfaction was stimulated first by the rise of economic and environmental agendas in international relations during the 1970s and 1980s and later by the rise of concerns with identity issues and transnational crime during the 1990s".[30] This more critical turn lead to the idea of 'securitization'. On this analysis, "security is about survival. It is when an issue is presented as posing an existential threat to a designated referent object".[31]

On the national security model, the nation is the referent object, and what matters is the survival or at least the persistence of the state. Thus, we have three interrelated ideas of security, first is the notion that the state must provide security to its citizens. Second is that security is about states and their militaries. Third is the idea of national security as the survival or persistence of the state.

In terms of the ethics of national security, all three interrelated areas indirectly or directly suggest a particular importance of national security:

> The special nature of security threats justifies the use of extraordinary measures to handle them... The invocation of security has been the key to legitimizing the use of force, but more generally it has opened the way for the state to mobilize, or to take special powers, to handle existential threats. Traditionally, by saying "security", a state representative declares and emergency condition, thus claiming a right to use whatever means are necessary to block a threatening development.[32]

The state has this special, perhaps overriding, responsibility to secure its citizens and its own persistence. This is the proper job of the state and security institutions like the military, police, intelligence and so on. Further, after the securitization turn, when security is invoked, it suggests that the normal rules or ethics do not apply. This is because of the special importance of what is being secured. Here, the moral importance of the nation trumps the normal moral constraints on what a state can do, the normal political processes and ethical constraints do not apply.

These are of course all highly contestable areas, and there is considerable disagreement on each of what ethics is, what nations and states are, and what security can mean. Rather than offer definitive accounts, my purpose here instead is to map some of the conceptual terrain, such that when talking about ethics and national security, there is some clarity about what I mean—*the justificatory reasons that are given to protect and preserve a state and its people*. This section should also raise some doubts about the first sceptical challenge—that there is no place for ethics in national security. In fact, I would suggest that discussions of national security are typically threaded through with attempts to justify the nation, its existence and what the state must do to protect either its people or its own persistence. That is, ethical reasoning is central to any discussion of national security.

An Open Question: Pluralism Versus Anything Goes[33]

All that said, there is a strong intuitive pull to the sceptical challenges of whether there is such a thing as 'an ethics of national security'. One form of the argument is this—'people have been arguing about these issues for millennia and have not come upon any single answer. Therefore, given the absence of a definitive answer to these questions, we ought to throw off such wasteful discussions'. To focus this specifically on the ethical issues, we can see the sceptical challenge as 'ethics does not provide an answer, so we ought not to waste our time with ethical discussions'. My preferred response is that the problem is not that there is no answer, but that there are many. Instead of looking for a single answer or single ethical theory that explains everything, we ought to be pluralistic. However, pluralism does not mean 'anything goes.' Following the idea of ethics as rigorous examination of the reasons that underpin our judgments of whether something is impermissible, permissible or obligatory, we can cast off a range of answers or reasons that do not justify particular decisions, actions or behaviours.

The position I am suggesting in this chapter is one of value pluralism. By that I mean that not only are there a plurality of values in play when considering national security, but that we need this plurality of values. "[N]o amount of philosophical argument can lead to a definitive victory of one account of value over the rest. Moral reflection is the effort to bring different dimensions of value to bear on specific occasions of judgment and to determine how they are best balanced or ordered, given the facts of the case".[34] Moreover, with a thoroughgoing value pluralism, it is likely an open question ought to be definitive in issues of national security, in what way, and how they interact and are weighed against each other. That is, it is unlikely that we will come to an agreement over the ultimate importance and role of these values in national security.

This value pluralism is ultimately built on reasonable moral pluralism, where we may agree on the importance of a set of morally relevant values, but there is no single agreed upon 'solution' to tensions or conflicts between those moral values. One approach would hold "the idea that there are many viable conceptions of the good life that neither represent different versions of some single, homogenous good, nor fall into any discernible hierarchy".[35] Expanding beyond a view that just looks at 'the good life', "a complete account will need to appeal to several foundational theories, each one of which is able to explain the basis of *some* of the normative factors, but no one of which explains all of them".[36] For instance, a utilitarian approach that maximises well-being will differ from one that takes individual rights to be sacrosanct, as advocated by libertarian philosophies:

> The problem with utilitarianism and libertarianism is that they each place extreme, and arguably implausible, weight on the values they emphasize. Utilitarianism holds that utility takes absolute priority—and that liberties must be compromised whenever liberty restriction is required to maximally promote utility overall (i.e., over the long run, all things considered). Libertarianism, on the other hand, calls for the opposite: (negative) liberty takes priority and must not be infringed for the sake of utility.[37]

Similarly, a deontological rights-based approach might preserve a rule like 'do not kill', which sits in contrast with a utilitarian's approach to maximise well-being. Applying this to national security, when faced with a situation where a nation's citizens lives are at risk, rather than choosing the option which minimises the number of casualties, a rights minded leader might decide that a principle like of 'do not let citizens die' is the operative principle, regardless of the numbers.

Likewise, those who understand justice to be concerned with fair distribution of costs and benefits will likely differ from those who understand justice to be concerned with equal treatment. Following Haidt, those who hold to the 'trinity of progressive values'; human dignity, suffering, and justice as fairness, will likely differ from those who hold more conservative beliefs; those with conservative beliefs see justice as equality, care about loyalty, the importance of social hierarchies and respect for the sacred.[38] On such an account, while reasonable people might disagree about *the* most important moral value, they can recognise there are other moral values, and that these are also important. The overall point is that any decisions, policies or laws around national security will factor these values in, but there will likely be ongoing reasonable disagreement about the ultimate form and weighting of those values.

Thus, on the 'ethics as reason giving' approach, we find a range of possible justificatory reasons that one can give in relation to any ethical situation. Yet, this does not mean that there is no answer to a given ethical issue, but that there are likely a range of different answers to a given issue. Importantly, however, on a pluralistic approach, it does not mean that anything goes. By holding that ethics is concerned with reason giving, one has to offer some justificatory reason for why a particular judgment was made. Taking norms to be about public accountability, we also find reasons playing a fundamental role in state-citizen relations and state-state relations. While there is likely disagreement about just what those reasons might be, I refer again to Haidt's work which sees as a matter of descriptive fact, that people do hold these six particular values to be authoritative. Any public justification would ultimately be founded in one or more of those values, and can be assessed by reference to them.

This also leads us some way to responding to the second sceptical challenge. That challenge centred on the idea that even if people, particularly political leaders, said they were acting on a given ethical reason, we ought to be sceptical about those motivations. Such statements are window dressing or rhetoric, used to convince a public or others to let one do what one will. Thus, on this second sceptical challenge, it is not that there are no ethics in national security, but rather that political leaders are in fact not motivated by those reasons.

In response to this, I acknowledge the accuracy of this challenge. First, there are many situations where people do not act in line with their publicly stated reasons for acting. This is, arguably, even more so when considering political leaders, who have a series of incentives to misrepresent their motivations. Second, it is often significantly problematic to actually ascertain and confirm what a person's motivations are. Thus, we do have reason to be sceptical about publicly stated reasons for acting. That said, this is where the notion of norms as public accountability become operative. Particularly in relation to liberal democracies, where a range of different public accountability measures have been developed to allow citizens some access to why particular decisions were made by their public representatives. Though we may not know the true motivations of a person's heart, insofar as there is public accountability, we can hold decision-makers accountable by reference to the publicly stated reasons.

Think here of decisions that are made by reference to national security. If, as I suggest, we take national security to be about either the state's responsibility to defend its people, the actions of the state and military or other national security institutions, or the protection and preservation of the nation against threats, then we have some measures to see if indeed those decisions or actions were made in line with national security. For instance, consider the case of 'Curveball', a secret informant whose intelligence on weapons of mass destruction provided much of the basis for the public justifications offered by the US and UK in their decision to go to war in Iraq in 2003.[39] As subsequent investigations has shown, not only were Curveball's information and motivations unreliable, this was not a sound basis on which political leaders should have decided to go to war.[40]

Second, as national security is itself wheeled out as a reason to go war and make other significant decisions, we are able to assess whether such claims are legitimate or not. This draws from the idea that national security is about the persistence or survival of the nation. Consider the 'war on terror'. The fear that Al Qaeda or so-called Islamic State or some other terrorist organisation poses an existential challenge to the US, the UK and so on is quite simply unfounded.[41] To put this in perspective, compare the existential threat posed by so-called IS to the UK with the existential threat posed by Nazi Germany to the UK during World War II. National security qua *national survival* does not hold water as a justifying reason for the UK's decision to join the US in invading Iraq in 2003. That said, national security qua a state's duty to *protect its citizens* is on more solid ground. But note that this likely justifies a significantly lesser degree of actions than existential risk, and also carries with it a set of constraints.[42] Similarly, while a single action or decision may not be indicative of the likely motivations, we can also see patterns of behaviour which allow us greater confidence to pass judgment on a person. Consider a political leader who does nothing to secure human rights generally but claims that human rights are their reasons for invading a country, and once the invasion has occurred, they plunder the target country's resources. This gives us reason to doubt the ethical foundation for the public reasons offered for their action.

The point here is that we can hold leaders and their decisions accountable, even if we cannot necessarily know a person's motivation. Responding to scandals is shown to play a major role in intelligence and national security sector reform in the US.[43] While these examples may involve accountability and criticism of the justificatory reasons offered for decisions and actions after the fact, the optimistic reading is that we can learn from these mistakes and install new processes to prevent similar mistakes from being repeated.

A DYNAMIC SPACE

A further challenge to the idea of ethical issues and national security is that this is a uniquely dynamic space: the conditions and factors around decision-making change. An example of this is Earth First, a radical environmental group who were engaged in high profile acts of property destruction to draw attention to environmental issues. The FBI considered them the highest US domestic terror threat in 2001. Then the 11 September Al Qaeda attacks occurred and everything in US counterterrorism policy shifted. Similarly, following the Al Qaeda attacks, many within the US were in strong support of new counter terrorism policies. The point here is twofold. First, that whether one is looking at the state protecting its citizens, the use of security institutions in response to threats, or the perceived need to protect the nation from threats, those *threats* change, evolve, emerge and recede. Second, in line with both the objective threat and subjective sense of those threats, people's *attitudes* to national security are also dynamic.

This is relevant to ethical issues in that it suggests that though particular ethical values and the principles derived from them might remain constant, the particular ways that those principles are interpreted and implemented will change. For instance, while a nation's citizens might see privacy as a key and fundamental value, they are also likely to see national security as an important value. Immediately following a major national security event, people are more likely to accept diminutions in their privacy if it may help or be seen to help reduce the threats. We see evidence of this following the Al Qaeda attacks on the US in 2001. The US is a country with a very strong sense of the value of privacy, and the values that privacy protects. Yet, following a major national security event, privacy receded in importance, compared to national security.

However, this does not mean that privacy evaporated or ceased to be valued. Following the revelations by Edward Snowden about widespread surveillance of people in the US and abroad by intelligence institutions like the US National Security Agency, the UK General Communication Headquarters, many in the US and abroad were now concerned that privacy was being unjustifiably overwhelmed by national security.[44] That is, for many people, privacy needed to be revisited and given more weight than national security. This pattern is common in issues of national security policy and oversight, in what Lester describes as the pendulum cycle.[45] On this, a failure in national security will drive greater powers for the government and national security institutions, and likely the diminution of legal or moral rights that liberal democracies consider important. On the other hand, a scandal in national security will drive stronger oversight and constraint on national security policies and practices, re-establishing the importance of legal and moral rights.

Further, following Lester's pendulum account, there this is a pluralism of values driving the swings of the pendulum. There are multiple values in play, and there is not only variation in which of those values are more or less important, but there is a dynamism in how these values are in fact valued. For instance, while we may take privacy to be fundamentally important for liberal democracies, a simple principle like 'privacy must be respected' needs to be interpreted. What does privacy consist in? What the reasons underpinning privacy's value? What does respect consist in? What happens if privacy must be reduced or violated, what recourse is open to those who have lost their privacy?[46] Moreover, how do we understand and value privacy in relation to other values? While privacy is important, and is likely necessary to protect or even secure other fundamental values, it is not the only thing that we think of as important. We need to understand privacy in relation to other values. Similarly, while we might agree that 'the state's first duty is the security of its citizens', we need to interpret that in context. What does security consist in? Even if the first duty is the security of its citizens, in liberal democratic nations, there are other responsibilities that a state has to its citizens, and it likely has moral responsibilities to non-citizens, within its borders and abroad. What are the reasons underpinning why national security takes importance at this time in this way? Again, while national security is important, and is likely necessary to protect or even secure other fundamental values, it is not the only thing that we think of as important. We need to understand national security in relation to other values.

This dynamism is important to recognise for two reasons. First, it helps explain some of the scepticism about ethics and national security. If people not only cannot give a single answer to how to resolve issues around ethics and national security, but constantly change their mind, then this breeds a scepticism about finding any answers at all. However, I would suggest here that this dynamism is not a bug but a feature. If we want our ethics, and indeed national security policies, to be applicable to reality, we need to be able to respond to changing facts. Second, it shows the importance of decision-making underpinned by publicly stated reasons. Given that it is so easy to change one's views, 'when the world changes, I change', it is perhaps easy to jettison what is of valuable for what is in a leader's short-term interest, and to dress changes up in rhetoric. However, this is where ethics as a sustained examination of the reasons that are given for a given action, decision or behaviour becomes so important and useful. By expecting reasons, we not only have the capacity to demand those reasons, but we can then hold decision-makers to account for their decisions, and we have some basis for actually holding them to account.

Where To? A Guide for Ethical Decision Making in National Security

The final point of this chapter is that ethics as reason giving provides tools that can help us both understand and criticise national security decision-making. We can look for and expect reasons to justify actions, decisions and behaviours provides a basis for enquiry, analysis and criticism. In terms of enquiry, in liberal democracies, there are expectations that our leaders and decision-makers will be held to account. There are typically paper or virtual trails, records and evidence of how certain decisions were made, and how those decisions led to policies, laws, and implementation. Thus, there is the capacity to enquire as to how and why decisions were made. In terms of analysis, ethics offers one way of analysing those decisions—it looks for the justificatory reasons that underpin the decisions. How does a particular national security decision engage with the responsibility to protect citizens, how were the national security institutions used, were they the best institutions to bring about the policy outcomes, and what was the actual threat environment that prompted or were claimed to justify those decisions?

We also have the tools to criticise those decisions. If, for instance, a particular national security policy violates individual's basic rights, causes unnecessary suffering, unfairly burdens one part of the population with the costs of the policy with little or no benefits or happens without due process, then we can criticise it. Also, given that there are multiple decisions being made by the same leaders or institutions, we have the capacity to compare different decisions for consistency in decision-making. This is where behaviours and patterns of decision-making become vital for analysis. If we can see a pattern of decision-making, while we may not know the actual motivations for an individual's decisions, we have the capacity to criticise patterns of decision-making. Consistency in reasoning, as I have argued elsewhere, can be a very powerful tool to criticise national security policies.[47]

This may seem somewhat idealistic, and it is true that ethics is the province of what we would like the world to be, rather than the way the world is. But, at least for liberal democracies, there are practices and mechanisms with which to hold decision-makers to account. This, however, places a responsibility on citizens to pay attention to what decisions are made, how they were made, and to hold those decision-makers and their institutions to account. While national security is often protected by a cloak of secrecy, as Lester shows, there are means by which even secret decision-making can be made somewhat accountable.[48]

With all this in mind, the questions to ask stem from the idea that ethics and national security is concerned with *the justificatory reasons that are given to protect and preserve a state and its people*. What were the reasons that were given to justify a given decision? How do those decisions track to values like care/harm, liberty/oppression, fairness/cheating, loyalty/betrayal, authority/subversion and sanctity/degradation? In what ways were these values weighed against each other? What was the actual threat to the nation and how serious was it? Have these calculations changed? If we cannot access these reasons, are there mechanisms by which those decision makers are held accountable?

To put those questions into a more structured form, what follows is a guide to ethical decision-making. The steps are adapted from Michael Davis' "Case Method".[49]

1. *State the Problem*: For example, 'there's something about this decision that makes me uncomfortable', or, 'there's a conflict of interest here' etc.

   The point of stating the problem is to get clarity on just what is actually causing the concern. It is not enough to simply say 'this is a problem' but to explain what the problem is. Issues in national security can seem like they are ethical issues because this is the first time we might have encountered this issue. Stating the problem clearly gives a better understanding of what is actually causing the moral concern.

2. *Check Facts*: Is this a real problem or are we confused about the facts?

   A number of ethical issues in national security may turn on the facts. For instance, you might be concerned about privacy implications of a particular policy, but perhaps this policy has no actual impact on privacy.

3. *Identify Relevant Factors*: For example, the people involved, laws, professional code or other constraints.

   This is essential to any ethical analysis of an issue—you need to be clear about who is affected by a particular decision, policy or application, how they are affected, what social norms, laws and other constraints are potentially at risk.

4. *Develop a List of Options*

This is an extension of the relevant factors—what are your options? What means do you have at your disposal, and who is best placed to pursue those means?

5. *Test Options*

Then for each of the options offered, we need to critically examine them.

5.1 *Harms Test*: does this option do more or less harm than others?

This is the basic notion of utilitarianism, in order to know what we should do, you need to know what the harms of different options are. On a simple utilitarian calculation, you would take the option that causes the least amount of harm. These harms may also need to include damage to sacred objects or particularly socially significant symbols.

5.2 *Publicity Test*: would I want my choice of this option published in the newspaper?

5.3 *Defensibility Test*: could I defend my reasoning when under professional scrutiny?

Steps 5.2 and 5.3 are quite similar. They both rely on the notion of being able to give justificatory reasons. What they ask of you is to first reflect on those reasons. And second, to consider whether you would be willing to stand by those reasons in public. This is not a foolproof way of ensuring that one's justificatory reasoning is as good as it could be, but it does give you way to reflect on those justifications. Importantly, if you are worried about those reasons going public, and/or would not be willing to stand by those reasons in public, this should give you significant pause, and to reconsider our reasoning. Moreover, public accountability is one of the aspects that tries to set liberal democracies apart from authoritarian nations is the notion of public accountability.

5.4 *Reversibility Test*: would I still think this was a good option if I was adversely affected by it?

This test goes to issues of fairness—if you would be unwilling to endure the outcomes, or if you would be unwilling to have those who you care about endure the outcomes, then it is likely that this option fails a basic test of fairness.

5.5 *Colleague Test*: what do my colleagues say when I tell them about my problem and proposed solution?

If, for example, your colleagues were to be significantly worried about a particular option, it is a good sign that option needs to be rethought. However, many institutions develop an institutional culture and can develop very similar values and ways of thinking. The risk of institutional culture narrowing one's considerations is why one must also consider what the public at large would say about this option.

5.6 *Professional Test*: what might my profession's governing body say about this?

5.7 *Organization Test*: what does the institution's legal officer say about this?

Steps 5.5, 5.6 and 5.7 are all quite similar. They are ways of using your institutional knowledge and expertise to test the options. They draw from the experience and moral authority of one's professional bodies, and the legal authority of the legal officer. However, what is legal is not necessarily ethical.

6. *Make a Choice*

You should then select from the options given. This is obvious, but needs to be stated. You cannot spend all their time reflecting on what to do and not actually do anything. This is particularly the case when certain national security threats or events require rapid decision-making.

7. *Review Steps 1–6*

This review step is quite important to see what can be learnt from the given experience, what could be done better, what went wrong and why? This also takes into account the dynamic nature of national security decision-making—that as the factors which play a role in decision-making shift, so too should your assessment of those decisions and the policies that arise from them.

While hardly foolproof or without controversy, this seven step guide to decision-making is an attempt to not only show that there are ethics in national security decision-making, but also that such ethics can be formalised and structured. This formalisation and structure make the public accountability feature of ethics as justificatory reasons both practical and useful. This is part of the case for seeing ethics as playing a key role in reasons for decision-making. Moreover, it gives something tangible to the idea that ethics and national security are *the justificatory reasons that are given to protect and preserve a state and its people*.

NOTES

1. I note that while many of the ethical issues about national security apply to non-liberal democracies, liberal democracies are the focus here. That said, with some adaptation, many of the issues and conceptual tools could be applied to non-liberal democracies.

2. *Inter arma silent leges* is attributed to the Roman politician, Cicero. Though his specific wording was *Silent enim lēgēs inter arma*. See Walzer, M. (2006). *Just War and Unjust Wars*, 4th Edition. New York: Basic Books, 3.

3. Coates, T. (1997). *The Ethics of War* (p. 1). Manchester: Manchester University Press.

4. Freeman, M. (2000). Universalism, Particularism and Cosmopolitan Justice. In Coates, T. (Ed.), *International Justice* (p. 65). Aldershot: Ashgate.

5. Quoted in Bickers, C. (2017). National Security COAG Meeting: Australian Airports to Get Facial Recognition Software. News.com, October 5. Accessed October 25, 2017. http://www.news.com.au/national/politics/give-gun-smugglers-life-jail-terms-bill-shorten-says-in-the-wake-of-las-vegas-massacre/news-story/acbdab7a741895204762825e7623a877.

6. Coates, T. (1997). *The Ethics of War* (p. 11).

7. Quoted in Bluth, C. (2004). The British Road to War: Blair, Bush and the Decision to Invade Iraq. *International Affairs*, 80 (5), 886.

8. I refer here to the Iraq Inquiry, chaired by John Chilcot, which showed that, not only were there not weapons of mass destruction found in Iraq, but that a main and perhaps decisive reason for Blair's decision was to maintain good relations with the US. Blair's note to President George W. Bush on July 28, 2002, where he said 'I will be with you, whatever'—as disclosed in the Iraq Inquiry (Chilcot 2016, 15)—indicates that Blair's decision to join the USA in Iraq was made independently of his publicly stated ethical motivations for action.

9. I have discussed this ethics/morality distinction in more detail in *Ethics in an Age of Surveillance* (Henschke 2017, 20–24).

10. This example of people setting fire to a cat is adapted from Gilbert Harmann (1977, 4), though he is making a slightly different point about ethics and observation.

11. See Smith, M. (1987). The Human Theory of Motivation. *Mind*, 96 (381), 38; and Smith, M. (1994). *The Moral Problem* (pp. 94–98). Malden: Blackwell Publishing.

12. There is a significant body of work looking at relations between metaethics, truth and epistemology. For more on these topics see: Jonsen, A. R., & Toulmin, S. E. (1988). *The Abuse of Casuistry: A History of Moral Reasoning*. Berkeley: University of California Press; Parfit, D. (1987). *Reasons and Persons*. Reprinted with corrections. Oxford: Clarendon Press; Parfit, D. (2011). *On What Matters*, Vol. 1. Oxford: Oxford University Press; Rachels, J. (1995). *The Elements of Moral Philosophy, 2nd Edition*. New York: McGraw-Hill International Editions; Smith, M. (1994). *The Moral Problem*; Ross, W. D. (1930). *The Right and the Good*. Oxford: The Clarendon Press; Blackburn, S. (1998). *Ruling Passions*. London: Oxford University Press; Mackie, J. L. (1977). *Ethics: Inventing Right and Wrong*. London: Penguin; Moore, G. E. (1959). *Principia Ethica*. Cambridge: Cambridge University Press; and Audi, R. (1997). *Moral Knowledge and Ethical Character*. New York: Oxford University Press.

13. Haidt, J. (2012). *The Righteous Mind: Why Good People Are Divided by Politics and Religion* (p. 211). London: Penguin.

14. Ibid., 211–214.

15. Brennan, G., Eriksson, L., Goodin, R. E., & Southwood, N. (2013). *Explaining Norms* (p. 36). Oxford: Oxford University Press. Emphasis in the original.

16. I note here that I will be using 'the nation' and 'the state' through this section. Given that the focus of this chapter is on ethics and national security, I will generally use 'nation', but many of the references that follow refer instead to 'the state'. Though they are complementary terms, we can treat them as referring to different aspects of the same collective. The nation is the people and the administrative or bureaucratic institutions that sit above the people.

The state, however, can refer instead to just those institutions as distinct from the people or citizens who they oversee. However, a number of the references that follow use the terms somewhat interchangeably, so I will be a little looser in my use here.

17. Vincent, A. (1987). *Theories of the State* (p. 3). London: Basil Blackwell.
18. Weber, M. (2012). *The Theory of Social and Economic Organization*. Martino Fine Books (p. 154, 165).
19. Vincent, A. (1987). *Theories of the State* (p. 7, 19).
20. At the peak of their military and geographic power, the so-called Islamic State of Iraq and Syria, ISIS, for instance, saw themselves as a state, providing a range of social services, including services like issuing passports. However, for a range of reasons, including their significant human rights violations, they were not granted legitimacy in the international arena.
21. Skinner, Q. (2009). A Genealogy of the Modern State. *Proceedings of the British Academy*, 162, 343.
22. Ibid., 346.
23. Quoted in Ibid., 353.
24. Ibid., 362. Emphasis in the original.
25. Vincent, A. (1987). *Theories of the State* (p. 20).
26. This idea, frequently attributed to Thomas Hobbes saw an earlier expression by British jurist Sir Edward Coke in the late sixteenth century. He described "the relationship between sovereign and subject in terms of a 'mutual bond and obligation,' under which the subject owed allegiance or obedience, while the sovereign was bound 'to govern and protect his subjects.'" The idea was perhaps given a concise formulation by US Representative John Farnsworth in 1867, when he said that "[t]he first duty of the Government is to afford protection to its citizens", both quoted in Heyman, S. (1991). The First Duty of Government: Protection, Liberty and the Fourteenth Amendment. *Duke Law Journal*, 41, 513 and 508.
27. Nagel, T. (2002). Rawls and Liberalism. In Freeman, S. (Ed.), *The Cambridge Companion to Rawls* (pp. 63–64). Cambridge: Cambridge University Press.
28. Buzan, B., Wæver, O., & De Wilde, J. (1998). *Security: A New Framework for Analysis* (p. 11). Boulder: Lynne Rienner.
29. McSweeney, B. (1999). *Security, Identity and Interests: A Sociology of International Relations* (p. 21). Cambridge: Cambridge University Press.
30. Buzan, Wæver, & De Wilde, (1998). *Security* (p. 2).
31. Ibid., 21.
32. Ibid.
33. Some of this discussion is taken from another paper where I develop a similar argument in favour of pluralism in the context of autonomous vehicle systems in Henschke, A. (Forthcoming-a). *Pluralism in the Design of Autonomous Vehicles*.
34. Galston, W. (2002). *Liberal Pluralism: The Implications of Value Pluralism for Political Theory and Practice* (p. 6). Cambridge: Cambridge University Press.
35. Larmore, C. (1987). *Patterns of Moral Complexity* (p. 23). Cambridge: Cambridge University Press.
36. Kagan, S. (1998). *Normative Ethics, Dimensions of Philosophy* (pp. 294–295). Boulder: Westview Press. Emphasis in the original.
37. Selgelid, M. J. (2009). A Moderate Pluralist Approach to Public Health Policy and Ethics. *Public Health Ethics*, 2 (2), 196.

38. As mentioned earlier, I am drawing from work by Jonathan Haidt here where he talks about six key common values that people take to be morally authoritative (Haidt 2012, 211–214). On his account, 'progressive' people typically value care/harm, individual liberty/oppression and fairness. In contrast, those who are more socially and politically 'conservative', value those three approaches but also see justice as equality, loyalty/betrayal, authority/subversion and sanctity/degradation as equally and at times more important than the values the progressives favour.

39. Drogin, B. (2007). *Curveball: Spies, Lies, and the Con Man Who Caused a War*. New York: Random House.

40. Chilcot, J. (2016). *The Report of the Iraq Enquiry*. Edited by Committee of Privy Counsellors.

41. I note here David Kilcullen's astute observation that such terrorist groups do pose much more of an existential threat to countries like Iraq, Syria and Libya and so on, see: Kilcullen, D. (2016). *Blood Year: The Unraveling of Western Counterterrorism*. Oxford: Oxford University Press.

42. Henschke, A., & Legrand, T. (2017). Locating the Ethical Limits of National Security: Counter-Terrorism Policy in Liberal Democratic Societies. *Australian Journal of International Affairs*, 71 (5), 554–561.

43. Lester, G. (2016). *When Should State Secrets Stay Secret?* (p. 197 and pp. 206–208). Cambridge: Cambridge University Press.

44. See Greenwald, G. (2014). *No Place to Hide: Edward Snowden, the NSA, and the U.S. Surveillance State*. New York: Metropolitan Books; and Harding, L. (2014). *The Snowden Files: The Inside Story of the World's Most Wanted Man*. New York: Vintage Books.

45. Lester, (2016). *When Should State Secrets Stay Secret?* (p. 163, 197, and pp. 206–208).

46. Privacy is another topic that has received considerable attention in the literature, and I cannot do it justice here. For more on this see: Solove, D. (2008). *Understanding Privacy*. Harvard: Harvard University Press; Koops, B. et al. (2016). A Typology of Privacy. *University of Pennsylvania Journal of International Law*, 38; Garon, J. M. (2016). Seeking to Promote Security Over Privacy and Achieving Neither. *SMU Science and Technology Law Review*, 19 (3), 351–374; and Henschke, A. (2017). *Ethics in an Age of Surveillance: Virtual Identities and Personal Information*. New York: Cambridge University Press.

47. Henschke, A. & Legrand, T. (2017).

48. Lester, (2016). *When Should State Secrets Stay Secret?*

49. I have adapted Michael Davis' original piece on this. In his piece, he sets out the seven steps to ethical decision making see: Davis, M. (1999). *Ethics and the University* (166–167). London: Routledge. What I offer here is a commentary and contextualisation on how these steps can be applied in a national security context.

Part II

Actors

CHAPTER 5

Nothing to Fear but Fear Itself: The National Security Policy of the United States

Christopher J. Fettweis

How difficult must it be for outsiders to understand the United States. The American people sometimes choose intellectual leaders with soaring rhetoric who transcend racial and class boundaries; at other times, they elect vulgarian showmen who pander to the worst instincts of the masses. For people in other countries—and increasingly for those in the United States too—America must seem like a confusing, vexing, and sometimes frightening place. The confusion and vexation would not be as disconcerting were the United States not an extremely powerful state. Similar swings in leadership styles occur elsewhere, but when they happen in the United States, power realities lend them more international significance. Hence, understanding American politics is more of an imperative for the rest of the world, for better or for worse.

No part of those politics is more urgent to understand for many observers around the world than foreign policy. The United States interacts with other countries from a different position: its status helps determine its foreign policy priorities and actions. Structural factors cannot explain everything the United States does, however. Indeed, Washington's foreign policy can change drastically from administration to administration, and never more so than in the transition from Obama to Trump. Examining policy over time, across presidents, can sometimes reveal common features that, if taken together, can present a fairly consistent approach to grand strategy and foreign affairs.

C. J. Fettweis (✉)
Department of Political Science, Tulane University, New Orleans, LA, USA
e-mail: fettweis@tulane.edu

© The Author(s), under exclusive license to Springer Nature Switzerland AG 2022

95

M. Clarke et al. (eds.), *The Palgrave Handbook of National Security*,
https://doi.org/10.1007/978-3-030-53494-3_5

This chapter reviews the evolution of U.S. strategic culture, seeking to explain the choices Washington makes today. It explains the influence of geography on the development of its approach to security, and the pathological obsession with complete safety that dominates its thinking. The world is a dangerous place, we are always told, which is true only to those without historical context or memory. Security is, after all, relative—no country is ever completely safe or free from danger—but the United States today is as close as any has ever been. It faces no existential threats, yet worries obsessively. Iran, North Korea, ISIS, electro-magnetic pulses, Vladimir Putin, Chinese bankers, Mexican migrants, and a variety of other minor irritants rise to the level of apocalyptic threats in the American marketplace of ideas. If there is one consistent element in the narrative of U.S. security, it is *fear*.

Why is this so? Why is it that the United States—the strongest power in the history of the world, in absolute and relative terms—is so worried about its security? The answer has multiple parts, but begins in the foundation of the country, and the mixed blessings provided by providence.

Free Security

The United States came of age, according to an apocryphal French diplomat, surrounded by Canada, Mexico, and fish.[1] The oceans provided "free security" for generations, shaping U.S. national security policy in ways large and small.[2] The United States had the spectacular fortune to be born in a relatively safe neighborhood, where no barbarians lurked just over the horizon eager to storm the gates. The first generation of U.S. strategists certainly appreciated the gifts bestowed by nature. National security was one of the very few issues on which the U.S. founding fathers spoke with one voice. With varying degrees of enthusiasm, and for somewhat different reasons, these men felt that the United States ought not squander the blessings provided by geography. They consistently and forcefully counseled restraint for their new nation instead of deep involvement in the affairs of Europe.[3] Washington was the most prominent advocate, arguing in his Farewell Address that "nothing is more essential" for America "than that permanent, inveterate antipathies against particular nations, and passionate attachments for others, should be excluded." His "great rule" of strategy was that the United States ought to extend its commercial relations with foreign nations, but have with them "as little political connection as possible."

All of his colleagues, even those with long-standing disagreements on nearly everything else, basically agreed with this sentiment. Alexander Hamilton advised Washington that "America's predisposition against involvement in Old World affairs" ought to be a "general principle of policy"[4]; Thomas Jefferson was "for free commerce with all nations, political connection with none, and little or no diplomatic establishment."[5] In his 1776 pamphlet *Common Sense*, Thomas Paine wrote that although "Europe is our market for trade, we ought to form no partial connection with any part of it. It is the true interest of

America to steer clear of European contentions." The second president agreed with the first: John Adams argued that "we should separate ourselves, as far as possible and for as long as possible, from all European politics and wars."[6] This recommendation was heeded by his son, President John Quincy Adams, who in 1821 issued his famous and eloquent warning against going abroad in search of monsters to destroy.

A number of recent works have argued that this common perception of the strategic guidance of the founders is mistaken, and that instead these men were pragmatists who did not counsel a course separate from the rest of the world.[7] These accounts do an admirable job of constructing and then knocking down the straw man of an isolationist United States. It is no great insight to point out that U.S. leaders have always lent rhetorical support to those who sought liberty and freedom abroad. It is also unsurprising that its policymakers carried out robust debates over the proper course of action and intervened in the affairs of other countries whenever it seemed wise to do so. The United States was never isolationist, and virtually no strategist today thinks it ought to be today.

These modern re-interpretations of history cannot wash away the obvious fact that for most of its existence, the United States defined threats, interests, and opportunities quite narrowly and maintained appropriately small militaries with which to address them.[8] The affairs of the Old World in particular held little more than a passing interest to U.S. strategists, who felt that the oceans provided adequate buffer from most ills. It was restraint, not isolationism, that dominated the grand strategy of this country for its first hundred and fifty years. During that time, the nation experienced steady economic growth and was unmolested by outside forces, eventually rising to become the strongest of the world's great powers. Strategic restraint seemed to serve the young nation quite well. Restraint, then and now, is a grand strategy with three rules. To paraphrase Eric Nordlinger, whose description remains the best, they are: minimal military and political engagement abroad, moderate activism on behalf of our ideals, and robust economic engagement.[9]

After the Second World War, a series of decisions were made that altered the traditional strategic approach, and the United States has followed an activist, internationalist path since. The turning point was a stark one: the era of restraint came to a sudden end on December 7, 1941. It had shown signs of cracking on occasion in the decades leading up to the Japanese attack on Pearl Harbor, but the constituency for nonintervention was always able to rein in America's growing internationalist impulses. President William McKinley had to be dragged into the brief war with Spain in 1898 by the combined power of a yellow press, bellicose public, and Teddy Roosevelt. Woodrow Wilson avoided involvement in the First World War for as long as he could— or as long as he decided to—and intervened after much of the butchery had already occurred. Afterward, the United States withdrew back to its hemisphere, renouncing Wilson's efforts to establish a liberal world order. The

Senate's repudiation of the Treaty of Versailles was a sure sign that restraint still dominated American foreign policy.

The Japanese—and then Hitler, who compounded his many mistakes by declaring war on the United States four days after Pearl Harbor—finally brought the era of restraint to a definitive end. The Japanese surprise attack did more than just tilt the scales in favor of the internationalists; it proved to be one of the formative events in U.S. strategic culture. Pearl Harbor demonstrated that the oceans no longer provided free security, and that the problems of the Old World could find their way to the New. The potential for danger arising out of nowhere, as a "bolt from the blue," has been a hallmark of U.S. strategic thinking ever since.[10]

Geography continues to afford Americans the luxury to forget about the problems of the world much of the time. When that isolation is shattered, greater-than-average shock follows. Arnold Wolfers once observed that "nations tend to be most sensitive to threats that have either experienced attacks in the recent past or, having passed through a prolonged period of an exceptionally high degree of security, suddenly find themselves thrust into a situation of danger."[11] Pearl Harbor was the type of "psychological hammer blow" that Brent Rutherford described as in 1966 as those that lead actors to "adopt several adaptive or maladaptive behaviors. The selection of these behaviors is based on the learning and internalization of these methods early in life, and is largely unconscious."[12] The U.S. strategic culture, and its high sensitivity to threat, has its origins in the decisions made in Tokyo in late 1941.

Pearl Harbor trained many American strategists to worry that surprise attack might come when they least expected it, which seemed to be confirmed by al Qaeda on September 11th, 2001. The terrorist attacks had a greater impact on the United States than they may have had elsewhere, and not just in the metaphorical, macro sense: depression and anxiety disorders were exceptionally common in their initial aftermath.[13] People became fixated on the possibility of another attack, waiting for the "other shoe to drop," a shoe that many worried would be even worse. "Worry about terrorism did not decline as time passed and the threatened onslaught failed to materialize," as journalist Daniel Gardner has noted. "Instead, it slowly rose."[14] Periods of apparent calm are not comforting to those societies who believe that surprise attacks can materialize out of nowhere, without warning. In the intervening years, it has hardly waned: the percentage of Americans who report anxiety regarding terrorism has remained essentially constant since 2001.[15]

For many analysts of U.S. foreign policy, one belief has remained constant since the Japanese attack awoke them to the potential for surprise attack: *We are living in dangerous times*. By the 1950s, communism had generated a level of national fear that inspired the United States to raise and maintain an enormous peacetime military for the first time in its history, an action that would have surely horrified its founding generation. The Cold War ended but the high perception of threat lived on; rogue states, terrorism and ethnic conflict rose to fill the void left by the Soviet Union, giving the American people no respite from anxiety. September 11th merely put a face on the danger that many already knew existed. When it came to fear, at least, Robert Kagan was correct when he noted that "America did not change on September 11," but "only became more itself."[16]

Many of those who make and/or comment upon U.S. foreign policy maintain that the world is full of enemies and evil, so this (whenever this is) is no time to relax. Former Speaker of the House Newt Gingrich is hardly alone in his oft-expressed, seemingly eternal belief that the world is a "fundamentally dangerous place," one to which our current leaders are underreacting, irresponsibly leaving the people vulnerable.[17] General Martin Dempsey repeatedly remarked that during his tenure as Chairman of the Joint Chief of Staff the world was more dangerous than at any point in his lifetime.[18] When John Bolton became Trump's third national security advisor, foreign policy *éminence grise* Walter Russell Mead opined that "not since the 1940s has a national security adviser [sic] faced an array of challenges this urgent, this numerous and this perplexing."[19] "We are now at maximum danger," agreed former Supreme Allied Commander in Europe Admiral James Stavridis.[20]

Constant repetition of this idea by elites has over time generated genuine belief in the public that the seas no longer can protect us from the dangers lurking everywhere. A 2009 poll found that nearly sixty percent of the public—and fully half of the membership of the Council on Foreign Relations—considered the world to be more dangerous than it was during the Cold War.[21] Nearly a decade later, the situation was no better. According to a 2017 Ipsos poll, 88% of Americans strongly or somewhat agree that, over the course of the previous year, the world became a more dangerous place.[22]

Since Pearl Harbor, then, the United States has been both the world's premier power and its supreme worrier. It has consistently detected more danger in faraway corners of the world than any other state, including its closest allies. Washington could find little support for its contention that the vital interests of the West were at stake in Southeast Asia in the 1960s, for example, or in Central America two decades later, or in Iraq to decades after that.

Paranoid countries are dangerous, and paranoid unipolar powers uniquely so. To paraphrase a wise and decidedly non-American thinker, fear leads to anger, and anger leads to hate.[23] Frightened actors take steps to assure their security; they build walls along their borders, or spend trillions countering terrorism, or invade countries to topple unfriendly regimes.[24] At home, they sacrifice civil liberties in hope of increasing security, and abroad they attack those they blame for their fear. They take action, in other words, to make themselves safer. When those fears are unwarranted, the actions they take are unnecessary. The dominant feature of twenty-first century U.S. national security has been fear, and as a result, there has been an unbroken line of acrimony, tragedy, waste, and unnecessary war.

Fear, more than any other single factor, helps explain the unbroken string of blunders upon which the United States has embarked over the course of the last few decades. Is this fear justified? What are the threats in the twenty-first century system? The next section reviews the major debates regarding threats to U.S. national security, as well as emergent and likely future challenges. The one after next speculates a bit about the sources of pathological fear in U.S. foreign policy.

What Are We Afraid Of? Issues and Debates in Twenty-First-Century U.S. National Security

While it is impossible to identify all the specific security issues with which U.S. leaders will deal as the century unfolds, a few broad themes and categories are likely to remain more or less constant. The bulk of U.S. security planning, as well as debates and analyses in the marketplace of ideas, tend to fall under a few major headings. Something of a consensus exists that dangers of the twenty-first century, such that they are, fall into four categories: the traditional, nontraditional, technological, and imagined perils.

Traditional Threats: Peer Competitors

Realists are not the only ones who believe that power is directly related to threat.[25] The stronger the rival, this logic goes, the greater the danger it poses. The United States faces a number of traditional challenges to its security, or may in the near future, the most obvious of which is China. For nearly two decades, a variety of analysts have identified the rise of China as the most dangerous development for the United States and its dominant position in the Pacific.[26] If indeed the relative power of the United States wanes over time, a "power transition" dynamic could take hold and lead to conflict.[27]

China may be the most likely potential peer competitor, but it is not alone. Russian resurgence has been predicted on-and-off for decades now, and Vladimir Putin might well be intent on making it a reality.[28] Other scholars worry about the potential for balancing over time against U.S. power by those countries with whom we currently have very good relations.[29] The main reason for continued high levels of U.S. military spending is the potential, even if far off down the road, for conventional war against great powers.

That road, for now, appears quite long. Furthermore, rising powers no longer pose the dire threat they once did. As most observers of international politics are (or should be) aware, the world is substantially less violent than it was even a generation ago. The impression, however widespread, that we live in a complex and chaotic era, one more dangerous than the past, is simply unsupportable: all forms of armed conflict, including major and minor international conflicts, civil wars, and ethnic conflicts are at record-low levels.[30] Large swaths of the globe are entirely at peace, including Europe, the Pacific Rim, and the entire Western Hemisphere. Sub-Saharan Africa has quietly just experienced its most peaceful decade in recorded history.[31] Warfare is an endangered species today, with its habitat now confined to an arc that runs from the Sahel through the Middle East into Pakistan.

Harvard psychologist Stephen Pinker labeled this remarkable (and remarkably underappreciated) trend in international security the "New Peace."[32] Raw conflict numbers tell only part of its story: by almost any measure the world has become significantly more peaceful, with measurable declines in coups, repression, the chances of dying in battle, territorial/border wars, conquest, genocide, and violence against civilians.[33] Whether these pacific trends represent a fundamental change in the rules that govern state behavior or a temporary respite between cataclysms is not yet clear, but there is no doubt that, thus far at least, the post-Cold War era has been far more stable and peaceful than any that preceded it.

The New Peace is not without its skeptics and critics. Popular (and political) perceptions about warfare certainly do not match empirical reality. Anxiety and unease about the state of the world remain high. The bloody mess in Syria in particular has blinded many observers to the broader security trends, which remain essentially unchanged. Whether or not this veritable golden age continues into the future is of course an open question. For now, however, there simply are no conventional threats to U.S. security. That U.S. leaders have not recognized these peaceful trends should not be surprising. "Between the happening of a historical process and its recognition by rulers," wrote historian Barbara Tuchman of the fourteenth century, "a lag stretches, full of pitfalls."[34] It then falls to outside observers to point out that ours is not a particularly dangerous world, no matter how conventional is the wisdom to the contrary. These are not dangerous times.

Today, the Department of Defense is euphemistically named; nothing it does actually *defends* the United States, since no state considers attacking it.[35] In fact, the idea that the military would ever be called upon actually to defend U.S. territory is beyond the imagination of even the most paranoid analyst, since invasion is utterly preposterous. And conventional conflicts, except for those of our own making, are less likely than ever before.

Nontraditional Threats: Terrorism, Rogue, and Failed States

Conventional war, much less outright assault, is not the leading security challenge facing the United States today in the minds of most. Instead, irregular or non-state actors, especially terrorists, appear at or near the top most lists of threats to the West. Other nontraditional threats, such as rogue states, also have risen to greater prominence in the aftermath of the Soviet collapse. There is a near-constant tension in defense circles about the order of priority here: Realists, as well as force planners for the Navy and Air Force, suggest that traditional threats, even if unlikely in the near future, ought to occupy the bulk of our planning, whereas a new generation of theorists suggest that we should look beyond state power and concentrate on the wide variety of challenges posed by the weak actors of the post-Cold War era. In this, they are joined by advocates for land power, especially the Army and Marines.

A completely different school of thought suggests that threats identified by both camps are relatively minor. International terrorism is not on the rise, hype, and fear notwithstanding.[36] The risk posed by terrorists to any individual is extremely low, less even than being struck by lightning or crushed by a cow.[37] National security officials tend to discount such statistics, at least in part because they conflict with their pre-existing beliefs about the ubiquity and danger of the threat. As Ambassador Philip Wilcox, the State Department coordinator for counterterrorism insisted, irrationally and pathologically, that when it comes to measuring terrorism "we shouldn't place too much emphasis on statistics."[38]

Despite their inability to inflict great damage, obviously Islamic fundamentalist terrorists pose some degree of danger to the United States. However, rational leaders would interpret this issue for what it is: a law enforcement challenge of the first order rather than an existential strategic threat. Fortunately, there is no meaningful dissent in the industrialized world about modern transnational problems like terrorism, weapons proliferation, human trafficking, drug smuggling, and piracy. Multilateral cooperation, coordination, and intelligence sharing are in the interest of every state and occur at high, if often underreported levels. Police action against terrorism is much less expensive than war and is likely to be far more productive as well.

For modern states, terrorism is a chronic rather than a life-threatening condition, one that causes problems and needs constant attention but is not fatal. Its practitioners can kill people and scare many more, but the localized damage they cause is by itself incapable of changing the character of Western civilization. Only the people of the West, largely through their own overreaction, can accomplish that. While U.S. analysts spend time worrying about such events, it is worth recalling that the diplomats of any prior age would likely have been quite grateful to have our problems. Terrorism and other irregular threats of the early twenty-first century are in reality quite minor in comparison with those of eras that came before, and certainly do not threaten the existence of this or any other country.

Second only to terrorism on the list of things that have animated the post-Cold War United States are those countries that operate outside of accepted behavioral norms, either because of illegitimate, tyrannical leaders, or the complete breakdown of governance. The Clinton administration spoke of "rogue states," many of which would find themselves part of President Bush's "Axis of Evil" a few years later. Today, it is often said, the United States seems to be threatened not by the strength of its adversaries, but by their weakness. "Disorder breeds disorder," argued neoconservative historian Frederick Kagan. "Just as disordered regions were a feeding ground for the Soviets during the Cold War, so now they are potential bases for the enemies of America and our way of life."[39] Those states that cannot control their borders, or that are too weak to stamp out non-state actors operating on their territory, are of major concern to Washington. The 2002 *National Security Strategy* made the case on its first page: "America is now threatened less by conquering states," it says, "than we are by failing ones."[40] "Of the world's more than 70 low-income nations," according to another analysis, "about 50 of them – excluding well-armed hostile nations such as North Korea – are weak in a way that threatens U.S. and international security" because of their general inability to control events on their soil.[41] After all, the thinking goes, al Qaeda thrived in the chaos of post-Soviet Afghanistan.

One might think that a major reconceptualization of the relationship between power and threat would have generated more controversy than it has. This new logic—which suggests that the weakest, most disorganized, and even pathetic regimes pose great danger to the strongest country in the history of the world—would demand an entirely new understanding of power in international politics. Minds from past ages would boggle at the suggestion that failed states present a greater threat to great power interests than do successful ones, or that the United States is more endangered by Afghanistan or Somalia than by China. Threat has traditionally been directly, not indirectly, related to power. Weak countries, even those that are actively hostile, should worry rational observers far less than strong. Rogue states do not pose serious risks to U.S. security.

Fears of "safe havens" arising out of the ashes of state failure are equally misplaced. For one thing, the training that a terrorist group needs is obviously rather minimal compared to that of a conventional army. Basic instruction on explosives is often the only necessary skill, and it does not require a safe haven, as Palestinian groups amply demonstrate. A shed is often sufficient. Those drills prominently displayed on al Qaeda propaganda videos, which feature recruits swinging from monkey bars and crawling under ropes for some reason, are of little utility for the modern terrorist, who usually seems able to function without much training at all. The instruction that Umar Farouk Abdulmutallab required before he stuffed a bomb into his underpants and walked onto an airplane was spiritual, not military.

Contrary to conventional wisdom, al Qaeda did not flourish in a failed state. It was sheltered by the most coherent government that Afghanistan has had since at least the mid-1970s. And an ungoverned region was hardly necessary to carry out the 9/11 attacks, since the cells that planned and perpetrated the hijackings could have presumably done so whether or not Osama was safe in Kandahar. Sanctuary for terrorists was also unnecessary for the multitude of attacks that have occurred since the deposition of the Taliban, from Paris to Bali to London. The vast majority of terrorist groups throughout history have proven able to operate in hostile territory, without any havens in which to train on monkey bars.

Finally, it is worth noting that the number of failed states is not increasing. In fact, the number of state failures remained essentially constant over the course of the second half of the twentieth century and has been declining

104   C. J. FETTWEIS

since a brief surge following the Soviet collapse.[42] It is not the case that globalization is leading to major disruptions of governance and that large swaths of the world have become lawless and anarchic. The strongest countries have little to fear from the weak.

Technological Threats: Nuclear, Cyber!, Killer Robots

If anything is more frightening than the various traditional and nontraditional actors of the twenty-first century, it is the tools they might use. The speed at which technology is changing society can be profoundly disorienting and disconcerting, especially for those who do not really understand the science behind it. "The hunger for stability is entirely natural," according to the philosopher William James. "Change is scary; uncharted change, demoralizing."[43] The pace of change does not wait for the anxious to adjust their expectations, however. A 2015 poll found that people are more afraid of evolutions in technology that they barely grasp, like robotics and artificial intelligence, than they are of death.[44] Technological change has always been accompanied by increases in anxiety and predictions of ill effects to come.[45] Since the speed of that change has never been greater, it should perhaps come as no surprise that the anxiety it has generated is greater as well.

The proliferation of scientific knowledge increases the potential mayhem the enemies of the future can perpetrate. The U.S. National Intelligence Council predicted in 1996 that "accelerating rates of change will make the future environment more unpredictable and less stable."[46] Weapon's proliferation is the most troubling, but other, seemingly benign scientific research can be destabilizing as well. The 2006 *Quadrennial Defense Review* suggested that the United States needed to shift its emphasis toward potentially catastrophic or merely "disruptive" technologies that future enemies might employ.[47] Few topics obsess U.S. planners as much as "cyberwarfare," or the potential of computer-based attack on the Western interests, which resulted in the creation of the U.S. Cybercommand in 2010.[48] "The world is applying digital technologies faster than our ability to understand the security implications and mitigate potential risks," warned a report of the U.S. Intelligence Community in 2013. "Compounding these developments are uncertainty and doubt as we face new and unpredictable cyber threats."[49]

Nuclear technology generated similar fears in the 1950s and 1960s, as well as apocalyptic visions of warfare or proliferation, neither of which have been borne out by events. In 1963, President Kennedy worried that by the early 1970s more than twenty-five countries might have the bomb; with the hindsight of a half-century, it is clear that his concerns were misplaced. Still, that fear lives on. The more countries with these weapons, the logic goes, the more likely they will be used or fall into the wrong hands. Today, no one has been discussing the dangers of nuclear proliferation and the attendant specter of their use more than Graham Allison and his "Managing the Atom" program at Harvard's Belfer Center, for whom the world is perpetually at the edge of a nuclear "tipping point" after which runaway proliferation will occur. That such a point has never arrived and shows no signs of doing so seems to offer little solace to those offering the most frightening warnings about mushroom clouds and fallout.

Other scholars have pointed out that there is far more proliferation pressure in imagination than in reality.[50] In fact, proliferation has slowed to a crawl since the end of the Cold War; today, its pace is essentially zero. In three decades, the number of countries with nuclear weapons has not changed, even if the membership roll in the "nuclear club" is different.

NUCLEAR WEAPONS STATES, 1988 AND 2018

1988	2018
United States	United States
USSR	Russia
China	China
United Kingdom	United Kingdom
France	France
India	India
Pakistan	Pakistan
Israel	Israel
South Africa	North Korea

Two states founded the club in the 1940s (the United States and the USSR), one joined in the 1950s (the United Kingdom), and two each in the sixties (France and China), seventies (India and Israel), and eighties (Pakistan and South Africa). In the 1990s, there were none. The over-hyped nuclear tests on the Indian subcontinent in 1998 merely confirmed what had been widely known for years, that both countries possessed nuclear arsenals. The nonproliferation regime suffered no consequences, since no other state followed their lead. North Korea has been the only new nuclear weapons state to emerge since the end of the Cold War, and its tests did not inspire others to go down that route, despite many breathless warnings to the contrary. Allison had predicted that if North Korea were to test a weapon, it would "unleash a proliferation chain reaction, with South Korea and Japan building their own nuclear weapons by the end of the decade. Taiwan would seriously consider following suit."[51] None of his feared consequences occurred. Proliferation "cascades" are the exception, not the rule.

Since the collapse of the USSR, trends in proliferation have actually been negative: three states that inherited part of the Soviet arsenal (Belarus, Ukraine, and Kazakhstan) peacefully surrendered the weapons to Russia. South Africa gave up its arsenal, and both Brazil and Argentina decided that the pursuit of nuclear weapons was not worth the cost.[52] Proliferation momentum has not only ground to a halt since the end of the Cold War, in other words, it has swung in the opposite direction. Allison's repeated warnings that "global trend lines in all things nuclear are worsening" fly in the face of the evidence.[53] There are simply not many countries that want nuclear weapons.

None of this will prove comforting to scholars like Allison, for whom warning lights are perpetually blinking in a world running out of time. He and his colleagues have provided the marketplace of ideas with some of its most disquieting images, of nuclear-armed terrorists and irradiated major cities. That nothing of the kind has come close to occurring does not seem to sap their motivation to scare. Facts about risk rarely alter the deeply held beliefs of those convinced about the dangers involved in nuclear proliferation, or any other of today's various bogeymen.

Imagined Threats: Unknown Unknowns

While the tangible threats of the post-Cold War world are rather minimal, the risk posed by intangible, vague, unknowable dangers that fecund Pentagon imaginations can devise are limitless. If one theme unifies the last two decades of U.S. strategic thinking, it is that the post-Cold War era is one marked by complexity, uncertainty and "unknown unknowns." Such vague concepts can be quite frightening, as long as they are not considered in any real depth. The threat to defense spending posed by the absence of threats to the country was first addressed by a group of analysts at RAND in the early 1990s. James Winnefeld and other "uncertainty hawks" pioneered the belief that the new system was not in fact any safer, appearances notwithstanding.[54] "Out with the old, in with the?????" and "Certitude vs. Uncertainty" were among Winnefeld's self-explanatory subheadings.[55] "Uncertainty is the dominating characteristic of the landscape," wrote Paul Davis, editor of a 1994 RAND volume on defense planning that focused on the dire challenges posed by the collapse of the lone actual threat to American security.[56] It did not take long for U.S. national security strategy documents to pick up the theme. "The real threat we now face," according to the 1992 *National Military Strategy*, "is the threat of the unknown, the uncertain."[57]

The message has been consistent, in both official and unofficial outlets, for more than two decades. The 2005 *National Defense Strategy* elevated uncertainty to the position of the "defining characteristic of today's strategic environment."[58] In 1997, Secretary of Defense William Cohen said that "while the prospect of a horrific, global war has receded, new threats and dangers – harder to define and more difficult to track – have gathered on the horizon."[59] At a press conference five years later, in the days leading up to the war in Iraq, his successor warned about "unknown unknowns," which are the threats that "we don't know we don't know," which "tend to be the difficult ones."[60] Such claims are rarely—if ever—questioned, much less subjected to scrutiny. That the world today is somehow more complex and therefore less predictable or knowable has become a belief, accepted on faith, without need of further justification.

Periods of apparent calm are not comforting to those societies conditioned to believe that danger can materialize out of nowhere, without warning. A seemingly safe world, where the sources of those inevitable surprises remain obscure, can seem more frightening than one with obvious threats. But the claims of uncertainty hawks contain a number of consistent elements that go beyond the American obsession with the possibility of a bolt-from-the-blue surprise attack. First and foremost, one of the more troubling aspects of unidentifiable threats is that little can be known about their relative intensity levels. Unknown unknowns might be rather benign, catastrophically severe or somewhere in between. For many observers of U.S. foreign policy, the possibility that unseen threats are exceptionally dangerous simply cannot be ruled out. "At present, Americans confront the most confusing and uncertain strategic environment in their history," writes historian Williamson Murray. "It may also be the most dangerous to the well-being of their republic."[61] Known knowns can be measured, understood, and combatted; those left to the imagination quickly expand to take on ominous proportions. "To make any thing very terrible, obscurity seems in general to be necessary," Edmund Burke noted centuries ago. "When we know the full extent of any danger, when we can accustom our eyes to it, a great deal of the apprehension vanishes."[62] The dangers posed by unknown unknowns, perhaps because of their obscurity, tend to appear unlimited and especially terrible.

Second, in a related point, since the present is so uncertain and frightening, these analyses tend to downplay the dangers of the past. The intangible threats of the present are often portrayed as more complex, uncertain, and unknowable than the tangible challenges of the past. The global security environment presents an "increasingly complex set of challenges," according to the 2012 *Defense Strategic Guidance*, compared to those that have come before.[63] Nostalgia for the Cold War, explicable once rosy retrospection and memory's positivity bias are understood, is quite common in official U.S. strategic documents.[64] The United States left a "time of reasonable predictability to an era of surprise and uncertainty," claimed the 2006 *Quadrennial Defense Review*.[65] Although the assertion that the Cold War was predictable might surprise those who waged it, to the strategists who came afterward the struggle against the Soviets seems to have been relatively uncomplicated, even quaint.

Finally, the obsession with the intangible prevents proper consideration of what is probably the most important force-planning question: How much is enough? How many supercarriers are enough to address the complex future, for instance? How many F-22s, cyberwarriors, spy satellites, or combat brigades does the United States need to keep its people safe from unknown unknowns? A security environment characterized primarily by drastic unknowables offers no guidance to those seeking to construct military forces. When danger is limited only by imagination, states invariably purchase far more than they need, wasting money on weapons systems that will never be used in the hopes of addressing threats they do not yet perceive.

Emily Goldman has argued that "unlike the prior interwar period, the uncertainty engendered by the end of the Cold War shows few signs of abating."[66] In this, she is essentially correct, even if her analysis is backward. The lack of identifiable, tangible, immediate threats to U.S. security has caused strategists to look toward intangible, unidentifiable, and future dangers, which are permanent and immutable. This age of uncertainty, however, is an age of relative safety. Until the day arrives when U.S. strategists are forced to replace vague threats with concrete ones, the basic security of the United States is assured.

Structure and Insecurity

If the threats of the twenty-first century are relatively minor, what explains persistent U.S. insecurity and fear? As it turns out, a state's perception of threat is directly related to power: as power expands, so too does the enemies list.[67] As Jack Snyder has explained, for history's most powerful states, "the preventive pacification of one turbulent frontier usually led to the creation of another one, adjacent to the first."[68] New enemies are always just over the horizon, awaiting discovery. The U.S. experience is not atypical, in other words; perception of threat expands with power, for at least four reasons.

First, great powers define their interests more broadly than do weak states. They participate in global as well as regional politics and take positions on many more issues as a result. Unipolar powers should be expected to take this phenomenon to an extreme, identifying more interests—as well as threats to those interests—than any other state in the system. "Most countries are primarily concerned with what happens in their neighborhoods," as Jervis has explained, "but the world is the unipole's neighborhood."[69] Today, the United States is the only country that participates in the geopolitics of every continent and expresses views on nearly every international dispute. States with relatively small numbers of interests face a simpler task in defending them and face a limited number of potential enemies. Great powers simply have broader concerns than do smaller powers, and a "hyperpower" should have the broadest of all.[70]

Examples of this dynamic are not hard to find. Two millennia after its collapse, it is easy to forget how much insecurity motivated Roman imperial expansion. Many of Rome's most prominent conquests, from Gaul to Dacia to Iberia, were driven not only by the desire for glory but also the sincere belief that untamed populations along its widening periphery represented threats to the empire.[71] Cicero explained that many Romans felt expansion was thrust upon them as part of a project to rid themselves of "frightening neighbors."[72] The fact that most of these neighbors were manifestly weaker did not matter; as its power grew, so too did Rome's insecurity and its expansion. The most powerful and in many ways safest society in the ancient world was never convinced that its security was assured as long as potential enemies existed anywhere.

Similar fears haunted the great European powers of the pre-modern and modern eras as well. The enormous size of the Spanish Empire, which at its height encompassed a quarter of the earth's land area, meant that its leaders could always detect a threat lurking somewhere. In 1626, King Philip IV was said to have lamented that "with as many kingdoms and lordships as have been linked to this crown, it is impossible to be without war in some area, either to defend what we have acquired or to divert our enemies."[73] Madrid spent itself into decline trying to address the many dangers it faced, whether real or imagined.[74] Great Britain also exhibited a high level of insecurity throughout the eighteenth and nineteenth centuries. As the boundaries of the empire expanded, new dangers consistently appeared just over the horizon. British politicians and strategists felt that turbulence on colonial borders "pulled them toward expansion," in words of a prominent historian of the era.[75] The notion that the empire could never be safe until all potential threats were addressed encouraged unnecessary forays into Afghanistan, Uganda, Zululand, the Crimea, and other places that served only to sap British strength.

The second reason that threat expands with power is that systemic disruptions can result in hierarchical alterations, or disruptions of status. For the power on top of the mountain, movement can only occur in one direction. Instability and conflict anywhere can appear to be the first steps toward systemic chaos and unpredictable status shake-ups. The United States can be expected to perceive threats quickly, therefore, often where other powers do not, and be more tempted to get involved in far-off turbulence that it imagines has the potential to challenge systemic stability. Its insecurity has no natural limits.[76]

Maintenance of the status quo, or preservation of the "unipolar moment," has been a central if often unstated goal of U.S. grand strategy since the end of the Cold War.[77] The goal has not always been unstated: the infamous and still classified 1992 *Defense Planning Guidance* made opposing the rise of peer competitors a central focus of its recommendations.[78] Successive administrations have not been as explicit about their status concerns, but none has shown a willingness to cede the top spot in the international hierarchy.

Rich people worry a great deal about their security. They build tall fences, install motion detectors, and hire private security guards to protect themselves and their belongings from the throngs of have-nots they assume are plotting to take what is theirs. Wealth creates insecurity in individuals, and it seems to do so in states as well, which is the third reason for American paranoia. Those who have more than what could be considered their fair share, perhaps bothered a bit by subconscious guilt, worry about security more than those who live in relative penury. In today's international system, the United States has the most and worries the most too, detecting enemies at a higher pace than other states. After all, to borrow Robert Kagan's memorable metaphor, the enemy of the outlaw is the sheriff, not the saloonkeeper.[79] Power and perceptions of insecurity are related, as counterintuitive as it may seem, since strong states believe they are the primary targets of those malevolent forces lurking in the dark corners of the world.

The final reason to expect that the power of the United States should be accompanied by intensified perceptions of threat is psychological, not structural. A large number of experiments have found that as actors grow in power and status, their evaluations of others, especially subordinates, become increasingly negative.[80] There is also some evidence, though admittedly not as robust, that power also affects the tendency to dehumanize others, muting reaction to their entreaties and/or suffering.[81] These and the other obstacles to empathy make asymmetric relationships fertile ground for the growth of enemy images, and suspicion of other actors. Not only do the strong misunderstand the weak, in other words, but they mistrust them as well.

Conclusions

The next disaster looms on the horizon. "There seems to be a curious American tendency," observed George Kennan toward the end of his life, "to search, at all times, for a single external center of evil, to which all out troubles can be attributed, rather than to recognize that there might be multiple sources of resistance to our purposes and undertakings, and that these sources might be relatively independent of each other."[82] During the Cold War, the root of the world's ills was obvious, and today, it appears equally plain for many American observers of international affairs. Iran has become to the twenty-first century what the Soviet Union was for the second half of the twentieth: evil's epicenter, the origin and supporter of the world's problems, from terrorism to radicalism to proliferation. The "road to victory" in the war on terror, therefore, goes through Tehran. President Trump's first national security advisor, Michael Flynn, wrote that Iran is the central actor in a nefarious alliance that includes Russia, Iran, China, ISIS, North Korea, Cuba, al Qaeda, Hamas, Hezbollah, Houthis, Venezuela, Syria, the Muslim Brotherhood, and a host of others, united by a shared hatred of freedom.[83] The perception is mutual; for many Iranian analysts, most of the evil in the world can be traced back to machinations emanating in Washington.[84]

The sense of insecurity that dominates the U.S. national security community is likely to lead to a showdown with Iran in the very near future unless more rational heads prevail. Where such heads could be found is not entirely clear; after all, the least hawkish principal on Donald Trump's national security team, General James Mattis, was fired by the previous administration for being too hawkish on Iran. If the day comes when the U.S. missiles are raining down on Tehran and its environs, the insecurity that comes with great power will share a big portion of the blame. Until then, the best the rest of us can do is point out that the United States is secure, by all reasonable historical measures, and can therefore afford patience in its foreign policy decisions. War, tragedy, and blunder need not result from insecurity, if perspective can keep it in check.

NOTES

1. This comment has been attributed to a variety of sources over the years. It is evocative and profound, whatever its origins.
2. That phrase first came from Woodward, C. V. (1960). The Age of Reinterpretation. *American Historical Review*, 66 (1), 1–19.
3. Gilbert, F. (1961). *To the Farewell Address: Ideas of Early American Foreign Policy*. Princeton, NJ: Princeton University Press; and Tucker, R. W. & Hendrickson, D. C. (1990). *Empire of Liberty: The Statecraft of Thomas Jefferson*. New York: Oxford University Press.
4. Quoted in Kupchan, C. A. (2002). *The End of the American Era: U.S. Foreign Policy and the Geopolitics of the Twenty-First Century*. New York: Knopf, 202.
5. From a letter to Elbridge Gerry in 1799. Bergh, Albert Ellery & Lipscomb, Andrew A. (Eds.) (2006). *The Writings of Thomas Jefferson*, Vol. 10. New York: Kessinger, 77.
6. Quoted in Dunn, D. H. (2005). Isolationism Revisited: Seven Persistent Myths in the Contemporary American Foreign Policy Debate. *Review of International Studies*, 31 (2), 253.
7. See especially Kagan, R. (2006). *Dangerous Nation*. New York: Knopf; Kagan, R. (2008). Neocon Nation: Neoconservatism, c. 1776. *World Affairs*, 170 (4), 13–35; Lind, M. (2006). *The American Way of Strategy*. New York: Oxford University Press; Gaddis, J. L. (2004). *Surprise, Security, and the American Experience*. Cambridge, MA: Harvard University Press; and Gaddis, J. L. (2008). Ending Tyranny: The Past and Future of an Idea. *The American Interest*, 4 (1), 11.
8. For a response to the new revisionism, see Fettweis, C. J. (2009). Dangerous Revisionism: On the Founders, 'Neocons' and the Importance of History. *Orbis*, 53 (3), 507–523.
9. Nordlinger, E. A. (1995). *Isolationism Reconfigured: American Foreign Policy for a New Century*. Princeton, NJ: Princeton University Press, 4. See also Gholz, E., Press, D. G., & Sapolsky, H. (1997). Come Home America: The Strategy of Restraint in the Face of Temptation. *International Security*, 21 (4), 5–48; Preble, C. (2009). *The Power Problem: How American Military Dominance Makes Us Less Safe, Less Prosperous and Less Free*. Ithaca, NY: Cornell University Press; and Posen, B. (2014). *Restraint: A New Foundation for U.S. Grand Strategy*. Ithaca, NY: Cornell University Press.
10. The literature is quite extensive. Good places to start include Betts, R. K. (1982). *Surprise Attack: Lessons for Defense Planning*. Washington, DC: The Brookings Institution Press; Gaddis (2004). *Surprise, Security, and the American Experience*; and Parker, C. F. & Stern, E. K. (2002). Blindsided? September 11 and the Origins of Strategic Surprise. *Political Psychology*, 23 (3), 601–630.
11. Wolfers, A. (1962). *Discord and Collaboration: Essays on International Politics*. Baltimore: Johns Hopkins Press, 151.
12. Rutherford, B. M. (1966). Psychopathology, Decision-Making, and Political Involvement. *Journal of Conflict Resolution*, 10 (4), 403.
13. Schuster, M. A. et al. (2001). A National Survey of Stress Reactions After the September 11, 2001, Terrorist Attacks. *New England Journal of Medicine*, 345 (20), 1507–1512.

14. Gardner, D. (2008). *The Science of Fear: How the Culture of Fear Manipulates Your Brain*. New York: Plume, 249.
15. Gallup has found that over 40% of Americans consistently report being worried that they will be the victim of terrorism. That number has not varied much since 9/11. See Gallup. Concern About Being Victim of Terrorism. Regularly updated and available at http://news.gallup.com/poll/4909/terrorism-united-states.aspx.
16. Kagan, R. (2003). *Of Paradise and Power: America and Europe in the New World Order*. New York: Knopf, 85.
17. Gingrich has made this argument throughout his long career. See Gingrich, N. (1995). *To Renew America*. New York: Harper Collins, 185, as well as virtually any speech or talk.
18. Dempsey, M. (2016). Notes from the Chairman. *Foreign Affairs*, 95 (5), 2. His long track record of nostalgia is critically addressed throughout the essays in Preble, C. A. & Mueller, J. (Eds.) (2014). *A Dangerous World? Threat Perception and U.S. National Security*. Washington, DC: Cato Institute.
19. Mead, W. R. (2018). Bolton Faces a Dangerous World. *Wall Street Journal*, 9 April, https://www.wsj.com/articles/bolton-faces-a-dangerous-world-1523315474.
20. Quoted in Wood, D. (2017). This Is How the Next World War Starts. *Huffington Post*, 4 April, https://highline.huffingtonpost.com/articles/en/trump-russia-putin-military-crisis/.
21. Another quarter (and a fifth of CFR members) consider the dangers to be equivalent. Pew Center for the People and the Press. 2009. America's Place in the World in 2009: An Investigation of Public and Leadership Opinion About International Affairs, http://www.people-press.org/files/legacy-pdf/569.pdf. See also Zenko, M. & Cohen, M. A. (2012). Clear and Present Safety: The United States is More Secure than Washington Thinks. *Foreign Affairs*, 91 (2), 79–93.
22. IPSOS (2017). Dangerous World. 13 June, https://www.ipsos.com/en/dangerous-world-2017.
23. No citation is needed for many people of a certain age; for the rest, the quotation is roughly what Master Yoda advises young Anakin Skywalker in *Star Wars I: The Phantom Menace*.
24. A study group from the Stimson Center calculated that the overall U.S. spending on counterterrorism from 2002 to 2017 was in the neighborhood of $2.8 trillion. See *Counterterrorism Spending*. Washington, DC: Stimson Center, May, https://www.stimson.org/content/counterterrorism-spending-protecting-america-while-promoting-efficiencies-and-accountability.
25. But they are among the most prominent. See Walt, S. (1987). *The Origin of Alliances*. Ithaca, NY: Cornell University Press.
26. Early entries in this literature include Gertz, B. (2000). *The China Threat: How the People's Republic Targets America*. New York: Regnery Publishing, Inc.; and Navarro, P. (2006). *The Coming China Wars: Where They Will Be Fought and How They Can Be Won*. Upper Saddle River, NJ: FT Press.
27. Power transition theory is usually credited to: Organski, A. F. K. (1958). *World Politics*. New York: Knopf. For a recent discussion with an application to China, see Allison, G. (2017). *Destined for War: Can America and China Escape Thucydides's Trap?* New York: Houghton-Mifflin.

28. Graham Allison worries about this too: Allison, G. & Simes, D. (2015). Russia and America: Stumbling Toward War. *The National Interest*, 10 (5), 9–21. See also this semi-fictional work by a senior NATO commander: Shirreff, R. (2016). *War with Russia: An Urgent Warning About the Immediate Threat from Russia.* London: Coronet.

29. The most consistent advocate for this position has been Christopher Layne. His position has changed little since it was first articulated, from: Layne, C. (1993). The Unipolar Illusion: Why New Great Powers Will Rise. *International Security*, 17 (4), 5–51; to Layne, C. (2012). This Time It's Real: The End of Unipolarity and the *Pax Americana. International Studies Quarterly*, 56 (1), 202–213.

30. See Human Security Report Project (2013). *Human Security Report 2013: The Decline in Global Violence.* Vancouver: Human Security Press; Marshall, M. G. & Cole, B. R. (2014). *Global Report 2014: Conflict, Governance, and State Fragility.* Vienna, VA: Center for Systemic Peace; and Backer, D. A., Bhavnani, R. & Huth, P. K. (Eds.) (2016). *Peace and Conflict 2016.* New York: Routledge.

31. See Williams, P. D. (2011). *War and Conflict in Africa.* Washington: Polity, chapter 2; Straus, S. (2012). Wars Do End! Changing Patterns of Political Violence in Sub-Saharan Africa. *African Affairs*, 111 (443), 179–201; and Burbach, D. & Fettweis, C. J. (2014). The Coming Stability? The Decline of Warfare in Africa and the Implications for International Security. *Contemporary Security Policy*, 35 (3), 421–445.

32. Pinker, S. (2011). *The Better Angels of Our Nature: Why Violence Has Declined.* New York: Viking. The phrase "Long Peace" is also occasionally used, but that can also refer to the period of great power stability following the Second World War. See Gaddis, J. L. (1986). The Long Peace: Elements of Stability in the Postwar International System. *International Security*, 10 (4), 99–142.

33. For reviews, see: Pinker, S. (2018). *Enlightenment Now: The Case for Reason, Science, Humanism, and Progress.* New York: Viking; Mueller, J. (2004). *The Remnants of War.* Ithaca, NY: Cornell University Press; and Goldstein, J. (2011). *Winning the War on War.* New York: Dutton. For a longer review of this literature, see: Fettweis, C. J. (2018). *Psychology of a Superpower: Security and Dominance in U.S. Foreign Policy.* New York: Columbia University Press, ch. 1.

34. Tuchman, B. W. (1978). *A Distant Mirror: The Calamitous 14th Century.* New York: Knopf, 211.

35. Andrew J. Bacevich makes this argument in: Bacevich, A. J. (2008). *The Limits of Power: The End of American Exceptionalism.* New York: Metropolitan Books, 53.

36. Terrorist incidents are tracked in the Global Terrorism Database by the National Consortium for the Study of Terrorism and the Responses to Terrorism at the University of Maryland. The data is accessible at http://www.start.umd.edu/gtd/.

37. Mueller, J. (2006). *Overblown: How Politicians and the Terrorism Industry Inflate National Security Threats, and Why We Believe Them.* New York: Free Press; and Mueller, J. & Stewart, M. (2011). *Terror, Security, and Money: Balancing the Risks, Benefits, and Costs of Homeland Security.* New York: Oxford University Press.

38. Quoted in Bacevich, A. J. (2002). *American Empire: The Realities and Consequences of U.S. Diplomacy*. Cambridge, MA: Harvard University Press, 119.
39. Kagan, F. W. (1999). Back to the Future: NSC-68 and the Right Course for America Today. *SAIS Review*, 19 (1), 69–70.
40. Were proper English as much a priority as failed states, this sentence would conclude with "than it is by failing ones". Bush, G. W. (2002). *The National Security Strategy of the United States of America*. Washington, DC: Government Printing Office, 1.
41. Eizenstat, S., Porter, J. E., & Weinstein, J. M. (2005). Rebuilding Weak States. *Foreign Affairs*, 84 (1), 136.
42. This was the main finding of the State Failure Task Force, whose observation still stands. See Goldstone, J. A. et al. (2000). *State Failure Task Force Report: Phase III Findings*. McLean, VA: Science Applications International Corporation [SAIC], http://globalpolicy.gmu.edu/pitf/SFTF%20Phase%20III%20Report%20Final.pdf.
43. Quoted in Schlesinger, A. M. (1986). *The Cycles of American History*. Boston: Houghton Mifflin Co., xi.
44. The 2017 poll found that "Corrupt Government Officials" was the #1 fear of the American people. All data and reports can be found at the website of the "Survey of American Fears," Chapman University, https://www.chapman.edu/wilkinson/research-centers/babbie-center/survey-american-fears.aspx.
45. For discussion of the effects of technological change on military organizations, see: Smith, M. R. (Ed.) (1985). *Military Enterprise and Technological Change: Perspectives on the American Experience*. Cambridge, MA: MIT Press.
46. National Intelligence Council (1996). *Joint Vision 2010*. Washington, DC: Government Printing Office, July, 8.
47. Office of the Secretary of Defense (2006). *Quadrennial Defense Review Report*. Washington, DC: Government Printing Office, February.
48. Reveron, D. S. (Ed.) (2012). *Cyberspace and National Security: Threats, Opportunities, and Power in a Virtual World*. Washington, DC: Georgetown University Press.
49. Clapper, J. R. (2013). Worldwide Threat Assessment of the US Intelligence Community. Report prepared for the Senate Select Committee on Intelligence, 12 March, http://www.dni.gov/files/documents/Intelligence%20Reports/2013%20ATA%20SFR%20for%20SSCI%2012%20Mar%202013.pdf, 1.
50. Mueller, J. (2009). *Atomic Obsession: Nuclear Alarmism from Hiroshima to Al-Qaeda*. New York: Oxford University Press.
51. Allison, G. T. (2004). *Nuclear Terrorism: The Ultimate Preventable Catastrophe*. New York: Henry Holt, 166.
52. For a discussion of the psychology of proliferation, see: Hymans, J. E. C. (2006). *The Psychology of Nuclear Proliferation*. New York: Cambridge University Press.
53. Allison, G. & Zedillo, E. (2008). The Fragility of the Global Nuclear Order. *Boston Globe*, 30 September, http://archive.boston.com/bostonglobe/editorial_opinion/oped/articles/2008/09/30/the_fragility_of_the_global_nuclear_order/.
54. This wonderful phrase was coined by Conetta, C. & Knight, C. (1998). Inventing Threats. *Bulletin of the Atomic Scientists*, 54 (2), 32–38. See also

Friedman, B. & Sapolsky, H. (2006). You Never Know(ism). *Breakthroughs*, 15 (1), 3–11.

55. James A. Winnefeld, *The Post-Cold War Sizing Debate: Paradigms, Metaphors, and Disconnects* (Santa Monica, CA: RAND, 1992), p. 12. Number of question marks in the original.

56. Conetta and Knight, "Inventing Threats," p. 34.

57. Powell, C. (1992). *The National Military Strategy of the United States.* Washington, DC: U.S. Government Printing Office, January, 4.

58. One might suggest that "stability" might have been a better choice. Office of the Secretary of Defense (2005). *The National Defense Strategy of the United States of America.* Washington, DC: U.S. Government Printing Office, March, 2.

59. Cohen, W. S. (1997). Quadrennial Defense Review: The Secretary's Message. Remarks made on 19 May 1997, www.disam.dsca.mil/pubs/INDEXES/Vol% 2019_4/Cohen.pdf. See also Conetta and Knight (1998). Inventing Threats.

60. DefenseLink (2002). DoD News Briefing. 12 February www.defenselink.mil/ transcripts/transcript.aspx?transcriptid=2636.

61. Murray, W. (2011). Thoughts on Grand Strategy. In Murray, W., Sinnreich, R. H. & Lacey, J. (Eds.) *The Shaping of Grand Strategy* (pp. 32–33) New York: Cambridge University Press.

62. Quoted in Robin, C. (2004). *Fear: The History of a Political Idea.* New York: Oxford University Press, 72.

63. Office of the Secretary of Defense (2012). *Sustaining U.S. Global Leadership: Priorities for 21st Century Defense.* Washington, DC: Government Printing Office, January, 1.

64. Both phenomena are discussed in Fettweis (2018). *Psychology of a Superpower*, ch. 2.

65. Office of the Secretary of Defense (2006). *Quadrennial Defense Review Report*, iv.

66. Goldman, E. O. (2011). *Power in Uncertain Times: Strategy in the Fog of Peace.* Stanford, CA: Stanford University Press, 125.

67. Karl W. Deutsch discusses a version of this in: Deutsch, K. W. (1968). *The Analysis of International Relations.* Englewood Cliffs, NJ: Prentice-Hall, 88; see also Fettweis, C. (2015). *The Pathologies of Power: Fear, Honor, Glory, and Hubris in U.S. Foreign Policy.* New York: Cambridge University Press, ch. 1.

68. Snyder, J. (2009). Imperial Myths and Threat Inflation. In Thrall, A. T. & Cramer, J. K. (Eds.) *American Foreign Policy and the Politics of Fear: Threat Inflation Since 9/11* (p. 41). New York: Routledge.

69. Jervis, R. (2009). Unipolarity: A Structural Perspective. *World Politics*, 61 (1), 200.

70. French Foreign Minister Hubert Védrine is widely credited with popularizing the term "hyperpower" to describe the United States.

71. For good reviews of what historians refer to as "defensive imperialism," see Errington, R. M. (1971). *The Dawn of Empire: Rome's Rise to Power.* London: Hamish Hamilton Ltd.; Gruen, E. S. (1986). *The Hellenistic World and the Coming of Rome.* Berkeley, CA: University of California Press; and Brunt, P. A. (1990). *Roman Imperial Themes.* Oxford: Clarendon Press, 1990, 102.

72. Quoted in Harris, W. V. (1985). *War and Imperialism in Republican Rome, 327–70 B.C.* Oxford: Clarendon Press, 164.

73. Quoted in Parker, G. (2000). The Making of Strategy in Hapsburg Spain: Philip II's 'Bid for Mastery,' 1559–1598. In Murray, W., Knox, M. & Bernstein, A. (Eds.) *The Making of Strategy: Rulers, States, and War* (p. 119). New York: Cambridge University Press.
74. Elliott, J. H. (1991). Managing Decline: Olivares and the Grand Strategy of Imperial Spain. In Kennedy, Paul (Ed.) *Grand Strategies in War and Peace* (pp. 87–104). New Haven, CT: Yale University Press.
75. Galbraith, J. S. (1960). The 'Turbulent Frontier' as a Factor in British Expansion. *Comparative Studies in Society and History*, 2 (2), 168. See also Robinson, R. & Gallagher, J. (1961). *Africa and the Victorians: The Official Mind of Imperialism*. London: Page.
76. This is related to the process Jack Snyder discussed in: Snyder, J. (1991). *Myths of Empire: Domestic Politics and International Ambition*. Ithaca, NY: Cornell University Press.
77. Krauthammer, C. (1990/1991). The Unipolar Moment. *Foreign Affairs*, 70 (1), 23–33.
78. Tyler, P. E. (1992). U.S. Strategy Plan Calls for Insuring No Rivals Develop. *New York Times*, 8 March, https://www.nytimes.com/1992/03/08/world/us-strategy-plan-calls-for-insuring-no-rivals-develop.html.
79. Kagan (2003). *Of Paradise and Power*, 34–36.
80. For meta-analysis of dozens of studies that draw this conclusion, see: Georgesen, J. C. & Harris, M. J. (1998). Why's My Boss Always Holding Me Down? A Meta-Analysis of Power on Performance Evaluations. *Personality and Social Psychology Review*, 2 (3), 184–195.
81. Lammers, J. & Stapel, D. A. (2011). Power Increases Dehumanization. *Group Processes and Intergroup Relations*, 14 (1), 113–126.
82. Kennan, G. F. (1996). *At a Century's Ending: Reflections 1982–1995*. New York: W. W. Norton, 87.
83. Flynn and his co-author throw around the term "alliance" rather loosely. Flynn, M. & Ledeen, M. (2016). *The Field of Fight: How We Can Win the Global War Against Radical Islam and Its Allies*. New York: St. Martin's Press.
84. See Mousavian, S. H. (2014). Iranian Perceptions of U.S. Policy Toward Iran: Ayatollah Khamenei's Mind Set. In Maleki, A. & Tirman, J. (Eds.) *U.S.-Iran Misperceptions: A Dialogue* (pp. 37–56) New York: Bloomsbury; and Barzegar, K. (2014). Iran's Perception of the U.S. Policy Toward the Region. In Maleki, A. & Tirman, J. (Eds.) *U.S.-Iran Misperceptions: A Dialogue* (pp. 89–110) New York: Bloomsbury.

CHAPTER 6

Chinese National Security: New Agendas and Emerging Challenges

Jingdong Yuan

The People's Republic of China's (PRC) growing economic power, military capabilities, and diplomatic influence are transforming the global and regional geo-economic and geo-political landscapes and pose significant challenges to the United States. Indeed, after decades during which Washington adopted an engagement policy hoping that cooperation and integration would transform China into a responsible stakeholder in the U.S.-dominated international system, the debate among U.S. policymakers and strategic analysts is now focused on whether that approach has ever worked.[1] Indeed, the Trump administration shifted gear and termed China as America's strategic rival that poses serious threats to U.S. interests.[2] The trade war that the administration had launched reflected this recognition. As China's power increases, so are its aspirations and ambitions, as well as growing expectations and concerns from the international community. Indeed, the past decades have witnessed Beijing's active diplomacy from the Six-Party Talks to climate change discussions, but also its assertiveness in maritime territorial disputes in the South and East China Seas.[3] Meanwhile, Chinese analysts are also engaged in heated debates on such critical issues as the country's grand strategy, the continued relevance of Deng Xiaoping's advice of 韬光养晦 [*taoguang yanghui* or "hide one's capabilities and bide one's time"] in guiding foreign policy conduct, and defining China's interests, role, and responsibility in the changing international

J. Yuan (✉)
University of Sydney, Sydney, NSW, Australia
e-mail: jingdong.yuan@sydney.edu.au

Stockholm International Peace Research Institute, Stockholm, Sweden

© The Author(s), under exclusive license to Springer Nature
Switzerland AG 2022
M. Clarke et al. (eds.), *The Palgrave Handbook of National Security*,
https://doi.org/10.1007/978-3-030-53494-3_6

117

environment. And China's national security policy making increasingly has to contend with growing demands from a multitude of actors within as much as it has to deal with external pressures, contingencies, and threats.[4]

Assessing the nature of China's rise and its likely trajectory in the coming decades requires a better understanding of the rationales behind China's growing global activism and the long-term economic and geostrategic implications of growing Chinese power in both global and regional contexts. Equally important is an analysis of China's national security since the end of the Cold War, which has undergone significant reconceptualization, structure, parameter, and policymaking process over the past three decades.[5] While continuing to emphasize traditional national security concerns such as sovereignty and territorial integrity, Beijing has reconceptualized national security, adopting a more comprehensive understanding and definition of what constitutes national security, and undertaken to restructure a policymaking process to address emerging security challenges. The new national security concept encompasses both external and domestic security threats, and expands security to include military, economic, and non-traditional issues, ranging from energy security to maritime piracy. Given the multiple sources of potential and real threats to national security interests, the restructured (and ongoing) policymaking process is aimed to anticipate and understand national security issues in strategic terms while at the same time coordinate and execute responses to threats in a more efficient and timely manner.

The End of the Cold War and Emerging Security Challenges

National security has always preoccupied generations of Chinese leaders from Mao Zedong to Xi Jinping. In the early years of the PRC, the country was confronted with the Korean War (1950–1953), the Taiwan Straits Crises (1954, 1958), the breakup of the Sino-Soviet alliance (1959), and the threats posed by the U.S.-led military alliances in Asia. In the 1960s, China fought a brief war with India, was indirectly involved in the Vietnam War, and had major border clashes with the Soviet Union. With the Sino-U.S. rapprochement in the early 1970s, China's security environment had become less precarious as Beijing and Washington joined forces in containing Soviet expansionism. Beginning in the 1980s, as Beijing adopted an independent foreign policy, and as Sino-Russian tensions receded, Deng Xiaoping confidently announced that "peace and development" rather than war and peace had become the theme of the time. China placed greater emphasis on economic development and reduced the size of the PLA by one million. China's national security perspectives and priorities underwent significant changes even as the core tenets remained intact. Political security, state sovereignty, and territorial integrity continued to be the dominant concepts in Chinese national security while the understanding of security expanded beyond defense against foreign invasions to ensure survival to include economic security and a whole range of traditional and non-traditional security issues.[6]

The end of the Cold War was a watershed event in the reconceptualization of China's security perspectives and national strategies. The normalization of Sino-Soviet relations in 1989 and the subsequent disintegration of the Soviet Union in 1991 effectively removed a major and at time existential external threat that had been the transfixion of Chinese security concerns since the late 1960s.[7] However, as an ancient Chinese axiom goes: "The nation that has no enemy in mind will perish." While the Soviet threat was receding, new challenges to China's security interests were emerging and had to be dealt with. These would include sovereignty in territorial waters, the Taiwan issue, and China's ultimate objective of national reunification, as well as residual border disputes with countries like India, the future orientation of Japan, and the potential threats from the United States.[8] Chinese analysts therefore considered three features of national security to be preeminent in the post-Cold War era: (1) military threats would no longer come from nuclear exchanges between superpowers but rather from regional conflicts of various types; (2) a broader conception of security that incorporated non-military elements such as economics and the environment would be required in order to better comprehend causes of insecurity; and (3) the development of a variety of military capabilities (such as rapid reaction forces) that would be necessary to ensure the country's national security interests under these conditions.[9]

Indeed, the decline and demise of the Soviet Union, the collapse of communism in Eastern Europe, the U.S.-led victory in the Gulf War, and the appearance if not the reality of a "unipolar moment" also meant the end to the relevance of China in the superpower balancing game.[10] While China could engage in various stratagems during the Cold War and act as a global power within the framework of the strategic triangle "without first having acquired the reach or the requisite normative and the material resources of a global power,"[11] the changing international geostrategic landscape meant that Beijing could no longer free ride in the international system. Three issues in particular presented themselves as serious challenges to the Chinese leadership. These were: (1) The likely evolution of the international order and the Asia-Pacific balance of power; (2) the direction to which this evolving international/regional order would be moving and how it might affect China'ssecurity interests; and (3) what role, if any, China could and should play in shaping this emerging international order and the regional balance of power, and what approaches suited Chinese interests better and therefore should be adopted and promoted. In addition, new security challenges emerged that threatened the core tenets of Chinese national security, from instability in Central Asia in the aftermath of the breakup of the Soviet Union and ethnic separatism in Xinjiang, the U.S.-led sanctions against China after the 1989 Tiananmen event, to territorial disputes in the South China Sea and growing concerns over energy security.[12]

While most Chinese analysts have described the transition from the current international system to the next as a process of multipolarization, there has not been an accepted definition of polarity nor an agreement on the implications of multipolarity for Chinese security. Most seem to acknowledge, either explicitly or implicitly, that in terms of 综合国力 *zonghe guoli* (comprehensive national strength embracing economic and technological power, military prowess, and political leadership), the United States by default had emerged since the end of the Cold War as a pole with no equals. This state of affairs was described as 一超多强 *yichao duoqiang* (one superpower, several major powers).[13] This "unipolar moment" and consequently the seemingly unchecked U.S. power politics posed serious threats to Chinese security interests, especially in the Asia-Pacific region with continued U.S. military ties with Taiwan through arms sales, the strengthening of the U.S. alliances even though the Soviet threats no long existed, and the deployment of military capabilities such as theater missile defense in Northeast Asia.[14]

And the nature and the sources of threats to China's national security had become multifarious and less clear-cut. The strategies of China's potential adversaries no longer were just military in nature; they could be economic, cultural, and presented in the forms of engagement, enlargement, as well as containment, and congagement.[15] Under such circumstances, it became imperative that national security perspectives should expand beyond focusing primarily on the military threats and territorial issues, but also involve analyses of and preparation for those challenges that threaten China's security interests in ideological terms so as to safeguard the CCP legitimacy as the ruling party and to maintain domestic social and political cohesion.[16]

Consequently, post-Cold War Chinese security policy aims to: (1) ensure a favorable international environment for economic development; (2) strive for national reunification and exercise protection of the country's territorial integrity; and (3) maintain political independence and firmly oppose any form of hegemonism.[17] Michael Swaine, at the time a senior analyst at RAND, thus observed:

> China's primary strategic objectives in the international arena are (1) to maintain an external environment conducive to the pursuit of economic reform, opening to the outside world, and economic construction, (2) to preserve or expand China's strategic independence and leverage in a complex multipolar environment, (3) to further China's efforts to reunify the nation, and (4) to strengthen China's ability to defend against external pressures or attacks emerging from a highly complex and uncertain yet arguably less immediately threatening security environment.[18]

Hence, the defining feature of China's understanding of post-Cold War international security environment remained clearly what is characterized as *parabellum*, or realpolitik. Not surprisingly, Beijing's response to perceived future security threats was one of realpolitik. States remained the key players in international relations and state sovereignty an ultimate concern. To achieve security and preserve sovereignty in an anarchical international system of constant change and flux required that one keep and enhance its capabilities. Security remained of paramount importance and a strong and prosperous state and a powerful military (富国强兵 *fuguo qiangbing*) therefore were viewed the only guarantor of national security.[19] During the Cold War, a minimum yet credible deterrence was crucial to China's security; in the post-Cold War era, the ability to preserve state sovereignty and territorial integrity broadly defined requires a military capability that can ensure victory in local conflicts. Interdependence and therefore an appreciation of cooperative security to enhance one's own security and the necessary change in foreign policy have not been accepted as the basic approach.[20] Again, to quote Swaine:

> At present, China's general line in external policy assumes a turbulent international environment associated with the transition from the Cold War bipolar confrontation to a more complex, multipolar configuration; the reduced likelihood of large-scale global or regional conflict; a growing number of limited regional threats and concerns demanding new types of conventional and unconventional military capabilities, including possible conflicts over disputed territories such as Taiwan; and the increasing importance of economic and technological factors to international security calculations.[21]

A long-term security concern was the fear that unless a stable international environment could be maintained, disruption of peace would hamper China's efforts in its modernization drive and therefore could widen the gap between China and the advanced industrialized countries and the newly industrialized economies (NIEs).[22] Chinese experts perceived economic and scientific challenges in the coming decades as constituting the major security threat to the country. Indeed, while constantly extolling the regional stability and economic prosperity in Asia–Pacific as compared to other regions, Beijing was (and remains) concerned that regional and local conflicts could seriously affect its modernization programs which, using the terminology of "comprehensive national strength," is regarded as the basis for national security.[23]

Economic security thus entails both securing a peaceful external environment for economic development and protecting the country's economic interests, including protecting its land, air space, and its territorial waters. The growing attention to maritime interests and the cultivation of a "conception of sea as territory" (海洋国土观 *Haiyang guotuguan*) reflects both a recognition of the potential of maritime resources for national economic development and a realization that China must enhance its ability to protect its perceived maritime territories.[24] In other words, the nature of international relations remains conflictual and threats ubiquitous. One Chinese analyst suggests:

> To make sure that such [maritime] resources are fully tapped and utilized, China needs to ensure the security of its maritime economic activities. A strong naval

defense is essential to reducing the threat posed by sea-borne smuggling and piracy to China's tariff incomes, ocean fishery and marine transportation.[25]

China's involvement in anti-piracy operations in the Gulf of Aden to protect Chinese and international cargo fleets since 2008 is a reflection of the emerging non-traditional security challenges that the country faces with its expanding international trade and dependence on imports of critical resources. Energy security, for instance, has since the early 1990s become an important item on China's national security agenda.[26]

National Security: Emerging Challenges

The end of the Cold War transformed China's external security environment for the better but also has presented Beijing with new security challenges, spanning both the traditional and non-traditional domains. While the country no longer faces the threat of foreign invasions, it is confronted with rising territorial disputes and growing instability in its periphery. Meanwhile, as the country has become ever more integrated into the global economy, its demands for raw materials and energy, and its interest in safeguarding commerce are placing greater emphasis on the non-military aspects of national security. Additionally, China's national security is also inextricably linked to great-power relations in the region and the evolution of the existing security architectures in the Indo-Pacific.[27]

From Beijing's perspective, the post-Cold War international and regional security environments have become more complicated even as they are largely seen as conducive to China's continued economic development. Indeed, as Andrew Nathan and Andrew Scobell, two astute watchers of China, point out, "[v]ulnerability to threats is the main driver of China's foreign policy."[28] This assessment is informed by an understanding of China's security from two different angles. One is a redefinition of China's security interests and strategic frontier. During the Cold War, national survival was the predominant concern and hence security policy hinged largely on preparing for "an early, major, and nuclear war," in particular in preparation against a land invasion from the Soviet Union. Today, however, national security interests not only involve sovereignty and territorial integrity, but also those that ensure the country's continued economic growth as well as its political and social stability. Some of these can be managed at home; others, such as the safe and stable supply of critical resources like oil and minerals imported from overseas, however, require active engagement abroad.[29]

A second angle derives from the expansion of China's national security interests. While a strong military remains critical in safeguarding national security, the development of the nation's comprehensive strength based on economic capabilities and scientific advancement is increasingly seen as equally important. These elements constitute critical components of a grand strategy that in turn informs and determines China's national security policy.[30] Indeed, this economic rationale has underpinned many of the domestic and foreign policy decisions Beijing has made over the past three decades—greater integration into the world economy, closer ties with the industrialized countries for markets, investments, and technology transfers, and seeking to develop a stable security environment in China's periphery through bilateral and multilateral diplomacy.[31]

The disintegration of the former Soviet Union in late 1991 and the newly independent Central Asian states posed security challenges to China's northwestern region, in particular the so-called "three evils"—ethnic separatism, religious extremism, and terrorism. The transnational nature of these threats (e.g., the East Turkestan Islamic Movement, or ETIM) required regional responses and multilateral cooperation. Beijing therefore responded to these threats by taking the lead in establishing a regional institution. This effort was made easy by years of border negotiation, military confidence building, and gradual development of mutual trust between China and its Central Asian neighbors and Russia, which in turn provided a foundation for the establishment of the Shanghai Cooperation Organization (SCO) in 2001. The organization has subsequently developed into a viable regional security institution that coordinates member states' (largely non-traditional) security policies, while building up its capacities and membership over the past 20 years.[32]

Territorial disputes have emerged as a major challenge to China's national security. Since 2007–2008, tension has risen between some of the key contending states to the long-standing territorial disputes in the South China Sea, principally China, Vietnam, and the Philippines.[33] Washington has long held a position of neutrality regarding the territorial disputes between China and the other five disputing parties. But in recent years, there has been a perceptible shift in the U.S. position in that it becomes more critical of Chinese policy, in particular, the latter's massive land reclamation efforts, resulting in Washington overtly siding with the other claimants despite public disavowals to the contrary.[34] The U.S. administrations also have rejected China's sovereignty claims to both the features it controls and the adjacent territorial waters, and the exclusive economic zones (EEZs). Both the Obama and Trump administrations have authorized freedom of navigation (FONOP) patrols either near or through the 12-nautical miles of China-controlled features, triggering strong Chinese protests. But it is the growing frequency of U.S. close-in intelligence gathering and reconnaissance activities on the one hand, and Chinese responses with maritime and aerial intercepts on the other, that are the most dangerous interactions. A number of incidents have already occurred in the past, with serious consequences, including loss of lives.[35]

Likewise, in the East China Sea, Tokyo's decision in September 2012 to nationalize three of the Senkaku/Diaoyu islands saw a rapid deterioration in bilateral relations. In late 2013, China unilaterally announced an Air Defence Identification Zone (ADIZ) covering the disputed territories and triggering strong rebuffs from Tokyo.[36] Even as it has surpassed Japan as the world's second largest economy, Beijing remains seriously concerned over the direction of Japan's security policy and its pursuit of greater military capabilities. One particular issue is whether the strengthening of the U.S.-Japan alliance will allow Tokyo to take advantage to introduce major changes and amend its constitution to permit it to become a "normal" military power capable of overseas deployment of military personnel, engagement in collective defense arrangements, modernization of the JSDF in both force structure and equipment, including possible acquisition of nuclear weapons.[37]

The U.S.-Japan alliance in recent years has been further consolidated with regular bilateral consultations such as 2+2 talks, joint military exercises, explicit references to U.S. commitment to the defense of Diaoyu/Senkaku islands under the U.S.-Japan security treaty, closer cooperation in joint intelligence gathering, reconnaissance, weapons development, defense technology cooperation, greater interoperability, and "seamless" joint operations between forward deployed U.S. troops and JSDF units. Within the alliance framework, Japan will play a more active and lead role in promoting an "free and openIndo-Pacific" (FOIP) strategy.[38]

Sino-Indian relations also form an important part of China's national security calculation. China's unresolved territorial disputes with India and its relations with Pakistan inform Beijing's South Asia policy, including sustained military competition in the region.[39] Beijing and New Delhi have yet to resolve their territorial disputes. After more than 20 rounds of negotiations, the two countries have failed to make any breakthroughs. Recent years have witnessed numerous incidents where the two troops face off each other, with the recent crisis in the Doklam area (2017) and the Galwan Valley clash (2020) risking escalation to more serious military confrontation. Beijing is also concerned about how a more confident India could affect Chinese security interests. From Beijing's perspective, these apprehensions include warming U.S.-India security ties since 2005; India's growing ties with Japan, Australia, and Vietnam and the revived Quadrilateral security alignment, or QUAD, consisting of Australia, India, Japan, and the United States; India's "Act East" policy toward expanding its presence in East Asia; and New Delhi's ambition to assert a prominent position in the Indian Ocean. These feed into a paranoia in China of encirclement by the United States and its allies. Beijing also harbors long-held concerns over India' support for Tibet, including providing a safe haven to the Dalai Lama and exiled Tibetans, which it views as meddling in China's internal affairs.[40]

In that context, the closer ties forged between New Delhi and Washington since the George W. Bush administration (2001–2009) and their continued consolidation under the Obama administration (2009–2017) and government of Narendra Modi have been the subject of growing discussion and analyses in Chinese military publications. Of particular note is their deepening bilateral defense cooperation where India has not only become the largest market for U.S. arms sales ($1.9 billion in 2013), but also benefitted from technology transfers. The PLA perceives the rationale behind such heightened security cooperation as reflecting U.S. intentions to strategically encircle China.[41]

Developments across the Taiwan Strait have been a core security interest for China. Since the end of the Cold War, cross-Strait relations have undergone periods of crises marked by Taipei's attempts to seek *de jure* independence, partly encouraged by the pro-Taiwan elements in the United Statas, which continues to provide major weapons systems to the island. During the 1995–1996 Taiwan Strait crisis, the Clinton administration even sent two aircraft carrier battle groups through the Taiwan Strait, a move that seriously threatened Beijing's security. While during the Ma Ying-jeou administration (2008–2016), cross-Strait ties stabilized with both sides seeking to promote trade and people-to-people exchanges, fundamental differences remained, and with the election of the DPP's Tsai Ing-wen, relations between the two have rapidly deteriorated.[42]

The North Korean nuclear and missile developments since the early 1990s have also posed a serious threat to Chinese security. This is due to the fact that Pyongyang's proliferation activities, if not firmly checked and reversed, could cause a domino effect in the region, with Japan and South Korea seeking to acquire their own nuclear weapons. Beijing initiated and played an active role in the Six-Party Talks (2003–2008) but in the end the negotiation collapsed due to major differences between the key parties, namely North Korea and the U.S. North Korea conducted six nuclear tests and about two dozens of missile tests between 2006 and 2017, causing enormous tensions on the Peninsula and in Northeast Asia. U.S.-led international sanctions threatened the very survival of the North Korean regime, with severe negative consequences for China. Concerns over further proliferation and stability close to home have presented Beijing with a serious dilemma of striking a delicate balance in its North Korea policy.[43]

China's expanding presence in all continents as its overseas investments and projects grow also exposes Chinese personnel to greater risks, which in turn poses another challenge to Beijing in protecting Chinese citizens and properties. This last point is closely related to the phenomenal expansion of what analysts have called China's international activism, driven largely by its growing activities in international trade and overseas investments, the search for energy and resources, and its contribution to international peacekeeping and anti-piracy operations.[44] To a significant extent, China's growing economic security interests—securing and safeguarding reliable supplies of raw materials and resources, and ensuring exports of Chinese goods to foreign markets—have elevated the importance of the Indian Ocean. China's perspectives on security developments and its growing interest in the Indian Ocean have been informed and influenced by three sets of key considerations. First, China's perceived maritime interests have expanded and constitute an increasingly crucial component of the country's overall economic development due to the rising international trade portion of its gross domestic product (GDP) and its growing energy and raw materials imports. Second, Beijing sees a "Malacca

Dilemma" in the form of a potential bottleneck or at a minimum a node of extreme vulnerability should hostile state(s) seek(s) to block transits of energy and other resources headed to China. And finally, as its dependence on, and stakes in, access to maritime traffic continues to rise China is witnessing an expanding internal debate about whether it is a continental or maritime power and, to the extent that it is the latter, how a balance can be struck between asserting China's maritime rights and interests by developing the necessary naval capabilities while not causing unnecessary alarm in the Indian Ocean Region.[45]

China has become increasingly aware of the emerging non-traditional security threats to its interests and the need to develop strategies for managing them. From Beijing's perspective, these include ethnic separatism, terrorism, internet and cyber security, mass unrest, natural disasters, public health and safety (e.g., SARS and Covid-19), overseas Chinese and properties, among others.[46] Indeed, economic development has exposed China to external vulnerabilities, from fluctuating prices of commodities to safety of Chinese citizens working overseas. It further widens income gaps in the country and therefore result in social instability. As a result, economic growth and prosperity highlight economic security issues, both internally and externally. This explains the expanding role of China's military in many emerging non-combat contingencies, from regime security (e.g., Tiananmen in 1989) to massive evacuation of Chinese citizens from a war-torn Libya in 2011.[47]

While Beijing faces many security challenges in the post-Cold War era, the most serious security challenge is the handling of its relationship with the United States. While China's rise has encouraged growing nationalism and Beijing has adopted a more active and at times more assertive foreign policy, its U.S. policy remains cautious and pragmatic. Beijing hard balances the United States only when it perceives its core interests threatened by America's predatory behavior seen as directly and deliberately to harm Chinese interests.[48] Clearly, how to manage its relationship with the United States—the reigning superpower—while continuing its ascendancy to great-power status is the most important national security priority for Chinese leaders. Developing a "new model of major-power relationship" [新型大国关系] with Washington therefore becomes Beijing's answer to the security dilemma of a potential "Thucydides trap" in Sino-U.S. relations. This reflects Chinese effort to address the growing concern that a rising China will pose a serious challenge to U.S. primacy in the region, leading to instability and conflict, and provide some reassurance to Washington that China recognizes the important role of the United States in the region and that it has no intention to seek its replacement. Beijing also hopes that its own interests would be recognized and respected by Washington.[49]

However, not only has Beijing's proposal not been accepted by Washington, during Obama's final years, Sino-U.S. rivalry only intensified and their differences over a range of regional issues effectively prevented the development of a "new model of major power relations," certainly not the kind envisioned by Beijing. In its place has emerged a new pattern of competitive relationship—cooperation and competition driven by divergent geostrategic interests, foreign and security policy priorities, and shared common concerns and challenges ranging from climate change to maritime piracy. Even as the U.S. and Chinese militaries recognize the importance of introducing crisis management mechanisms, Beijing and Washington continue to differ over maritime territorial disputes in East and South China Seas, alliances and security architectures in the region, and how to best promote regional trade and investment.[50]

The election of Trump as U.S. president in November 2016 also posed serious challenges to Beijing. Trump's acceptance of a call from Taiwan's leader Tsai Ing-wen and his casual comment why the United States should be bound by the "One China Policy" caused significant concerns in Beijing. Despite two summits (April and November 2017) between Xi and Trump, bilateral relations remained unsettled and were further aggravated by a series of policy announcements by the United States. The National Security Strategy of 2017 for the first time in years explicitly named China as America's key challenger and threat. The Trump administration's June 2017 announcement of arms sales to Taiwan, the Taiwan Travel Act, and the 2019 National Defence Authorization Act represent the most serious threat to China's core interests over the past four decades since bilateral diplomatic ties were established.[51] Three issues stand out as particularly concerning: (1) the Trump administration (or perhaps more accurately a pro-Taiwan Congress) posed a serious threat to the One China principle by elevating the level of exchanges between Washington and Taipei; (2) the administration's arms sales policy to Taiwan directly challenged China's sovereignty and a violation of the Sino-U.S. August 17, 1982, Joint Communique; and (3) the new U.S. policy could embolden Taipei, further aggravating an already tense relationship across the Taiwan Strait. Under the Biden administration, U.S.-China relations have continued be defined by their strategic rivalry.

Reconceptualizing Security: New Structures

The 2007–2008 global financial crisis (GFC) arguably marked the arrival of China as a great power. It became the second largest economy in the world in 2010 and is projected to become number one before 2030. In fact, measured in purchasing power parity (PPP) terms, China has already overtaken the United States.[52] Analyses of China's rise and its implications—whether it is framed by realist, liberal, or constructivist international relations paradigms—have focused predominantly on the structural opportunities, incentives, and constraints that can affect Beijing's foreign and national security policy strategies and behaviors.[53] What has transpired since 2012–2013 when Xi Jinping became China's top leader are a much more confident and assertive foreign policy initiatives from engagement in global and regional multilateral diplomacy, promotion of grand strategic designs such as the Belt and Road Initiative (BRI), to a more proactive role in international security (peacekeeping and nuclear nonproliferation) and firmer (and hardline) positions on territorial disputes in the South and East China Seas. In particular, Xi Jinping, in his call for rejuvenation of the great Chinese nation and the realization of the China Dream, has undertaken an ambitious great-power agenda that has driven Chinese foreign policy in the past few years.[54]

However, even as China becomes stronger, it remains anxious and insecure in many aspects. It is concerned over the political legitimacy of the CCP rule; it worries about and indeed is feeling the attempts by the United States and the West as a whole to keep it down; and it is fraught with domestic instability, primary among them ethnic unrest and ever-expanding socio-economic inequality. That explains why Beijing's concept of national security really is, first and foremost, about domestic political and regime security, and only secondarily about external threats albeit at times the latter could pose serious problems for Chinese leaders. These factors have significantly influenced Beijing's threat perceptions and hence its national security goals, priorities, and strategies.[55] Domestic factors such as ideas, players, policy-making processes, and the extent to which these variables are expressed and how they inform and influence policy options have received less attention than is warranted. Granted, it still remains extremely difficult to look into the "black box" of Chinese national security policymaking, yet researchers today have much greater access than before to information and debates in China that can provide the basis for informed analysis.[56] From the official propaganda, one gets the sense that debates in China on the country's rise are by and large guided by the concepts of revitalization and rejuvenation of a great civilization and its return to its rightful place in the world; determination to right the wrongs inflicted on China during its 100 years of humiliation—and hence a strong emphasis on sovereignty and territorial integrity, and the path to great-power status: continued economic growth and the development of comprehensive national strength, which, as we pointed out earlier, depend on a stable international environment and the ability to secure critical inputs—capital, technologies, labor, and resources.[57]

Since President Xi took the reins in 2012–2013, China has undertaken an overhaul of the country's national security apparatuses. First, a new concept of national security has been presented as the overall guideline for assessing contemporary security challenges and for formulating effective strategies to manage these challenges. It places greater emphasis on the holistic and comprehensive understanding of national security, the increasing blurring of internal and external security challenges, and the growing non-traditional security issues. It also recognizes that as China's growing overseas presence and interests expand, they would inevitably encounter and be perceived as encroaching established interests of western powers, in particular the United States. Domestic issues such as growing income gaps between regions, environmental degradation, natural disasters, ethnic unrest and separatist activities, mass protests, as well as overall economic slowdown constitute major security challenges for the CCP that depends on economic growth for legitimacy and political survival.[58]

Beijing has been trying to adjust and adapt to these new challenges and demands with better coordination between different government agencies at both the central and local levels, and enterprises operating in foreign countries, even though a truly centralizing and coordinating body the like of U.S. National Security Council has yet to be introduced.[59] While various Chinese leaderships from Jiang Zemin to Hu Jintao had toyed with the idea of establishing a centralized national security structure, it was not until January 2014 that the "National Security Commission" with Xi as the head was finally set up. In January 2015, the first comprehensive national security strategy guideline was adopted by the CCP Politburo. The concept of "comprehensive, common, cooperation and sustainable security" was presented as setting the overall Chinese national security objectives. The concept proposes five key principles emphasizing (1) people; (2) political; (3) economic; (4) military, culture, and society; and (5) international security. Also included are security of information, science and technology, ecology, and energy, an approach that reflects the comprehensive nature of national security in the Chinese conception. Political and military security clearly stand out, judged by Xi Jinping's various statements on national security and the analyses and commentaries by Chinese scholars. Furthermore, safeguarding national security requires better management of five relationships—between (1) domestic and external security; (2) territorial and people's security; (3) traditional and non-traditional security; (4) development and security; and (5) one's own security and common security for all.[60]

The establishment of the National Security Commission in 2014 was followed by a major restructuring of the People's Liberation Army to centralize command and control in the Central Military Commission (CMC) and in particular in Chairman Xi Jinping, who for the first time was conferred the title of "Commander-in-Chief" of the newly launched PLA Joint Command Centre. Meanwhile, the previous four PLA general headquarters were dissolved and re-organized into four new joint departments, together with the other newly established departments, all under the CMC. The seven military regions were also re-organized into five war zones or commands modeled after the U.S. system. All these were meant to streamline the command structure of the Chinese military, bringing it firmly under the CCP control, with Xi being given unprecedented power since Mao. At the same time, China's maritime law enforcement and para-military agencies also underwent re-organization to effect better coordination in executing the country's maritime policies.[61]

The national security overhaul follows from four decades of economic reforms and opening up that have resulted in a gradual decentralization process that now has to accommodate the increasing number of actors in China's foreign and national security policymaking, who pursue multiple interests that are not always compatible with what can be described as Chinese national interests. On the contrary, some of China's biggest state-owned companies, and indeed the national oil companies (NOCs), pursue strategies that sometimes can undermine Chinese foreign policy goals and tarnish Beijing's reputation. At the same time, because of the emerging and ongoing debates within China on what the country should do as its power grows, it becomes harder to pin down what the dominating ideas are, whether and to what extent they can actually influence and shape foreign policy.[62] Indeed, Chinese leaders from Jiang Zemin on have sought to restructure the country's foreign and national security policymaking structure to better confront the challenges it faces. Various models have been tried out, in particular the various leading small groups (LSGs). The growing numbers of actors—from the powerful state-owned enterprises (SOEs) to the various government agencies at both the national and sub-national levels in the policymaking processes—created discordance and diluted central control.[63]

To what extent China's new national security apparatuses will improve Beijing's ability to manage a multitude of security challenges, both domestic and external, in both responding to major crises and designing and developing long-term strategies, remains to be seen. In fact, apart from a few and brief references to the NSC, there is really not so much daylight on how the organization is structured, what its briefs are, who staff them, and how it coordinates national security activities horizontally (coordination of various relevant government departments as well as the typically opaque PLA) and vertically (implementation of adopted policies top-down). In fact, since January 2014, there have been only two reported NSC meetings (2014 and more recently, March 2018). However, the overhaul has laid the foundation that, when fully integrated and operational, the NSC could significantly reshape how decisions are made, with an improved process and better coordination of various stakeholders and a capacity in crisis management and top-design national security policy formulation.[64]

The Chinese military's role in the new national security process will remain critical in military aspects of the national security policy but likely with reduced direct influence over its domestic political dimensions.[65] On the one hand, China's growing power and the new historic missions that the Party has assigned to the military enable the PLA to have a bigger voice on national security as it demands and receives greater resources for modernization. On the other hand, the restructuring of the PLA means that the Party and Xi himself are reasserting control of the military in the aftermath of recent uncovering of corruption cases involving a number of top PLA generals. Nonetheless, military security is one of the top priorities of the new security concept and a foundation of the nation's core security interests. This explains the resources and efforts being put into building a lean but strong military. In recent years, the PLA has achieved major milestones and breakthroughs. These include new weapons systems, including the launch of its first domestic aircraft carriers, advanced fighter aircraft and surface battle ships, modernization of its small but growing nuclear arsenal and ballistic and cruise missiles;

better and more realistic training and joint exercises with the foreign militaries; and dispatches of naval escort fleets to the Gulf of Aden that provide real-time experiences of long-distance operations and logistic support.[66]

Beijing's emphasis on cooperative security has led to more active diplomatic initiatives to engage China's counterparts and promote Chinese voices and solutions regarding global and regional security issues.[67] Apart from seeking solutions to nuclear proliferation challenges (North Korea, Iran) and participating in international peacekeeping operations, China has sought to consolidate regional security organizations such as the SCO where it plays a lead role, and made efforts to revive and strengthen others such as the Conference on Interaction and Confidence Building Measures in Asia (CICA). At the 2014 CICA summit, which China hosted as the chair, President Xi called for Asians to tackle Asia's security problems.[68] Together with other multilateral events that Beijing hosts (so-called "主场外交 [host diplomacy]"), from BRICS and APEC summits to the SCO and G-20 gatherings, China uses these platforms to advocate its concept of Asian security: common, cooperative, and comprehensive security and sustainable development. Recognizing the diversity of security architectures and institutions in the region—ASEAN-led initiatives such as ARF, EAS, and the ADMM Plus (ASEAN Defence Minister's Meeting), the U.S.-led alliance systems, and multilateral security dialogues such as the IISS-Shangri-La Dialogue, the 香山论坛 [Xiangshan Forum], Beijing argues that future Asian security architecture requires the participation of all concerned, must be one that is based on consensus, and provides security for all. It emphasizes the importance of economic cooperation and economic integration as conducive to the development of security architecture. It advocates multilateralism and calls for dialogues in addressing security issues and non-traditional security challenges. It promotes a new Asian security architecture that is inclusive, cooperative, and win–win, with states in the region encouraged to pursue partnerships than military alliances.[69]

Media and public opinions have often played very important roles in democratic societies. However, the relationship between media, public opinions, and foreign policy can be viewed as a continuous loop and interactive.[70] It is increasingly difficult for the Chinese authority to completely control or censor news or information these days on issues of public interests, such as relations with the United States, Japan, India, or territorial disputes in the East and South China Seas. The commercialization of media means there are more outlets for news coverage. More citizens are interested in international affairs and their perceptions and sentiments on certain events and public opinions become pressure points on the government. Indeed, Beijing can ill afford to be seen as weak-kneed in its handling of sensitive issues such as sovereignty and territorial integrity. Certain media such as *Global Times* often publish articles that reinforce the public's nationalist sentiments. All of these impose considerable constraints on policymakers and at times become impediments to effective execution of diplomacy.[71]

Conclusion

China's national security has evolved from the early days of a near exclusive focus on political and military security in the sense of defending the nation's sovereignty and territorial integrity against foreign invasions, to the post-Cold War shift toward economic development and building up of the country's comprehensive national strength (综合国力) as the foundation of national security. Deng Xiaoping's advice for the country to keep a low profile served as an important guidance during the trying periods of the late 1980s in the aftermath of Tiananmen and the collapse of communism. However, while China no longer faces foreign invasions, Beijing has adopted a more expansive and comprehensive national security concept that addresses an entire spectrum of security challenges, domestic as well as external, both traditional and non-traditional.

China's arrival as a great power has enabled the country to engage in more active diplomacy at both global and regional levels, and Beijing seeks to play a more prominent role in addressing various external challenges impinging on its national security interests while boosting its image as a responsible stakeholder in international affairs. These range from combating global terrorism to managing nuclear proliferation, to mediating regional conflicts through its participating in and contributing to international peacekeeping operations. At the same time, China's ever-expanding global presence and growing economic footprints also expose the country to emerging threats in terms of the security and safety of its citizens and interests overseas. Meanwhile, recent economic slowdown and ethnic unrest have resulted in domestic instability and that could threaten the CCP's legitimacy and staying power. Beijing's new national security concept and organizational structures highlight both the continuity (political and military security) and changes (people, economic, and non-traditional security). China's national security concept and practice remain unique in that the emphasis continues to be placed on domestic as well as external security, and the holistic way whereby the CCP seeks to understand and address various challenges. It remains to be seen whether the system that has been put in place in recent years will stand the tests given both the uncertain international environment and the rapidly changing domestic socio-economic and ethnic conditions.

Notes

1. See Campbell, K. M. & Ratner, E. (2018). The China Reckoning: How Beijing Defied American Expectations. *Foreign Affairs* 97 (2), 60–70, and the responses from Wang, J. et al. (2018). Did America Get China Wrong? The Engagement Debate. *Foreign Affairs* 97 (4), 183–195. See also Harding, H. (2015). Has U.S. China Policy Failed? *The Washington Quarterly* 38 (3), 95–122; Friedberg, A. (2018). Competing with China. *Survival* 60 (3), 7–64; Brands, H. & Cooper, Z. (2019). After the Responsible Stakeholder, What?

Debating America's China Strategy. *Texas National Security Review* 2 (2), 68–81.

2. The White House, *National Security Strategy of the United States of America*, December 2017, https://www.whitehouse.gov/wp-content/uploads/2017/12/NSS-Final-12-18-2017-0905.pdf.

3. Rudolph, J. & Szonyi, M. eds. (2018). *The China Questions: Critical Insights into a Rising Power*. Cambridge: Harvard University Press; Toje, A. ed. (2017). *Will China's Rise Be Peaceful? Security, Stability, and Legitimacy*. New York: Oxford University Press; and Hawksley, H. (2018). *Asian Waters: The Struggle over the South China Sea and the Strategy of Chinese Expansion*. New York: Overlook Press.

4. 刘慧等编 [Liu Hui et al., eds.]. (2018).《国际安全蓝皮书: 中国国家安全报告(2017)》[*Bluebook of International Security: Annual Report on China's International Security Studies (2017)*]. 北京 [Beijing]: 社会科学文献出版社 [Social Sciences Academic Press]; 王帆 [Wang Fan]. (2016).《大国外交》[*China's Diplomacy*]. 北京 [Beijing]: 北京联合出版公司 [Beijing United Publishing Co. Ltd]; Lampton, D. M. ed. (2002). *The Making of Chinese Foreign and Security Policy in the Era of Reform*. Stanford: Stanford University Press.

5. An important work is Nathan, A. J. & Scobell, A. (2012). *China's Search for Security*. New York: Columbia University Press.

6. Segal, G. & Tow, W. T. eds. (1984). *Chinese Defence Policy*. New York: Palgrave Macmillan; 林利民 [Lin Limin]. (2017). 新中国成立以来国家安全观念发展演变评析 [A Review of the Evolution of National Security Concept Since the Founding of the PRC].《中国军事科学》[*Chinese Military Science*] 5, 87–95.

7. Luthi, L. M. (2008). *The Sino-Soviet Split: Cold War in the Communist World*. Princeton, NJ: Princeton University Press.

8. Shambaugh, D. (1994) The Insecurity of Security: The PLA's Evolving Doctrine and Threat Perceptions Towards 2000. *Journal of Northeast Asian Studies* 13 (1), 3–25; Whiting, A. S. (1996). The PLA and China's Threat Perceptions. *The China Quarterly* 146 (June), 596–615.

9. 郭震远 [Guo Zhenyuan]. (1992). 世界格局中大变化的几点思考 [SomeThoughts on the Major Changes in the Global Structure].《学术交流》[*Academic Exchanges*] 2, 6.

10. Ross, R. S. ed. (1993). *China, the United States, and the Soviet Union: Tripolarity and Policy Making During the Cold War*. Armonk, NY: M.E. Sharpe; Dittmer, L. (1981). The Strategic Triangle: An Elementary Game-Theoretical Analysis. *World Politics* 33 (4), 485–515.

11. Shambaugh, D. (1992). China's Security Policy in the Post-Cold War Era. *Survival* 34 (2), 88–106; and Kim, S. S. (1995). China's Pacific Policy: Reconciling the Irreconcilable. *International Journal* 50 (3), 466.

12. Nathan, A. J. & Ross, R. S. (1997). *The Great Wall and the Empty Fortress: China's Search for Security*. New York: Columbia University Press.

13. 萨本望 [Sa Benwang]. (1996). 关于世界格局'多极化'的几点思考 [Some Perceptions on "Multipolarization" of World Structure].《和平与发展》[*Peace and Development*] 2 (June), 1.

14. Pillsbury, M. 2000. *China Debates the Future Security Environment*. Washington, DC: National Defense University Press; Goldstein, A. (2013). U.S.-China Interactions in Asia. In Shambaugh, D. (Ed). *Tangled Titans: The United States and China*. (pp. 263–291). Lanham: Rowman & Littlefield; and Rigger,

S. (2013). Taiwan in U.S.-China Relations. In Shambaugh, D. (Ed). *Tangled Titans: The United States and China*. (pp. 293–311). Lanham: Rowman & Littlefield.

15. Khalilzad, Z. (2017). The Case for Congagement. *The National Interest* 150 (July/August), 15–20.

16. See, for example, Forney, M. (1996). Patriotic Game. *Far Eastern Economic Review* 3 (October), 22–28.

17. Hu, W. (1995). China's Security Agenda After the Cold War. *Pacific Review* 8 (1), 117 –35.

18. Swaine, M. D. (1996). *The Role of the Chinese Military in National Security Policymaking*. Santa Monica, CA : R AND, 9.

19. Rozman, G. (2010). *Chinese Strategic Thought Toward Asia*. New York: Palgrave Macmillan; and Johnston, A. I. (1995). *Cultural Realism: Strategic Culture and Grand Strategy in Chinese History*. Princeton, NJ: Princeton University Press.

20. Shambaugh, D. (1994). Growing Strong : C hina's Challenge to Asian Security. *Survival* 36 (2), 43 –59.

21. Swaine, *The Role of the Chinese Military in National Security Policymaking*, 9.

22. Glaser, B. S. (1993). China's Security Perceptions : I nterests and Ambitions. *Asian Survey* 33 (3), 253.

23. Chen, Q. (1993). New Approaches in China's Foreign Policy : T he Post-Cold War Era. *Asian Survey* 33 (3), 240–241.

24. 张文木 [Zhang Wenmu]. (2014). 论中国海权 [*On China's Sea Power*], 3rd Edition. 北京 [Beijing]: 海洋出版社 [Ocean Press].

25. Xuetong, Y. (1995). Economic Security, Good-Neighbor Policy Emphasized in Post-Cold War Security Strategy. *Contemporary International Relations* (8), 10.

26. Erickson, A. S. & Strange, A. M. (2016). *Six Years at Sea … and Counting: Gulf of Aden Anti-Piracy and China's Maritime Commons*. Washington, DC: The Jamestown Foundation; Economy, E. C. & Levi, M. (2014). *By All Means Necessary: How China's Resource Quest Is Changing the World*. New York: Oxford University Press.

27. For an early assessment, see Swaine, M. D. & Tellis, A. J. (2000). *Interpreting China's Grand Strategy: Past, Present, and Future*. Santa Monica, CA: RAND.

28. Nathan & Scobell. (2012). *China's Search for Security*, 3.

29. Holslag, J. (2011). China's Vulnerability Trap. *Survival* 53 (2), 77–88; and Dannreuther, R. (2011). China and Global Oil: Vulnerability and Opportunity. *International Affairs* 87 (6), 1345–1364.

30. Jisi, W. (2011). China's Search for a Grand Strategy. *Foreign Affairs* 90 (2), 68–79.

31. Economy, E. C. & Oksenberg, M. eds. (1999). *China Joins the World*. New York: Council on Foreign Relations; and Gill, B. (2007). *Rising Star: China's New Security Diplomacy*. Washington, DC: Brookings Institution Press.

32. Song, W. (2016). *China's Approach to Central Asia: The Shanghai Cooperation Organization*. Abington: Routledge; and Howell, D. (2018). Take the Shanghai Cooperation Organization Seriously. *Japan Times*, 7 June.

33. Special Focus (2011). The South China Sea Dispute. *Contemporary Southeast Asia* 33 (3).

34. 杨毅 [Yang Yi] (2015). 警惕! 中国崛起正面临 '安全困境' [Be Alert! China's Rise Is Facing 'Security Dilemma'].《国防参考》[*National Defense Reference*], 7 January.

35. 周琪 [Zhou Qi]. 冷战后美国南海政策的演变及其根源 [Source of Change in U.S. South China Sea Policy After the Cold War].《世界经济与政治》[*World Economics & Politics*] (6), 23–44.

36. Smith, S. A. (2013). *A Sino-Japanese Clash in the East China Sea*. New York: Council on Foreign Relations; Liff, A. P. & Erickson, A. S. (2017). From Management Crisis to Crisis Management? Japan's Post-2012 Institutional Reforms and Sino-Japanese (In)Stability. *Journal of Strategic Studies* 40 (5), 604–638.

37. 郭丽立 [Guo Lili]. (2005). 日本的'自主防卫'与日美同盟发展趋势 [Japan's 'Self-Defense' and Development Trends in U.S.-Japan Alliance].《国际问题研究》[*International Studies*] (2), 52–55.

38. 卢昊 [Lu Hao]. 2018. 日美关系: 政军互动与印太战略下的政策协调 [Japan-U.S. Relations: Political and Security Exchanges and Strategic Coordination in the Context of 'Indo-Pacific Strategy']. In 杨伯江等编 [Yang Bojiang et al.] (Eds.)《日本研究报告 (2018)》[*Annual Report of Research of Japan (2018)*] (pp. 158–175). Beijing: Social Sciences Academic Press; 王广涛 [Wang Guangtao]. (2017). 军工利益集团与日本的安全政策 [Military-Industrial Interest Group and Japan's Security Policy].《世界经济与政治》[*World Economics and Politics*] (12), 26–47.

39. Holslag, J. (2009). The Persistent Military Security Dilemma Between China and India. *Journal of Strategic Studies* 32 (6), 811–840.

40. Garver, J. W. & Wang, F. (2010). China's Anti-Encirclement Struggle. *Asian Security* 6 (3), 238–261; and 宋德星 [Song Dexing]. (2016).《印度海洋战略研究 [*India's Maritime Strategy*]. 北京 [Beijing]: 时事出版社 [Current Affairs Press].

41. 王涛 [Wang Tao]. (2015). '印太'地缘政治概念视角下的美印防务关系 [U.S.-India Defense Ties Under the Prism of Indo-Pacific Geopolitics].《现代军事 [*Conlimit*] (7), 38–44.

42. See Bush, R. C. 2013. *Uncharted Strait: The Future of China-Taiwan Relations*. Washington, DC: The Brookings Institution; Womack, B. & Hao, Y. eds. *Rethinking the Triangle: Washington-Beijing-Taipei*. Singapore: World Scientific Publishing; and Kastner, S. (2018). China-U.S.-Taiwan Relations Are in Choppy Waters: Here's What's Going On. *Washington Post*, 30 April, https://www.washingtonpost.com/news/monkey-cage/wp/2018/04/30/china-u-s-taiwan-relations-are-in-choppy-waters-heres-whats-going-on/.

43. Snyder, S. A. (2016). Will China Change Its North Korea Policy? *Council on Foreign Relations*, 31 March; Yuan, J. (2016). Managing the Hermit Kingdom: China, North Korea and the Arts of Strategic Patience. In Zhiyue, B. (Ed.) *China-US Relations in Global Perspective* (pp. 173–195) Wellington: Victoria University Press.

44. See Medeiros, E. S. (2009). *China's International Behaviour: Activism, Opportunism, and Diversification*. Santa Monica: RAND; and Saunders, P. C. (2006). *China's Global Activism: Strategy, Drivers, and Tools*. Washington, DC: National University Press; and Dittmer, L. & Yu, G. T. eds. *China, the Developing World, and the New Global Dynamic*. Boulder and London: Lynne Rienner.

45. See Yuan, J. (2013). China and the Indian Ocean: New Departures in Regional Balancing. In Garofano, J. & Dew, A. J. (Eds.) *Deep Currents and Rising Tides: the Indian Ocean and International Security* (pp. 157–183). Washington, DC: Georgetown University Press; and Brewster, D. ed. (2018). *China and India at Sea: Competition for Naval Dominance in the Indian Ocean.* New Delhi: Oxford University Press.

46. 耿志强 郑守华 [Geng Zhiqiang and Zheng Shouhua]. (2017). 中国非传统安全威胁研究 [A Study of Non-traditional Security Threats Facing China].《中国军事科学》[*Chinese Military Sciences*] (4), 105–112; and Thornton, P. (2015). China's Non-traditional Security. In Dittmer, L. & Yu, M. (Eds.) *Routledge Handbook of Chinese Security.* New York: Routledge.

47. Fravel, M. T. (2011). Economic Growth, Regime Security, and Military Strategy: Explaining the Rise of Noncombat Operations in China. *Asian Security* 7 (3), 177–200; and Zerba, S. H. (2014). China's Libya Evacuation Operation: A Diplomatic Imperative—Overseas Citizen Protection. *Journal of Contemporary China* 23 (90), 1093–1112.

48. Kucharski, M. (2011). China in the Age of American Primacy. *International Relations* 26 (1), 60–77; and Wang, Y. (2010). China's Response to the Unipolar World: The Strategic Logic of Peaceful Development. *Journal of Asian and African Studies* 45 (5), 554–567.

49. Steinberg, J. B. & O'Hanlon, M. (2014). *Strategic Reassurance and Resolve: U.S.-China Relations in the Twenty-First Century.* Princeton, NJ: Princeton University Press; and Allison, G. (2017). *Destined for War: Can America and China Escape Thucydides's Trap?* New York: HMH.

50. On this emerging competition or even rivalry between the United States and China, see International Institute for Strategic Studies. (2017). *Asia-Pacific Regional Security Assessment 2017.* London: IISS; on how to manage such a rivalry and promote stability in the region, see Swaine, M. D., Deng, W., & Lescure, A. R. (2016). *Creating a Stable Asia: An Agenda for a U.S.-China Balance of Power.* Washington, DC: Carnegie Endowment for International Peace.

51. See Pickrell, R. (2018). The US 'Must Not Let This Bill Become Law': Beijing Blasts Bill Designed to Counter China. *Business Insider.* 3 August, https://www.businessinsider.com.au/beijing-blasts-us-defense-bill-designed-to-check-china-2018-8; and Chen, D. P. (2019). The Trump Administration's One-China Policy: Tilting toward Taiwan in an Era of US-PRC Rivalry? *Asian Politics & Policy* 11 (2), 250–278.

52. PWC. (2017). *The World in 2050: How Will the Global Economic Order Change by 2050?,* https://www.pwc.com/gx/en/world-2050/assets/pwc-the-world-in-2050-full-report-feb-2017.pdf.

53. Mahbubani, K. (2018). *Has the West Lost It?* London: Penguin; and Rachman, G. (2017). *Easternisation: War and Peace in the Asian Century.* London: Vintage.

54. See Tobin, L. (2018). Xi's Vision for Transforming Global Governance: A Strategic Challenge for Washington and Its Allies. *Texas National Security Review* 2 (1), 155–166; Plobberger, C. (2017). One Belt, One Road—China's New Grand Strategy. *Journal of Chinese Economic and Business Studies* 15 (3), 289–305; Huotari, M. et al. (2017). *China's Emergence as a Global Security Actor.* Berlin: Mercator Institute for China Studies; Wang, J.

(2019). Xi Jinping's 'Major Country Diplomacy': A Paradigm Shift? *Journal of Contemporary China* 28 (115), 15–30; Hawksley, *Asian Waters*.

55. Babones, S. (2019). Mandate from Heaven? *The National Interest* 164 (November/December), 40–51; Anon. (2011). Rising Power, Anxious State—Special Report. *The Economist* 25 June, 1–14; Khan, S. W. (2018). *Haunted by Chaos: China's Grand Strategy from Mao Zedong to Xi Jinping*. Cambridge: Harvard University; Ratner, E. (2011). The Emergent Security Threats Reshaping China's Rise. *The Washington Quarterly* 34 (1), 29–44.

56. Lampton (2002). *The Making of Chinese Foreign and Security Policy*.

57. Legro, J. W. (2007). What China Will Want: The Future Intentions of a Rising Power. *Perspectives on Politics* 5 (3), 515–533; Hart, A. F. & Jones, B. D. How Do Rising Powers Rise? *Survival* 52 (6), 63–88.

58. 门洪华 肖晞 [Men Honghua and Xiao Yi] (2016). 总体国家安全观与中国特色国家安全道路 [Holistic National Security Perspective and a Path to National Security with Chinese Characteristics].《攀登》[*New Heights*] 35 (1), 2–8; and Xi, X. (2016). China's National Security: Strategic Challenges and Choices. *China: An International Journal* 14 (1), 171–181.

59. Cabestan, J. P. (2009). China's Foreign- and Security-Policy Decision-making Processes Under Hu Jintao. *Journal of Current Chinese Affairs* 38 (3), 63–97.

60. 徐光顺 [Xu Guangshun] (2018). 习近平新时代国家安全战略思想探析 [An Analysis of Xi Jinping's Thoughts on National Security Strategy in the New Era].《邓小平研究》[*Deng Xiaoping Research*] (2), 54–61; and 陈启音 [Chen Qiyin] (2017). 深入贯彻总体国家安全观走新时代中国特色的国家安全道路 [Thoroughly Implement the Holistic View on National Security and Take the Path of National Security with Chinese Characteristics in the New Era].《中国军事科学》[*Chinese Military Sciences*], (4), 95–104.

61. See Saunders, P., Ding, A. S., Scobell, A., Yang, A. N. D. & Wuthnow, J. eds. (2019). *Chairman Xi Remakes the PLA: Assessing Chinese Military Reforms*. Washington, DC: National Defense University Press; Cabestan, J. P. (2017). China's Institutional Changes in the Foreign and Security Policy Realm Under Xi Jinping: Power Concentration vs. Fragmentation Without Institutionalization. *East Asia* 34 (2), 113–131; Wuthnow, J. & Saunders, P. C. (2017). *Chinese Military Reforms in the Age of Xi Jinping: Drivers, Challenges, and Implications*. Washington, DC: Institute for National Strategic Studies, National Defense University; and Lyle J. Goldstein. Five Dragons Stirring up the Sea: Challenge and Opportunity in China's Improving Maritime Enforcement Capabilities. *China Maritime Study* (5). Newport, RI: China Maritimes Studies Institute, Naval War College.

62. See Jakobson, L. & Know, D. (2010). New Foreign Policy Actors in China. *SIPRI Policy Paper* 26. Stockholm: SIPRI, September; Shambaugh, D. (2011). Coping with a Conflicted China. *The Washington Quarterly* 34 (1), 7–27; Changhe, S. (2010). Understanding Chinese Diplomatic Transformation: A Multi-actor's Perspective. *The Hague Journal of Diplomacy* 5, 313–329; and Chen Zhemin, C., Junbo, J. & Diyu, C. (2010). The Provinces and China's Multi-Layered Diplomacy: The Cases of GMS and Africa. *The Hague Journal of Diplomacy* 5, 331–356.

63. Cabestan. (2009). China's Foreign- and Security-Policy Decision-making Processes Under Hu Jintao.

64. Wuthnow, J. (2017). China's New 'Black Box': Problems and Prospects for the Central National Security Commission. *The China Quarterly* 232 (December),

886–903; and Ji, Y. (2016). China's National Security Commission: Theory, Evolution and Operations. *Journal of Contemporary China* 25 (98), 178–196.

65. Saunders, P. C. & Scobell, A. eds. (2015). *PLA Influence on China's National Security Policymaking*. Stanford, CA: Stanford University Press.

66. These developments have been described in studies undertaken by the U.S. National Defense University's National Institute of Strategic Studies, Center for Naval Analysis, U.S. Army War College's Strategic Studies Institute, Congressional Research Service, U.S. Naval War College's China Maritime Studies Institute, and the National Bureau of Asian Research. For the latest overall assessment, see Office of the Secretary of Defense. (2018). *Annual Report to Congress: Military and Security Developments Involving the People's Republic of China 2018*. Washington, DC: Department of Defense.

67. See, for example, Fung, C. J. (2019). *China and Intervention at the UN Security Council: Reconciling Status*. New York: Oxford University Press.

68. Ng, T. (2014). Xi Calls Asian People to Uphold Asia's Security as He Aims to Sideline US. *South China Morning Post*, 21 May, https://www.scmp.com/art icle/1517256/xi-calls-asian-people-uphold-asias-security-he-aims-shut-out-us.

69. China State Council Information Office. (2017). *China's Policies on Asia-Pacific Security Cooperation*, http://english.gov.cn/archive/white_paper/ 2017/01/11/content_281475539078636.htm.

70. Baum, M. A. & Potter, P. (2008). The Relationships Between Mass Media, Public Opinion, and Foreign Policy: Toward a Theoretical Synthesis. *Annual Review of Political Science* 11 (June), 39–59.

71. Shirk, S. L. (2011). Changing Media, Changing Foreign Policy. In Shirk, S. L. (Ed.). *Changing Media, Changing China* (pp. 225–252). New York: Oxford University Press.

CHAPTER 7

Russia's National Security Posture

Matthew Sussex

Of all the major powers in contemporary international politics, Russia's national security policy has appeared—on the face of it—the most unstable. Following the dissolution of the USSR nearly thirty years ago, Russia's trajectory shifted initially from a pro-Western orientation to a strategy of multipolarism, where cooperation with the West was conditional on national interests coinciding. More recently, its national security posture has adopted a theme that has quickly become familiar: an often bellicose and muscular actor unafraid of using military force, offensive cyber weapons and information warfare, hybrid capabilities, espionage and sabotage, and a role as a spoiler against Western liberal democracies. At the same time Russia's relationship with China, while hardly a partnership of co-equals, has matured to the point where many commentators see it as a de facto anti-Western alliance.[1]

Why has Russian national security policy followed this path? Is it more accurate to see Russian interests as being shaped by rational material factors, the external environment, its own internal turmoil and frequent lawlessness, the adoption of a virulently nationalistic identity, the machinations of elites, or a combination of these factors? To answer these questions, this chapter explores the sources of Russian national security policy, its main rationales, and the constraints and limitations on Russian choices in future. In doing so it makes an argument that some readers may find surprising or confronting: that even

M. Sussex (✉)
Centre for Defence Research, Australian Defence College, Canberra, ACT, Australia
e-mail: matthew.sussex@anu.edu.au

Griffith Asia Institute, Griffith University, Brisbane, QLD, Australia

© The Author(s), under exclusive license to Springer Nature Switzerland AG 2022
M. Clarke et al. (eds.), *The Palgrave Handbook of National Security*,
https://doi.org/10.1007/978-3-030-53494-3_7

139

though its methods have become much more assertive over time, there has actually been remarkable consistency in Russian national interests since the Soviet collapse.

And while Russia will probably continue to utilise the various instruments at its disposal in attempts to disrupt and fragment Western nations—which includes meddling in its elections, Machiavellian diplomacy and using the economic, technological, and military forces at its disposal—it is important to note that Russian assertiveness stems in many ways from a fear of future weakness. Having concluded that a rising China will overtake the United States as the world's most influential actor, Russia faces a new set of security dilemmas on its vulnerable southern flank, in its relatively undeveloped Far East, and in the potential for being sidelined as the PRC's economic juggernaut moves on.

As a result, fears of entrapment or irrelevance[2] will be powerful drivers of Russian policy in the years to come. This means that we should not consider Russia's current national security stance to be fixed, unchanging or irrevocable. Indeed, Russia has long favoured a pivot state role between Europe and Asia, to maintain its great power status as well as insulating it from major global power blocs.[3] Of course, much of this will depend on external forces that Russia cannot control, and it equally relies on domestic political stability. This is by no means assured. But at the very least it suggests analysts should be cautious in making convenient assumptions about Russian behaviour, either in terms of how it will react to international events, or how it attempts to shape them itself.

THE ROOTS OF RUSSIAN CONDUCT

In order to understand Russia's national security posture, an awareness of its historical post-communist experience is fundamental. To begin with, the collapse of the USSR was in many respects a series of nationalist revolutions, where former republics recaptured self-determination after decades of being subsumed into the Soviet experiment.[4] As the largest former Soviet republic—in physical terms, in population, as the centre of the USSR's politics and economy, and the national embodiment of the Soviet project—it was not hard to see the Russian Federation as the inheritor of all that had been lost from the collapse of the USSR. And although it retained many of the trappings of Soviet power, including the USSR's Permanent seat on the UN Security Council and its nuclear arsenal, Russia effectively lost a third of its territory as well as a third of its people. Fundamentally it also lost the sense of a unifying national idea. For all its flaws, the USSR had represented a national project that Russians took pride in, and has become a nostalgic myth recalling past power and greatness.[5]

Of course, these sentiments were not always mirrored in other former Soviet republics. For many Ukrainians, the end of the USSR meant the end of political repression. The new post-Soviet government in Kiev sought to retain ways to protect it from the prospect of Russian dominance, which included a desire to keep the Soviet nuclear weapons stored on Ukrainian soil. Whereas Kazakhstan promptly handed the nuclear arsenal on its own territory back to Russia, it took an intervention by the United States, as well as a sizeable aid and reassurance package, to convince Kiev that the end of the Cold War should not also be a proliferation event, resulting in the emergence of new nuclear powers.[6]

It is also worth remembering that Russia also inherited the Soviet economy, which had ossified to the point of collapse. The new Russian economy suffered almost instantly the decision to move to from the plan to the market was introduced. The 500-day Shatalin Plan, a voucher privatisation scheme, saw prices for goods skyrocket, and an informal grey economy emerge that favoured hard currency (or even barter exchange) over the rouble.[7] And because the logistics of the administrative transition were hurried, a small number of Russians grew immensely wealthy, positioning themselves as directors of new private companies that had formerly been state assets. The rise of a new economic and political class—the oligarchs—with close ties to President Boris Yeltsin's administration meant corruption was embedded in the Russian state from the outset.

Russia also experienced deep political turmoil in the early years of its transition. Former leading members of the Soviet Communist Party, as well as influential figures in the national security apparatus, articulated a strong nationalistic and anti-Yeltsin line as parliamentarians in the Congress of People's Deputies.[8] As tensions between the legislature and the executive grew, the Congress voted to re-establish the Brezhnevite Constitution, and declared the office of Russian President defunct, after Yeltsin had attempted to dissolve the parliament and call fresh elections.[9] A power struggle ensued, with Deputies arming and barricading themselves inside the White House. Yeltsin enlisted the support of his Defence Minister Pavel Grachev to put down what he characterised as an attempted coup. Russians were then confronted with the image of their own government using tanks against their parliament.[10]

The upshot of the constitutional Russia's constitutional crisis was that it provided Yeltsin with the opportunity to hold a referendum on the powers of the Presidency. In it, which Russians grudgingly endorsed, he asked for a popular mandate to rule by decree if necessary. In effect he created what was termed a 'superpresidential' constitution allowing him to bypass the parliament, appoint the Constitutional Court, and disband the legislative branch if it failed to endorse his legislative agenda.[11] As a result the Duma (the new Russian parliament) became a hub for popular protest votes during the 1990s, and was dominated by the Communist Party of the Russian Federation (CPRF) as well as nationalist parties like the proto-fascist Liberal Democratic Party of Russia (LDPR), in what became termed a 'red–brown' alliance.[12] Hence Yeltsin often needed to issue decrees for major policy initiatives and appointments. He also found it necessary to sack Prime Ministers and hold new elections on a number of occasions.

As the last decade of the twentieth century progressed, Russia's security situation also deteriorated. Tensions with the United States and the broader West increased, especially after NATO expansion started to become vigorously pursued by the Clinton Administration. One of the chief sources of Russia's sense of betrayal by the West has been the narrative that the George H. W. Bush administration had promised not to expand NATO. But by the mid-1990s, with expansion firmly on the agenda, the Visegrad states (Poland, Hungary, and the Czech Republic) that had been agitating for membership were admitted to the alliance. Russian objections became even more strident when it became evident that Moscow would only be admitted to NATO as a second tier member, with a voice but no veto[13]—a status that every other member of the alliance enjoyed.

Hence by the mid-1990s a new 'Cold Peace' had emerged between Russia and the West. Moscow altered its foreign and security policy direction, abandoning the 'Friends with Everyone' approach that had been championed by Foreign Minister Andrei Kozyrev,[14] and envisioned Russia as a leading upholder of international law as well as a responsible aspirant member of the European Union. Instead Russia's new Foreign Minister (and later Prime Minister) Yevgenyi Primakov adopted a new policy of 'multipolarism', which sought to diversify Russian attention away from the West, and compete directly with the United States if necessary.[15] By the time NATO intervened militarily in the Kosovo crisis in 1999, Russian attitudes had hardened considerably: over 80% of Russians saw NATO expansion and involvement in humanitarian interventions as a threat to Russian interests, and an incursion into its sphere of influence.[16]

Aside from symbolic expressions of disapproval, however, Russia was both unable and unwilling to respond more vigorously to what it saw as deeply unfair treatment by the United States and the EU. Russian room to manoeuvre was also constrained by the fact that it relied heavily on Western support to navigate its own deepening internal economic woes. It suffered particularly acutely from the knock-on effects of the Asian Financial Crisis, which caused a number of banks to collapse and inflation soar to a point that brought the economy to the brink of collapse. Stabilisation measures, including printing more money, withdrawing the 50-ruble note from circulation, and attempting to increase tax receipts did little to resolve the underlying weakness of the Russian economy, and Russia was forced to rely on numerous IMF and World Bank bailouts to maintain essential government spending.[17]

Hence in the first decade after the collapse of the USSR, Russia effectively underwent a process of demodernisation. A yawning gap between a small number of extremely wealthy 'New Russians' and the rest of the population meant that for the vast majority, life was harder under Russia's economic 'shock therapy' than even during the dying days of the USSR.[18] Organised crime had flourished under a weak state, and Russian political elites offered few choices beyond a return to the past (in the case of the CPRF) and more of the same chaos (in the case of Yeltsin's government). The first war in Chechnya, from 1994 to 1996, had raised the spectre of Russia disintegrating into a rump state surrounded by impoverished former regions, many of which featured simmering ethno-nationalist tensions. Yeltsin's own health deteriorated (due at least partly to chronic alcoholism), he repeatedly underwent major heart surgery, and often appeared at major international events in a state of complete incoherence.[19]

It is little wonder, therefore, that Russians came to associate democracy, the West and capitalism with deep mistrust. It was also understandable that when Yeltsin decided to yield power to his new and relatively unknown Prime Minister Vladimir Putin, Russians greeted the news with relief. In articulating a vague agenda around restoring Russia to stability and order, Putin's first steps were remarkably unambitious. He promised to clean up corruption, make Russia a great power again, and instituted a flat tax rate to stimulate growth.[20] Even so, he set a cautious timeframe for recovery, arguing that it would be seven years before Russia's GDP would be the same size as Portugal's.[21] After the events of 9/11 he was the first foreign leader to call George W. Bush and offer Russian assistance, especially by facilitating US access to Manas airbase in Kyrgyzstan, an important staging-post for US coalition strikes into Afghanistan. Doing so also helped Putin convey the image that he was fighting radical Islamic terrorism in Chechnya, where alleged Russian human rights abuses had prompted the suspension of Russia's participation in the Council of Europe.[22] As Bush put it during a meeting at Camp David, he had looked into Putin's soul and seen a man of God with whom he could do business.[23]

Yet any prospect of a sustained Russia–West rapprochement largely dissipated by the time of the Iraq war in 2003. Russia led a number of nations in rejecting US pressure for the UNSC to endorse a pre-emptive conflict against Saddam Hussein, on the pretext that Iraq posed a danger to US security through a clandestine WMD program and sponsorship of radical Islamic terrorism. Both were flimsy pretexts subsequently proven to be false or exaggerated. Russia's main concern here was for Middle Eastern security, where the universally reviled Hussein regime played a circuit-breaker role for regional tensions. It was also concerned that the United States was seeking to monopolise trade in the Middle East, cutting Russia off from potential partners. By 2005, then, the relationship between Russia and the West had deteriorated again, to the point where analysts were speaking of a new Cold War.[24]

Closer to home, Putin had made progress both domestically as well as in his goal of bringing the so-called 'Near Abroad' of former Soviet republics into Russia's sphere of influence. Although Yeltsin's constitution afforded him sweeping powers, he nonetheless began dismantling Russian democracy as well as civil society. Crackdowns on the media began in 2004, silencing many critics of the regime. Putin's renovation of the Russian Upper House (the Federation Council) included removing a number of provincial governors—many of whom were corrupt—and replacing them with selectorates.[25] An important check and balance in Russian democracy therefore became beholden to the President. Putin also embarked on the renationalisation of Russian energy companies. This took place between 2003 and 2005 with the Yukos affair, where the company—which was responsible for 20% of Russia's oil output—was accused of tax evasion and presented with a US$28 billion bill.[26] Unable to pay, its assets were frozen and then sold to the government at a fraction of their value; while Mikhail Khordokovsky, the Yukos CEO, was arrested and jailed for fraud.

One of the main benefits of a renationalised oil and gas sector was that energy could be used more effectively as a strategic weapon. One year after Yukos Russia escalated a dispute over gas with Ukraine and Belarus. Moscow accused both nations—but particularly Ukraine—of siphoning off Russian gas transiting to Europe. Russia cut off all gas supplies to Ukraine in 2006 to force it to pay its debts. This occurred again in 2009, when Gazprom insisted that it was entitled to seize ownership of Ukrainian gas infrastructure, in lieu of payment for the transition to market-based pricing and an end to Soviet-era subsidies.[27] The vulnerability of EU nations to Russian gas-tap diplomacy was later apparent in the reticence of leading actors (such as Germany, which relies on Russia for about 35% of its gas) to include bans on Russian gas in subsequent EU sanctions regimes in protest of Russian behaviour in Crimea.[28]

Emboldened by its successes in the gas wars, Russia also sought to revamp its military after the 2008 Five Day War against Georgia. The conflict, which had been sparked by Georgian encroachment into the Russian-protected enclaves of South Ossetia and Abkhazia (whose residents considered themselves Russian citizens), revealed—for Putin at least—sizeable deficiencies in the Russian military. He therefore ordered an ambitious USD$600 billion modernisation program, paid for by increased revenue from energy sales, which had significantly eased economic pressure.[29]

The Russian military also began investing in the use of technology as an instrument of national power. Although it lacked the military research and development budgets of the West, Moscow paid particular attention to using cyber tools as offensive weapons, backed up by military deception measures to mask intentions and operations. The 'Gerasimov Doctrine', named in 2012 after the Chief of the General Staff, prompted Russian national security policy planners to examine how conflicts could be shaped without relying on kinetic force: in other words, to win wars without fighting.[30] As its strategists argued, the Western conception of war had become increasingly rules-bound, constrained by laws of combat, the need for a clear rationale, and clear exit strategies. Conversely, they noted, war was a totalising phenomenon that incorporated politics, economics, and society. And within a world increasingly reliant on digital communications, control of the information battlespace could make the need for overt hostilities almost redundant.

The debut performance of Russia's new hybrid war doctrine came in February and March 2014, when armed forces with no unit insignia occupied Crimea, in response to the overthrow of the pro-Russian Ukrainian President Viktor Yanukovich, and the groundswell of popular Ukrainian support for an association agreement with the EU. The transfer of power in Kiev, which led to violence at Maidan Square, put Russia at a strategic disadvantage: a pro-EU government could cut off the Crimean peninsula, effectively shutting Russia out of the Black Sea. Russia's takeover was decisive and swift: confusion about the 'friendly green men' on the streets of Simferapol and Sevastopol stymied Ukrainian counter-mobilisations, and a series of cyber attacks against military and civilian infrastructure crippled the ability of the Ukrainian military to respond.[31] Having established itself in Crimea, the Russian government then backed separatist rebels in Ukraine's Donbas region, in a bloody conflict that shows no sign of abating. With Ukraine effectively split in two, Putin also began referring to the Donbas as 'Novorossiya' (new Russia), echoing phrasing that had been used by Catherine the Great.[32]

Russia also employed non-linear warfare in other theatres, in ways that were not anticipated in the West. Its intervention in Syria, in support of Bashar Al Asad targeted those who might represent a viable alternative to the Syrian dictator. It also radicalised them, tacitly assisting in the creation of new ISIS supporters in the West who would go on to attack civilian targets. Russia's bombing campaign contributed to the wave of refugees emptying out of Syria and heading for the EU, where Russia deliberately assisted Far Right parties to push statist and anti-immigration narratives, thus weakening the European Union from within. And Russian support for Asad sent a powerful message to authoritarian leaders that Moscow stood by its allies, in contradistinction to the West, which Moscow noted had abandoned Hussein, Hosni Mubarak, and Muamar Gaddafi. When the Trump White House took the much-criticised step of withdrawing US troops from northern Syria in 2019, Russia filled the vacuum, brokering a safe zone involving Syrian regular forces and a Turkish military advancing on Kurdish safe havens.[33]

Hence from the end of the USSR to the end of 2019 the Russian state had moved from a position where it sought friendship with the United States and integration into Europe, to the West's most ardent adversary. In the process Russian democracy was derailed: first by Yeltsin, and then by Putin. Russia became a highly managed electoral democracy where excessive dissent was criminalised, and journalists and regime critics were routinely jailed or even killed. In articulating Russian interests Putin continued the momentum begun under Primakov by enunciating a much more nationalistic tone in Russian national security policy, deeply hostile to the West and building on the narrative that Russia had been deliberately weakened by the West. Having concluded that the Western order was moribund and European unity was an anachronism, Putin turned to China, forging a close relationship with Xi Jinping and prompting speculation about a new 'axis of authoritarians'.[34] And yet, with the EU suffering from internal malaise prompted by the Global Financial Crisis, the Brexit fiasco, and an upsurge in support for anti-EU parties, at the end of the twenty-first century's second decade Putin appeared to have been prescient. With the United States left effectively rudderless, torn by infighting and intrigue about the chaotic Trump presidency, it is not surprising that Putin came to be viewed—through both its words and alleged deeds—as the international community's chief spoiler.

Understanding Russian National Security Policy

How, therefore, can we understand Russian national security policy? What are its key drivers, and how is Russian national security policy best conceptualised? Answering these questions is important, because the primary purpose of assessing national security policy in any state requires an assessment of its motivations. This allows the analyst to explain its behaviour through a conceptual lens, examine the leading forces influencing its behaviour, and put forward prescriptions or predictions about its future national security trajectory. In the case of the Russian Federation, there is no shortage of ways to make such an assessment. Accordingly, this section examines three explanations for Russian behaviour from leading paradigms in international relations theory. Each has its relative strengths and weaknesses, but each also offers a potentially useful conceptual framework for the analysis of Russia's motivations and intentions.

Constructivist Approaches

To begin with, constructivist approaches that focus on the significance of ideas and identity in shaping how nations behave, have much to contribute in attempts to understand Russian national security policy. These assessments have focus heavily on the gradual emergence of a radicalised Russian national identity under Putin, and the shift in internal discourses from a moderate position to an assertive nationalistic consensus. The result has been an anti-Western narrative that reinforces the need for Russia, betrayed by the United States and the EU, to be a great power in its region and the world.[35]

A leading constructivist contribution here has been Andrey Tsygankov's[36] work on the role of identity in shaping Russia's national interests. Tsygankov divided schools of Russian thought into three categories: liberal Westernisers; Statists, and Civilisationists, although others have framed it more simply as a dual narrative between a pro-Western approach to Russian interests, and those who favoured Eurasianism.[37] Analyses such as these have drawn inspiration from Russian myth, memory, and socio-cultural totems as markers of how a neo-imperial Russian identity emerged under Putin. Constructivist approaches stress that the traditional contest between the 'Westernisers' and 'Eurasnianists' (or 'Civilisationists' for Tsygankov) has been decided strongly in favour of the latter. This implies a Russian construction of identity occupying a separate and distinct region: neither Western nor Asian, but a crucial geopolitical bridge between the two. Occupying what Halford Makinder called the 'heartland' of the Eurasian landmass,[38] Russia—by virtue of its size and ethnic composition—thus sees itself as a civilisational bridge between East and West.

This is convenient for Russian nationalists for several reasons. First it allows them to argue that Russia is by nature a unifier of peoples: a 'Third Rome', as many of its proponents argue.[39] Second, if Russia is indeed a bridge between East and West, then it is the natural meeting point of a variety of different civilisational groups, each of which has a long and sometimes bloody history with the others. Hence to keep Islamic, Judeo-Christian, and Sinic civilisations from conflict—so the argument goes—Russia must inevitably be a great power in world affairs. If it is weak and fractured, the alternative is civilisational chaos.

In many respects a view like this is not too unusual. In fact, it is a civilisational form of the same logic used by US neoconservatives to justify American primary: that liberal hegemony is the only assured way to prevent international order from breaking down.[40] But when used instrumentally, as nationalist narratives tend to be, they can also be a justification for empire, the mistreatment of minority populations, and a rhetorical justification for policies that advance national interests under a zero-sum formulation. And regardless of whether Russia's internal debates are framed in three categories or only two, it is clear that the most assertive strand has come to dominate Russian messaging on its foreign and security policy, as well as its internal narratives to justify them.

Hence under a constructivist conception of Russian national security and national interests, the key in predicting how policy preferences are shaped and change can be found in tracing the transformation of its ideas and identity. Following the reforms of the Gorbachev period, which Russians blame for the collapse of the USSR, the lack of a core idea about what Russia's national purpose was subjected to strenuous debate. The Russian periodical *International Affairs* featured numerous contests over the issue of whether Russia was a great power, or whether during the 1990s that it had actually become 'Upper Volta with ballistic missiles', as a popular saying put it.[41] And while the overall purpose of Russian nationhood was being debated, so too was the scope and purpose of Russian policy in its neighbourhood and beyond. What, for instance, should its role be in the so-called 'Near Abroad' (the former republics of the USSR, which Russians hesitated to regard as independent states)? What should be its attitude to European integration, NATO membership, and relations with Asian nations? What would justify Russia using force to protect its interests, and how closely should it follow international law in making those judgements?

In each of these debates, the initial view from Kozyrev was that Russia should join what Gorbachev had earlier called the 'Common European Home'.[42] But it quickly became evident to Russian elites that the West seemed unsympathetic to its struggles as it navigated the post-Soviet political and economic landscape. The mood in the West was not one of triumphalism, but certainly one of relief, with priorities turning to 'peace dividends'. NATO expansion, previously regarded a strategic misstep that could alienate Russia, was put back on the agenda by the Clinton administration as a way to promote collective security and assuage the fears of new democracies in Central and Eastern Europe. At the same time, the economic frailty of the Russian transition project, which exacerbated its political turmoil, was regarded by many in the West as putting an unnecessary financial burden on global liberal institutions. When Russia pivoted to a more multipolar orientation to its foreign and security policy in 1996, Clinton's response was to move away from the language of partnership. Instead, he cast Russia as a problem to be managed in his 1998 State of the Union address.[43]

Hence, from a constructivist perspective, the changes to Russian identity were already taking shape under the Presidency of Boris Yeltsin. This was aggravated by the success of Far Right parties in the regions and the Russian parliament, as well as by the Russian Communist Party. Once Putin took over, he quietly extended the statism that Yeltsin had begun to espouse, and strengthened civilisationist (or Eurasianist) agendas by appealing to Russian nationalist tropes once it became evident that his reset of the Russia–US relationship with Bush Jnr was not bearing fruit. He made public his admiration for Peter the Great; reached out to domestic fascist ideologues like Alexander Dugin; adopted the notion of 'sovereign democracy'; spoke wistfully about the Soviet Union; tightened his control over the state apparatus; and repeatedly articulated a much more nationalistic vision for the pursuit of Russian interests.[44] This was particularly evident in his speech at the 2007 Munich Security Conference, in which he cast the West as a potential threat to Russian interests, and warned it from interfering in the former Soviet space, which he characterised as Russia's privileged sphere of influence.[45]

In many respects, a constructivist reading of Russia's move from liberalism to an assertive civilisational posture is a persuasive one. Yet it also is open to challenge. The notion that identity is a normative force that can act as a determinant of national interests, although seemingly useful on the surface, is problematic when it comes to actually demonstrating this to be the case. First, it is not always conclusively clear which conception of identity is ascendant at a particular time, which aspects of behaviour they have shaped, and under what circumstances. Nor is it guaranteed that researchers who seek to identify what are essentially ideological cleavages in society are correct in identifying the contours of a particular viewpoint.

Second, the proposition by constructivists that identity and interests are mutually and normatively constituted is effectively a tautology: in order to understand ideas we must understand interests, and vice-versa. Third, ideas and identity are clearly tied to systems and structures. This was neatly demonstrated by Stephen Brooks and William Wohlforth in a landmark article which took issue with the constructivist claim that the end of the Cold War was brought about by shifts in Soviet ideas and identity (particularly Gorbachev's).[46] As Brooks and Wohlforth showed, ideas change when material circumstances do, rather than the other way around. This explains the realisation by Gorbachev that the state of the Soviet economy—which was nearing total collapse—required a different approach to how the USSR engaged with the West. In order words, for Gorbachev necessity was the mother of his invention. His decision to unilaterally change the combative nature of US–Soviet rivalry was thus more the product of his pragmatic realisation that the USSR had effectively lost the Cold War and needed an exit strategy, rather than a fundamental shift in Soviet identity.[47]

This logic can be applied to other constructivist explanations for Russia's move to a more assertive anti-Western posture. How can we be sure that it is a radicalised identity—amongst leaders, the Russian people or both—that is driving its behaviour? Would it not be equally persuasive, if not even more so, to see Putin as a pragmatist who uses identity and nationalism as rhetorical justifications for a policy determined by Russia's material capabilities (or lack of them)? And what does characterising Russian foreign and security policy as 'neoimperial', really mean in practice? What specific differences are there, for instance between a neoimperial approach and one that is merely assertive? Finally, focusing on ideas and identity—normative factors that are difficult to prove are determinants of behaviour at any given time—can give rise to cartoonish depictions of a state's policy platforms, which are influenced by a number of stakeholders, agencies, ministries, and informal as well as formal networks with competencies in security policy making.

Neoliberal Approaches

An alternative to the constructivist approach can be found in neoliberal explanations for Russian foreign and security policy. The emphasis here has less to do with identity as a factor driving behaviour. In fact, liberals tend to agree with realists that states are rational utility maximisers. Rather, liberals focus on the negative effects of economic and political dislocation and chaos on the way that elites and publics engage with policy processes.[48] In other words, liberals explain Russia's posture through the prism of bad leaders and bad institutions, instead of problems associated with democracy or the market per se.

For liberals, understanding Putin's Russia rests on an understanding of how its democracy was derailed. To begin with, the economic transition was mishandled from the outset. This created a bifurcated society in which a very few rich oligarchs—such as Boris Berezovsky and Roman Abramovich—benefitted immensely from the transition process, and exerted undue influence over economic and political decision-making in order to protect their interests.[49] As a result, democracy never really had a chance in Russia, which became riven with corruption, nepotism, and a weak state apparatus that failed to regulate the excesses of the economic elite. With ordinary Russians facing structural obstacles to participating in the market (paying off organised crime gangs, for instance, was an endemic problem for Russian businesses), it is little wonder that a politics of resentment set in. In this way, a negative experience with robber capitalism became linked in popular perceptions to an inherent failing of democracy, rather than placing the blame where it should have fallen: on the political elites that enabled such practices, and who benefitted personally from their relationships with Russia's new wealthy class.[50]

Liberals also tend to explain Russian hostility to NATO expansion and its evolution into an anti-Western actor as the product of this political chaos. Since the old Soviet elite had not been provided with 'golden parachutes' to soften their fall from positions of power, they sought to recapture their privileged roles by becoming influential political actors. As Edward Mansfield and Jack Snyder noted, the transitional phase of any fledgling democracy makes it particularly vulnerable to co-option if former elites are not carefully managed.[51] In the example of the Russian Federation, it was in the interests of former Communist Party bosses to articulate a radical nationalistic and anti-Western line, which appealed to the popular view that many of the Russian Federation's problems were the fault of the West. In this way, not only could a process of transition be derailed, but the risk of conflict was also magnified. Moscow's deliberate attempt in 1999 to stymie the NATO occupation force in Kosovo by seizing Pristina airport with Russian forces[52] was illustrative of this tendency: that by framing the relationship between the West and Russia as fundamentally adversarial, old elites could push the two towards war.

Liberal explanations for Russian national security policy under Putin also focus on how entrenched corruption has become. For them, far from cleaning up corruption in the post-Yeltsin era, Putin made the problem worse by institutionalising it, ruling over a series of rich clans by periodically switching favour from one to another, and scapegoating individuals such as Khordokovsky to serve as a warning to others who might deviate from the official Kremlin line. Putin's closeness to a number of extremely rich individuals (and his own unreported but suspected massive personal fortune),[53] thus creates a series of informal networks to circumvent the normal bureaucratic policy process of negotiation and compromise.

In other words, for liberals, Putin has created an authoritarian kleptocracy that thrives especially off the increased receipts that flow from a nationalised energy industry.[54] The fact that ministers, politicians, and leading policymakers in the decision-making apparatus also have numerous ties to financial barons means that the entire process of Russian politics—and by extension its national security policy—becomes an extension of the personal financial preferences of the elite, and a mechanism to serve the constant enrichment of powerful individuals rather than the Russian people. Russian democracy is a sham, featuring vote-rigging, the suppression of dissent with black PR, tough laws constraining the expression of alternative views, and the subjugation of society to the leader's whims. The wealthy then are responsible for capital flight, sending profits from the Russian energy industry offshore, buying property in the United States and exotic European locales, and educating their children at Western universities.[55]

These explanations are also potentially useful in seeking to frame Russian national security policy. However, while they describe real and lasting problems in Russian society, economics, and politics, they are also not immune to criticism. Chief amongst these is that a liberal approach leaves the United States and the West blameless in Russia's slide to authoritarianism. As critics of NATO expansion have pointed out, although the original intention may have been to foster collective security, the result has been to marginalise Russia from European security affairs. That Russia was presented with a unique downgraded form of association with the alliance deepened Russian hostility from an early stage, and also contributed towards the framing of powerful anti-Western narratives.[56] That the West was sympathetic to the 'colour revolutions'[57] that swept the post-Soviet space in the mid-2000s was also regarded as proof of its inherent hostility, as were the events in Ukraine during 2013, when the EU made a closer economic association agreement with Kiev conditional on Ukraine not participating in Russia's rival Eurasian Union.[58] The political upheaval this unleashed—in which Ukraine was prompted to choose between two major poles of regional power—can be identified as a strong contributing factor behind Russia's decision to reoccupy Crimea.

Similarly, the West's enthusiasm for humanitarian intervention during the late 1990s and early 2000s was regarded by Russia—with some justification—as a fundamental challenge to the principle of state sovereignty, on which Russia depended as the primary consideration in international law. For Moscow, not only was Article 2 of the UN Charter threatened by Western activities, but intervening on human rights grounds also allowed it to benefit considerably from post-conflict state building efforts, fostering compliance from grateful new leaders under the pretext of democracy promotion by force.[59]

The war in Iraq is a good example of this, where reconstruction contracts went overwhelmingly to states that participated in the 'Coalition of the Willing'. Similarly the civil war in Libya, where NATO was used as a de facto air arm of Gaddafi's opponents is indicative of mission creep, with a UN resolution to protect civilians becoming an argument for regime change. The fact that Gaddafi was hauled from his palace, tortured, and then executed on the street rather than tried in an international court was, for many Russians, an indication of the moral hazards of interventions, not to mention the dangers of power vacuums in their aftermath.[60] The same Libyan example, where the ongoing civil war claimed more lives in its aftermath than during the struggle against Gaddafi, is again instructive here. Hence for Russians the moralising of Western liberal governments was a way to preserve and extend their hegemony. It enabled them to rid themselves of leaders they disapproved of; represented a form of 'empire lite' under the cover of liberal justifications; allowed them to enjoy the spoils of victory; created dangerous precedents for international law; and embedded double standards whereby other legitimate human rights concerns (such as over the treatment of ethnic Russians in the Baltics and the Caucasus) were ignored.

Realist Approaches

Although it arguably has the richest tradition on national security matters, realism's record on explaining Russia's posture is mixed. The main realist tenet—that world politics can be understood in terms of competition for power between actors whose interests do not intersect—is largely uncontroversial. This formulation puts Russia, which retains many of the factors that make up national power such as nuclear weapons, a large landmass, and an abundance of national resources, as a nation struggling for influence against others in a region that has historically been an important geostrategic crossroads. Its chief obstacle has been its loss of significant power in the aftermath of the collapse of the USSR, and its ensuing weakness which has allowed other actors, from the EU to the United States and more recently the PRC, that have exerted pressure on Russia and its post-Soviet sphere of influence.

For realists Russia's assertive and revisionist posture is largely due to the systemic transformation in world politics that occurred through the collapse of bipolarity.[61] Fearful of being relegated to the status of a mere raw materials appendage and buffer zone by either China or the EU, realists see Russia as adopting a stance that vigorously defends its national interests against a world order inimical to Russian preferences. This has obvious implications for its ability to shape regional and global affairs, as well as for its own stability and prosperity. Because of the power imbalance with the United States and the PRC, Russia has adopted a defensive posture regionally, but an aggressive one in relation to the West, seeking to degrade the EU from within and deploying cyber weapons and information warfare to reshape EU and US politics. And although it has frequently been forced to default to Chinese interests in its regional sphere of influence, it has nonetheless decided to bandwagon with Beijing as the next prospective global leader.[62]

While this is potentially useful, it is important to note that realist claims rely fundamentally in practice on choices by leaders and their elites. And yet structural realism (or neorealism) has little to say about the domestic preferences of states where choices are made. For neorealists, the nature of the international system explains the behaviour of states within it, which are treated as like units that differ only on the basis of their material power.[63] In this way neorealists seek to make high-level assumptions and predictions. For instance, bipolar configurations can be stable because they feature power structures that are more or less balanced. Thus the risk of war (especially between nuclear-armed great powers) becomes too high. By contrast, multipolar systems tend to be more fluid since the option of temporarily aligning with different power blocs can permit states to profit against others.[64] But since allies cannot be trusted, intensely competitive blocs tend to emerge. Under those conditions the risk of conflict is heightened unless international security is managed by some form of concert system to manage great power behaviour.[65]

Although neorealism has some advantages as a broad way to can conceptualise international interaction, it is arguably less helpful in explaining why certain states make the national security choices that they do. It is for this reason that constructivist accounts have gained significant ground in the aftermath of the Cold War: because neorealists treat states effectively as billiard balls or black boxes,[66] little insight can be gained either into their interpretation of the external environment, or how domestic forces like history and identity shape their preferences. And while neorealists counter these arguments by claiming that the levels-of-analysis problem makes determining when domestic variables shape international policy and vice-versa impossible, they are nonetheless largely unable to account for why Russia (for instance) should choose to compete with the West rather than bandwagoning with it.

Another variant of realism, referred to as neoclassical realism, is arguably more helpful in this respect. Neoclassical realists accept much of the neorealist canon: namely, that international relations is essentially anarchical; that material power is the main factor determining a state's national interests; and that cooperation in world politics is often the exception rather than the norm. However, they also stress the importance of how domestic decision-makers interpret the policy choices that states can make.[67] This can be on the basis of cultural and social factors like identity, their own political, financial or institutional interests (or both), or factors like public opinion and domestic and international prestige.

Like constructivists, then, neoclassical realists seek to go beyond structural explanations for states' behaviour by unpacking the complex mix of internal and external influences on decision-makers. Unlike constructivists, though, they see normative forces as largely secondary to material ones when it comes to determining national interests.[68] In other words, neoclassical realists regard ideology and national values as factors that are used instrumentally by elites: justifying policy and drumming up public support for a nation's rational policy objectives, rather than acting as causal factors in themselves. And while the shortcomings of such an approach are often highlighted by neorealists—that neoclassical realism becomes a theory of foreign policy rather than a theory of international relations—it is nonetheless frequently employed as an alternative analytical frame to understand national security decision-making.[69]

Applied to the case of Russia, neoclassical realists produce a view that is in some ways a hybrid of neorealism and constructivism. They see the evolution of Russian policy as the product of poor choices by the West in unintentionally marginalising Moscow, as well as poor management of Russia's internal political and economic affairs that facilitated the evolution of an authoritarian elite with strong interests in maintaining their privileged positions.[70] This creates powerful incentive structures for Russian elites to limit public freedoms, while blaming the West for its ills. Hence identity and ideology become important tools to motivate the population and marginalise dissent. But this does not mean that Russia is free to pursue whatever policies its leaders choose. On the contrary, for neoclassical realists the scope of Russian national interests is heavily influenced by its ability to pursue them. In other words, it is not sufficient to have the will: rather it is necessary to have the wherewithal. On this issue they agree with neorealists that Russia's long-term trajectory is essentially downward, and point to the efforts by the Putin administration to simultaneously court the PRC as well as fragment the West as a way to overcome the potential of being caught in a geopolitical pincer between East and West.[71]

In this way, while Russia welcomes its new relationship with China, it is simultaneously wary of it, seeking alternative trade routes to the Belt and Road Initiative at the same time as it relies heavily on Chinese investment in its energy sector. When Putin made the decision in 2013 to pivot to the East, this was much more about geoeconomics than any sense of a Eurasian identity. Having surmised that China and Asia would be the epicentre of global power in the twenty-first century, it made logical sense for Russia to try and establish the same type of energy monopolies it had constructed in Europe in the aftermath of the Cold War.[72] By the same token, a Russian desire to hamper Western encroachment into its sphere of influence manifested itself in increasingly bellicose rhetoric that drew on a sense of betrayal, the beefing up of its military, and the deployment of non-traditional levers of power—from resource wars to hybrid warfare in Crimea and cyber-enabled information operations—against former Soviet states as well as Western democracies. But as the PRC continues to develop its capacity to influence Russia's southern flank in Central Asia, neoclassical realists foresee the Sino-Russian as having the potential for tension. This highlights the complex nature of both the domestic environment as well as the external security policy challenges facing Russia's rulers.

Power and Weakness: Enablers and Constraints

While these explanations are all potentially useful ways to help us understand Russia's national security trajectory, it is important to also make some assessment of Russia's future prospects, both internally and externally, as a way of mapping out the choices that will confront future Russian policy makers. Hence the remainder of this chapter focuses on sources of potential strength and weakness that will affect the scope as well as the nature of Russian national security policy for the foreseeable future.

Military Power

One of the frequent reasons Russia is typecast as a neoimperial actor has been its desire to minimise interference by potential adversaries with Russian military power. Putin has made frequent references to the former communist nations as falling within Moscow's orbit, and has voiced his expectation for a free hand in Russia's 'Near Abroad', especially given its importance to his Eurasian Union.[73] Yet two important factors make such a characterisation problematic. The first is that great powers have typically sought to carve out geopolitical space where they are the dominant actors. The United States, for instance, pursued regional primacy under the auspices of the Monroe Doctrine, which sought to exclude European powers from Central and Latin

America, and provided diplomatic cover for frequent US military and political interventions.[74] By the same token, the PRC's Belt and Road Initiative seeks to create continental zones of privileged interest by controlling trade corridors. Its development of militarised islands in the South China Sea, and courting of regional actors in the Pacific for PLAN basing rights, represents the maritime aspect of that strategy: an attempt to break out of the so-called 'First Island Chain' of US military balancing.[75]

A second reason why buffer zones are by no means exclusively a neoimperial form of regional dominance is that Russia has sought to consolidate control over the former USSR for long before Putin. As early as 1992, during the formulation of Russia's first Foreign Policy Concept, Boris Yeltsin was urged to establish a 'zone of interest' in the former Soviet territories.[76] A year later he echoed that sentiment, calling for 'special recognition' of Russia's role as a 'guarantor of peace and stability' in the former USSR. He went on to note that Russia could not simply determine its own national security interests because 'responsibility for peace around us is not just a strategic, but a moral agenda, even a family one'.[77]

Of course, Yeltsin was unable to see that goal to fruition, given the weakness of the Russian state during his time in office, and that the West began to swiftly fill the power vacuum via NATO expansion. It has only been relatively recently that Russia has developed the military means to directly challenge the West in its own backyard. Thus a more useful way of viewing Russia's regional aspirations in terms of its national security policy is to assess to what extent Moscow is actually able to project power, both as a global actor as well as closer to home.

On this question, an assessment of Russia's capabilities yields mixed conclusions. To an extent its military modernisation campaign after 2008 has resulted in the creation of some impressive new military hardware. This includes the renovation of Russia's SSBN fleet with its development of the *Borei* class ballistic missile submarines, the renovation of the Pacific Fleet, its S-400 surface-to-air missile system, the T-14 Armata tank, and the rollout of new equipment for both ground and air forces in the Northern theatre and in Russia's Western military districts.[78] It has also deployed the short-range *Iskander* nuclear missile to its Kaliningrad enclave, giving it a deterrent capability that reaches into Poland, Germany, and the Baltic States, as well as the capacity for anti-access and area denial (A2AD) against potential NATO deployments.[79]

Russia has also boosted its nuclear doctrine to give it flexible strike options, moving from a 'no first use' policy during the Soviet era to 'assured first use' in its Military Blueprint of 2008, and finally to embracing the controversial 'escalate to de-escalate' posture outlined by the Russian ministry of defence in 2015.[80] This would see Russia threatening to swiftly escalate any conflict to the use of nuclear weapons; with the logic being that the threat of 'going nuclear' would deter Russia's foes from considering even small-scale hostilities. And in addition to these renovations in military hardware and doctrine,

Putin publicly unveiled a new suite of 'doomsday weapons' during his State of the Nation address in March 2018. These included the *Burevestnik* cruise missile, equipped with a nuclear propulsion system that theoretically gives it unlimited range; the *Sarmat* ICBM; the unmanned *Poseidon* drone submarine that can carry a 100 megaton nuclear warhead to devastate coastal cities; and the hypersonic *Avengard* hypersonic missile system with intercontinental range, and a forecast speed of Mach 20. 'Nobody listened to Russia', Putin theatrically intoned before introducing the new weapons systems. 'Well, listen up now'.[81]

But for all Moscow's bravado about its military capabilities, they are much more reflective of weakness than strength. Russia has been forced to rely increasingly on weapons of mass destruction (WMD), and its new weapons systems are tools of brinkmanship. Put simply, Russia's calculation is that the West is not prepared to risk war against it, and this gives the Kremlin the opportunity to assert escalation dominance (and hence deter the West in the process) via the message that it will use any option available to secure its interests. Yet Russia is being overtaken on capabilities, especially on military spending. According to the ISS *Military Balance*, Russia's 2017 defence budget was US$61 billion.[82] This was less than a tenth of the US total, far behind the PRC's estimated $250 billion, and behind Saudi Arabia, India, and France respectively.[83] Moreover, it should be noted that Russia's territory (spanning 11 time zones) is difficult to protect, let alone use as a base to project power. Flanked by states it considers hostile to its West, weak actors with internal tensions in Central Asia and the Caucasus, and simultaneously seeking to develop greater capacity for military deployments in the Pacific, Russia will arguably be less capable of securing its interests as other nations—especially the PRC—spend comparatively more.

Information Operations and Hybrid Warfare Capabilities

One area where Russia maintains a substantial advantage over its rivals is in information operations. Russia's blurring of the lines between military and non-military forms of coercion has resulted in the development of cyber-enabled information warfare capabilities that are currently unmatched. As one cyber security observer put it in 2019, at the Cycon conference in Estonia, for many years the West has focused its efforts to inoculate vulnerable groups from online radicalisation associated with Islamic terrorism. In contrast, Russia has prioritised digital advertising to divide and fragment societies, both close to home as well as amongst the transatlantic Western democracies, and combine compromising information (termed *kompromat* in Russia), with networks of pressure and digital messaging.[84] This creates plausible deniability because the viral nature of messaging means that spreading of misinformation comes from the target population itself, and is often curated by regular citizens, rather than stemming from state-directed and controlled agencies in Russia.

Russia's information warfare in Ukraine and the Baltic states in particular has taken on a hybrid character, from its hack of the Ukrainian power grid in 2016 coupled to its operations in Crimea and the Donbas,[85] a steady stream of digital propaganda directed at the Baltic states, and regular incursions into NATO airspace.[86] Allegations of Russian information warfare and hybrid campaigns date back as early as 2004, when Lithuania's President Roland Paksas in 2004 decided to grant citizenship to Yuri Borisov, a leading alleged Russian crime figure, and leaked to Borisov that he was under investigation (Paksas was later impeached for this). It also included the hacks that shut down Estonia's internet in 2007 after it joined NATO,[87] and against Georgia during the Five Day War.

While Russian information operations in the United States have received the most attention, it should also be noted that Moscow has been accused of meddling in the affairs of many European nations, often using far-right organisations as proxies. This includes France, where a failed Russian-backed media campaign in 2016 tried to tarnish the Presidential candidate Emmanuel Macron using fake emails[88]; alleged support for proto-fascist groups in Germany, Austria, and Spain[89]; and suggestions it was involved in amplifying the 'Vote Leave' campaign's messaging prior to the UK's 2016 Brexit referendum.[90]

In addition to honing its capacity to disrupt and influence political outcomes in the EU, the greatest perceived triumph of Russian information operations came via the hack of the 2016 Democratic National Convention, particularly the emails of John Podesta that showed a clear effort by the DNC to discredit Bernie Sanders, Hilary Clinton's rival for the Democratic Party's Presidential nomination.[91] The release of the emails to Wikileaks was attributed by numerous internal US agencies to a Russian attempt to sway the election in favour of Donald Trump, who had numerous business links to Russian oligarchs that potentially included compromising information, and had articulated a strongly pro-Russian foreign policy agenda. This was assisted by a large-scale Russian information warfare campaign that used right-wing media and websites such as Breitbart, InfoWars, and 4chan to amplify conspiracy theories about Clinton, as well as its much-documented purchase of around $100,000 of Facebook advertisements that reached an estimated 120 million Americans.[92]

Following Trump's surprise election in 2016, well-documented allegations continued about Russian influence over the US President, as well as its interference in the 2018 mid-term Congressional elections. They encompassed the Mueller report, a US Department of Justice indictment of the Russian-based Internet Research Agency (considered the information warfare division of the Russian Federation); and the Congressional inquiry into Trump's impeachment over claims that he had put pressure on the Ukrainian government—thus serving Russian interests as well—in order to investigate alleged corruption by Joe Biden, his likely Democratic rival in the 2020 US Presidential elections.

Energy: Encouraging Vulnerable Over-Dependencies

Central to Russia's pivot to Asia has been a desire to capitalise on the main commodity Russia possesses in abundance—energy—to develop the same type of dependencies in the East as it has in the West. Asia's oil and gas imports are set to rise dramatically over the next twenty years, with China and India the region's top two consumers. Russia has made progress here since 2014, when China surpassed Germany as Russia's biggest customer.[93] And with Asia's oil imports alone likely to exceed the OPEC nations' overall output by 2035, a primary area of focus by Russian energy planners in developing its 2019 energy strategy has been to ensure that Russia has the capacity to meet that demand.[94]

While oil is important to Russian prosperity—and hence central to its national security posture—gas is even more crucial. With Asia set to consume 50 per cent of the world's gas,[95] Russia has sought to meet the increase in demand by developing gas fields in the eastern and southern areas of Pacific Russia, and seeking foreign investment to do so, which it has largely obtained from the PRC. Its abandonment of the South Stream pipeline in favour of a gas line to Turkey has also been important in allowing it to continue to sell gas into European markets, as well as to re-route its supply to Asia.[96] In the Far East, in order to service its US$400 billion deal to supply the PRC with gas for twenty-five years, it has sought to open new transport corridors into China. This foresees four separate pipeline distribution points: the link to Western China via Gorno-Altaisk, and three separate conduits in the Far East (at Blagoveschensk, Dalnorechensk, and Vladivostok).[97]

Yet a major challenge here is that pipelines need to be secured. This can be risky, especially in regions such as northern Pakistan, as well as Afghanistan, and has limited the potential flexibility of Russian energy sales. Hence it has attempted to diversify towards a more balanced mix by developing LNG plants for seaborne transit, especially near the Far Eastern port of Vladivostok.[98] Cutting the transit distance for Russian energy to nearby potential clients like the ROK, Japan, and Southeast Asian nations has the advantage of making significant savings on infrastructure and maintenance costs. Even so, the economies of Russian energy sales and distribution are complex. With Russia's Far Eastern gas fields lagging behind existing plants in Western Siberia (which have boosted their output), the only viable means of transportation to Asian transit nodes (either by pipeline or by sea) has been by rail. This makes Russian gas in Asia from Western Siberia less commercially viable, considering it must travel over 5,000 kilometres to reach a point where it can be transported to client nations.

A further complicating factor in Russia's energy strategy has been that much of its infrastructure development has relied heavily on Chinese capital. Russian concerns that BRI effectively bypasses Russia, thus locking it in to Chinese-dominated trade routes to transport energy, have prompted it to seek a number of alternatives. One of these has been the Arctic Northern Sea

Route. Global warming has assisted this: already in 2018 a Russian ship made the crossing unassisted. But for much of the year the region is frozen, so to ensure reliable supply nuclear-powered icebreakers are needed to clear paths over the Arctic Circle. The relatively low cost of gas (which is expected to fall further) also makes the route problematic in terms of its future viability. Nonetheless, Russia has continued to invest heavily in both onshore and offshore oil and gas developments on the Yamal Peninsula, where in 2018 the energy company Novatek completed construction of a US$27 billion LNG plant, capable of handling 60 million tons of natural gas by 2030.[99]

There should therefore be no doubting Russia's ambition to become Asia's premier energy supplier. But it is unclear whether Asian clients will permit it to establish the types of strategic leverage it has enjoyed in Europe. For one thing, Moscow's habit of using energy as an instrument of its national security policy has not escaped governments in the region. Nor has the future availability of alternatives: the United States, for instance, intends to also become a major gas and oil supplier in the region due to its decision to scale up fracking efforts in its domestic oil and gas fields. Another major gas supplier is Australia, which also has an ambitious agenda to compete in Asian energy markets.[100] Hence the benefits of Russia's large-scale energy pivot, although impressive in scope, remains contingent in large part to forces beyond its control.

Institutional Underdevelopment, Sub-regional Weakness, and Political Vulnerability

While military power, political warfare capabilities, and energy sales can be regarded (albeit to varying extents) as potential enablers of Russia's national security policy in the future, its political and economic vulnerabilities will in all likelihood constrain it. To begin with, Russia has clearly abandoned its attempts to reset its relationship with Western actors, and such an eventuality is highly unlikely for the foreseeable future. And despite some success in assisting the EU's fragmentation alongside a region-wide shift towards nationalism, there is little trust between mainstream EU parties and the Kremlin.

The Skripal Novichok poisoning affair in 2017, the use of polonium on FSB agent Alexsandr Litvinenko in 2006 and a host of deaths amongst Russian dissidents has made the UK government unequivocally hostile to Russian interference. So too are the Baltic and Nordic nations, as well as amongst mainstream French and German political parties, where Moscow is tacitly regarded as the greatest existential threat to EU unity. And despite the puzzling warmth of the Trump White House towards Putin, it is clear that Trump's successor—whether Republican or Democrat—will likely articulate a much more assertive US posture with respect to Russia. This is because Republicans will want to distance themselves from the accusation that they were complicit in a foreign interference campaign, while Democrats will have the added motivation of revenge for the alleged events of 2016.

The relationship between China and Russia, while often touted as a nascent alliance, is also not without potential future pressure points. Although Putin and Xi meet frequently, the Kremlin is concerned at the extent to which it has become beholden to PRC preferences. The Shanghai Cooperation Organisation, for instance, has shifted from a Russian-promoted 'Asian NATO'[101] to a subset of China's BRI, where infrastructure and energy programs are largely distributed to Central Asian members. Putin's own Eurasian Union has also failed to generate significant traction, even though it received Beijing's rhetorical blessing as a complementary venture running on a parallel path to the BRI. At the same time, Chinese investment in Central Asia has given it substantial leverage over sub-regional actors, which Russia cannot match. Hence, while Russia has accepted the status of junior partner in its relationship with the PRC, becoming a convenient Chinese buffer between East and West does not suit its national security preferences as an independent great power.

Domestic vulnerability is also a problem for Russian national security planners. In raw demographic terms life expectancy for Russians, according to 2018 World Health Organisation data, sat at 66.4 years for males and 77 years for females, ranking Russia at 105th globally.[102] Social problems, alcoholism, and other negative development indicators are also widespread, especially in the regions. Russia's population has declined at an average rate of 0.5% annually, with numbers falling more sharply in the vital Far Eastern region.[103] Economically, Russia remains heavily dependent on energy sales, and the widely expected Chinese injections of development funding into Russian services and businesses beyond the energy sector have not materialised, due mainly to Beijing's concerns about corruption and viability of investment.

Finally, Russia's political vulnerability will be a source of future concern. Putin is acutely aware of the potential for 'colour revolutions' to sweep into Russia, and his domestic strategies have been designed to protect his leadership against that eventuality.[104] But he will not remain Russia's President forever. By 2019 Putin had been Russia's leader for longer than Leonid Brezhnev led the USSR, and it is by no means clear who his successor might be. After nearly two decades in power, Putin has shaped its political class to view strong vertical Presidential power as the norm. Hence it is unlikely that democracy will suddenly take root after Putin's passing. But neither can Russia's complex networks of political patronage and institutionalised mistrust, which Putin created, be trusted to produce a consensus candidate who might act as a benign autocrat. Instead, it is more likely that Putin's successor will be more nationalistic but politically much weaker. Those looking to a more stable and predictable Russia after Putin leaves the Presidency may therefore be disappointed.

Conclusions

Russia's turbulent history after the collapse of the USSR explains much about its current national security posture. Whichever analytical frame one might choose to employ—constructivist, liberal, or realist—it is clear that identifying the key drivers of Russian national security policy, much less making predictions about future Russian behaviour, is a complex undertaking. What should be equally disturbing is that for each of the conceptual approaches offered in this chapter, rapprochement between Russia and the West is unlikely. A constructivist lens sees Russian identity drifting further towards Eurasian/Civilisationist narratives. Liberal approaches offer gloomy assessments of both Russian political and economic prospects. And while realists do not discount the potential for a more convention Euro-Pacific pivot, they tend to see the likelihood of entrapment by the PRC as a difficult prospect for Russia to resist.

Yet whereas the story of Russia's national security posture and its evolution has been one of flux and perturbation, it is also paradoxically one where significant continuity can be found. In many respects, Russia's national interests have not changed appreciably since the collapse of the USSR—and even before that, in fact. First, Russia has sought to secure its borders, as well as its regional sphere of influence, consistent with the posture of a great power. Second, it has sought stability and order within its own population. Third, it has sought to achieve a pathway to increasing prosperity for its citizens. And although the way in which it has sought to realise those objectives has changed markedly over time, we should be cautious about ascribing Russian behaviour to uniqueness, difference, and a tragic search for greatness, rather than commonalities with other nations in similar positions. By doing so, we run the risk of stylising Russia as the product of all its stereotypes, thus reducing our own ability to make informed judgements about its prospects and intentions.

NOTES

1. See for instance Melinda Liu. 2019. 'Xi Jinping Has Embraced Vladimir Putin, for Now', *Foreign Policy*, October 3. https://foreignpolicy.com/2019/10/03/xi-jinping-has-embraced-vladimir-putin-for-now/; Nadege Rolland. 2019. 'A China-Russia Condominium over Eurasia', *Survival*, 61 (1), 7–22; and Artyom Lukin. 2019. 'The Implications of a True Russia–China Alliance', *Australian Outlook*, July 14. http://www.internationalaffairs.org.au/australianoutlook/implications-true-russia-china-alliance/.
2. On entrapment see Victor Cha. 2000. 'Abandonment, Entrapment and Neoclassical Realism in Asia: The United States, Japan and Korea', *International Studies Quarterly*, 44 (2), 261–291; and Michael Clarke and Matthew Sussex. 2020. 'BRI and the Sino-Russian Security Relationship: Navigating Accommodation and Entrapment Dilemmas in Central Asia', in Michael Clarke, Matthew Sussex and Nick Bisley (eds), *BRI and the Future of Regional Order in the Indo-Pacific*. Lanham: Lexington Books.
3. Matthew Sussex. 2012. 'The Shape of the Security Order in the Former USSR', in Matthew Sussex (ed), *Conflict in the Former USSR*. Cambridge: Cambridge University Press; and Matthew Sussex. 2012. 'Continuity and

Change in Russian Foreign Policy', *Global Peace, Change and Security*, 24 (2), 202–213.

4. Peter Shearman and Matthew Sussex. 2009. 'The Roots of Russian Conduct', *Small Wars and Insurgencies*, Special Issue on 'Russia, Georgia and the West', 20 (2), 251–275.

5. In 2018 the Levada polling agency reported that some 66% of Russians felt the collapse of the USSR was something to regret—the highest figure since 2004. See *Moscow Times*. 2018. 'Nostalgia for the USSR Hits 14-Year High in Russia', December 18. https://www.themoscowtimes.com/2018/12/19/nostalgia-for-soviet-union-hits-14-year-high-russia-poll-says-a63884.

6. Steven Pifer. 2011. 'The Trilateral Process: The United States, Ukraine, Russia and Nuclear Weapons', *Brookings Institution Arms Control Series*, no. 6, May. https://www.brookings.edu/research/the-trilateral-process-the-united-states-ukraine-russia-and-nuclear-weapons/.

7. Marie Lavigne. 1991. 'Financing the Transition: The Shatalin Plan and the Soviet Union', *Institute of East–West Studies*, New York: Westview.

8. Lilia Shevtsova. 2013. '1993: Russia's "Small" Civil War', *Carnegie Moscow Centre*, March. https://carnegie.ru/commentary/53189.

9. Brian D. Taylor, 2001. *Politics and the Russian Army: Civil-Military Relations 1689–2000*. Cambridge: Cambridge University Press, 234–239.

10. The coup plotters were led away, and many received jail terms in Lefortovo prison, although several later re-emerged to play prominent roles in Russian regional politics. This included figures like Ruslan Khasbulatov, the speaker of the Supreme Soviet, who went on to become influential in Chechen politics, and a leading academic commentator on the Russian economy. See Mikhail Sokolov and Anastacia Kirilenko. 2013. 'Twenty Years Ago Russia Had Its Biggest Political Crisis Since the Bolshevik Revolution', *The Atlantic*, October 4. https://www.theatlantic.com/international/archive/2013/10/20-years-ago-russia-had-its-biggest-political-crisis-since-the-bolshevik-revolution/280237/.

11. Stephen Fish. 1997. 'The Pitfalls of Superpresidentialism', *Current History*, October, 326–330.

12. Stephen White, Richard Rose and Ian McAllister. 1996. *How Russia Votes*. London: Sage, 255–257.

13. Tuomas Forsberg and Graeme Herd. 2015. 'Russia and NATO: From Windows of Opportunities to Closed Doors', *Journal of Contemporary European Studies*, 23 (1), 41–57.

14. On Kozyrev's approach, see Suzanne Crow. 1993. *The Making of Foreign Policy in Russia Under Yeltsin*. Washington, DC: Radio Free Europe/Radio Liberty Inc.

15. J. Michael Waller. 1997. 'Primakov's Imperial Line', *Perspective* 8 (3), 1–8.

16. 'Perspectives on the war in Kosovo'. 1999. *Fond Obshestvoennoye Mnieniye*, September 16.

17. Thane Gustaffson. 1999. *Capitalism Russian-Style*. Cambridge: Cambridge University Press, 217.

18. On 'shock therapy' and the idea's originator Jeffrey Sachs, see David Kotz and Fred Weir. 1997. *Revolution from Above: The Demise of The Soviet System*, London: Routledge, 161–3.

19. The memoirs of Yeltsin's bodyguard are instructive here. See Andrei Korzhakov. 1997. *From Dawn to Dusk*. Moscow: Interbook.

20. Anna Ivanova, Michael Keen, and Alexander Klemm. 2005. 'The Russian Flat Tax Reform', *International Monetary Fund*, Fiscal Affairs Department Working Paper, January. https://www.imf.org/external/pubs/ft/wp/2005/wp0516.pdf.
21. Vladimir Putin. 2000. 'Millennium Manifesto', *Vital Speeches of the Day*, 9 July.
22. Pamela A. Jordan. 2003. 'Russia's Accession to the Council of Europe and Compliance with Human Rights Norms', *Demokratizatsiya*, 11 (2), 281–296.
23. Peter Baker. 2003. 'The Seduction of George W. Bush', *Foreign Policy*, November 6. https://foreignpolicy.com/2013/11/06/the-seduction-of-geo rge-w-bush/.
24. Michael Lind. 2018. 'America Versus Russia and China: Welcome to Cold War II', *National Interest*, April 15. https://nationalinterest.org/feature/america-vs-russia-china-welcome-cold-war-ii-25382.
25. On Russia's selectorates, see William Zimmerman. 2014. *Ruling Russia: Authoritarianism from the Revolution to Putin*. Princeton: Princeton University Press.
26. Peter Brooks. 2004. 'The Yukos Affair', *Heritage Foundation*, December 28. https://www.heritage.org/europe/commentary/the-yukos-affair.
27. Matthew Sussex. 2012. 'Strategy, Security, and Russian Resource Diplomacy', in Roger E. Kanet and Marie Racquel Freire (eds), *Russia and Its Near Neighbours*. New York: Palgrave.
28. Ibid.
29. Matthew Sussex. 2015. 'Russia's Next Big Strategic Move (And It Has Nothing to Do with Ukraine)', *National Interest*, June 10. http://nation alinterest.org/blog/the-buzz/russias-next-big-strategic-move-it-has-nothing-do-ukraine-13081.
30. It is also worth noting that the impact of the Gerasimov Doctrine is highly debated. One of the most influential commentators on Russia, Mark Galeotti, suggests that it is a complete fiction. See Mark Galeotti. 2018. 'The Mythical "Gerasimov Doctrine" and the Language of Threat', *Critical Studies on Security*, February 27. This has not prevented it becoming accepted orthodoxy in studies of Russian warfighting, however. See for instance Charles K. Bartles. 2016. 'Getting Gerasimov Right', *Military Review*, US Army Combined Arms Centre, January–February. http://usacac.army.mil/CAC2/MilitaryReview/Archives/English/MilitaryReview_20160228_art009.pdf.
31. Tad A. Schnaufer. 2017. 'Redefining Hybrid Warfare: Russia's Non-linear War Against the West', *Journal of Strategic Security* 10 (1), 17–31.
32. Ibid.
33. Kareem Fakhim, Karen De Young and Missy Ryan. 2019. 'Russia and Turkey Reach Deal to push Kurdish Forces Out of Northern Syria', *Washington Post*, October 23. https://www.washingtonpost.com/world/middle_east/turkeys-erdogan-meets-with-putin-in-russia-to-discuss-syrian-operation/2019/10/22/764abcea-f43f-11e9-b2d2-1f37c9d82dbb_story.html.
34. Richard Ellings, Robert Sutter, Angela Stent, Charles Ziegler, Richard Weitz, Peter Mattis and James Steinberg. 2018. *Axis of Authoritarians: Implications of China–Russia cooperation*. Washington, DC: National Bureau of Asian Research.
35. See for instance Geoffrey Checkel. 1993. 'Ideas, Institutions, and Gorbachev's Foreign Policy Revolution', *World Politics*, 45 (1), 271–300; Thomas

Risse-Kappan, 1994. 'Ideas Do Not Float Freely: Transnational Coalitions, Domestic Structures, and the End of the Cold War', *International Organisation*, 48 (2), 185–214; and Janice Gross Stein. 1995. 'Political Learning by Doing: Gorbachev as Uncommitted Thinker and Motivated Learner', in Richard Ned Lebow and Thomas Risse-Kappan (eds), *International Relations Theory and the End of the Cold War*. New York: Columbia University Press, 223–258.

36. Andrei Tsygankov. 2012. *Russia's Foreign Policy: Change and Continuity in National Identity* (2nd edn). London: Lanham, Rowman & Littlefield.

37. Hans Adomeit. 1995. 'Russia as a "Great Power" in World Affairs: Images and Reality', *International Affairs*, 71 (2), 35–68. See also Margot Light. 1996. 'Foreign Policy Thinking', in Neil Malcolm, Alex Pravda and Margot Light, *Internal Factors in Russian Foreign Policy*. New York: Oxford University Press, 33–100 (especially pp. 44–46); and Roland Suny. 1999. 'Provisional Stabilities: The Politics of Identities in Post-Soviet Eurasia', *Review of International Studies* 24 (3), 139–178 (p. 151).

38. Halford Makinder. 1904. 'The Geographical Pivot of History', *The Geographical Journal*, April.

39. Areg Galstyan. 2016. 'Third Rome Rising: The Ideologues Calling for a New Russian Empire', *National Interest*, June 27. https://nationalinterest.org/feature/third-rome-rising-the-ideologues-calling-new-russian-empire-16748.

40. William Kristol and Robert Kagan, 1996. 'Toward a Neo-Reaganite Foreign Policy', *Foreign Affairs* 75 (July/August), 18–32.

41. Peter Rutland rejected the reference, drily claiming that this was an insult to Upper Volta.In Russian, the phrase is 'Verkhnaya Vol'ta, nachinennaya ballisticheskimi raketami' ('Upper Volta with ballistic rockets'). See *Johnson Russia List*, no. 3033, January 29, 1999.

42. Neil Malcolm. 1989. 'The Common European Home and Soviet European Policy', *International Affairs*, 65 (4), 659–676.

43. 'President Clinton's 1998 State of the Union Address'. 1998. *Washington Post*, January 27.

44. David Kerr. 1995. 'The New Eurasianism: The Rise of Geopolitics in Russia's Foreign Policy', *Europe–Asia Studies*, 47 (6), 977–988.

45. Andrew Monahan. 2008. 'An Enemy at the Gates, or "From Victory to Victory"? Russian Foreign Policy', *International Affairs*, 84 (4), 717–733.

46. Stephen Brooks and William Wohlforth. 2001. 'Power, Globalisation and the end of the Cold War: Re-evaluating a Landmarks Test Case for Ideas', *International Security*, 25 (3), 5–53.

47. Ibid.

48. See for instance John Mearsheimer. 1994. 'The False Promise of International Institutions', *International Security*, 19 (3), 5–49.

49. See for instance Sergei Guriev and Andrei Rachinsky. 2005. 'The Role of Oligarchs in Russian Capitalism', *Journal of Economic Perspectives*, 19 (1), 131–150.

50. Stephen Handelman. 1997. *Comrade Criminal: Russia's New Mafia*. New York: Yale University Press.

51. Edward Mansfield and Jack Snyder. 1995. 'Democratization and the Danger of War', *International Security*, 20 (1), 5–38; see also Jack Snyder. 2002. *From Voting to Violence: Democratization and Nationalist Conflict*. New York: W. W. Norton.

52. Barry Posen. 2000. 'The War for Kosovo: Serbia's Political-Military Strategy', *International Security* 24 (4), 39–84.
53. Bill Browder, one of Putin's leading critics, has put his net worth at around US$200 billion. See Adam Taylor. 2018. 'Ahead of Russian Elections, Putin Releases Official Details of Wealth and Income', *Washington Post*, February 8. https://www.washingtonpost.com/news/worldviews/wp/2018/02/07/ahead-of-russian-elections-putin-releases-official-details-of-wealth-and-income/.
54. Anders Aslund. 2016. 'Russia's Gloomy Prospects', *Project Syndicate*, May 9. https://www.project-syndicate.org/commentary/crony-capitalism-hurting-russian-economy-by-anders-aslund-and-simon-commander-2016-05?barrier=accessreg.
55. *Moscow Times*. 2019. 'Russia's Capital Flight More Than Doubled in 2018 to $68 Billion', January 18. https://www.themoscowtimes.com/2019/01/18/russias-capital-outflow-more-than-doubled-2018-68-billion-reports-a64193.
56. Thomas Ambrosio. 2007. 'Insulating Russia from a Colour Revolution: How the Kremlin Resists Regional Democratic Trends', *Democratization*, 14 (2), 232–252.
57. Ibid.
58. Ivan Krastev. 2014. 'Russian Revisionism: Putin's plan for Overturning the European Order', *Foreign Affairs*, March 3. https://www.foreignaffairs.com/articles/russia-fsu/2014-03-03/russian-revisionism.
59. For instance Phillip Spasso. 2014. 'NATO, Russia and European Security: Lessons Learned from Conflicts in Kosovo and Libya', *Connections* 13 (3), 21–40.
60. Alan Kuperman. 2013. 'A Model Humanitarian Intervention? Reassessing NATO's Libya Campaign', *International Security*, 38 (1), 105–136.
61. See William Wohlforth. 1994. 'Realism and the End of the Cold War', *International Security*, 19 (3), 91–129.
62. Matthew Sussex. 2015. 'From Retrenchment to Revanchism… and Back Again?', in Roger E. Kanet and Matthew Sussex (eds), *Russia, Eurasia and the New Geopolitics of Energy. Confrontation and Consolidation*, Houndmills, Basingstoke, and Hampshire: Palgrave Macmillan, 19–41.
63. Kenneth Waltz. 1979. *Theory of International Politics*. New York: Addison-Wesley, 93.
64. Randall Schweller. 1997. 'A Tale of Two Realisms: Expanding the Institutions Debate', *Mershon International Studies Review*, 41 (1), 1–32.
65. Benjamin Miller. 1994. 'Explaining the Emergence of Great Power Concerts', *Review of International Studies*, 20 (4), 327–348.
66. See for example Brian C. Schmidt. 2004. 'Realism as Tragedy', *Review of International Studies* 30 (3), 427–441.
67. For example, Gideon Rose. 1998. 'Neoclassical Realism and Theories of Foreign Policy', *World Politics*, 51 (1), 144–172; Steven Lobell, Norrin Ripsman and Jennifer Taliaferro (eds). 2009. *Neoclassical Realism, the State and Foreign Policy*. Cambridge: Cambridge University Press; and Jennifer Sterling-Folker. 1997. 'Realist Environment, Liberal Process and Domestic-Level Variables', *International Studies Quarterly*, 41 (1), 1–25.
68. Rose. 1998. 'Neoclassical Realism and Theories of Foreign Policy', 152.
69. Lobell et al. 2009. *Neoclassical Realism, the State and Foreign Policy*, 16–19.

70. See for example Elena Kropatcheva. 2012. 'Russian Foreign Policy in the Realm of European Security Through the Lens of Neoclassical Realism', *Journal of Eurasian Studies*, 3, 30–40.
71. This recalls Jennifer Sterling-Folker's observation that irrational identity politics at the domestic level can coincide with rational policy choices on the international level. See Jennifer Sterling-Folker. 2002. *Theories of International Cooperation and the Primacy of Anarchy: Explaining U.S. International Policy-Making After Bretton Woods*. New York: State University of New York, 103.
72. Matthew Sussex. 2017. 'The Triumph of Russian National Security Policy? Russia's Rapid Rebound', *Australian Journal of International Affairs*, 71 (5), 499–515.
73. For an in-depth discussion, see Gerard Toal. 2018. *Near Abroad: Putin, the West and the Contest over Ukraine and the Caucasus*. Oxford: Oxford University Press.
74. On linkages between the Monroe Doctrine and notions of empire in US foreign policy thought, see Michael Cox. 2004. 'Empire, Imperialism and the Bush Doctrine', *Review of International Studies* 30 (4), 585–608.
75. For an early analysis of this, see James R. Holmes. 2012. 'China's Monroe Doctrine', *The Diplomat*, June 22. https://thediplomat.com/2012/06/chinas-monroe-doctrine/.
76. *Nezavisimaya gazeta*, April 10, 1992, p. 1.
77. Boris Yeltsin. 1994. *The Struggle for Russia*. New York: Random House, 289–290.
78. Rod Thornton. 2017. 'The Russian Military's New "Main Emphasis"', *The RUSI Journal*, 162 (4), 18–28.
79. Jack Stubbs. 2018. 'Russia Deploys Iskander Nuclear-Capable Missiles to Kaliningrad'. *Reuters*, February 6. https://www.reuters.com/article/us-russia-nato-missiles/russia-deploys-iskander-nuclear-capable-missiles-to-kaliningrad-ria-idUSKBN1FP21Y.
80. Phil Ewing. 2015. 'Is Russia's Brinkmanship the New Norm?', *NATOSource*, June 15. http://www.atlanticcouncil.org/blogs/natosource/is-russia-brinkmanship-the-new-norm.
81. Tony Wesolowsky. 2018. 'Listen to Us Now: Putin Unveils Weapons, Vows to Raise Living Standards in Fiery Address', *RFE/RL Monitor*, March 1. https://www.rferl.org/a/putin-set-give-annual-address-amid-presidential-election-campaign/29069948.html.
82. International Institute for Strategic Studies. 2019. *The Military Balance*. London: Routledge.
83. Ibid.
84. Jason Healey. 2019. 'Cyber Deterrence and NATO', Silent Battle: 11th International Conference on Cyber Conflict, NATO CCDOE, Tallinn, Estonia, May 28–31.
85. James Condliffe. 2016. 'Ukraine's Power Grid Gets Hacked Again: A Worrying Sign for Infrastructure Attacks', *MIT Technology Review*, December 22. https://www.technologyreview.com/s/603262/ukraines-power-grid-gets-hacked-again-a-worrying-sign-for-infrastructure-attacks/.
86. Stephen J. Flanagan et al. 2019. 'Deterring Russian Aggression in the Baltic States Through Resilience and Resistance', *RAND Research*

Reports. https://www.rand.org/content/dam/rand/pubs/research_reports/RR2700/RR2779/RAND_RR2779.pdf.

87. Richard Krickus. 2011. 'The Presidential Crisis in Lithuania: Its Roots and the Russian Factor', *Wilson Centre Global Europe Program*, 292, July 7. https://www.wilsoncenter.org/publication/292-the-presidential-crisis-lithuania-its-roots-and-the-russian-factor.

88. Heather A. Conley. 2018. 'Successfully Countering Russian Election Interference', *CSIS Briefs*, June 21. https://www.csis.org/analysis/successfully-countering-russian-electoral-interference.

89. For instance, Matthew Karnitschnig. 2019. 'Austrian Government Collapses over Russia Scandal', *Politico*, May 18. https://www.politico.eu/article/sebastian-kurz-triggers-austrian-election-after-far-right-scandal/; Todd C. Helmus et al. 2018. 'Russian Social Media Influence', *RAND Corporation*, Santa Monica, CA; and Alina Polyakovo and Spencer P. Boyer. 2018. 'The Future of Political Warfare: Russia, the West and the Coming Age of Global Digital Competition', Brookings Institution, Brookings-Robert Bosch Foundation, March. https://www.brookings.edu/wp-content/uploads/2018/03/the-future-of-political-warfare.pdf.

90. House of Commons Select Committee on Digital Culture, Media and Sport. 2019. *Disinformation and Fake News: Final Report*. London: UK Parliament. https://publications.parliament.uk/pa/cm201719/cmselect/cmcumeds/1791/179102.htm.

91. See Robert Mueller. 2019. *The Mueller Report: The Final Report of the Special Counsel into Donald Trump, Russia and Collusion*. Washington, DC: The Washington Post Writers Group, April 18; Julia Ioffe. 2016. 'Is Trump a Russian Stooge?', *Foreign Policy*, July 25. https://foreignpolicy.com/2016/07/25/is-trump-a-russian-stooge-putin-dnc-wikileaks/; and Uri Friedman. 2016. 'What the DNC Hack Could Mean for Democracy', *The Atlantic*, August 2. https://www.theatlantic.com/international/archive/2016/08/dnc-hack-russia-election/493685/.

92. For a primer, see Ryan Broderick. 2019. 'Here's Everything the Mueller Report Says About How Russian Trolls Used Social Media', *BuzzFeed News*, April 18. https://www.buzzfeednews.com/article/ryanhatesthis/mueller-report-internet-research-agency-detailed-2016.

93. Emma Graham Harrison et al. 2015. 'China and Russia: The World's New Superpower Axis?', *Guardian*, July 7. http://www.theguardian.com/world/2015/jul/07/china-russia-superpower-axis.

94. British Petroleum, *BP Energy Outlook 2035*, BP, February 2015. http://www.bp.com/content/dam/bp/pdf/Energy-economics/energy-outlook-2015/Energy_Outlook_2035_booklet.pdf.

95. *BP Energy Outlook 2035*. http://www.bp.com/content/dam/bp/pdf/Energy-economics/energy-outlook-2015/Energy_Outlook_2035_booklet.pdf.

96. Orfan Gafarli. 2015. 'Turkish Stream: A Bluff or Not?', *Eurasia Daily Monitor*, 12 (32), February 20.

97. Nicholas Newman. 2015. 'Russia's Pipeline Dreams Under Threat', *Pipeline and Gas Journal*, 242 (3), March.

98. *Reuters*. 2015. 'Russia's Rosneft Says Considering Moving LNG Project Away from Sakhalin', May 28. http://www.downstreamtoday.com/(X(1)S(zffz10mj533ouj45czrmson2))/news/article.aspx?a_id=47876&AspxAutoDetectCookieSupport=1.

99. Joel K. Byrne. 2019. 'Russia's Massive New Gas Plant on the Arctic Coast', *National Geographic*, March 22. https://www.nationalgeographic.com/environment/2019/03/sabetta-yamal-largest-gas-field/
100. Matthew Sussex. 2016. *Russia's Asian Rebalance*. Sydney: Lowy Institute for International Policy.
101. See for example Roy Allison. 2018. 'Protective Integration and Security Policy Coordination: Comparing the SCO and CSTO', *The Chinese Journal of International Politics*, 11 (3), 297–338.
102. World Health Organisation (WHO). 2018. 'Russian Federation', WHO Global Health Observatory. http://apps.who.int/gho/data/node.country.country-RUS.
103. Matthew Luxmoore. 2019. 'Rising Mortality Rates Challenge Russia's Efforts to Kick-Start Population Growth'. *RFE-RL*, April 4. https://www.rferl.org/a/rising-mortality-rates-challenge-population-growth-decline-putin-demographics/29861882.html.
104. Evgeny Finkel and Yitzhak M. Brudny. 2012. 'Russia and the Colour Revolutions', *Democratization*, 19 (1), 15–36.

CHAPTER 8

Between Aspiration and Reality: Evolution of Japanese National Security Policy

Yuki Tatsumi

Throughout its post-World War Ii history, Japan has struggled to reconcile two contradictory elements when it comes to its national security policy. On the one hand, its experience of the complete defeat in World War II—ended in its unconditional surrender, followed by the Allied occupation until it regained its sovereignty in 1951—deeply scarred its national psyche. In fact, the impact of the defeat was so profound that the country eventually adopted the Constitution which, in its Article Nine, declared that Japan would not possess "land, sea, and air forces, as well as other war potential, will never be maintained".[1]

On the other hand, shortly after the end of the World War II, it had quickly become clear that Japan is at the forefront of the Cold War rivalry between the United States and then the Soviet Union in East Asia. When the Korean War broke out in 1950, Japan found itself in a position to have to defend itself from potential military threat from outside the country as US forces stationed in Japan was mobilized to fight a war on the Korean Peninsula, while having already disbanded its Imperial Army and Navy.

Japan at the time chose to bridge this gap by creating the organization that looked, was equipped and behaved like a professional military organization without calling them one: the National Police Reserve (*Keisatsu Yobi-tai*)—precursor of today's Japan Ground Self-Defense Force (JGSDF)—and Japan Maritime Security Safety Force (*Kaijou Keibi-tai*)—precursor of today's Japan Maritime Self-Defense Force (JMSDF)—were respectively created in 1950 and

Y. Tatsumi (✉)
The Stimson Center, Washington, DC, USA
e-mail: ytatsumi@stimson.org

© The Author(s), under exclusive license to Springer Nature Switzerland AG 2022
M. Clarke et al. (eds.), *The Palgrave Handbook of National Security*,
https://doi.org/10.1007/978-3-030-53494-3_8

169

1952. The National Police Reserve then briefly changed its name to National Safety Force (*Hoan-tai*) in 1952. The National Safety Force and Maritime Safety Security Force merged and, with Air Self-Defense Force (JASDF) added, became Japan Self-Defense Force (JSDF) in 1954. Although the JSDF was a professional military organization by international standard, the justification for its creation was not as an armed force. Rather its creation was justified as an enforcement organization that possesses minimally necessary self-defense capability.

Since then, Japan has been struggling to bridge the gap between what it needs to do to effectively defend itself from external security threat and what its Constitution allows it to do. This struggle continued after it regained its status as a sovereign state in 1951 and signed the Mutual Security Treaty with the United States, joining the US alliance system. Furthermore, as Japan regained its economy strength and has grown to be the world's leading economic power, the initial step it took to bridge the gap began to show its limitations due to an emerging criticism against Japan of being a free-rider of security in its alliance relationship with the United States. The criticism against Japan's inability to contribute to the common cause for international peace and security in a way other than financial contribution was coined as "checkbook diplomacy" during the 1991 Gulf War, and its belated dispatch of JMSDF minesweepers at the end of the conflict discredited as "too little, too late".

Japan's national security policy was anchored in three fundamental principles—reliance on the United States as its ultimate security guarantor (maintenance of a strong US–Japan alliance), exclusively defense-oriented posture for the JSDF, and minimization of the role military (Japan Self-Defense Force in this case) plays in its national efforts to promote and protect its national interests. Furthermore, Japan also imposed additional restrictions on its national security policy. These restrictions included: Three Non-Nuclear Principles (no possession, no production, or no introduction of nuclear weapons onto Japanese soil); Three Principles of Arms Exports (effectively a total ban of the exports of defense equipment from Japan), and limiting the use of space only to peaceful purposes (such as weather monitoring and communications).

Since the end of the Cold War, all of these principles have been challenged. As noted above, the 1991 Gulf War demonstrated to Japan that economic might alone will not help Japan increase its influence in international stage. Rising tension in East China Sea, North Korea, South China Sea, and other parts of the world is forcing Japan to revise its stance of minimizing the role played by JSDF in its national security policy. Finally, the perceived decline of the United States, coupled with the inclination toward the isolationism recently demonstrated by the Trump Administration, Tokyo finds itself less and less uncertain about the sustainability of US's staying power as a dominant player in Indo-Pacific region, let alone the guarantor of Tokyo's own security. In order to effectively respond to the evolving security challenges that Japan faces, it will have to change the way that the existing national security institutions, created based on the three principles mentioned above—have been established. And that is the direction that Prime Minister Shinzo Abe has been taking Japan into since 2012.

However, while public is growing more aware of the security challenges Japan faces and more appreciative of the JSDF, normative constraints on Japan's national security policy remains powerful. This chapter examines how, even as Japan's national security policy has evolved since the end of the Cold War, the persisting normative constraints has, and will likely continue to, frustrate the efforts to reform its national security policy and its national security establishment which will have to execute these policies.

Background: Basic Elements of Japan's National Security Policy

The most basic principle of Japan's national security policy can be found in the Article Nine of Japanese constitution. Standing alone under the Chapter Two entitled "Renunciation of War", the article reads as follows:

> Aspiring sincerely to an international peace based on justice and order, the Japanese people forever renounce war as a sovereign right of the nation and the threat or use of force as means of settling international disputes. In order to accomplish the aim of the preceding paragraph, land, sea, and air forces, as well as other war potential, will never be maintained. The right of belligerency of the state will not be recognized.[2]

The Article Nine of the Japanese constitution is reflective of Japan's national sentiment when the Constitution took effect. Overwhelming population in Japan at the time was deeply suspicious of the military and were happy to no longer depend on its military institution to play a major role in their government's effort to ensure their safety. This culture of anti-militarism—persists as one of the enduring legacies that constrains Japanese national security policy up to today[3] in the form of Japan's self-identity as a "nation of peace" that manifests itself in an utter unwillingness to change Article Nine of the Constitution and reluctance to see the JSDF in combat except for the defense of Japan—created the foundation on which Japan established the architecture of its national security policy.

The national strategy commonly referred to as the "Yoshida Doctrine"— a concept shaped by Shigeru Yoshida who served as Japanese prime minister three different periods between the years 1946 and 1954—was the manifestation of Japan's anti-military sentiment at that time. The Doctrine offered three basic pillars for Japan's external policy—primary focus on Japan's own economic development, minimal investment in Japan's own military, and reliance on the alliance with the United States as a means to ensure Japan's security.[4] Based on this conceptual framework, Japan established the following legal framework and made other key declaratory policy decisions for its national security policy which were firmly maintained throughout the Cold War period.

As a legal framework, the Self-Defense Force Law (*Jiei-tai Ho*) was enacted in 1954, which formally authorized the establishment of the Japan Self-Defense Force (JSDF). The JSDF was allowed to only undertake the activities that were explicitly authorized in the SDF Law under various circumstances, and even then, their use of weapons was strictly restricted so that they would be only used for self-defense. In addition, the Japan Defense Agency Establishment Law (*Bouei-sho Secchi Ho*) was also enacted to create the Japan Defense Agency (*Bouei-sho*)[5] as a civilian agency to provide a strict oversight over the management and operations of the JSDF. Furthermore, a subtle yet an important differentiation was made at the establishment of the JDA—it was positioned as one of subordinating agency to the Cabinet Office and as such, the status of JDA was not equal to other full-fledged government agencies such as the Ministry of Foreign Affairs (MOFA), Ministry of Finance, (MOF), or Ministry of International Trade and Industry (MITI).

Furthermore, consistent with the minimization of the roles to be played by JDA and SDF in the country's security policy, Japan made a few important declaratory policy decisions on other key areas related to national security. First, the government adopted the *Basic Principles of National Defense* (*kokubou no kihon houshin*) in 1957 as the basic principles of Japan's national security policy.[6] The *Basic Principles* included (1) support for the United Nations and its activities to achieve international peace, (2) establishment of the foundation necessary to heighten patriotism, safety of its people, and secure nation's security, (3) gradual build-up of the defense capability that is minimally necessary for national defense, and (4) reliance on the US–Japan alliance to counter external aggression until the UN-led collective security system begins to effectively function.[7] It also established the baseline that Japan's defense build-up would be "exclusively defense-oriented (*senshu boei*)"—in order to be consistent with the argument that the JSDF is constitutional because it is not an armed force but rather an enforcement organization that possess the capability that is just enough for self-defense, the government needed to declare that the SDF were to possess the capability that is "minimally necessary for self-defense" so that Japan would not become the area of power vacuum in East Asia.

Following the adoption of the *Basic Principles of National Defense,* Japan adopted a few more declaratory policies in the 1960s. One is the Three Principles of Arms Exports, which was set as the government's policy based on then Prime Minister Eisaku Sato's statement during the Diet session in 1967. Technically, these non-legal binding principles prohibited Japan from exporting weapons to (1) the communist bloc countries, (2) the countries that are subject to UN sanctions, and (3) the countries that are in conflict. However, subsequent statements made not only by Sato's successor Takeo

Miki and other senior government officials established the operational principles that Japan would also refrain from arms exports that did not fall into any of those three cases.

The other policy was on the peaceful use of outer space. On May 9, 1969, Japanese Diet passed a resolution that declared that Japan should limit the purpose of developing space launch vehicles and related technologies to peaceful purposes such as academic progress, improvement of the quality of life, and welfare of international community and advancement of technology that would benefit international cooperation.[8] In addition, Japan committed itself to the policy of not becoming a nuclear weapon state despite its desire to pursue robust indigenous civil nuclear power capability as an alternative source of energy to crude oil. Even prior to signing Nuclear Non-Proliferation Treaty in 1970, Japan legally committed itself to the path of non-nuclear weapon state by (1) signing US–Japan Cooperative Agreement on Nuclear Power in 1955 and (2) enacting the Nuclear Power Basic Law in 1955. The broader principles of Japan's decision not to pursue nuclear weapons were then articulated when the Prime Minister Eisaku Sato delivered a policy speech to the Diet in 1968 in which he laid out four major tenets for this policy—(1) Three Non-Nuclear principles (no possession, production, or introduction of nuclear weapons), (2) strong advocacy for nuclear disarmament and arms control, (3) reliance on US nuclear deterrence, and (4) peaceful use of nuclear energy.[9]

Finally, Japanese government demonstrated its unwillingness to invest in defense through its budgeting practice. The practice of keeping Japanese defense spending to the maximum of 1% of its Gross Domestic Production (GNP) was first formally established by then Miki cabinet in 1976 through cabinet decision, as Japan adopted its first National Defense Program Outline (NDPO), a long-term defense policy and acquisition document. Although this ceiling was eliminated by the Nakasone cabinet in 1986, there has been only a handful of years in which Japan has spent more than 1% of GDP on defense since then.

Taken together, these constitutional, legal, institutional, and policy frameworks that were established in the first 20 years of Japan's postwar history placed strict constraints on Japan's ability to utilize the SDF to promote its national interests, particularly outside Japan. Rather, by focusing on non-military means to advance Japan's national interests abroad, they labeled their approach as "comprehensive security policy (*sougou anzen* hosho)".[10] To be fair, these frameworks for Japan's national security policy suited Japan's foreign policy priority during the Cold War. Even though Japan rejoined the international community following the signing of the San Francisco Peace Treaty in 1951, its foreign policy prioritized the restoration of its diplomatic relations with the international community: for instance, it could not become the UN member state until 1956 after its diplomatic relations with the Soviet Union was normalized following the Japan–Soviet Joint Declaration. Furthermore, Japan had to settle the issue of wartime reparation with the countries in Asia it either colonized and/or invaded prior to 1945. All of this required Japan

174   Y. TATSUMI

to focus on economic development and post-war reconstruction at home. In other words, investing in the military capability was simply not the priority for Japan, at least until 1970s.

A Framework Challenged: Japan's Security Policy in Post-Cold War and Post-9/11 Years

The basic framework for Japan's national security policy described above had begun to face challenges in the 1980s. By then, Japan was no longer a country that was trying to recover from the destruction of war; rather, it has ascended to become one of the world's biggest economic powers. And as Japan's standing in international community changes, the multi-layer constraints it had imposed on its national security policy—its inability to send JSDF to the missions in overseas, in particular—had come under greater scrutiny.

Such a scrutiny over Japan's inability to commit JSDF to the international operation hit Japan in full force at the time of the 1991 Gulf War. Given that the creation of JSDF was justified as the organization for homeland defense, Japan had no legal framework to allow the JSDF to participate in the operations overseas at the time of the Gulf War. Although then Prime Minister Toshiki Kaifu tried to look for ways to dispatch the JSDF even with a limited capacity and mandate,[11] his effort did not materialize. Instead, Japan was only able to provide financial assistance while the United States and England worked with other permanent members on the United National Security Council to form multinational force to repel Iraqi invasion out of Kuwait based on the UN Security Council Resolution 678. Even though Japan's financial contribution to the war effort was substantial (totaling thirteen billion dollars), this contribution by and large went unappreciated. Indeed, the size of Japan's financial contribution led to criticism against Japan's "checkbook diplomacy", implying Japan is evading its responsibility as the world's major power by buying its way out of having to commit people to multinational force. When Japan was finally able to dispatch JMSDF minesweepers to clear mines in the Persian Gulf after the conflict ended, it still met a muted criticism as "too little, too late". Underappreciation for Japanese support for the Gulf War became abundantly clear when Kuwaiti government published a full-page advertisement on the world's major newspapers, Japan was not included in the list of the countries that Kuwait thanked. This experience was an extremely bitter pill to swallow for Japan, demonstrating that Japan, having emerged as the world's leading economic power, would be expected to play a more robust role in the area of international security as well. This experience also deeply traumatized Japanese government officials and lawmakers, making them determined to do things different about a decade later in the aftermath of the 9/11 terrorist attacks.

In addition, other international and domestic incidents following the Gulf War further challenged Japan to shift its national security policy to better respond to the security environment that Japan faced. In particular, the first

North Korea nuclear crisis that began with North Korea's withdrawal from Nuclear Non-proliferation Treaty (NPT) in 1993 exposed Japan's inability to support US military operations in East Asia. The 1995 Sarin Gas attack against Tokyo subway by the indigenous cult Aum Shinrikyo also reminded Japan that the crisis that would require mobilization of the JSDF may not be a military invasion from foreign power. Clearly, the legal and policy frameworks that were established during the Cold War based on the premise of relatively static major power competition between the United States and Soviet Union were proving to be inadequate for Japan to navigate the evolving security environment in Asia and beyond.

Japan tries to respond to this challenge by changing the existing legal framework and revising policy just enough to navigate through the changes that were happening, rather than fundamentally changing them. On legal front, in the days immediately followed the Gulf War, Japanese lawmakers reluctantly began to discuss the possible legal framework under which the JSDF could be dispatched to overseas missions. Given the basic principle that the JSDF maintains an exclusively defense-oriented posture, it was very important that any activities that the JSDF would be allowed to conduct outside Japan be (1) not engaging in combat activities or any activities that feeds into combat, and (2) use of weapons by the dispatched JSDF forces would be restricted only to self-defense. After a protracted debate due to strong opposition by the opposition parties led by the Social Democratic Party of Japan (which was the largest opposition party at that time), the Japanese Diet approved the United National Peace Keeping Operations Cooperation Law (commonly referred to as PKO Law) in June 1992.

The enactment of the PKO Law did not make the JSDF dispatch for UN PKO missions easier, however. In fact, as the Japanese Diet approved the PKO Law, it attached what is known as "PKO Participation Five Principles" as the conditions which would have to be met for the dispatch of the JSDF to move forward. These principles included (1) a cease-fire agreement on the ground; (2) an agreement by all parties to the cease-fire about accepting the deployment of PKO forces; (3) political impartiality for the PKO forces can be sustained; (4) reservation of the right for Japan to withdraw the JSDF if any of the conditions (1)–(3) are not met; and (5) the dispatched JSDF force would be restricted in its ability to use weapons to self-defense.

In addition, given the JSDF's history in providing disaster relief assistance within Japan, Japanese government also determined that the humanitarian assistance/disaster relief operations (HA/DR) is additional area which the JSDF can conduct overseas. In September 1992, the international Disaster Relief Law (IDR Law) was revised to allow the JSDF to be dispatched overseas to conduct HA/DR operations where civilian disaster assistance team may not be able to reach due to extremely austere conditions on the ground.

On the policy front, the effort to assess how to adjust to the changes began with the deliberation by the Advisory Council on Security (commonly known as the Higuchi Commission) which, in its final report *Modality of the Security and Defense Capability of Japan: The Outlook for the 21st Century*, argued that Japan should move away from its Cold War-ear security policy which was described as "passive" and reconstruct its security policy into an "active" one, so that Japan can play a role in shaping a post-Cold War international order. It also advocated for Japan to have a defense capability that has a stronger intelligence and better equipped with crisis management capability. Based on the recommendation put forward by the Higuchi Commission, Japanese government revised the National Defense Program Outline (NDPO), a defense policy and acquisition planning document, for the first time since it first determined it in 1976. While the original NDPO solely focused on the defense of Japan and the JSDF capability necessary for that mission, the 1995 NDPO expanded the scope of Japan's defense policy goals to include Japan playing a role in the international efforts for peace and security. As such, the JSDF capability was also to be adjusted so that it would be able to conduct operations overseas.[12]

Combined with the efforts in the mid-1990s to redefine the US–Japan alliance to meet the post-Cold War security environment by repositioning it a stabilizer for regional peace and security rather than a part of US-led anti-communist bloc, these initial set of adjustments restarted Japan's process to bridge the gap between what it is allowed to do within the basic framework of its national security policy established soon after the war with what it is required to do to effectively defend the country and its national interests. By the end of 1990s, Japan was able to send the JSDF and other personnel to UN-mandated the peacekeeping operations when a certain set of conditions are met. The JSDF had explicit legal authorization to provide a certain type of logistical support for US military operations in case of emergencies near Japan. In addition, the JSDF had become able to conduct HA/DR operations overseas.

However, the 9/11 terrorist attacks in 2001 quickly proved that the limited adjustments that Japan made in the previous decade were not sufficient for Japan to adapt to the major change in security environment that the threat of international terrorism brought. Indeed, in order to stay as an "active" player in international effort to counter the threat presented by Al-Qaeda, Japan had to take further legislative actions to ensure that the JSDF would be able to take part in the international responses. Japanese government officials and lawmakers were determined not to repeat the experience of the Gulf War.[13] In particular, they wanted to make sure that the JSDF can be dispatched in support of the coalition forces' operation, and the dispatch would not be criticized as "too little, too late". Japanese government's decision to pass two special measures laws (*tokubetu sochi ho*)—the 2001 Anti-Terrorism Special Measures Law and the 2004 Iraq Reconstruction Support Special Measures Law—instead of trying to use the existing laws as the legal justification for authorizing the JSDF dispatch for these missions were based on the judgement on the part of the government that the special measures law that explicitly defines the types of anticipated JSDF activities on the ground that the JSDF will be engaged in and the period of deployment to authorize the JSDF participation in the Operation Enduring Freedom and Operation Iraqi Freedom would result in a more timely deployment of relevant JSDF units.

In addition, it is also during the first decade of the twenty-first century that Japan enacted legislation that would provide the JSDF legal authorization to take the actions that are against Japanese domestic law in peacetime should Japan faces an armed attack. This set of laws, called contingency legislation (*yuuji hosei*), allowed the JSDF to override some Japanese domestic laws (i.e., following the traffic signals) while conducting operations to defend Japan against those attacks.

As Japan shored up the legal framework to allow the JSDF to respond to the attempt of attacks against Japan and also began its experiment of allowing the JSDF to engage in the overseas operation other than HA/DR and UN PKO by first enacting case-specific special measures laws that authorized such participation, it also launched a new process to revise its defense policy priorities given the new challenges presented by the rise of international terrorism symbolized by 9/11. Similar to the post-Cold War policy revision process, this effort also began with the deliberation by the advisory group for the prime minister, the Council on Security and Defense Capabilities (referred to as the Araki Commission). The Commission's final report *Japan's Visions for Future Security and Defense Capability,* released in October 2004, advocated a multi-layer approach to achieve two main security policy goals for Japan that the Commission identified—defense of Japan and prevention of threats in the international security environment that can threaten Japan's security. The Commission report argued that such a multi-layer approach should stand on the three legs: (1) Japan's own enhanced efforts to build-up its defense capability, (2) even more robust US–Japan alliance, and (3) cooperation with potential partners beyond the United States. Although the Commission report did not recommend constitutional revision or reinterpretation, it did suggest that some of the declaratory policies Japan adopted between 1950 and 1970s might benefit from revision given the new security challenges, and identified the Three Principles of Arms Exports as and example.

The revised *National Defense Program Guidelines,* approved by the cabinet in December 2004, incorporated the ideas put forth in the Araki Commission Report, calling the transnational threats such as international terrorism and proliferation of weapons of mass destruction (WMD) as the most serious security challenge Japan would face in the post-9/11 security environment. What was most notable about the 2004 NDPG was that it suggested that the time might have come for Japan to revisit its approach to the JSDF capability and its force build-up. While it stopped short of suggesting that the constitutional revision or reinterpretation might be necessary, the 2004 NDPG emphasized the importance of the JSDF engagement in overseas missions. It also suggested that the time may have come for Japan to move beyond the long-held principle of exclusively defense-oriented posture for the JSDF build-up, advocating for "multi-functional, flexible, and effective force".

Another symbolically significant institutional changes took place soon after 9/11 as well. In April 200X, JDA was granted the status of full ministery, and it became the Ministry of Defense (MOD). While most of the changes caused by this status change was administrative and procedural (such as MOD, as a full-status ministry, can now submit its annual budget proposal to and directly negotiate with the Ministry of Finance, rather than going through Cabinet Affairs Office), it signaled an important institutional change in Japan's national security policy toward allowing MOD and the JSDF to play more pronounced role in security policy-making and its implementation. The JSDF Law was also revised to reflect the policy guidance in the 2004 NDPG, clearly defining JSDF's overseas operation as its primary mission alongside with homeland defense.

Japan also went through a new round of consultation—known as the Defense Policy Review Initiative (DPRI)—with the United States on ways in which the two countries can deepen bilateral defense ties, as Washington, under the Bush Administration, seeks to realign the force posture of forward-deployed forces. Under DPRI, Japan clarified that it has the primary responsibility in defending homeland, agreed that the JSDF would share a greater role in supporting US operations in East Asia, and further agreed to allow the JSDF to play a more robust role in the international operations that are occurring beyond the Asia-Pacific region.

Japan Transformed? Changes Made Under the Second Abe Cabinet (December 2012–Present)

Incremental changes in Japan's national security policy as well as the legal and institutional frameworks that have been put in place since the end of the Cold War through the first decade of the twenty-first century laid the groundwork for Prime Minister Shinzo Abe to push for further changes when he became the prime minister for the second time in December 2012. After assuming the office, Abe re-energized a number of efforts that he began when he first became the prime minister in 2006. One of such efforts was to enhance the National Security Secretariat (NSS), dubbed as Japanese version of National Security Council. He recruited retired top diplomat Shotaro Yachi to be the director of the secretariat, and accelerated the process of consolidating the decision-making process to the Office of the Prime Minister (*kantei*), including the NSS. This provided incentive to the ministries and agencies that send detailees to the NSS—MOFA, MOD, METI, National Police Agency, etc.—to send a highly-qualified officials to NSS.

With the enhanced NSS staff, Abe also set out to craft Japan's first-ever National Security Strategy. The completed National Security Strategy, issued in December 2013, replaced the 1957 Basic Principles of National Defense as the document to set the overarching principles for Japan's national security policy. While the document did not abandon the principle of exclusively defense-oriented posture for Japan's defense build-up, it also set forth the concept of "proactive contribution to peace (*Sekkyoku-teki Heiwa-shugi*) as the guiding principle of Japan's national security policy. The 2013 NDPG, issued in tandem with the National Security Strategy in December 2013, called for "joint and mobile defense force" as the goal that the JSDF strives to achieve in its defense build-up. Under this banner, it advocated the JSDF to continue improving on jointness, acquire amphibious capability, and enhanced ballistic missile defense capability.

Based on these policy guidance, Japan has strengthened its security relationship not only within the context of the US–Japan alliance as symbolized by completing the revision of the Guidelines for US–Japan Defense Cooperation under which Japan committed itself not only to play a greater role in its own defense and in support of US military operations in the Asia-Pacific region, but also in international operations outside the region. Japan also proceeded with institutionalizing its security partnership with many US allies such as Australia, England, France, Republic of Korea, India, and the Philippines by signing either the Acquisition and Cross-Service Agreement (ACSA), General Security of Military Information Agreement (GSOMIA)/Information Sharing Agreement (ISA), or agreement on defense equipment and technology transfer and cooperation (or any combination of them).

Abe also revisited some of the declaratory policy that constrained Japan's national security policy since the Cold-War. For instance, under his watch, Japanese government changed its long-time policy of peaceful use of outer space to authorize Japanese government's use of space to benefit Japan's national security. More significantly, Japan replaced the Three Principles of Arms Exports (3Ps) with the Three Principles of Defense Equipment Transfer (commonly referred to as the New 3Ps), considerably easing the restriction on the Japanese companies not only to export the defense equipment they produce overseas, but also to partner with foreign defense industry. Although Japan did not win, its bid in Australia's next-generation submarine acquisition program and England's reconnaissance aircraft acquisition program are early indicators to demonstrate the appetite for defense equipment export on the side of Japanese industry.

Most significantly, Abe reactivated the private advisory panel to explore the overhaul of Japan's national security-related legislation, including whether to revise Article 9 of the Constitution. Abe launched this panel, led by the former Japanese Ambassador to the US Shunji Yanai (therefore commonly referred to as the Yanai Commission) when he first became the prime minister in 2007. Although the Commission finished the preliminary report in June 2008, by the time of the completion of the report, Abe's first term as the prime minister had abruptly ended in 2007, and their report was essentially ignored by his successors. The commission, reactivated by Abe in 2013, recommended in April 2014 that Japanese government consider re-interpret Article 9 of the Constitution to allow conditional exercise of the right of collective self-defense. The panel's recommendations culminated in the 2014 Cabinet decision of re-interpreting the Article 9 of the Constitution that Japan is constitutionally allowed to exercise the right of collective self-defense under a limited set of circumstances. This reinterpretation of Article 9 of the Constitution led to Japan enacting a group of national security-related laws (referred to as Peace and Security Legislation as the package) to translate the constitutional reinterpretation into the legal framework that authorizes the JSDF activities.

Conclusion: A Glass Ceiling for Japan's National Security Policy

Since the end of the World War II, Japan's national security policy has demonstrated significant evolution. The evolution did not happen by Japan's choice: rather, it was driven by Japan's need to continue to adapt to its changing circumstances. In the years that followed the end of World War II, Japan found itself unable to rely on UN-centered collective security system despite its wariness of military power as an instrument to advance national interests. Its choice to depend on the alliance with the United States for its security also put Japan under the pressure to share due burden in the context of the US–Japan alliance in order to avoid the criticism of being a free-rider in the alliance relationship. Moreover, their aspirational approach, symbolized by Article 9 of its Constitution, of minimizing the role the military power plays in its national security policy turned out to be simply not sustainable after its emergence as one of the world's leading economic power.

Thus, as Japan tried to adapt to the reality it faced, the evolution of its national security policy most clearly manifested itself in Japan's efforts to find ways to allow the JSDF to play more visible role externally. However, in the absence of national consensus on how Japan should use the JSDF as a means to promote and secure its national security interests, it tried to do so without fundamentally changing the constitutional framework. To be fair, Japan has been successful in making incremental changes to the ways in which the JSDF can be used. Despite started as the organization that was supposed to have the capability just enough to defend Japan from external aggression, the JSDF today is among the world's most-advanced and best-trained professional military organization. Although the JSDF was not anticipated to operate overseas at all when it was first established The JSDF today regularly participates in HA/DR operations in the Indo-Pacific region, participate in UN PKOs (although with limitations), engage in the coalition operation beyond the Indo-Pacific region such as the counter-piracy operation in the Gulf of Aden, and is on the trajectory of playing a bigger role in working not only with the United States but with other US allies and partners in the region to maintain free and open global commons in the region, as demonstrated by Japan's increasing interest in intensifying Quad cooperation with the US, Australia and India.

As such, Many expects Japan to have a more robust defense capability and continue to play a more prominent role in the multinational effort to maintain peace and security.[14] For one, Prime Minister and the ruling Liberal Democratic Party (LDP) certainly are interested in bringing Japan into that direction. When Abe returned to power in December 2012, he spoke about "departure from post-war regime (*Sengo Rejiimu kara no Dakkyaku*)" to which constitutional revision is central.[15] Indeed, in the last several years, Abe has taken concrete steps to prepare for the constitutional revision process to kick in. One of the important legislative steps that began most recently is that the Panel on Constitution in the Japanese Diet began to deliberate on the reform on National Referendum Law to align its content with the Public Election Law.[16]

Furthermore, there has been a growing desire, particularly within the ruling LDP, but also many in the opposition, to see the JSDF to equip itself with more robust capabilities and maintain strong defense industrial base that could support it. After all, it was during the rule of the Democratic Party of Japan (DPJ) that Japan took a clear first step toward revising the Three Principles of Arms Export that had previously existed as Japan decided to introduce F-35 to the JASDF. More recently, the LDP's Committee on National Defense released the recommendation for the National Defense Policy Guidelines that is to be revised by December 2018 in which they pushed for "active defense" that would allow Japan to have a "cross-domain defense posture".[17] These developments suggest that there is a desire within Japan to see that Japan would stay on its current path on defense reform that will eventually result in Japan revising its Constitution (including Article 9) and free the JSDF from the existing constraints that are place on their ability to operate.

However, as considerable as the incremental changes of last six decades represents, closer observation of what appears to be epoch-making changes in Japan's nations national security policy in the last several years suggests that Japan's self-identity as "nation of peace" and the persistent public perception of the JSDF primarily as the HA/DR responder and homeland defender rather than a professional military that can be expeditionary and engage in the missions overseas has not changed much. And these elements will likely remain powerful constraints against Japan's national security policy to maintain the current pace of evolution, particularly in post-Abe era Japan.

First is the evolution of the debate on whether Article 9 of the constitution should be revised or reviewed under Abe's watch. As mentioned earlier in the chapter, Abe launched the Yanai Commission, a private advisory panel to explore the most appropriate constitutional and legal framework for Japan's national security policy in 2007 when he first became the prime minister. The focus of the Yanai Commission was on whether it would be appropriate for Japan to maintain its prohibition of exercising the right of collective self-defense. In the final report published by the Commission in June 2008, it identified four specific cased in which Japan ought to be allowed to exercise the right of collective self-defense: (1) escorting US vessels in high sea; (2) intercept ballistic missiles that may be targeting the US; (3) use of weapons by the JSDF personnel participating in UN PKO missions; and (4) rear-area support for the other PKO participating militaries. At the same time, the Commission report explicitly recommended that Japan would put legislation in place that would maintain a certain level of "restrain" on the JSDF's activities, including the continuing prohibition of JSDF participation in UN PKOs whose primary mission includes combat operations.[18]

When the Commission was reactivated in 2013, the Commission revisited the four scenarios it identified in its 2008 report and further identified six cases in which the Commission viewed that either Japan should be able to exercise the right of collective self-defense, or new legislation to authorize JSDF operation would be necessary: (1) support (including defending US ships) in case of regional contingency; (2) support for the United States in case United States came under attack; (3) minesweeping in the waters that are critical for Japan's national security; (4) participation in multinational coalition operations that are based on US resolutions; (5) response to the submarines that continue submerged operations in Japan's territorial waters despite Japan's repeated warnings; and (6) response to the illegal activities by armed groups against ships and civilians that are beyond the response capacity owned by Japan Coast Guard.[19] Based on the Commission's recommendation, Abe Cabinet made the decision on July 1, 2014 in which it officially reinterpreted the Article 9 of the Constitution to allow Japan to exercise the right of collective self-defense under three circumstances—when the situation is considered to significantly impact Japan's National Security (*Juuyou Eikyou Jitai*), when the situation, if left unattended, will endanger Japan's national security (*Sonritu Kiki Jitai*), and when the JSDF is dispatched to participate in support of multinational coalition operations (*Kokusai Heiwa Kyoudou Taisho Jitai*).[20]

What is noticeable here is that, with this interpretation, the Abe Cabinet continued to emphasize that Japan would remain "nation of peace" and the need to steadfastly maintain this identity. During the press conference to announced the July 1 Cabinet Decision, he stressed that the basic interpretation of the Article 9, such as prohibition of the JSDF to engage in combat activities overseas, would remain intact. He also argued that his cabinet's re-interpretation of the Article 9 was fundamentally to benefit Japan's own security, using the example of the JSDF, with the new interpretation of Article 9, would now be able to defend US ships that are evacuating Japanese citizens from foreign countries where conflict began.[21]

The Peace and Security Legislation that the Japanese Diet passed in the fall of 2015 has two-components. One is the overarching law that dictates the revision of 10 existing national security-related laws (i.e., the JSDF Law, the Ship Inspection Activities Law, the PKO Cooperation Law) and is called Peace and Security Legislation Arrangement Law (*Heiwa Anzen Housei Seibi Hou*). The other is a new legislation that authorizes the JSDF to participate in the multinational coalition operations and called International Peace Support Law

(*Kokusai Heiwa Shien Hou*).[22] However, even with these legislation to reflect the constitutional reinterpretation enacted, a few critical constrains continued to exist. For one, the Prime Minister can make an initial determination on whether a certain situation merits to be recognized as one of the three conditions that would allow Japan to exercise the right of collective self-defense, but his/her decision has to be endorsed by the Diet in the form of pre-authorization of JSDF actions to be taken in those circumstances. Secondly, although the JSDF can technically participate in the multinational coalition operation in addition to UN PKOs, the benchmark with which the Diet approves JSDF participation in UN PKOs remains to be based on the Five Principles of PKO participation. Japan's withdrawal of the JSDF from UN Mission in South Sudan (UNMISS) in March 2017—a decision was effectively made because of the deteriorating security situation in South Sudan—only several months after Japanese Diet made the changes to the list of authorized activities that the JSDF can conduct to reflect the new constitutional interpretation was a clear reminder that the constitutional reinterpretation would not necessarily result in Japan's participation in multinational operations that are higher-risk.[23]

Finally, significant questions remain on whether Japanese public will support the changes that Abe and the LDP envisions. According to the public opinion poll conducted every 2–3 years by the Cabinet Affairs Office on the JSDF and defense issues, although close to 90%[24] of the public have favorable perception of the JSDF—clear improvement from 1971, for example, when only 60% of the public deemed the JSDF favorably[25]—such a favorable impression is largely shaped by the HA/DR operation that the JSDF engages domestically as well as internationally.[26] Furthermore, even the most recent poll—conducted in 2017 after public has seen the increased Chinese assertive activities in East China Sea as well as provocation by North Korea that includes nuclear test and missiles—shows that the public does not have an appetite for considerable expansion of Japan's military capability with only a little less than 30% advocating for enhancing the capability while approximately 60% think the current level of defense build-up is sufficient.[27]

Evolution in Japan's national security policy has shown significant evolution from immediate post-war years. These changes, while incremental and moving at glacial pace, represents considerable changes in aggregate. However, these changes have one element in common: with the exception of the passage of PKO Cooperation Law, all the significant institutional and legislative changes to Japan's national security policy have been made under the leadership of the prime ministers who either enjoys high public approval rating, or have strong footing within the Liberal Democratic Party. Junichiro Koizumi, who oversaw the enactment of two special measures laws to support coalition operations in the Middle East, elevation of the Japan Defense Agency to the Ministry of Defense, and enactment of contingency legislation, was the example of the former. Shinzo Abe, whose popular support has never been as high as Koizumi enjoyed but has a solid footing within the LDP, is the example of the latter. But even these leaders so far have not been able to overcome the fundamental principle of Japan's national security policy that was established in the years immediately after the World War II—Japan's identity as a "nation of peace", unwillingness to revise Article 9, and reluctance to see the JSDF in combat except for when defending Japan from armed attack. And these three fundamental elements in Japan's post-war security policy will likely remain as powerful normative constraints as Japan continues its attempt to adapt to the changing security environment.

NOTES

1. Constitution of Japan. (1947). Article 9. Enacted 3 May. https://japan.kantei. go.jp/constitution_and_government_of_japan/constitution_e.html.
2. Ibid.
3. Introduction to the enduring legacies in Japanese security policy can be found in: Oros, A. L. (2017). *Japan's Security Renaissance*. Columbia University Press, 24–32. For a more thorough discussion of the culture of anti-militarism in Japan, see: Berger, T. (1996). Norms, Identity and National Security in Germany and Japan. In Peter Katzenstein (ed.), *The Culture of National Security* (pp. 317–356). New York: Columbia University Press.
4. For the discussion of the Yoshida Doctrine, see, for example: Kosaka, M. (1968). *Saishou Yoshida Shigeru* (Premier Shigeru Yoshida). Chukou Zensho, 128–146.
5. As an agency subordinate to Cabinet Affairs Office, JDA lacked some of the prerogatives that other full ministries had, such as the ability to directly negotiate its budget with the Ministry of Finance. Director-General of JDA was also considered "junior' and less important compared to other cabinet ministers. When the JDA became the Ministry of Defense in 2010, it achieved the equal status with other ministries.
6. The 1957 *Basic Principles of National Defense* guided Japan's defense policy until the Abe government adopted *National Security Strategy of Japan* in December 2013.
7. Government of Japan. 1957. *Kokubou no Kihon Houshin* (Basic Principles of National Defense). Adopted by the cabinet decision, 20 May. https://rnavi. ndl.go.jp/politics/entry/bib01269.php.
8. House of Representative. (1969). *Waga kuni-ni okeru Uchuu-no Kaihatsu oyobi Riyou no Kihon ni kansuru Ketsugi* (Resolution on the Basic Principle in the Development and Use of Outer Space). Adopted 9 May. http://www.jaxa.jp/library/space_law/chapter_1/1-1-1-4_j.html.
9. Tatsumi, Y. (2008). *Japan's National Security Policy Infrastructure: Can Tokyo Meet Washington's Expectation?* Washington, DC: Stimson Center, 18.
10. For good summary of Japan's security policy between immediate post-war years and the Cold War, see: Hughes, C. W. (2004). *Japan's Security Agenda*. Boulder: Lynne Rienner, 119–158.
11. For instance, dispatching the JASDF transport aircraft to fly Japanese hostages held by the Iraq government back to Japan was identified as a possible way to allow the JSDF to play some role, albeit limited.
12. Tatsumi, Y. (2008). *Japan's National Security Policy Infrastructure*, 23.

13. Hisae, M. (2002). *9/11 to Nihon Gaikou* (9/11 and Japanese Diplomacy). Kodansha Gendai Shinsho. This provides detailed narrative accounts of the thinking among Japanese officials and lawmakers at the time.
14. For instance, see Samuels, R. & Heginbotham, E. (2018). A New Military Strategy for Japan: Active Denial Will Increase Security in Northeast Asia. *Foreign Affairs*. The authors argue that Japan should reform its defense posture and adopt an "active denial strategy" which would include tactically offensive weapons.
15. Takahashi, K. (2014). *Abe Chouki Seiken, Sengo Rejiimu Dakkyaku Kasoku he: Kenpou Kaisei no Hatajirushi Senmei ni* (Abe's long-term government to accelerate departure from post-post-war regime: push for constitutional revision becoming clear). *The Huffington Post Japan*, 14 December. https://www.huffingtonpost.jp/kosuke-takahashi/post_8759_b_6323538.html.
16. "*Kokumin Touhyou Hou Kaisei-an Shingi-Iri: Yotou Jiki Kokkai Seiritsu Mezasu* (Deliberation of the Revision on the National Referendum Law Begins: Ruling Parties Looks to Pass it at the Next Diet Session) *Mainichi Shimbun*, July 5, 2018. https://mainichi.jp/articles/20180705/k00/00e/010/242000c.
17. Liberal Democratic Party Committee on National Defense. (2018). Aratana Bouei Keikaku no Taikou oyobi Chuuki Boueiryoku Seibi Keikaku no Sakutei ni Muketa Teigen—Tajigen Oudan (Kurosu Domain) Bouei Kousou no Jitsugen ni Mukete (Recommendation for the next National Defense Policy Guidelines and the Mid-Term Defense Program—Toward the Realization of Cross-Domain Defense Posture) 29 May. https://jimin.jp-east-2.os.cloud.nifty.com/pdf/news/policy/137478_1.pdf?_ga=2.161048509.1889899540.1532809961-1055908956.1532809961.
18. *Anzen Hoshou no Houteki Kiban ni Kansuru Kondan-kai* (Advisory Panel on the Legal Foundation for National Security). (2008). *Anzen Hosho no Houteki Kiban ni Kansuru Kondan-kai Houkoku-sho* (The Report of the Advisory Panel on the Legal Foundation for National Security) 24 June. http://www.kantei.go.jp/jp/singi/anzenhosyou/houkokusho.pdf.
19. *Anzen Hoshou no Houteki Kiban ni Kansuru Kondan-kai* (Advisory Panel on the Legal Foundation for National Security). (2014). *Anzen Hosho no Houteki Kiban ni Kansuru Kondan-kai Houkoku-sho* (The Report of the Advisory Panel on the Legal Foundation for National Security) 15 May. https://www.kantei.go.jp/jp/singi/anzenhosyou2/dai7/houkoku.pdf.
20. Office of the Prime Minister. (2014). *Anzen Hoshou Housei ni kansuru Kakugi Kettei* (Cabinet Decision on National Security Legislation) 1 July. The entire text of the decision reported by *Huffington Post Japan* can be found at: https://www.huffingtonpost.jp/2014/07/01/right-of-collective-self-defense_n_5549648.html.
21. Office of the Prime Minister. (2014). Press Conference by Prime Minister Shinzo Abe, 1 July. https://www.kantei.go.jp/jp/96_abe/statement/2014/0701kaiken.html.
22. Cabinet Affairs Office. *Heiwa Anzen Housei no Gaiyou* (Overview of Peace and Security Legislation). https://www.cas.go.jp/jp/houan/150515_1/siryou1.pdf.
23. Tatsumi, Y. (2017). Japan Self Defense Force Withdraws from Sudan. *The Diplomat*, 13 March, https://thediplomat.com/2017/03/japan-self-defense-force-withdraws-from-south-sudan/.

24. Cabinet Affairs Office. (2018). *Heisei 29-Nendo Jieitai Bouei ni Kansuru Yoron Chosa* (The 2017 Public Opinion Poll on the JSDF and Defense Issues). https://survey.gov-online.go.jp/h29/h29-bouei/zh/z04.html.
25. Cabinet Affairs Office. (2017). *Heisei 26-Nendo Jieitai Bouei ni Kansuru Yoron Chosa* (The 2014 Public Opinion Poll on the JSDF and Defense Issues). https://survey.gov-online.go.jp/h26/h26-bouei/zh/z07.html.
26. For instance, in the 2017 Public Opinion Poll on the JSDF and Defense Issues, the role of the JSDF that the public most identified with is disaster relief operations—approximately 80% of the respondents referred to disaster relief as the role they expect from the JSDF. https://survey.gov-online.go.jp/h29/h29-bouei/zh/z06.html.
27. The 2017 Public Opinion Poll on the JSDF and Defense Issues. https://survey.gov-online.go.jp/h29/h29-bouei/zh/z05.html.

CHAPTER 9

India's National Security Challenges and the State Response

Harsh V. Pant and Akshay Ranade

India, unlike other major democracies, does not have a formally declared national security policy or strategy. Non-Alignment, which survived through the Cold War years as a grand strategy for India to safeguard its national interest, started eroding with the structural changes after the fall of the Soviet Union. The end of the Cold War and concurrent economic and strategic developments compelled India to adopt a renewed framework for not just its economic policy but also its foreign policy. Though New Delhi adjusted to these new developments, the quest for a politically aligned and formally declared security policy that would concretely define India's security environment and responses continues.

For years, Indian security responses were characterized as reactionary; that attempted to address security threats sporadically as and when they arose. One of the major impediments in articulating an agreed national security strategy has been a lack of political consensus in not only understanding the nature of security threats, but also in ways of addressing them. This lack of consensus has occasioned ad hoc responses to security challenges which are driven prominently by the nature and instincts of the top political leadership.

This chapter examines emergent and likely future security challenges facing India and the pattern of Indian policy responses. By enquiring into debates

---

H. V. Pant (✉)
King's College London, London, UK
e-mail: harsh.pant@kcl.ac.uk

A. Ranade
Symbiosis International University, Pune, India

© The Author(s), under exclusive license to Springer Nature
Switzerland AG 2022
M. Clarke et al. (eds.), *The Palgrave Handbook of National Security*,
https://doi.org/10.1007/978-3-030-53494-3_9

187

that emerged while formulating responses to security threats, it seeks to highlight the underlying factors that have been central in shaping India's response to its security environment. In understanding these debates, special focus is on ideological shifts and institutional capabilities that continue to shape India's approach to its national security policy. First, a brief overview of the political and institutional context in which India's security policy is formulated is provided. Subsequently, this chapter delves into key security challenges facing India and policy responses to these challenges.

A Gradual Evolution in Indian National Security Policy

A nation's security policy is essentially aimed at creating and sustaining the space—regionally and globally—which enables it to pursue its national interests. Devising such a policy requires an assessment of external environment, the nature, and intensity of the threat as well as the means, both internal and external, to mitigate such a threat. Post-independence, India charted for itself a path free of power rivalries by not getting associated with any power-blocks and thereby retaining its 'independent foreign policy'. This 'Non-Aligned' policy framework constituted for India its grand strategy for the entire Cold War period. The crux of Non-Alignment was to stay aloof from alliances of the Cold War and retain the manoeuvring space with both the super-powers. The limitations of such a policy in a world fraught with power rivalries soon became apparent with countries like Pakistan entering into alliances with US and thereby changing the power dynamics in the region.

The first decisive blow to the essence of Non-Alignment was the Indo–Soviet Treaty of Peace, Friendship and Cooperation which was signed on 9th August, 1971 to counter the strategic affinity between Washington–Beijing–and Islamabad. The Indo–Soviet Treaty was signed at a critical juncture when Asian geo-political situation was in flux with the evolving developments, the most critical of which was the unfolding cordiality between US and China. To contain US and Chinese influence in Asia, the Soviet Union needed a strong security arrangement in the region which would serve Soviet interests. General Secretary Brezhnev's 1969 proposal to develop a collective security system in Asia was essentially aimed at this objective in Asia. The proposal however did not receive positive support from any of the Asian countries, including India which was unwilling to enter in any arrangement which would be seen as "anti-China". Yet, in a matter of two years, India entered into a security arrangement with the USSR, overcoming its initial hesitations. The deteriorating situation in East Pakistan (now Bangladesh) and the evolving US–China relations after Kissinger's secret visit to China in July 1971 accelerated the process of India entering into any security arrangement with the Soviet Union. The likelihood of external interference in a possible Indo–Pakistan conflict, the evolving Sino-US entente and the US–Pakistan alliance also played a key role in overcoming India's resistance to enter into security arrangements. The rationale for India signing the treaty was aptly summarized by then External Affairs Minister Swaran Singh, when he stated in Lok Sabha:

> We shall not allow any other country or combination of countries to dominate us or to interfere in our internal affairs. We shall, to our maximum ability, help other countries to maintain their freedom from outside domination, and their sovereignty. We have no desire to interfere in the internal affairs of other countries, but this does not mean that we shall look on as silent spectators if third countries come and interfere in the internal affairs of other countries, particularly our neighbours, as our own national interest could be adversely affected.[1]

Though the treaty was essentially a security agreement with the USSR that marked a decisive deviation from India's stated non-aligned posture, the text made sure that the rhetorical component of Non-Alignment was adhered to. Article IV of the treaty, for instance, stated that "the Union of Soviet Socialist Republics respects India's policy of non-alignment and reaffirms that this policy constitutes an important factor in the maintenance of universal peace and international security and in the lessening of tensions in the world". Article VIII restricted the two countries from "enter[ing] into or participat[ing] in any military alliance directed against the other party" and "to abstain from any aggression against the other Party and to prevent the use of its territory for the commission of any act which might inflict military damage". And Article IX stated in the "event of either Party being subjected to and attach or a threat thereof" had provision to "immediately enter into mutual consultations in order to remove such threat and to take appropriate effective measures to ensure peace and the security of their countries"[2] in effect gave this 'friendship treaty' the identity of a 'soft-alliance'. When seen from the Soviet perspective, the treaty was critical in its strategy to balance the Asian power equations which were in considerable flux. Though Brezhnev's effort at materializing collective security for Asia did not see any considerable success, this 'special friendship' with India remained a critical component of his strategy for Asia.

The Treaty was also important from a regional security point of view as when seen from the Indian perspective it enabled it to keep regional security intact by balancing and pre-empting any external dominance in the region. The utility of such a 'treaty' was not lost upon the political elite, and this 'friendship' remained the cornerstone of India's security policy until the disintegration of the Soviet Union. After the Friendship Treaty with the USSR, India used the rhetoric of Non Alignment essentially as a cover to maintain its position of a Third World Leader, even as the essence of the policy became progressively diluted.

The withering of non-alignment as a grand strategy saw its logical next step in the early 1990s, beginning with the Narasimha Rao government. Arguably, it was more a consequence of both structural changes globally and economic compulsions domestically. Structurally, the end of Cold War ushered in a unipolar world dominated by the US, not just militarily but also ideologically.[3] This in effect made the strategic logic of remaining non-aligned redundant. The fall of the Soviet Union was also a strategic setback for India. Throughout the Cold War years India had relied heavily on the USSR for its diplomatic and strategic manoeuvring. Domestically, India faced a dire economic crisis which was culmination of decades of socialist driven economic model and gross fiscal mismanagement that drained India's foreign exchanges reserves, and resulting into a severe balance of payment crisis. The end of the Cold War therefore coincided with a series of changes in India's economic and foreign policy approach and to a considerable extent, the two reinforced each other.

Strategically, two significant changes were evident in the post-Cold War era. First, India's ties with the US assumed a more positive trajectory. The economic liberalization of India in the early 1990s provided an incentive to mend ties with the US with whom India had troubled relations during most part of the Cold War. For India, to mend ties with the US made strategic as well as economic sense, especially since the new economic model India was adopting resonated with the American system. The second was India's burgeoning engagement with countries which hitherto had received less attention. The initiation of India's Look East Policy (LEP) and upgrading Israel to full ambassadorial level relations were the highlights of the Rao government. Yet while Rao began the process of dismantling the Nehruvian model, it was still a subtle process which retained the rhetorical component of Non-Alignment intact.

The advent of the BJP and its assumption of power in New Delhi in effect took the next step of distancing India's strategic approach from the Nehruvian model. An ideological opponent of the Congress, it had no hesitation in explicitly re-orienting towards a new foreign policy framework. Thus, under the leadership of Atal Behari Vajpayee, the possibility of an Indo–US strategic partnership was talked about openly for the first time. For instance, during his Speech to the Asia Society, just months after India's 1998 nuclear tests, Vajpayee for the first time called India and the US natural allies.[4] Similarly Brajesh Mishra in 2003, then the National Security Advisor, spoke openly of a probable 'axis' between India, the US, and Israel in tackling the common threat of terrorism, noting that "such an alliance would have the political will and moral authority to take bold decisions in extreme cases of terrorist provocation"[5] The new approach had two critical components: a desire to forge and strengthen strategic partnerships; and a broader scope in which no country was off the strategic radar.

The policy broadly continued with the next Manmohan Singh government as he continued the path of strengthening India's relations with major powers. The US–India civil nuclear deal of 2005 was a major reordering of the global nuclear order. Domestically this drew political fissures into the open, with the Left withdrawing its support from the government over the decision, and forcing Singh's government to face a no-confidence vote, which it eventually overcame.[6] PM Singh's government also invested in strengthening India's relations with Japan, which has seen considerable development since then. The second term of the government, however, was plagued with political indecisiveness and was riddled with multiple scandals that had an adverse impact on India's foreign policy as well.

The government led by Narendra Modi came to power in 2014 promising a decisive and focussed foreign policy without any assumptions about the need for alliance politics. A tough policy vis-à-vis Pakistan and China was spoken in many circles with emphasis on application of 'hard power' for strategic needs. The most prominent change with the new government under PM Modi, however, has been the emphasis on deepening strategic ties with major powers like US, Japan, France, and Germany (among others). The relationship with the US has been the highlight of the new government with critical developments in their bilateral relations. But the Modi government's approach has also been to focus on developing meaningful security and strategic partnerships with the major powers, but not at the cost of India's 'strategic autonomy'. This was demonstrated by India's independent position regarding trade issues,[7] its vote with regards to Jerusalem in General Assembly,[8] and also in India's pursuit of relations with countries like Russia.

India's response to its strategic environment has therefore been a function of the nature of its political leadership, their ideological preferences and the contemporary issues that needed to be tackled. There has not been a single, coherent, comprehensive assessment of India's strategic environment and its responses consequently have been episodic and ad hoc. This fact becomes even starker when the response to the individual security and strategic threats are examined, be it in the realm of interstate threats or intrastate threats. Since independence, two prominent state-level strategic threats for India have emerged: from Pakistan and China respectively. It is to these issues that the chapter now turns.

India's Relationship with Pakistan

One of the enduring inheritances of India's independence has been its rivalry with Pakistan and the threat Islamabad has posed to Indian security. Speaking strictly in hard power terms, Pakistan lags substantially behind India in terms of military strength,[9] except in numbers of nuclear weapons (where Pakistan is estimated to have more than India).[10] Conventionally, however, India has always maintained an advantage over Pakistan. Yet Pakistan has been a constant source of irritation, and it continues to be a major source of India's insecurity. So far, India has fought four wars with Pakistan: in 1948, in 1965, 1971, and 1999, and border skirmishes continue perpetually. At the heart is the unsettled issue of Kashmir. Pakistan continues to look at Kashmir, a Muslim majority state right at its border, as unfinished territorial division. Some scholars have also argued that the problem between the two states moves beyond the Kashmir conundrum and the root cause of the persisting rivalry is the ideological moorings of Pakistan, which essentially are revisionist—ideologically and even religiously—and anti-status quoist. Therefore to assume that a solution to the Kashmir issue will ensure peace between the countries is misplaced, as the problem transcends the Kashmir problem where goal of Pakistan is "to undermine India's position in the region and beyond".[11] Given the nature of the conflict and the individual country's position on various issues, most particularly on Kashmir, India–Pakistan continues to be one of the most intractable conflicts and it is unlikely that full normalization of relations will be achieved in the near future.[12] The tensions are likely to get aggravated with the change of status-quo is Kashmir after the revocation of the special status of the region in the Indian constitution, a promise on which BJP has campaigned for long. The revocation of the special status attracted provocative response from the Pakistan Army which pledged to "go to any extent to support people in the contested Kashmir region".[13] While government in New Delhi saw it as the 'full integration'[14] of the Jammu & Kashmir to India, the Indian Home Minister was categorical in stating that Pakistan Occupied Kashmir (PoK) and Aksai Chin are part of Kashmir too,[15] which reportedly as irked Chinese.[16]

In light of its obvious military disadvantage, Pakistan has worked on a two pronged-strategy to respond to its strategic rivalry with India. First, it has sought to engage with major powers in an attempt to gain strategic equivalence with India. Its geopolitical significance made Pakistan an invaluable ally for the US during the entire Cold War where the US had bases to watch over Soviet moves in South Asia. Pakistan was also part of the SEATO and CENTO security alliances which offered a military umbrella to Pakistan. It was also critical to the US during the Afghanistan conflict. After a relative decline in its importance in the post-Cold War era, the indispensability of Pakistan for American War on Terror thrust Pakistan again into the global spotlight. Pakistan also cultivated a special relationship with China, and has continued to do so even when its relationship with US has appeared strained. This has Pakistan with additional leverage in the region. Beyond geo-economics, Pakistan has also been critical in allowing China to contain India's desire for regional dominance, which has served as an additional rationale for China's policy.

The second component of Pakistan's strategy has been its continued attempt to wage sub-conventional war on India by using proxies, including terrorists, and supporting various insurgent and separatist movements in India. Pakistan did that in the Khalistan movement during the 1980s in Punjab and continues to do so in Kashmir today. The policy of using proxies became more attractive after the war in Afghanistan, where disenchanted Islamists from Afghanistan were strategically used in Pakistan's efforts to destabilize Kashmir. Afghani militants received ISI training, and were provided with the support necessary to use them as agents in Kashmir.[17] This policy attained a new dynamic under the nuclear umbrella where the possibility of a full scale Indian conventional retaliation became ill-advised. Nuclear weapons, being the most potent equalizers, have made full conventional war between India and Pakistan highly unlikely, if not outright impossible. The asymmetric war-games have thus become a routine Pakistani approach to bleed India by thousand cuts.

India's response to Pakistan's continued proxy war has reflected primarily a three-fold approach: defence, diplomacy, and dialogue. New Delhi has tried to build defensive capabilities against anticipated attacks from Pakistan by using intelligence and military means. India's diplomacy has included attempts at coercive approaches, along with raising the issue of terrorism in multi-lateral forums like the UN, ASEAN, and others, with the aim of creating an international discourse favourable to Indian sensitivities. The second component, however, has only occasionally yielded results given Pakistan's use of its global and regional allies. The third component of Indian strategy—dialogue—has been geared around engaging Pakistan on a range of issues to keep channels of negotiation open. However, a major problem in dealing with Pakistan through dialogue has been the existence of diarchy in the Pakistani state, whereby its Army wields a disproportionate say in foreign and security matters, often bypassing the civilian leadership. The existence of two power structures in Pakistan creates prolonged socio-political instability, and has made it difficult for New Delhi to directly engage with the government to discuss the issue.

India's response across various governments has therefore primarily been defensive and reactionary. The difficulty of framing a military response is the 'fear of escalation' which might breach the nuclear threshold between the two rivals. Even after 26/11 attacks, when there was no dearth of proof to link terrorist and proxy attacks directly to Pakistan, India reconsidered its initial decision to attack Pakistan, finally settling on diplomatic and other means.[18] There has however been an occasional change of course in the Indian approach. Operation Parakram, for instance, was an attempt at coercive military diplomacy by the Indian government after the terrorist attacks on Indian Parliament in 2001 which took the form of a full-scale mobilization of armed forces across the border for nearly ten months. The effectiveness of Parakram continues to be debated,[19] however it was a first attempt at Indian retaliation which brought the two nations almost to the brink of war. Similarly, the doctrine of Cold Start had its roots in the Indian response after the Parliament Attack, and was aimed at allowing Indian forces to conduct sustained attacks across the border while preventing nuclear retaliation from Pakistan. The essence of the doctrine was swift movement of forces, thereby retaining the element of surprise, while carrying out attacks. The doctrine was seen as a departure from previous defensive strategies and heralded a new attempt to craft a proactive response, even though the Indian Army denied the existence of such a doctrine[20] until the Army Chief General Bipin Rawat accepted its existence in 2017.[21] In the absence of any comprehensive doctrine of response to Pakistani provocation, the Indian approach is generally summed up as that of 'strategic restraint', where overt military retaliation was consciously eschewed in favour of relying mostly on diplomatic and defensive means.

The Modi government however attempted a change of course. In response to the Uri Terrorist Attack, Indian Army conducted 'surgical strikes' via cross-border military operations against terror launch-pads in Pakistan Occupied Kashmir, killing "terrorists and those providing support to them".[22] It was a more decisive military response to unprovoked Pakistani aggression through its proxy terror networks in the form of a highly publicized attack, with the government coming out in open acknowledgement of its operations. Similarly, in response to the Jaish orchestrated terror attacks in Pulwama, which killed more than 40 CRPF men, India conducted 'non-military pre-emptive' surgical Air Strikes in Balakot in Khyber Pakhtunkhwa region of Pakistan and destroyed one of the largest terror installations run by Jaish.[23] The significance of the Balakot strike was that the strikes were in the sovereign territory of Pakistan, implicitly implying that an armed response to unprovoked aggression by Pakistani state through proxies is conceivable. The critical aspect to note of these surgical strikes is the justification of the Indian army that these were 'anti-terror' operations rather than military retaliation against Pakistan per se, and that it was the legitimate right of any sovereign state to pre-empt such terror attacks.[24]

The new response framework attempted by the Modi government is significant with two critical components. One, the military response was well co-ordinated with the diplomatic manoeuvrings. A largely favourable international response towards India after the surgical strike and the Balakot air strikes points to this fact. It also hinted towards Pakistan's diplomatic vulnerability with regard to its support to terrorism. And second, it exposed Pakistan's nuclear bluff—the blackmail under which Pakistan has continued the relentless export of terrorism to India and managed to avert any punitive armed retaliation. Apart from this, the approach challenged the 'strategic restraint' paradigm and attested that an armed response which doesn't cross the nuclear threshold is possible. While it may be argued that such 'strikes' are unlikely to prevent Pakistan from supporting terrorism, the utility of the new approach in increasing the cost for perpetrators to wage such a war is significant to note. The credible deterrence disproportionately increases the costs of an operation than the expected benefits. Such armed strikes, apart from neutralizing imminent threat, would be critical for increasing the costs for those instigating and supporting this asymmetric conflict. The success of this new approach however depends heavily on India's defence preparedness and the capacity differential between the two militaries.

Sino-Indian Tensions

India's relations with China have been turbulent since the 1962 Sino-Indian War. Although cordiality is often expressed in the political level as well as in diplomatic circles, the realization of the threat emanating from an increasingly assertive and aggressive China has recently become more acute in New Delhi. This has become further aggravated with the intermittent border skirmishes and the open diplomatic one-upmanship the two countries often indulge in. For India, China poses a two-fold strategic threat. Firstly, it is a direct military threat. Overall militarily, the power differential between the two is disproportionately in favour of China. China today has around 2.3 million personnel active in service with around 6,457 in combat tanks, 4,788 armoured fighting vehicles and 6,246 towered artillery and 1,770 rocket batteries. India lags far behind at around 1.2 million active personnel with 4,426 combat tanks, 6,704 armoured fighting vehicles and 7,414 towered artillery and 290 rocket batteries.[25] Similarly, China's naval assets include 714 vessels with two air craft carriers in service and one under construction, along with 68 submarines. India's navy comprises 295 vessels with one aircraft carrier in service, and one expected to be commissioned by 2020,[26] along with 15 submarines. China also recently commissioned its new fifth generation aircraft into service, which marks a substantial leap in its air defence capabilities,[27] a sign which has worried New Delhi, along with its ongoing rollout of the Russian-built S400 surface to air missile system. While the aforementioned Chinese conventional and nuclear inventory help assuage Chinese threat concerns emanating from the US and Japan on its Eastern front, the growing Chinese assertiveness on the Indian side—as was evident during the Doklam standoff, the rapid infrastructural build up on the border areas and a proactive, offensive military restructuring within the PLA,[28] has intensified apprehensions in New Delhi. And though India is working to augment its defensive and offensive capabilities, it still lags behind China on conventional as well nuclear parameters. Even India's infrastructural preparedness along the border lacks sophistication when compared to China's ability to mobilize. The unsettled and often troubling border dispute with Beijing, its increasing defence budget (which is now almost three times more that of India) and its improved logistics capabilities along the border compounds the military threat China poses to India, which is likely to endure for the foreseeable future.

The second component in India's threat perceptions concerns China's increasing influence in the India's neighbourhood. The most critical component of this is the China–Pakistan axis. In its effort to keep the South Asian space divided and contain the Indian presence in the region, China has cultivated a special relationship with Pakistan which includes direct military and diplomatic support, help in building critical infrastructure and its open siding with Pakistan over major international issues. China has also thwarted India's attempts to list Pakistani-based terrorists on the UN sanctions list, thereby giving Pakistan a sense of impunity. But the most significant and arguably most worrying development for India from this interaction is the China–Pakistan Economic Corridor (CPEC), a part of China's ambitious Belt and Road Initiative (BRI) project, which passes through the Indian territory of Jammu and Kashmir occupied by Pakistan. India has strongly opposed CPEC, arguing that it violates India's sovereignty,[29] thereby becoming the most vocal opponents to China's BRI.

Along with Pakistan, China has also proved to be an external balancer for other South Asian countries. China's rapid strategic inroads in countries like Sri Lanka, Bangladesh, the Maldives, and Nepal has exacerbated New Delhi's concerns of perceived Chinese encirclement. Chinese influence also extends to other Indian Ocean littoral states where it is fast expanding its footprint to increase its oceanic presence.[30] Along with its growing influence in the South Asian region, China has also sought to contain India's presence in multilateral forums like the NSG and continue to be an obstacle in India's quest towards permanent membership at Security Council.

Under Xi's leadership, China is making no secret of its expansionist ambitions. Xi's address to the 19th Congress of Chinese Communist Party was an exposition of the distinctive 'Chinese dream' which focussed not only on the domestic reformation but had global ambitions of 'exporting Chinese model of governance' to world and the intent of applying hard power for domestic as well as global ambitions. The BRI project is seen as a way to establish economic and strategic supremacy over China's peers. For New Delhi, expanding Chinese influence, backed by its strong military along with an open adversarial international posturing is a direct security threat. And as China's influence grows it is likely to constrain India's strategic capacity to pursue its interests.

While the perception of the Chinese threat has been well-recognized in New Delhi, it is yet to evolve a strong, cohesive strategic rejoinder. Mostly its response has been tactical and episodic, often changing with the change in governments. Apart from the differing approaches of the governments, two other factors directly impact India's China policy. First, the structural environment which essentially implies the nature of global and regional balance of power. During the post-Cold war for instance, with hegemonic US the relative structural stability helped Indo–China relations to grow. The change in the structural dynamics with the rise of China altered the equations substantially. Second, and arguably more important, is India's strategic equations with other major powers. Given the capacity differential between the two, the possibility to internally balance China in the short run is limited. India therefore needs strong strategic partners to frame a concrete response. The impact of all these variables has resulted in a seemingly fluctuating China policy.

The Cold War period saw a troubled phase for bi-lateral relations with a major defeat in 1962, which is generally attributed to the inability of India to correctly predict Chinese intentions.[31] Subsequently, India primarily attempted to internally balance China by augmenting its own capabilities and at times relying on Soviet diplomatic support.[32] The end of the Cold War saw a steady improvement in India–China relations as both nations attempted to create a framework to peacefully solve outstanding disputes. With domestic reforms ongoing in both countries, they primarily focussed on developing good economic relations and boosting trade cooperation. America's undisputed hegemony initially provided relative structural stability in the immediate post-Cold War period that enabled states like India to pursue foreign policy without the compulsions of power-rivalries.

Yet the rise of China, especially after the 2008 economic melt-down and relative decline of the US, has changed the structural calculus drastically, and has altered the strategic environment for India both regionally as well as globally. China's rise has also translated into growing assertiveness in the South China Sea, and it is now attempting to exert its influence across the Indo-Pacific. In dealing with China, New Delhi's approach has been markedly ad hoc and non-linear, and has oscillated from attempting to align with China to hedging as well as soft-balancing. Primarily, India has attempted to reach out to China to ease the tensions by hedging its options. There was a practical consideration behind such an approach. First, given the power differential between the two, internal balancing against China in short run was not possible. The other significant component was India's scepticism regarding America's utility as a probable balancer against China, especially against the backdrop of US showing signs of getting closer to China and attempting to build partnerships on global issues. In the absence of a possible 'external balancer', India attempted to build cordial relations with Beijing, alongside exploring the possibility of deeper strategic partnerships with the US and Japan.

The Modi government in 2014 attempted a new direction which slanted towards what can be generally assumed as 'soft-balancing'. To that effect, the emphasis of the new administration was on building ties with like-minded states such as the US, Japan, and Vietnam which has direct implications for its China policy. The most significant indication of this was India's attempt to upgrade ties with US by overcoming its "historical hesitations".[33] The implication was clear—India was willing to move beyond the rhetoric of Non-Alignment. This was first reflected in India and the US signing and operationalizing the bilateral Logistics Exchange Memorandum of Agreement (LEMOA) which extends the General Security of Military Information Agreement (GSOMIA) of 2002[34] by giving the militaries of both countries access to each other's facilities for supplies and repairs.[35] The agreement was dubbed as a kind of 'soft-alliance' since it was one of only four similar arrangements between the US and those nations it considers close defence partners. In 2018, the two countries also signed the third of the 'foundational agreements', Communications Compatibility and Security Agreement (COMCASA)' which resulted in the first-ever secure communication link between the Indian Naval Headquarters and the US Central as well as Pacific Naval Commands.[36]

The intent of adopting a 'soft-balancing' approach also became clear with the re-emergence of the "Quad" grouping, and regularizing the Indian-sponsored Malabar exercises, along with the participation of Japan. India also consciously evolved its relationship with Japan to deepen security and defence ties. In a significant development, India and Japan also plan to develop India's North-Eastern states as a "concrete symbol of developing synergies", which irked Beijing.[37] Normatively too, India and Japan have attempted to counter the Chinese model of BRI by providing an 'inclusive alternative' to it in the form of the Asia Africa Growth Corridor (AAGC). India also signed a 'LEMOA-like' agreement with France, which enables the use of each other's military facilities including opening of naval bases to warships.[38] This is significant considering the stakes France has in the Indian Ocean region and common concerns of an expansionist China.

A relatively troubled phase in Indo–US partnership with increasingly inward looking and protectionist US and arguably unpredictable President Trump along with a protracted US–China trade war has actually led India to reorient its approach vis-à-vis China from attempting to balance to hedging. Since the Wuhan informal summit in 2018, India's attempt to sustain cordiality with China has been very visible with India's conspicuous silence in the recent China–Vietnam stand-off, its perceived indifference regarding China's South China Sea manoeuvrings[39] and an apparent lack of interest in operationalizing QUAD into a strong defence grouping. Though China is seen to be reciprocating the cordiality, it is not readily evident if India's hedging can sustain given a recalcitrant China's growing assertiveness. Even in its 2019 defence white paper, China has made no secret of its military ambitions in the South China Sea when it declared that "the South China Sea islands and Diaoyu Islands are inalienable parts of the Chinese territory. China exercises its national sovereignty to build infrastructure and deploy necessary defensive capabilities on the islands and reefs in the South China Sea".[40] The indications are therefore clear: in the absence of the possibility to internally balance China in short term, New Delhi needs to forge strong strategic and defence partnerships with major powers and with other states that have a direct stake in balancing the rise of China. But given India's concerns regarding the 'prospective strong partner' and the accompanying structural dynamics impacting India's strategic calculations, India's approach is likely to respond to these realities. Moreover, apart from external security challenges, India continues to face significant internal security challenges, which consume a large portion of the Indian state's resources, and are important in any assessment of its national security posture.

Left Wing Extremism

Left Wing Extremism (LWE), primarily identified with the armed insurgency by Maoist rebels, has had a long history in India. The Political Communist Movement emerged in India in the early 1920s, and since then it has branched into numerous offshoots. Some of these, like Communist Party of India (CPI) and Communist Party of India (Marxist) (CPI-M) have adopted the democratic processes of the country and participate in elections, while others have rejected the legitimacy of the Indian state and have waged an armed struggle to overthrow it. The most prominent among the latter is the Communist Party of India (Maoist). Designated as a terrorist organization under Unlawful Activities (Prevention) Act and thereby banned, the CPI (Maoists) came to prominence in 2004 by merging within itself various ultra-radical, armed rebel groups like Maoist Communist Centre of India (MCCI) and the People's War Group.[41] The rise the CPI (Maoist) ushered in one of the most violent phases in the history of independent India. In 2006 Manmohan Singh, then Prime Minister, said that "it would not be an exaggeration to say that the problem of Naxalism is the single biggest internal security challenge ever faced by our country".[42]

The origin of the armed Maoist struggle is generally traced back to the Telangana Revolt which saw large-scale Communist participation.[43] The radical ideological influences of Maoism thereafter started spreading in different parts of country, prominently in West Bengal and Andhra Pradesh thereby giving momentum to its more radical and violent brand. The influence resonated most with the peasants and the labourers who occasionally resorted to violence for seizure of land and revolting against the local landowners.[44] The first manifestation of a violent uprising was in response to the killing of 11 people in a police shooting in the village of Naxalbari in West Bengal on May 25, 1967, which soon spread to parts of Andhra Pradesh, Bihar, Orissa, the Punjab, and Uttar Pradesh.[45] However, a more organized and concerted revolt was facilitated by the formation of Communist Party of India (Marxist–Leninist) under the leadership of Charu Majumdar in 1969. Within a few years of the formation of CPI-ML, the violent movement had spread, engulfing the entire state of West Bengal, along with a sizeable footprint in Bihar and Andhra Pradesh, among others. The violence reached a peak in 1971 with an estimate of over 3,650 violent incidents involving the killing of over 850 "class-enemies" (landlords, money lenders, police officials, and informers).[46]

The movement seemed to fizzle out in the mid-1970s with a state led counter-insurgency campaign comprising of joint operations involving police, central paramilitary forces and army. But it re-emerged with the formation of People's War Group (PWG) in Andhra Pradesh in the early 1980s under the leadership of K. Seetharamaiah. With the help of its armed squads referred to as *Dalams*, the PWG primarily indulged in attacks on the police, kidnappings, and killing of political leaders and civilians. The 'struggle' was complemented by groups like the Maoist Communist Centre (MCC), which was active primarily in Bihar. These contributed to the resurgence of the Maoist violence, which peaked again in the early 1990s. Affected states assisted by the Centre renewed their counterinsurgency efforts that targeted these different Maoist outfits. Bans were imposed on organizations suspected to be complicit in violence, and force was used to address the new wave of violence. These efforts apparently yielded results in terms of reducing the Naxal violence by either eliminating the rebels or by forcing them to surrender.[47]

With violence largely contained, the movement nonetheless remained strong underground. The decades of the 1990s and the early 2000s were marked by a phase of mergers and consolidation whereby different groups coordinated their strategies and attempted to form common ground to rebuild the movement.[48] The most significant and arguably most concerning merger for India's internal security was the formation of Communist Party of India (Maoist) which was formed primarily by merging of PWG and MCCI. The CPI (Maoist) continues to be the biggest, most influential and lethal Left Wing Extremist organization to date, ranking fourth among the world's deadliest terror outfits after the Taliban, IS, and Boko Haram.[49] CPI (Maoist) unleashed a new phase of terror which spread rapidly throughout the areas referred to as the "Red Corridor". The attacks on security personnel and police, kidnappings, and extortions increased significantly as the movement acquired greater sophistication and lethality. An estimated US$18.4 million has been extorted annually from government offices, contractors, businessmen, and industrialists from the period of 2004 to 2011, the time when the movement was at its peak.[50] Almost 5,800 people, including civilians and security forces, were killed during the same period, the bloodiest year being 2010 where an estimate of 1,100 died as a result of Naxal violence in a single year.[51] Since then, there has been a downward trajectory in LWE in India though there still continue to be around 90 Naxal-affected districts, including 30 which the government is focusing on. Yet any government approach which is devoid of plans to cater the realities that drive people to LWE is unlikely to yield results. These include low social-economic status, education deficits, and 'negative externalities' coming from developmental projects like land grabbing and displacement, which continue to be main drivers for the movement.

State Responses to LWE

There appears to be a general recognition that the issues which instigated and strengthened the Naxal movement was the state's inability to provide a healthy socio-economic environment, resulting in the marginalization of certain sections of society. This was amplified by feelings among peasants and labourers regarding the 'imperial tendencies' of the state, which on one hand encroached upon the rights of the tribal people, and on the other was seen as complicit in the activities of those whom Naxals identified as 'class enemies'. It has also been argued that Maoist violence is the consequence of commercialization of forest resources resulting into widespread tribal unrest.[52] Those arguing that such causes are at the root of Naxal unrest maintain that the solution for this problem should essentially be political rather than via the use of force. The Indian government on the other hand, though recognizing the socio-economic causes behind the insurgency, broadly appears to have seen it as essentially a law and order problem, and has tried to deal it primarily by coercion, along with keeping political channels open from time to time. But on each occasion, although the use of force has yielded temporary results, the movements keep returning. This has led to the questioning of the approach successive governments have taken in addressing the issue of LWE.

One expression that is most commonly observed in the government narratives regarding tackling LWE is that it has employed a 'holistic approach' to the problem of Maoist violence. The contours and specifics of the government response, however, have largely been episodic, at times reactionary, and also undifferentiated. Here the state's response can broadly be characterized as a two-pronged approach: first, developing legal structures and using force; and second, providing special developmental assistance to the region. Arguably the first aspect has dominated, which inevitably involves banning radical organizations (thereby enabling security agencies to act against them), and devising counterinsurgency plans for attending the problems. A significant operation in this context was Operation Steepalchase in 1971, which was followed by imposing Presidential rule in West Bengal, and bringing in the Army to address Naxal violence.[53] The operation yielded results, as a large number of Naxalites were killed and many more were arrested—including the leader of the movement, Charu Majumdar, who eventually died in custody.[54] Operation Greenhunt was other major operation which originated in 2009 to take on Naxalism institutionally across India's regional states in a co-ordinated approach involving central paramilitary forces along with local forces.[55] Again, while operations such as these seemed initially to produce results, they were only temporary, with the Maoists responded back strongly with increased violence and high profile attacks on each occasion.

Considering the fact that broadly, the government viewed this problem as a law and order issue, the responsiveness of the individual affected states in the overall counter-insurgency operation was an important determinant of the overall effectiveness of State's response to left wing extremism. The responses of the states however has revealed varying degrees of success and even willingness to counter Naxal violence. There is no unanimity among the states regarding the way they viewed the issue of Maoist violence. So, while states such as Chhattisgarh and Tamil Nadu have proscribed the CPI (Maoist), West Bengal for long appeared to be dragging its feet.[56] Even the capacities differ from state to state. For instance, Andhra Pradesh's elite state level special force (called the 'Grey Hound' forces, specializing in anti-insurgency operations against the Maoists), are considered to be the finest anti-insurgency force conducting anti-Maoist operations, supported by their expertise in jungle warfare.[57] Other states do not necessarily have such trained combat forces to deal with Maoists and therefore rely on the centre's support, along with the local police. The differentiated state responses have also sometimes produced methods that received heavy criticism from various human rights organizations and other related institutions. For instance, the infamous *Salwa Judum* was one such initiative where state government in Chhattisgarh was found to be sponsoring counter-militias by offering guns, money, and other required logistical support. Apart from fostering human rights abuses, the move backfired also because the Maoist gained local sympathies due to the abuse of power by the local rival tribes supported by the government. The *Salwa Judum* was eventually banned by the Supreme Court, and the state government was ordered to disband its forces immediately.[58]

While India's states have continued to devise their own counter-insurgency plans, the centre plays the role of supporting state efforts. Within the Ministry of Home Affairs, a separate division established in 2006 called the Left Wing Extremism Division has the primary purpose of monitoring the LWE situation and the counter-measures being taken by the affected States. Apart from the deployment of Central Armed Police Forces (CAPFs) in LWE-affected States, the division also looks at the capacity building efforts of states to combat LWE though the Ministry of Home Affairs Security Related Expenditure (SRE) scheme, the Special Infrastructure Scheme, and Special Central Assistance, all of which provide support for initiatives to combat LWE in the form of funding and other assistance.[59] The creation of this division has led to an institutionalization of a more coordinated and cohesive state response to the Maoist challenge. Yet questions about its efficiency remain.

The NDA government in 2015 launched the National Policy and Action Plan in 2015, covering security, development, ensuring rights, and the entitlements of local communities. Under the new policy roadmap, the government has incorporated various programs and schemes dealing with the security and development aspects for the affected districts in the state. The new policy direction, incorporating a 'multi-pronged' approach, according to the government, is yielding results. Indeed, official statistics do indicate that since 2014 there has been a steady decline in the number of attacks. For instance, there has been an overall 26.7% reduction in violent incidents (1136 to 833) and 39.5% reduction (397 to 240) in LWE related deaths since end-2013. In comparison to 2017, the year 2018 saw a decline of 8.3% (908 to 833) in incidents of violence and the number of deaths by 8.7% (263 to 240). Even developmental outreach, the government claims, has resulted in an increasingly large number of LWE cadres shunning the path of violence based on the improvement in the numbers of those who have been arrested and forced to surrender.[60]

While there are signs of an evolving institutionalized and co-ordinated approach to tackle LWE, it is not readily evident if the same of pattern of violence will resurface after a period of decline, as in the past. Ad hocism in state response and differentiated approaches persist within the establishment which point towards a lack of well-defined and long term strategic goal to address the problem of LWE. So far, the trend shows that the approach is dependent of incumbent state and central governments. This can pose a serious challenge to the sustainability of current trends.

Insurgency in the Northeast

Insurgency in the north-eastern part of India affects the seven states of Assam, Meghalaya, Tripura, Arunachal Pradesh, Mizoram, Manipur, and Nagaland (often referred as ''Seven Sisters''). Though conventionally the insurgency is collectively referred as the 'northeast insurgency', the reality is quite complex in each of the seven states owing to multiple demands from insurgents in each of them, ranging from claims to autonomy to insistence on a separate independent state. Even the level of violence has differed spatially. The history of insurgency in the northeast goes back to the time of Indian independence where it was first manifested in Nagaland. At the root of the insurgency is the assertion of a distinct identity separate from the Indian nation. Consequently, many groups from the north-eastern part of India opposed the incorporation of their territories within the Indian state, pointing out that even administratively they were separate during colonial times.[61] Geographically too, the northeast is connected to India by the slim 28 km Siliguri Corridor, and the region shares almost 98% of its borders with Bangladesh, Bhutan, Myanmar, and China. This slim geographical contiguity, complemented by historical factors linked to ethnic identities, accentuates the feeling of distinctiveness that led to the emergence of different insurgent movements in these states.

The northeast is also characterized by incredible diversity in terms of ethnicity and language, with a conglomeration of around 475 ethnic groups and sub-groups speaking over 400 languages and dialects.[62] Often the cause of resentment has been inter-ethnic rivalries, exacerbated by the perceived demographic tension caused by the large-scale 'migration' of 'outsiders'. These issues have been aggravated by the overall poor state of socio-economic development and a widespread feeling of exploitation and alienation.[63] A prominent narrative north-eastern insurgents have sought to build concerns the distinctiveness of their identity and New Delhi's indifference towards the genuine concerns of the local people. As the insurgency turned increasingly violent, the Indian state resorted to the use of force against rebel groups, further intensifying anti-New Delhi sentiments among the locals. Repressive laws like the Armed Forces Special Powers Act (AFSPA) have been routinely subjected to criticism by not just locals, but also by the various human rights groups and civic and political leaders.[64]

When seen from the perspective of the state, the instability in these areas represents a grave threat in India's overall security calculations. All states in the northeast share borders with countries like China, Bangladesh (earlier East Pakistan), Myanmar and Bhutan. To maintain order in these strategically crucial areas is imperative. Furthermore, insurgent groups in the northeast have developed external linkages and were receiving active and also indirect support from neighbouring countries.[65] As violence escalated and insurgent groups started forming inter-linkages, the use of force has turned into a necessity.

Indian Responses to Insurgencies in the Northeast

India's response to the insurgency in the northeast has broadly followed the pattern which was for the first time articulated by the Indian Army as the Doctrine of Sub-conventional Operations in 2006. The doctrine articulated an apparently sequential approach[66] which employs "various elements of national power to gain control of the affected area and address root causes of the conflict". The first component of the doctrine is the "Creation of Secure Environment", which in effect means to quell upsurges in violence, and to compel the rebels to give up their arms, thereby paving way for a political process. The second component of the doctrine is "Isolation of Conflict Zone" which is aimed at preventing any external or internal support which may help in prolonging the insurgency. The first component essentially entails the role of army and other security forces, while the second requires diplomatic as well as security dimensions. The third component of the doctrine is "Addressing Local Aspirations and Winning Hearts and Minds" which seeks to create an enduring environment for peace ensuring full liberties alongside the effective functioning of the state. This naturally entails initiating the political process of negotiation. And the fourth component, which runs in parallel to all the other above-mentioned components, is "Public Information and Perception Management" where the diplomatic channels to shape international opinion as well as state channels for doing so internally are involved.

A careful study of Indian responses to northeast insurgency reveals that India has indeed applied the above formulation in the region. The emphasis on the security aspect, however, has been more pronounced. Political negotiations, for instance, always have two non-negotiable components—of territorial integrity and the ambit of India's constitutional framework. Thus the question of allowing a separate State has never been seriously entertained.[67] So when the insurgency first broke in the Nagaland in early 1950s, after unsuccessful attempts by the Assam police to restore order, the Indian Army was sent in April 1956 to destroy rebel bases and infrastructure. In the intensive operation that followed an estimated 4,000 people were arrested, while a further 3,000 surrendered voluntarily.[68] To create a legal foundation and enable the Army to carry out counter-insurgency operations within the State, India's government passed the Armed Forces Special Powers Act (AFSPA) in 1958. Once a troubled part was designated as a "disturbed area" the army was then delegated special powers to maintain law and order within the areas affected. As per the provisions of the Act, the armed forces are also permitted, if reasonable suspicion exists regarding possibility of a possible breakdown of law and order, to open fire, arrest people without a warrant, and can enter and search any premises to make any arrests.[69] AFSPA has been under heavy criticism due to the alleged excesses committed by the armed forces under the cover of AFSPA in these areas towards the locals.[70]

This can be demonstrated by the insurgency that broke out in Mizoram, when the Mizo National Front (MNF) declared independence after its famed Operation Jericho in 1966. In response, India's Army was sent in to crush the revolt. Even the Air Force was used for airstrikes in the places like Aizwal.[71] Arguably, it was in Mizoram where the Army was seen to be most active and at times brutal. Following the squashing of the revolt, the insurgency continued, and so did the state's counter-insurgency. After the first ground and air attacks, those who survived the assault went in hiding in jungles and hills to continue guerrilla attacks. In the process the rebels mixed with the civilian population so that effective counter-insurgency operation without civilian casualties became extremely difficult. To tackle this, government launched an alternative strategy to quell insurgency called *Operation Accomplishment*. Under this, a large scale resettlement of the villages was adopted in three phases beginning in January 1967. The idea was to isolate the insurgents from the local population and carry out a targeted counter-insurgency operation to minimize civilian casualties. Almost 240,000 persons constituting some 80% of the total population in the Mizo Hills were relocated to what were termed "Protected and Progressive Villages" (PPV) in the years until 1972.[72] *Operation Accomplishment* was eventually abandoned due to mounting protests from political parties and human rights organizations. Violence continued and so did the army operation within the state, and by 1975 the insurgents were forced to negotiate with the centre. By 1986, a peace accord was signed and insurgent commander Laldenga won the local election for the position of Chief Minister of Mizoram, effectively ending the protracted insurgency in the state.[73]

A similar approach was evident in other troubled north-eastern states. With the onset of insurgency in Manipur during the 1980s, the entire Imphal valley was declared a "disturbed" area and the Army was brought in. The insurgency still endures in the state of Manipur with AFSPA applicable throughout the state, excluding seven assembly constituencies of Imphal. Similarly, in Assam, the army has maintained a presence since the late 1970s. With an improvement in the situation within the state of Tripura, the AFSPA was revoked in 2015 after being in force for almost 18 years,[74] and similar decisions were made about Meghalaya and parts of Arunachal Pradesh in 2018.[75]

India's government has also used other methods to pacify insurgents and bring them to the negotiating table. These have included negotiating the levels of autonomy to be accorded to the different regions, announcing development packages, granting amnesty, and releasing arrested rebels to generate goodwill.[76] It has been suggested that emphasis on using such a developmental governance-led model to tackle insurgency was more a recent phenomenon when strategic considerations weighed more heavily in overall decision making. The key component here has been the initiation of India's Look East Policy in 1991 that necessitated a peaceful northeast as a bridge for India to connect its eastern and south-eastern neighbours.[77] While this may be true, attempts at brokering peace were made even before the 1990s with different rebel groups. The success of these negotiations has largely been dependent on the efficiency of the local administration,[78] the soundness of centre-state equations, and the will of the local leaders and populace in general to be part of the peace process.

The quest for a stable and peaceful northeast continues to this day, with states like Nagaland, Assam and Manipur still under the AFSPA, and insurgent factions still active in pockets. The Indian state's reliance on the army and other central forces to carry out counter-insurgency operations has been aimed at raising the opportunity cost for rebels of using violence, thereby making peace a viable option in attempts to tackle this issue. Even so, local misgovernance and heavy government intervention continues to lead to the re-emergence of the problem.

Terrorism in Punjab

Terrorism in Punjab is rooted in the demand for a separate state of Khalistan for the Sikhs. The assertion of Sikh identity manifested for the first time just after partition with a demand for separate state for Sikhs within India. While the grievances of certain Sikh factions over issues like the sharing of rivers and declaring Chandigarh as the capital of Punjab were settled politically, the situation was aggravated when radical groups within the Sikhs started demanding a separate state of Khalistan from India. The movement was spearheaded by Jarnail Singh Bhindranwale, who launched a militant movement to demand for Sikhs a separate State. Though in the initial phases, Bhindranwale was helped by the ruling Congress party which attempted to stoke Bhindranwale to outdo the Akali Dal in Punjab,[79] the nature of his demands and the accompanying violence soon spiralled out of control, resulting in one of the most violent insurgencies in India.

The first violent outburst in Punjab was the clash in April 1978 between the Nirankaris, a Sikh sect accused of apostasy, and a Bhindranwale's group of radical Sikhs. The clash resulted in death of 13 Sikhs along with Fauja Singh, who was accomplice of Bhindranwale. Radical Sikh groups went on to wage an extremely violent and bloody campaign, killing civilians, politicians, and the security forces. There was also an external dimension to the terrorist movement with the extremists getting direct support from Pakistan.[80] By 1984, Bhindranwale had made the Golden Temple (one of the most sacred places in Sikhism) as his refuge, and controlled all the terrorist activities from the Akal Takht within the Golden Temple. 1984 saw growing violence with terrorists killing an estimated 298 people between January 1 and June 3.[81] On June 3rd, the Indian Prime Minister Indira Gandhi ordered one of the most controversial operations, *Operation Blue Star*, with an aim to clear the Golden Temple of terrorists. Bhindrawale was eventually killed along with more than hundreds of security forces and almost 500 civilians in the crossfire.[82]

But *Operation Blue Star* did not achieve its desired results. Instead, it further estranged the already discontented Sikhs. As an act of revenge, two Sikh bodyguards assassinated Prime Minister Indira Gandhi, which was followed by massive anti-Sikh riots across Delhi and in parts of Punjab which killed nearly 3,000 members of India's Sikh community.[83] These events led to the second wave of Khalistani terrorism. K.P.S. Gill who is credited to have controlled and eventually suppressed the separatist movement in Punjab described Operation Blue Star and the anti-Sikh riots as "the two most significant victories for the cause of 'Khalistan'…not won by the militants, but inflicted…. upon the nation by its own Government… These two events, in combination, gave a new lease of life to a movement which could easily have been contained in 1984 itself".[84] The Rajiv Gandhi Government initiated peace process and tried to reach out the separatists and the Rajiv Gandhi–Longowal Accord was signed in July 1985 which temporarily halted the turbulence. The next decade was followed by concerted counter-insurgency operation led primarily by the Punjab Police and the movement was controlled and largely eliminated by the mid-1990s.

In dealing with the Khalistan movement, the Indian state's response fluctuated between "attempting to talk" and "use of force", both of which had no predetermined roadmap. The political intervention was detrimental at times to the process of counter-insurgency as it diluted military-security operations and gave time and space for the insurgents to regroup.[85] When force was used, for instance in *Blue Star*, its aftereffects were miscalculated, and ultimately proved counter-productive. By the mid-1980s the Punjab Police took over the entirety of counter-insurgency operations, and were ultimately much more successful in suppressing the separatist movement.

Terrorism in Jammu and Kashmir

Jammu and Kashmir was the first place in India where the strategies of resorting to terror for political objectives were witnessed, in the form of Pakistani-sponsored tribal aggression in 1948. Since then, Kashmir has been a centre of state-sponsored terrorism in India where proxies trained, financed and supported by Pakistan have been instrumental in creating a perpetual state of instability, especially after the 1980s. At the core of the Kashmir problem are separatist tendencies within a section of the Kashmiri population, and resentment with the central government in general, which was then instrumentalized by Pakistan to create and sustain the unrest. Since 1948, India and Pakistan have fought three wars, with two of them—in 1965 and 1999 respectively—being fought over Kashmir. Though the intervening decades after the Bangladesh war witnessed a relative calm, the peace was disturbed in the late 1980s with the trigger point being allegedly rigged state elections in 1987. The interference of Delhi in state affairs was resented heavily by the locals, and the rigging of elections intensified this. This was effectively used by Pakistan to trigger further unrest in the valley.

Two factors made the use of proxies to wage sub-conventional war a natural choice for Pakistan. First, successive defeats in conventional wars had rendered the utility of conventional war redundant. The second was the ready availability of 'agents' for sub-conventional wars to Pakistan in the form of Mujahideen after the Soviet departure from Afghanistan. This was arguably a simple task. All Pakistan had to do was to channel the Islamist narrative and integrate it with resentment in Kashmir to foment unrest. Pakistan thus started supporting the terrorism in Kashmir—by helping import the terrorist from outside Kashmir and also by supporting local rebels.[86]

The nature of Kashmir unrest changed from purely a demand for a separate state for ethnic Kashmiris to an apparently Islamist movement extensively controlled and abetted by Pakistan. Pakistan used the area of Kashmir controlled by its army to set up training camps, where terrorists were subsequently infiltrated into the areas under Indian control.[87] This continuous influx of terrorists and the resulting instability has affected the state adversely with poor socio economic conditions, low investments in the region, and lack of development. Tourism, which is the primary source of livelihood for most people is also severely affected due to the terrorist menace. And while there have been instances when the situation was fairly controlled, the peace has always been temporary with unrest resurfacing at regular intervals.

Indian position on Kashmir held by the subsequent governments largely had one basic pre-condition—the solution to the Kashmir issue will essentially be under the ambit of Indian constitution. This pre-empted the possibility of creation of separate state as Indian constitution has no provision for secession. The state of Jammu & Kashmir however since independence enjoyed a special status through the provision of Article 370 of Indian Constitution which accorded autonomy to the state government in all matters except defence, foreign policy and communications. Along with the Article 35 A of the Indian constitution—which defined the permanent citizens of the state—the state of Jammu and Kashmir enjoyed substantial power by considerably restricting the powers of central government in the state. Despite the 'Temporary and Transitional' nature of the Article,[88] it was almost assumed as the permanent feature until the Modi government revoked its special status by a Presidential order and bifurcated the state into two Union Territories—Jammu & Kashmir and Ladakh.[89]

Terrorism in Kashmir has an internal as well as an external dimension. The approach adopted by the subsequent governments primarily centred around the use of force to quell uprisings, deploying paramilitary forces to control the region, and the use of the Army for counter-insurgency operations.[90] The legal provisions like AFSPA enabled the Army to work in the state for counter-insurgency operations. Special constitutional provisions, economic packages, and government developmental schemes have been the other ways the government has attempted to address the problem in Kashmir.[91]

As far as the external dimension of the problem arising out of Pakistan is concerned, India's approach has mostly been defensive. Intermittently, the government has tried to address the issue through dialogue with Pakistan, but that has not resulted in anything substantial barring temporary arrangements to keep the peace. There is a deep-rooted feeling in New Delhi that a powerful constituency in the Pakistani Army is against any peace overtures with India, and attempts at peaceful dialogue have been regularly disturbed by a terrorist event in their lead-up. For instance, the UPA government under PM Manmohan Singh engaged in a sustained dialogue with his Pakistani counterparts which was said to have been on a positive track to resolve the problem of Kashmir.[92] But 2008 terror attacks on Mumbai disturbed the process and since then there has not been any such sustained attempt. Successive governments in New Delhi have attempted to continue with dialogue, but with the basic precondition that Pakistan works proactively in dismantling its terror network.

In absence of any substantial development on that front, it is unlikely that such a dialogue will produce any substantive outcome.

One of the biggest challenges in Kashmir has been to counter the separatist narrative within the state. This becomes even more pertinent with the revocation of the special status. While the decision is positively received in the Jammu and the Ladakh region of the state, there are concerns that it might aggravate tensions in the Kashmir Valley. Though the revocation of the special status is seen as a bold step, its success will largely depend on the way New Delhi is able to manage both—internal and external—dimensions of the problem.

India's response to the Kashmir issue has largely lacked a pre-determined road-maps with clear milestones. This is partly also because of the nature of conflict, where its external component is extremely active. And the changes in India's governments have impeded consistency in approach to Kashmir. As a result the pattern of cyclic violence and counter-violence from security forces and the terrorists has in effect been normalized, resulting in an unfortunate status quo which has prevented lasting peace in the region.

Conclusion

The pattern of India's response to its security challenges underscores its episodic and ad hoc nature, lacking in long term strategic direction and deliberate strategic goals. Two reasons can broadly be attributed to this. One is the lack of political consensus on major security challenges. This is most pronounced in the cases of relations with Pakistan and China. With regards to Pakistan, the public discourse in the country is sharply polarized between the necessities for a hard security response to any provocation by the state-backed terrorists on the one hand, versus calls for unrestricted diplomatic negotiations with Pakistan on the other. Stephen Cohen, for instance, identifies five different schools of thought regarding Pakistan in India, which range from the most accommodating to the most hard-line, all containing a mixture of pragmatic and idealistic approaches, and each raising specific implementation problems.[93] As argued thus far, the Indian response has oscillated between these extremes. It has also been mostly driven by the personality of the leader. The same problem is replicated even in the Kashmir issue, with different political parties approaching the Kashmir problem differently. In the absence of consensus, the policy has often changed along with changes in government, with each leader adding his own particular imprint.

Similarly, there is no consensus with regard to India's response to the perceived threat of China. While each of India's political parties has called for a peaceful and meaningful bilateral relations, there are still differing opinions on two counts: whether China really is a threat to India; and how to deal with it. The spectrum of opinion again involves viewing China as the most significant threat on one end, to China being a benevolent power and a trusted neighbour on the other. This lack of clarity too has occasioned an incoherent policy framework vis-a-vis Beijing, characterized by tactical shifts in policy responses.

A differentiated approach can also be witnessed concerning the Naxal/Maoist problem, where different Indian states have tended to adopt different approaches according to the ideological inclinations of the state governments. While the existence of diverging opinions in a democracy is healthy, these divergences, especially on strategic issues, have often been a major impediment in drafting coherent national security policy for India.

The lack of institutionalization of the security apparatus is a further impediment here, preventing a coordinated and systematic approach to national security that is operationalized at both the top and local levels. The security environment in and around India remains highly challenging, yet the institutional apparatus that is required to address it continues to remain weak. The most critical institution, the National Security Council (NSC), created in late 1990s, is still plagued with a lack of resources and the necessary powers to enforce decisions.[94] Successive governments have made promises to reform and revamp India's institutional capacity on this score, but each have failed to deliver. The Modi government came to office in May 2014 with a promise of reforming "the National Security Council to make it the hub of all sector-related assessments", and to "ensure greater participation of Armed Forces in the decision-making process of the Ministry of Defence". It also promised to "study in detail India's nuclear doctrine, and revise and update it, to make it relevant to challenges of current".[95]

Some steps to that effect have been initiated by the government with an intent to strengthen the existing institutionalized security architecture, and also create new institutions to complement existing ones. The most significant of those has been the creation of the Defence Planning Committee, which was set up by the government in 2018 to "to facilitate comprehensive planning for the defence forces besides focusing on military doctrines to deal with emerging security challenges for India".[96] Apart from concentrating on the issues of improving the defence manufacturing ecosystem as well as defence diplomacy, one of the critical issues which the Committee, chaired by the NSA, will look into is the drafting of a National Security Strategy, along with an international defence engagement strategy.[97] Another curious development has been the creation of Centre for Contemporary Chinese Studies (CCCS), a dedicated in-house think-tank of MEA focusing entirely on the developments within China and its implications for India. And within the existing National Security Council, the NSA will now be assisted by three Deputy NSAs, concentrating on external and technical intelligence, internal security matters, and on the handling diplomatic affairs respectively. The government also increased the budget of the National Security Council Secretariat (NSCS), tenfold from ₹ 33 crore in 2016–2017 to ₹333 crore in 2017–2018.[98]

These initial steps aimed at reforming the existing architecture are a welcome sign. But the efficacy of these new institutions will depend largely on the way India's political leadership allows them to evolve. The evidence so far suggests that there is general apathy in the political leadership towards institutional soundness. For instance, the Modi government took almost three years to re-constitute the National Security Advisory Board (NSAB) after the tenure of the previous one ended in 2015.[99] Also, the major reforms which have taken place over the years have mostly been triggered by crises like the 1999 Kargil War, the attack on the Indian Parliament in 2001 and the 26/11 terrorist attacks in Mumbai during 2008. These crises led to a serious public debate, prompting a reactive governmental response in terms of setting up of committees to review the security situation in the country. But even as that happened, the significant institutional shakeup which was expected has not materialized.

In the absence of a strong institutional setup, the NSC is therefore driven primarily by the National Security Advisor (NSA) and less by consistent institutional priorities. Personality thus dominates decision making, and given the fact the NSA is appointed by the Prime Minister, the approaches of each individual NSA have largely followed the approach of their respective Prime Minister. India even today continues to be highly under-staffed in terms of the external affairs ministry in New Delhi, and also in missions abroad. Considering India's growing stature and also its stakes in the global order, an understaffed foreign ministry continues to be a major impediment to India's ability to engage with the world. A direct implication of the lack of political consensus and a weak institutional framework has been the inability of India to come up with a politically acceptable, viable and coherent a National Security Strategy, much less generating the necessary political consensus to do so.

For a rising power like India, not having a defined strategy continues to be a significant challenge, especially when its neighbourhood is riddled with strategic competitions and it faces security threats emanating from non-conventional threats like terrorism (both state-backed and the non-state), left-wing extremism, piracy, drug trafficking, and others. The other major concern is an absence of a substantive public discourse on national security challenges facing the nation. Thus the conventionally low electoral salience of defence and security issues within the Indian populace also contribute to the relative neglect of these issues in public debate. National security never forms the core electoral agenda for any political party, except for rhetorical positioning vis-à-vis Pakistan or China, with discussion on these issues limited to Delhi-based elites in policy think- tanks, and only occasionally in the mainstream media. Without promoting a substantive public discussion, including among the major political parties, it is unlikely that the issue will be taken up seriously at the political level. Yet this only underscores the urgency for India to have a well-defined security strategy, which spells out the present and future security threats and clearly lays out a roadmap for policy direction.

Notes

1. Quoted in: Bhasin, A. S. (2018). *India and Pakistan: Neighbours at Odds*. London: Bloomsbury.
2. Excerpts from the text of Treaty of Peace, Friendship and Co-operation, 1971. For the full text of the Treaty, see https://mea.gov.in/bilateral-documents. htm?dtl/5139/Treaty+of+.
3. The disintegration of communist USSR that ended the Cold War was also translated as the victory of liberal democratic order led by the US. The most popular of such pronouncement came in the form of Fukuyama's famous thesis of 'End of History' which argued that the fall of the Soviet Union would lead to the universalization of Western liberal democracy as the final form of human government. See, Fukuyama, F. (1992). *The End of History and the Last Man*. New York: Free Press.
4. See for instance: Mohan, C. Raja. (2013). Beyond Non-Alignment. In Bajpai, K. P. & Pant H. V. (Eds.) *India's Foreign Policy: A Reader* (pp. 27–50) Oxford University Press.
5. Tillin, L. (2003). 'US–Israel–India: Strategic axis?' *BBC News*, 9 September, http://news.bbc.co.uk/2/hi/south_asia/3092726.stm.
6. The government, which was supported by the Left, had to face the vote of confidence after the Left withdrew its support over India's nuclear deal with US. See: BBC News. (2008). Indian government survives vote, 22 July, http://news.bbc.co.uk/2/hi/south_asia/7519860.stm.
7. India has complained about unfavourable trade treatment from US and has raised tariffs on 29 goods imported from the US. See: *Economic Times*. (2018). India to raise duties on 29 goods from US, 22 June, https://economictimes.indiatimes.com/news/economy/policy/india-to-raise-duties-on-29-goods-from-us/articleshow/64690730.cms.
8. *Indian Express*. (2017). India joins majority to vote against US move to recognize Jerusalem as Israel's capital, 22 December, https://indianexpress.com/article/world/india-vote-against-us-move-to-recognise-jerusalem-as-israels-capital-united-nations-4993529/.
9. For the comparison, see *Indian Express*. (2017). Military strength: How do India, China, and Pakistan compare?, 18 July, https://indianexpress.com/article/world/military-strengths-how-do-india-china-and-pakistan-compare-4749146/.
10. For details on estimated global nuclear warhead inventories, see https://www.armscontrol.org/factsheets/Nuclearweaponswhohaswhat.
11. Fair, C. C. (2014). *Fighting to the End: The Pakistan Army's Way of War*. Oxford: Oxford University Press.
12. The sentiment that India–Pakistan rivalry will continue has been suggested by many scholars. See for instance: Cohen, S. P. (2013). *Shooting for Century: The India–Pakistan Conundrum*. Washington, DC: Brookings Institution Press.
13. Shahzad, A. (2019). Pakistan army chief says military will 'go to any extent' to support Kashmir cause. *Reuters*, 6 August, https://www.reuters.com/article/us-india-kashmir-pakistan-army/pakistan-army-chief-says-military-will-go-to-any-extent-to-support-kashmir-cause-idUSKCN1UW0ZM.
14. There was a sentiment that Article 370, which accorded special status to Jammu & Kashmir was a major impediment in fully integrating the State to Indian Union. Revocation was thus hailed as full integration of the Jammu

and Kashmir. For such reactions, see The Hindu Bureau. (2019). Centre scraps Article 370, bifurcates J&K into two Union Territories. *The Hindu*, 5 August, https://www.thehindubusinessline.com/news/jammu-and-kashmir-to-be-separate-union-territory/article28819858.ece.

15. *The Hindu*. (2019). PoK, Aksai Chin part of Kashmir, says Amit Shah in Lok Sabha, 6 August.
16. Choudhary, D. R. (2019). China raked up status of Aksai Chin at UNSC informal session. *The Economic Times*, 20 August.
17. See for instance: Cohen, S. P. (2004). *The Idea of Pakistan*. Washington, DC: Brookings Institution Press.
18. Menon, S. (2016). *Choices: Inside Making of India's Foreign Policy*. Washington, DC: Brookings Institution Press.
19. See for instance: Kanwal, Brig. Gurmeet. (2011). Lost opportunities in Operation Parakram. *Indian Defence Review*, 13 December, http://www.indiandefencereview.com/spotlights/lost-opportunities-in-operation-parakram/.
20. Pubby, M. (2010). No 'Cold Start' doctrine, India tells US. *Indian Express*, 9 September, http://archive.indianexpress.com/news/no-cold-start-doctrine-india-tells-us/679273/.
21. India Today Executive Editor Sandeep Unnithan's interview with India's newly appointed Army chief General Bipin Rawat. For the full text, see https://www.indiatoday.in/magazine/interview/story/20170116-lt-general-bipin-rawat-surgical-strikes-indian-army-985527-2017-01-04.
22. The following phrase was used in the Army Statement after the Surgical Strike. For full text, see https://indianexpress.com/article/india/india-news-india/pakistan-infiltration-attempts-indian-army-surgical-strikes-line-of-control-jammu-and-kashmir-uri-poonch-pok-3055874/.
23. *India Today*. (2019). India strikes back again: This is what happened in Surgical Strike 2, 26 February, https://www.indiatoday.in/india/story/indian-air-force-airstrike-pakistan-destroys-jaish-terror-camp-developments-1465490-2019-02-26.
24. For Indian Army Statement, see https://indianexpress.com/article/india/india-news-india/pakistan-infiltration-attempts-indian-army-surgical-strikes-line-of-control-jammu-and-kashmir-uri-poonch-pok-3055874/.
25. Chakraborty, S. (2017). How India stacks up against China, and why China can't win despite its military superiority. *Economic Times*, 20 July, https://economictimes.indiatimes.com/news/defence/why-china-cant-subdue-india-despite-its-obvious-military-superiority/articleshow/59679615.cms.
26. Peri, D. (2018). Navy confident of commissioning aircraft carrier Vikrant in two years. *The Hindu*, 19 January, http://www.thehindu.com/news/national/navy-confident-of-commissioning-aircraft-carrier-vikrant-in-two-years/article22474986.ece.
27. Gady, F. S. (2017). China's first 5th generation fighter jet is operational. *The Diplomat*, 2 October, https://thediplomat.com/2017/10/chinas-first-5th-generation-fighter-jet-is-operational/.
28. For detailed comparative study of Indian and Chinese military preparedness and the current approaches, see: O'Donnell, F. (2018). *Stabilizing Sino-Indian Security Relations: Managing Strategic Rivalry After Doklam*. Carnegie–Tsinghua Center for Global Policy, June.

29. *Indian Express*. (2017). CPEC violates sovereignty: S Jaishankar tells China, 22 February, https://indianexpress.com/article/india/cpec-violates-sovereignty-s-jaishankar-tells-china-4538588/.
30. See for instance: Pant, H. V. & Das, P. (2018). China's Military Rise and the Indian Challenge. In Pant, H. V. & Das, P. (Eds.) *Defence Primer: An Indian Military in Transition* (pp. 4–15) New Delhi: Observer Research Foundation.
31. For instance, see: Mansingh, S. (2013). Rising China and Emergent India in Twenty-First Century. In Bajpai, K. P. & Pany, H. V. (Eds.) *India's Foreign Policy: A Reader* (pp. 281–302) Oxford: Oxford University Press.
32. See, Rajagopalan, R. (2017). *India's Strategic Choices: China and the Balance of Power in Asia*. Washington, DC: Carnegie Endowment for International Peace.
33. The phrase 'hesitations of history' was first used by PM Modi in his address to US Congress in 2016. The address was dubbed as willingness of India to upgrade its ties with US. See, Roy, S. (2016). Shedding 'hesitations of history', PM Modi points to future in his address to US Congress. *Indian Express*, 9 June, https://www.google.co.in/search?q=modi+us+historical+hesitation&oq=modi+us+historical+hesitation&aqs=chrome..69i57.5230j0j4&sourceid=chrome&ie=UTF-8.
34. Ibid.
35. For details of LEMOA, see George, V. K. (2016). India, US sign military logistics pact. *The Hindu*, 30 August, http://www.thehindu.com/news/international/India-US-sign-military-logistics-pact/article14598282.ece. The first indication of its operationalization was seen when in 2017, US Navy tanker refuelled an Indian Navy ship in the Sea of Japan. See Singh, S. (2017). LEMOA in place, US tanker refuels Indian Navy ship in Sea of Japan. *Indian Express*, 11 November, https://indianexpress.com/article/india/lemoa-in-place-us-tanker-refuels-indian-navy-ship-in-sea-of-japan-4932082/.
36. Samanta, P. D. (2019). First secure link between India, US navies set up. *Economic Times*, 2 April.
37. Patranobis, S. (2017). China reacts to India–Japan cooperation in northeast, says no room for 'third party'. *Hindustan Times*, 15 September, https://www.hindustantimes.com/india-news/japan-should-not-get-involved-in-china-india-border-dispute-beijing/story-IE9M3uxuTGTT6j4HHgVCcM.html.
38. See *Business Standard*. (2018). India, France sign strategic pact on use of each other's military bases, 10 March, https://www.business-standard.com/article/pti-stories/india-france-sign-strategic-pact-on-use-of-each-other-s-military-bases-118031000416_1.html
39. India has not been explicitly vocal about China's moves in the South China Sea lately. This is an apparent departure when India not only used joint statements with like-minded countries to refer to Chinese assertiveness in the seas but also used multiple multilateral fora to raise similar concerns. See for instance India official communique after the May 2019, QUAD meeting in Bangkok. Full text https://www.mea.gov.in/press-releases.htm?dtl/31403/IndiaAustraliaJapanUnited_States_Consultations.
40. For the full text of the Defence White Paper, see http://www.xinhuanet.com/english/2019-07/24/c_138253389.htm.
41. See Kumar, A. (2004). PWG and MCC merge to form new party. *The Times of India*, 14 October, https://timesofindia.indiatimes.com/city/patna/PWG-and-MCC-merge-to-form-new-party/articleshow/885422.cms.

42. See Singh, M. (2006). PM's speech at the Chief Minister's meet on Naxalism, 13 April, http://archivepmo.nic.in/drmanmohansingh/speech-details.php?nodeid=302#.
43. See for instance: Menon, A. K. (2007). The red revolt. *India Today*, 20 December, https://www.indiatoday.in/magazine/cover-story/story/20071231-the-red-revolt-734843-2007-12-20.
44. Oetken, J. L. (2009). Counterinsurgency Against Naxalites in India. In Ganguly, S. & Fidler, D. P. (Eds.) *India and Counterinsurgency: Lessons Learned* (pp. 127–152) London: Routledge.
45. Robbins, S. (2015). Searching for Solution to a Conundrum. In Fremont-Barnes, G. (ed.) *A History of Counter-Insurgency (Vol. II)* (pp. 21–48) London: Praeger Security International.
46. See, Singh, K. P. (2008). The Trajectory of the Movement. In Ramanna, P. V. (ed.) *The Naxal Challenge: Causes, Linkages and Policy Options* (pp. 10–17) London: Pearson Longman.
47. See for instance, Lynch, T. S. (2016). India's Naxalite Insurgency: History, Trajectory, and Implications for U.S.–India Security Cooperation on Domestic Counterinsurgency. *Strategic Perspectives* (22) (Center for Strategic Research Institute for National Strategic Studies, National Defense University), http://ndupress.ndu.edu/Portals/68/Documents/stratperspective/inss/Strategic-Perspectives-22.pdf Thomas mentions almost 9000 Naxals surrendering during the process.
48. For the details of various mergers of different Naxal Organizations, see Ramana, P. V. (2011). India's Maoist Insurgency: Evolution, Current Trends, and Responses. In Kugelman, M. (ed.) *India's Contemporary Security Challenges* (pp. 29–45) Woodrow Wilson International Center for Scholars, Asia Program.
49. Chauhan, N. (2016). Maoists fourth deadliest terror outfit after Taliban, IS, Boko Haram: Report. *The Times of India*, 16 September, https://timesofindia.indiatimes.com/india/Maoists-fourth-deadliest-terror-outfit-after-Taliban-IS-Boko-Haram-Report/articleshow/54354196.cms.
50. Lynch, T. S. (2016). India's Naxalite Insurgency.
51. Data Compiled from the report: *Indian Express*. (2014). Over 12,000 killed in Naxal violence in past 20 years. 12 March, https://indianexpress.com/article/india/india-others/over-12000-killed-in-naxal-violence-in-past-20-years/.
52. See for instance: Subramanian, K. S. (2010). *Economic & Political Weekly* xlv (32).
53. Lynch, T. S. (2016). India's Naxalite Insurgency.
54. Singh, P. (2007). *The Naxalite Movement in India*. New Delhi: Rupa & Co.
55. Adhikari, S. (2012). The Resurgence of Naxalism: Implications for India's Security. *Air Power Journal* 7 (1), 29–30.
56. See Ramana, P. V. (2011). India's Maoist Insurgency.
57. Bhattacharjee, B. (2017). Greyhounds among the best anti-insurgency forces: Experts. *The Hindu*, 22 March, http://www.thehindu.com/todays-paper/tp-national/tp-andhrapradesh/greyhounds-among-the-best-anti-insurgency-forces-experts/article17568627.ece.
58. Venkatesan, J. (2011). Salwa Judum is illegal, says Supreme Court. *The Hindu*, 5 July, http://www.thehindu.com/news/national/Salwa-Judum-is-illegal-says-Supreme-Court/article13639702.ece.

59. For a detailed understanding of the functioning of the Left Wing Extremism Division of MHA, see https://mha.gov.in/division_of_mha/left-wing-extremism-division.
60. For a detailed report see: Ministry of Home Affairs (2019). *Annual Report 2018–19*. New Delhi: Government of India.
61. For a brief historical overview see: Bhaumik, S. (2007). Insurgencies in India's Northeast: Conflict, Co-option, and Change. Washington, DC: Working Paper, East–West Centre Washington, July.
62. Bhaumik, S, (2009). *Troubled Periphery: The Crisis of India's North East*. London: Sage.
63. The mentioned factors are listed in most of the official MHA documents. For instance, see https://mha.gov.in/division_of_mha/north-east-division.
64. AFSPA, an act passed in 1958, gives special powers to Armed forces to carry out counter insurgency operation and in effect maintain law and order in the states designated as 'disturbed areas'. It has been criticized on the grounds that in a democracy, to accord arbitrary powers to Armed forces to deal with its own citizens is contradictory to the spirit of democracy.
65. For details regarding external linkages of these insurgent groups see: Routray, B. P. (2016). Insurgencies in India's North–East: Rise, Fall and the Rise? In Pant H. V. (ed.) *Handbook of Indian Defence Policy: Themes, Structures and Doctrines* (pp. 304–320) London: Routledge.
66. Though the doctrine is not explicit in its enunciation that the approach will be 'sequential', the nature of the doctrine is such that the flow of the doctrine will be sequential.
67. For instance, Jawaharlal Nehru is said to have considered the demand for a separate state of Nagaland almost absurd. See for instance: Routray, B. P. (2016). Insurgencies in India's North–east.
68. Robbins, S. (2015). Searching for a Solution to a Conundrum.
69. For the details of the act, see http://nagapol.gov.in/PDF/The%20Armed%20Forces%20Special%20Powers%20Act%201958.pdf.
70. For instance see: Chadha, V. (2012). *Armed Forces Special Powers Act: The Debate*. New Delhi: IDSA Monograph Series No. 7.
71. Lintner, B. (2012). *The Great Game East: India, China, and the Struggle for Asia's Most Volatile Frontier*. Yale: Yale University Press, 93.
72. For details, see http://www.satp.org/satporgtp/countries/india/states/mizoram/backgrounder/index.html.
73. Robbins, S. (2015). Searching for a Solution to a Conundrum.
74. Ali, S. S. (2015). Tripura withdraws AFSPA, says insurgency on the wane. *The Hindu*, 28 May, http://www.thehindu.com/news/national/other-states/tripura-withdraws-afspa-says-insurgency-on-the-wane/article7252919.ece.
75. Singh, V. (2018). AFSPA revoked in Meghalaya, parts of Arunachal. *The Hindu*, 23 April, http://www.thehindu.com/news/national/afspa-removed-from-meghalaya-parts-of-arunachal/article23647009.ece.
76. These different approaches have been tried at various times in different states. Various ceasefire agreements with Naga rebels and also in Mizoram have been attempted.
77. For instance see: Bhaumik, S. (2014). 'Look East through Northeast': Challenges and Prospects for India. *ORF Occasional Paper* 51 (June).

78. It has been observed that the development packages have been diverted by the insurgent groups and never really reached their desired goals. For instance, see Thapliyal, S. (2016). Insurgency in The Northeast: Is There Light at the End of the Tunnel? *Indian Defence Review*, 31 (4).

79. For the political intervention that helped the movement of Bhindranwale see: Gill, K. P. S (1997). *Punjab: The Knights of Falsehoods*. New Delhi: Har Anand Publications.

80. See for instance: Singh, T. (1986). Pakistan involvement in Sikh terrorism in Punjab based on solid evidence: India. *India Today*, 15 May, https://www.indiatoday.in/magazine/special-report/story/19860515-pakistan-involvement-in-sikh-terrorism-in-punjab-based-on-solid-evidence-india-800879-1986-05-15.

81. For details on the South Asia Terrorism Portal See, http://www.satp.org/backgrounder/india-punjab.

82. Ibid.

83. Bedi, R. (2009). Indira Gandhi's death remembered. *BBC News*, 1 November, http://news.bbc.co.uk/2/hi/south_asia/8306420.stm.

84. Gill, K. P. S. (2013). Endgame in Punjab. In Bajpai, K. & Pant, H. V. (Eds.) *India's National Security: A Reader* (pp. 55–106) Oxford: Oxford University Press.

85. This view has been emphatically put forward by K. P. S Gill that the political intervention created disruption in the counter-insurgency operation. See Ibid.

86. See for instance, Haqqani, H. (2003). Pakistan's Endgame in Kashmir. In Ganguly, S. (ed.) *The Kashmir Question: Retrospect and Prospect* (pp. 27–42) London: Frank Cass.

87. There have several documented evidences which suggest the existence of these camps in the PoK. See for instance: Krishnaswami, S. (2006). FBI identifies terror camp in Pakistan through satellite pictures. *DNA*, 1 August, https://web.archive.org/web/20070310220755/http://www.dnaindia.com/report.asp?NewsID=1044850. These terror camps have also been causing problems for the locals in the PoK regions. See for instance: Neelakantan, S. (2016). Terrorist training camps making our life hell, PoK residents say. *The Times of India*, 6 October, https://timesofindia.indiatimes.com/india/Terrorist-training-camps-making-our-life-hell-Pakistan-Occupied-Kashmir-residents-say/articleshow/54711939.cms.

88. Article 370 of Indian Constitution is drafted Under Part XXI of Indian Constitution which is tiled as "Temporary Transitional and Special Provision".

89. *India Today*. (2019). Article 370 powers gone, Lok Sabha passes J&K bifurcation bill, 7 August, https://www.indiatoday.in/india/story/article-370-jammu-kashmir-ladakh-bifurcation-all-you-need-to-know-1578034-2019-08-07.

90. The Armed Forces Special Power's Act is applicable in Jammu and Kashmir since 90 when the region was designated as Disturbed Area.

91. For instance, in 2010 the death of young Kashmiri Tufail Mattoo has sparked series of protests in the Valley thereby disturbing the peace in the region. See: Polgreen, L. (2010). A youth's death in Kashmir renews a familiar pattern of crisis. *New York Times*, 11 July, https://www.nytimes.com/2010/07/12/world/asia/12kashmir.html. The killing of Burhan Wani, an identified militant with Hizbul Mujahideen, led to violent protests by the Kashmiris which

renewed the cycle of violence. See *Indian Express*. (2016). Curfew imposed in three areas of Kashmir Valley, separatists continue shutdown, 1 September, https://indianexpress.com/article/india/india-news-india/curfew-imposed-in-three-areas-of-kashmir-valley-separatists-continue-shutdown-3007452/.

92. For details on these developments see: Kasuri, K. M. (2015). *Neither a Hawk Nor a Dove: An Insider's Account of Pakistan's Foreign Policy*. Oxford: Oxford University Press.
93. See Cohen, S. (2013). *Shooting for a Century*, 73–83.
94. See for instance: Gupta, A. (2011). A National Security Strategy Document for India. *IDSA Comments*, 20 October, https://idsa.in/idsacomments/ANationalSecurityStrategyDocumentforIndia_arvindgupta_201011.
95. These excerpts are taken from BJP's election Manifesto for 2014 election.
96. See the *New Indian Express*. (2018). Defence Planning Committee holds first meeting; decides to make action plan to deal with security challenges, 4 May, http://www.newindianexpress.com/nation/2018/may/04/defence-planning-committee-holds-first-meeting-decides-to-make-action-plan-to-deal-with-security-ch-1809890.html.
97. Shreyas, A. (2018). Modi government eyes new national security strategy: NSA Doval to spearhead Defence Planning Committee. *Financial Express*, 19 April, https://www.financialexpress.com/defence/modi-government-eyes-new-national-security-strategy-nsa-doval-to-spearhead-defence-planning-committee/1138021/.
98. Singh, V. (2017). Security Council Secretariat gets Rs.333 crore, a tenfold hike. *The Hindu*, 2 February, https://www.thehindu.com/news/national/Security-council-secretariat-gets-Rs.333-crore-a-tenfold-hike/article17148272.ece.
99. *Economic Times*. (2018). National Security Advisory Board reconstituted with ex-envoy to Russia Raghavan as head, 13 July, https://economictimes.indiatimes.com/news/defence/national-security-advisory-board-reconstituted-with-ex-envoy-to-russia-raghavan-as-head/articleshow/54765284.cms.

CHAPTER 10

Turkey: The Security Policy of a 'Lonely' State

Bill Park

Introduction: With a Neighbourhood like Turkey's, Who Needs Enemies?

The security policy of each state is rooted in a uniquely blended range of factors. Geopolitical and geostrategic circumstance, historical experience, domestic political system and culture, level of economic development, the regional and global political orders, and 'constructed' and subjective national narratives, all play a role. This is no less true for the 'new' state of Turkey that emerged from the Ottoman ruins in 1923, and this chapter will touch on each of those drivers. Yet one could also argue that few countries have quite so complex a security context as Turkey. This stems largely from its geopolitical location. It is simultaneously a European and in particular Balkan, Middle Eastern, Caucasian, Mediterranean, Black Sea, Eurasian, and Turkic country. Developments in its multiple neighbourhoods can offer opportunities, threats, or both simultaneously. Furthermore, the ways in which Turkey's neighbourhoods shape the country's security agenda have depended on larger regional and global dynamics over which Turkey has little control. Since its inception, the security policy of the republic has been obliged to adapt to British and French colonial presence, the emergence of the Soviet Union, decolonisation, the creation of the state of Israel, the Iranian revolution, the cold war, and its demise, the invasion of Iraq, the 'war on terror', and the 'Arab Spring'. Today much of Turkey's neighbourhood, and the Middle East especially, remains

B. Park (✉)
King's College London, London, UK
e-mail: william.h.park@kcl.ac.uk

© The Author(s), under exclusive license to Springer Nature Switzerland AG 2022
M. Clarke et al. (eds.), *The Palgrave Handbook of National Security*,
https://doi.org/10.1007/978-3-030-53494-3_10

219

220   B. PARK

unstable and unpredictable. The quantity, complexity, and dynamic nature of the security issues that are thrown up by the sheer march of events across its various borders are almost impossible to encapsulate, and can give a manic quality to Turkish endeavours to cope with them. Furthermore, Turkey is as much an echo chamber of this tumult as actor. Security policy towards what, when, who, and in what order of priority?

Turkey, Existentially: Who Are Turks and What Is Turkey?[1]

All states and societies are rooted in and shaped by their past, and by the way that past has been mythologised. The Turkish republic emerged from the ruins of the Ottoman empire, which variously incorporated most of the Arab world and north Africa, parts of the Caucasus, and the Balkans. Its European possessions were particularly highly valued and left their mark on the Ottoman governing elite. In the decades preceding its demise it was dubbed 'the sick man'—of Europe. 'Turks' are descendants of nomadic tribes originating in Central Asia, and are linguistically akin to Kazhaks, Uzbeks, Kyrgyz, Turkmen, and Azeris. These origins shaped the Turkish republic's founding mythology, and provide the basis for the 'pan-Turkism' or Eurasianism that intermittently surfaces there. Turks arrived in Anatolia a thousand years ago and intermingled with the Greek, Armenian and Syriac Christians, Muslim Kurds and Arabs and other peoples that had long inhabited it. The Byzantine empire, with Constantinople as its capital (later renamed Istanbul), fell to Ottoman Turks in 1453, but Anatolia itself—with the empire as a whole—remained demographically multi-ethnic and multi-faith. However, as a result of conversion, assimilation, genocide, wars, population exchanges, and emigration, few Christians remain in today's Turkey. This demographic shift was augmented by the arrival of Muslims fleeing from the Balkans, the Caucasus, and Central Asia. The pre-Turkic and non-Muslim Anatolian past has for the most part been not so much absorbed, let alone revered, as supplanted and largely forgotten.

So, until recently, was its Ottoman past. Many of the 'Young Turks' who formed the basis of the new republic's elite under the leadership of Mustafa Kemal—or Ataturk, the father of the Turks—were rooted in the European parts of the empire. They saw their mission as the creation of a new 'Turkish' state in the Anatolian lands they were left with, and of a nation that would identify with it. They embarked upon a top-down programme of modernisation aimed at dragging a socially conservative, mostly Muslim, economically backward, and illiterate population towards European 'modernity'. This aspiration was driven in no small degree by their conviction that the Ottoman empire had ultimately been destroyed as a consequence of its backwardness relative to its European counterparts, and of its internal divisions. From this perspective, the Kemalist modernisation project, and its insistence on national 'unity', were in effect elements in the new republic's security policy.[2] Furthermore, Ataturk explained Turkey's 'backwardness' by reference to the hold of a 'superstitious' Islam.[3] In order to soften this hold, the caliphate, or leadership of the Islamic world, which had been held by successive Ottoman sultans, was abolished in 1924, religious brotherhoods were banned and their assets confiscated, formal religious education all but disappeared, the secular basis of law was extended, and a Directorate of Religious Affairs (Diyanet) was established in 1924, to ensure state control over imams and the content of their sermons. Islam in Turkey would now be subordinated to political control and even direction.

Despite these efforts, 'the rural and pious masses of Anatolia remained largely unaffected by the cultural re-engineering' of Kemalism.[4] Samuel Huntington described Turkey as 'the most obvious and prototypical torn country',[5] split between its European-leaning secular establishment and its devout hinterland. Islamism was framed as an internal 'security' threat to the state's secularity.[6] On the other hand, the 'new' Turkish nation was to be unified by its 'Turkishness'. To generate this identity, the Latin alphabet replaced the Arabic in a mass literacy campaign, and many pre-Turkish place names were erased, as was reference to Anatolia's pre- and non-Turkic and even Ottoman past. This campaign of 'Turkification' is still ongoing, and has left its mark. It is illegal to 'insult' Turkishness, children are daily obliged to recite the words 'Happy is he who can call himself a Turk', the national flag is everywhere, and exaggerated displays of nationalism permeate education, popular culture, and state and media discourse.[7] In this atmosphere, non-Turks— notably the mostly Sunni Muslim Kurds, who constitute around one-fifth of the population—can be readily presented as internal security threats.

Once Turkey embarked on its halting process of democratisation, these polarities became ever more difficult to paper over. In the country's first ever free election in 1950 the Democratic Party (DP) emerged victorious, gaining most of its electoral support from rural and small town Anatolia. It lifted the ban on the Arabic call to prayer, embarked on a mosque-building programme, and took other measures to limit Kemalist arch-secularism. The consequent military coup of 1960 heralded the emergence of the Turkish General Staff (TGS) as the ultimate 'guardians' of state secularism and the Kemalist order, expressed by coups in 1971 and 1980,[8] and the so-called 'post-modern' coup of 1997 that forced an Islamist-led coalition government from office. A new constitution was drafted and the National Security Council (NSC) formed in 1961, which enabled the military to steer the country's domestic and external security policies. Key to this, in legislative terms, was the Turkish Armed Forces Internal Service Law of 1961 which endowed the armed forces with the responsibility 'for defending both the Turkish fatherland and the Turkish republic as defined by the Constitution'. This responsibility was also enshrined in the 1982 Constitution drawn up in the wake of the 1980 coup, and in the 1983 National Security Council Law. Its understanding of security focused on internal as well as external 'threats', on protecting 'Turkishness' and 'secularism'. Along the way, the DP and all successor political parties that challenged official secular ideology were banned. The Welfare

Party of Necmettin Erbakan, from which emerged the current ruling party, the *Adelet ve Kalkinma Partisi* (or AKP), was banned in 1998. The TGS could make its voice heard across the whole economic, political, social, and cultural spectrum. Turkey's secular elites often welcomed the military's political dominance, and happily deferred to its leading role in determining external security policy,[9] notably towards relations with the US and Israel, and with regard to the Cyprus and Kurdish issues. The TGS's tutelary role, and the ideology that accompanied it, produced a 'national security regime' in Turkey which inhibited the growth of democracy in the country.[10]

Paradoxically the post-1980 coup era saw the encouragement of the so-called 'Turkish-Islamic synthesis', which was reflected by the reintroduction of compulsory religious education in schools, the expansion of Diyanet, and the growth of specifically religious *Imam Hatip* schools. Religious brotherhoods made a comeback, and an economic boom brought an explosion of religiously oriented media outlets alongside the emergence of a better educated Muslim middle class. The aim had been to wean Turkey's youth from radical leftism, but Turkey's increased pluralism enabled Turkey's conservative and devout 'periphery' to challenge the secular, 'westernising' and urban 'centre'.[11] This manifested itself in 2002 when the newly formed AKP, led by Recep Tayyip Erdogan, won the election and was able to form a single-party government. In the June 2011 and November 2015 elections the party's electoral support reached 50%. Erdogan was elected president in June 2018 with over 52% of the vote. Such impressive popular support, combined with a divided opposition and the military purges and resignations that followed the 2008–2013 '*Ergenekon*' and '*Balyoz*' trials of 'deep state' activities[12] eroded the secular elite's capacity, and the TGS's in particular, to resist the AKP's de-secularisation of Turkish politics and society. The purges that came in the wake of the failed 2016 coup attempt eroded the military's functional capacity too.

Progressively since 2002 but especially in more recent years, AKP governments have managed to weaken the domestic political role of the TGS; raise the profile of Islam in the social, economic, and political life of the country; shake the hold of secularists over the bureaucracy, the legal system and much of the educational sector; establish a presidential system with few checks and balances; intimidate and marginalise much of the opposition; and take control over most of the media. Turkey's domestic political system has shifted from rule by a secular and largely unrepresentative elite, guaranteed by a powerful and interventionist military establishment, to an authoritarian majoritarianism and centralised presidentialism organised around the personality of Erdogan.[13] Competent professionals in government service, including in the upper echelons of the military, have been replaced by cronies and loyalists. It is hard to identify anything that might be understood as a 'strategy' emerging from so personalised, de-institutionalised and impulsive governmental and decision-making system. Furthermore, a somewhat concocted version of the late Ottoman era has been glorified, alongside a general revival of Ottomanism in education, popular media, and political discourse. In a commemoration marking the death of Sultan Abdulhamid 11, whose reputation as a Turkish nationalist and devout Muslim has been deliberately cultivated, Erdogan declared the republic to be 'a continuation of the Ottomans' and condemned those who 'try to break us from our roots and ancient values'.[14] He champions Sunni Islamism, and the Muslim Brotherhood in particular, and seems to derive much of his belief system from Erbakan and associated Turkish Islamist thinkers.[15] Erdogan's republic is in many ways very different from what its founders envisaged, and unsurprisingly it pursues a security agenda that reflects its own values and circumstances.

THE INTER-WAR YEARS: SECURITY POLICY FOUNDATIONS[16]

The so-called 'Sevres syndrome', which informs Turkish security policy to this day and is integral to the country's nationalist discourse, has its origins in the great power machinations surrounding the dismemberment of the Ottoman empire. The Treaty of Sevres, drawn up by British and French officials in 1920, foresaw an independent Armenian state, held out the prospect of a Kurdish state, envisaged the enlargement of Greece to include parts of Anatolia, suggested the establishment of foreign protectorates over parts of Anatolia, and allowed for the imposition of other financial and military restrictions on Turkey. In fact Ataturk's victory over Greece in what Turks call their 'War of Independence' ensured it was never imposed. Nevertheless it created in Turkey a lasting conviction that even its closest allies were bent on its dismemberment. The syndrome has been described as a 'virtual siege mentality',[17] and has survived Turkey's long-standing membership of NATO and EU accession candidate status. As Kenan Evren, the leader of the 1980 coup and president of the country from 1980 until 1989 put it, Turkey is 'bound to be strong since she has very few friends'.[18] This worldview, integral to the 'national security regime' ethos, is propagated via the educational system, the media, and by leading politicians and bureaucrats, for whom its precepts are a constant refrain.[19] The TGS has been one of its most constant propagators, illustrated by the head of Turkey's Military Academy in 2000, when he informed its new intake that 'you will see that Turkey has the most internal and external enemies of any country in the world. You will learn about the dirty aspirations of those who hide behind values such as democracy and human rights and who want to take revenge on the republic of Ataturk'.[20] The current AKP government draws on this mentality no less than its Kemalist predecessors.

Overlapping with the 'Sevres syndrome', and rooted in Kurdish resistance to 'Turkification' and centralised rule, the 'Kurdish issue' is Turkey's most serious and persistent security problem. It is often presented as the work of external 'enemies', bent on fanning the flames of Kurdish identity in pursuit of a weakened Turkey. Following a Kurdish tribal revolt in the 1920s, and a series of localised rebellions in the years that followed, the state embarked upon a brutal campaign of repression. The 1934 Law on Resettlement aimed to disperse Kurds around the country in an attempt to enforce cultural homogenisation. The massacres, executions, deportations, incarcerations, destruction of villages and the imposition of martial law that was a feature of Turkey's campaigns during the 1920s and 1930s established a pattern that has continued, on and off, right up to the present day. Linguistic, cultural, and political expressions of Kurdish identity were banned and the very existence of Kurds as a distinct ethnic identity was denied. In a foretaste of Turkey's incursions into neighbouring Iraq in the 1980s and 1990s and into Syria more recently, in 1929 Turkish forces even violated the territory of Iran in its pursuit of Kurdish rebels. Many of today's Syrian Kurdish population are the descendants of those who fled Turkish repression in the 1920s and 1930s. Particularly hard hit was the rebellious Alevi (Shia) Kurdish Dersim province, renamed Tunceli in 1936. In 1937 and 1938 it was subjected to a vicious military campaign involving the deployment of tens of thousands of troops, sustained aerial bombardment, and thousands of deaths. Before Ataturk's death in 1938, tens of thousands of Kurds had lost their lives, their feudal leadership was decimated, the population dispersed, and the economic infrastructure of southeastern Turkey ruined.[21] Kurdish disaffection and alienation has been a persistent feature of the republic's life since its birth,[22] and fears that it could result in the country's fragmentation its most enduring security concern.

Contemporary commentary on the security policies and strategic significance of Turkey are typically infused with reference to its location. However, the salience of Turkey's geography is a function of the prevailing global and regional order. During the republic's first two decades, its posture towards the outside world was isolationist and it was generally ignored by Europe's major powers, although economic interaction with the Soviet Union was considerable. As a WWI adversary it was excluded from the League of Nations until 1932. Turkey's WWII neutrality, which was generally respected by the combatants, was indicative of its isolation. Given British and French predominance in the Middle East, and the consolidation of Soviet control over the Caucasus and Central Asia, Ankara had little room for manoeuvre in its neighbourhood. Ankara's major differences with the great powers during this period related to the final determination of its borders. Ataturk sought to incorporate the former Ottoman province of Mosul, which had a large Kurdish and also a Turkmen population, but lost out to the British insistence that it be attached to what in 1932 became the independent state of Iraq. Ankara has never fully resigned itself to this 'loss'. Conversely, in 1938 Turkey acquired Hatay, in Turkey's southeast, from the French Syrian protectorate, in a French bid to win favour with Ankara should war break out in Europe. The independent Syrian state that was established in 1946 has persisted in its resentment of this border revision. Today the borders with Iraq and Syria are central to Turkey's 'securitised' approach to the place of Kurds in the region. The 1934 Balkan Pact, signed with Greece, Romania, and Yugoslavia, and the

1937 Saadabad Pact with Iran, Iraq, and Afghanistan, indicated little more than Ankara's commitment to mutual non-interference in its relationships with its neighbours and its opposition to great power meddling in its neighbourhood(s). However, the 1936 Montreux Convention, which conferred to Turkey maritime control of the Dardanelles and Bosphorus, through which all Black Sea traffic is obliged to transit, offered a foretaste of the importance geopolitical circumstances could have for Turkey's external relations.

The Security Policy of the Pre-AKP Republic: The Cold War Years

This indifference to Turkey's location ended with the Cold War, when Turkey acquired geostrategic value owing to its proximity to the Soviet Union's southern flank. The Cold War's emergence was crucial in enabling Turkey to pursue its 'destiny' to become part of the west. Post-1945 Soviet territorial demands on Turkey and pressure to revise the Montreux Convention prompted Ankara to reconsider its stance of neutrality. Turkey obtained US military aid via the 1947 Truman Doctrine which aimed to contain Soviet expansion by bolstering countries around its perimeter, and Turkish lobbying, continued Soviet provocation, the 1949 signing of the North Atlantic Treaty—which led by 1951 to the formation of the North Atlantic Treaty Organisation (NATO)—and the Turkish contribution of 5000 troops to the Korean War, all led to Turkey joining NATO in 1952, along with Greece. Turkey was now deluged with US military and economic aid, and progressively tied to the US via a plethora of bilateral and often secret agreements. Turkey's armed forces grew to become NATO's second largest, at around half a million strong. US air and missile bases, naval port facilities, military storage sites, and communications stations proliferated. U2 spy planes, nuclear armed bombers, battlefield nuclear weapons, and in the late 1950s Jupiter medium range missiles were all located on Turkish territory. These geopolitical factors reinforced, and were reinforced by, the domestic political status of the TGS. Although the US–Turkey relationship was prisoner of a narrow geopolitical concept, derived from Turkey's location, the bipolar nature of the Cold War also enabled Turkey to join the Organisation for European Economic Cooperation (OEEC) in 1948, the Council of Europe in 1949, and even to become an associate member of the European Economic Community (EEC) in 1963. These organisations symbolised the 'western community' aspect of the Cold War's bipolarity, and notably its 'European' dimension, even though Cold War exigencies further entrenched Turkey's 'national security regime'. Economically semi-developed, imperfectly democratic and Muslim, Turkey was now part of the 'west' and even of 'Europe'.[23] This encouraged the Turkish state's inclination to turn its back on the Arab world, and equally encouraged much of the Arab world to frame Turkey as a neo-Ottoman threat and Trojan horse for external regional meddling.[24] The UK-sponsored Baghdad Pact of 1955, incorporating Turkey, Iraq, Iran, and Pakistan, and the TGS's cultivation of a close security relationship with Israel in the mid-1990s[25] helped stimulate this sentiment. Such policies also encouraged the view that Turkish policy was characterised by a 'hard security' approach.

However, Turkey's western security alignment was vulnerable to disagreements in Turkey's immediate neighbourhood. Most notably, when Turkey threatened to intervene on behalf of the Turkish Cypriot minority when the Greek side's abrogation of the island's power-sharing arrangements sparked intercommunal violence, Washington forcefully protested. A repeat crisis in Turkey–US (and Turkey–EU) relations occurred in the wake of Ankara's 1974 invasion of the island to forestall its annexation by the military junta in Athens. Ankara retaliated to the consequent US congressional embargo on military transfers to Turkey by suspending US operations at military installations across the country. To this day Turkey retains around 30,000 troops in the Turkish Republic of Northern Cyprus (TRNC)—an entity recognised by Ankara alone. The unresolved division of Cyprus has served to block Turkey's thin hopes of accession to the EU.[26] Turkey–EU relations are further threatened by Turkey's forceful obstruction of European energy exploration vessels off the Cypriot coast.[27] There are too frequent incidents between the militaries of Turkey and fellow NATO neighbour Greece over their disputed territorial claims in the Aegean.[28]

TURKISH SECURITY POLICY, THE END OF THE COLD WAR AND THE RISE OF THE AKP

Just as the Cold War broadly coincided with secular prevalence on the Turkish domestic political scene, so the AKP's advent to power in November 2002 roughly corresponded to the lifting of the 'iron curtain', making it difficult to assess the extent to which recent rifts between Turkey and its western allies are primarily a consequence of AKP policies or of post-Cold War dynamics. In fact, the Cold War's demise enabled even pre-AKP Turkey to embark on a 'new activism' in its foreign and security policies,[29] characterised by benign 'soft politics' initiatives in regional relationships, such as the Black Sea Naval Cooperation Task Group (BLACKSEAFOR) in 1991 and Black Sea Economic Cooperation (BSEC) in 1992. Ankara encouraged aid, trade, cultural cooperation, communications links, and other confidence-building measures in the Balkans, the Caucasus, and in central Asia, where Turks rediscovered their distant ethnic Turkic cousins. However, little could be built upon these modest initiatives, whether as a consequence of Turkey's weak capacity, negative regional memories of the Ottoman past, or because post-communist states had alternative options. Turkey's multilateral engagements during this period were more in keeping with its broadly western orientation. In the Yugoslav crises Ankara contributed air, naval, and ground forces to UN, NATO, and EU-led peacekeeping forces that were deployed there. Turkey also made significant contributions to multilateral efforts in Afghanistan, twice heading the UN (and then NATO)-mandated International Security Assistance Force (ISAF), taking command of the Kabul Regional Command, and establishing its own Provincial Reconstruction Team.[30] Turkey also made peacekeeping and monitoring contributions in Lebanon, Georgia, and throughout Africa.[31]

However, it was the US-led invasion of Iraq in 2003, just months after the AKP came to power, that really challenged Turkish security perspectives. As one analyst put it, the US 'in one bold stroke managed to push Turkey back into the Middle East'.[32] In effect, the invasion heralded a new paradigm in Turkish security thinking—or, perhaps more accurately, a succession of new paradigms. From Washington's angle, Turkey's geostrategic virtue had shifted from its location on the Soviet southern flank to its proximity to the Middle East's trouble spots. However, neither the Turkish government, nor the TGS, nor public opinion, approved of the military intervention to overthrow Saddam Hussein's regime. As the invasion approached, in October 2001 Turkish Prime Minister Bulent Ecevit argued that 'the operation may lead to Turkey's dismemberment. It also will disrupt all the balances in the Middle East'.[33] US disappointment with Ankara's disapproval was intensified by Washington's aspiration to promote Turkey as a 'model' for pro-western democratisation in the Middle East[34] and in the Muslim former Soviet republics, and as a 'bridge' between 'east' and 'west'. That the US then proceeded to arm, train, and operate alongside the Kurdish *peshmerga* forces of an increasingly consolidated Kurdistan Regional Government (KRG) confirmed Turkey's worst fears. Worse still, the US presence in Iraq now inhibited Turkey's 'hot pursuit' of PKK forces that based themselves in northern Iraq and that in June 2004 called off their ceasefire in their struggle against the Turkish state. The Iraq invasion unambiguously demonstrated the mismatch between Washington's expectations of its NATO ally and Ankara's vulnerability to regional crises.[35]

The ideological roots of the AKP are quite distinct from those of the republic's secular founders, and this extends to its external policies. In particular, the AKP frames Turkey as an integral part of the Middle East region, even if not exclusively so, and as more tangentially 'western'. Although the evolution of Turkish security policy under the AKP has also reflected more pragmatic adjustments to the torrent of events in its neighbourhood, this ideological shift is paramount. In more recent years—certainly since around 2013—Erdogan's increasing domination of the political scene have also meant that his personality and preferences have emerged as key determining factors in Turkish security policy. He has brought to Turkey's external interactions a volatility and pugnaciousness that renders definitive comment problematic. However, the intellectual underpinnings of the AKP government's approach was provided by Ahmet Davutoglu, who was successively Erdogan's foreign policy advisor, foreign minister, and prime minister until he fell out of favour with Erdogan in 2016. Davutoglu's thinking is associated with catchy phrases such as 'strategic depth', as the foreign policy of a rising trading state,[36] and 'zero problems with the neighbourhood'.[37] This 'soft power' thinking spawned a myriad of confidence-building and visa free regimes and a boom in Turkey's regional trade.[38] Indeed, Turkey's 'soft power' outreach extended to sub-Saharan Africa and other parts of the globe too. Less comfortably, the AKP's new direction has also been described as 'neo-Ottoman',[39] 'Turkish Gaullism',[40] and as 'pan-Islamist'.[41] In a sense it is all of these things. However, three core ideas that lie at the heart of his thinking, and that of Erdogan, help explain current Turkish foreign and security policy. The first is that Turkey is, or should be, a 'central' country rather than one peripheral to other regions, able to exploit its history, geography, culture, religion, and economic prowess to put itself at the heart of a set of interlocking regions that roughly corresponds to the former Ottoman empire. This conceptualisation has more than a whiff of geostrategic overtone and 'regional power' ambition. His second idea was that Islam should function as a unifying factor. The 'Arab Spring' raised the hope that the region might be re-engineered in accordance with the interests of its inhabitants, which encouraged Ankara's policy switch away from the existing regimes and towards the pro-Islamist forces and especially (Sunni) Muslim Brotherhood forces in Tunisia, Libya, Egypt, Palestine, and Syria. It also explains the AKP government's antipathy towards Israel, which is seen as foreign to the region's cultural geography.[42] The third assumption is that the global system is undergoing a shift towards a more multipolar arrangement, and to Eurasia's emergence in particular, in which Washington cannot expect to successfully impose its will. This is an inevitable evolution, and explains Turkey's apparent if problematic embrace of Russia, Iran, and China, and its distancing from the west. Turkey's own rise as an economically dynamic 'trading state' is itself evidence of this shift.

However, other countries, such as the US, Russia, the UK, France, Iran, Egypt, and Saudi Arabia also have considerable influence and capacity in the regions abutting Turkey. Ankara's conviction that it could play a major role in re-engineering the region through the pursuit of an independent foreign policy was always likely to collide with larger realities. The 'Arab Spring' has exposed some of those realities, but events such as Russia's use of force against Georgia in 2008—which Ankara had been assiduously cultivating—and its annexation of Crimea, including its Turkic Tartar minority, delivered similar messages. The middle east and north African (MENA) region is in uproar, from Iraq to Syria to Yemen to Libya. The very viability of the regional map, and of any sustainable political stability, is open to question.[43] For Turkey, MENA's turmoil is existentially threatening. It has brought floods of refugees, terrorist attacks, a downturn in trade, and has added to its own domestic Kurdish travails. External interventions in the region have frequently contradicted Ankara's preferences. Turkey's policies have at times been ill-judged, but the region's dysfunctionalities and external interventions provide a difficult backdrop for Turkey's efforts to pursue any coherent security agenda.

The 'Arab Spring' raised the question, among others, of precisely which 'neighbours' Turkey 'zero problems' approach should target—the states and governments of the region, or their populations? In Egypt and Tunisia, Ankara quickly switched its support to Muslim Brotherhood (MB) factions in their opposition to autocratic rule. However, Ankara's relationship with Cairo has yet to recover from Turkey's condemnation of MB leader Mohamed Morsi's July 2013 overthrow in a coup led by General Abdel Fatah al-Sisi. Ankara's decision to side with Qatar in its stand-off with a Saudi-led alliance of Arab states has similarly reflected the MB sympathies Erdogan shares with the Qatari leadership. Turkey has acquired a military base there, and one in Somalia too—Turkey's largest overseas military base—which suggest a 'neo-Ottoman', regional power dimension to Turkish policy towards the region.[44] Libya's Muammar Gaddafi had developed a close relationship to Erdogan and Ankara was initially reluctant to swing behind the west's military campaign against the regime. Ankara eventually accepted the realities of Gaddafi's demise, but its continued meddling in Libyan affairs has aroused hostility and mistrust of Turkey on the part of some of the country's leading factions.[45] In Bahrain, in contrast, Ankara supported the Saudi-led suppression of a revolt on the part of the country's Shia majority population by its Sunni minority government, suggesting a pro-Sunni bias in Turkish policy. In short, Turkey's somewhat revisionist reactions to the 'Arab Spring' have left it with few Arab friends. However, developments in Syria and Iraq have been more compelling, as they involve the Kurdish issue.

The Kurdish Issue, Again

In 1984 the leftist Kurdish nationalist PKK, formed in 1978, embarked on a still-ongoing armed campaign for Kurdish self-determination. The Turkish state responded with its characteristic repressiveness, and a 'dirty war' ensued. Around one-third of Turkey's army was located in the predominantly Kurdish southeast at any one time, which was in whole or in part under martial law until 2002. The fighting was at its most intense during the 1990s, and included multiple Turkish bombing raids and cross-border operations against PKK forces in northern Iraq, some of them involving tens of thousands of soldiers.[46] However, in August 2005 Prime Minister Erdogan conceded that Turkey had a 'Kurdish issue' and that 'mistakes' had been made in the handling of it, implying a new and de-securitised approach to the problem. Erdogan believed that economic improvements, some cultural freedom, and an emphasis on the Islamic values of many Kurds, could be sufficient and might even attract more Kurdish voters to the AKP.[47] The first stab at progress, in 2009, ended in acrimony and an outbreak of violence in which around seven hundred people are estimated to have been killed in the fourteen months up to August 2012—the highest level of PKK-related violence for thirteen years.[48] A second attempt, launched in 2013, revealed just how far apart on issues of substance that the two sides remained.[49] The preeminent Kurdish demand, for some kind of 'democratic autonomy' that would, in effect, introduce something tantamount to a federal political system in Turkey[50] and which challenged Turkey's 'Turkishness', met with little response. The lesson

Erdogan took from a national election in June 2015, in which the Kurdish People's Democratic Party (*Halklarin Demokratik Partisi*, or HDP) vote increased and denied the AKP a parliamentary majority, was that a 'peace process' might benefit the Kurdish party, but that he might benefit politically from a return to violence. In the run-up to a repeat election in November 2015 Turkey's security forces engaged in a resumption of fighting against the PKK which involved enforced curfews, the flattening of Kurdish towns and cities, and intensified bombing of PKK targets in northern Iraq. Casualties on all sides rocketed, and up to half a million Kurds were displaced from their homes.[51] In the elections, the HDP vote fell, the AKP's increased, and AKP single-party rule was ensured. Soon, the national and regional leaderships of the HDP and its affiliates were arrested, elected Kurdish-run councils were taken over by state trustees, academics and journalists deemed sympathetic to the Kurdish struggle were detained and media outlets closed down.[52] This was hard to square with a belief that Erdogan had ever been much committed to a genuine resolution of Turkey's Kurdish problem, was reminiscent of previous dark eras in Ankara's handling of the issue, and suggested that maintenance of the country's 'unitary' nature remained the pre-eminent security concern.

Simultaneously, Turkey's Kurds had been profoundly influenced by events in neighbouring Syria.[53] The evolution in Turkey's relations with Syria perfectly illustrate the volatility of Turkish foreign and security policy. Finding themselves at odds over the Cold War, water resources, relations with Israel, and over Damascus's hosting of PKK training camps and PKK leader Abdullah Ocalan, Turkey–Syrian relations had long been in a deep freeze. However, relations softened following a Turkish threat to use force against Syria in 1998 in order to force Ocalan's expulsion. Syria complied, withdrew its support for the PKK and expelled Ocalan, who was captured and remains in a Turkish prison. Syria soon emerged as the centrepiece of Ankara's new region-friendly 'zero problems' foreign policy, much to the annoyance of Washington.[54] Yet Turkey converted almost overnight from being Bashir al-Assad's most assiduous courtier into his most determined adversary in the wake of his regime's harsh crackdown against Syria's 'Arab Spring' protestors in 2011. Ankara quickly began to work for his overthrow, sponsored opposition to his rule, and joined the Arab League, the EU and the US in imposing sanctions on the Damascus regime. However, once it became evident that the Assad regime was not about to fall, and also that there was little support from Turkey's western allies for direct intervention, Ankara was exposed. Turkey's western allies also became wary of Ankara's overly close relationships with al-Qaeda affiliated and other radical *jihadi* groups that were fighting against the regime, and by its failure to shut down the so-called '*jihadi* highway' that brought IS and other radicalised fighters to Syria via Turkey. This suspicion has never quite evaporated,[55] and is seen as an indication of an 'Islamist' agenda on Ankara's part.

Furthermore, Ankara failed to anticipate the emergence of the PKK-affiliated Democratic Union Party (*Partiya Yekitiya Demokrat*, or PYD) as a key element in the Syrian conflict.[56] In early 2013 the PYD established *Rojava*, consisting of three geographically discontiguous self-governing Kurdish cantons along Syria's border with Turkey. This seriously rattled Ankara as it implied the establishment of PKK-controlled havens on its southern border.[57] When Islamic State (IS) forces embarked on a siege of the Kurdish border town of Kobane in 2014, the Turkish military looked on impassively as US forces dropped military supplies to the PYD defenders from distant bases due to Ankara's denial of US access to the NATO base at Incirlik. Washington was by now more committed to the defeat of IS than to Assad's overthrow and, frustrated both by the inadequacy of 'moderate' Syrian fighters and by Ankara's unhelpfulness, elected instead to ramp up its support for the Kurdish-led Syrian Democratic Force (SDF). This contributed to a serious downturn in the Turkey–US relationship. Russian and Iranian backing for the Assad regime added to Ankara's problems, made worse by Turkey's downing of a Russian jet in November 2015. However, Ankara's apology—and its softening of its opposition to Assad—freed Turkey to launch its Operation Euphrates Shield in September 2016. Composed of a small contingent of Turkish forces and a larger number of radical Syrian rebel fighters, by early 2017 Turkey had established a 'safe zone'—in effect a Turkish protectorate— where Syrian rebels could be based and which obstructed the merging of the PYD's Kurdish cantons.[58] In January 2018 Turkey also sent forces into Kurdish-controlled Afrin, obliging its Kurdish militia to vacate the area.[59] More dramatically still, in October 2019 Turkey launched Operation Spring Peace into north–eastern Syria, which aimed to clear SDF—and IS—fighters from a 'safe zone' extending up to thirty kilometres from Turkey's border, and to create the conditions for a return of some of the millions of Syrian refuges that Turkey now hosted. Both Moscow and the US acquiesced, but Turkey's engagement in Syria was now dependent on a fragile understanding with Russia that was at the mercy of the Damascus government's opposition—and that of Syria's Kurds—to the Turkish presence on Syrian soil, and to Russian and Syrian hostility to Ankara's radical Syrian allies.[60] This will surely constitute a major security headache for Ankara in the future, yet Turkish infrastructure investments, promises of more to come, and some 'cleansing' of Kurdish inhabitants in Afrin and now in Syria's northeast, suggested that a long stay is envisaged.[61]

The KRG

Relations with the Kurdistan Regional Government (KRG) offers another example of the turbulence in Turkey's foreign and security policy in recent years, and Ankara's persisting preoccupation with the Kurdish question. Ankara held the US responsible for the emergence of the KRG in 1991, and refused to deal with Erbil formally.[62] Yet, and notwithstanding the KRG's emergence as a Kurdish quasi-state with its own border controls, armed forces, constitution, and government, by 2010 Turkey was opening a consulate in

Erbil, was beginning to dominate the Iraqi Kurdish economy, and treating KRG president Massoud Barzani like a head of state in Ankara. The KRG's dynamic approach to the development of its energy resources synergised with Ankara's desire to limit its energy dependency on Russia and Iran and with its aspiration to develop as an energy 'hub'. By early 2014 the KRG was exporting oil via a newly constructed pipeline for export from the Turkish port of Ceyhan, in the face of opposition from both Baghdad and Washington.[63] This shift in Ankara's approach was spurred by several factors. Burgeoning trade with the KRG, Ankara's realisation that its struggle with the PKK might stand a better chance of success if it could gain Erbil's cooperation, a shared antipathy towards Iraqi prime minister Nouri al-Maliki's increasingly Shia sectarian tendencies, a wariness about Iranian influence, Davutoglu's pursuit of 'zero problems' relationships, and the discovery of ever-greater reserves of oil and gas within the KRG area, all provided impetus. The decline of the TGS's role in Turkish policy towards the KRG was a key enabling factor.[64]

The paradox was that Ankara remained uncomfortable with the prospect of Iraqi Kurdish independence, and opposed its territorial expansion to include areas disputed between Erbil and Baghdad, most notably oil-rich and partly Turkmen-populated Kirkuk.[65] Turkey's delicate stance was severely challenged by a Kurdish independence referendum held on 25 September 2017, including in the disputed territories, which resulted in a resounding 'yes' vote. Erdogan's response was to threaten the KRG with an economic embargo that could include shutting down the oil pipeline, to declare that Turkey's relations with Iraq would henceforth be conducted exclusively via Baghdad, and to enter into security understandings vis-à-vis Iraqi Kurdistan with both Iraq and Iran.[66] Ankara could only applaud when, in October, Iraqi government forces, backed by Shia militias and Iran, took back all disputed territories from Kurdish control. The establishment of an independent Iraqi Kurdistan now looked less likely, but Turkey's relationship with Iraq's Kurds was undermined, Shia domination of and Iranian influence in Iraq now seemed greater than ever, and the Erbil–Ankara energy relationship was put at risk.[67]

Many Iraqi Kurds were now disillusioned with Turkey, the PKK and its Syrian affiliates were intact and still able to utilise Iraqi Kurdish territory, and Turkey's Kurds were as alienated as ever. Turkey was now engaged in armed conflict against Kurdish forces on its own territory and in neighbouring Syria and Iraq, with no end in sight. Baghdad and Damascus were critical of Turkey's military activities and unwanted presence on their sovereign territory—Turkey is reckoned to have around twenty bases in northern Iraq dating back to the 1980s.[68] Ankara's alliance with the US and its western allies had been corroded by its behaviour in Syria and excesses towards its own Kurds, and Ankara had become dependent on the uncertain goodwill of Moscow and, to a degree, Tehran. In the process, Turkish security policy has returned to its familiar pattern of reliance on force, and Erdogan has increasingly surrounded himself with a bevy of security officials. Turkey has long regarded Kurdish self-determination as its biggest security challenge, yet it is hard to argue that its 'securitised' approach has actually enhanced its security. Ankara's behaviour has alienated its friends, handed opportunities to its rivals, and committed it to a three-front and unwinnable war. Turkey has never seriously considered alternative approaches to the Kurdish question, which is indicative of how security policy can be an expression more of a country's inner dynamics than of an objective search for greater security.

Conclusion: Turkey's Loneliness

In the years following the establishment of the republic in 1923, Turkey had little scope to develop relationships with many former Ottoman lands. The cold war put up further barriers to interaction as some of the regions surrounding Turkey were either shut away behind the 'iron curtain' or adopted radical or, in much of the Middle East, Arab nationalist postures. Indeed, Arabs often saw Turkey as a former coloniser and a non-Arab 'outsider'.[69] In any case, for much of its history Turkey had neither the economic basis nor the political inclination to engage with its Islamic 'near abroad'. In recent years this has changed, but turmoil in the Arab world has prevented the development of more structured interactions. Davutoglu's confidence-building strategy of 'zero problems' might over time have improved Turkey's diplomatic fortunes, but it did not survive the 'Arab Spring' and Erdogan's confrontational and impulsive style. Yet Turkey's relationships with its western partners were also constrained. US interest in Turkey barely extended beyond its geostrategic utility, and many Europeans refused to recognise it as part of Europe.[70] Turkey's 'hard security' culture and its arch-nationalism and paranoia do little to ease its diplomatic dealings. Turkey is currently on a search for new alignments. Erdogan has expressed his interest in the Shanghai Cooperation Organisation (SCO), in the BRICS (Brazil–Russia–India–China–South Africa) group of countries, and is cultivating both Russia and China, but there is a long way to go before these initiatives meet with success, if ever they do. Simultaneously, Erdogan's anti-western rhetoric and behaviour—symbolised by the proposed purchase of Russians-400 anti-air missiles, and the US threat to retaliate by denying Turkey the F35 fighter jets—further alienated Turkey's western partners. It has sought to deepen its bonds with its fellow Turkic states, but the scope for more fully developed interaction is again limited. Even with respect to energy supply and transit, the Central Asians are geographically too distant, too intertwined with Russian energy networks, or too drawn towards China, and the political and technical problems too great, for Turkish ambitions to be assured to succeed.[71] Turkey remains heavily dependent on Russia and Iran for its growing energy needs, which reinforces its inclination to cultivate them.

In short, Turkey has a foot in many camps but is not truly integral to any of them. It is an odd fit in all the regions it abuts. This 'loneliness' suggests that, over time, the best Turkey can hope for are functioning transactional bilateral and multilateral relationships. A deeper 'belonging' to any of the political and cultural constellations and states that it neighbours will likely remain elusive. It has even been argued that Turkey's main function has been to insulate regional 'security complexes' by virtue of its constrained interactions with each of the regions that surround it.[72] It has similarly been defined as a 'cusp state', defined as 'states that lie uneasily on the political and/or normative edge of what is widely believed to be an established region'.[73] Of course, Turkey does 'bridge' different regions, either by virtue of its geography—for example, with respect to the flow of Syrian refugees, energy resources or narcotics westwards, or of European *jihadis* eastwards; or by virtue of its political nature or policies—as a semi-democratised and relatively economically developed Muslim country; or as a result of initiatives such as the Alliance of Civilisations.[74] But it has equally been regarded as a potential bridgehead for US interventions in the Middle East or against the Soviet southern flank, or as a potential drawbridge that can be raised against unwanted flows westwards.[75] However characterised, Turkey's geography seems to expose it to buffetings and pressures from forces beyond its borders. As a security actor it is so frequently constrained and, for reasons related to its own narratives and make-up, so often unhelpful to its own best interests. Under Erdogan, the personalisation and unpredictability of Turkish external policy raises the question of whether the country now pursues anything resembling a 'strategy' at all. This circumstance looks unlikely to alter until Erdogan falls from grace. However, even a post-Erdogan Turkish security policy will be shaped by the peculiarities in the country's essence, by its past, and by its unforgiving neighbourhood.

NOTES

1. For an overview on Turkey see: Park, B. (2012). *Modern Turkey: People, State and Foreign Policy in a Globalised World*. London: Routledge.
2. For background material see: Findley, C. V. (2010). *Turkey, Islam, Nationalism, and Modernity: A History, 1789–2007*. Yale: Yale University Press; Lewis, B. (2002). *The Emergence of Modern Turkey*, 3rd edition. Oxford: Oxford University Press; and Zurcher, E. J. (2017). *Turkey: A Modern History*, 4th edition. London: I.B.Tauris.
3. See: Jenkins, G. (2008). *Political Islam in Turkey: Running West, Heading East?* London: Palgrave Macmillan; and Kuru, A. (2012). *Democracy, Islam and Secularism in Turkey*. New York: Columbia University Press.
4. Taspiner, O. (2007). The Old Turks' Revolt: When Radical Secularism Endangers Democracy. *Foreign Affairs*, 86 (6), 118.
5. Huntington, S. The Clash of Civilisations. *Foreign Affairs*, 72 (3), 141. See also: Cornell, S., & Karaveli, H. M. (2008). *Prospects for a 'Torn' Turkey: A Secular and Unitary Future?* Central Asia-Caucasus Institute, Silk Road Paper, October, http://www.silkroadstudies.org/resources/pdf/SilkRo adPapers/2008_10_SRP_CornellKaraveli_Turkey.pdf.
6. See: Bilgin, P. (2008). The Securityness of Secularism? The Case of Turkey. *Security Dialogue*, 39 (6), 593–614.
7. Poulton, H. (1997). *Top Hat, the Grey Wolf, and the Crescent: Turkish Nationalism and the Turkish Republic*. London: Hurst and Co.

8. See: Ozbudun, E. (2000). *Contemporary Turkish Politics: Challenges to Democratic Consolidation*. Boulder: Lynne Rienner, 24–43.

9. Ozcan, G. (2011). The Military and the Making of Foreign Policy in Turkey. In Rubin, B., & Kirisci, H. (Eds.) *Turkey in World Politics: An Emerging Multiregional Power*, (pp.13–30) Boulder: Lynne Rienner.

10. See: Jenkins, G. (2001). Context and Circumstance: The Turkish Military and Politics. *Adelphi Papers* 337; Jenkins, G. Continuity and Change: Prospects for Civil-Military Relations in Turkey. *International Relations*, 8 (2), 339–355; and Narli, N. (2000). Civil-Military Relationships in Turkey. *Turkish Studies*, 1 (1), 107–127.

11. This much-quoted 'centre-periphery' approach to understanding Turkish politics and society was first enunciated by Mardin, S. (1973). Centre-Periphery Relations: A Key to Turkish Politics? *Daedalus*, 102 (1).

12. See Jenkins, G. (2009). *Between Fact and Fantasy: Turkey's Ergenekon Investigation*. Silk Road Paper, Central Asia-Caucasus Institute, August; Jenkins, G. (2014). The Balyoz Trial and the Changing Politics of Turkish Justice. *Turkey Analyst*, 7 (12); and Kapakci, M. (2009). Turkey's Test with Its Deep State. *Mediterranean Quarterly*, 20 (4), 83–97.

13. See: George, E. (2018). A Tyranny Establishes Itself. *London Review of Books*, 24 May; Cagaptay, S. (2017). *The New Sultan: Erdogan and the Crisis of Modern Turkey*. London; I.B.Tauris.

14. Guldogan, D. (2018). Turkish Republic Continuation of Ottoman Empire. *Anadolu Agency*, 10 February, https://www.aa.com.tr/en/todays-headlines/turkish-republic-continuation-of-ottoman-empire/1059924.

15. Cornell, S. (2018). Erbakan, Kisakurak, and the Mainstreaming of Extremism in Turkey. *Hudson Institute*, 4 June, https://www.hudson.org/research/14375-erbakan-k-sak-rek-and-the-mainstreaming-of-extremism-in-turkey. See also: Yilmaz, I., Barton, G., & Barry, J. (2017). The Decline and Resurgence of Turkish Islamism: The Story of Tayyip Erdogan's AKP. *Journal of Citizenship and Globalisation Studies*, 1 (1), 48–62.

16. For an overview of Turkish foreign policy see: Hale, W. (2012). *Turkish Foreign Policy since 1774*, 3rd edition. London: Routledge.

17. Jenkins. (2001). Context and Circumstance.

18. Quoted in: Berdal, A. (1997). Turkey's Insecure Identity from the Perspective of Nationalism. *Mediterranean Quarterly*, 8 (1), 87.

19. Guida, M. (2008). The Sevres Syndrome and 'Komplo' Theories in the Islamist and Secular Press. *Turkish Studies*, 9 (1), 37–52.

20. Jenkins, 2001, *op.cit.*, p.90.

21. See: McDowell, D. (1996). *A Modern History of the Kurds*. London: I.B. Tauris, 184–213 and 395–417; Natali, D. (2005). *The Kurds and the State: Evolving National Identity in Iraq, Turkey, and Iran*. Syracuse, NY: Syracuse University Press, 70–116.

22. See: Saracoglu, C. (2010). *Kurds of Modern Turkey: Migration, Neoliberalism and Exclusion in Turkish Society*. London: I.B. Tauris.

23. See; Calis, S. B. (2017). *Turkey's Cold War: Foreign Policy and Western Alignment in the Modern Republic*. London: I. B. Tauris; Cetiner, Y. T. (2015). *Turkey and the West: from Neutrality to Commitment*. Lanham: University Press of America; and Karpat, K. H. (ed.). (1975). *Turkey's Foreign Policy in Transition, 1950–1974*. Leiden: Brill Publishers.

24. Barkey, H. J. (ed.). (1996). *Reluctant Neighbour: Turkey's Role in the Middle East*. US Institute of Peace.
25. See: Abadi, J. (1995). Israel and Turkey: From Covert to Overt Relations. *Journal of Conflict Studies*, 15 (2), 104–128; Lochery, N. (1998). Israel and Turkey: Deepening Ties and Strategic Implications, 1995–1998. *Israel Affairs*, 5 (1), 45–62.
26. See: Ker-Lindsay, J. (2011). *The Cyprus Problem: What Everyone Needs to Know*. New York: Oxford University Press.
27. Carlson, S. (2016). Pivoting Energy Relations in the Eastern Mediterranean. *Turkish Policy Quarterly*, 15 (1), 67–78.
28. International Crisis Group. (2011). Turkey and Greece: Time to Settle the Aegean Dispute. *Europe Briefing* 64 (19 July), http://www.crisisgroup.org/~/media/Files/europe/turkey-cyprus/turkey/B64-%20Turkey%20and%20Greece-%20Time%20to%20Settle%20the%20Aegean%20Dispute.pdf.
29. Makovsky, A. (2009). *Daring and Caution in Turkish Strategic Culture: Republic at Sea*. London: Palgrave Macmillan. See also: Robins, P. (2003). *Suits and Uniforms: Turkish Foreign Policy since the Cold War*. London: Hurst and Co.
30. Guney, N. A. (2007). The New Security Environment and Turkey's ISAF Experience. In Guney, N. (Ed.) *Contentious Issues of Security and the Future of Turkey* (pp.177–189) London: Ashgate.
31. Gruen, G. E. (2006). Turkey's Role in Peacekeeping Missions. *American Foreign Policy Interests*, 28 (6), 435–449.
32. Barkey, H. (2008). The Effect of US Policy in the Middle East on EU–Turkey Relations. *International Spectator*, 43 (4), 31.
33. Quoted in: Candar, C. (2002). Regime Change in Iraq: Repercussions for Turkey. *Western Policy Centre*, July, www.patrides.com/july02/enregime.htm.
34. Altunisik, M. B. (2005). The Turkish Model and Democratisation in the Middle East. *Arab Studies Quarterly*, 27 (1–2), 45–63.
35. Hale, W. (2007). *Turkey, the US and Iraq*. London: SAQI.
36. Kirisci, K. The Transformation of Turkish Foreign Policy: The Rise of the Trading State. *New Perspectives on Turkey*, 40, 29–57.
37. See: Grigoriadis, I. N. (2010). The Davutoglu Doctrine and Turkish Foreign Policy. *Working Paper* 8. Hellenic Foundation for European and Foreign Policy (ELIAMEP), April, http://www.eliamep.gr/en/all-publications/working-papers/the-davutoglu-doctrine-and-turkish-foreign-policy/; Murinson, A. (2006). The Strategic Depth Doctrine of Turkish Foreign Policy. *Middle Eastern Studies*, 42 (6), 945–964; and Ozkan, B. (2014). Turkey, Davutoglu and the Idea of Pan-Islamism. *Survival*, 56 (4), 119–140.
38. See: Altinay, H. (2008). Turkey's Soft Power: An Unpolished Gem or an Elusive Mirage? *Insight Turkey*, 10 (2), 55–66; Altunisik, M. B. (2008). The Possibilities and Limits of Turkey's Soft Power in the Middle East. *Insight Turkey*, 10 (2), 41–54.
39. Taspinar, O. (2008). Turkey's Middle East Policies: Between Neo-Ottomanism and Kemalism. *Carnegie Papers* 10. Washington, DC: Carnegie Endowment for International Peace, 7 October, https://carnegieendowment.org/files/cmec10_taspinar_final.pdf.
40. Taspinar, O. (2011). The Rise of Turkish Gaullism: Getting Turkish–American Relations Right. *Insight Turkey*, 13 (1), 19–25.

41. Ozkan. (2014). Turkey, Davutoglu and the Idea of Pan-Islamism.
42. See: Bengio, O. (2010). *The Turkish–Israeli Relationship: Changing Ties of Middle Eastern Outsiders*. New York: Palgrave Macmillan.
43. Fisk, R., Cockburn, P., & Sengupta, K. (2016). *Arab Spring Then and Now: from Hope to Despair*. London: The Independent Press.
44. Cochrane, P. (2016). Secret Details of Turkey's New Military Pact with Qatar. *Middle East Eye*, 27 January.
45. See: Gurbuz, M. (2017). *Turkey's Policy Towards a Fractured Libya*. Washington, DC: Arab Center, 12 December; Schanzer, J. (2015). Turkey's Secret Proxy War in Libya? *The National Interest*, 17 March; and Stein, A. (2015). Turkey's Proxy War in Libya. *War on the Rocks*, 15 January, http://waronther ocks.com/2015/01/turkeys-proxy-war-in-libya/.
46. See: Akkaya, A. H., & Jongerden, J. (2011). Born from the Left: The Making of the PKK. In Casier, M., & Jongerden, J. (Eds.) *Nationalism and Politics in Turkey: Political Islam, Kemalism and the Kurdish Issue* (pp. 123–142) London: Routledge; Akkaya, A. H., & Jongerden, J. (2011). The PKK in the 2000s: Continuity through Breaks? In Casier, M., & Jongerden, J. (Eds.) *Nationalism and Politics in Turkey: Political Islam, Kemalism and the Kurdish Issue* (pp.143–162). London: Routledge.
    Sarihan, A. (2013). The Two Periods of the PKK Conflict: 1994–1999 and 2004–2010. In Bilgin, F., & Sarihan, A. (Eds.) *Understanding Turkey's Kurdish Question* (pp. 89–102). Lanham: Lexington Books; Tezcur, G. M. (2014). The Ebb and Flow of Armed Conflict in Turkey: An Elusive Peace. In Romano, D., & Gurses, M. (Eds.) *Conflict, Democratisation and the Kurds in the Middle East* (pp.171–188) London: Palgrave Macmillan.
47. See: Bahcheli, T., & Noel, S. (2011). The Justice and Development Party and the Kurdish Question. In Casier, M., & Jongerden, J. (Eds.) *Nationalism and Politics in Turkey: Political Islam, Kemalism and the Kurdish Issue* (pp.101–120). London: Routledge; Cizre, U. (2009). The Emergence of the Government's Perspective on the Kurdish Issue. *Insight Turkey*, 11 (4), 1–12; Candar, K. (2009). The Kurdish Question: The Reasons and Fortunes of the 'Opening'. *Insight Turkey*, 11 (4), 13–19; Pope, H. (2013). Turkey and the Democratic Opening for the Kurds. In Bilgin, F., & Sarihan, A. (Eds.) *Understanding Turkey's Kurdish Question* (pp. 117–140). Lanham: Lexington Books; and International Crisis Group. (2014). Turkey and the PKK: Saving the Peace Process. *Europe Report* 234 (6 November).
48. International Crisis Group. (2012). Turkey: The PKK and a Kurdish Settlement.
49. See: Yilmaz, E. (2013). Turkey's Kurdish Question and the Peace Process. *Insight Turkey*, 15 (2), 7–17; Gunter, M. M. (2014). The Turkish-Kurdish Peace Process Stalled in Neutral. *Insight Turkey*, 16 (1), 19–26; Villellas, A. (2013). New Peace Talks in Turkey: Opportunities and Challenges in Conflict Resolution. *Insight Turkey*, 15 (2), 19–26; and Nykanen, J. (2013). Identity, Narrative and Frames: Assessing Turkey's Kurdish Initiatives. *Insight Turkey*, 15 (2), 85–101.
50. *Today's Zaman*. (2013). Kurdish Conference Ends with List of Demands from Gov't, 17 June, http://www.todayszaman.com/news-318516-kurdish-confer ence-ends-with-list-of-demands-from-govt.html.
51. See: International Crisis Group. (2016). Turkey's PKK Conflict: The Rising Toll, 20 July, http://www.crisisgroup.be/interactives/turkey/; International

Crisis Group. (2017). The Human Cost of the PKK Conflict in Turkey: The Case of Sur, 17 March, https://d2071andvip0wj.cloudfront.net/b80-the-human-cost-of-the-pkk-conflict-in-turkey-the-case-of-sur.pdf; and Mandiraci, B. (2016). Turkey's PKK Conflict Veers onto a More Violent Path. *International Crisis Group*, 10 November, https://www.crisisgroup.org/europe-central-asia/western-europemediterranean/turkey/turkeys-pkk-conflict-veers-more-violent-path.

52. Human Rights Watch. (2017). Turkey: Crackdown on Kurdish Opposition, 20 March, https://www.hrw.org/news/2017/03/20/turkey-crackdown-kurdish-opposition.

53. Heller, S. (2017). Turkey's 'Turkey First' Syria Policy. *The Century Foundation*, 12 April, https://tcf.org/content/report/turkeys-turkey-first-syria-policy/; Park, B. (2019). Turkey's Kurdish Complexes and Its Syrian Quagmire. In Gunter, M. M. (ed.) *Routledge Handbook on the Kurds* (pp. 282–295) London: Routledge.

54. Altunisik, M. B., & Tur, O. (2006). From Distant Neighbours to Partners? Changing Syrian–Turkish Relations. *Security Dialogue*, 37 (2), 229–248.

55. See: Bozkurt, A. (2017). ISIS Suspects Released in Big Numbers under Erdogan's Rule. *Stockholm Center for Freedom*, 24 April, http://stockholmcf.org/isil-suspects-released-in-big-numbers-under-erdogans-rule/; Bekdil, B. (2016). Turkey's Double Game with ISIS. *Middle East Quarterly* 22 (3), 1–8; Philips, D. L. (2016). ISIS–Turkey Links. *Huffington Post*, 8 September, https://www.huffingtonpost.com/entry/research-paper-isis-turke_b_6128950.html; and Tahiroglu, M. & Schanzer, J. (2017). Islamic State Networks in Turkey. *Foundation for Defense of Democracies*, March.

56. See; International Crisis Group. (2014). Flight of Icarus? The PYD's Precarious Rise in Syria. *Middle East Report* 151 (8 May), https://www.crisisgroup.org/middle-east-north-africa/eastern-mediterranean/syria/flight-icarus-pyd-s-precarious-rise-syria; Gunter, M. (2014). *Out of Nowhere: the Kurds of Syria in Peace and War*. London: Hurst and Co.

57. Erkus, S. (2015). Erdogan Vows to Prevent Kurdish State in Northern Syria, as Iran Warns Turkey. *Hurriyet Daily News*, 27 June, http://www.hurriyetdailynews.com/erdogan-vows-to-prevent-kurdish-state-in-northern-syria-as-iran-warns-turkey.aspx?pageID=238&nID=84630&NewsCatID=338.

58. Candar, C. (2017). Operation Euphrates Shield: A Post-Mortem. *Al Monitor*, 5 April, http://www.al-monitor.com/pulse/originals/2017/04/turkey-post-mortem-in-syria.html?utm_source=Boomtrain&utm_medium=manual&utm_campaign=20170406&bt_ee=uUVbVCsHX3BpTkikUz5rRueZ57bvbM/ikC8vws7hOsux48LUcOyF7omE+5QVd5q+&bt_ts=1491498185749.

59. Kasapoglu, C., & and Ulgen, S. (2018). Operation Olive Branch: A Political-military Assessment. *The Centre for Economics and Foreign Policy Studies (EDAM)*, 30 January, https://edam.org.tr/en/operation-olive-branch-a-political-military-assessment/.

60. See for example: Park, B. (2019). Operation Spring Peace: A Deepening Syrian Chaos? *Platform for Peace and Justice*, 12 October, http://www.platformpj.org/operation-spring-peace-a-deepening-syrian-chaos/; Park, B. (2019). There Are no Clear 'Winners' and 'Losers' Yet in Syria. *Platform for Peace and Justice*, 30 October, http://www.platformpj.org/there-are-no-clear-winners-and-losers-yet-in-syria/.

61. al-Tamimi, A. J. (2018). In Syria, Its Either Reconciliation or Annexation. *The American Spectator*, 23 August, https://spectator.org/in-syria-its-either-reconciliation-or-annexation/; Eytan, H., & Yanarock, C. (2018). The Cypriotisation of Northern Syria. *The Jerusalem Institute for Strategic Studies*, 20 June, https://jiss.org.il/en/yanarocak-the-cypriotization-of-northern-syria/#:~:text=The%20Cypriotization%20of%20Northern%20Syria%20Dr.%20Hay%20Eytan,a%20Turkish%20protectorate%20through%20military%20and%20economic%20domination.

62. See: Lundgren, A. (2007). *The Unwelcome Neighbour: Turkey's Kurdish Policy*. London: I.B. Tauris; Park, B. (2005). Turkey's Policy Towards Northern Iraq: Problems and Perspectives. *Adelphi Papers*, 45 (374), 11–27.

63. Robin Mills, R. (2018). A Rocky Road: Kurdish Oil and Independence. *Iraq Energy Institute*, 19 February, https://iraqenergy.org/rocky-road-kurdish-oil-and-independence; Paasche, T. F., & Mansurbeg, H. (2014). Kurdistan Regional Government–Turkish Energy Relations: A Complex Partnership. *Eurasian Geography and Economics*, 55 (2), 111–132; Balci, A. (2014). 'Energized' Neighbourliness: Relations Between Turkey and the Kurdish Regional Government. *Analysis 9*, Foundation for Political, Economic and Social Research (SETA), September; and Borroz, N. (2014). Turkey's Energy Strategy: Kurdistan Over Iraq. *Turkish Policy Quarterly*, 13 (2), 103–110.

64. See: Park, B. (2014). *Turkey-KRG Relations after the US Withdrawal from Iraq: Putting the Kurds on the Map*. Carlisle, PA: Strategic Studies Institute, US Army War College, March.

65. Bartu, P. (2010). Wrestling with the Integrity of a Nation: the Disputed Internal Boundaries of Iraq. *International Affairs*, 86 (6), 1329–1343; Kay, S. (2011). *Iraq's Disputed Territories: A View of the Political Horizon and Implications for US Policy*. Washington, DC: United States Institute of Peace, March, https://www.usip.org/publications/2011/04/iraqs-disputed-territories.

66. Park, B., Jongerden, J., Owtram, F., & Yoshioka, A. (2017). On the Independence Referendum in the Kurdistan Region of Iraq and Disputed Territories. *Kurdish Studies*, 5 (2), 199–2014.

67. Usten, K., & Dudden, L. (2017). Turkey-KRG Relationship: Mutual Interests, Geopolitical Challenges. *SETA Report*, September, http://setadc.org/turkey-krg-relationship-mutual-interests-geopolitical-challenges/; Uyanik, M. (2017). Turkey and the KRG After the Referendum: Blocking the Path to Independence. *Center for Strategic and International Studies*, 22 November, https://csis-prod.s3.amazonaws.com/s3fs-public/publication/171122_Turkey_and_the_KRG.pdf?59mZTTCAofHDZVpg.M6jYR6uf4d5ovUi.

68. Iddon, P. (2019). Turkish Military in for the Long Haul in Iraqi Kurdistan. *Ahval*, 16 November, https://ahvalnews.com/iraq/turkish-military-long-haul-iraqi-kurdistan.

69. Jung, D. (2005). Turkey and the Arab World: Historical Narratives and New Political Realities. *Mediterranean Politics*, 10 (10), 1–17.

70. Onis, Z. (1999). Turkey, Europe, and the Paradoxes of Identity. *Mediterranean Quarterly*, 10 (3), 107–136.

71. Richert, J. (2015). *Is Turkey's Energy Leadership Over Before It Began?* Istanbul Policy Centre-Stiftung Mercator Initiative, January; Winrow, G. (2014). Realization of Turkey's Energy Aspirations: Pipe Dreams or Real Projects? *Turkey Project Policy Paper* 4. Centre on the US and Europe, Brookings Institution, April.

72. See Buzan, B., & Diez, T. (1999). The European Union and Turkey. *Survival*, 41 (1), 41–57; Diez, T. (2005). Turkey, the European Union and Security Complexes Revisited. *Mediterranean Politics*, 10 (2), 167–180.
73. See for example: Herzog, M., & Robins, P. (Eds.). *The Role, Position and Agency of Cusp States in International Relations*. London: Routledge.
74. Balci, A., & Mis, N. (2008). Turkey's Role in the Alliance of Civilisations: A New Perspective in Turkish Foreign Policy? *Turkish Studies*, 9 (3), 387–406.
75. Lesser, I. O. (1992). *Bridge or Barrier? Turkey and the West After the Cold War*. Santa Monica, CA: RAND, Report R-4202-AF/A.

CHAPTER 11

Securing Iran in the Internet age

Dara Conduit

The Islamic Republic of Iran has been consumed by the question of security since its establishment in 1979. In its founding years, Iran was invaded by Iraq, isolated by the international community, and weakened by domestic jostling over the future shape of the Republic. Fierce and bloody battles with internal and external Others have occupied the country ever since. Iran is an important case study of national security because it is one of the most powerful states in the Middle East. It has a large population, a diverse (although severely mismanaged) economy, and strong regular, and irregular armed forces. Yet the Islamic Republic has always felt a keen sense of vulnerability from both domestic and international bogeymen, and thus has enacted policies including the harsh repression of domestic opponents, efforts to export its model of revolution, the cultivation of proxy non-state actors across the region, and the pursuit of nuclear technology. These strategies have in turn heightened regional security dilemmas, prompting counter-measures by neighbours and foes including Saddam Hussein-era Iraq, Saudi Arabia, Israel, and the US, and feeding the cycles of regional insecurity that have characterised the international relations of the Middle East for decades.

Scholars of security have urged authors to think more deeply about both the referent object of security, and what it is that renders that object insecure. Initially, this began with problematising the nation-state as the primary

---

D. Conduit (✉)
Alfred Deakin Institute for Citizenship and Globalisation, Deakin University, VIC, Australia
e-mail: dara.conduit@deakin.edu.au

© The Author(s), under exclusive license to Springer Nature
Switzerland AG 2022
M. Clarke et al. (eds.), *The Palgrave Handbook of National Security*,
https://doi.org/10.1007/978-3-030-53494-3_11

241

object of security. Mohammed Ayoob noted that in the developing world, 'the sense of insecurity from which these states—and, more particularly, their regimes—suffer, emanates to a substantial extent from within their boundaries rather than from outside.'[1] Kevin Krause and Michael C. Williams argued: 'to understand security from a broader perspective means to look at ways in which the objects to be secured, the perceptions of threats to them, and the available means of securing them (both intellectual and material) have shifted over time.'[2] Indeed, it became clear that neither the referent object of security nor the nature of threats was universal or static. It varied from jurisdiction to jurisdiction, and changed with time. Threat environments would also evolve dramatically over the coming decades alongside technological innovation, the mass movement of refugees across borders, and increasingly extreme weather events linked to climate change.

For much of Iran's contemporary existence, the country's leadership has prioritised securing the regime—and the Islamic Republic system as a whole—from threats inside and outside the country. Although the regime has always maintained a firm grip on power, its threat calculus has been shaped by a deep-seated fear of societal strength. Gregory Koblentz has explained that in such cases, 'the interests of the regime may diverge from those of the nation as a whole and, when it does, the regime will prioritise its own security and prosperity to the detriment of the rest of the nation.'[3] Scholars have identified the value of analysing states that subjugate state-wide interests in favour of parochial regime interests through the lens of 'regime security.'[4] This approach differs to neo-realist and neo-classical realist approaches to security, because of the important distinction between *regime* and *state* as the referent object, and its recognition that external and internal threats can both independently pose serious threats to regime security.[5]

This chapter therefore examines Iran through the lens of regime security, first looking at the founding moments of the Islamic Republic to identify key drivers of regime insecurity, before turning to an overview of the key features of Iranian regime security over the past four decades. Recent technological innovation has fomented significant changes in regime security in Iran. The spread of the internet—and social media in particular—was initially viewed as a panacea for the country's opposition, with observers breathlessly (and prematurely) proclaiming a 'Twitter Revolution' in the weeks after the disputed 2009 presidential election. But with time the Internet has proven a valuable tool through which the country's intelligence apparatus has also been able to counter its internal and external Others. Hence the chapter argues that while many of Iran's founding regime security challenges remain unresolved, the twenty-first century has provided it with new mechanisms to counter perceived threats.

Security in the Founding
Moments of the Islamic Republic

The contemporary Iranian state was formed through the machinations that followed the 1979 revolution, which saw millions of Iranians take to the streets to call for an end to the corruption, decadence and violence that had characterised Mohammad Reza Shah's regime; as well as independence from foreign powers, especially the US. While the revolution is often portrayed as an Islamic Revolution, it was a popular uprising made up of a broad range of opposition groups that included Marxists, nationalists, democrats, students, and both traditional and radical clerics.[6] The opposition was highly fragmented, characterised by fighting between and within factions.[7] It was in this context of in-fighting that the country's future Supreme Leader Ayatollah Ruhollah Khomeini and his supporters came to dominate and eventually unite the opposition. But as Ziba Moshaver observed: clerical rule was 'by no means the natural outcome of the revolution.'[8] Khomeini's leadership of the revolution did not automatically translate into acceptance of his vision for the post-revolutionary state, and the conflicts that took place in these founding moments set the scene for many of the challenges that the country's leaders would face in the future.

A shaky secularist-Islamist alliance was established in an interim government in 1979, but its term was characterised by vicious infighting and power struggles, as well as serious challenges to its rule by excluded opposition members and ethnic minorities demanding autonomy. By June 1981 the first two revolutionary governments had collapsed, while anti-statist opposition challenges persisted, including in the bombing of the Iranian Revolutionary Party headquarters, which killed 72 people,[9] as well as mounting pressure from separatist movements in the Turkoman Sahra and Kurdish areas.[10]

Nonetheless, Khomeini eventually succeeded in establishing a new political system in line with his radical vision of *Velayat e-faqih,* defining Iran as an Islamic state with a hierarchical system that delimited power between clerical and civilian governance. This saw the appointment of a Supreme Leader who is constitutionally and ideologically empowered to both determine 'the overall politics of the Islamic Republic' and supervise 'the proper implementation of the general policies of the system.'[11] In parallel, the country's president and parliament were to be elected by the people, with checks on their power from institutions including the Guardian Council (half of which is appointed by the Supreme Leader), which vets electoral candidates and approves parliamentary legislation. Iran was therefore a hybrid authoritarian regime from its moment of birth, with its system of government based on an uneasy division between societal and authoritarian clerical power.[12] This set the scene for many of the challenges Iran would face over the subsequent decades, with its contradictions pointing to what Shahram Akbarzadeh described as a 'dual personality.'[13] Indeed, the idea of Iran as an Islamic state made the country perhaps the greatest 'imagined community' of all.[14] This left the new Iranian

244   D. CONDUIT

regime highly insecure as Khomeini and his supporters struggled to drown out dissenting voices.

Key Events and Issues

Foreign and domestic policy-making in the Islamic Republic is rooted in the regime's rational synthesis of the country's contemporary historical experiences, its memories of state building and the nature of the threats that it faces. Post-revolution Iran settled in to a relatively stable pattern of security seeking that centred around several key themes, including leveraging international events for domestic advantage, achieving independence and self-sufficiency, and neutralising internal threats. These themes emerged early in the life of the Islamic Republic, and would guide future threat perception and decision-making in the ever-evolving politics of the Middle East.

The 1979 US hostage crisis was a seminal moment in regime security policy as it revealed the fierceness of the regime's anti-Americanism and drive for independence, and gave an indication of the intense interplay between the internal and external in the regime's worldview. Anti-US sentiment had been the cornerstone of the 1979 revolution because the Shah was viewed as a puppet of the US, having been installed as monarch following the CIA and MI6-backed coup that toppled the country's elected prime minister Mohammad Mosaddeq in 1953.[15] On November 4, 1979, Iranian student demonstrators took over the US Embassy in Tehran, taking 52 US diplomats and citizens hostage for 444 days, sparking the Islamic Republic's first major international crisis. The events that followed set Iran and the US on a collision course for decades to come.

The hostage crisis was also important because it demonstrated the Iranian regime's willingness to use international events for domestic gain. Consistent with other states where regime security takes primacy, the Iranian regime has rarely differentiated between the inside and outside: developments in the international arena are frequently used to unite the population against a common foe, while dissidents inside the country are almost always framed as pawns in the pay of international powers. Both are viewed equally as serious threats to the regime. The then-US Secretary of State Cyrus Vance quickly sensed that the crisis was being drawn out to galvanise the Supreme Leader's own position, opining: 'you will not get your hostages until Khomeini has put all the institutions of the Islamic Revolution' into place.'[16] Whether or not Khomeini's intent was so overt, the events nonetheless enabled him to secure the support of the population behind the ailing state and against the 'Great Satan,' the moniker used to describe the US. Mahmood Monshipouri and Ali Assarreh similarly concluded that 'since its inception, the Islamic Republic has almost always guaranteed its political longevity by defending itself against "real" or "imagined" enemies.'[17] The international arena would change substantially after these heady early days of the revolution, but the events of 1979 and 1980 nonetheless became an early example of the regime's willingness to leverage foreign events and enemies for domestic gain.

The hostage crisis also strengthened Iran's drive to seek independence and self-sufficiency away from the great powers. Although the US and the UK had been focal points of popular ire during the revolution, it was only decades before that Russia had occupied Iran. In the Cold War context, the new regime sought independence from all powers, with Khomeini popularising the term 'Neither East Nor West.' Iran became an enthusiastic member of the Non-Aligned Movement, and has subsequently sought membership from regional bodies such as the Shanghai Cooperation Organisation, which it perceives as a counterweight to Western influence.[18]

The Iran–Iraq war too had a path-defining impact on the posture of the Islamic Republic. Pledging to export the Islamic Revolution was a rhetorical device used by Khomeini and his followers, with Iraq provocatively depicted as an early target because President Saddam Hussein's despotic minority government oversaw a downtrodden majority Shi'ite population. Deeply threatened by Iran's posturing, Saddam Hussein invaded Iran in September 1980. The war represented a defining historical moment for Iran that vindicated the regime's fear of external and internal threats. Iraq had opportunistically invaded at Iran's point of greatest domestic weakness, even supplying weapons to the Kurdish Democratic Party of Iran (KDPI) to exacerbate domestic unrest.[19] Despite that Iraq was the initial aggressor in the war and would subsequently use weapons of mass destruction against Iranian troops and its own population, it still enjoyed the backing of most of the Arab states and the international community, including the US and Saudi Arabia.[20]

To the Iranian regime, the war therefore underlined that self-help and self-reliance would be imperative to its own survival. It could not rely on another state to guarantee its own security, and in fact its neighbours had now actively conspired against it. Iran would need to actively protect itself given the presence of Iraq, Saudi Arabia, Israel, and the US in its own backyard. In practice, this saw Iran develop large and capable conventional forces, as well as the Islamic Revolutionary Guards Corps (IRGC), which was charged with protecting the Islamic system (or put another way, the regime itself) from domestic and international threats. Within years, the IRGC expanded its operations across the region, establishing a Lebanese proxy group following the 1982 invasion of Lebanon that eventually became Hezbollah.[21] Iran forged a close relationship with Syria as a bulwark against both Israeli and Iraqi ambitions, and would later establish relations with non-state actors in Israel/Palestine, Yemen and Iraq, shoring up its position vis-à-vis its regional rivals Israel and Saudi Arabia. At the same time, Iran's naval resources patrolled the Persian Gulf, periodically harassing commercial traffic to remind Iran's sea traffic-reliant neighbours on the Arabian Peninsula that the Islamic Republic enjoyed a geographic and military advantage over the Hormuz Strait. Iran would also make efforts to acquire nuclear technology. Although the Shah himself had purportedly attempted to acquire nuclear weapons long before the revolution, Iran took tangible steps towards a nuclear capability from the 1990s until 2015. This drive probably reflected a desire to obtain regional prestige, as well as an effort to balance Israel's nuclear capacity and enhance its own position as a powerful state in the region.

The Iran–Iraq war, however, also demonstrated the regime's willingness to subjugate national interests in favour of the interests of the regime. By 1982, Iran had successfully repelled Iraq from its territory, but it controversially decided to go on the offensive by invading Iraq. Although this may have reflected a rational fear that Saddam Hussein would regroup and re-invade, Ray Takeyh argued that:

> For the clerical rulers, the war was not just about territorial restoration but also about defending Islam and spreading the revolution. Thus, the ideal outcome was an extension of Iran's Islamist template to Iraq.[22]

This was not a decision based on the rational interests of the Iranian state, which had already suffered significantly in the first two years of the war. Hundreds of thousands died over the nearly six years of brutal conflict that followed, with Iran also sustaining massive economic damage, the direct and indirect costs of which Hooshang Amirahmadi estimated could have amounted to US\$592 billion for Iran.[23]

Finally, the Islamic Republic has faced a persistent threat from within throughout its lifetime. This has included periodic, but serious violent challenges from ethnic-based separatist groups such as the Baluch Jaish al-Adl, the Kurdistan Free Life Party and the Arab Struggle Movement for the Liberation of Ahwaz, some of which the Iranian regime has viewed as fifth-columns for its foreign rivals.[24] Iran has also faced armed challenges from actors such as the Mujahideen al-Khalq (MeK) which targeted Iranian interests both inside and outside the country, as well as recent attacks by the Islamic State group.[25] The Iranian regime has responded to such threats with massive violence: in a matter of weeks in 1988, the regime undertook the extra-judicial execution of up to 5,000 dissidents in Iranian jails, most of whom belonged to the MeK.[26] But the Iranian regime's fear of its domestic foes extends beyond violent actors and is also based on the securitisation of the myriad non-violent dissident and civil society groups that exist inside and outside the country. Consistent with Koblentz's observations on regime security,[27] these societal threats have been taken as seriously as external threats and vigorously countered, representing a prioritisation of regime interests over the broader interests of the Iranian state and its population. This has led to the violent repression of citizens mobilised against regime policy, including the killing of student protesters in 1999, and the jailing and harassment of women's activists taking part in the historic One Million Signatures campaign that called for gender equality during the 2000s.[28] In 1999, the Ministry of Intelligence and Security announced that 'rogue elements' had been involved in the assassination of several political figures and activists who supported the elected president Mohammad Khatami.[29]

The regime's worst fears were realised following the 2009 presidential election. After what was perceived to be a closely contested campaign between the hard-line incumbent Mahmoud Ahmadinejad and the reformist Mir Hossein Mousavi, Iran's state news agency announced that Ahmadinejad had won the poll by a large margin. The following day, hundreds of thousands of protesters took to the streets, marking the formation of the Green Movement.[30] The regime attempted to discredit the protesters by linking them to foreign conspirators. Nine local staff members from the British Embassy were arrested, with an editorial by *Fars News Agency* declaring that British Embassy staff were the 'main elements' behind the protests.[31] But the regime's counter-narrative did little to quell the demonstrations, which continued at key junctures over the following six months, at their peak drawing more than three million protesters. It was only with brute force that the regime was eventually able to wrest back control of the streets. At the time of writing a decade later, the movement's leaders including presidential candidate Mir Hossein Mousavi remained under house arrest, highlighting ongoing regime concerns about societal threats.

These key themes of independence, self-reliance and a deep-seated paranoia about the enemy within that emerged in the founding years of the Islamic Republic would become the defining feature of regime threat perceptions and responses. They would often override the overarching interests of the Iranian state and its people. The regime would face myriad new challenges over the coming decades, including the US invasion of Iraq and the toppling of Saddam Hussein, the imposition of debilitating international sanctions, and the 2009 protests. The regime's response to every crisis was deeply influenced by these three themes, which would shape its approach to emerging technology and particularly the internet.

IRANIAN REGIME SECURITY
AND THE INTERNET: A DOUBLE-EDGED SWORD

The internet arrived in Iran in the early 1990s as the country attempted to rebuild and rehabilitate following the Iran–Iraq war. It was initially embraced by the Iranian regime, who recognised its potential as a tool for the country's much-needed post-war economic recovery. But the internet quickly became viewed around the world as a 'liberation technology' that would threaten the very foundation of authoritarian regimes.[32] Bill Clinton famously declared: 'in the new century, liberty will spread by cell phone and cable modem [...] Now, there's no question China has been trying to crack down on the Internet—good luck. That's sort of like trying to nail Jello to the wall.'[33] The subsequent emergence of social media was seen to compound this challenge. Yet the spread of the internet has proven a more mixed phenomenon for Iran, providing both opportunities for—and threats against—regime security.

This is consistent with pluralist developments in other hybrid authoritarian regimes, which as Andreas Schedler has noted are neither categorically good nor bad for regimes or oppositions, but usually occupy a space somewhere in between.[34] The following section examines the Iranian regime's evolving relationship with the internet, which has been variously viewed as a benign economic tool, a highly securitised domestic threat, and a useful instrument to serve regime domestic and foreign interests. Indeed, although the internet has facilitated the greatest domestic (and at times international) threat in the regime's 40-year history, it has also been instrumental in ensuring the regime's international and domestic salvation.

The internet was not initially securitised by the Iranian regime: little consideration was given to its potential as a vehicle for mass political upheaval as it was viewed mainly as an economic tool.[35] Its introduction in Iran was followed soon after by the election of President Mohammad Khatami, who was elected with a mandate of almost 70% of the vote.[36] He campaigned on a reform platform, pledging to assure 'civil rights and freedoms of citizens,' to reduce censorship, respect the 'variety and diversity of attitudes' inside Iran, and to challenge the idea 'that politics should be monopolised by a specific group.'[37] The period represented a high water mark for the country's pluralist institutions, and a time of online innovation and personal expression.

It was in the context of a relatively open political environment, stark post-war economic imperatives and a lack of regime technological knowledge that the internet in Iran was initially able to flourish. Within a year of the internet's arrival in Iran, several government agencies had established websites.[38] During the 1999 student protests, some students reportedly used chatrooms to organise, while the following year the key Supreme Leader critic Ayatollah Montazeri uploaded his 600-page memoir onto his personal website.[39] By 2008, there were an estimated 60,000 Iranian blogs that were regularly updated.[40] But it was not just young people who embraced the internet in this period, with some close to the regime also sensing its potential. Here, Ali Ansari observed that:

> Internet use has been given a boost in the belief that it is the ideal vehicle for 'exporting the revolution'...Far from advocating an insular purity, many clerics began to argue that by embracing the new technology and harnessing it to good use as they saw it, a more confident Islamic Revolution would be better able to spread the word.[41]

This would be an early indication of how the regime would seek to weaponise the internet decades later. Nonetheless, the first years of the internet in Iran represented somewhat of a golden era in which citizens, government, and business were free to innovate online, largely unhindered by the authoritarian aspects of the state. For a short period, the internet existed independently of notions of regime security in Iran.

The regime's approach to the internet changed dramatically in the late 1990s and early 2000s, as it began to securitise the online sphere, cognisant that online technologies posed a threat. This change took place amid the broader crackdown against pluralism across the country briefly noted above. Alongside the arrests, repression and targeted assassinations, hundreds of media outlets were forced to close. The websites of some of those targeted opposition newspapers were also taken offline.[42] President Khatami and his supporters had become increasingly marginalised by regime elements by his second term, with decrees by the Supreme Council of the Cultural Revolution in 2001 providing the legal framework for new web filtering practices. By 2004, more than one-third of 1477 websites tested in one study were blocked in Iran.[43] By 2007, the Islamic Republic was acknowledged to have 'one of the most extensive technical filtering systems in the world.'[44] Subsequent legislation including the 2009 Computer Crimes Law provided the regime with further coercive instruments.[45] Nonetheless, the number of Iranians connected to the internet continued to increase faster than most other states in the region, with Iran recording a 2,900 per cent increase in internet connections between 2000 and 2005.[46]

The 2009 presidential election protests took place in this context of an already highly securitised online environment. The Green Movement protesters combined street protests with an innovative online campaign across social media platforms, particularly Twitter. The movement's mastery of social media in this period prompted observers to breathlessly declare that 'The Revolution will be Twittered'[47] and note the rise of the 'Twitter Revolution.'[48] Later analysis would downplay the significance of social media as a singular force for political change,[49] but it nonetheless played a very visible role in helping oppositions organise, and would represent a key point of learning for the Iranian regime. Social media remains important for Iranian activists, including members of the women's movement's White Wednesday campaign against compulsory veiling, and for protesters who participated in the countrywide 2017/18 bread riots. Iranians also became enthusiastic users of encrypted smartphone messaging apps: in 2017, the CEO of the company that makes the encrypted private messaging app Telegram claimed that 40 million Iranians used the app each month.[50]

The spread of the Stuxnet worm in 2010 highlighted that the Iranian regime would also face cyber threats from outside the country. The worm was designed to target Iran's nuclear program by infiltrating computer networks to disable machines that managed uranium enrichment processes.[51] Stuxnet is thought to have been co-developed by Israel and the US as part of *Operation Olympic Games*, although neither country has publicly confirmed their involvement in the operation. Tehran downplayed the impact of Stuxnet, with Communications Minister Reza Taghipour initially maintaining that 'the effect and damage of this spy worm in government systems is not serious.' President Ahmadinejad later acknowledged that Stuxnet had interrupted the country's nuclear program, but that it only impacted a 'limited number of centrifuges.'[52]

External sources estimated that Stuxnet could have destroyed as many as 1,000 centrifuges at the Nanatz nuclear facility, setting Iran's nuclear program 'back by at least two years.'[53] Iran would face further attacks in the coming years from state-built malware including DuQu, which was an espionage tool that infiltrated computers in Iran and Sudan with the aim of stealing data, and the highly sophisticated Flame malware that was found on computers inside the Iranian oil ministry and in countries including Syria and Lebanon.[54]

The events of 2009 and 2010 therefore acted as a watershed moment in the Iranian regime's cybersecurity policy, highlighting that the internet posed a grave internal and external risk to the regime. Cognisance of this prompted Iran to take a considerably more offensive cyber posture, enacting three new strategies that enhanced its ability to watch its citizens, and weaponise the internet against internal and external opponents. This meant (1) Substantially expanding its domestic coercive apparatus, (2) Developing a significant cyber-warfare capacity, and (3) Leveraging the internet's soft power potential. The seriousness of this commitment was underlined by the decision by the IRGC's Mobin Trust Consortium to purchase a 50 per cent stake in the Telecommunications Infrastructure Company (TIC) just three months after the 2009 election.[55] TIC provides the country's internet infrastructure, with the purchase enhancing the Guards' influence over the country's technology systems and intelligence gathering activities.

The Iranian regime took immediate steps to enhance its control of the internet, prioritising the security of the regime over broader state interests and international norms, including freedom of expression online.[56] By 2012, Freedom House's 'Freedom on the Net' report ranked the country as having the least free internet in the world, noting that over the previous three years, 'Iranian authorities waged an active campaign against internet freedom, employing extensive and sophisticated methods of control that went well beyond simple content filtering.'[57] The 2009 Computer Crimes Law had facilitated stricter content bans, as well as the establishment of the Commission to Determine the Instances of Criminal Content (CDICC), which met fortnightly to make decisions on website filtering. This included unpopular attempts to block encrypted smartphone messaging apps such as Whatsapp, Telegram, and Viber. The regime's enhanced legislative architecture also enabled the widespread arrest of internet users.[58] These practices continued unabated under the comparatively moderate presidency of Hassan Rouhani, who demonstrated little ability to influence internet policy despite committing to online freedoms during his election campaign.[59] Indeed, regime practices online were often at odds with the priorities of elected officials: ICT Minister Vaezi announced in 2017 that seven million websites were banned during Rouhani's 2013 presidential term.[60] This included six media organisations that were blocked for publishing stories on corruption in the Tehran construction industry.[61] The regime also implemented other strategies to prevent access to online content, including throttling data transfer rates during politically sensitive periods such as elections in order to make the internet unusable. Collin

Anderson described the strategy thus: 'Rather than shut down networks, which would draw attention and controversy, the government was rumoured to have slowed connection speeds to rates that would render the Internet nearly unusable, especially for the consumption and distribution of multimedia content.'[62]

In close consultation with China, Iran developed the National Information Network, a state-wide intranet that promised faster and cheaper connections, but also facilitated closer monitoring of the internet by authorities. The Network violated the principle of net neutrality by creating a two-tier internet system in which access to content hosted outside Iran would become more expensive and slower. The regime also developed its own parallel social networking and instant messaging tools such as Soroush, which is a smartphone app that boasts most of the features of Telegram, but also provides the government unimpeded access to user content. Indeed, as the Iranian regime gained mastery over the tools of online coercion, it would begin to see the benefits of the internet. The exponential increase of Iranian internet users had given the regime access to a huge tranche of communications material that would previously have required a sophisticated and resource-heavy human intelligence network. In short, the internet was in some ways making the regime more secure.

The second key area of post-2009/2010 expansion was Iran's development of a significant cyberwarfare capability. Although this reflected the increasing importance of cyberwarfare as a tool of non-conventional warfare globally, Iran quickly became one of the most aggressive state actors online. These new tools would prove indispensable in the never-ending struggle against domestic and foreign adversaries. They were 'almost exclusively overseen by the IRGC—likely without the oversight of the country's publicly "elected" officials.'[63] Indeed, the internet's potential was seen as too significant to leave in the remit of state institutions: those charged with protecting the regime itself would exercise the most influence over internet strategy. The IRGC had purportedly broached the idea of establishing a 'cyber army' as early as 2005, but these efforts expanded significantly after 2009.[64] By 2013, it claimed to have the fourth largest cyberCyber army in the world.[65] Iran's capabilities would develop across a range of decentralised groups and contractors inside the country, with varying levels of sophistication and connection to Iranian intelligence services. By 2017, Iran was thought to have spent US$1 billion to resource its cyberwarfare operations.[66] This shift has been widely linked to the events of 2010, with the chief of the US Air Force's cyber operations General William Shelton explaining:

> It's clear that the Natanz situation generated reaction by them. They are going to be a force to be reckoned with, with the potential capabilities that they will develop over the years and the potential threat that will represent to the United States.[67]

This assessment was echoed in a leaked 2013 NSA document, which suggested that the US intelligence community believed that Iranian cyberattacks were 'retaliation to Western activities against Iran's nuclear sector.'[68]

In line with broader practices of regime security in Iran, the country's enhanced cyberwarfare capabilities were simultaneously designed to target threats both at home and abroad. Its domestic efforts were visible during the 2009 protests, when regime-linked cyber actors hijacked opposition websites, distributed spyware ans undertook Distributed Denial of Service (DDoS) attacks on websites related to opposition organising.[69] In December that year, regime-linked cyber actors successfully targeted Twitter and Baidu, as well as local news websites.[70] The IRGC subsequently took responsibility for defacing the websites of nine local human rights organisations and independent media outlets.[71] Hackers from the 'Charming Kitten' group linked to the state have also been held responsible for spear phishing campaigns targeting Iranian activists and US officials.[72]

Iran's cyberwarfare capabilities have also been used extensively as a tool for asymmetric warfare to deter and retaliate against Iran's international foes. In this context Jaclyn Kerr has noted the internet's utility in such situations as it enables states to work towards strategic goals without risking armed conflict.[73] In particular, Iran has attacked entities and institutions linked to the global crackdown on its nuclear program, including international organisations and financial institutions. Between 2011 and 2013, Iranian cyber actors carried out *Operation Ababil*, which targeted 46 US financial institutions with DDoS attacks that brought down websites and prevented customers from accessing accounts.[74] Those targeted included JP Morgan, Wells Fargo and American Express, with Anderson and Sadjadpour warning that the internet had become 'the newest frontier in the four-decade-long US–Iran cold war.'[75] In 2012, a group linked to the IRGC hacked into servers at the International Atomic Energy Agency (IAEA), which is the international organisation charged with policing nuclear proliferation. The hackers demanded an IAEA investigation into Israel's nuclear program.[76] Iranian threat actors also targeted Iran's regional rivals, especially Saudi Arabia. In 2012, Iran released Shamoon malware that destroyed tens-of-thousands of computers at the Saudi state-run oil company Aramco.[77] Indeed, Iran had become a major international cyber actor by the 2010s, capable of causing significant damage and interruption-to states and businesses globally. The unilateral US withdrawal from the Iran nuclear deal in May 2018 raised the prospect warned that Iran may once again use its cyberwarfare capabilities to retaliate against companies and institutions involved in the re-enforcement of sanctions.[78]

Although these cyber-attacks involved varying levels of sophistication, ranging from the relatively simple DDoS attacks and phishing campaigns, to more advanced malware such as Shamoon, Iran's cyberwarfare strategies also highlighted the ongoing interaction between internal and external regime threats. Anderson and Sadjadpour observed that Iran's cyber operations:

Do not maintain clear boundaries between operations directed against its internal opposition and those directed against foreign adversaries. The same infrastructure and tools used by Iranian threat actors for campaigns against the American defense industry are also used to target Persian-language women's development programs; the same malware used in destructive attacks against Saudi government institutions had been previously used for surveillance against members of the Green Movement opposition.[79]

Indeed, threat perceptions and responses on the internet echoed patterns seen in conventional aspects of Iranian regime security more generally.

But the events of 2009 also prompted the regime to recognise the soft power value of the internet, representing perhaps the most innovative aspect of Iran's post-2009 internet strategy. A senior state broadcaster told Narges Bajoghli soon after the 2009 protests that 'state television is no longer the way. We need to figure out new ways to influence the narrative and bring the story back to our side.'[80] The regime soon enacted a massive and innovative online soft power campaign to target Iran's enemies both home and abroad, and foment competing counter-narratives to serve regime interests.

Some aspects of the new Iranian strategy closely resembled traditional soft power strategies by producing online content to shape political narratives. On the eve of the signing of the 2015 nuclear deal for example, a high budget music video titled 'Nuclear Energy' was released that featured the prominent Iranian rapper Amir Tataloo singing it is 'our absolute right / to have an armed Persian Gulf.'[81] The regime implemented a similar strategy during the 2017–18 bread riots as protests took place across the country against inflation and unemployment. Days into the protests, a new 'independent' production company called Avant TV released a video interviewing emotional and disgruntled Iranians about the country's economic situation. Each interviewee blamed President Hassan Rouhani. It was later revealed that Avant TV was operated by the IRGC,[82] representing a strategy that attempted to galvanise regime security at the expense of the country's elected officials.

Iran also began to use the internet and social media in a covert manner, establishing thousands of fake social media accounts and websites to foment pro-regime narratives. This strategy took place alongside a broader trend of online innovation by other hybrid authoritarian regimes, exemplified in the findings of the investigation undertaken by the US Special Counsel Robert Mueller, which concluded that Moscow had used social media to 'sow discord in the US political system through what it termed "information warfare".'[83] Indeed, Michael Michaelsen, and Marlies Glasius have found that social media platforms might be predisposed to manipulation by autocrats because of the non-transparent and authoritarian manner in which social media algorithms analyse and target users.[84] With the Russian campaign that targeted the US election thought to have cost just US\$4 million,[85] the weaponisation of social media seemed particularly well suited to hybrid authoritarian regimes such as Iran, offering it a relatively low-tech and cheap tool for innovative cyber war.

Analysts of Russia in particular identified the congruence between social media and the Russian military doctrine of *maskirovka* (military arts by deception), enabling authoritarian regimes to act aggressively online, while maintaining an element of plausible deniability.[86] This would also complement the hybrid Iranian political system, with the element of deniability enabling the regime to bypass the transparency demanded by some aspects of its pluralist system, including its elected leaders.

As early as 2012, Iran had developed an extensive ecosystem of websites that covertly disseminated regime propaganda across multiple languages.[87] One investigation found more than 70 websites targeting 15 countries, including Yemen, Syria, and the US: three countries that play a central role in Iran's foreign policy priorities more broadly.[88] An example of this was Nile Net Online, which is a news website targeting Egyptians. It claimed to have headquarters in Cairo and promised Egyptians 'true news' via its websites and 110,000-follower social media accounts, which often contradicted official Egyptian state media narratives, particularly on the US. An investigation revealed that the website was based in Tehran. The 70 websites fomented Iranian regime messaging that was anti-Israel and anti-US President Donald Trump, while pro-nuclear deal and pro-liberal US political figures.[89]

At the same time, Iran was setting in motion a large scale covert social media campaign that leveraged social media's in-built algorithms to deliver its messaging to target audiences. Analysis of Iranian-regime linked Facebook pages found that activity had started as early as 2010, with two fake Facebook pages created that year and five in 2011. A further 30 pages had been active since 2014, suggesting a gradual expansion of the program. Consistent with other aspects of the regime's cyber strategy, the accounts targeted both domestic and international audiences, although the majority of pages were geared towards the latter.[90] Iranian actors also targeted Twitter, with the social media giant in 2018 and 2019 releasing details of 3,090 fake accounts that it believed were operated by actors linked to the authoritarian regime. Preliminary analysis of 770 of these accounts identified a focus on disseminating regime messages internationally by promoting content from more than 100 pro-regime websites, as well as recycling content produced by activist groups on Twitter. The ten most popular terms used by the accounts included: 'Saudi', 'Trump', 'Palestin*', 'Israel', and 'Syria.'[91] Similar to Iran's fake websites, the content was anti-Saudi, pro-Houthi, anti-Israel, and pro-US Democratic presidential candidate hopeful Bernie Sanders. Account activity peaked in late 2014 as momentum was building behind the July 2015 signing of the nuclear deal.[92] Digital Forensics Lab, however, noted that in comparison to Russia's social media strategies, Iran's 'purpose was much less pernicious. This was an attempt to spread regime messaging through covert channels, alongside the overt ones, not to spread division.'[93] It nonetheless marked a new point of innovation in Iranian cyber strategy that would mark it as one of the most sophisticated and feared online actors in the world. The internet's soft power characteristics now served regime interests at home and abroad.

Conclusions

Iran's threat environment changed dramatically over the first four decades of the Islamic Republic, characterised by the fall of its most immediate threat Saddam Hussein, the Israeli withdrawal from Lebanon and the spread of online technologies. Nonetheless, the regime's threat perceptions and responses remained relatively stable, centred around self-help, independence and cognisance of the dual internal and external threat, as well as ensuring the survival of the regime above all else.

The spread of the internet in Iran heralded a new range of threats by both empowering societal actors and providing a new avenue for Iran's myriad foreign enemies to infiltrate the Islamic Republic. But with time the Iranian regime was able to gain mastery over its online sphere, which came to represent a key plank in the regime's security architecture. The internet enabled it to gather far superior intelligence on its own population than previous manual HUMINT efforts, and provided a vehicle through which to engage in non-conventional offensives at home and abroad. These offensives inflicted significant damage on Iran's foes without risking a retaliatory war. It also enabled it to operate and have influence in countries far beyond its immediate neighbourhood such as the US. In short, the internet has become central to Iranian regime's interests, contributing no small way to securing the regime at home and abroad.

The Iran case also demonstrates that the answers to questions about national security can vary from state to state. State security has never been the central focus of the Iranian regime, which has consistently prioritised its own security over the interests and needs of the Iranian state. At times regime security has even been at odds with state interests and the goals of its elected officials, highlighting the importance of nuance in the examination of questions of security.

Notes

1. Ayoob, M. (1983). Security in the Third World: The Worm About to Turn? *International Affairs* 60 (1), 43.
2. Krause, K. & Williams, M. C. (1997). From Strategy to Security: Foundations of Critical Security Studies. In Krause, K. & Williams, M. C. (Eds.). *Critical Security Studies: Concepts and Cases* (p. 49). Minneapolis: University of Minnesota Press.
3. Koblentz, G. D. (2013). Regime Security: A New Theory for Understanding the Proliferation of Chemical and Biological Weapons. *Contemporary Security Policy* 34 (3), 507.
4. Jackson, R. (2007). Regime Security. In Collins, A. (Ed.). *Contemporary Security Studies* (pp. 185–201). Oxford: Oxford University Press.

5. Koblentz, G. D. (2013). Regime Security, 507.
6. Saidabadi, M. R. (1996). Islam and Foreign Policy in the Contemporary Secular World: The Case of Post-Revolutionary Iran. *Pacifica Review* 8 (2), 32–44.
7. Katouzian, H. (2009). The Iranian Revolution of February 1979. In *The Iranian Revolution at 30* (p. 21). Washington, DC: The Middle East Institute.
8. Moshaver, Z. (2005). Revolution, Theocratic Leadership and Iran's Foreign Policy: Implications for Iran–EU Relations. In *Analyzing Middle East Foreign Policies and the Relationship with Europe* (p. 177). London: Routledge.
9. Ramazani, R. K. (1983). Khumayni's Islam in Iran's Foreign Policy. In *Islam in Foreign Policy*. London: Royal Institute of International Affairs.
10. Vaziri, M. (1993). *Iran as Imagined Nation: The Construction of National Identity*. New York: Paragon House.
11. Constitution of the Islamic Republic of Iran. (1989). *Iran Data Portal*, http://www.wipo.int/edocs/lexdocs/laws/en/ir/ir001en.pdf. p. 23.
12. Letivsky, S. & Way, L. A. (2010). *Competitive Authoritarianism: Hybrid Regimes After the Cold War*. Cambridge: Cambridge University Press.
13. Akbarzadeh, S. (2005). Where Is the Islamic Republic of Iran Heading? *Australian Journal of International Affairs* 59 (1), 25.
14. Anderson, B. (2006). *Imagined Communities: Reflections on the Origin and Spread of Nationalism*. London: Verso.
15. Dehghan, S. K. & Norton-Taylor, R. (2013). CIA Admits Role in 1953 Iranian Coup. *The Guardian*, https://www.theguardian.com/world/2013/aug/19/cia-admits-role-1953-iranian-coup.
16. Milani, M. M. (1994). *Iran's Islamic Revolution: From Monarchy to Islamic Republic* (2nd ed., p. 172). Boulder: Westview Press.
17. Monshipouri, M. & Assareh, A. (2009). The Islamic Republic and the 'Green Movement': Coming Full Circle. *Middle East Policy* 16 (4), 27.
18. Akbarzadeh, S. (2015). Iran and the Shanghai Cooperation Organisation: Ideology and Realpolitik in Iranian Foreign Policy. *Australian Journal of International Affairs* 69 (1), 88–103.
19. Middle East Institute. (no date). The Kurdish Factor in Iran–Iraq Relations https://www.mei.edu/publications/kurdish-factor-iran-iraq-relations.
20. Rubin, B. The Gulf States and the Iran-Iraq War. In *The Iran–Iraq War: Impact and Implications* (pp. 121–132). Tel Aviv: The Jafee Center for Strategic Studies.
21. Conduit, D. (2014). Hizballah in Syria: The Limits of the Democracy/Moderation Paradigm. *Ortadoğu Etütleri* 5 (2), 81–114.
22. Takeyh, R. 2010. The Iran–Iraq War: A Reassessment. *Middle East Policy* 64 (3), 371.
23. Amirahmadi, H. (1990). Economic Reconstruction of Iran: Costing the War Damage. *Third World Quarterly* 12 (1), 30.
24. Gourlay, W. (2016). Mesopotamian Nexus: Iran, Turkey, and the Kurds. In Akbarzadeh, S. & Conduit, D. (Eds.). *Iran in the World: President Rouhani's Foreign Poicy* (pp. 111–132). New York: Palgrave Macmillan.
25. Akbarzadeh, S. (2015). Iran and Daesh: The Case of a Reluctant Shia Power. *Middle East Policy* 22 (3), 44–54.
26. Amnesty International (2013). Iran Still Seeks to Erase the '1988 Prison Massacre' from Memories, 25 Years On. https://www.amnesty.org/en/latest/news/2013/08/iran-still-seeks-erase-prison-massacre-memories-years/.

27. Koblentz, G. D. (2013). Regime Security, 507.
28. Barlow, R. (2012). *Women's Human Rights and the Muslim Question: Iran's One Million Signatures Campaign*. Melbourne: Melbourne University Press.
29. Smith, C. (1999). Return to Tehran: Twenty Years On, Iran's Veils Fall. *The Observer*, 1999.
30. Milani, A. (2010). The Green Movement. United States Institute of Peace: The Iran Primer, http://iranprimer.usip.org/resource/green-movement.
31. Blitz, J. (2009). Iran Accuses Detained Embassy Staff. *Financial Times*, https://www.ft.com/content/cbe7aa64-6598-11de-8e34-00144feabdc0.
32. Diamond, L. & Plattner, M. F. (2012). *Liberation Technology*. Baltimore: Johns Hopkins Press.
33. Clinton, B. (2000). Clinton's Words on China: Trade Is the Smart Thing. *New York Times*, https://www.nytimes.com/2000/03/09/world/clinton-s-words-on-china-trade-is-the-smart-thing.html.
34. Schedler, A. (2010). Authoritarianism's Last Line of Defense. *Journal of Democracy* 21 (1), 77.
35. OpenNet (2013). After the Green Movement: Internet Controls in Iran 2009–2012. https://opennet.net/sites/opennet.net/files/iranreport.pdf.
36. Kinzer, S. (1997). Moderate Leader Elected in Iran with Wide Margin. *New York Times*, 25 May. http://www.nytimes.com/1997/05/25/world/moderate-leader-is-elected-in-iran-by-a-wide-margin.html.
37. Parsa, M. *Democracy in Iran: Why It Failed and How It Might Succeed* (p. 150). Cambridge: Harvard University Press.
38. Rahimi, B. (2003). Cyberdissent: The Internet in Revolutionary Iran. *Middle East Review of International Affairs* 7 (3), 5.
39. Rahimi, B. (2003). Cyberdissent, 7.
40. Etling, B. & Kelly, J. (2008). Mapping Iran's Online Public: Politics and Culture in the Persian Blogosphere. Berkman-Klein Center for Internet & Society, Harvard University, https://cyber.harvard.edu/publications/2008/Mapping_Irans_Online_Public.
41. Ansari, A. (2000). *Iran, Islam, and Democracy: The Politics of Managing Change* (p. 66). London: Royal Institute of International Affairs.
42. Rahimi, B. (2003). Cyberdissent, 8.
43. OpenNet. (no date). Country Study: Internet Filtering in Iran 2004–2005. https://opennet.net/studies/iran.
44. OpenNet. 2007. Internet Filtering in Iran in 2006–2007. Opennet Initiative, https://opennet.net/studies/iran2007#footnote3_hlidr4p.
45. "Islamic Republic of Iran: Computer Crimes Law" (London, 2012), https://www.article19.org/data/files/medialibrary/2921/12-01-30-FINAL-iran-WEB[4].pdf.
46. OpenNet. 2007. Internet Filtering in Iran in 2006–2007.
47. Ambinder, M. (2009). The Revolution Will Be Twittered. *The Atlantic*, 15 June, https://www.theatlantic.com/politics/archive/2009/06/the-revolution-will-be-twittered/19376/.
48. Grossman, L. (2009). Iran Protests: Twitter, the Medium of the Movement. *Time*, 17 June, http://content.time.com/time/world/article/0,8599,1905125,00.html.
49. Esfandiari, G. (2010). The Twitter Devolution. *Foreign Policy*, 8 June, https://foreignpolicy.com/2010/06/08/the-twitter-devolution/.

50. Durov, P. (2017). 25 Mln Daily, 40 Mln Monthly. *Twitter*, https://twitter.com/durov/status/854472773137256448.
51. Aboul-Enein, S. (2017). *Cybersecurity Challenges in the Middle East*. Geneva: Geneva Centre for Security Policy, 17. https://dam.gcsp.ch/files/2y10Nth6z Pq3L46mSmNHjDCHu0dHgIRQpn3vynHt587WqRL4WBwP1ta.
52. Cited in: Farwell, J. P. & Rohozinski, R. Stuxnet and the Future of Cyber War. *Global Politics and Strategy* 53 (1), 29.
53. Katz, Y. (2010). 'Stuxnet Virus Set Back Iran's Nuclear Program by 2 Years'. *Jerusalem Post*, 15 October. https://www.jpost.com/Iranian-Threat/News/Stuxnet-virus-set-back-Irans-nuclear-program-by-2-years.
54. Zetter, K. (2012). Meet 'Flame,' The Massive Spy Malware Infiltrating Iranian Computers. *Wired*. https://www.wired.com/2012/05/flame/.
55. "After the Green Movement: Internet Controls in Iran 2009–2012."
56. Freedom on the internet is a relatively new aspect of international human rights law, having been added to Article 19 of the Universal Declaration of Human Rights in 2016 to recognise 'The promotion, protection and enjoyment of human rights on the Internet.' See: UNHRC (2016). The Promotion, Protection and Enjoyment of Human Rights on the Internet. https://digitallibrary.un.org/record/845728?ln=en.
57. Freedom House. (2012). Freedom on the Net 2012. https://freedomhouse.org/report/freedom-net/2012/iran.
58. See US Department of State. (2016). 2016 Country Reports on Human Rights Practice: Iran. Bureau of Labor, Human Rights and Labor, https://www.state.gov/j/drl/rls/hrrpt/2016/nea/265496.htm.; Dehghanpisheh, B. (2017). Arrests in Iran Show Rouhani's Difficulty Shielding Reformists Ahead of Vote. *Reuters*, 4 April, http://www.reuters.com/article/us-iran-politics-pri soners-idUSKBN1761IW.
59. Conduit, D. & Akbarzadeh, S. (2018). The 'Inside-Track'Approach to Change in Iran Under President Rouhani: The Case of Freedom on the Internet. In Barlow, R. & Akbarzadeh, S. (Eds). *Human Rights and Agents of Change in Iran* (pp. 27–50) New York: Palgrave Macmillan.
60. Center for Human Rights in Iran. (2017). Rouhani Government 'Closed Seven Million' Websites in First Term. https://www.iranhumanrights.org/2017/06/rouhani-government-closed-seven-million-websites/.
61. U.S. Virtual Embassy Iran. (2016). Human Rights Report: Iran-2016, https://ir.usembassy.gov/human-rights-report-iran-2016/.
62. Anderson, C. (2012). *Dimming the Internet: Detecting Throttling as a Mechanism of Censorship in Iran*. University of Pennsylvania: Center for Global Communication, 1.
63. Anderson, C. & Sadjadpour, K. (2018). Iran's Cyber Threat: Espionage, Sabotage, and Revenge. *Carnegie Endowment for International Peace*, https://car negieendowment.org/files/Iran_Cyber_Final_Full_v2.pdf. p. 17.
64. Rezbaniyeh, F. (2010). Pulling the Strings of the Net: Iran's Cyber Army. *Frontline: Tehran Bureau*, https://www.pbs.org/wgbh/pages/frontline/teh ranbureau/2010/02/pulling-the-strings-of-the-net-irans-cyber-army.html.
65. Fars News. (2013). IRGC Official: Iran Enjoys 4th Biggest Cyber Army in World. http://en.farsnews.com/newstext.php?nn=9107141074.
66. Aboul-Enein (2017). Cybersecurity Challenges in the Middle East, 23.

67. Shalal-Esa, A. (2013). Iran Strengthened Cyber Capabilities after Stuxnet: U.S. General. *Reuters*, https://ca.reuters.com/article/technologyNews/idCABRE90G1C420130117.
68. The Intercept. 2015. Iran—Current Topics, Interaction with GCHQ. https://theintercept.com/document/2015/02/10/iran-current-topics-interaction-gchq/
69. Anderson, C. & Sadjadpour, K. (2018). Iran's Cyber Threat, 11.
70. Rezbaniyeh. (2010). *Pulling the Strings of the Net*.
71. Anderson, C. & Sadjadpour, K. (2018). Iran's Cyber Threat, 11.
72. Certfa Lab (2018). The Return of The Charming Kitten: A Review of the Latest Wave of Organized Phishing Attacks by Iranian State-Backed Hackers. https://blog.certfa.com/posts/the-return-of-the-charming-kitten/.
73. Kerr, J. A. (2018). *The Russian Model of Internet Control and Its Significance*. Lawrence Livermore Laboratory: Department of Energy National Nuclear Security Administration, 7, https://www.osti.gov/servlets/purl/1491981.
74. Volz, D. & Finkle, J. (2016). U.S. Indicts Iranians for Hacking Dozens of Banks, New York Dam. *Reuters*, https://www.reuters.com/article/us-usa-iran-cyber/u-s-indicts-iranians-for-hacking-dozens-of-banks-new-york-dam-idUSKCN0WQ1JF.
75. Anderson, C. & Sadjadpour, K. (2018). Iran's Cyber Threat, 5.
76. Lake, E. (2012). Did Iran's Cyber-Army Hack Into the IAEA's Computers? *Daily Beast*, https://www.thedailybeast.com/did-irans-cyber-army-hack-into-the-iaeas-computers.
77. BBC News. (2012). Shamoon Virus Targets Energy Sector Infrastructure. https://www.bbc.com/news/technology-19293797.
78. Newman, L. H. (2018). The Iran Hacks Cybersecurity Experts Feared May Be Here. *Wired*, https://www.wired.com/story/iran-hacks-nuclear-deal-shamoon-charming-kitten/.
79. Anderson, C. & Sadjadpour, K. (2018). Iran's Cyber Threat, 12.
80. Bajoghli, N. (2018). IRGC Media Producers Open New Front against Rouhani. *Al-Monitor*, 3 January, https://www.al-monitor.com/pulse/originals/2018/01/iran-protests-irgc-media-producers-landscape-avant-tv.html.
81. McKay, T. (2017). Iranian Propaganda Has Pivoted To Video. *Gizmodo*, https://www.gizmodo.com.au/2017/08/iran-has-pivoted-to-video/.
82. Bajoghli. (2018). IRGC Media Producers Open New Front.
83. Mueller, R. (2019). *Report On The Investigation Into Russian Interference In The 2016 Presidential Election*. Washington, DC, 4 https://www.justice.gov/storage/report_volume2.pdf.
84. Michaelsen, M. & Glasius, M. (2018). Authoritarian Practices in the Digital Age—Introduction. *International Journal of Communication* 12, 3788–3794.
85. Polyakova, A. (2018). *Weapons of the Weak: Russia and AI-Driven Asymmetric Warfare*. Washington, DC: Brookings Institution, https://www.brookings.edu/research/weapons-of-the-weak-russia-and-ai-driven-asymmetric-warfare/.
86. Kerr, J. A. (2018). *The Russian Model of Internet Control*.
87. Stubbs, J. & Bing, C. (2018). Special Report: How Iran Spreads Disinformation around the World. *Reuters*, https://uk.reuters.com/article/uk-cyber-iran-specialreport/special-report-how-iran-spreads-disinformation-around-the-world-idUKKCN1NZ1FH.
88. Stubbs and Bing. (2018).

89. FireEye (2018). Suspected Iranian Influence Operation Leverages Network of Inauthentic News Sites & Social Media Targeting Audiences in U.S., UK, Latin America, Middle East. 21 August, https://www.fireeye.com/blog/threat-res earch/2018/08/suspected-iranian-influence-operation.html
90. Barojan, D. (2019). Eight Takeaways From Iranian Information Operations. *The Cyber Edge*, 1 April, https://www.afcea.org/content/eight-takeaways-ira nian-information-operations.
91. Digital Forensic Lab. (2018) #TrollTracker: Twitter Troll Farm Archives, Part Three. 17 October, https://medium.com/dfrlab/trolltracker-twitters-troll-farm-archives-17a6d5f13635.
92. Digital Forensic Lab. (2018).
93. Digital Forensic Lab. (2018).

CHAPTER 12

Brazil: In Search of a Security Space

Vinícius G. Rodrigues Vieira

INTRODUCTION

It may seem obvious nowadays that South America—comprising all states in the Western Hemisphere south of Panama—is the "natural" security space for Brazil. However, it was not until late 1970s that Brasilia started to pursue more in-depth relations with neighboring states other than those in the so-called Southern Cone, which comprises Argentina, Paraguay, Uruguay, and Chile— the latter with no border with Brazil. As the region where a power is located serves as a frame for acting in the world,[1] Brazilian security policy therefore shifted as its conception of region evolved, including even the South Atlantic and, hence, South-West Africa. Region, in this respect, can be understood as a meta-concept since it shapes how other aspects of national security are framed. That is, domestic and systemic factors vary across time in defining what region

---

Parts of this chapter have been adapted from my M.A. thesis in Latin American Studies submitted in May 2010 to the University of California at Berkeley, entitled "*Reinventing the Wheel: A Comparative Study* of the Political Economy of Brazilian Foreign Policy under Cardoso and Lula", and the paper "The Limits of the Neighborhood: South-West Africa, the South Atlantic, and the Concept of Region in Brazilian Foreign Policy", presented at the 34th LASA Meeting, New York, May 2016. This research was supported by a São Paulo Research Foundation (FAPESP) grant (no. 2014/26455-7).

V. G. R. Vieira (✉)
Economics and International Relations, Armando Alvares Penteado Foundation (FAAP), São Paulo, Brazil

© The Author(s), under exclusive license to Springer Nature Switzerland AG 2022
M. Clarke et al. (eds.), *The Palgrave Handbook of National Security*, https://doi.org/10.1007/978-3-030-53494-3_12

means to Brazilian policymakers. In addition, the actors conceived as threats also change across time.

In-between those two concepts—regions and actors—Brazil's national security policy has evolved over time and, as new systemic and domestic challenges emerge, those elements are likely to keep shaping the minds of diplomats and defense policymakers in Brasilia. As I argue below, from independence in 1822 until the Military Dictatorship (1964–1985), the focus of Brazilian security concerns was related to actors with interests in the Southern Cone. As industrialization advanced so did Brazil's material capabilities, prompting Brazil to pursue stronger ties with the Andean countries in South America's Pacific Coast as well as to look across the Atlantic to recover ties with post-colonial Africa. As redemocratization was consolidated, national security then became a public policy like any other, being subject to the demands from domestic civil society, on the one hand, and challenged by transnational actors, like cross-border crime syndicates, on the other.

In all those moments, Brazil had to rely on either competition or consent with its major Southern Cone challenger—Argentina. Without collaboration between Brasilia and Buenos Aires, no regional intergovernmental organization (IGO) comprising a majority of states in the landmass below Panamá (where Central America ends) would be possible. However, since the turn of the millennium Venezuela's rising profile as a petrostate with revisionist ambitions at the international level seems to have also been crucial in bridging for the first time the two main groups of countries into which South America has been traditionally divided: the Southern Cone and the Andean Region, which is closer to the Pacific and the Caribbean in an arc formed from Bolivia to Venezuela. Also located in South America, Guiana and Suriname had never been integrated in the region due to their non-Iberian heritage and late independence from European powers (United Kingdom and the Netherlands, respectively). By contrast, all other South American states acquired sovereignty in the first half of the nineteenth century and had their territories colonized by either Spain or Portugal. The only colonial enclave that remains in the region is French Guiana, officially an overseas department where France's sovereignty applies as much as in Europe, which may bring in the long-run an external challenge to Brazil's dominance in the region.

The chapter reviews those debates and suggests that a convergence of systemic and domestic factors constrained the institutionalization of Brazilian leadership in the region as the recently-dead Union of South American Nations (UNASUR) and its South American Defense Council (SADC) became ineffective due to diverging interests with key states in the region, particularly Argentina, Chile, Colombia, and Venezuela. Such a divergence, in turn, stems from the silent competition between China and the US for influence in the Western Hemisphere from the 2000s onward, which includes the use of financial statecraft, in particularly the provision of development finance.[2] This competition echoes the quest for influence in Latin America between

Britain and the US during the "Belle Epoque" in which Brazil took Washington's side before flexing its muscles to pursue autonomy. Brazil therefore faces a "reverse spiral" consisting of the de-escalation of military strength as the country does not have its leadership recognized by neither neighbors nor great powers and has its sovereignty de facto complicated by illegal non-state actors. Yet, Brasilia remains focused on South America and the South Atlantic as the means of preserving sovereignty and autonomy in a world that appears to be moving toward bipolarity.

I organize the discussion as follows. The first section of the chapter comprises the history of Brazilian national security from independence until the end of the military dictatorship in 1985. We then focus on the challenges the redemocratization amid globalization brought to both civilian and military policymakers, who had to also manage the legacy of the authoritarian regime's doctrine of autonomy in diplomacy and defense. The last section discusses whether the election of Jair Bolsonaro, a retired army captain, as president in 2018 represents a new turning point in Brazil's security policies, specifically his support for re-alignment with the US in a reversal of Brazil's pursuit for more than half-century of autonomy in foreign policy and, hence, in security affairs. The conclusion recasts the argument and outlines a research agenda focused on non-state actors—particularly transnational crime—as the main challengers to Brazilian security in the twenty-first century.

FROM INDEPENDENCE TO GLOBALIZATION: THE PATHWAY TOWARD AUTONOMY

As with other countries in Latin America, Brazil's post-colonial experience has specific elements that do not match the trajectories of the Global South and more specifically of emerging powers in Asia. Unlike BRICS partners China and India, Brazil cannot claim status as an ancient civilization. The country started to be formed in the sixteenth century—there was not any unified political entity before the Portuguese arrived, and so it was colonial rule that built the nation-state. The landowners who were working on the behalf of the Portuguese crown became, in practice, the rulers of the lands where they had settled and became the forefathers of the elite that would later achieve autonomy from Lisbon. Yet the political independence of Brazil in 1822 did not represent a substantial change domestically or internationally. Under the leadership of the heir to Portugal's throne, the Empire of Brazil kept the former Portuguese colony united under a weak state, although it was strong enough to be able to quash separatist movements. It maintained an agricultural economy oriented toward exportation and based on large plantations, monocropping, and slave labor, while encouraging investment in railroads, banks, and other institutions designed to facilitate the export-oriented economy.[3] Strategically, this retained Lisbon's policy of alignment with Britain.

Despite the abolition of slavery in 1888 and the inauguration of the Republic in 1889 led by a military coup, the Brazilian economy did not change substantially, although the accumulation produced by coffee plantations enabled an incipient industrialization.[4] In combination with immigration from Europe and migration from the countryside, industrialization began to foster an urban class that gained political strength. In 1930, in the aftermath of the collapse of exports due to the crisis of 1929, a military-supported political coup overthrew the national governing coalition formed by landowners and oligarchs. In contrast to domestic instability, Brazil faced a relative external stable environment during the Belle Époque, during which the world was ravaged by imperial competition. Thanks to the leadership of the Baron of Rio Branco, head of the Ministry of Foreign Affairs (known as Itamaraty) during five presidential governments (1902–1912), the country consolidated its borders without major military conflicts—with the War of the Triple Alliance (1865–1870), in which Argentina, Brazil, and Uruguay allied against Paraguay the most notable exception.

Therefore, a non-bellicose tradition and reliance on international law emerged as the core features of Brazilian foreign policy in the twentieth century and remained salient at least until the beginning of the 2010s. Until the 1950s, aversion to war implied an automatic alignment with the hegemonic power in the international system: first, the United Kingdom, and, second, with the US. In the first decade of the twentieth century, Rio Branco fostered the institutionalization of foreign policy as a state issue which would reside in a stable bureaucratic corps. He also perceived that the configuration of the international system during the liberal order was changing, with the ascension of new powers, most notably the US. Thus, he engineered a shift in the focus of Brazilian diplomacy from the United Kingdom to the US,[5] which was consolidated in the aftermath of World War I (1914–1918). Nonetheless, the erosion of British hegemony does not explain alone this change. In aligning Brazil with the US in the international arena, Rio Branco looked forward to balance US influence in South America, insofar as US hegemony would undermine Brazilian aspirations in the region. Getting closer to the US was therefore a strategy to soft-balance its influence over South America, which already had a more powerful player—at least in economic terms—than Brazil: the then fast-growing, export-oriented Argentina.

Even with industrialization, which gained momentum after the Great Depression of 1929 and finally took over in the aftermath of World War II, Brazil has not become a typical "monster" country in Kennan's definition—nations with great populations, economies, and territorial areas, and faced with extensive challenges.[6] Unlike other "monsters"—among them China, Russia, and India—Brazil has never played a central role in world security coordination debates, due to its geographical location in South America, which was not on the front lines of the Cold War and so has not been strategically important to the Global North, at least when compared to capitalist East Asia.[7] Here, it is necessary to make a geopolitical caveat that also makes Brazil different from other monsters: its localization, in the Americas, implies that it is in the sphere of influence of the US—the post-World War II capitalist hegemon.

Indeed, the Brazilian-American relationship has to be understood within the context of US-Latin American international dynamic. Schoultz says that US foreign policy toward its Southern hemispheric neighbors serves national interests related to internal security, domestic politics, and economic development. As he points out, the US identity, whose roots lie in the supposed superiority of the white race over civilizations with any degree of non-European influence, shapes that policy.[8] Besides ideology/identity issues, state capabilities matter as well. Smith argues that the reactive character of US foreign policy in Latin America is based on the overall structure of the world system. In the context of imperialism and liberalism in the international economy (from the nineteenth century to the 1930s), the US focused its efforts in Latin America to attain mainly economic interests of American entrepreneurs, using imperialist methods and by putting in practice Monroe's Doctrine (1823) statement "the Americas for the Americans." Afterward, there was Franklin Roosevelt's good neighbor policy—with less asymmetrical rhetoric. Soon it was replaced by the contingencies of the Cold War, which led American policy-takers to keep its influence over Latin America at any cost in order to contain a possible advance of communism in the periphery.[9]

The constraints that arise from U.S. interests and identity in the Western Hemisphere therefore explain at least in part what the "moderated constructiveness" of Brazilian foreign policy, characterized by the use of both diplomacy and international law to solve conflicts with other nations.[10] Such a tradition goes back to the end of the nineteenth century and the beginning of the twentieth century, when, as described above, Brazil solved its border problems with its neighbors mainly through diplomacy. If structural factors hindered Brazil's potential as a monster country and, consequently, military ambitions, the inauguration of the ISI strategy in the 1930s and the empowerment of the federal government vis-à-vis the regional oligarchies that controlled de facto military personnel improved state and economic capabilities and, thus, prompted changes in Brazilian foreign policy—including in the security realm. Even before World War II, the Brazil had already demonstrated autonomy vis-à-vis the US in military issues. Under Getúlio Vargas's leadership, the presidency played a stronger role in Brazilian diplomacy,[11] reflecting the increasing industrialization of Brazilian economy. Vargas took advantage of the turbulence in the international system provoked by Nazi Germany's rise and expanded its bargaining power with the US,[12] delaying as much as possible the adherence to the Allies in World War II, which happened only in 1942, and requiring US diplomats to "court" Brazil with incentives.

With the Allied victory and the start of Cold War, Brazil sided—along with the rest of Latin America—with the US-led capitalist bloc politically and economically. However, the strategy of negotiated alignment with the developed world, especially with the US, to attract inflows proved to be flawed due to the fact that it reduced the bargaining power of Brazil in relation to other countries.[13] So there were adjustments in the subsequent years, which, nonetheless, did not remove Brazil from the American political sphere of influence. In the aftermath of World War II, defense policy was developed in function of the National Security Doctrine that shaped most of the Latin American strategic thought during the Cold War. According to that doctrine, the enemies—namely the communists and other left-wing factions that would be Moscow-leaning—were not external, but instead internal. In such a context, being ready for eventual war was no longer a matter concerning just the armed forces, but society as a whole since individuals could (and should) fight the communist threat.[14] Essential for advancing such a policy was the foundation in 1949 of the Advanced School of War (ESG in the original acronym), an army-sponsored institution that nevertheless provided training for civilians.

Pursuing autonomy vis-à-vis hegemonic powers was an economic need instead of a military-motivated change. As Almeida says, "the Brazilian foreign policy, since the 1960s, at least, has been described by many specialists and even by professional diplomats as 'diplomacy of development'...," based upon a high institutionalized diplomatic corps.[15] Such diplomacy intends to satisfy the interests of the political and economic endogenous-based forces which led the Brazilian development process: the state, the national and international capital.[16] The diplomacy of development became evident with the Independent Foreign Policy (PEI in the Portuguese acronym), inaugurated by President Janio Quadros, who resigned less than seven months after having taken office, in 1961. Although the PEI is usually portrayed as the first Brazilian attempt of independence in foreign relations, Brazil started to take its path toward more autonomy in international relations few years before. In 1958, President Juscelino Kubitschek proposed to the US the so-called Pan American Operation, a project to promote economic development in Latin American countries analogous to the Marshall Plan that rebuilt Europe after World War II. Nonetheless, the American government did not accept the proposition.[17] At same time, Latin America launched the first projects of regional integration, among them the Latin American Association of Free Trade (ALALC), founded in 1960 and renamed as ALADI in 1980. None of those initiatives, however, had military purposes.

In the military-strategic realm, the PEI logic only emerged after the beginning of the military dictatorship. Thanks to economic liberalization and reforms between 1964 and 1967,[18] the dictatorship left aside PEI principles and launched a new foreign policy, based on an "interdependent" approach to international relations. It was when Brazil collaborated the first and only time ever with the US in a non-UN-backed military intervention in the Dominican Republic that was nevertheless supported by the Washington-centered Organization of American States (OAS).[19] In the following years, amid the Brazilian miracle and the beginning of the export-promotion growth strategy,[20] the military government returned to a more autonomous orientation with nationalistic tones, which culminated at the pragmatismo responsável (responsible pragmatism) doctrine during Ernesto Geisel's government (1974–1979). Such an approach remains rather controversial: whereas for some it pursued practical interests related to the new industrialization phase in Brazil,[21] other scholars argue that it consisted more of an ideologically driven approach. The origins of such an ideology are found in the "Brazil Grande" (Great Brazil) project, through which the military wanted to convert Brazil into great power.[22] Geisel indeed dismantled a military-cooperation agreement with the US in 1977, as a response to the American government's criticism on human rights in Brazil, and signed a nuclear partnership with West Germany in 1975.[23] Relations with the US would remain complicated in the 1980s amid debt crisis and redemocratization.

At this stage, it is worth noting that it was only within the framework of responsible pragmatism that parts of the South America other than the Southern Cone (including Chile) became part of the Brazilian conception of region in foreign policy. Notwithstanding the resolution of border issues with Bolivia, Peru, Colombia, and Venezuela in the transition from the nineteenth century to the twentieth century under Rio Branco's leadership, the Northern borders only gain prominence under the doctrine of National Security that framed strategic thought in Brasilia during the Military Dictatorship (1964–1985). Also, in the same period—more specifically during the Responsible Pragmatism approach in foreign policy between 1974 and 1979—Africa's Atlantic coast regained prominence in Brazil's foreign affairs after more than a century of minimum relations across the Southern Atlantic. The creation of the Amazon Cooperation Treaty (TCA) in 1978 signaled the beginning of the actual incorporation of the rest of South America into the Brazilian conception of region for foreign policy purposes. Following Brasilia's initiative, Bolivia, Colombia, Ecuador, Guiana, Peru, Suriname, and Venezuela joined the agreement. Concerns with the Amazon and national security became paramount in the 1970s thanks to the expansion of the agricultural frontier toward the rainforest while growing awareness with environmental issues in the international community.

The combination of domestic and systemic changes therefore led Brasilia to look beyond the Southern Cone, pursuing stronger ties with the so-called Andean countries of South America. Yet, as detailed in the next section, South America as the Brazilian main regional space only became effective more than 20 years after the TCA was established following the consolidation of the redemocratization process and the appeasement with Argentina—the long-standing rival in the Southern Cone—amid economic multipolarity and military unipolarity. With this, South America became a regional security complex (RSC) de facto, given that the countries in the region were finally converted into "…a set of units whose major process of securitization, desecuritization, or both are so interlinked that their security problems cannot reasonably be analyzed or resolved apart from one another."[24]

Re-democratization: From Great Power to Middle Power

With the end of the Military Dictatorship in 1985, Brazil progressively put aside its nuclear military ambitions on the global stage and pursued through institutional means the construction of a RSC de facto in South America. In the meantime, however, as democratization and globalization advanced, the state recognized, albeit implicitly, the loss of monopoly over security issues. Moreover, economic and political developments related to the South Atlantic expanded the Brazilian strategic interests toward Western and Southern Africa. In conceptual terms, however, security was not a straightforward matter in the first years after redemocratization. The 1988 Constitution—approved in the aftermath of authoritarian rule—no longer referred to the concept "national security," which was mentioned in the undemocratic 1967 charter the military dictatorship imposed.[25] This was the case because democratic leaders had problems in defining and, hence, dealing with the concept of security, which became associated with repression during the dictatorship.[26] Amid this gap, Brazilian policymakers and security community operated a transition of the country as pursuing the great power status toward a condition of middle power that relies more on soft power than any other means of influencing the international arena.

The democratic charter also prohibited the use of nuclear technology except for peaceful ends. More than a purely endogenous change—understood as a potential consequence of civil society's demands—such a development reflected systemic constraints. As the world moved toward military unipolarity led by the US and reaffirmed economic multipolarity under the market model, Brazil was left with little room of maneuver in security issues except on affairs within South America and the Southern Atlantic. To understand how domestic and systemic factors converged to reframe Brazil's conception of region, I first reassess the factors that led the country to look beyond the Southern Cone.

Brazil competed with Argentina for hydroelectric projects on the Parana River (part of the River Plate basin), then triggering regional tensions.[27] That was the case in particular because Buenos Aires considered that the construction of the Itaipu Dam—build at the border with Paraguay in the Parana River—could be used as a war weapon by Brasilia: opening the dam's stop gates would certainly inundate Northern Argentina and its capital.[28] The historical disputes between the two regional powers only diminished in 1979 as Brazil, Argentina, and Paraguay signed an agreement with Paraguay on the use of the River Plate and its tributaries.[29] In 1980, Buenos Aires and Brasilia agreed upon launching mechanisms of nuclear cooperation in order to restrict the use of this technology to peaceful purposes.

Thanks to this, the civilian government (elected indirectly) inaugurated in 1985 could sign with Buenos Aires in the following year a series of agreements that would lead in 1991 to the institutionalization of peace within the Southern Cone through the establishment of the Common Market of the

South (MERCOSUR) and the Brazil-Argentina Agency for Accounting and Control of Nuclear Materials (ABACC). In the meantime, Brasilia kept an eye on its Northern border. A direct offspring from the initiatives taken during the dictatorship to integrate the Amazon with the rest of country, the *Calha Norte* project was created in December 1985 in the first year after the end of military rule.[30] It first aimed to improve infrastructure in Brazil's Northern border, starting in its Northwestern portion (near Colombia) and moving Eastward toward French Guiana.

Only in the government of Fernando Henrique Cardoso (1995–2003), the country managed to establish an National Defense Policy (PDN in the original acronym), launched in 1996.[31] The PDN defined the topic as relevant for the whole society and as subject to the Constitution,[32] which had established the pursuit of peaceful solutions for international grievances and the promotion of peace and security at the international level—the pillars of a middle power profile that contrasted with the Great Brazil project. In the PDN, South America was described as distant for conflict hotspots and as the "most de-militarized region of the world."[33] Moreover, according to the document, the Brazilian regional space comprised not just South America, but also the South Atlantic.[34] Cardoso, a former opponent to the dictatorship and Marxist-leaning sociologist who had lost his chair at the University of São Paulo in 1969 due to his opposition to the regime, faced a silent opposition from within the military, who lost power and prestige in Brazilian politics due to the creation of the Ministry of Defense in 1999 just after the president's reelection based on a neoliberal political platform mixed with social concerns. Until then, the commander of each armed force (Air Force, Landed Army, and the Navy) held a seat in the presidential cabinet as a minister. With the new ministry, the military chiefs would be placed under the leadership of a civilian, then setting the stage for further interaction with the civil society on this issue-area. Yet, more than Cardoso's leftist past and willingness to open security policy to civilian scrutiny while reducing Brazil's military, the reduction of the budget for the armed forces from 18 billion USD in 1995 to 11 billion USD in 2002 (according to values in that year) was the most crucial factor for triggering grievances from the military against the president.[35]

However, the major blow to the military-nationalistic *Great Brazil* policies had already taken place by then as Brazil acceded and ratified the Non-Proliferation Treaty (NPT) in 1998 as part of its strategy of confidence building with the West, particularly with the aim of attracting investments to stabilize its economy after a decade of hyperinflation between early 1980s and mid-1990s.[36] Certainly, Brazil had already signaled its commitment to not play the nuclear card in security by creating the ABAAC with Argentina. However, agreeing with what in the third world came to be known as a "nuclear apartheid" at the multilateral level was a step that those with nationalist views in both the left and the right could not accept. Acceding to the NPT was first and foremost a domestic decision as, in regional terms, the nuclear threat had diminished not just because of the creation of ABAAC, but also because Argentina joined the treaty in 1994. In systemic terms, incentives for nuclearization in South America were never as strong as in other regions of the world. That is the case because, along with other Latin American countries and the US, Brazil belongs to the Inter-American Treaty of Reciprocal Assistance (TIAR). In place since 1947 (just after the dawn of the nuclear age) and known as Rio Pact, TIAR formally implies in obligations of mutual defense in the case of third-part attacks. However, TIAR has not constrained either Brazil or Argentina to engage in a nuclear race in the Southern Cone.

The emphasis on soft power and, hence, on a middle power identity became evident as Cardoso's optimism with neoliberal globalization vanished and, more than confidence-building with the Global North, his government sought to enhance regional ties. Following a strategy that Burges labels "leading by doing,"[37] Cardoso was the first Brazilian president to call a meeting of the presidents of South American nations, a sign of strengthening regional leadership. Due to this meeting, the countries launched a program to integrate regional infrastructure, the IIRSA,[38] and thus fostering economic integration. This meeting took place in 2000—that is, before the 9/11 terrorist attacks, which, as many scholars argue, led the US to focus on Middle Eastern and security issues, and to ignore the economic agenda in Latin America, such as the creation of the Free Trade Area of the Americas.[39] The IIRSA should be understood not just in economic terms, but also in strategic ones insofar as improving regional infrastructure tends to enhance development and, hence, stability in South America, then mitigating security challenges Brazil could eventually face. Not coincidently, Brazil's emphasis in the region took place just two years after the creation in 1998 of the Amazon Cooperation Treaty Organization (OTCA), a TCA offspring. The organization has a permanent secretariat in Brazil, focusing on cooperation related to the Amazon among member-states.[40]

Emphasis on South America only increased during Luiz Inácio Lula da Silva's Workers' Party's (PT) center-of-left government (2003–2011), which also recovered ties with the other side of the South Atlantic. Lula expanded *Calha Norte* to cover municipalities in all border states in the North and the Center-West regions, then including also the borders with Bolivia and Peru.[41] In line with the emphasis on South-South relations, Lula reactivated an initiative launched just after the end of the dictatorship. The South Atlantic Zone of Peace and Cooperation (ZOPACAS) resulted from a Brazilian initiative at the United Nations General Assembly (UNGA), having been approved in 1986. The main goal consists of keeping the South Atlantic as a Nuclear-Free Zone, following regional commitments in Latin America and the Caribbean (the Treaty of Tlateloco, established in 1968) and Africa (the Treaty of Pelindaba), apart from the Antarctic Treaty.[42] ZOPACAS has 24 members: Angola, Argentina, Benin, Brazil, Cape Verde, Cameroon, Congo, Equatorial, Guinea, Gabon, Gambia, Ghana, Guinea, Guinea Bissau, Ivory Coast, Liberia, Namibia, Nigeria, Democratic Republic of Congo, São Tomé and Príncipe, Senegal, Sierra Leone, South Africa, Togo, and Uruguay.[43] At a first glance, the creation of ZOPACAS contradicts the argument that the Ministry of Foreign Affairs does not coordinate with Defense sectors on security issues, playing with them in light of broader foreign policy concerns. Yet, a series of bilateral initiatives in the years after ZOPACAS had been established corroborates that defense ties with Africa prevail over diplomatic ones. The most salient is the naval agreement Brazil-Namibia established in 1994 for aiding that country to structure its Navy after the independence from South Africa.[44] The agreement was renewed in 2001, having been in force since 2003. In 2009, a new agreement was established covering military exchange in general.[45]

Hence, while in economic terms Brazil entered the twenty-first-century skeptical of the so-called neoliberal globalization that eventually exposed the country to exogenous shocks in late 1990s,[46] in the military realm the country begun to foresee opportunities to enhance its status as a middle power. The most emblematic of those initiatives was the Brazilian leadership role in the United Nations Stabilization Mission in Haiti (MINUSTAH), the UN peacekeeping operations in that Caribbean nation between 2004 and 2017. The operation was crucial for improving the capacity of Brazilian troops to participate in peacekeeping missions as well as to signal to the international community (particularly the West and P5 UNSC members) that Brasilia was ready to bear the costs that being a regional power implies. Yet, as explained above, even before 2001, Brasilia had already launched initiatives to consolidate Brazilian power in South America and guarantee stability in the region, within which Brazil emerged as the major economic powerhouse and, hence, most likely regional hegemon in a multipolar world from an economic standpoint. Those initiatives paved the way for Brazil to reclaim in late 2000s status as the main regional power even in military terms, then consolidating South America as an RSC.

Moreover, analysts envisioned the formation of an axis Caracas-Brasilia-Buenos Aires in 2002, that is, before the rise of the pink-tied left in Brazil under Lula's leadership and its neighbors.[47] This axis would dominate the region in the 2000s, with the institutionalization of regional integration and the consolidation of Brazilian hegemonic pretensions in all South America advanced. Both processes led to the creation of the South American Community of Nations (CASA in the Portuguese and Spanish acronyms) in 2004, which three years later was converted into the UNASUR, becoming effective in 2008. Both CASA and UNASUR exemplify how Brazil's strategy for building strategic cooperation in South America depended on a long-standing network of regional integration efforts that were at their origins more focused on economic rather than security-related issues. That is the case of MERCOSUR and the Andean Community, both of which, as UNASUR's constitutive treaty recognizes, should be the basis for the organization aims.[48] Moreover, UNASUR member-states also integrated IGOs comprising countries in adjacent regions in the Western Hemisphere, including the OAS, founded in 1947 and, as explained before, led by the global hegemon, the US.

Brazil would not have been successful in pushing for deeper integration among all South America without the collaboration of Argentina. The regional competitor, however, only accepted the formation of UNASUR after a long negotiation, in which Buenos Aires was assured the organization's "…institutional design and multiaxial profile would allow it to develop its own regional cooperation and integration agenda without major restrictions being placed on the definition of its foreign policy goal."[49] Indeed, by the time Brazil convened the first South American regional meeting in 2000 and launched IIRSA, Argentina postponed as much as possible the confirmation that it would send a representative. One of the reasons is that the exclusion of Mexico—the second largest Latin American economy—"… from the participants was perceived by many within the Argentinean government as being a part of Itamaraty's strategy for strengthening Brazil's own position as the regional leader."[50] Thus, perhaps not coincidently, Mexico joined UNASUR as an observer in 2012: it was a means for balancing Brasilia's regional leadership pretensions.

Briceño-Ruiz and Hoffmann, however, disagree with the view that Brazil's leadership and Argentina's ambition to lead the region were crucial for the formation of UNASUR.[51] Instead, they emphasize the role of Venezuela in converting the CASA into UNASUR. Under such an account, Venezuelan President Hugo Chávez gained strength within CASA with the election of the leftists Evo Morales in Bolivia (2005) and Rafael Correa in Ecuador (2006). Along with Argentina's President Kirchner, those three countries prompted CASA to downplay trade-related issues in favor of strategic factors as the organization gave origin to UNASUR. The argument, however, ignores that any change in CASA would not have happened without the consent of the largest member-state (Brazil), not to say that the pre-CASA initiatives, such as IIRSA, focused on security and infrastructure. All this indicates that, from its origins, UNASUR and, hence, Brasilia's regional leadership ambitions in the twenty-first century went well beyond economic integration, serving first and foremost security purposes. Moreover, the creation of the SADC in 2008 under UNASUR's umbrella followed a proposal by then-president Luiz Inácio Lula da Silva. The SADC clearly aimed to prevent US interference on regional questions, particularly the long-standing partnership with Colombia to fight drug trafficking and, therefore, the FARC left-wing guerrilla.[52]

In the preamble of UNASUR constitutive treaty, the organization's core principles are "unconditional respect to state sovereignty, as well as to states' territorial integrity and inviolability; people's auto determination; solidarity; cooperation; peace; democracy; popular participation and pluralism; universal human rights – all indivisible and interdependent; reduction of asymmetries and harmony with the nature for sustainable development."[53] That is, notwithstanding the organization's commitment to democracy, UNASUR defends first and foremost state sovereignty. In the case of UNASUR, the intention to hinder US influence also becomes clear in the statements the IGO issued opposing Washington's positions on member-states domestic affairs. For instance, in 2015, the 12 members of the organization opposed the US sanctions on Venezuelan officials. They had been issued under the justification that the political instability in Venezuela presented a threat to US national security and foreign policy.[54]

Notwithstanding all those efforts, Brazil still lacked effective regional leadership in South America, being a "...leader without followers." [55] That is the case as Brazil lacks solid ties with Spanish-speaking South America and the broad Hispanic world that makes up most of Latin America from Mexico's border with the US to Patagonia. In 2014, only 4% of all Brazilians identify themselves as part of Latin America.[56] By contrast, in Argentina, Chile, Colombia, Ecuador, Mexico, and Peru, the average reached 43%. The limits of Brazilian leadership in Latin America and more specifically in South America became evident once the "pink tide" left declined in region, first with the end of the *peronista* rule in Argentina as then-President Cristina Fernandez de Kirchner did not make her successor in the 2015 and later with the controversial impeachment Brazil's president Dilma Rousseff from the PT faced in 2016.[57]

The same happened in the South Atlantic, notwithstanding the fact that in Africa, Brazil "...enjoys an important 'cultural advantage' in comparison to China, Russia or India, especially in Portuguese-speaking Africa."[58] This would be the case due to the fact that Brazil hosts the largest African-descent population outside Africa largely because of the slave trade in the South Atlantic that took place between the sixteenth and nineteenth centuries, first under Portugal's colonial leadership and after under the Empire of Brazil. If de facto existent, such advantage has yet to yield benefits for Brazilian diplomatic and defense strategists as the South Atlantic still has a dubious status in Brazilian security policy. That is the case because of a split between defense and other issue-areas in Brazilian foreign policymaking, with the Ministry of Defense dominating the first and the Ministry of Foreign Affairs controlling the latter, including economic diplomacy. In military terms, Brazilian authorities conceive such ocean as a vital space for Brazilian sovereignty.

Yet, South-West Africa (broadly defined as the states ranging from Senegal to South Africa) is not considered part of Brazil's regional complex. That is the case due to the relative low participation of that group of states in Brazilian international economic relations—a pattern that even Lula's government emphasis on South-South relations could not reverse. Such a pattern, in turn, persists only because security issues in foreign policy remain mainly in the hands of the Ministry of Defense, without coordination with other issue-areas in external affairs, which are still under Itamaraty's auspices. The fact is that South Atlantic gained further prominence in defense affairs not just because diplomatic approximation with Africa, but also due to the discovery and exploration of pre-salt oil basins from 2007 onward. In a demonstration of national pride amidst security concerns, the Navy dubbed the Brazilian territorial sea as "Blue Amazon." As the Defense White Paper published in 2013 summarizes:

> Considering the abovementioned maritime segments and projections, it may be affirmed that Brazil's strong link to the sea is substantial, from both political and economic perspectives. This has induced the country to exert a natural influence over the South Atlantic. The strong dependence on maritime traffic for foreign trade constitutes a relevant challenge to defense. The South Atlantic region over which Brazil has territorial rights and other exploration and control prerogatives is the country's jurisdictional waters. These waters have recently been labeled as the Blue Amazon, and are roughly equal, in terms of geographic area, to the Brazilian Green Amazon. Oil reserves in deep water and ultra-deep water, so important for the country's development, can be found under this region. Hence, the need to intensify monitoring and control of maritime traffic and of incidents in areas that are subject to Brazilian authority.[59]

Ironically, it was under left-leaning PT's government that Brazilian security concerns started to be framed again under a nationalistic framework like that the Military Dictatorship had adopted. Indeed, Rousseff herself appointed a Communist, Aldo Rebelo (a former speaker of the lower house) as Ministry of Defense during her last months in office. Rebelo had nationalistic positions like his high-ranked military subordinates, many of whom would be selected for Bolsonaro's government.

In sum, the period 1985–2015 resulted in the consolidation of expanding Brazil's region from the Southern Cone to the whole South America. Yet, as explained in the next section, the subsequent years would bring setbacks not in the Brazilian conception of regional identity, but instead in the capacity of Brasilia to exert regional leadership and, hence, to control potential threats to the national sovereignty.

AN EXHAUSTED DEMOCRACY: BACK TO PRE-AUTONOMY DAYS?

With rising power competition and multipolarity at the world stage, one could expect that Brazil could reassert its claims for regional hegemony and/or leadership in South America. Yet, declining economic growth and political instability since 2013 ruled out such hypotheses. The election of retired captain Bolsonaro—a backbencher member of the parliament between 1991 and 2018—only reduced the chances that Brazil would retain its focus over South America and eventually its status as a rising power. In the meantime, for both ideological and practical reasons, Bolsonaro tends to emphasize the role of the military in fighting domestic security threats, while downplaying international pressure for preserving the Amazon, a topic that has led the Brazilian president to be involved in a public feud with his French colleague, the centrist Emmanuel Macron, during most of 2019. Instead of a breakthrough with previous governments' practices, securitizing public safety is a direct consequence of changes that happened outside Brazil almost two decades ago, when the emergence of terrorism demanded new strategies that did not match the state-centric Cold War doctrines on national security.[60]

The key for understanding the return of the military in Brazilian politics under Bolsonaro and the impact of such a process in Brazilian national security lie in a series of junctures that took place in the PT's years in power. Veterans from the MINUSTAH acquired experience in dealing with complex issues in the front in Haiti and once at home became involved in domestic politics, first in contributing to the law and order operations in Rio de Janeiro's favelas dominated by drug gangs under PT's governments. That was a remarkable change in relation to the first years after redemocratization. By the end of Cardoso's presidency, the military were still reluctant to fight drug trafficking except by backing actions led by the Federal Police.[61] Moreover, in the last year of Lula's government (2010), the president established a shared military command between the three armed forces (the EMCFA), which is de facto above the Minister of Defense. Civilian oversight over the military appears to have diminished since then and, considering the first measures taken under Bolsonaro's administration, one would not exaggerate in claiming that democratic rule failed to place military authority under civilian control given that since 2017 a military has been ahead of the Ministry of Defense.

The long-term trend of Military-as-protagonists in Latin America therefore re-emerged in Brazil well before Bolsonaro's election, which thus far has brought a unique situation of securitization of society within democracy, including the resurgence of sovereignty concerns over the Amazon. In opposition to what happened under military rule during the Cold War, internal enemies are no longer defined in partisan terms. Instead, the enemies are now those who threaten state sovereignty regardless of their placement in the left–right political spectrum—under the diffused right-wing, conservative ideology of *Bolsonarismo* official enemies may range from drug cartels to environmental activists who, allied with foreign powers, may compromise Brazilian territorial integrity. In May 2019, when disputes between conservatives and pragmatists reached their highest level, former Army Commander and Bolsonaro special advisor general Eduardo Vilas-Boas published a comment on Twitter condemning both left- and right-wing extremists.[62] After Bolsonaro's inauguration, the military begun influencing fields other than defense and public safety, generating tensions not just with civilian politicians, but also with bureaucrats and the civil society. The lack of coordination between defense and diplomacy became evident during the Venezuelan crisis, with the military ruling out from the beginning any action in the neighbor and the Itamaraty suggesting that Brazil would side with the US in the case of intervention. Minister of Foreign Affairs Ernesto Araújo even offered to American officials just after Bolsonaro's inauguration the possibility of installing a military basis in Northern Brazil. As high-ranked military members of the cabinet expressed their discontent, Araújo—who espouses the view that Brazil should classify itself as a Western country—withdrew the offer.

Following Colombia's decision, other South American nations with either centrist or right-wing government left the UNASUR, which is now a defunct organization awaiting to be replaced by the PROSUR, a new club announced for the pursuit of cooperation among South American nations with a liberal orientation in economic matters.[63] The dismissal of UNASUR only crowned the declining relevance of South America for Brazilian foreign policy and the potential of consolidating a RSC under Brasilia's leadership. Although Brazil's military acts behind the scenes for building a diplomatic solution for Venezuela's crisis, the protagonists are not regional powers. Instead, Caracas became the battleground of two external powers—the US and Russia, who support its ally Maduro. This indicates relative loss of prestige for Brazil within its own region, which, in turn, will pose further challenges to the country for reassessing its national security policy in the years to come.

Likewise, the lack of deeper institutionalization in the relations among Southern Atlantic states may leave the region pray to the interests of great powers. The concept of Atlantic Rim—an area encompassing both North and South Atlantic—has historically been at the sidelines yet has gained traction in the last decade in policy circles in the US.[64] Apart from traditional strategic issues related to navigation and natural resources, the South Atlantic has attracted attention from the centers of power in the Global North because West Africa became crucial for illicit drug trafficking between Latin America and Europe.[65] Thanks to their status as emerging powers, Brazil and South Africa tend to regard the Atlantic not as a locus of cooperation with EU and the US, but rather as a region where their influence will inevitably grow.[66] China has become a significant player in the South Atlantic as well, given the growth of economic ties with both Latin America and Africa over the 2000s.[67]

The 2019 Venezuelan crisis, indeed, illustrates the risks of the scenario above not in the South Atlantic, but within South America itself. The direct interference of out-of-the-region powers signals to the return to a Cold War logic that closes the space of action for regional powers like Brazil unless they take sides at the macro-level. The left-wing, anti-US Venezuelan dictator Nicolás Maduro receives Vladimir Putin's Russia's ostensive support, while also counting on Beijing and Ankara at the sidelines. By contrast, the US under Trump has managed to exert direct pressure over Maduro and, more than relying on Brazil, prefers aligning with the American long-standing ally in South America: Colombia. Indeed, the fact that the later along with liberal-turned Peru were the de facto leaders of the Lima Group that gathers the Western Hemisphere's opponents to Maduro and not Brazil exemplify how weak is Brasilia's leadership within its own neighborhood at the dawn of the 2020s.

While Bolsonaro himself and other conservatives who love criticizing the so-called globalist project that would threaten people's will, the military clearly favors a more pragmatic approach. No wonder why Bolsonaro suspects his

Vice-President General Hamilton Mourão wants his seat. Yet, more than following the domestic struggle for power, one must pay attention at systemic factors to predict where Brazil is heading to considering systemic developments. In 2017, the federal government published the Defense Scenarios for the period 2020–2039, indicating that it is possible that there will be an increasing multipolarity as the center of global power moves eastward. Moreover, rivalries among states tend to expand in parallel with the relative reduction of US power and the potential rising relevance of regional IGOs.[68] Specifically in what concerns Brazil's regional setting—conceived as being formed by both South America and sub-Saharan Africa—the governed envisioned risks associated with the potential scarcity of natural resources.[69] As the report states, threats like piracy in West Africa's shore would jeopardize Brazilian interests if involving the supply of oil from Nigeria.[70] If this diagnosis makes any sense, the project Calha Norte has not, however, prevented Northern Brazil from being impacted by Venezuela's humanitarian crisis as the state still lacks effective presence in the Amazonic borders. The program was still in place as of 2019,[71] notwithstanding the intention to expand austerity measures to the armed forces.

The assessment summarized above suggests more continuity in relation to the trends that had emerged by end of the Military Dictatorship than rupture that changes in the Brazilian government may trigger. Regardless of who holds power in Brasilia, she tends to retain the international identity of a regional power autonomous vis-à-vis great powers in the North of the Equator. As Burges summarizes:

> A central precept of Brazilian foreign policy beyond being a major power or major power-to-be is that the country is not part of the dominant North-Atlantic bloc set up and managed by the United States. The Brazilian view of how international society should be structured and operate deviates from the United States-led bloc's turn towards strengthened international regimes and institutions, remaining instead fixated on the preservation of sovereignty and maintenance of the principle of non-intervention.[72]

The Venezuelan crisis again reflected the persistence of such an identity. Although the military who support Bolsonaro do not oppose strengthening ties with the US, they do not favor at all automatic alignment with Washington or any other power. Vice-President General Hamilton Mourão publicly opposed the idea of offering support to US troops for an eventual intervention in Caracas to oust Maduro from power.[73] Also, in a trip to China without President Bolsonaro, Mourão ruled out breaking ties with Huawai—a clear signal that Brasilia will take no sides in the technology war that Washington declared over Beijing.[74] This, however, does not mean breaking ties with the US, with which Brazil may want to pursue further collaboration in the field of military technology, as the proximity between Bolsonaro and his American counterpart Donald J. Trump suggested as of July 2020.

From the facts above, Brazil clearly still stands as a regional power as much as a pivot state even under a right-wing, US-leaning government and is likely to retain such a status notwithstanding the sluggish economic growth that compromises the improvement of defense capabilities. Yet, when it comes to Brazilian identity as an emerging power, BRICS member, one can expect more nuance as sympathy to the US may imply in hindering revisionist pretensions[75] that had arisen under PT's government but nevertheless had never translated into any type of in-depth military exchange with China, Russia, and even India—Brazil's long-standing ally in other issue-areas, particularly trade.[76]

Conclusion

The Brazilian experience in conceptualizing national security suggests that, prior to identifying which actors nations target to defend themselves, their policymakers must define the limits of the neighborhood. Across almost two centuries of sovereign life, Brazil has only recently looked beyond the Southern Cone and strengthened ties with the rest of South America and looked to the other side of the Atlantic to seek cooperation with Africa. The 2013 Brazilian Defense White Paper summarizes the extra-borders' concerns as follows, keeping the priorities established at the PND in 1996: "With regards to other countries, Brazil gives priority to its immediate neighbors in South America, the South Atlantic region and Africa's western coast."[77] Regional stability is listed among the priorities of National Defense.

The literature on Brazilian Foreign Policy has been almost unanimous in pointing out that the country tends to be reluctant in assuming the costs of being a regional and emerging power even though Brasilia reclaims at least since late 1990s higher status in international affairs. In the meantime, Brazil lacked state capacity to fight crime within its borders—a domestic security threat much more dangerous than the communist specter that haunted Latin America during the Cold War. Consequently, local cartels became transnational and now operate in neighboring countries, then posing a challenge to national security in the long term. Therefore, exchange with Armed forces in both South America and West Africa coast does not, however, seem to suffice for attaining Brazilian defense goals in the South Atlantic.

A research agenda covering such challenges needs to be developed prior to deciding on the future of Brazilian strategic capabilities. Apart from that, it is worth noting that the creation of a National Council of Foreign Relations could mitigate the effects of a de facto fragmentation of Brazilian security policy as those in charge of warfare remain apart from civilian control and only interacts with diplomats on a case-by-case basis. Only with this, Brazil shall be able to consolidate ties within its "natural region"—South America, which has been subject to China's and Russia's assertiveness in the US "natural space," the Western Hemisphere. A united South America shall be able to hinder great power influence over the region while satisfying the resurgence of concerns about foreign appetite for Amazon's biological and mineral resources. Brazil's neighbors, however, must consent on Brazilian leadership. Brazil, in turn, must be more willing to bear the costs that being a hegemon in its "security space" implies.[78] If not, considering the state of affairs under the Bolsonaro administration as of July 2021—when the country was regarded as the epicenter of the COVID-19 pandemic and nevertheless did not coordinate in-depth efforts with neighbors to fight the greatest global health crisis ever seen—Brasilia runs the risk of definitely losing its status within South America and the world, jeopardizing its sovereignty in the dawn of what seems to be a new age of great power competition.

NOTES

1. Ramanzini Júnior, Haroldo, and Vinicius Rodrigues Vieira. 2017. Regions and the Globe: A Spatial–Temporal Framework for Foreign Policy Analysis. *Brazilian Political Science Review*, http://dx.doi.org/10.1590/1981-382120 1700030005.
2. On hegemonic transitions and financial statecraft, see Obydenkova, Anastassia V., and Vinícius G. Rodrigues Vieira. 2019. The Limits of Collective Financial Statecraft: Regional Development Banks and Voting Alignment with the United States at the United Nations General Assembly. *International Studies Quarterly*, https://doi.org/10.1093/isq/sqz080.
3. Carvalho, José Murilo de. 2001. *Cidadania no Brasil: o longo caminho*. Rio de Janeiro: Civilização Brasileira.
4. Furtado, Celso. 1961. *Formação Econômica do Brasil*. São Paulo: Companhia Editora Nacional.
5. Danese, Sergio. 1999. *Diplomacia Presidencial: História e Crítica*, 250–284. Rio de Janeiro: Top Books.
6. Lafer, Celso. 2000. Brasil: dilemas e desafios da política externa. *Estudos Avançados*. http://dx.doi.org/10.1590/S0103-40142000000100014.
7. Ibid.
8. Schoultz, Lars. 1998. *Beneath the United States: a history of U.S. Policy Toward Latin America*, xvi. Cambridge, MA: Harvard University Press.
9. Smith, Peter H. 2008. *Talons of the Eagle: Latin America, the United States, and the World*. 3rd ed. New York: Oxford University Press.
10. Lafer 2000.
11. Danese 1999, 285–331.
12. Moniz-Bandeira, Luiz Alberto. 1973. *Presença dos Estados Unidos no Brasil: Dois séculos de História*, 249. Rio de Janeiro: Civilização Brasileira.
13. Hirst, Monica 1996. A Política Externa do Segundo Governo Vargas. In *Crescimento, modernização e política externa*, ed. José Augusto Guilhon Albuquerque, 217. São Paulo: Cultura Editores Associados.
14. Campos, Iris Valquiria. 2002. Defesa nacional. In *Era FHC: um Balanço*, ed. Bolivar Lamounier, and Rubens Figueiredo, 460. São Paulo: Cultura.
15. Almeida, Paulo Roberto de. 2003. A Política Internacional do Partido dos Trabalhadores: da Fundação à Diplomacia do Governo Lula. *Revista Sociologia e Política*, 20: 98.
16. Evans, Peter. 1979. *Dependent Development: The Alliance of Multinational, State and Local Capital in Brazil*. Princeton, NJ: Princeton University Press.

280 V. G. R. VIEIRA

17. Moniz-Bandeira 1973.
18. Souto Maior, Luiz Augusto. 1996. A Diplomacia Econômica Brasileira no Pós-Guerra. In *Diplomacia para o Desenvolvimento*, ed. José Augusto Guilhon Albuquerque, 272. São Paulo: Cultura Editores Associados.
19. Sposito, Ítalo Beltrão. 2013. Foreign policy change in Brazil: comparing Castelo Branco (1964–1967) and Fernando Collor (1990–1992). *Brazilian Political Science Review*, 7: 133.
20. Visentini, Paulo Fagundes. 2004. *A Política Externa do Regime Militar Brasileiro*, 31. Porto Alegre: Editora UFRGS.
21. Flecha de Lima, Paulo Tarso. 1996. Diplomacia e Comércio: Notas sobre a Política Externa Brasileira nos Anos 70. In *Diplomacia para o Desenvolvimento*, ed. José Augusto Guilhon Albuquerque, 234–235. São Paulo: Cultura Editores Associados.
22. About the Great Brazil project, read Garcia, Eugênio Vargas. 1997. O pensamento dos militares em política internacional (1961–1989). *Revista Brasileira de Política Internacional*, 40: 25.
23. Garcia, Eugênio Vargas. 2005. *Cronologia das Relações Internacionais do Brasil*, 211 and 2015. Rio de Janeiro: Contraponto.
24. Buzan, Barry, and Ole Waever. 2003. *Regions and Powers: The Structure of International Security*, 44. Cambridge: Cambridge University Press.
25. Campos 2002, 459.
26. Campos 2002, 473.
27. Oelsner, Andrea. 2005. *International Relations in Latin America: Peace and Security in the Southern Cone*. New York and London: Routledge.
28. Hurrell, Andrew. 1992. Brazil as a Regional Great Power: A Study in Ambivalence. In *Regional Great Powers in International Politics*, ed. Iver B. Neummann, 34. Basingstoke: Macmillan.
29. Mallea, Rodrigo, Matias Spektor, and Nicholas J Wheeler. 2015. *The Origins of Nuclear Cooperation: A Critical Oral History of Argentina and Brazil*, 84. Washington, DC, and Rio de Janeiro: Woodrow Wilson International Center for Scholars and Fundação Getúlio Vargas.
30. Campos 2002.
31. Campos 2002, 459.
32. Presidência da República. 1996. Política de Defesa Nacional, 3. http://www.biblioteca.presidencia.gov.br/publicacoes-oficiais/catalogo/fhc/politica-de-defesa-nacional-1996.pdf. Accessed 10 June 2019.
33. Ibid., 5.
34. Ibid.
35. Campos 2002, 458.
36. Rodrigues Vieira 2014.
37. Burges, Sean W. 2009. *Brazilian Foreign Policy after the Cold War*, 62–63. Gainesville: University Press of Florida.
38. Ibid.
39. For further discussion about the impact of 9/11 in Brazilian foreign relations, please read Barbosa, Rubens Antônio. 2002. Os Estados Unidos pós 11 de setembro de 2001: implicações para a ordem mundial e para o Brasil. *Revista Brasileira de Política Internacional*, 45: 72–91; Grandin, Greg. 2006. *Empire's Workshop: Latin America, the United States, and the Rise of the New Imperialism*. New York: Metropolitan Books; Smith (2008).

40. Ministério das Relações Exteriores. 2016. Organização do Tratado de Cooperação Amazônica. http://www.itamaraty.gov.br/index.php?option=com_con tent&view=article&id=691&catid=146&Itemid=434&lang=pt-BR. Accessed 10 June 2019.
41. O Globo. 2004. Apesar da falta de verbas, Calha Norte é ampliado, January 10.
42. Ministério das Relações Exteriores. 2016. Zona de Paz e Cooperação do Atlântico Sul. http://www.itamaraty.gov.br/index.php?option=com_tags& view=tag&id=567-zopacas-zona-de-paz-e-cooperacao-do-atlantico-sul&lang= pt-BR. Accessed 10 June 2019.
43. Ministério da Defesa. 2013. Defense White Paper, 39. http://www.defesa.gov. br/arquivos/estado_e_defesa/livro_branco/lbdn_2013_ing_net.pdf. Accessed 10 June 2019.
44. Brazil. 1994. Acordo de Cooperação entre o Governo da República da Namíbia e o Governo da República Federativa do Brasil. http://dai-mre.serpro.gov.br/ atos-internacionais/bilaterais/1994/b_13/at_download/arquivo. Accessed 10 June 2019.
45. Brazil. 2009. Acordo entre o Governo da República Federativa do Brasil e o Governo da República da Namíbia sobre Cooperação no Domínio da Defesa. http://dai-mre.serpro.gov.br/atos-internacionais/bilaterais/2009/ b_6362/at_download/arquivo. Accessed 10 June 2019.
46. Rodrigues Vieira, Vinícius. 2014. Is Politics Behind Trade? The Impact of International Trends and Diplomatic Action on Brazil's Exports during Globalisation. *Bulletin of Latin American Research*, 33: 140–157.
47. Campos 2002, 488.
48. UNASUR. 2008. Tratado Constitutivo de la Unión de Naciones Suramericanas, 8. http://www.unasursg.org/images/descargas/DOCUMENTOS% 20CONSTITUTIVOS%20DE%20UNASUR/Tratado-UNASUR-solo.pdf. Accessed 10 June 2019.
49. Nolte, Detlef, and Nicolás Matías Comini. 2016. UNASUR: Regional Pluralism as a Strategic Outcome. *Contexto Internacional*, 38: 546.
50. Ibid., 554.
51. Briceño-Ruiz, José, and Andrea Ribeiro Hoffmann. 2015. Post-hegemonic regionalism, UNASUR, and the reconfiguration of regional cooperation in South America. *Canadian Journal of Latin American and Caribbean Studies*, 40: 48–62.
52. Santos, Fabio Luis Barbosa dos. 2016. UNASUL à Luz de um Contraste: As Relações com Venezuela e Colômbia. *Austral: Revista Brasileira de Estratégia e Relações Internacionais*, 5: 240–263.
53. UNASUR 2008, 8.
54. Duddy, Patrick. 2015. Venezuela's Crisis, U.S. Sanctions and the UNASUR Reaction. *American Diplomacy*, April 15, www.americandiplomacy.org. Accessed 10 June 2019.
55. Malamud, Andrés. 2011. A Leader Without Followers? The Growing Divergence Between the Regional and Global Performance of Brazilian Foreign Policy. *Latin American Politics and Society*, 53: 1–24.
56. Guimarães, Thiago. 2015. Brasileiro despreza identidade latina, mas quer liderança regional, aponta pesquisa. https://www.bbc.com/portuguese/noticias/ 2015/12/151217_brasil_latinos_tg. Accessed 10 June 2019.

57. Rodrigues Vieira, Vinícius. 2018. Symbolic Power in an Age of Globalism and Populism. In *Civil Society in the Global South*, ed. Palash Kamruzzaman. London: Routledge.
58. Bartesaghi, Ignacio, and Susana Mangana. 2013. Trade relations between Africa and Mercosur: Brazil as a case study. Bridges Africa, 2. http://www.ictsd.org/bridges-news/bridges-africa/news/trade-relations-between-africa-and-mercosur-brazil-as-a-case-study. Accessed 29 March 2016.
59. Ministério da Defesa 2013, 21.
60. Campos 2002, 484.
61. Campos 2002, 457.
62. Godoy, Marcelo. 2019. Villas Bôas em cena é aviso contundente para rede bolsonarista. *O Estado de S. Paulo*, May 7. https://politica.estadao.com.br/noticias/geral,villas-boas-quer-pacificar-o-palacio-de-bolsonaro,70002818504.
63. Agência Brasil. 2019. Brazil officially leaves Unasur to join Prosur. Apr. 17. http://agenciabrasil.ebc.com.br/en/internacional/noticia/2019-04/brazil-officially-leaves-unasur-join-prosur. Accessed 11 June 2019.
64. Alcaro, Riccardo, and Emiliano Alessandri. 2013. A Deeper and Wider Atlantic. Istituto Affari Internazionali. Document IAI 13.01, 18. http://www19.iadb.org/intal/intalcdi/PE/2014/13716.pdf. Accessed 28 March 2016.
65. Ibid.; Williams, Phil. 2012. Illicit Threats: organized crime, drugs, and small arms. In *Routledge Handbook of Latin American Security*, ed. David Mares, and Aire M. Kacowicz, 266–75. New York: Routledge.
66. Alcaro and Alessandri 2013, 19.
67. Ibid.
68. Ministério da Defesa. 2017. Cenários de Defesa: 2020–2039, 17. https://www.defesa.gov.br/arquivos/ensino_e_pesquisa/defesa_academia/cadn/pal estra_cadn_xi/xiv_cadn/cenarios_de_defesa_2039.pdf. Accessed 16 May 2019.
69. Ibid., 25.
70. Ibid., 25.
71. Ministério da Defesa. 2019. Calha Norte. https://www.defesa.gov.br/progra mas-sociais/programa-calha-norte. Accessed 10 June 2019.
72. Burges, Sean. 2013. Brazil as a bridge between old and new powers? *International Affairs*, 287. https://doi.org/10.1111/1468-2346.12034.
73. Della Coletta, Ricardo, and Gustavo Uribe. 2019. Vice-President Rules Out An Intervention in Venezuela. *Folha de S. Paulo*, February 26. https://www1.folha.uol.com.br/internacional/en/world/2019/02/vice-president-rules-out-an-intervention-in-venezuela.shtml. Accessed 11 June 2019.
74. Schipani, Andres, Jude Webber, and Benedict Mander. 2019. Latin America resists US pressure to exclude Huawei. Financial Times, June 9. https://www.ft.com/content/38257b66-83c5-11e9-b592-5fe435b57a3b. Accessed 9 June 2019.
75. Here I consider that emerging powers are states that have four characteristics: (1) capacity to influence the world order; (2) a strong international identity; (3) the pursuit of revisionism (changes) in the international society, but not in a contentious manner, with revolutionary claims; and (4) regional leadership, that is, some degree of influence over neighboring states (adapted from Gómez Bruera, Hernán F. 2015. To Be or Not to Be: Has Mexico Got What It Takes to be an Emerging Power? *South African Journal of International Affairs*, 22: 227–248. https://doi.org/10.1080/10220461.2015.1053978).

76. Rodrigues Vieira, Vinícius. 2015. The 'Eastern Brother': Brazil's View of India as a Diplomatic Partner in World Trade. In *Competing Visions of India in World Politics*, ed. Kate Sullivan, 111–127. Basingstoke: Palgrave.
77. Ministério da Defesa 2013, 16.
78. Rodrigues Vieira, Vinícius. 2020. Hegemonia benevolente e empreendedorismo político como pressuposto para o desenvolvimento regional. In *Desenvolvimento e Cooperação na América Latina: A Urgência de uma Estratégia Renovada*, ed. Enrique García, 671–686. São Paulo: Edusp.

Part III

Issues

CHAPTER 13

Nuclear Weapons and National Security: From the Cold War to the "Second Nuclear Age" and Beyond

Matthew Sussex and Michael Clarke

When it comes to nuclear weapons, strategic thinkers tend to prefer certainty and simplicity to ambiguity and complexity. For all its nuclear horrors—from Mutually Assured Destruction (MAD) to counterforce doctrines and plans to fight and win a nuclear war—the Cold War represented a relative straightforward dynamic that could dampen nuclear dangers via a combination of arms control and deterrence. The global nuclear "club" was effectively managed by the Non-Proliferation Treaty (NPT), which delegitimised the development of nuclear weapons, except for a privileged few major powers.[1] The overlay of bipolar competition also made for relatively straightforward dyadic nuclear relationships. Within the US alliance system, there were certainly debates about Washington's commitment to extended nuclear guarantees,[2]

M. Sussex · M. Clarke (✉)
Centre for Defence Research, Australian Defence College, Canberra, ACT, Australia
e-mail: Michael.clarke@anu.edu.au; Michael.clarke@uts.edu.au

M. Sussex
e-mail: matthew.sussex@anu.edu.au

M. Sussex
Griffith Asia Institute, Griffith University, Brisbane, Australia

M. Clarke
Australia-China Relations Institute, University of Technology Sydney, Ultimo, NSW, Australia

Strategic and Defence Studies Centre, Australian National University, Canberra, ACT, Australia

© The Author(s), under exclusive license to Springer Nature Switzerland AG 2022
M. Clarke et al. (eds.), *The Palgrave Handbook of National Security*,
https://doi.org/10.1007/978-3-030-53494-3_13

287

but since both superpowers took steps to untie nuclear weapons from potential conventional flashpoints there were relatively few real crises during the period where nuclear use was likely, except perhaps by accident. And despite some attempts at brinkmanship—including the Cuban Missile Crisis and the stationing of intermediate nuclear forces in Turkey—both the US and USSR generally sought to engender a situation that was characterised by mutually clear communication of capabilities and intentions, as well as nuclear postures that incorporated graduated and flexible steps to facilitate de-escalation.

But the end of the Cold War did more than free nuclear weapons from the global power structure. It created perverse incentives for states to consider developing their own nuclear capabilities to maximise power (in the case of the DPRK, for instance), or escalate strategic competition to a new level (in the case of India and Pakistan). By the second decade of the twenty-first century, advances in modernised nuclear capabilities, as well as non-nuclear defence technologies, put pressure on nuclear weapons states to increase their arsenals to ensure they were sophisticated. Missile defence systems, once described by former US Secretary of State Colin Powell as little more than a pipe dream during the Reagan era,[3] have become a reality. But in the process they have been seen by other nations as attempts to attain nuclear primacy, eroding US credibility and undermining its ability to reassure other nuclear states that it has a continued stake in more traditional mechanisms of stabilisation.

The effect has been that nuclear complexities are outpacing the ability of arms control regimes to respond, not to mention attempts to manage them within competitive dyads. Not only is it now commonplace to refer to nuclear "trilemmas",[4] but the six established nuclear weapons states (as well as new ones) have each exacerbated the complexities of deterrence relationships. Asia has become the engine room of globalisation as well as the main locus of major power competition, and has been described by one leading author as the site of the "second nuclear age".[5] Indeed, it is clear that there are a number of complex nuclear relationships in Asia, giving rise to the notion of a multipolar nuclear region. The clearest expression of this has been in the refusal of the US under the Trump administration to renegotiate the New START Treaty (NST), with the view that it should include the People's Republic of China (PRC) as well as Russia and the US.[6] And at the same time, the lines between nuclear and conventional deterrence have become blurred, especially given the emergence of "escalate-to-de-escalate" nuclear doctrines.[7] This has retied nuclear weapons to conventional war-fighting capabilities, with the logic that the first state to use (or threaten to use) nuclear weapons obtains a strategic edge.

For national security policy planners, the return of nuclear politics adds to the challenges of an increasingly crowded threat terrain. Among US allies in Europe and Asia, the transactional Trump administration has shaken confidence in American security commitments, much less extended nuclear deterrence guarantees. The fact that states especially vulnerable to nuclear dangers (such as Japan and the Republic of Korea) have begun—even tentatively—to consider future scenarios under which they might be prompted to proliferate,[8] indicates how unstable the global nuclear balance has become. The temptation for Iran and Saudi Arabia to do so as well threatens to add new layers of complexity in a geopolitical region that has historically been a troublesome flashpoint. In China, growing ambitions for a Sino-centric order in the Belt and Road space is beginning to meet robust US resistance, creating the impetus for Beijing to increase its own nuclear arsenal. Even Russia and the United States, as the two major nuclear players, have no incentive to reduce their nuclear stockpiles. For Moscow, nuclear weapons have become a critical component of national defence, matched by a strategy of brinkmanship in an attempt to level the playing field with the US.[9] In Washington, meanwhile, there is a consensus that nuclear weapons remain a fundamental element of the US deterrence mix.[10]

In this chapter, we examine the conditions that have given rise to these new global and regional nuclear complexities. We begin by tracing the evolution of nuclear politics from the Cold War to the immediate post-Cold War environment, and then to the new and arguably more dangerous nuclear milieu characterised by great power competition, a global leadership vacuum and an increasingly moribund non-proliferation regime. We then survey the nuclear doctrines of three major states—the US, Russia and the PRC—to identify motives, rationales and prospects for nuclear tension in future. Finally, we identify some potential nuclear flashpoints that underscore the challenges nuclear weapons pose to strategic stability in future.[11]

The Evolution of Nuclear Politics: Between MAD and "Nuclear Abstinence"

As Bernard Brodie once observed, nuclear weapons are overshadowed by two things: they exist in the first place, and they are so destructive. It is axiomatic, but nonetheless worth recalling that nuclear weapons are more destructive—by many orders of magnitude—than any previously developed instrument of war. This has made managing them, whether in terms of proliferation, accumulation or even use one of the key strategic challenges for major powers since 1945. As Kenneth Waltz noted, nuclear weapons are especially attractive for second tier actors because of the massive security guarantees they offer, potentially reversing the fates of small and weak states.[12] For Waltz, nuclear weapons were a strong element of stability in international relations, because their use (or even the conditions that could give rise to their use) entailed "preposterous risk". Hence, for Waltz, there would remain significant temptations for states to try and obtain greater security as opposed to large and expensive conventional forces.[13]

As the twentieth century played out, the US and USSR—as the main protagonists during the Cold War—developed extensive mechanisms for managing nuclear weapons. These were accompanied by changes in the global non-proliferation regime, which sought to regulate the use of nuclear technologies, advance the nuclear non-use norm and ultimately lead to global nuclear disarmament. But after a brief interregnum that followed the end of Cold War bipolarity, in which there was significant enthusiasm about the prospects for tighter governance of nuclear security questions, it quickly became evident that just as the emerging security dynamics of the twenty-first century would be fluid and complex, so would the role of nuclear weapons within them.

Nuclear Weapons and the Cold War: Toward MAD

The development of stable nuclear deterrence formed the basis of a nuclear order focused on reducing the enmity of the Cold War "to a more benign and contained rivalry".[14] Central to this was the establishment of the Non-Proliferation Treaty (NPT) in 1968 and its augmentation through superpower arms control agreements such as the Strategic Arms Limitations Talks (SALT). As William Walker noted, the nuclear order of the Cold War had two components: (i) a system of "managed deterrence" wherein the recognised nuclear weapons states (NWS) undertook to limit further horizontal proliferation, and (ii) a system of "nuclear abstinence" codified in the rules and norms of the NPT by which non-nuclear weapons states (NNWS) committed to refrain from acquiring nuclear weapons in return for access to the "peaceful" applications of nuclear technology. This system, however, emerged in fits and starts, and was both constrained and encouraged by superpower competition.

Central to the initial considerations of the "nuclear age" were the exigencies of the Second World War. Not only had it provided the impetus for the creation of nuclear weapons but also initial doctrinal frameworks and technical means with which to harness their military potential. Thus, when the United States dropped atomic bombs on Hiroshima and Nagasaki in August 1945, they were guided by the same strategic logic and intent as the conventional "firebombing" air raids undertaken by the allies on German and Japanese cities. In other words, they were initially envisaged as another weapon of war—albeit of immensely enhanced destructive capability. Much of the next decade or more was characterised by widespread debate by both policy-makers and scholars as to the impact of the nuclear age on national security policy and in the practicality of applying Clausewitzian principles to nuclear weapons. Thus, such questions as to what political purpose could nuclear weapons be put, which circumstance warranted their use, and how such weapons could be deployed exercised substantial mental energies from the late 1940s onward.[15]

The "delicate balance of terror" of nuclear deterrence between the US and USSR took some time to develop.[16] In the immediate years after Hiroshima and Nagasaki, it was potential offensive applications that exercised the imaginations (and nightmares) of strategists and policy-makers. In the American context, for example, a "nuclear Pearl Harbor" animated early debate about the impact of nuclear weapons on American national security.[17] This may seem incongruous given that the United States in the immediate post-war years retained a nuclear monopoly. But fears of the offensive potentialities of the new technology were framed by recent experiences—what if a similarly "irrational" leader such as Hitler were to acquire this new weapon?—and the rapid acceleration of technological development. Jet engines and ballistic missiles, which had made their appearance in the final year of the Second World War, made it seem a question of not if but when such propulsion systems were married to atomic weapons.[18] In classic security dilemma and arms spiral fashion, the Soviet Union relatively quickly broke the American nuclear monopoly with its own successful atomic test in 1949. This spurred not only further technological development in the form of the development of thermonuclear weapons and their delivery vehicles of ballistic missiles and long-range bombers in the 1950s, but also further iterations of nuclear doctrine which sought to identify the conditions under which using nuclear weapons would be contemplated.

The Truman administration (1945–1952), after the breakdown of negotiation with the Soviet Union and a number of other states on establishing international controls on nuclear technology under the auspices of the UN, slowly began to build up its nuclear arsenal. As relations with Moscow deteriorated rapidly in 1947 and 1948, the administration more actively contemplated how and when to use nuclear weapons.[19] American military planners viewed a Soviet invasion of Western Europe, with Moscow leveraging its advantage in conventional forces, as the most likely scenario in which nuclear use would be contemplated as a means to compensate for American and Allied conventional inferiority.[20] Significantly, the Soviet Union envisaged a future war in the same fashion, comprised of "an atomic air offensive by the United States, which would not succeed in defeating the Soviet Union, and large-scale Soviet offensive operations to push the Western powers out of Europe and the Middle East".[21]

Thus, even at this early stage, both American and Soviet planners did not conceive of nuclear weapons as necessarily constituting the "winning weapon" in a possible World War 3. This was underlined by the successful testing of thermonuclear weapons by the United States and the Soviets in August–September 1953, which prompted both President Eisenhower and new Soviet Premier Georgii M. Malenkov to acknowledge that a new world war would likely threaten the existence of civilisation.[22] This situation appeared to confirm Bernard Brodie's prescient observation of 1946 regarding the significance of the nuclear age. "Thus far", he noted, "the purpose of our military establishment has been to win wars. From now on its chief purpose must be to avert them. It can have almost no other useful purpose".[23]

Yet policy-makers and military planners were slow to accept the veracity of Brodie's observation. President Eisenhower's (1953–1960) approach to national security, for example, resulted in doctrinal development that *enhanced* the role of nuclear weapons in American national security policy and *accelerated* the nuclear arms race with the USSR. Eisenhower fundamentally believed that national security was not just about the physical defence of the United

States but also the protection of its values, economic system and domestic institutions. This core belief resulted in an approach that emphasised the need to strike a balance between the "cost of an adequate defense and the need to maintain a healthy, solvent economy".[24] His subsequent "New Look" strategy put those principles into practice, cutting ground and naval forces considerably and resting America's deterrent on "massive atomic capability".[25] The doctrine of "massive retaliation", whereby the United States would effectively "threaten to go to a nuclear war to deter conventional Soviet challenges", was born.[26]

Although promising more "bang" for the American defence "buck", it quickly became apparent that massive retaliation introduced a number of problems that contradicted Eisenhower's objectives. First, it rested on a problematic premise: its promise to avert nuclear war could only hold so long as the United States could *credibly* threaten to use its deterrent. Would the United States, for instance, effectively commit suicide, escalating to general nuclear war to protect Western Europe from Soviet attack?[27] Second, the doctrine was based on the asymmetrical application of American power regardless of the level of threat or "aggression". Third, deterring Soviet "aggression" by relying on offensive retaliatory strength entailed American commitment to a significant *build-up* of nuclear weapons and their delivery systems, including inter-continental ballistic missiles (ICBMs) and submarine-launched ballistic missiles (SLBMs). This actually *added* rather than subtracted from the defence budget. Fourth, massive retaliation committed the United States to a nuclear arms race of indefinite duration just to stay ahead of the Soviets.[28]

Eisenhower's approach thus introduced dilemmas that would recur throughout the Cold War: could "credibility" of nuclear threats be assured; were the budgetary effects of the "military-industrial complex" sustainable; and was there a way out of the nuclear arms race? The issue of credibility was particularly troublesome given the expansion of the United States' security perimeter to the global level implicit in the strategy of containment. Here, as demonstrated by crises throughout the 1950s over Berlin, the islands of Quemoy and Matsu in the Taiwan Straits, and Indo-China, assuring adversaries (and allies) of the credibility of "massive retaliation" entailed acceptance of significant risks by the United States.[29] These included consideration of use of "tactical", low-yield nuclear weapons in response to low-level conventional attacks and placement of small American "trip-wire" forces in contested regions such as Berlin. The purpose of the latter, as Thomas Schelling bluntly observed, would simply be to "die heroically, dramatically, in a way that guarantees that action cannot stop there".[30] More broadly, Eisenhower had set the United States up for two worst-case choices in the event of a major crisis: "either risk a major foreign-policy defeat, and the loss of credibility that would have resulted from a failure to follow through on earlier threats" or "risk the likely international revulsion that would greet another crossing of the nuclear threshold".[31]

In the Soviet Union, too, the combination of perceived threat of encirclement by the United States and its allies and a desire to achieve parity with the United States spurred Moscow to develop its own nuclear arsenal and delivery systems.[32] After Stalin's death in 1953, Soviet policy ran to an extent parallel to that in the United States. Moscow, too, sought to decrease its reliance on conventional forces in favour of nuclear weapons and bolstered its air defences to counter the threat of long-range American strategic bombing.[33] This was accelerated by Nikita Khrushchev, who emerged as Stalin's successor in 1955–56. Khrushchev's approach, much like Eisenhower's, was in part ideologically-informed and "derived from his belief that the Soviet Union could afford to reduce its reliance on military power and benefit from a demilitarization of the Cold War" as the superiority of communism would ultimately prevail over the capitalist West if "peaceful coexistence" could be struck.[34]

This was also informed by recognition of the Soviet Union's distinct inferiority in the nuclear arms race, both in numbers and in delivery systems. The American nuclear arsenal grew from 369 in 1950 to over 27,000 in 1962, while the Soviet arsenal "grew from a handful of bombs to about 3,300" over the same period.[35] Additionally, while the United States by the end of the 1950s possessed long-range bombers and military bases within striking distance of the Soviet Union, and increasing ICBM and SLBM capabilities, the Soviet Union had significantly fewer nuclear weapons and had limited means with which to deliver them.[36]

"Mutual destruction" was thus not "assured". Eisenhower's conception of deterrence, wherein he maintained that the United States should have enough "retaliatory power" to destroy Soviet cities and "government concentrations" (what would subsequently be termed "countervalue" targeting), was also clearly premised on continued American nuclear superiority in both quantitative and qualitative terms.[37] As Albert Wohlstetter noted, the American commitment to "overmatch Soviet technology and, specifically, Soviet offense technology" meant "confusing deterrence with matching or exceeding the enemy's ability to strike first".[38] What was required for deterrence, however, was the ability to retaliate *after* being struck. This recognition led, in turn, to both sides becoming "obsessed with the actual or imagined risk of first strikes" and "encouraging the establishment of retaliatory, "second-strike" capacities to ensure that deterrence would hold everywhere".[39]

The Soviet Union's successful launch of *Sputnik* in October 1957 prompted much domestic posturing in the United States about a supposed "missile gap" between the US and USSR.[40] This was used particularly effectively by John F. Kennedy in the presidential election of 1960, as a sustained critique of the alleged "complacency" of the Eisenhower administration's national security policy.[41] Once in the White House JFK's administration sought an alternative to "massive retaliation", which came to be termed "flexible response".[42] It focused on developing a proportional range of nuclear and conventional strike options as the path to escape from the worst-case choices of defeat/capitulation or nuclear war presented by "massive retaliation".[43] Kennedy's "flexible response" strategy would be based on a greater focus on conventional forces, renewed emphasis on developing the nuclear "triad" (ICBMs; SLCBMs; strategic bombers) and development of counter-insurgency capabilities.

Yet the crux of the problem, as Kennedy's Deputy National Security Adviser Walt Rostow noted in March 1962, was that the Eisenhower policy had meant that the United States was not only "often caught in circumstances where our only available riposte is so disproportionate to the immediate provocation that its use risks unwanted escalation or serious political costs" but this "asymmetry makes it attractive for Communists to apply limited debilitating pressures upon us in situations where we find it difficult to impose on them an equivalent price".[44] In essence, the administration was substituting a symmetrical response for the asymmetrical one under Eisenhower, which they judged had increased the risk of nuclear war and created openings for adversaries to manipulate the ambiguities of American deterrent threats or commitments.[45]

Much like "massive retaliation" however, "flexible response" also created problematic dynamics. One was the significant increase in the Defense budget to build up both conventional and nuclear capabilities. With respect to nuclear doctrine, "flexible response" also theoretically encompassed the possibility of "limited" nuclear war. Under Secretary of State Robert McNamara, the Department of Defence initially explored development of a counterforce (direct targeting of Soviet military installations) rather than countervalue doctrine. However, after studies revealed that counterforce would likely result in the deaths of 28 million Americans and 60 million Western Europeans, McNamara returned to a largely countervalue strategy.[46] The 1962 Single Integrated Operational Plan (SIOP) presented to President Kennedy contained fourteen options that would launch "all available strategic forces" against "military and urban-industrial targets throughout the Sino-Soviet bloc".[47] By the end of the Kennedy administration, as John Lewis Gaddis notes, the "peculiar logic" of "mutually assured destruction"—"the idea that one's population could best be protected by leaving it vulnerable, so long as the other side faced comparable vulnerabilities"—was taking shape.[48]

Two crises in particular demonstrated the limits of flexible response. On the positive side of the ledger stands Kennedy's handling of the Cuban Missile Crisis which has been widely seen as having demonstrated American "credibility" while limiting the risk of escalation.[49] On the other side was American intervention in Vietnam, which was, as John Lewis Gaddis notes, "derived quite logically" from "flexible response".[50] Here, the desire for "calibration" of American responses led to first the commitment of military advisers in May 1961 under JFK to the "Rolling Thunder" bombing campaign of North Vietnam in March 1965, and the ultimate commitment of over 500,000 American troops by 1967. "Calibration" arguably worked in the Cuban Missile Crisis and not in Vietnam for the simple fact that to function such an approach required the accurate measurement of the commitment of the adversary. In Cuba, the Soviet Union's commitment to keeping missiles there was limited, while North Vietnam's commitment to unify Vietnam under its control clearly was not.[51]

However, MacNamara's "Flexible Response" doctrine was not the final refinement made to US nuclear strategy during the Cold War. Indeed, during the Carter administration (1977–1980), a number of amendments were made to boost the selective targeting options available to US nuclear forces, with an emphasis on a balance between counterforce and countervalue. The so-called Schlesinger Doctrine, named after the US Defence Secretary at the time, evolved into the Single Integrated Operational Plan 5 (SIOP-5), which sought to prevent escalation into an all-out nuclear war by withholding attacks on Soviet cities in favour of military targets.[52] Refined further by Carter's Presidential Directive 59,[53] the US sought to harden its own command and control facilities so that they could withstand a Soviet first strike and still be able to respond massively against the USSR if necessary.

Carter's nuclear posture renovations effectively shifted the US towards a "war-fighting" approach, which the Reagan administration adapted into a "war winning" posture. This envisaged deliberately targeting Soviet command and control centres with a decapitating first strike, sowing so much chaos and confusion that the USSR was prevented from responding in kind. As part of a deliberate campaign to increase pressure on Moscow, Reagan also oversaw a significant hike in the US defence budget, pursuing a technological edge to both the American deterrent and its ability to withstand nuclear attacks. The most prominent of these was the Strategic Defence Initiative (SDI), nicknamed the "Star Wars" program, which aimed to develop a suite of sophisticated US antimissile capabilities. Prominent Western strategists were divided on the issue: some, like Colin Gray, saw a war-fighting posture as a logical evolution of nuclear strategy,[54] whereas others regarded it as a dangerous weakening of deterrence that created the incentive for further arms races.[55]

Beyond the US, other Western nuclear weapons states took differing approaches to deterrence. The United Kingdom integrated its own relatively small nuclear forces, primarily deployed on submarines via the Polaris and then Trident nuclear missile systems, into the central NATO command and control structure.[56] France, on the other hand, stressed the importance of independent nuclear forces—the *force de frappe*—with the logic that ambiguity about each Western power centre's tipping point on nuclear use would ultimately strengthen deterrence. Critics of that view argued that since the cornerstone of nuclear deterrence was clear central control, Paris was in fact engaging in nuclear brinkmanship—and that its strategy was more reflective of a broader reticence to commit firmly to the NATO alliance.[57]

China's acquisition of nuclear weapons and subsequent elucidation of its nuclear doctrine demonstrated some similarities with that of the French example. Rather than being primarily concerned with deterring an existential threat, China's decision to acquire nuclear weapons was driven by a desire to prevent the United States and the Soviet Union from using their nuclear capabilities to coerce Beijing in crisis situations, as Washington had done during the Korean War and the Taiwan Straits crises of the 1950s.[58] Yet it took a different approach to the superpowers, focusing instead on "minimum" or "limited deterrence". In order to achieve the strategic objective of deterrence, it was sufficient for China to develop and deploy a small number of weapons in such a manner as to ensure that if attacked first, China would still retain the capacity to inflict unacceptable damage on its attacker.[59]

In parallel to these developments, the superpowers also engaged in a variety of arms control negotiations and treaties throughout the Cold War. The initial impetus for this was an outcome of the crises of the 1958–1962 period which "fostered the view in Washington, Moscow and other capitals that security and survival could henceforth only be achieved through greater practice and insti-tutionalization of restraint, and through strategic developments that brought a more stable balance of power and diminished risks of escalation to all-out nuclear war".[60] A major contribution to ensuring "restraint" within the arms race was the stabilisation of deterrence through establishing the condi-tions under which both parties would have secure "second-strike" capabilities. Limiting or controlling the development of new types of nuclear weapons and new systems thus became a particular focus from the 1960s onward. The first step along this path was the Limited Test Ban Treaty of August 1963 that prohibited nuclear testing in the atmosphere, underwater or in outer-space.[61] TheLTBT's failure to prohibit underground nuclear testing, however, limited its effect on the superpower arms race.[62]

Due to a variety of factors, including leadership changes in Washington and Moscow and American entanglements in Vietnam, the next major round of superpower arms control negotiations did not occur until the Strategic Arms Limitation Talks (SALT) in Helsinki in 1969. An Interim Agreement included the SALT I Treaty and the Anti-Ballistic Missile (ABM) Treaty in 1972. The ABM Treaty limited each party to two ABM sites in order to prevent missile defences undermining confidence in "second-strike" capability and thus the deterrence relationship between the United States and the Soviet Union. "It was", Avis Bohlen noted, "a significant and indeed unique achievement in that it closed off an expensive arms race in one area of technology".[63]

The issue of "offensive" weapons, however, proved to be more problematic than missile defence as American and Soviet arsenals had diverged in the 1960s in terms of the types of weapons and delivery systems each relied upon. The United States had focused on sea-based systems to ensure its "second-strike" capability, increased missile accuracy, warhead miniaturisation and develop-ment of multiple independent re-entry vehicles (MIRVs). Moscow, in contrast, based its arsenal on land-based missiles, emphasised increased missile payloads and sought to rapidly increase missile numbers. SALT I placed a "five-year freeze on the ICBM and SLBM launchers of both sides" but did little to address the MIRV issue as the United States already had deployed the tech-nology on *Minuteman* (1970) and *Poseidon* missiles (1971) while Soviet MIRV technology was in development.[64] Negotiations for SALT II, begun almost immediately upon conclusion of SALT I, were not completed until

1979. Although ultimately a victim of the deterioration of US-Soviet relations with the Soviet invasion of Afghanistan, SALT II had proposed "limiting not only the total number of delivery vehicles on each side, but also the crucial subcategories of MIRVed missiles, MIRVed ICBMs and heavy missiles".[65]

While the emergence of nuclear arms control from the early 1960s onward has been seen by some as evidence that American and Soviet policy-makers had accepted the desirability of "mutual vulnerability", it is perhaps more accurate to note that US and Soviet arms control was based on the recognition of the *reality* of "mutual vulnerability".[66] On the American side of the equation although the Nixon and Ford administration acceded to numerical parity in SALT I, they nonetheless consistently sought to "transcend parity" through pursuit of a range of qualitative advantages through the modernisation and innovation of the US nuclear arsenal, command and control and intelligence innovations and anti-submarine capabilities.[67] This amounted to an "holistic offset" strategy that combined arms racing and arms control whereby the US "raced the Soviets in military technologies where the United States was perceived to enjoy significant advantages, while simultaneously entangling the Soviet Union in an arms control regime that would limit areas of Soviet strength".[68]

Nuclear Non-Proliferation Treaty: An Imperfect Nuclear Abstinence?

In addition to the nuclear arms race, a global nuclear non-proliferation regime developed slowly. The development of stable nuclear deterrence between the superpowers by the mid-to-late 1960s formed the basis of a nuclear order focused on reducing the enmity of the Cold War "to a more benign and contained rivalry".[69] Central to the containment of that enmity was the establishment of the Non-Proliferation Treaty (NPT) in 1968 and its augmentation through superpower arms control agreements such as SALT. The non-proliferation regime (centred on the NPT) and arms control agreements formed the basis of a relatively stable nuclear order defined by a "managed system of deterrence" and "abstinence".[70] The former (i.e. "managed system of deterrence") functioned through the dynamics of superpower balancing and self-interest to limit the further expansion of the NWS "club" (noted in the previous section) while the latter (i.e. "managed system of abstinence") operated via the rules and norms embedded in the NPT.

The NPT established a bargain between the NWS and NNWS signatories. Under the NPT, the NWS committed to guaranteeing NNWS access to the "peaceful uses" of nuclear technology, not to proliferate to NNWS and "eventual" nuclear disarmament. In return, the NNWS committed to not seek nuclear weapons and to access the "peaceful uses" of nuclear technology under international supervision.[71] Thus, as the superpower's dampened "the dynamics of their own competition" by the late 1960s, they "gradually refocused to nonproliferation" which revolved around controlling access to critical technology and establishing a "norm of condemning nations that pursued nuclear weapons".[72] Indeed, the functioning of the non-proliferation system during the Cold War reflected the interests of the recognised NWS by privileging the goal of preventing further horizontal proliferation than to the goals of nuclear disarmament or access for NNWS to civilian applications of nuclear technology.

During the 1970s, two major developments—an unprecedented growth in civilian nuclear power generation in the US, Japan and Western Europe and the testing of a nuclear device by India in 1974—converged to exert major pressure on the "managed systems of deterrence and abstinence". A major question raised by these dynamics was whether expanded use of nuclear power to meet increasing energy demand would ultimately increase the likelihood of nuclear weapons proliferation. India's "peaceful nuclear explosion" (PNE) of May 1974 was taken by many to be a harbinger of things to come in this regard. India's diversion of plutonium extracted from the spent fuel rods of a Canadian-supplied CIRUS reactor, and heavy-water supplied by the US, brought into stark relief the need for the development of more stringent export controls and safeguards for nuclear materials and technology in order to limit further horizontal proliferation.[73] In the wake of this event, it emerged that a key policy choice for the US, and other major suppliers of nuclear materials and technology with an interest in slowing or halting further nuclear proliferation, was whether to attempt to achieve non-proliferation goals through multilateral cooperation, or through unilateral measures to deny potential proliferators access to nuclear technology (nuclear reactors, uranium enrichment and/or reprocessing plants) and materials (enriched uranium or plutonium).[74]

The responses of the Nixon (1968–1974), Ford (1974-1977) and Carter administrations (1978–1982) to this question oscillated between these poles, creating significant dilemmas for both consumers and suppliers of nuclear materials and technology. Throughout the 1970s, the US retained three significant elements of leverage through which it could attempt to influence the development of the economic domain of global nuclear affairs: possession of the world's most advanced nuclear technology; its position as a primary source of financing for the construction of nuclear facilities (including reactors); and its near monopoly status as supplier of low enriched uranium fuel in the "free world".[75] This dominant position, or "civilian nuclear suzerainty" as William Walker has termed it, was, however, increasingly challenged by the emergence of new suppliers such as France, West Germany and Japan.[76] These states were expanding their own nuclear power programs and, as their domestic markets did not appear large enough to support such expansion alone, they sought to sell not only reactor technology but also the full range of nuclear fuel cycle facilities abroad.

While the concern that expanding civilian nuclear energy programs would increase the risk of further nuclear proliferation was eased for a time with the declining fortunes of the nuclear industry after disasters such as Three Mile Island (1981), the broader challenge represented by India's nuclear test did not. Bracken notes that India's 1974 test can be seen as the beginning of a "second nuclear age" whereby primarily Asian states would directly challenge the NPT system established in 1968 in order to mitigate "national insecurities" whether material (direct threats to national security) or ideational (to achieve a "rightful" claim to status and prestige).[77] Significantly, the major proliferation challengers from the 1970s to the end of the Cold War such as South Korea, North Korea, Pakistan, Iraq, Brazil and Argentina were driven by such "national insecurities" rather than ideological commitment to either major superpower protagonist.[78]

THE POST-COLD WAR NUCLEAR INTERREGNUM AND THE "SECOND NUCLEAR AGE"

In the immediate post-Cold War period, the enthusiasm for democratisation and the "peace dividends" flowing from the end of bipolarity witnessed a new optimism about the prospects for non-proliferation. The successful handover of former Soviet nuclear weapons from Ukraine and Kazakhstan to Russia seemed to indicate that in addition to a powerful "non-use" norm, the NPT had also engendered a growing non-proliferation norm. And while many of the treaties making up the non-proliferation regime—including the Comprehensive Test Ban Treaty (CTBT), the Fissile Material Cut-off Treaty (FMCT) and the Missile Technology Control Regime (MTCR)—continued to suffer from problems that stemmed from lack of ratification to outright cheating, there was nonetheless a sense in the early 1990s that the eventual goal of the NPT—global nuclear disarmament—might be in reach.

However, these developments were counterbalanced by the nuclear tests conducted by India and Pakistan in 1996 that formally announced them as nuclear weapons states, but outside of the NPT. So too did the development of a crude nuclear capability by the DPRK, which saw such weapons as important components of both its power maximisation stance and regime security. In the West, debates over nuclear weapons continued to be animated by the fear that further arms reductions between the US and Russia might actually make a nuclear war winnable (and hence encourage first strikes). Some, like Kenneth Waltz, articulated the view that more nuclear weapons were better.[79] Others like John Mearsheimer called for selective proliferation to what he saw as "stable" states (in particular a unified Germany) in order to maintain the European balance of power.[80]

The very fact these debates continued during the 1990s is instructive with respect to how quickly the initial enthusiasm for arms control, institutional mechanisms and disarmament dissipated after the dawn of the twenty-first century. The twin problems of the NPT—that it had made no progress on superpower disarmament while at the same time effectively facilitating opaque proliferation—meant that the main accomplishments in arms control were bilateral, in the form of the New START Treaty. Even the goal of counter-proliferation was effectively taken away from the non-proliferation regime after the US, under George W. Bush, embarked on the Proliferation Security Initiative (PSI), a series of bilateral arrangements that permitted US warships to stop and search vessels suspected of smuggling nuclear weapons components by sea. And yet even though the US and Russia managed to maintain their respective commitments to reduce nuclear stockpiles, in spite of an frosty relationship, other aspects of superpower cooperation in related fields diminished. As part of its commitment to missile defence, the US withdrew from the Anti-Ballistic Missile Treaty in 2002 and repeated cheating by Russia prompted it to abrogate the Intermediate Nuclear Forces Treaty in 2019. In June 2020, the Trump administration signalled its intention to withdraw from the 1992 Open Skies Treaty, which permitted each both Russia and the US to conduct high altitude reconnaissance flights over each other's territory.

Hence, one of the defining features of nuclear politics in the twenty-first century has been that many of the mechanisms that contributed to stability in the Cold War era—as John Lewis Gaddis had pointed out—were absent in respect of the US-Russia nuclear dyad.[81] More crucially, global and regional balances were often more reflective of unstable multipolar nuclear relationships, as well as a complex mix of conventional deterrence postures coupled with the temptation of nuclear use. In South Asia, for instance, a nuclear triangle involving India, the PRC and China has emerged, which overlays existing security dilemmas that incorporate India-Pakistan hostilities over Kashmir and radical Islamic insurgencies, Sino-Indian strategic rivalry in the maritime Indian ocean space and in the Himalayas, and the broadening of Chinese geostrategic ambitions via the China-Pakistan Economic Corridor (CPEC) as part of Beijing's Belt and Road Initiative.

The policy and posture of the US have also pivoted to embrace strategic competition with China as well as Russia. The Nuclear Posture Review process has tended to serve the specific political goals of different US administrations, rather than suggesting a clear sense of strategic direction. Created soon after the events of September 11, 2001, the 2002 NPR stipulated the development of scenarios for potential US nuclear use against a variety of nations identified by the Bush administration as part of an "axis of evil", including Iran, Iraq and the DPRK.[82] But it also saw Russia, China, Libya and Syria as potential aggressor states that might require the US to use nuclear weapons during a future conflict. In contrast, Barack Obama's 2010 NPR was designed to support his push for "nuclear zero": an attempt to reinvigorate a desire to wind back nuclear weapons within the NPT framework.[83] Accordingly, it developed a more minimalist posture based on reasonable sufficiency on nuclear arms, and explicitly stressed that states in compliance with the NPT would not be the targets of US nuclear attack.[84]

Nuclear Postures of Major Powers

Given that the defining feature of the twenty-first-century nuclear security environment is complexity and chaos rather than stability, what roles are each of the major nuclear weapons states playing in the process? Is nuclear deterrence still feasible under these conditions? And what do they see as the main threats and opportunities in the nuclear domain? Below we assess the postures of the three main nuclear powers in the twenty-first century—the US, Russia and the PRC—in order to shed some light on these questions.

United States

American nuclear doctrine, posture and practice during the Cold War challenges what Francis Gavin terms the conventional "nuclear revolution" school of nuclear politics.[85] This is based on two basic arguments: (i) nuclear weapons "provide states with the ability to protect their sovereignty and independence not via direct defense but rather through deterrence", and (ii) hence ""nuclear superiority" was a meaningless concept" as a "handful of survivable weapons makes it very unlikely that another state will attack you directly".[86] These fundamental arguments have been central to interpretations of the causal factors for the "long peace" of the Cold War. It is, as John Lewis Gaddis argues, "inescapable" that what induced "unaccustomed caution" in superpower competition was "the workings of the nuclear deterrent".[87]

However, the "nuclear revolution" school does not necessarily explain why the United States sought quantitative and qualitative superiority over the Soviet Union (and other NWS) or to limit horizontal proliferation.[88] Explanations for this arguably lie in the broader and more ambitious objectives of American grand strategy since 1945 to "de-volatise" international politics through establishment of American primacy which entailed not only the containment of outright adversaries such as the Soviet Union but also the management of the independent capabilities of allies.[89]

The purpose envisaged for the American nuclear arsenal by successive administrations was therefore as an instrument to underpin not simply American national security but by extension international security. Here, the central assumption was that "unchallenged US military power underwrote global security commitments, dampened long-standing rivalries in key regions and gave Washington immense diplomatic leverage".[90]

It is therefore not surprising that nuclear weapons have retained a central place in US national security policy. This has been reflected in successive National Security Strategy (NSS), Nuclear Posture Review (NPR) and Quadrennial Defense Review (QDR) documents since the end of the Cold War. US policy in this regard since 1991 has been characterised by the emergence of a number of major inter-related themes or directions. Successive US administrations since 1991 have identified the prospect of "rogue" states such as Iraq, Iran, Syria or North Korea acquiring WMD capabilities (nuclear, chemical and biological weapons) as the gravest threat to US national security and international security more broadly.[91] This in turn resulted in the retention of the US nuclear arsenal as a central plank of national security policy.

Nuclear weapons thus came to be viewed by US administrations, particularly by the Bush Snr and Clinton administrations, as a counter-proliferation tool. Moreover, this also created stimulus for a more flexible nuclear arsenal, including the development of "low yield, precision-guided" nuclear weapons that could be used in "regional wars" to avoid destabilising conflicts.[92]

Related to these concerns about the proliferation of WMD capabilities to "rogue" states was the parallel proliferation of ballistic missile technology and systems that would deliver WMD, leading the Clinton administration to countenance Ballistic Missile Defence (BMD).[93] Domestically, the Republican's victory in the US mid-term elections of 1994 resulted in their concerted promotion of the concept of BMD to ensure maximum freedom of action for the US in combating hostile powers and "rogue" states. This was intensified by further nuclear and ballistic missile proliferation in 1998, including the Indian and Pakistani nuclear tests of May, and the ballistic missile testing of North Korea and Iran later that year.[94] Clinton committed US$6.6 billion in the 1999 budget for the development of a BMD capability, and the US Senate rejected the ratification of the Comprehensive Test Ban Treaty (CTBT).[95]

These developments to some analysts were a response to the dynamics of the "second nuclear age".[96] Paul Bracken has argued here that in contrast to the first, the second nuclear age was defined by multiple nuclear weapons aspirants; nuclear weapons programs linked to state-building; nuclear aspirants confronted an existing non-proliferation architecture; its geopolitical centre of gravity was Asia; and costs of nuclear weapons acquisition had decreased.[97] In such a world, a hedging strategy predicated on the primacy of nuclear weapons was deemed a prudent necessity.[98] Clinton's 1997 QDR further refined the US quest to identify the pre-eminent threats to its security emanating from what it termed a "highly uncertain world". Once more "rogues" such as Iraq, Iran and North Korea were singled out as potential threats, closely followed by WMD proliferation, "failed states" and international terrorism. The goal of US pre-eminence was also further underlined in the same document by stressing the need for the US to develop and maintain "full spectrum dominance" in military affairs—including maintenance of nuclear superiority—that would permit it to deter potential adversaries and intervene whenever and wherever on the globe in the defence of US interests.[99] However, the US attachment of increased utility to nuclear weapons and commitment to strategies such as BMD also contributed to the stresses on the international non-proliferation regime and other supporting treaties such as the ABM Treaty and the CTBT.[100]

For George W. Bush, 9/11 acted as a "trigger" for the further development of these tendencies within the US' approach to nuclear proliferation.[101] Concern that "rogue states" would either be tempted to use nuclear weapons themselves, or pass them to terrorists eroded the administration's belief that a traditional conception of deterrence was now sufficient to ensure American national security. This resulted in shifts in nuclear doctrine that made nuclear weapons more important in American national security policy, held potential to stimulate new arms racing dynamics and further weakened the non-proliferation regime.

The administration's December 2001 NPR, for example, began by reiterating the "fundamental" role nuclear weapon played in deterring attack on the United States. However, the document also emphasised the need to maintain and enhance American "military flexibility", develop a new "triad" of offensive strike systems, defensive systems and a responsive defence infrastructure, and maintain a large stockpile of nuclear weapons.[102] TheNPR also signalled the administration's desire to abandon key institutions of arms control and restraint, including the ABM Treaty in order to pursue BMD and consideration of development of "mininukes" for possible use in pre-emptive strikes against nuclear weapons systems housed in hardened underground bunkers. Critics noted that such policies were destabilising, with the former potentially undercutting others' "second-strike" capability and the latter potentially introducing a new spur to vertical proliferation (the development of new types of nuclear weapons by existing nuclear weapons states).[103]

9/11, in conjunction with the perceived failures of the non-proliferation regime in the late 1990s (e.g. continuation of DPRK nuclear ambitions, India and Pakistan's nuclear tests), also prompted the Bush administration to adopt a more assertive posture vis-à-vis nuclear (and other WMD) proliferation based on either unilateral or "coalition of the willing" pre-emption and "regime change" rather than the multilateral framework of arms control.[104] MuchUS policy here was based on the view that multilateral arms control and non-proliferation agreements were in fact "disciplinary measures above all else...cages for holding states within established legal frameworks and to the legal obligations that followed".[105]

While the Obama administration came to office promising a return of American commitment to arms control, non-proliferation and nuclear disarmament, it nonetheless maintained the need to maintain and modernise the country's nuclear arsenal. While Obama called for a world free of nuclear weapons in his famous speech of April 2009 in Prague, he also, in the same speech, declared that, "As long as nuclear weapons exist, the United States will maintain a safe, secure, and effective nuclear arsenal to deter any adversary, and guarantee the defense of our allies". Obama thus subscribed to the "dominant strategic dualism" evident in post-Cold War American nuclear policy that "nuclear war would be a catastrophe but the country had to be prepared to engage in it in order to prevent it".[106]

The administration achieved some limited success on reviving nuclear arms control with the signing of New START, signed by Presidents Obama and Russian President Dmitri Medvedev in Moscow on 8 April 2010. Under this agreement, both parties committed to reduce their deployed arsenals to 1,550 strategic warheads by 2017. However, the treaty's accounting rules meant that reductions would likely be much less than claimed. For example, heavy bombers—one key leg of the US nuclear triad—would be counted as one warhead despite the fact that such bombers often carry multiple nuclear-armed missiles or bombs. The treaty's accounting rules also permitted both a significant "upload" capacity by omitting the US's arsenal of "reserve" warheads awaiting dismantlement and Russia's "several thousand" tactical nuclear weapons.[107]

The Obama administration's 2010 NPR signalled a major shift in US declaratory policy and nuclear posture by assigning to the US' nuclear arsenal the "sole purpose" of deterring a nuclear attack by a hostile nuclear weapons state and making a "no first use" declaration.[108] However, it only signalled that it would move in this direction at some undisclosed point in future.[109] The NPR also asserted that the US would only consider it "in extreme circumstances" and would "not use or threaten to use nuclear weapons against non-nuclear weapons states that are *party to the NPT* and in *compliance* with their nuclear non-proliferation obligations".[110] The effect of this statement was threefold. First, the US still threatened to use nuclear weapons against nuclear weapons states that are party to the NPT (China, Russia) if they were to attack with nuclear, biological or chemical weapons. Second, it implied that the US reserved the right to use nuclear weapons against states that are not party to the NPT, and explicitly disavowed its negative security assurance to those in violation of the treaty. Third, as the new policy did not explicitly identify what it meant for a state to be "in compliance" with the NPT, the administration reserved the right to determine for itself what constituted "compliance".[111]

The 2010 NPR also identified the maintenance of "strategic deterrence and stability at reduced nuclear force levels" and the "strengthening of regional deterrence and reassurance of US allies" as core objectives. To maintain "strategic deterrence and stability at reduced nuclear force levels", the NPR reasserted the US' retention of the traditional triad of SLBMs, ICBMs and heavy bombers and contemplates the "possible addition of non-nuclear prompt-global strike capabilities" (i.e. conventionally armed ICBMS or SLBMs).[112] The retention of these capabilities was clearly linked to concerns regarding the continued nuclear modernisation efforts and strategic doctrines of both Russia and China.

This was also designed to allay the fears of allies that the administration's stated goal of reducing the role of nuclear weapons in US national security strategy would result in the erosion of the credibility of US security commitments. Simultaneously, however, the continued development of such non-nuclear capabilities as BMD and PGS was viewed by both Beijing and Moscow as potentially threatening to strategic stability in their nuclear relationships with Washington.[113] Taken together, the administration sought to strike a balance between its desire to reduce the role of nuclear weapons in American national security and maintain its commitments to allies via "to make sure that non-nuclear weapons, much more capable of discriminate and proportionate use, would increasingly bear the lion's share of the country's deterrent as well as defense needs".[114]

Finally, under the Trump administration (2017-present), the nuclear posture of the United States has shifted towards one reminiscent of the Eisenhower and Kennedy years. The Obama administration's commitment to reduce and limit the role of nuclear weapons has been replaced by an enthusiasm for the multiple roles that the American nuclear arsenal can play in ensuring the country's national security interests. The 2018 NPR was notable in this respect in a number of ways. First, it broadened the circumstances for potential use by asserting that nuclear weapons could be used in response to any actor that "supports or enables terrorist efforts to obtain nuclear devices" or in response to "significant non-nuclear strategic attacks" including attacks on "civilian population or infrastructure".[115] Second, with respect to extended nuclear deterrent commitments, the NPR claimed—somewhat incongruously given Trump's public doubting of the utility of the United States' alliances— that "no one" should doubt its commitments and capabilities to provide it. Third, the NPR demonstrated a disdain for previous American commitments to arms control by reserving the right to "resume nuclear testing if necessary to meet severe technological or geopolitical challenges".[116]

In terms of force structure, the NPR called for the development of a "flexible and tailored" modernised nuclear arsenal. "The United States", it asserted, "will sustain and replace its nuclear capabilities, modernize NC3 [nuclear command and control and communications], and strengthen the integration of nuclear and non-nuclear military planning".[117] This emphasis on "flexibility" was to be "facilitated by a greater-than-ever reliance on "dual capacity" weapons–especially new or modernized cruise missiles launched by fighter-bombers or submarines, with either (or both) nuclear or non-nuclear warheads".[118] The desire for "flexibility" not only frames the NPR's apparent commitment to modernise and replace the existing nuclear triad—at the cost of approximately $US1.25 trillion over the next 30 years—but also develops new types of warheads, particularly "low-yield" SLBMs and sea-launched cruise missiles (SLCMs).[119]

One assessment of the 2018 NPR asserts that its "basic stance–conceptually and in its recommendation of specific weapon systems–is of a machismo posture of readiness to nuke it out with any WMD-armed adversary who deigns to cross any vital national interest red line the United States has drawn".[120] Yet, given the history of American policy reviewed here, one may ask whether this in fact constitutes such a far-reaching change from previous policy. Indeed, the 2018 NPR's statement that a "flexible" and modernized arsenal "will enhance deterrence by denying potential adversaries any mistaken confidence that limited nuclear employment can provide a useful advantage over the United States and its allies" is strikingly similar to the language about dissuading *potential* adversaries used in successive NPRs from 1990 onward.

Russia

Russian nuclear doctrine has shifted considerably since the end of the Cold War. During the bipolar era, the USSR—unlike the US and NATO—maintained a "no first use" policy for its nuclear arsenal. The general thinking by Soviet strategists was that the significant size advantages of the Warsaw Pact (if not overall their qualitative edge) made it largely unnecessary to resort to nuclear weapons as a first resort. In terms of other potential nuclear challengers during the Cold War such as the PRC, Moscow relied on a conventional force advantage as well as superior logistics and manoeuvrability. That said, it is obvious that this posture was never tested. Moreover, Soviet blitzkrieg theory certainly saw an important role for tactical nuclear weapons in the event of a NATO escalation to blunt any large-scale Soviet invasion of Western Europe, with graduated and flexible responses designed to try and retain the upper hand in subsequent attempts at de-escalation.[121] In addition, the Soviet position was complicated by alliance commitments to the USSR's Warsaw pact allies in Central and Eastern Europe, where there remained significant questions about the nature and extent of Soviet extended deterrence guarantees. Nonetheless, Moscow's logic in adopting a formal "no first use posture" was that the Soviet Union could clearly communicate its preference for deterrence and arms control as the main mechanisms to manage the US-Soviet nuclear dyad, while retaining the option of altering its position should circumstances make it necessary.

Yet after the collapse of the Soviet Union, nuclear weapons came to occupy an increasingly important place in Russian strategic thinking. The primary reason for this, at least initially, was defensive and linked to the degradation of Russian relative conventional capabilities during the 1990s. This made Moscow increasingly reliant on its nuclear arsenal in order to underwrite its territorial integrity against the risk of major power war. Concerned that the Russian armed forces would be unable to withstand a concerted campaign by either NATO or a swiftly modernising PLA, the Russian Federation first moved to a "first use if necessary" posture in the early to mid-1990s.[122] Then, as the extent of its economic dislocation became more apparent, Moscow pivoted to a position of "assured first use": a clear warning to potential adversaries that a serious threat to Russian sovereignty would be tempered by with the possibility that Moscow would turn to nuclear weapons.[123]

This was again partly due to the continued centrality of nuclear deterrence in Russian strategic thought. Under circumstances where a conventionally weaker Russia faced potential future scenarios in which its armed forces would not be able to deter an attack, a more assertive posture came to assume a more important role, with the logic that it would make would-be aggressors think twice before engaging in conventional hostilities. But the pace and scale of technological change was also an important factor in Moscow's thinking. While it continued to strenuously resist effort by the US to develop missile defences, arguing that this upset the balance created by deterrence under the

START II accords,[124] the effect of gradual deployments of these defensive capabilities by the US throughout the first decade of the twenty-first century paradoxically made Russia even more reliant on its nuclear arsenal. Given that the US approach to missile defence was holistic, from theatre-based systems such as Aegis and THAAD to heavy investment by George W. Bush's administration in sophisticated tracking platforms, airborne lasers and killer satellites, the risk for Moscow was that its nuclear forces faced the prospect of obsolescence in the face of a fully functioning US National Missile Defence (NMD) capabilities.[125] Even more concerning for Russia was that in addition to undermining deterrence, US missile defences actually made nuclear war *more* likely, providing Washington with a shield behind which it could then strike at the Russian homeland with impunity.

The increasing sophistication of US defences as well as its conventional military capabilities during the early 2000s, sometimes referred to as the Revolution in Military Affairs (RMA), provided an urgent need for Russia to modernise its own military, in which both nuclear weapons and their delivery systems formed a key component. The 5 Day War between Russia and Georgia in 2008 over the disputed territories of South Ossetia and Abkhazia was widely regarded as providing the impetus for Russian military modernisation, but the desire to revamp the Russian military had been present for some time earlier. The difference in 2008, however, was that the Russian economy had rebounded following Vladimir Putin's de facto nationalisation of the Russian energy industry. This gave Moscow the wherewithal to embark on an ambitious $600 billion program to update its conventional as well as nuclear forces.[126] They included funds to accelerate production and deployment of the SS-26 *Iskander* short-range nuclear missile system, as well as the Borei-class SSBN which was intended for deployment in the Russian Northern and Pacific Fleets.[127] Russia also covertly developed the SSC-8 ground-based cruise missile system, with a range of 2,500 kms, in violation of the Intermediate Nuclear Forces (INF) Treaty. Indeed, it was the SSC-8, in addition to fears that the PRC was developing intermediate nuclear forces that it was under no international legal obligation to curtail, which prompted the Trump administration to withdraw from the INF Treaty in 2019.[128]

Here, it is instructive to note that the modernisation of its conventional forces has not reassured Russian strategic elites of the need to rely heavily on nuclear weapons. If anything, the reverse has been the case. At his 2018 annual address, similar to US State of the Union speeches by American Presidents, Putin unveiled a suite of new nuclear delivery systems in order to showcase Russian military technological prowess. Putin noted dramatically that "for years nobody listened to Russia. Well listen to us now".[129] These new platforms, swiftly dubbed Putin's "doomsday weapons", included the Burevestnik cruise missile, a nuclear-powered rocket with technically unlimited range; the Avengard hypersonic missile capable of speeds of up to Mach 20 (in other words, fast enough to defeat any Western surface-to-air missile system); the Sarmat ICBM with the capacity to carry 10-15 MIRVs or Avengard glide vehicles; and the Poseidon autonomous undersea drone that can carry a 200 megaton warhead.[130]

Each of these weapons systems serves to highlight the Russian preference that nuclear weapons are a key component of its overall military posture. The Burevestnik, Avengard, Sarmat and Poseidon are all first strike weapons. The Burevestnik, as a nuclear-powered missile, can conceivably be perpetually in flight, significantly cutting the time normally needed to generate nuclear forces (as well as reducing warning times for their targets). The Avengard is specifically designed to overcome US missile defences and can be mated to either an ICBM or a smaller cruise missile. The Sarmat, a massive nuclear weapons delivery system, is a response to the US development of Prompt Global Strike[131] weapons that will have the capacity to deliver a payload anywhere in the world within an hour. And the Poseidon raises the prospect that quiet and unmanned Russian drone submarines could be deployed off the coasts of large US cities, with the ability to devastate them at short notice.[132]

Why has Russia become so keen to engage in nuclear brinkmanship? In addition to its relative weakness, the key reason concerns the complex twenty-first-century threat environment that Russia faces. In June 2020, Russia unveiled its new nuclear doctrine, which made a number of amendments to its previous posture. These included non-nuclear attacks that went beyond conventional forces and also incorporate cyber attacks: in the words of the doctrine, this also includes a potential pre-emptive response to "enemy impact on critically important government or military facilities, the incapacitation of which could result in the failure of retaliatory action of nuclear forces".[133] The document also clarified the "escalate to de-escalate" strategy[134] hinted at by Russia since 2015, by noting that it reserved the right to respond with nuclear weapons in the event of an attack with conventional forces that threatened the "very existence of the state".[135]

For Moscow, the challenges of managing nuclear weapons in order not to upset regional strategic balances are less important than the extent to which this is seen as a priority by both the US and the PRC. This is because Russia really only has two significant nuclear deterrence dyads: Russia-US and Russia-China. Hence, its fortunes are much more tied to the effects of Sino-US competition than having a fundamental stake in driving how global order takes shape. If anything, its preferred outcome would be for regional strategic conditions to be as chaotic as possible. This serves its broader agenda in Europe and Asia to try and prevent dominance by any one particular state.

China

China's nuclear journey has undergone three significant phases of development since 1949 in relation to China's perception of the utility and importance of nuclear weapons, acceptance of the norm of non-proliferation and engagement with the evolving international nuclear non-proliferation framework. The first phase between 1949 and 1959 could be viewed as a period of China's "coming to grips" with the reality of nuclear weapons in terms of their political, military and strategic significance, and reconciling this to the state's revolutionary worldview.[136] The subsequent 1960 to 1978 period, encompassing the intensive phase of Chinese nuclear development program and acquisition in 1964, not coincidentally saw China opposed to both the Soviet Union and the US. With respect to nuclear weapons, this phase witnessed China's declaratory statements emphasise the right of sovereign states to develop nuclear weapons capabilities for self-defence and to break the superpower nuclear "monopoly".[137] Moreover, from the point of acquisition onward, China opposed the emerging bilateral US-Soviet disarmament and strategic arms agreements, and ultimately the elucidation of the Non-Proliferation Treaty in 1968 and institutionalisation of the norm of non-proliferation. In effect, China deemed that its national and security interests would not be served, and could in fact be harmed, by acceding to such agreements in the face of strategic encirclement by the Soviet Union and the US. This perspective was, like much to do with China, substantially re-evaluated following Mao Zedong's death in 1976 and the re-emergence of Deng Xiaoping to leadership of the CCP thereafter in 1978.

The subsequent 1978 to 1991 period, framed by Deng's return to leadership of the CCP and the collapse of the Soviet Union, saw China gradually reassess its approach to nuclear weapons, arms control and proliferation and the international regimes and agreements that had evolved in response to these issues. This process was highlighted, for example, in 1984 when China joined the IAEA, beginning a process that would see China become more engaged with, and accepting of, the international nuclear framework as it began to perceive that the political, security and strategic benefits of this significantly outweighed those of remaining on the "outside".[138]

The final 1992 to the present has seen the completion of this process, with China acceding to the NPT as a NWS in 1992 and signing the CTBT in 1996. Since that time, Beijing has consistently reiterated its strong support for the non-proliferation regime based on the NPT and IAEA.[139] In the same period, however, Beijing pursued a range of activities that ran counter to its declared commitments to non-proliferation. It pursued exports of ICBM and short-range ballistic missile (SRBM) technology and components throughout the 1990s to a range of states such as DPRK, Iraq, Iran, Saudi Arabia and Pakistan long considered by the United States and others as nuclear proliferation risks.[140] Additionally, it also engaged in the export of nuclear weapons-related technology and components to Pakistan.[141] China's motivations for such activities were based on a desire to generate export earnings from its expanding arms manufacturing sector and broad strategic objectives to keep rivals off balance or distracted in the Persian Gulf and South Asia.[142]

Beijing released new export control regulations that covered missile technology, chemical weapons precursors and technology, and biological agents in August and October 2002 that many observers assessed as prompted by the events of 9/11—and the subsequent increase in international concern that

WMD technology could be acquired by terrorists—and a desire to improve relations with the George W. Bush administration that had imposed a range of sanctions on Chinese entities suspected of involvement in arms transfers to Iran.[143] Beijing's subsequent White Paper on Non-Proliferation in December 2002 sought to downplay China's differences with the United States and highlighted its new export control regime and its agreement to abide by the guidelines set out by the Missile Technology Control Regime (MTCR) even though Beijing was not a member.[144] However, just as China appeared to have accepted the norm of non-proliferation and begun to demonstrate some effort to engage with arms and technology control regimes, the evolution of US nuclear posture and the emphasis of the George W. Bush administration on "counter-proliferation" efforts outside of the NPT system (e.g. PSI) contributed to Chinese ambivalence on arms control and a desire to continue the modernisation of its own nuclear arsenal.[145]

Since the early 2000s, China has consistently viewed American force posture developments as especially troubling due to its enduring reliance on a posture focused on maintaining, in Jeffrey Lewis' phrase, the "minimum means of reprisal"—i.e. ensuring a secure, second-strike capability.[146] The endurance of this posture has been reflected not only in the modest size of China's nuclear arsenal and ICBM force—which in 2019 stood at approximately 290 nuclear warheads for delivery by 180 to 190 land-based ballistic missiles, 48 sea-based ballistic missiles, and bombers—but also in its declared "no-first-use" policy that stipulates China's commitment to only use its nuclear force in response to a nuclear strike upon it.[147]

In contrast to the United States and to some extent Russia, China has relied almost exclusively on land-based ICBMS and intermediate range ballistic missiles under the command of the Second Artillery Force (SAF) to ensure its "second-strike" capability, resulting in significant recent modernisation efforts for its missile forces to transition from silo-based liquid-fuel missiles to mobile solid-fuel missiles. While the US Department of Defense' 2019 "Missile Defense Review" noted that China "can now potentially threaten the United States with about 125 nuclear missiles", one independent assessment suggests that only 80 of these missiles "have sufficient range to target the continental United States from their deployment areas in China".[148] China has sought to augment this reliance on land-based missiles with investments in modernisation of its bomber capabilities and development of a limited SLBM capability in order to establish a "credible" nuclear "triad".[149] In 2012, the PLA Air Force (PLAAF) was assigned a "strategic deterrence" mission, prompting speculation that the PLAAF would soon field nuclear capable cruise missiles on its medium-range bombers and fighter-bombers.[150] The US Department of Defense's May 2019 report to Congress on Chinese military modernisation and capabilities noted, however, that China's development of an air-launched ballistic missile (ALBM)—once deployed and integrated into PLA forces—"would for the first time, provide China with a viable nuclear "triad" of delivery systems dispersed across land, sea, and air forces".[151]

Beijing has thus arguably begun to transition away from reliance on its minimum deterrent posture by increasing and modernising its ICBM force and augmenting it through modernisation of its bomber forces and development of SLBM capability as a means enhancing survivability. In terms of nuclear doctrine while declaratory policy has remained remarkably consistent in maintaining China's "no-first use" policy, "its evolving capabilities are opening up new strategic options".[152] This is particularly the case since the elevation of the SAF to a full "service" within the PLA as the PLA Rocket Force (PLARF) on 31 December 2015. The PLARF is to "possess both nuclear and conventional" capabilities and to conduct "comprehensive deterrence and warfighting" operations.[153] The "comprehensive" nature of the "deterrence" envisaged, as Bates Gill and Adam Ni note, "includes a geographic element that requires the PLARF to be able to fight and deter enemies across different regions and distances" and "a domain element that requires the PLARF to conduct operations with effects across land, sea, aerospace and electromagnetic spectrums".[154] The modernisation of China's arsenal, emergent nuclear triad and organisational pre-eminence of the PLARF thus arguably "boosts Beijing's ability to deter the United States and its allies across a wider spectrum of the escalation ladder, up to and including nuclear use, thus possibly limiting American and allied options in an escalating crisis".[155]

From China's perspective, it has been the evolution of US force posture since the end of the Cold War and its expanded conventional counterforce capabilities that have been a major stimulus to here. Chinese observers have suggested that Washington was seeking to attain "absolute security" and thereby escape mutual vulnerability within the Sino-US nuclear relationship, posing a clear security dilemma for Beijing.[156] China's response illustrates both the manner in which the evolution of American nuclear posture and the increasing overlap in nuclear and conventional capabilities has provided incentives for vertical proliferation and force modernisation. Moreover, China's shifting nuclear force posture and doctrine, while enough to potentially deter an American conventional counterforce strike, may also encourage worst-case American assumptions about China's threshold for nuclear use in a crisis.[157]

Nuclear Flashpoints

It is therefore clear that changes in power relativities, and the associated reshaping of world and regional order, are having a significant impact on the way the most powerful nuclear weapons states view the role of deterrence. For the US, nuclear weapons remain an important part of the deterrence mix. But they fit uneasily with the development of offensive cyber tools and missile defences that may blunt an adversary's capabilities while undermining the strategic reassurance associated with deterrence. Coupled to US retrenchment and the turbulent Trump presidency, this has the additional effect of diminishing the confidence of allies in extended US nuclear security guarantees. Russia, on the other hand, has come to see nuclear weapons as an instrument for power politics and a means to challenge transatlantic resolve, albeit by necessity rather than design. The PRC, meanwhile, has realised that in order to maximise its capabilities in strategic competition with the US, it will be necessary to develop larger, more modern and more diversified nuclear forces. And yet these changes to power dynamics are also having an effect on smaller nuclear powers as well. Hence, in this section, we turn to consider how traditional nuclear flashpoints are being impacted by these changing global and regional power realities.

Nuclear Instability on the Korean Peninsula

The development of nuclear weapons by the DPRK is not a fundamentally new development. A decade before its first test in 2006, the Clinton administration had considered airstrikes on the Yongbyon uranium enrichment facility in order to delay and disrupt Pyongyang's proliferation project. The delicate nature of DPRK-ROK relations, not to mention the interests of China and Japan in strategic stability, played an important role in channelling US responses towards a more conventional sanctions regime. But by 2020 the DPRK had developed a small nuclear arsenal in addition to at least an IRBM delivery system through its Nodong rocket program, and made numerous attempts to develop ICBM capability in order to threaten the continental United States. Failed attempts at diplomacy by the Trump administration via a summit with Kim Jong Un in Singapore during 2018—which set back US interests in demonstrating firmness on the Korean Peninsula while at the same time giving the DPRK an unexpected propaganda coup—were juxtaposed with bellicose American rhetoric from Trump. He called Kim "rocket man", threatened "fire and fury" against the DPRK and petulantly claimed that his nuclear button was bigger and better than Kim's.[158]

In addition to impeding Washington's ability to develop a coherent American diplomatic strategy for the Korean Peninsula, the optics of the chaotic US position on the DPRK also gave Xi Jinping the opportunity to play the role of elder statesman on the issue. Frequent visits by Kim to meet with Xi have been portrayed by the CCP as the Beijing having a smoothing influence on its "younger brother", as well as promoting Chinese diplomacy as favouring a more measured line based on maintaining the status quo.

These episodes are reflective of the changing order in North-East Asia, marked by a (largely self-imposed) diminution of US reach, with the vacuum filled by the PRC. Japan has notably expressed alarm at Washington's erratic diplomacy, with Shinzo Abe—normally a strong supporter of Trump's Korea policy in public—hinting in 2019 that the US and Japan were not necessarily on the same page over the severity of North Korean missile tests.[159] For its part, the ROK has had its confidence in the US further shaken over a public spat in 2019, during which Trump threatened to withdraw 4,000 US military personnel from the ROK unless Seoul contributed more to hosting them.[160] And although Russia has been a minor player on the Korean nuclear issue, the previous US decision in 2016 to station the THAAD missile system in the ROK had the effect of driving Moscow and Beijing closer together, with the two moving to harmonise missile defences in the Russian Far East military district with China's Northern Theatre Command around Shenyang.[161]

Hence, there is a real risk that a combination of insecurity over US commitments as well as fear over the DPRK's increasingly modernising nuclear arsenal might prompt decision-makers in Seoul and Tokyo to seek a nuclear capability of their own. This prospect was raised as a real possibility in 2019 by Stephen Biegun, the US Special Representative for North Korea, and has been the subject of recent quiet discussions in Tokyo.[162] And, given the historical animosity between the ROK and Japan, it has long been assumed that if one acquired a nuclear capability, the other would follow suit. This gives rise to the unpalatable prospect of proliferation chain reactions in North-East Asia, which is already becoming a locus for great power competition.[163]

A nuclear cascade in the sub-region would produce at least five new nuclear dyads in close physical proximity: Japan-ROK; Japan-PRC; Japan-DPRK; ROK-DPRK; ROK-PRC; and possibly Japan-Russia as well. It would also result in a variety of triangular and multipolar nuclear relationships, drawing the major regional nuclear players into a complex system marked by uncertain alliances, major power rivalry, rogue states, irredentist disputes and middle power-great power tensions. Under those circumstances, even the most ardent defender of nuclear weapons as strategic stabilisers would find it difficult to argue that such an eventuality would diminish tensions, rather than exacerbating them.

The South Asian Nuclear Triangle

It is well known that South Asia hosts a number of territorial disputes involving nuclear-armed powers, and each can be considered a potential flashpoint in its own right. One of these concerns the contested border area between the PRC and India in the Himalayas, dating back to the Chinese invasion of Aksai Chin in 1962 and the resultant Sino-Indian war. Whereas the region has often been tense, repeated physical clashes along the Line of Actual Control (LAC) between PLA and Indian troops in 2019 and 2020 led to the killing of service personnel on both sides. And while there has been little attempt by either the PRC or India to escalate tensions to the point of war, both have used it for domestic political purposes.

In doing so, they have highlighted the deepening strategic rivalry between the two nations. The Indian media has been particularly vociferous in stirring up Indian nationalism and internal anti-Chinese sentiment, whereas the PRC's *Global Times* used the episode to construct a narrative around the PLA as highly organised and trained, in contrast to an impulsive and ill-disciplined Indian side.[164] In terms of efforts to mediate a resolution to the crisis, the US declined to participate, while Russia was quick to offer itself as an honest broker.

The second major flashpoint in South Asia concerns the India-Pakistan border regions in the disputed territory of Jammu and Kashmir. While the region has long been characterised by periodic clashes between Indian and Pakistani forces, both sides have consistently stopped short of all-out war, although each has also utilised the conflict for domestic political purposes. The role of nuclear deterrence as a stabilising factor in the conflict has also been raised as a potential factor, creating the incentive for both Pakistan and India to dampen tensions down relatively quickly after they have flared up.[165]

Yet the examples of the Himalayas and Kashmir reflect assumptions that conflicts can be kept conventional in nature, and are best seen as dyadic. In reality, the nuclear politics of South Asia are triangular, in which India's deterrent is intended for two audiences: China and Pakistan. This is made more problematic by the fact that major power interests have altered significantly over the last two decades: Washington heavily courted Islamabad after the events of 9/11, swiftly turning former PM Pervez Musharraf into a partner of the US rather than an international pariah following Musharraf's military-led coup in 1999. But more recently US influence over Pakistan has been almost completely supplanted by the PRC. Beijing has made significant investments along the strategically important China-Pakistan Economic Corridor (CPEC) linking China's restive territory in Xinjiang to the key port at Gwadar, as part of its Belt and Road Initiative.[166]

This means that interests and allegiances in South Asia have become much more opaque. It is certainly the case that China uses Pakistan as a proxy for its interests, but more importantly it sees it as an important spoiler in its ability to keep India occupied, drawing New Delhi's capacity as well as its attention away from direct Sino-Indian rivalry.[167] This forces India to acquire significant numbers of mobile platforms—from aircraft to ships and missile silos—in order to guard against the possibility of two-front conflict. The resultant conventional imbalance in the India-Pakistan relationship therefore adds increased pressure on Islamabad to increase its nuclear stockpiles in order to maximise its deterrent, with the dangerous potential for nuclear arms races.[168] By the same token, a modernised and expanded PRC deterrent creates additional incentive for New Delhi to try and match China's nuclear capabilities, turning a series of arms races into a nuclear arms spiral.

Testing Transatlantic Cohesion: Russian Adventurism in Ukraine and the Baltics

Any assessment of future flashpoints would not be complete without a scenario that brings NATO and Russian forces into potential hostilities. There are many candidates for such an outcome, from a deepening of the civil conflict in Ukraine to Russian adventurism in both the Arctic and Nordic maritime space, as well as instability in the Caucasus. But the Baltic arena has proven to be probably the most visible centre of gravity in Russia-West tensions.

In particular, Estonia has been the target of numerous Russian misinformation and disinformation campaigns, as well as cyber attacks. Russian military aircraft have repeatedly violated Estonian airspace and prompted NATO to scramble fighters by approaching the border and then turning away at the last minute.[169]

These provocations have several aims. Some are related to capability assessments about NATO readiness and force posture. Others pertain to electronic intelligence gathering. But more broadly they are designed to test the resolve of the transatlantic West. This follows a pattern of behaviour that the Kremlin has engaged in since its seizure of the Crimean Peninsula in 2013, and the ongoing civil war in Ukraine, where Russian-backed militias in the Donbas region have sought to create *Novorossiya*—a territorial entity sympathetic to Moscow, in an echo of Russian imperial thinking under Catherine the Great.[170]

The West's response to Russia has been interpreted in Moscow as largely feeble and uncoordinated. While the sanctions packages imposed by the EU and US have had some effect, they were considerably diluted from initial proposals that would have seen the EU impose more wide-ranging restrictions on the sale of Russian energy. But given that key powerbrokers in the EU—especially Germany—are vulnerably over-dependent on supplies from Gazprom, Russia was able to use its strategic economic heft in order to ensure that the sanctions were less impressive than they may have been.[171] Moreover, NATO's response to the civil war in Ukraine was relatively muted. NATO not extend membership to Kiev, or do more than station a small rapid reaction force near Ukraine. The US response also became mired in internal arguments about selling Kiev anti-tank weapons, later made conditional by Donald Trump on an investigation into Hunter Biden, the son of the US Democratic Presidential nominee.

This is important because the perception in Moscow that the West is divided and weak gives it an incentive to push for greater concessions in the so-called "near abroad". It has long been the intention of Russia to establish itself as the primary security guarantor over the former Soviet space.[172] And its recent renovations to its nuclear doctrine raise the potential for Russia to threaten war—including the limited use of tactical nuclear weapons—in order to strengthen its hand in terms of achieving this objective.

When this is considered alongside the fact that Moscow has stationed intermediate range nuclear weapons in its Kaliningrad enclave, along with S-400 surface to air missile systems, Russia is clearly attempting to develop an anti-access area denial (A2AD) capability that extends as far West as Poland and Germany.[173] Hence, the concern is that Russia's employment of nuclear brinkmanship through its new nuclear forces and doctrine will come to be regarded as an additional tool through which to exercise strategic leverage against the West. Absent a concerted response by NATO members, and especially considering the preference of the Trump White House for a closer relationship with Russia, the prospects for ongoing strategic destabilisation in Ukraine and the Baltic States remain high.

Conclusions

As this chapter has demonstrated, nuclear rivalries and proliferation dangers will remain significant drivers of tension in international security politics for the foreseeable future. This is due to three key hallmarks of nuclear politics in the twenty-first century, which distinguish it from the relative stability of deterrence relationships during the Cold War. First, nuclear weapons are now characteristic of multipolar power dynamics rather than bipolar ones. This makes nuclear relationships more complex, more multifaceted and increasingly tied to both existing and new security dilemmas. Second, the way that major actors have responded to these changing realities militates against the reconstruction of strategic stability.

Both the US and Russia have taken steps to undermine deterrence in their own ways. The US continues to rely on nuclear forces but with associated defences and increasing cyber capabilities to potentially stymie the development or deployment of nuclear weapons by its adversaries. Russia, meanwhile, has utilised its nuclear arsenal for offensive purposes, as a means to increase its heft in geopolitical struggles with the transatlantic West. And the expansion of the PRC's zone of interest and power has also brought with it the potential for deepened conventional and nuclear rivalries in South Asia and Northeast Asia in particular. The upshot is that initial visions of limited proliferation in the post-Cold War as a panacea are unlikely to be borne out. On the contrary, nuclear weapons are likely to deepen uncertainties and insecurities as the twenty-first century continues, rather than ameliorating them.

Notes

1. Wesley, M. (2005). It's Time to Scrap the NPT. *Australian Journal of International Affairs*, 59 (3), 283–299.
2. Schelling, T. (1960). *The Strategy of Conflict*. Cambridge, MA: Harvard University Press and Schelling, T. (1966). *Arms and Influence*. Cambridge, MA: Harvard University Press. On extended deterrence see also Huth, P. (1989). *Extended Deterrence and the Prevention of War*. New Haven: Yale University Press; and Crawford, T. W. (2009). The Endurance of Extended Deterrence: Continuity, Change, and Complexity in Theory and Policy. In Paul, T. V., Morgan, P. M. & Wirtz, J. J. (Eds.) *Complex Deterrence: Strategy in the Global* Age. Chicago, IL: Chicago University Press and O'Neil, A. (2011). Extended Nuclear Deterrence in East Asia: Redundant or Resurgent? *International Affairs*, 87 (6), 1439–1457.
3. Powell, C. & Persico, J. E. (1995). *A Soldier's Way*. London: Hutchinson, 223–224.
4. See for instance: Koblentz, G. D. (2014). *Strategic Stability in the Second Nuclear Age*. Council on Foreign Relations, special report no. 71 and

Anderson, N. D. (2017). America's North Korean Nuclear Trilemma. *The Washington Quarterly*, 40 (4), 153–164.

5. Bracken, P. (2013). *The Second Nuclear Age: Strategy, Danger and the New Power Politics*. London: St Martins Press.

6. Vaddi, P. (2019). The Importance of the New Start Treaty. Testimony to the House of Representatives Foreign Affairs Committee, Carnegie Endowment for International Peace. https://carnegieendowment.org/2019/12/04/importance-of-new-start-treaty-pub-80834.

7. Tertrais, B. (2018). Russia's Nuclear Policy: Worrying for the Wrong Reasons. *Survival*, 60 (2), 33–44.

8. Fuhrmann, M. & Sechser, T. (2014). Nuclear Strategy, Nonproliferation, and the Causes of Foreign Nuclear Deployments. *The Journal of Conflict Resolution*, 58 (3), 455–480.

9. See for instance: Podvig, P. (2018). Russia's Current Nuclear Modernization and Arms Control. *Journal for Peace and Nuclear Disarmament*, 1 (2), 256–267.

10. This does not mean that the role of nuclear weapons in US strategy is uncontested. See for instance: Glaser, C. S. & Fetter, S. (2016). Should the United States Reject MAD? Damage Limitation and US Nuclear Strategy Towards China. *International Security*, 41 (1), 49–98.

11. Schelling, T. & Halperin, M. (1985). *Strategy and Arms Control*. New York: Pergammon-Brassey's.

12. Watz, K. (1981). The Spread of Nuclear Weapons: More May Be Better. In *Adelphi Papers* (p. 171). London: International Institute for Strategic Studies.

13. Ibid.

14. Walker, W. (2004). Weapons of Mass Destruction and International Order. *Adelphi Papers*, 370, 10. See also: Walker, W. (2012). *A Perpetual Menace: Nuclear Weapons and International Order*. London: Routledge.

15. See, for example: Brodie, B. (ed.) *The Absolute Weapon*. New York: Harcourt, Brace and Company; Kissinger, H. (1957). *Nuclear Weapons and Foreign Policy*. New York: Harper; Osgood, R. (1957). *Limited War: The Challenge to American Strategy*. Chicago: University of Chicago Press; and Brodie, B. (1957). *Strategy in the Missile Age*. Princeton, NJ: Princeton University.

16. The phrase is of course Albert Wohlstetter's seminal description of the emerging concept of nuclear deterrence. See: Wohlstetter, A. (1958). The Delicate Balance of Terror. *Foreign Affairs*, 37.

17. See, for example: Brodie, B. (1946). Implications for Military Strategy. In Brodie, B. (Ed.) *The Absolute Weapon* (p. 76). New York: Harcourt, Brace and Company; and Oakes, G. & Grossman, A. (1992). Managing Nuclear Terror: The Genesis of American Civil Defence Strategy. *International Journal of Politics, Culture, and Society*, 5 (3), 361–403.

18. For a discussion of the impact of such considerations on American national security policy in the late 1940s, see: Friedberg, A. A. (2000). *In the Shadow of the Garrison State: America's Anti-Statism and Its Cold War Strategy*. Princeton, NJ: Princeton University Press, 36–38; and Mandelbaum, M. (1979). *The Nuclear Question: The United States and Nuclear Weapons, 1946–1976*. Cambridge: Cambridge University Press.

19. In September 1948, President Truman endorsed National Security Council paper (NSC 30) that stated simply that the country must "utilize promptly

and effectively all appropriate means available, including atomic weapons, in the interest of national security and must therefore plan accordingly". See NSC 30: United States Policy on Atomic Warfare,

20. Holloway, D. (2010). Nuclear Weapons and the Escalation of the Cold War, 1945–1962. In Leffler, M. & Westad, O. A. (Eds.) *Cambridge History of the Cold War, Vol. 1*. (pp. 376–378). Cambridge: Cambridge University Press.

21. Ibid, 379.
22. Ibid, 383.
23. Brodie. (1946). *The Absolute Weapon*, 76.
24. See: Friedberg. (2000). *In the Shadow of the Garrison State*, 124–132. This was also based on a tradition of political thought in the United States stemming back to Founding Fathers, Thomas Jefferson and James Madison, that viewed maintenance of a large, standing military establishment as a pathway to "statism" and tyranny through the extensive taxation required for the development and maintenance of such an establishment and concentration of political power that usually went hand-in-hand with it. See, for example: Burch,K.T. (2020). To Protect Against Standing Armies. In *Jefferson's Revolutionary Theory and the Reconstruction of Educational Purpose: The Cultural and Social Foundations of Education*. New York: Palgrave; Hickey, D. R. (1981). Federalist Defense Policy in the Age of Jefferson, 1801–1812. *Journal of Military History*, 45 (2); and Read, J. H. (2000). *Power versus Liberty: Madison, Hamilton, Wilson, and Jefferson*. University of Virginia Press.
25. See NSC162/2. (1953). Basic National Security Policy. Report to the National Security Council, 30 October, https://fas.org/irp/offdocs/nsc-hst/nsc-162-2.pdf.
26. Hemmer, C. (2016). *American Pendulum: Recurring Debates in US Grand Strategy*. Ithaca: Cornell University Press, 67.
27. Walker. (2012). *A Perpetual Menace*, 60.
28. See: Gaddis, J.L. (2005). *Strategies of Containment: A Critical Reappraisal of American National Security Policy during the Cold War*. New York: Oxford University Press, 119–121; Chernus, I. (2008). *Apocalypse Management: Eisenhower and the Discourse of National Insecurity*. Stanford: Stanford University Press, 61–66; Wells, S.F. (1981). The Origins of Massive Retaliation. *Political Science Quarterly*, 96 (1), 31–52; and Leighton, R.M. (2001). *Strategy, Money, and the New Look, 1953–1956*. Washington, DC: Office of the Secretary of Defense.
29. See, for example: Hanania, R. (2017). Tracing the Development of the Nuclear Taboo: The Eisenhower Administration and Four Crises in East Asia. *Journal of Cold War Studies*, 19 (2), 43–83; and Burr, W. (1994). Avoiding the Slippery Slope: The Eisenhower Administration and the Berlin Crisis, November 1958–January 1959. *Diplomatic History*, 18 (2), 177–205.
30. Schelling. (1966). *Arms and Influence*, 47.
31. McMahon. (2010). US National Security Policy from Eisenhower to Kennedy, 297.
32. See: Holloway, D. (1994). *Stalin and the Bomb: The Soviet Union and Atomic Energy*, 1939–1956. New Haven, CT, 335–345.
33. Holloway. (2010). Nuclear Weapons and the Escalation of the Cold War, 1945–1962, 386.

34. See Mastny, V. (2010). Soviet Foreign Policy, 1953–1962. In Leffler, M. & Westad, O. A. (Eds.) *Cambridge History of the Cold War, Vol. I*. (pp. 317–320). Cambridge: Cambridge University Press. Mastny notes in this context that Khrushchev's attempts to demonstrate a conciliatory posture to the West—including at the Geneva summit of 1958—were based on "his belief in the [Soviet] system's fundamental strength".
35. Holloway. (2010). Nuclear Weapons and the Escalation of the Cold War, 1945–1962, 387.
36. Hemmer. (2016). *American Pendulum, 71.*
37. Chernus. (2008). *Apocalypse Management*, 189–190.
38. Wohlsetter. (1959). The Delicate Balance of Terror.
39. Walker. (2012). *A Perpetual Menace*, 60.
40. See, for example: Renshon, J. (2009). Assessing Capabilities in International Politics: Biased Overestimation and the Case of the Imaginary "Missile Gap". *Journal of Strategic Studies*, 32 (1), 115–147; and Wenger, A. (1997). Eisenhower, Kennedy, and the Missile Gap: Determinants of US Military Expenditure in the Wake of the Sputnik Shock. *Defence and Peace Economics*, 8 (1), 77–100.
41. See: Preble, C.A. ""Who Ever Believed in the "Missile Gap"?": John F. Kennedy and the Politics of National Security. *Presidential Studies Quarterly*, 33 (4), 801–826.
42. The term itself was closely associated with former Army Chief of Staff, and subsequent Kennedy advisor, General Maxwell Taylor, who had advocated for reinvestment in conventional capabilities, augmented by nuclear weapons, as an alternative to reliance on "general" nuclear war to deter the Soviet Union. See Taylor, M. (1960). *The Uncertain Trumpet*. New York: Harper.
43. Kennedy, J.F. (1961). Special Message to the Congress on the Defense Budget. *The American Presidency Project*, 28 March, http://www.presidency.ucsb.edu/ws/?pid=8554.
44. Quoted in Gaddis. (2005). *Strategies of Containment*, 213.
45. Ibid.
46. Rosenberg, D.A. (1994). Constraining Overkill: Contending Approaches to Nuclear Strategy, 1955–1965. In "More Bang for the Buck": U.S. Nuclear Strategy and Missile Development 1945–1965. *Naval History and Heritage Command*, January 12, https://www.history.navy.mil/research/library/online-reading-room/title-list-alphabetically/m/more-bang-buck.html.
47. Sagan, S. (1987). SIOP-62: The Nuclear War Plan Briefing to President Kennedy. *International Security*, 12 (1), 37.
48. Gaddis. (2005). *Strategies of Containment*, 218.
49. See Allison, G. *Essence of Decision.*
50. Gaddis. (2005) *Strategies of Containment*, 236.
51. See Ibid., 242–248; and Hemmer. (2016). *American Pendulum*, 76–77.
52. For an excellent overview of the development of US nuclear posture from SIOP-62 to SIOP-5, see the latest edition of Lawrence Freedman's classic text on the topic. Lawrence Freedman and Jeffrey Michaels (2019). *The Evolution of Nuclear Strategy*, London: Springer.
53. On PD-59, see William Burr. (2012). How to Fight a Nuclear War: Jimmy Carter's Strategy for Armageddon (we're still using it)' *Foreign Policy*, September 14. https://foreignpolicy.com/2012/09/14/how-to-fight-a-nuclear-war/.

54. Colin Gray and Keith Payne. (1980). Victory Is Possible. *Foreign Policy*, 39 (1), 14–27.
55. Desmond Ball and Robert C. Toth. (1990). Revising the SIOP: Taking War-Fighting to Dangerous Extremes. *International Security*, 14 (4), 65–92.
56. See, for example: Heuser, B. (1993). Containing Uncertainty: Options for British Nuclear Strategy. *Review of International Studies*, 19 (3), 245–267.
57. Haglund, D. G. (1995). France's Nuclear Posture: Adjusting to the Post-Cold War Era. *Contemporary Security Policy*, 16 (2), 140–162.
58. See, for example: Lewis, J. W., & Litai, X. (1988). *China Builds the Bomb*. Stanford: Stanford University Press; Ryan, M. (1989). *Chinese Attitudes Toward Nuclear Weapons: China and the United States During the Korean War*. New York: M. E. Sharpe; and Goldstein, L. J. (2003). When China Was a "Rogue State': The Impact of China's Nuclear Weapons Program on US-China Relations During the 1960s. *Journal of Contemporary China*, 37 (12).
59. See: Lewis, J. (2007). *The Minimal Means of Reprisal: China's Search for Security in the Nuclear Age*. Cambridge, Mass.: The MIT Press, 10–11; and Roberts, B., Manning, R. & Montaperto, R. (2000). China: The Forgotten Nuclear Power. *Foreign Affairs*, 79.
60. Walker. (2012). *A Perpetual Menace*, 64.
61. For a detailed analysis of American and Soviet motivations for the LTBT, see: Mastny, V. (2008). The 1963 Nuclear Test Ban Treaty: A Missed Opportunity for Détente? *Journal of Cold War Studies* 10 (1), 3–25.
62. Rhodes, R. (2008). *Arsenals of Folly: The Making of the Nuclear Arms Race*. New York: Knopf Doubleday.
63. Bohlen, A. (2003). The Rise and Fall of Arms Control. *Survival*, 45 (3), 10.
64. See Ibid., 11–13; and Garthoff, R. L. (1978). SALT I: An Evaluation. *World Politics*, 31 (1), 1–25.
65. Bohlen. (2003). The Rise and Fall of Arms Control, 14–15.
66. Ibid.
67. See: Petrelli, N., & Pulcini, G. (2018). Nuclear Superiority in the Age of Parity: US Planning, Intelligence Analysis, Weapons Innovation and the Search for a Qualitative Edge, 1969–1976. *International History Review*, 40 (5), 1191–1209; and Long, A., & Green, B. (2015). Stalking the Secure Second Strike: Intelligence, Counterforce and Nuclear Strategy. *Journal of Strategic Studies*, 38 (1/2), 38–73.
68. Maurer, J. D. (2018). The Forgotten Side of Arms Control: Enhancing U.S. Competitive Advantage, Offsetting Enemy Strengths. *War on the Rocks*, 27 June. https://warontherocks.com/2018/06/the-forgotten-side-of-arms-con trol-enhancing-u-s-competitive-advantage-offsetting-enemy-strengths/.
69. Walker, W. (2004). Weapons of Mass Destruction and International Order. *The Adelphi Papers*, 370, 10.
70. Ibid.
71. For overviews of the bargain at the heart of the NPT, see: Smith, R. K. (1987). Explaining the Non-Proliferation Regime: Anomalies for Contemporary International Relations Theory. *International Organization*, 41 (2) 253–81; and Rathbun, N. S. (2006). The Role of Legitimacy in Strengthening the Non-Proliferation Regime. *Nonproliferation Review*, 13 (2), 227–52.
72. Bracken, P. (2003). The Structure of the Second Nuclear Age. *Orbis*, 47 (3), 410.

73. See, for example: Power, P. F. (1979). The Indo-American Nuclear Controversy. *Asian Survey*, 19 (6), 574–596.
74. For a detailed overview of the effect of the PNE on US policy, see: Walker, J. S. (2001). Nuclear Power and Nonproliferation: The Controversy over Nuclear Exports, 1974–1980. *Diplomatic History*, 25 (2), 215–249.
75. Some estimates suggest the US supplied 70 percent of the "free world's" nuclear fuel and technology in the mid-1970s. See Walker. (2001). Nuclear Power and Nonproliferation; and Tzeng, P. (2013). Nuclear Leverage: US Intervention in Sensitive Technology Transfers in the 1970s. *Nonproliferation Review*, 20 (2), 482–484.
76. Walker, W. (2012). *A Perpetual Menace: Nuclear Weapons and International Order*. London: Routledge, 87.
77. Bracken, P. (1999). *Fire in the East: The Rise of Asian Military Power and the Second Nuclear Age*. New York: Harper Collins, 109–112. Bracken acknowledges that China's first test in 1964 and Israel's probable first test in 1968 could also be seen as harbingers of this new era. However, he justifies his identification of India's first test on the basis of that it acquired nuclear weapons entirely "outside the legalistic Western arms control system". China also benefited from the fact that its test preceded the conclusion of the NPT itself, under whose terms it became a recognized NWS having successfully tested prior to 1968.
78. See, for example: Bracken. (2003). The Structure of the Second Nuclear Age; Redick, J., Carasales, J. C., & Wrobel, P. S. (1995). Nuclear Rapprochement: Argentina, Brazil, and the Nonproliferation Regime. *Washington Quarterly*, 18 (1), 107–122; and Kapur, A. (1981). Nuclear Proliferation in the 1980s. *International Journal*, 36 (3), 535–555.
79. Watz, K. (1981). The Spread of Nuclear Weapons: More May Be Better. *Adelphi Papers*, 171. London: International Institute for Strategic Studies.
80. Measheimer, J. (1992). Back to the Future Part II: Instability in Europe after the Cold War. *International Security*, 5 (1), 5–56.
81. Gaddis, J. L. (1986). The Long Peace: Elements of Stability in the Postwar International System. *International Security*, 10 (4), 99–142.
82. Narang, N., Gartzke, E., and Kroenig, M. (2015). *Nonproliferation Policy and Nuclear Posture*. New York: Routledge.
83. Tertrais, B. (2010). The Illogic of Zero. *The Washington Quarterly*, 33 (2), 125–138.
84. US Department of Defense. (2010). *Nuclear Posture Review Report*. April, http://www.defense.gov/npr/docs/2010%20nuclear%20posture%20review%20report.pdf.
85. Gavin, F. (2019). Rethinking the Bomb: Nuclear Weapons and American Grand Strategy. *Texas National Security Review*, 2 (2). https://tnsr.org/2019/01/rethinking-the-bomb-nuclear-weapons-and-american-grand-strategy/#_ftnref29.
86. Walt, S. (2010). Rethinking the "Nuclear Revolution". *Foreign Policy*, 3 August, https://foreignpolicy.com/2010/08/03/rethinking-the-nuclear-revolution/. Preeminent representatives of the "nuclear revolution" school are: Jervis, R. (1990). *The Meaning of the Nuclear Revolution: Statecraft and the Prospect of Armageddon*. Ithaca, NY: Cornell University Press; and Freedman, L. (2003). *The Evolution of Nuclear Strategy*. New York: Palgrave Macmillan.

87. Gaddis, J. L. (1986). The Long Peace: Elements of Stability in the Postwar International System. *International Security*, 10 (4), 121.
88. Rovner, J. (2018). Was There a Nuclear Revolution? Strategy, Grand Strategy, and the Ultimate Weapon. *War on the Rocks*, 6 March. https://waronther ocks.com/2018/03/was-there-a-nuclear-revolution-strategy-grand-strategy-and-the-ultimate-weapon/.
89. See: Layne, C. (2005). *Peace of Illusions: American Grand Strategy since 1940*. Ithaca: Cornell University Press; and Quinn, A. (2011). *American Foreign Policy in Context: National Ideology and Grand Strategy from the Founders to the Bush Doctrine*. London: Routledge.
90. Brands, H. (2018). Choosing Primacy: US Strategy and Global Order at the Dawn of the Post-Cold War Era. *Texas National Security Review*, 1 (2), 15.
91. Russell J. A. & Wirtz, J. J. (2004). United States Nuclear Strategy in the Twenty-first Century. *Contemporary Security Policy*, 25, 91–108.
92. Perry, W. (1995). *US Secretary of Defense: Annual Report to the President and the Congress*. Washington, DC, February http://www.dod.mil/exe csec/adr95/npr_html; and Christensen & Handler. (1996). The USA and Counter-Proliferation, 389.
93. Lewis, G., Gronlund, L. & Wright, D. (1999/2000). National Missile Defense: An Indefensible System. *Foreign Policy*, (Winter), 121–122.
94. O'Hanlon, M. (1999). Star Wars Strikes Back. *Foreign Affairs*, 78 (6), 78; and Walker. W. (1998). International Nuclear Relations after the Indian and Pakistani Nuclear Tests. *International Affairs*, 74 (3), 508–509.
95. Kubbig, B. W. (2005). America: Escaping the Legacy of the ABM Treaty. *Contemporary Security Policy*, 26 (3), 415.
96. See: Bracken, P. (1999). *Fire in the East: The Rise of Asian Military Power and the Second Nuclear Age*. New York: Harper Collins; and Gray, C. S. (1999). *The Second Nuclear Age*. Boulder: Lynne Reinner.
97. Bracken, P. (2003). The Structure of the Second Nuclear Age. *Orbis*, 47 (3), 403–408.
98. See: Perry, W. J. (1995). *US Secretary of Defense: Annual Report to the President and the Congress*. Washington, DC: US Government Printing Office, February, https://history.defense.gov/Portals/70/Documents/ann ual_reports/1995_DoD_AR.pdf?ver=2014-06-24-152712-81384–85.
99. See: Cohen, W. A. (1997). *Secretary of Defense: Report of the Quadrennial Defense Review*, May, https://history.defense.gov/Portals/70/Documents/ quadrennial/QDR1997.pdf?ver=2014-06-25-110930-527.
100. Walker. (1998). International Nuclear Relations after the Indian and Pakistani Nuclear Tests, 409.
101. Bracken. (2003). The Structure of the Second Nuclear Age, 412.
102. See for example: Ferguson, C. (2002). Nuclear Posture Review. *NTI Analysis*, 1 August, https://www.nti.org/analysis/articles/nuclear-posture-review/; and Kristensen, H. (2005). The Role of U.S. Nuclear Weapons: New Doctrine Falls Short Of Bush Pledge. *Arms Control Today*, 35 (7), 13–19.
103. Kubbig. (2005). America: Escaping the Legacy of the ABM Treaty, 424.
104. Joseph, J. (2005). The Exercise of National Sovereignty: The Bush Administration's Approach to Combating Weapons of Mass Destruction Proliferation. *Nonproliferation Review*, 12 (2).
105. Walker. (2012). *A Perpetual Menace*, 142.

106. Brown, S. (2018). The Trump Administration's Nuclear Posture Review (NPR): In Historical Perspective. *Journal for Peace and Nuclear Disarmament*, 1 (2), 273–274.
107. Chalmers, M. (2010). Numbers and Words: Prospects for Nuclear Arms Control. *RUSI Journal*, 155 (2), 28.
108. Cossa, R. (2010). Nuclear Posture Review: Moving Toward "No First Use". *PacNet Newsletter*, 17 (6 April).
109. US Department of Defense. (2010). *Nuclear Posture Review Report*, April, http://www.defense.gov/npr/docs/2010%20nuclear%20posture%20r eview%20report.pdf, viii–ix.
110. Ibid., ix.
111. See, for example: Feaver, P. (2010). Obama's Nuclear Modesty. *New York Times*, 9 April. http://www.nytimes.com/2010/04/09/opinion/09feaver. html; and Sagan, S. & Vaynman, J. (2011). Reviewing the Nuclear Posture Review. *Nonproliferation Review*, 18 (1), 20–23.
112. US Department of Defense. (2010). *Nuclear Posture Review Report*, 20.
113. For example, see: Anin, A. (2011). Prompt Global Strike Weapons and Strategic Instability. *Security Index: A Russian Journal on International Security*, 17 (2), 15–25; Bartles, C. K. (2017). Russian Threat Perception and the Ballistic Missile Defense System. *Journal of Slavic Military Studies*, 30 (2), 152–169; and Zhao, T. (2011). Conventional Counterforce Strike: An Option for Damage Limitation in Conflicts with Nuclear-armed Adversaries? *Science & Global Security*, 19 (3), 195–222.
114. Brown. (2018). The Trump Administration's Nuclear Posture Review (NPR), 276.
115. US Department of Defense. (2018). *Nuclear Posture Review Report*. Washington, DC, February, 59 and 28–31 https://media.defense.gov/2018/Feb/02/2001872886/-1/-1/1/2018-NUCLEAR-POSTURE-REVIEW-FINAL-REPORT.PDF; see also Perkovich, G. (2018). Really? We're Gonna Nuke Russia for a Cyberattack? *Politico*, 18 January, https://www.politico.com/magazine/story/2018/01/18/donald-trump-russia-nuclear-cybera ttack-216477.
116. Ibid.
117. Ibid.
118. Brown. (2018). The Trump Administration's Nuclear Posture Review (NPR), 277.
119. US Department of Defense. (2018). *Nuclear Posture Review Report*, 12 and 50.
120. Brown. (2018). The Trump Administration's Nuclear Posture Review (NPR), 277.
121. Vigor, P. H. (1983). *Soviet Blitzkrieg Theory*. New York: Palgrave.
122. Sussex, M. (2018). Russia and Nuclear Instability in Asia. In *Paradigm Shift: Nuclear Asia*. Australian National University: College of Asia and the Pacific. http://asiapacific.anu.edu.au/nuclearasia.
123. Ibid.
124. Gottemoeller, R. (2020). Russia Is Updating Their Nuclear Weapons: What Does that Mean for the Rest of Us? Carnegie Endowment for International Peace, January 29. https://carnegieendowment.org/2020/01/29/russia-is-updating-their-nuclear-weapons-what-does-that-mean-for-rest-of-us-pub-80895.

125. Cordesman, A. (2018). Russia's Nuclear Weapons: Whomever Dies with the Most Toys Wins? Washington, DC: Centre for Strategic and International Studies, 8 March, https://www.csis.org/analysis/russias-new-nuclear-weapons-whoever-dies-most-toys-wins.

126. Sussex, M. (2017). The Triumph of Russian National Security Policy? Russia's Rapid Rebound. *Australian Journal of International Affairs*, 71 (5), 499–515,

127. Sussex, M. (2015). Russia's Asian Rebalance. *Lowy Institute Analysis*, 7 December, https://www.lowyinstitute.org/publications/russia's-asian-reb alance.

128. Missile Defense Project. (2020). SSC-8 (9M729). *Missile Threat*, Center for Strategic and International Studies, 23 June. https://missilethreat.csis.org/missile/ssc-8-novator-9m729/.

129. Wesslowsky, T. (2018). Listen to Us Now: Putin Unveils Weapons, Vows to Raise Living Standards in Fiery Annual Address. *RFE-RL News*, 1 March. https://www.rferl.org/a/putin-set-give-annual-address-amid-presid ential-election-campaign/29069948.html.

130. Sussex, M. (2018). Is Vladimir Putin bluffing, or Should We Be Worried About His New Miracle Weapons. *ABC News*, 2 March. https://www.abc. net.au/news/2018-03-02/is-vladimir-putin-bluffing-on-nuclear-weapons/9502240.

131. Congressional Research Service (2020). Conventional Prompt Global Strike and Long-Range Ballistic Missiles: Background and Issues. *CRS Report* R41464, 14 February. https://fas.org/sgp/crs/nuke/R41464.pdf. See also: Pollack, J. (2009). Evaluating Conventional Prompt Global Strike. *Bulletin of the Atomic Scientists*, (January/February). https://journals.sagepub.com/doi/pdf/10.2968/065001003.

132. Geist, E. & Massicot, D. (2019). Understanding Putin's Nuclear Super-weapons. *SAIS Review*, 39 (2), 103–117.

133. Panda, A. (2020). What's in Russia's New Nuclear Deterrence "Basic Principles?" *The Diplomat*, 9 June. https://thediplomat.com/2020/06/whats-in-russias-new-nuclear-deterrence-basic-principles/.

134. See for instance: Baev, P. (2015). Apocalypse a Bit Later: The Meaning of Putin's Nuclear Threats. Washington, DC: Brookings Institution, 1 April. http://www.brookings.edu/blogs/order-from-chaos/posts/2015/04/01-putin-nuclear-threats-meaning; Colby, E. (2015). *Nuclear Weapons in the Third Offset Strategy: Avoiding a Nuclear Blind Spot in the Pentagon's New Initiative*. Washington, DC: Center for a New American Security, January; Sokov, N. (2014). Why Russia Calls a Limited Nuclear Strike "De-escalation". *Bulletin of the Atomic Scientists*, 13 March; and Olikar, O. (2016). Russia's Nuclear Doctrine: What We Know, What We Don't, and What that Means. *CSIS Russia and Eurasia Program*, Center for Strategic and International Studies (CSIS), Washington, DC. https://csis-website-prod.s3.amazonaws.com/s3fs-public/pub lication/160504_Oliker_RussiasNuclearDoctrine_Web.pdf.

135. Isachenkov, V. (2020). New Russian Policy Allows Use of Atomic Weapons Against Non-nuclear Strike. *Defense News*, 2 June. https://www.defens enews.com/global/europe/2020/06/02/new-russian-policy-allows-use-of-atomic-weapons-against-non-nuclear-strike/.

136. See: Ryan. (1989). Chinese Attitudes Toward Nuclear Weapons; and Lewis, J. W. & Litai, X. (1987). Strategic Weapons and Chinese Power: The Formative Years. *China Quarterly*, 112, (December), 541–554.

137. Medeiros, E. S. (2006). Evolving Nuclear Doctrine. In Bolt, P. J. & Willner, A. S. (Eds.) *China's Nuclear Future* (pp. 46–47). Boulder: Lynne Reinner.

138. Frieman, W. (2014). *China, Arms Control, and Non-Proliferation*. London: Routledge.

139. Chan, G. (2006). *China's Compliance in Global Affairs: Trade, Arms Control, Environmental Protection, Human Rights*. Singapore: World Scientific Press, 115–116.

140. Liff, R. (1999). *China's Arms Sales: Motivations and Implications*. Santa Monica, CA: RAND Corporation, 8–15.

141. See, for example: Malik, M. (1999). Nuclear Proliferation in Asia: The China Factor. *Australian Journal of International Affairs*, 53 (1), 31–41.

142. See, for example: Paul, T. V. (2003). Chinese-Pakistani Nuclear/Missile Ties and Balance of Power Politics. *Nonproliferation Review*, 10 (2), 21–29; and Yuan, J., Saunders, P., & Lieggi, S. (2002). Recent Developments in China's Export Controls: New Regulations and New Challenges. *Nonproliferation Review*, 9 (3), 153–167.

143. See Yuan, J. (2002). The Evolution of China's Nonproliferation Policy since the 1990s: Progress, Problems, and Prospects. *Journal of Contemporary China*, 11 (31), 209–233; and Lieggi, S. (2010). From Proliferator to Model Citizen? China's Recent Enforcement of Nonproliferation-Related Trade Controls and Its Potential Positive Impact in the Region. *Strategic Studies Quarterly*, 4 (2), 40–41.

144. Kerr, P. (2003). China Stresses Common Approach with Bush Administration's Nonproliferation Policy. *Arms Control Today*, 34 (1), 36.

145. Carranza, M. (2006). Can the NPT Survive? The Theory and Practice of US Nuclear Non-proliferation Policy after September 11. *Contemporary Security Policy*, 27 (3), 489–525.

146. Lewis. (2007). *The Minimal Means of Reprisal*.

147. Kristensen, H. & Korda, M. (2019). China's Nuclear Forces 2019. *Bulletin of the Atomic Scientist*, 75 (4), 171.

148. See: US Defense Department. (2019). *Missile Defense Review*. Washington, DC: Office of the Secretary of Defense, 17 January. https://media.defense.gov/2019/Jan/17/2002080666/-1/-1/1/2019-MISSILE-DEFENSE-REVIEW.PDF; and Kristensen & Korda. (2019). China's Nuclear Forces 2019, 173.

149. Kristensen & Korda. (2019). China's Nuclear Forces 2019, 175. China currently has a fleet of four Jin-class (Type 094) nuclear-powered ballistic missile submarines (SSBNs), with an additional two Jin-class SSBNs under construction.

150. For example: Roblin, S. (2016). China's H-6 Bomber: Everything You Want to Know about Beijing's "B-52" Circling Taiwan. *The National Interest*, 18 December. https://nationalinterest.org/blog/the-buzz/chinas-h-6-bomber-everything-you-want-know-about-beijings-b-18772.

151. Department of Defense. (2019). Annual Report to Congress: Military and Security Developments Involving the People's Republic of China 2019. Washington, DC: Office of the Secretary of Defense, May. https://media.

defense.gov/2019/May/02/2002127082/1/1/1/2019_CHINA_MILI TARY_POWER_REPORT.

152. Gill, B. & Ni, A. (2019). The People's Liberation Army Rocket Force: Reshaping China's Approach to Strategic Deterrence. *Australian Journal of International Affairs*, 73 (2), 165.

153. Tao, Z. (2016). China establishes Rocket Force and Strategic Support Force. 1 January, http://english.chinamil.com.cn/news-channels/china-mil itary-news/2016-01/01/content_6839967.htm.

154. Gill & Ni. (2019). The People's Liberation Army Rocket Force, 162.

155. Ibid., 173.

156. Zhang, B. (2011). US Missile Defence and China's Nuclear Posture: Changing Dynamics of an Offence–Defence Arms Race. *International Affairs*, 87 (3), 555–569.

157. See: Goldstein, A. (2013). First Things First: The Pressing Danger of Crisis Instability in US-China Relations. *International Security*, 37 (4), 49–89.

158. Stevens, M. (2018). Trump and Kim Jong Un, and the Names They've Called each Other. *New York Times*, 9 March. https://www.nytimes.com/2018/03/09/world/asia/trump-kim-jong-un.html.

159. Asahi Shimbun. (2019). Trump, Abe at Odds on North Korean Missile Launches, 26 August. http://www.asahi.com/ajw/articles/AJ2019 08260012.html.

160. Lee, J. & Stewart, P. (2019). Pentagon Denies Report US Mulls Pulling up to 4,000 Troops from South Korea. *Reuters*, 21 November. https://www.reuters.com/article/us-southkorea-usa-military/us-considers-pulling-up-to-4000-troops-from-south-korea-chosun-ilbo-idUSKBN1XU2V4.

161. Gady, F. (2017). China, Russia Kick of Anti-ballistic Missile Defence Exercise. *The Diplomat*, 12 December. https://thediplomat.com/2017/12/china-rus sia-kick-off-anti-ballistic-missile-defense-exercise/.

162. Fitzpatrick, M. (2019). How Japan Could Go Nuclear. *Foreign Affairs*, 3 October. https://www.foreignaffairs.com/articles/asia/2019-10-03/how-japan-could-go-nuclear. See also Kelly, T. & Kubo, N. (2017). Allowing Nuclear Weapons in Japan Could Defuse North Korean Threat, Say Some Policy-makers. *Reuters*, 6 September. https://www.reuters.com/article/us-northkorea-missiles-japan/allowing-nuclear-weapons-in-japan-could-defuse-north-korean-threat-say-some-policy-makers-idUSKCN1BH1FO.

163. See for instance: Bekanic, E. et al. (2008). *Preventing Nuclear Proliferation Chain Reactions: Japan, South Korea and Egypt*. Princeton, NJ: Woodrow Wilson School of Public and International Affairs.

164. Griffiths, J. & Sud, V. (2020). India's Modi Responds to Violent Face-off with China over Himalayan Border. *CNN*, 18 June. https://edition.cnn.com/2020/06/17/asia/china-india-himalayas-conflict-intl-hnk/index.html.

165. Sasikumar, K. (2019). India-Pakistan Crises under the Nuclear Shadow: The Role of Reassurance. *Journal for Peace and Nuclear Disarmament*, 2 (1), 151–169.

166. See: Chan, L. (2020). Can China's Belt and Road Initiative build a peaceful regional order? Acquiescence and resistance in South Asia. In Clarke, M., Sussex, M. & Bisley, N. (Eds.) *The Belt and Road Initiative and the Future of Regional Order in the Indo-Pacific* (pp. 23–40). Lanham: Lexington, pp. 23–40; and Clarke, M. (2017). The Belt and Road Initiative: China's New Grand Strategy? *Asia Policy*, 24, 71–79.

167. Clary, C. & Narang, V. (2019). India's Counterforce Temptations: Strategic Dilemmas, Doctrine and Capabilities. *International Security*, 43 (3), 7–52.
168. Panda, A. (2019). Shifting Nuclear Sands in South Asia: Understanding India's Counterforce Temptations. *The Diplomat*, 23 April. https://thediplomat.com/2019/04/shifting-nuclear-sands-in-south-asia-understanding-indias-counterforce-temptations/.
169. Oliphant, R. (2016). Mapped: Just How Many Incursions into NATO Airspace Has Russia Made? *Telegraph*, 15 May. http://www.telegraph.co.uk/news/worldnews/europe/russia/11,609,783/Mapped-Just-how-many-incursions-into-Nato-airspace-has-Russian-military-made.html.
170. Schnaufer, T. A. (2017). Redefining Hybrid Warfare: Russia's Non-linear War Against the West. *Journal of Strategic Security*, 10 (1), 17–31.
171. Sussex, M. (2017). Russia's Next Big Strategic Move (And It Has Nothing to Do with Ukraine). *The National Interest*, 10 June. http://nationalinterest.org/blog/the-buzz/russias-next-big-strategic-move-it-has-nothing-do-ukraine-13081.
172. Monahan, A. (2008). An Enemy at the Gates, or "from Victory to Victory"? Russian Foreign Policy. *International Affairs*, 84 (4), 717–733.
173. Dalsjo, R., Berglund, C. & Jonsson, M. (2019). Don't Believe the Russian Hype. *Foreign Policy*, 7 March. https://foreignpolicy.com/2019/03/07/dont-believe-the-russian-hype-a2-ad-missiles-sweden-kaliningrad-baltic-states-annexation-nato/.

CHAPTER 14

Maritime Security: Problems and Prospects for National Security Policymakers

Carolin Liss

INTRODUCTION

Today, maritime security is an integral part of national security considerations, not only for coastal states but for all states engaged in international trade. In the maritime security domain, what threats are considered relevant to national security changed over time, as did the role and practices of naval forces. This chapter discusses the link between national and maritime security over time. The first part provides a historical overview, which situates maritime security in the context of national security. It discusses the relationship between the emergence of nation states, control of water areas by states, the monopoly of violence at sea, maritime trade and national security. Particular attention is paid to how the distinctions between the political and economic, the national and international, and the private and public emerged and changed in the maritime sphere, shaping national maritime interests. By tracing how interests in the maritime sphere have changed over time, the historical overview explains how the current understanding of maritime security and its relationship with national security emerged.

The second part offers an overview of maritime security issues that are today of concern for national security, with a special focus on the 'rise' of non-traditional maritime security threats. The third part discusses how navies and other government agencies have adapted their operations to face these challenges, considering the special nature of the maritime sphere and the need to address problems in cooperation with other states. It further examines

C. Liss (✉)
Department of International Affairs, Vesalius College, Ixelles, Belgium

© The Author(s), under exclusive license to Springer Nature Switzerland AG 2022
M. Clarke et al. (eds.), *The Palgrave Handbook of National Security*,
https://doi.org/10.1007/978-3-030-53494-3_14

329

how, and why, new actors such as Private Military and Security Companies (PMSCs) are today engaged in addressing maritime security threats and how they work alongside state agencies. It demonstrates that non-state actors again play a role in addressing maritime security threats that are of national security concern–even if their motivations are not necessarily in line with national interest. The conclusion summarises that maritime security is today an integral part of national security and state agencies are adapting their operations to the changing security environment. However, current developments indicate that we may witness, at least to some extent, a return to a system in which the private and political and the national and international begin to blur once again.

Situating 'Maritime Security'

This section will discuss how maritime security has been incorporated in, or is related to, national security. The first step in this process is to define the term maritime security as it will be used in this chapter. As scholars such as Bueger[1] and Germond[2] have pointed out, there is currently no internationally accepted definition of maritime security. For the purpose of this chapter, maritime security encompasses all security issues (including traditional and non-traditional issues) that originate in or affect the maritime domain. Maritime security threats in turn are challenges to the survival and well-being of states, people and the environment that arise out of military and non-military sources that originate in or affect the maritime sphere.[3] These threats include inter-state conflicts at sea, maritime resource depletion, climate change, marine pollution, smuggling and trafficking at sea, piracy and illegal fishing. Not all maritime security threats are always part of national security considerations, as threat perception changes over time and varies between nations.

The link between maritime security and national security is both simple and complex. From a simplistic vantage point, any part of the maritime environment that is part of a nation state should by default be of national interest and be included in national security considerations. However, while land borders are (with some notable exceptions) generally established and clearly define national territory, maritime borders and zones of influence have been subject to change in recent decades and are often more diffuse, including zones with different levels of jurisdiction and responsibilities of nation states. These differences are a result of the historical processes that led to increased state control in the maritime sphere.

Extending state control to the sea was a prolonged process and a distinction has to be made between a state monopoly of violence at sea (which will be discussed later) and state control over water areas. State control over water areas only gradually started to gather pace in the eighteenth and nineteenth centuries. Since then, states have tried to control ever-larger maritime areas and thus increase the 'territory' that falls "within their sovereign reach and jurisdiction".[4] States initially only aimed to control port areas, bays and estuaries, but this changed with the emergence of the territorial sea as a recognised maritime zone. As Rothwell and Stephens explain:

> As the territorial sea became important, in the eighteenth and nineteenth centuries for the control of the flow of goods in and out of a state, and customs laws became more sophisticated, an additional layer was added to coastal state interests in the application and enforcement of laws and regulations within that zone.[5]

The size of the territorial waters, however, was contested from the outset, with suggestions ranging from a cannon-shot range to larger water areas. In the twentieth century, state ambition to expand control over bigger water areas grew apace. With the United Nations Law of the Sea Conventions (UNCLOS), adopted in 1982 and coming into force in 1994,[6] new maritime zones were recognised and defined, including the 12 nautical miles (nm) territorial seas and the Exclusive Economic Zones (EEZs), which stretch up to 200 nm from the shoreline. Waters beyond the EEZs are the high seas and fall outside the jurisdiction of coastal states. Significantly, not all maritime zones are sovereign territories of the coastal state. For example, coastal states have sovereignty over the territorial sea, but not over their EEZ. However, coastal states have over the past decades tried to increase their rights in water areas not under sovereignty, a process often referred to as creeping jurisdiction.[7] As a result of this process, national influence and jurisdiction are more diffuse at sea than on land. This, however, does not imply that water areas relatively close to the shore are not of 'national interest' or not part of national security considerations.

Moreover, national interest in the maritime environment clearly extends further than the protection of waters under national jurisdiction. The oceans are today crucial for international trade, with ships carrying more than 90 per cent of goods by volume. They are also an important source of food, oil, gas and other resources.[8] Maritime security is therefore also tied to other aspects of national security, such as economic, energy and food security, which are discussed in detail in other chapters in this volume. The safety and security of international shipping and maritime installations are consequently of importance to nations around the world, including those that do not border the ocean. The protection of international maritime infrastructure and shipping relies on the ability and authority of states to secure and police water areas beyond a state's borders, which emerged in a prolonged process starting in the sixteenth century. This process was until the twentieth century largely dominated by European powers, which built trade and political empires relying on naval coercion and power projection.[9]

In the past, the now conventional categories separating public and private, commercial and political were blurred in the maritime sphere. For example, vessels were used for fighting and trade interchangeably and rulers relied on private violent actors, such as privateers who were authorised by governments through a *letter of marque* to attack enemy ships in times of war. When European states grew stronger from the sixteenth century onwards, rulers increasingly showed an interest in controlling violence at sea to enforce more ambitious maritime policies. They began to introduce laws that distinguished between the legal and illegal use of private violence at sea, increased the control of private maritime resources and established permanent navies.[10] However, states continued to rely on private actors in the maritime sphere, such as privateers to further their ends.[11] It was only with the consolidation of state power in the nineteenth century that the use of violent private actors in the maritime sphere declined and eventually halted entirely. With the emergence of a state monopoly of violence at sea and the establishment of permanent navies, states became the basic security actors in the maritime sphere–at least for some time. Janice Thomson argues that the "elimination of nonstate violence from global politics" facilitated the emergence of the "state's monopolization of the authority to deploy violence beyond its borders".[12] In the nineteenth century, she suggests, a transformation in the institution of sovereignty occurred resulting in the de-legitimisation of non-state violence and with it the drawing of boundaries between the international and domestic, the political and economic and the realms of state and non-state authority:

> Because states authorized nonstate violence, it was difficult to determine which acts of nonstate violence were state sanctioned and which were private, independent, or free-lance. Because individual rulers personally profited from nonstate enterprises, it is difficult to say whether such enterprises were driven by economic or political motives. Because military forces were multinational, the distinction between the domestic and the international was unclear. What the institutional change in sovereignty produced was a clarification of the boundaries – both authoritative and territorial – that characterize the modern national state-system.[13]

The distinction between economic and political motives was exemplified by the emergence of the private shipping industry, which became gradually independent from politics and states. The first step in that direction was the creation of charter companies for long-distance sea trade in the early seventeenth century. While a strong connection between state interests and the companies remained, these joint-stock companies financed by shareholders had a stronger emphasis on commercial operations than on political or religious ideals, aiming primarily at the creation of personal wealth.[14] However, it was only in the nineteenth century that the maritime industry as we know it today emerged.

Driven by economic, political and technological developments, the speed of change accelerated in the nineteenth century and "shipping (in that century) changed more than in the previous two millennia".[15] The use of steamships allowed vessels to sail independent of the wind, travel faster and on schedule.

Industrial cargoes such as coal were for the first time transported in large quantities by vessels. Ships became more specialised, with dedicated tankers, cargo liners and passenger vessels starting to emerge at the time. Maritime trade increased rapidly, rising from 20 million tons in 1840 to 140 million tons in 1887. From the 1870s, a network of cargo liners encircled the globe, servicing the routes between Europe and its colonies. The new liner companies such as P&O and Hamburg Süd became household names and symbols of national pride.[16] As Stopford writes:

> Naturally the ships were registered locally, and the companies were generally publicly quoted, even though the stock was usually held by family members. In short, liner shipping became a prominent and highly respectable business, and young men joined the industry confident in the knowledge that they were serving national institutions.[17]

The link between shipping and nations, however, eroded further in the following decades. One important factor was the emergence of the flag-of-convenience (FOC) system, which emerged between the First and Second World Wars.[18] The FOC system offered shipowners an alternative to national registers. The main difference is that national registers only accept vessels from their own country, while open registers accept vessels from virtually any nation without significant restrictions. Shipowners are thus able to choose a flag, and with it a set of laws that is financially beneficial for their companies.[19] Being convenient for shipowners, open registers flourished:

> In 1950, 71% of the world fleet was registered in Europe and the United States, and 29% under overseas flags. By 2005, the share of the European and US flags had fallen to 11%, whilst other countries, particularly flags of convenience such as Liberia and Panama, accounted for 89%.[20]

With the introduction of the FOC system, the nationality of shipowners, or where they are based, no longer determined the nationality of a vessel.[21] Indeed, in some FOC countries, the beneficial ownership of a vessel (the person or company who receives the profits) does not even have to be revealed.[22] The FOC system was driven by and facilitated the rise of independent shipowners, such as Onassis and Pao, who reflagged their ships in open registers to cut costs. Their businesses were private enterprises that outsourced many operations traditionally performed by shipping companies.[23] As a result, the image of shipping companies changed from prestigious enterprises linked to national identity to increasingly secretive business operations.

These changes in international shipping changed the bond between states and shipping and with it the link between national interest and maritime security. On the one hand, maritime trade remained crucial for states. Indeed, trade by sea has become even more important after the Second World War when the ideals of free trade and access to global markets were institutionalised at the Bretton Woods Conference and the foundation for the General Agreement on Tariffs and Trade (GATT) was laid. This new system depended on trade, and efficient and safe shipping "played a central part in creating this new global economy".[24] The shipping industry also became more global in the distribution of powerful shipping nations, with Japan establishing itself as the world's leading maritime nation from the 1960s to the 1970s and South Korea followed by China also increasing their shipping power in line with their rising economies.[25] The protection of the world's shipping lanes has hence become increasingly important in national security considerations around the world.

On the other hand, international shipping has become more independent from states. The ownership of vessels has become blurred and many strong shipping nations, such as the United Kingdom, the United States, Japan or Germany, no longer have their own strong merchant fleet. Indeed, the out flagging of vessels has been identified as a risk in emergency situations as states can no longer direct the use of merchant ships if they do not fly their flag. They can no longer restrict these vessels' trade with enemy countries or ensure that a sufficient number of vessels are available to fulfil national trade requirements.[26] With the changes in ship registration, the connection between navies and merchant shipping also changed.

Protecting National (Maritime) Security—The Navies

National security cannot be completely divorced from 'traditional' interpretations, in which policy is shaped by agencies, ministries, and other institutions tasked with the protection of national interests from external threats. At sea, navies (and later also other state agencies) are predominantly tasked with the protection of national security and interests. The attention maritime security and navies received waxed and waned over time, as states and strategists placed different emphasis on the maritime sphere. In the late nineteenth century and early twentieth century, prominent naval strategists such as Rear Admiral Alfred Thayer Mahan (1840–1914) and Sir Julian Corbett (1854–1922) stressed the importance of naval strength, with Mahan for example suggesting that "Control of the sea by maritime commerce and naval supremacy means predominant influence in the world".[27] Even though the ideas of Mahan and Corbett are still influential today, the link between national security, seapower[28] and maritime trade remains contested and ideas and practices changed over time. As a result, the role of navies, their engagement in warfare and their relationship with merchant shipping also changed.

In the past, the distinction between navies and merchant shipping was blurred. For a long period, states were not able to create sufficiently large navies and even states with comparatively strong navies relied on merchant ships for warfare.[29] The use of merchant ships by navies was possible because merchant ships began to carry guns/cannons from the fifteenth century even at times of peace. As Howards writes:

> With guns mounted along flush decks, even merchantmen could more than hold their own against war galleys whose guns could only be mounted in prow and stern. So for a time the distinction between warship and merchantmen almost disappeared. It was to reappear in the eighteenth century when gun powder became all important and warships had to crowd on board as many guns as the decks would hold if they were to take their place in the battle line; but in the meantime it was hardly worth putting a ship to sea unless it could both carry a cargo *and* fight. It was a period when war, discovery, and trade were almost interchangeable terms.[30]

The hiring of merchant ships for war purposes, however, became increasingly difficult over time. Especially after the introduction of steam vessels, merchant ships could no longer compete with purpose-built warships. Furthermore, from the second half of the nineteenth century, merchant ships began to become more specialised, resulting in the introduction of the highly specialist ships, such as supertankers.[31] These specialist vessels were less suitable for warfare than the earlier merchant sailing ships.[32] Furthermore, with the emergence of FOC registers after the Second World War:

> shipowners realized that the obligations imposed by their flag States by far outweighed the benefits offered by them. (…) shipowners were no more willing to have their vessels removed from trade for national security reasons (e.g. transport of troops, military equipment), because these vessels would have found it exceedingly difficult, if not impossible, to re-enter the trade.[33]

Registering a vessel in an FOC country became more appealing as they do not require the same commitment from shipowners. As a result of these developments, merchant trade and navies drifted apart, with merchant shipping no longer contributing directly to the defence of national interests and national security through the use of their vessels.

The link between merchant shipping and the navy, however, remains strong. Navies continue to protect merchant ships and maritime infrastructure and consequently enable extensive trade by sea.[34] Navies, in the past and today, have clearly benefited from the maritime infrastructure created by merchant shipping, and international sea trade has generated income for states to establish and finance permanent navies.[35] After merchant shipping stopped to benefit rulers directly financially, states gained their revenue through taxation. From the mid-seventeenth century, "the European naval scene was dominated by the development of large sailing battle fleets, bureaucratically organised officer corps and warfare supported by taxes and customs duties raised by territorial states".[36] The income created through taxation allowed European powers to establish permanent navies. These navies supported wars in Europe, with sea battles an integral part of many conflicts. Navies were also deemed necessary to further European expansion overseas–in the Americas, Africa and Asia. Till points out that:

> For better or worse, the Europeans created new empires and changed the world. And they did it by sea. To make it all possible, they developed navies and a strategy, a set of concepts of how to use them from which all of the classic functions of seapower derived: Assuring sea control, projecting power ashore in peace and war, attacking and defending trade, directly and indirectly, and maintaining good order at sea.[37]

The role of navies therefore was not only the protection of national security in a narrow sense to defend against threats to the nation but also the expansion of national power and national interests well beyond its borders.

After the Second World War, changes in the role and tasks of navies followed. While the protection of maritime trade became even more important with the emergence of the post-war global economy, the acquisition of colonies and the navies' role in the process became obsolete with the end of European imperialism.[38] In the Cold War era, security concerns focused mainly on the rivalry between the two superpowers, the United States and the Soviet Union, or their proxy-states. On land and at sea, little attention was paid to non-state threats and the provision of security was firmly in the hand of state agencies. At sea, the rapid build-up of the Soviet navy challenged American naval strengths, causing concern about the Soviet fleet's ability to threaten "transatlantic routes and (to conduct) a submarine-launched missile attack on the USA".[39] The naval strengths of other formerly strong naval countries such as Britain and France declined in the Cold War era often due to financial constraints as funds were invested in other sections of the armed forces. The weakening of their individual naval strengths was for many Western countries somewhat offset by alliances with the US, especially the North Atlantic Treaty Organisation (NATO).[40]

Warfare at sea also changed in the Cold War era, symbolised by the demise of battleships. Indeed, despite the naval war race between the Soviet Union and the United States (and its allies), conflict at sea remained rare during the Cold War. In the three decades following the end of the Second World War, no major naval conflicts were fought and in the 1980s, only the Falklands War saw major (and crucial) naval involvement. The Falklands War, however, remained an exception and the navy build-up during the Cold War was largely "unmediated by conflict".[41] Navies, if they played a role in wars or other conflicts, were mainly used for transport or for sea-to-land operations. As a result, ships such as aircraft carriers that were required for such operations became more important to fulfil the new role of the navies. After the break-up of the Soviet Union, the Soviet fleet declined rapidly, leaving the US as the sole naval superpower.[42]

Overall, in the Cold War era, naval power changed, and the importance of naval forces declined relative to other military forces, even in the USA where the lack of naval conflict was one contributing factor that supported the argument that the navy was losing "its function as a fighting service".[43] The domestic support for the navy in the US, and in other countries, was weaker than in past centuries, when naval power in states such as Britain, was more central to the nations' interests and self-image. The relationship between national security and maritime security therefore changed: as navies played a different, more supportive, role, battles at sea became a thing of the past and less emphasis was placed on national defence at sea.[44]

CONTEMPORARY NATIONAL SECURITY THREATS: THE MARITIME SPHERE

The term 'maritime security' has risen to prominence after the end of the Cold War and has become a buzzword in international relations. States and multilateral organisations have since launched maritime security strategies and have re-focused their activities to increasingly address 'maritime security' challenges.[45] One prominent example is the United States' *Cooperative Strategy for the 21st Century Seapower*, which was launched in 2007 (and updated in 2015). This superseded the previous maritime strategy published in 1986, at the height of the Cold War.[46] A second example that demonstrates the increasing importance of cooperation in the maritime sphere is the EU's *Maritime Security Strategy* which was adopted by the Council of the European Union in 2014.[47] Both documents address traditional security threats in the maritime sphere that are of national security concern, but also have a stronger emphasis on non-traditional security issues.

Even though the focus shifted towards non-traditional security issues in the post-Cold War era, traditional security concerns remained of importance. The rivalry between states in the maritime sphere has been triggered, for example, by the growth of navies and naval power outside of Europe and the USA. In Southeast Asia, for example, the scale of purchases of new (and the modernisation of old) naval equipment triggered fears of a naval arms race in the region by the mid 1990s. While this naval build-up created regional concern, these developments were not regarded as threats internationally because these countries remained only modest maritime powers despite modernisation programmes.[48] Much more attention has been paid to the rise and strengthening of the Chinese (and to a lesser extent the Indian) navy, and more recently the Russian navy. These rivalries between states, such as the USA (and its allies) and China or the USA and Russia, that emerge in the maritime sphere are one segment of larger power struggles between these countries. For example, the modernisation and expansion of the Chinese Navy are linked to the rise of China and its growing international military and economic might. The emergent US–Chinese naval rivalry is but one part of the (hostile) competition between these two powers and their allies. Of concern for the US and its allies are, for instance, the growing global reach of the Chinese navy and its role in maritime boundary conflicts, especially the disputes in the East and South China Seas.[49]

Indeed, disputes over maritime boundaries and ownership of water areas and islands have also been part of national security concerns, especially for the countries involved and their allies. The demarcation of boundaries at sea and the extension of national waters in line with UNCLOS have led to disputes, due to overlapping claims of ownership of ocean areas and islands. These disputes have primarily emerged over islands in strategic locations, access to fishing grounds, and, most importantly, over areas in which natural resources such as oil or gas are located. To legitimate and enforce their claims and to protect their borders and natural resources from foreign actors, states have built up their naval strengths. The periodic flare-up of tensions over ownership of the Spratley Islands involving China and several Southeast Asian countries is one of the most prominent examples today.[50]

National Security and Non-Traditional Maritime Security Threats

Since the end of the Cold War, governments and government agencies have increasingly focused on non-traditional security threats, such as terrorism and climate change. There is, in some cases an overlap between traditional and non-traditional security concerns, with (maritime) cybersecurity, for example, today regarded as a national security risk[51] including attacks from states as well as non-state actors such as terrorists. The distinction, however, is nonetheless made here as the shift in focus from traditional to also include non-traditional security threats is also prevalent in the maritime sphere. This is demonstrated in maritime strategy papers, issued by states or regional organisations such as the EU, which includes piracy, terrorism, organised crime and climate change in its considerations.[52] This section will provide a brief overview of some of the most important 'new' security issues and why they are considered by many states as national security issues before the role of state agencies and non-state actors in combatting these threats is discussed.

Today, more and more attention is being paid to 'soft' security issues in the maritime sphere. Some of these, such as climate change and natural disasters, are environmental challenges that are difficult to address as security concerns by naval forces. The focus of navies (and other maritime agencies) is therefore often on addressing the consequences of threats such as natural disasters.[53] Most of the non-traditional security concerns, however, are posed by (violent) non-state actors. These include criminals, such as smugglers and pirates, as well as radical politically motivated groups such as terrorists. Their targets include ports, vessels, energy installations and underwater cables. Among the most prominent non-traditional maritime security threats are at present Illegal Unregulated and Underreported (IUU) fishing, the smuggling of goods and people, piracy, and maritime terrorism.

IUU is a serious security concern in waters around the world. It includes activities such as fishing illegally in protected waters, fishing without a valid licence, underreporting catch, and using banned fishing gear.[54] IUU fishing leads to the depletion of fish stocks and the destruction of the marine environment and causes substantial financial losses to affected communities and countries. A 2009 worldwide study estimates that "the overall loss from our studied fisheries is 13–31% (…) worth some \$5–11 bn in 2003".[55] The rising global demand for fish and marine products has driven illegal fishing activities resulting in the destruction and pollution of marine areas and overfishing due to the introduction of highly effective fishing technology. Also significant were the changes caused by the implementation of UNCLOS, which endorsed the establishment of different maritime zones, including EEZs that reach up to 200 nm offshore.[56] As a result, water areas under the jurisdiction of individual countries were considerably extended and with this, fishers became, at least legally, ever more restricted in their movements.[57] IUU fishing is of national security concern because it threatens food security, incurs substantial financial losses for states, and interferes with state control of water areas. It can also cause tensions and conflict between states, triggering sovereignty concerns.[58]

Smuggling is a worldwide concern, with goods such as prohibited drugs, fake medicine, weapons and cigarettes illicitly transported by sea between countries and regions. Drug trafficking, from Latin American and Southeast Asian countries to Europe and the USA, is a case in point. In recent years, the activities of people smugglers and traffickers also received substantial attention. The refugee boats sailing from northern Africa to Europe, or from the Middle East to Australia are prominent examples.[59] Smuggling of goods and people is a national security consideration mainly because the protection and safeguarding of national (or, for example, EU) borders are of key interest to states for economic and security reasons.[60] Also of concern are the illegal goods smuggled, especially weapons and drugs, and the consequences of unregulated movement of people (at sea). Indeed, since right wing and populist movements have become increasingly influential in many states around the world, unregulated migration (at sea) has been pushed forward as an eminent threat to national security.[61]

Pirates are another category of criminals active in the maritime sphere. Contemporary piracy has first been a concern in Southeast Asia. Between the 1990s and the mid-2000s, this region has been regarded as *the* global 'hot spot' of pirate attacks on commercial vessels and fishing boats. The waters and ports of Indonesia, Malaysia and the Philippines have been particularly affected, but international concern was caused primarily by the increase in reported attacks in the strategically important Malacca Strait. In this strategic waterway, reported attacks jumped from two actual and attempted attacks in the area in 1999 to 75 the following year.[62] Unfounded speculation that terrorists may collude with pirates in the Malacca Strait further increased international concern.[63] When the number of reported attacks in Southeast Asia declined from the mid-2000s, piracy in the wider Gulf of Aden area became the focus of attention.

340   C. LISS

Since 2008, the large number of serious pirate attacks in the wider Gulf of Aden area has been cause for international concern. The number of actual and attempted attacks in the wider Gulf of Aden area rose from 51 in 2007 to 111 in 2008, 218 in 2009, 219 in 2010 and peaking at 237 attacks in 2011.[64] Somali pirates have been responsible for these attacks and have targeted vessels of all types and nationalities, ranging from fishing boats and yachts to UN supply ships and supertankers. Unlike their Southeast Asian counterparts, Somali pirates have hijacked a large number of ships and held them and the crew on board for ransom. While estimates vary, a World Bank study found that between April 2005 and December 2012, Somali pirates hijacked a total of 179 ships and collected between US$339 million and US$413 million in ransom.[65] The severity of attacks and the substantial financial losses triggered international responses to combat piracy, and as a result, the number of incidents began to decline drastically. In 2012, the number of reported, attempted and actual attacks dropped to 75, went down to 15 in 2013, and dropped further in the following years.[66] As Somali piracy declined, the number of attacks in Southeast Asia began to increase again and in 2013, Southeast Asia became the most 'pirate infested' region again. The vast majority of pirate attacks in Southeast Asia are, however, simple 'hit and run robberies'.[67] Piracy resurfaces as a national and international security concern periodically, whenever a high(er) number of attacks is reported in strategic waterways and shipping lanes, such as the Malacca Strait or the Gulf of Aden.[68] The attacks are not a direct threat to national security, but they pose a threat to international shipping, energy supply and the safety of Sea lines of Communication (SLOC) that are of national interest to states around the globe.

In addition to profit-driven criminals, a range of radical politically motivated groups such as terrorists and insurgents have played an increasingly important part in national security considerations. Such groups target maritime assets such as vessels, port facilities and offshore oil and gas installations. After the 11 September 2001 terrorist attacks, terrorism was propelled to the top of the security agenda and fears of a maritime terrorist attack heightened. Fighting terrorism and preventing attacks in the maritime sphere became of national and international importance, resulting in the implementation of new vessel, container, and port safety and security regulations. The US Government was the driving force behind many of these initiatives, including the 2002 Container Security Initiative (CSI), the Proliferation Security Initiative (PSI) launched in May 2003 and the International Ship and Port Security Code (ISPS).[69] However, according to the RAND-MIPT Terrorism Incident database, only 2 per cent of terrorist attacks have targeted maritime installations or vessels in the past thirty years.[70] But even though the threat is low, maritime facilities have been targeted. Prominent examples are the 2004 bombing of the *SuperFerry 14* by the Abu Sayyaf in the southern Philippines, which killed more than 100 people,[71] and the attacks on the *USSCole* in October 2000 and the French tanker *Limburg* in 2002 in Yemen by al-Qaeda.[72]

Safeguarding National Security: Addressing Non-Traditional Maritime Security Threats

With the change in national security threat perception after the end of the Cold War, national agencies, especially navies, had to adapt to the new security environment and take on new roles. As a result, navies have become more involved in addressing non-traditional security threats and in maintaining the safe and sustainable use of the ocean. They share the responsibility with other maritime agencies and non-state organisations, which have re-emerged as active players in the maritime sphere after the end of the Cold War. Till describes the new role of navies as follows:

> Navies, coastguards and other maritime agencies have an increasingly vital contribution to make in support of good order at sea. Until very recently, however, such activities have been almost totally ignored by the main maritime thinkers. They were regarded as something that navies could do when nothing more important was occupying their attention; usually other maritime agencies bore the main burden. Nonetheless, the need for navies to address such issues more seriously grew steadily through the last century and seems likely to develop even faster in this one.[73]

By addressing non-traditional threats such as piracy, terrorism and illegal fishing, navies take on more constabulary functions and have to coordinate their activities increasingly with other maritime agencies such as coast guards.[74] Such agencies have traditionally focused more on safety and law enforcement while navies have been concerned with national security. As the distinction between law enforcement and national security has become increasingly blurred, with non-traditional threats today regarded as challenges to national security and the sovereignty of states, the work of navies and other maritime agencies has become increasingly intertwined.[75]

Due to the nature of non-traditional security threats, the operations of navies and other maritime agencies have also changed. Operations today increasingly take place 'far away from home' and because they address transnational problems they are often cooperative efforts. As a result, navies from different countries frequently work together to achieve a common aim. Civilian maritime agencies are also playing an increasingly important role in such cooperative efforts as they carry less 'political baggage' than navies. Furthermore, the focus of naval operations has shifted from the protection of specific national assets to safeguarding the system. For example, because of the current ship registration system, it makes little sense for states to secure only the vessels flying their own flag, as national trade generally depends not only on these vessels.[76] The international efforts to combat Somali piracy illustrate many of these characteristics of contemporary naval operations. As the number of attacks in the wider Gulf of Aden area increased, nations from around the world began to deploy warships to address piracy off the coast of

Somalia. Many of these navy vessels were part of missions sanctioned or organised by multilateral organisations, such as NATO and the EU. These included EU NAVFOR Operation Atalanta, NATO Operation Ocean Shield and the Combined Task Force-151 (CTF 151). As part of these missions, warships and aircraft patrolled waters in the high-risk area, convoys for merchant ships were organised, and an Internationally Recommended Transit Corridor (IRTC) was established.[77] These anti-piracy operations took place off the coast of Africa 'far away from home' for most navies involved, addressed a transnational problem and were largely cooperative efforts. The navies involved generally did not only protect ships under their own flag but shipping itself and with it the freedom of navigation. However, the responses were nonetheless driven by national interests, in this case mainly the economic and energy security of countries heavily dependent on global shipping.

The extended responsibilities of navies have caused some difficulties, as additional and often task-specific resources are needed. In a time of austerity, choices have to be made and priorities set. While this applies to all navies, these concerns are even more severe for navies of developing countries, where resources are sparse. This lack of resources of navies and other maritime agencies is one factor why non-state actors have become increasingly involved in addressing non-traditional maritime security threats.

Defending National Security? the Rise of Non-State Actors

Since the end of the Cold War, non-state actors have played an ever more important role in responding to national and international (maritime) security threats. The nature and scale of their involvement depend on the non-state actors' motivations, capacities and interests. Their activities can be violent or non-violent and can focus on local concerns or on international problems. The active involvement of non-state actors in addressing security threats since the end of the Cold War challenges "the 'monopoly' of the nation state in the legitimate provision of security".[78] Among the non-state actors involved in security governance are for-profit actors, such as private security companies, and not-for-profit actors, such as NGOs. They work alongside state agencies, and their activities are at times welcomed by states and not welcomed at other times.

For national security considerations, armed services provided by non-state actors are arguably most important. Such services are provided by Private Military and Security Companies (PMSCs), private businesses that offer a range of military or security services. Most PMSCs have emerged after the end of the Cold War and are best known for their activities on land, especially their operations in wars and conflict zones in places such as Iraq and Afghanistan. Their employers include governments, such as the US or British governments, the UN, NGOs and multinational corporations; but PMSCs have also worked for rebel groups and international criminal syndicates.[79] PMSCs are today also active in the maritime sphere., unlike in the past, where for-profit actors such as privateers were used for offensive operations such as the disruption of trade, today's PMSCs largely offer defensive (or protective) maritime services. These can roughly be divided into services provided on land or at sea. On land, PMSCs are active in ports where they provide services ranging from access control and screening of containers to emergency responses–roles previously performed by state agencies. The employment of PMSCs in ports was facilitated by the increasing privatisation of ports.[80] Among the PMSC services that are predominantly conducted at sea are the protection of offshore energy installations, fishing grounds and vessels such as merchant ships, yachts and cruise ships. PMSCs' businesses are in demand for a variety of reasons, including changes in national laws, that allow these companies to replace or supplement state personnel. Some countries have, for example, in recent years changed their laws and now allow not only state but also private forces to protect oil and gas installations. A more prominent example is anti-piracy services.

PMSCs began to offer and conduct anti-piracy services in Southeast Asia at the beginning of this century and demand skyrocketed after the surge in Somali piracy from 2008 onwards. Anti-piracy services offered by PMSCs include risk assessment, consulting, training of crews, provision of armed guards on board vessels, and the recovery of hijacked ships and cargoes. Mostly, PMSCs are hired to provide protection for vessels such as merchant ships, fishing boats and pleasure crafts, by stationing armed guards on board the protected ship or, in rare cases, by using armed escort vessels. While the provision of armed services by PMSCs was initially criticised by governments, maritime industry representatives and international organisations, their involvement has been accepted, if not supported, by many earlier critics since the rise of Somali piracy threat. Indeed, governments around the world have introduced new laws and regulations that allow, or at least do not prohibit, the use of armed PMSC personnel on ships flying their flags. Concerns remain, however, about the use of firearms by PMSCs, on the acquisition, transport, and storage of weapons, and the dearth of public oversight of PMSC activities.[81] The acceptance of armed PMSC services indicates that governments and their agencies have become willing to outsource some tasks that are associated with national interests and security to non-state actors, given that they operate within the legal framework established by states. While the task they perform within this framework is in line with national security interests, the motivation of these companies is possibly not. Indeed, PMSCs are in it for the money, not to enhance national security.

Conclusion

After the end of the Cold War, the absence of open rivalry between major powers has made traditional naval competition less important. Perhaps as a result and because of a new, broader understanding of security, non-traditional maritime security threats, such as piracy and illegal fishing, have featured more prominently in national (maritime) security considerations. Government agencies such as navies and coast guards have hence adapted their operations and focus much more on addressing such 'soft', transnational threats. The focus has also shifted from the protection of national assets to the protection of the 'system'. To combat these security issues and protect the system, a strong emphasis has been placed on naval cooperation between states.[82] Furthermore, state agencies increasingly share the burden with non-state actors such as PMSCs, which have become accepted (or at least tolerated) security providers in the maritime sphere. The focus on transnational threats as 'national security concerns', the protection of the system, the emphasis on cooperation, and the acceptance of non-state actors in addressing security concerns all suggest that the distinction between the private and public and the national and international are becoming blurred again.

Threat perception, however, is ever evolving and changing—and with it the roles of navies and other maritime agencies and actors. With China's rise, for example, US national security and grand strategy considerations have focused on the maritime balance of power in the Western Pacific.[83] Similar concerns are arising from the strengthening of the Russian navy, especially after the Russian annexation of Crimea in 2014.[84] Indeed, it has been argued that "Long-term strategic competition from China and Russia is profoundly more threatening to maritime security compared to the threat of non-state terrorists".[85] This suggests that the focus on non-traditional security threats that emerged after the Cold War may be superseded by a stronger focus on major-power competition in the future.

Notes

1. Bueger, C. (2015). What is Maritime Security? *Marine Policy* 53 (March), 159–164.
2. Germond, B. 2015. The Geopolitical Dimension of Maritime Security. *Marine Policy* 54 (June), 137–142.
3. This definition borrows some ideas from the definition of non-traditional security threats used by Mely Caballero-Anthony. Caballero-Anthony, M. (2007). Non-Traditional Security Challenges, Regional Governance, and the ASEAN Political-Security Community (APSC). *Asia Security Initiative Policy Series Working Paper* No. 7. https://www.rsis.edu.sg/wp-content/uploads/rsis-pubs/NTS/resources/research_papers/MacArthur_working_paper_Mely_Caballero-Anthony.pdf. Accessed 24 May 2019.
4. Rothwell, D. R. & Stephens, T. (2012). *The International Law of the Sea.* Oxford and Portland: Hart Publishing, 412.
5. Rothwell & Stephens. (2012). *The International Law of the Sea*, 412.
6. Stopford, M. (2004). *Maritime Economics*, 2nd edn. London: Routledge, 429–30.
7. Rothwell & Stephens. (2012). *The International Law of the Sea*, 422, 428.
8. European Commission. (2019). *European Union Maritime Security Strategy: Responding Together to Global Challenges. A Guide for Stakeholders.* https://ec.

europa.eu/maritimeaffairs/sites/maritimeaffairs/files/leaflet-european-union-maritime-security-strategy_en.pdf. Accessed 1 June 2019.

9. See: Sharman, J. C. (2019). Power and Profit at Sea. The Rise of the West in the Making of the International System. *International Security* 43(4),163–196.

10. Glete, J. (1999). *Warfare at Sea, 1500–1650: Maritime Conflicts and the Transformation of Europe*. London: Routledge, 60 and 134.

11. See: Sechrest, L. J. (2004). Public Goods and Private Solutions in Maritime History. *Quarterly Journal of Austrian Economics* 7(2), 6–7; and Anderson, G. M. & Gifford Jr, A. (1991). Privateering and the Private Production of Naval Power. *Cato Journal* 11(1), 104–5.

12. Thomson, J. E. 1994. *Pirates, Sovereigns, and Mercenaries*. Princeton: Princeton University Press, 3–4.

13. Ibid, 19.

14. Bohn, R. (2011). *Geschichte der Seefahrt*. München, Verlag C.H. Beck, 92.

15. Stopford. (2009). *Maritime Economics*, 23.

16. Ibid, 23–32.

17. Ibid, 32.

18. Ibid, 46.

19. See: International Labour Office. (2004). *The Global Seafarer. Living and Working Conditions in a Globalized Industry*. Geneva, 39–40 and 49; and Alderton, T. and Winchester, N. (2002). Regulation, Representation and the Flag Market. *Journal for Maritime Research*, September. http://www.tandfonline.com/doi/pdf/10.1080/21533369.2002.9668323. Accessed 2 August 2013.

20. Stopford. (2009). *Maritime Economics*, 43.

21. See: Carlisle, R. P. (1981). *Sovereignty for Sale. The Origins and Evolution of the Panamanian and Liberian Flags of Convenience*. Annapolis, Maryland: Naval Institute Press.

22. Stopford. (2009). *Maritime Economics*, 438.

23. Ibid, 434; and Ekberg, E., Lange, E. & Merok, E. (2012). Building the Networks of Trade: Perspectives on Twentieth-Century Maritime History. In Harlaftis, C., Tenold, S. & Valdaliso, J. M. (Eds.) *The World's Key Industry. History and Economics of International Shipping* (p. 90). Houndmills: Palgrave Macmillan, 90.

24. Stopford. (2009). *Maritime Economics*, 37.

25. Ibid, 38–9; and Bohn. (2011). *Geschichte der Seefahrt*, 115.

26. See for example: Security and Defence Committee (Finnland) (2006). The Strategy for Securing the Functions Vital to Society. Government Resolution 23.11.2006, Government of Finnland, https://www.defmin.fi/files/858/06_12_12_YETTS__in_english.pdf. Accessed 27 May 2019); and Wendel, P. (2007). *State Responsibility for Interferences with the Freedom of Navigation in Public International Law*. Berlin: Springer, 10–11.

27. Alfred Thayer Mahan cited in: Till, G. (2013). *Seapower: A Guide for the Twenty-First Century*, 3rd edition, London: Routledge, 1.

28. The meaning of seapower changed over time. Seapower, in its narrower interpretation, refers to naval capacities, represented by the number and capabilities of naval ships, submarines and manpower. Maritime power, on the other hand, includes not only naval capacities but also the broader use of the sea–for example the sea as a resource or a place for trade. The common practice,

however, is to use the terms maritime and seapower interchangeably and include the non-military aspects of sea-use. See: Ibid, 25–26; and Sakhuja, V. (2011). *Asian Maritime Power in the 21stCentury: Strategic Transactions China, India and Southeast Asia*. ISEAS, Singapore, 4–5.

29. See: Till, *Seapower*, 89; Howard, M. (2009). *War in European History*. Oxford University Press, 49–50; and Anderson & Gifford. (1991). Privateering and the Private Production of Naval Power, 114–115.
30. Howard. (2009). *War in European History*, 41.
31. Stopford. (2009). *Maritime Economics*, 23–24.
32. However, merchant ships continued to be used as cruisers, convoy escorts, rescue ships, landing ships, or to transport troops during the First and Second World Wars and even in the Falklands War in 1982. See: Anderson & Gifford. (1991). Privateering and the Private Production of Naval Power, 114–115; and Black, J. (2009). *Naval Power: A History of Warfare and the Sea from 1500*. London: Red Globe Press, 200.
33. Wendel. (2007). *State Responsibility*, 11.
34. Till. (2013). *Seapower*, 19.
35. Ibid, 89; and Howard. (2009). *War in European History*, 17.
36. Glete. (1999). *Warfare at Sea*, 2–3.
37. Till. (2013). *Seapower*, 89; Howard. (2009). *War in European History*, 15.
38. Till. (2013). *Seapower*, 16.
39. Black. (2009). *Naval Power*, 193.
40. Ibid, 193–203.
41. Ibid, 201.
42. Ibid, 193–203.
43. Ibid, 206.
44. Ibid, 203–207.
45. Bueger. (2015). *What is Maritime Security?*, 159; and Germond. (2015). *The Geopolitical Dimension of Maritime Security*, 138.
46. Department of the Navy. (2015). A Cooperative Strategy for the 21st Century Seapower, United States of America. United States Coast Guard, March, https://www.navy.mil/local/maritime/150227-CS21R-Final.pdf. Accessed 4 June 2019.
47. Council of the European Union. (2014). *European Union Maritime Security Strategy*. Brussels, 24 June.
48. Bateman, S.(1997). ASEAN's Tiger Navies. *Jane's Navy International* 102(3), n. p.; and Bateman, S. (1996). Sea Change in Asia-Pacific. *Jane's Navy International* 101(8), n. p.
49. Kim, T. (2016). US Alliance Obligations in the Disputes in the East and South China Seas: Issues of Applicability and Interpretations. *PRIF Report*, 1–34; and Kim, T. (2018). U.S. Rebalancing Strategy and Disputes in the South China Sea: A Legacy for America's Pacific Century. In Anders Corr (ed.) *Great Powers, Grand Strategies: The New Game in the South China Sea*, 174–98. Annapolis: US Naval Institute Press.
50. See: Kim. (2018). U.S. Rebalancing Strategy; and Leng, L. Y. (1982). *Southeast Asia: Essays in Political Geography*. Singapore: Singapore University Press, 54–7.
51. See for example: Council of the European Union. (2014).*European Union Maritime Security Strategy*, Brussels, 24 June; and Hayes, C. R. (2016).

Maritime Cybersecurity: The Future of National Security. Masters Thesis, Monterey, California: Naval Postgraduate School.

52. See: Council of the European Union.
53. Germond, B. & Mazaris, A. D. (2019). Climate Change and Maritime Security. *Marine Policy* 99, 262–266.
54. See: High Seas Task Force. (2006). *Closing the Net: Stopping Illegal Fishing on the High Seas*. Governments of Australia, Canada, Chile, Namibia, New Zealand, and the United Kingdom. WWF, IUCN and the Earth Institute at Columbia University, 23; and Organization for Economic Co-operation and Development. (2004). *Fish Piracy: Combating Illegal, Unreported and Unregulated Fishing*, Paris: OECD.
55. Agnew, D. et al. (2009). Estimating the Worldwide Extent of Illegal Fishing. *PLoS ONE* 4(2), 2.
56. United Nations. (1982). United Nations Convention on the Law of the Sea of 10 December, http://www.un.org/Depts/los/convention_agreements/convention_overview_convention.htm. Accessed 9 June 2019.
57. See: Butcher, J. G. (2004). *The Closing of the Frontier: A History of the Marine Fisheries of Southeast Asia c.1850–2000*. Singapore: ISEAS Publications.
58. For examples see: Ibid; Ganesan, N. (2001). Illegal Fishing and Illegal Migration in Thailand's Bilateral Relations with Malaysia and Myanmar. In Tan, A. & Boutin, J. (Eds.) *Non-Traditional Security Issues in Southeast Asia* (pp. 507–27) Singapore: Select Publishing.
59. See: Tagliacozzo, E. (2002). Smuggling in Southeast Asia. History and its Contemporary Vectors in an Unbounded Region. *Critical Asian Studies* 34(2), 193–220; Bruni, J. (2010). Border Crossing: People-Smuggling into Australia. *Jane's Intelligence Review*, 29 October, n.p.; and Liss, C. (2019). Turning a Blind Eye? The Rescue of Migrants in the Mediterranean. *PRIF Spotlight* 3.
60. See, for example: Council of the European Union. Department of the Navy et al.
61. Reynolds, J. (2018). Matteo Salvini: Can Italy trust this man? *BBC News*, 5 August, https://www.bbc.com/news/world-europe-44921974. Accessed 22 March 2019.
62. ICC. (2006). *Piracy and Armed Robbery against Ships*. Report for the Period 1 January–31 December 2005. International Maritime Bureau, London, p.5.
63. Liss, C. (2011). *Oceans of Crime: Maritime Piracy and Transnational Security in Southeast Asia and Bangladesh*. Singapore: Institute of Southeast Asian Studies and International Institute for Asian Studies.
64. ICC. (2012). Piracy and Armed Robbery against Ships. Report for the Period 1 January–31 December 2011. International Maritime Bureau, London, pp.5–6.
65. World Bank. (2013). *Pirate Trails: Tracking the Illicit Financial Flows from Piracy off the Horn of Africa*. Washington DC: United Nations Office on Drugs and Crime and World Bank.
66. ICC. (2014). Piracy and Armed Robbery against Ships. Report for the Period 1 January–31 December 2013. International Maritime Bureau, London, p. 20.
67. See: ICC annual piracy reports 1992–2012.
68. High financial losses caused by piracy and pressure from the maritime industry also play a role in pushing piracy to the front of the security agenda.
69. See: Ho, J. & Raymond, C. Z. (Eds.) (2005). *The Best of Times, the Worst of Times. Maritime Security in the Asia Pacific*. Singapore: Institute of Defence

and Strategic Studies; Persbo, A. & Davis, I. (2004). *Sailing Into Uncharted Waters? The Proliferation Security Initiative and the Law of the Sea*. BASIC Research Report, British American Security Information Council. International Maritime Organisation. N.d. IMO Adopts Comprehensive Maritime Security Measures. http://www.imo.org/Newsroom/mainframe.asp?topic_id=583&doc_id=2689. Accessed 5 February 2006.

70. Chalk, P. (2006). Maritime Terrorism in the Contemporary Era: Threat and Potential Future Contingencies. In *The MIPT Terrorism Annual 2006*, National Memorial Institute for the Prevention of Terrorism ed., Oklahoma City: National Memorial Institute for the Prevention of Terrorism, p. 21.

71. Labog-Javellana, J. & Tubeza, P. (2004). SuperFerry 14 Bombing Solved, Says Arroyo. *Philippine Daily Inquirer*, 12 October, A1.

72. Bradford, J. F. (2005). The Growing Prospects for Maritime Security Cooperation in Southeast Asia. *Naval War College Review* 2005 (6), 67, 71; and Nincic, D. K. 2012. Maritime Terrorism: How Real is the Threat. *Fair Observer*, July 16, http://www.fairobserver.com/region/north_america/maritime-terrorism-how-real-threat/. Accessed 1 August 2014.

73. Till. (2013). *Seapower*, 305.

74. There are, however, major differences between the organization and responsibilities of navies and other maritime agencies between countries.

75. Till. (2013). *Seapower*, 315–6.

76. For an overview of the new roles of navies see: Ibid, 31–38 and 282–300.

77. Ehrhart, H. G., Petretto, K. & Schneider, P. (2010). Security Governance als Rahmenkonzept für die Analyse von Piraterie und maritimem Terrorismus. Konzeptionelle und Empirische Grundlagen.*PiraT-Arbeitspapiere zur Maritimen Sicherheit*, Nr. 1, 40–5.

78. Krahmann, E. (2005). From State to Non-state Actors: The Emergence of Security Governance. In Krahmann, E. (ed.) *New Threats and New Actors in International Security*. London: Palgrave Macmillan, 9.

79. See: Singer, P. W. (2003). *Corporate Warriors: The Rise of the Privatized Military Industry*, Cornell: Cornell University Press; and Avant, D. (2005). *The Market for Force: The Consequences of Privatizing Security*. Cambridge: Cambridge University Press.

80. See: Reveley, J. & Tull, M. (Eds.) (2008). *Port Privatisation: The Asia–Pacific Experience*. London: Edward Elgar.

81. See: Liss, C. & Schneider, P. (Eds.) (2015). Regulating Private Maritime Security Providers, Special Issue. *Ocean Development and International Law*, 46(2).

82. This cooperation in non-traditional maritime security activities, have been a politically non-provocative way to improve military cooperation among states.

83. "Maritime security" is mentioned 21 times in a recent report on the Indo-Pacific, issued by the Pentagon. The report also discusses "The People's Republic of China as a Revisionist Power" and "Russia as a Revitalized Malign Actor." U.S. Department of Defense. 2019. Indo-Pacific Strategy Report: Preparedness, Partnerships, and Promoting a Networked Region. June 1, https://media.defense.gov/2019/May/31/2002139210/-1/-1/1/DOD_INDO_PACIFIC_STRATEGY_REPORT_JUNE_2019.PDF. Accessed 8 June 2019.

84. Burkovskyi, P. & Haran, O. (2018). Dire Strait: Russian naval aggression and Ukrainian politics. *European Council on Foreign RelationsCommentary*, 5 December,https://www.ecfr.eu/article/commentary_dire_strait_russian_naval_aggression_and_ukrainian_politics. Accessed 7 June 2019.
85. McKechnie, J. (2018). *What do the New National Security and Defense Strategies Mean for Maritime Security?* Center for International Maritime Security, June 13, http://cimsec.org/what-do-the-new-national-security-and-defense-strategies-mean-for-maritime-security/36746. Accessed 7 June 2019.

CHAPTER 15

Intelligence and National Security: The National Security Problematique

Paul Burke

The defence of "national security" has been used by different countries as a justification for taking military action, introducing new policies and legislation or amending existing ones. The difficulty in clearly defining the concept of national security is similar to that of defining terrorism, given that how a nation defines its national security has a direct bearing on the actions and measures which it takes to protect it.[1] To paraphrase Davies, the tendency of countries to employ different definitions of national security has both conceptual and substantive implications.[2] The concepts of national security and terrorism are also similar in that many people feel that they know what these two concepts embody, but struggle to elucidate them. The concept of national security is equally politicised, with the attachment of this term becoming a powerful tool in claiming international legitimacy for one side or the other. This naturally depends on which side can most convincingly apply the label to the opposition and thus "the more confused a concept, the more it lends itself to opportunistic appropriation".[3]

Recent years have witnessed an expansion in scale, scope, audacity and impact of the threats to the national security of liberal democracies in particular: highly credible suspicions of attempted state-level interference in elections, referendums and other important votes in democracies, sophisticated manipulation of the major social media platforms to support distinct agendas, assassinations of dissenters abroad, coordinated hacking attacks ranging from

P. Burke (✉)
Delft University, Delft, The Netherlands
e-mail: p.j.burke@tudelft.nl

© The Author(s), under exclusive license to Springer Nature
Switzerland AG 2022
M. Clarke et al. (eds.), *The Palgrave Handbook of National Security*,
https://doi.org/10.1007/978-3-030-53494-3_15

351

cyber-vandalism, and data theft through to the disruption of essential services. The Intelligence process of countries that were NATO members during the cold war has had to adapt from targeting the fixed, monolithic threat posed by the former Soviet Union, to covering threats that include terrorism, transnational organised crime, energy/food/water/cyber/information security, climate change, narcotics/weapons/people trafficking and natural and man-made disasters, to name a few.

Parallel to this evolution in threats and vulnerabilities, we have seen an increasing role played by intelligence agencies in public discussions of national security. Consider the definition of national security coined by Secretary of Defence Harold Brown: "the ability to preserve the nation's physical integrity and territory; to maintain its economic relations with the rest of the world on reasonable terms; to protect its nature, institutions and governance from disruption from outside; and to control its borders".[4] Running in parallel with a notion of national security like this is the need for those decision-makers tasked with preservation of a nation's integrity and territory to be properly informed about how to protect the nation. As David Omand notes, *"the most basic purpose of intelligence is to improve the quality of decision-making by reducing ignorance"*.[5] Thus we improve the odds of acting in line with our goals beyond what we would have achieved had we simply "tossed a coin to decide between courses of action, acted on hunch or wrong information, or allowed events in the absence of decision to decide the outcome". Information differs from Intelligence in a number of ways, one of which is that it has been subjected to a process (as this chapter describes in more detail), including evaluation. Omand and Pythian contend that another difference separating the two concepts is that "the environments in which intelligence is required are fundamentally competitive ones".[6] Thus intelligence is both necessary for national security but also needs to be understood within a national security context.

This chapter presents an overview of the intelligence cycle. The purpose is to give an overview of the different formalised aspects of intelligence tasking, gathering, and use and to gesture at some of the contextual aspects of intelligence for national security.

Approaches to the Intelligence Cycle

The effective collection of Intelligence requires some form of a formalised process to be used. This might be a cyclical model, a linear model or even a more intricate, process-flow diagram, but the absence of any formalised process will make it difficult to collect and process Intelligence effectively or efficiently. Different models are in use across the world and even different agencies with the same country are known to use different models. A UK model popular in the last two decades has been the six-stage cycle, as depicted Fig. 15.1 below.

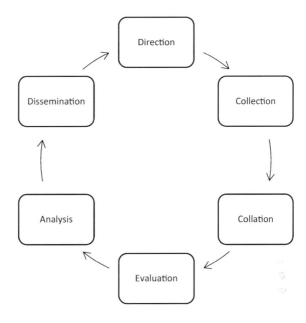

Fig. 15.1 UK 6-stage intelligence cycle (National Policing Improvement Agency, 2008, p. 11)

In this model, the cycle begins with direction, which then triggers the collection process. There are various schools of thought regarding the applicability of all of the above components, and more besides, such as planning (absent in this model, as it is considered to form an integral part of direction). By comparison, US models such as the CIA's Intelligence cycle have traditionally favoured starting the process with planning, either as a standalone component or pairing it with direction.[7] While this model contains the planning component, evaluation does not feature in it. As many Intelligence and law enforcement agencies and bodies have studied the concept of the Intelligence cycle as a model for their operational work, various lessons have been learned along the way and some have re-shaped their models accordingly.[8] Similar differences can be seen in the absence of planning in some UK models and similarly the absence of evaluation in some US models such as the Federal Bureau of Investigation (FBI) Intelligence cycle(2020).[9]

Direction

Once a requirement has been identified, Intelligence agencies are then directed, or tasked, to begin collection against it. In the case of the target requirement being an individual or individuals residing in, or a national of, the country in which the collection is taking place, this process can often begin quickly, due to the potential amount of existing information available to the authorities, such as name, address, mobile phone number, passport number, bank account details, vehicles owned, passport details, upcoming travel, etc.

354   P. BURKE

Any or all of these information sources can provide a start point for the collection to begin.

The tasking process can additionally establish any priorities for the collection process, an essential factor in organisations with limited resources. This allocation of resources can help to ensure that agencies do not simply collect unilaterally with no regulated process behind such decisions, and to avoid any duplication of effort.[10] Direction can come from the top-down, where a strategic priority may be set by the political leadership, for example, deciding that a requirement is sufficiently important to the nation's security for the Intelligence and law enforcement agencies to be tasked with collection. Direction can also come from the bottom up, and it may be generated from the collectors, analysts and specialists during ongoing collection. A HUMINT handler, for example, may uncover time-sensitive Intelligence while debriefing a source and this may require the immediate tasking of other assets, possibly to confirm the accuracy of the Intelligence or to begin preparations for a short-notice operation.

Planning

The planning element often includes the drafting of a collection plan that identifies which assets, sources and methods are best positioned to conduct collection against a requirement. This planning provides the link between the direction of the effort, and the instigation of the actual collection processes. It is heavily used in military Intelligence, especially in theatres of conflict, largely due to a deployed military command being the effective owner of an array of collection assets that may include Human Intelligence (HUMINT), Signals Intelligence (SIGINT), Imagery Intelligence (IMINT), Open Source Intelligence (OSINT), Geospatial Intelligence (GEOINT), Counter-Intelligence (CI) and possibly more. In large-scale deployments such as those in Afghanistan and Iraq, these assets may also cover a full spectrum of domains, such as land, sea, air, sub-surface, space and cyber. Describing the importance of full-spectrum Intelligence support on operations during the allied invasion of Iraq in 2003, Harris (2009) notes that "the entire intelligence community and each intelligence discipline - human intelligence (HUMINT), signals intelligence (SIGINT), geospatial or imagery intelligence (GEOINT), as well as intelligence, surveillance, and reconnaissance (ISR) systems - primarily unmanned aerial vehicles - have contributed in varying degrees to the effort in Iraq".

The collection plan helps in formalising the Intelligence Requirements (IRs) which are to be collected against, and this process helps to narrow the specific questions which the collection should help to answer. Once the IRs have been agreed upon and collection assets have been allocated, the plan helps to identify any potential gaps of IRs which do not have suitable or available assets to support them. The plan can also be used to plan more complex levels of overlap in the overall collection strategy. Such an overlapping approach is a more intensive use of resources and thus requires more careful management of the collection. The collection plan is then used to match IRs with capabilities, taking into account their suitability, effectiveness, potential access and other factors.

Collection and Collation

The collection of Intelligence relies upon a variety of sources and methods that span the spectrum from overt, through discrete, to covert disciplines. Overt sources can include news reports, presentations given provided during public conferences, media interviews, government reports, commercial documents released publicly, academic and technical, peer-reviewed journals, trade exhibitions and blogs. Discrete sources and methods do not use subterfuge to collect information, although the actual collection itself is generally conducted away from the public gaze, such as the debriefing of refugees in an overseas conflict zone. Schroeder provides another example, that of conducting a surveillance flight close to an international border, while the aircraft remains in international airspace.[11]

Covert sources and methods employ more sensitive and intrusive elements, such as the use of covert human Intelligence sources (CHIS) to collect human Intelligence, the interference with property or vehicles in order to conduct audio and/or video surveillance or the covert penetration of a terrorist group.[12] There are considerable national security advantages for those nations able to conduct full-spectrum or multi-source Intelligence collection.[13] It can provide the ability to confirm Intelligence through two or more sources that can strengthen the evaluation process, giving analysts and policymakers a potentially higher degree of confidence about the veracity of a piece of Intelligence. One source can "cue" or trigger another, providing steering so the second source knows when and where and what to collect.[14] It also allows the strengths of each source to be synergised. The following diagram, which is not exhaustive, shows some of the major disciplines and their sub-categories (Fig. 15.2).

Not all requirements will need all-source collection. Collection against a hostile, the foreign country may not require an intensive, multi-source collection effort due to the geopolitical situation regarding relations with it, whereas in an ongoing counter-terrorism operation dealing with an active plot and a threat to life, the complete span of available sources is more likely to be used, given the much higher risk to public safety.

The strengths and weaknesses of the various sources and methods must be fully understood by collection managers. Each of the three primary sources of SIGINT, HUMINT and GEOINT have their own benefits and drawbacks and they are not all equal in every collection strategy.[15] In the author's experience, these sources and methods function more effectively when they are aligned, which ensures that an IR has the fullest possible coverage, in line with available resources. Each of these sources can potentially be used to trigger

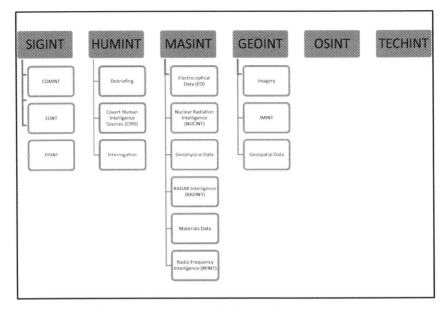

Fig. 15.2 Intelligence sources and methods overview

or "cue" a range of options, such as additional collection, or the start of a disruption operation. Collection management has expanded rapidly, from a unitary, unglamorous task into a distinct discipline complete with dedicated training courses and the retention of experienced staff.[16] This progression is a testament to how important this function has become in the contemporary Intelligence process.

Collation is not always included in Intelligence cycles, depending upon country or agency, but it remains an integral part of the Intelligence process as it collects into one location all the existing knowledge about a target at the start of the collection process.[17] This enables the collection to begin, while knowing with a high degree of certainty that the designated target is the correct one. It also helps to expand the initial picture of the target, using a range of techniques and tools such as "charts; Spreadsheets; Tables; Databases; Maps; Commodity flows including financial material; Communication flow and frequency charts. It is essential that such products are not considered to be the final analytical product. The evaluation and subsequent interpretation of collated material are the key processes that change material into analysis".[18] The rapid advancement of IT-based tools has resulted in less clear boundaries between collation and de facto analysis but the importance of collation as a component of the process remains.

SIGINT is primarily concerned with the identification, collection and analysis of information contained within signals emanating from a range of communication systems such as radios, RADAR, mobile telephony and similar platforms. Satellites now generate a large percentage of technical SIGINT collection for the US and UK Intelligence agencies (Satellite Observation, 2017). The employment of SIGINT as a resource can differ greatly depending on the theatre in which the operations are conducted. In a developed country with no ongoing conflict, a greater use may be made of mobile telephony as a collection source, whereas in a less permissive environment such as a fragile or conflicted state, other elements of SIGINT may be more appropriate for delivering the required collection profile, such as HF or VHF radios. Due to the sensitivities of the SIGINT environment, some of the previous writing on SIGINT has included varying degrees of inaccuracy, but work by Aid,[19] Richelson[20] and Dover and Goodman[21] in particular provide an excellent source of accurate, scholarly work on the subject. The lawful interception of communications is usually one of the most sensitive areas of Intelligence collection by the UK government, and it is only natural that technical details about this capability are protected from unauthorised public disclosure.

The collection and management of SIGINT by the "Five Eyes" partner nations (USA, UK, Canada, Australia and New Zealand) is conducted by the respective national agencies of these countries (the National Security Agency (NSA) in the USA, Government Communications Headquarters (GCHQ) in the UK, the Communications Security Agency (CSE) in Canada, the Australian Signals Directorate (ASD) and the Government Communications Security Bureau (GCSB) in New Zealand). The Five Eyes agreement came into being after the Second World War, as a result of the Allied countries examining what a post-war world might look like and how it might be monitored.[22] The five-eyes alliance brings with it a number of benefits for the participating countries, one of which is the division of Intelligence effort regarding large tracts of the globe. To avoid the duplication of effort in monitoring some target countries or regions, it made sense in the post-war years to divide the number of areas among the alliance members. Such an arrangement can only work if there is significant trust between the partner countries, and this trust has been a cornerstone of this unique partnership. In allocating a division of effort and working in an environment of mutual trust and sharing, the sum of the alliance becomes stronger than its constituent parts.

During the Cold War, the ability to gain an accurate picture of troop dispositions, aircraft flight profiles, naval deployments, readiness states, equipment holdings, weapon system capabilities and politico-military intentions provided a large segment of the Intelligence used to create strategic assessments on both sides. While contemporary debate tends to be concentrated on the collection of bulk data, the interception of mobile cellular data and the use of metadata,[23] the capability to intercept more traditional forms of communication such as HF/VHF/UHF remains, as does the ability to access parts of the frequency spectrum other than mobile telephony and the internet.[24] The range of platforms from which SIGINT can be conducted has expanded continuously since telephonic and electronic communications began to be intercepted. Interception is now conducted across the entire land-sea-air-subsurface domain, as well as from space, since the advent of one of the most significant technological innovations in SIGINT, viz. the operationalising of space-based satellites for Intelligence collection.

As human beings are creatures of habit, they often take the path of least effort and this can apply equally to individuals and to governments. Whilst a terrorist operative may be instructed to minimise their communications for reasons of security, they might still phone their spouse at the same time each week to make their own life easier.[25] In the same way, a national government may put in place a fully joined-up policy for communications security (COMSEC), including usage limitations, encryption and similar measures.[26] The weaknesses in the system traditionally come from individuals taking shortcuts, ignoring COMSEC policy or breaking the rules.[27] Thus, while governments know that other nations will attempt to access their high-level communications, the measure of success for their COMSEC efforts often stands or falls largely on the willingness of individual users to follow policy rules such as user verification. As Jacobs observes, "Nobody likes manual key verification, but no technical solution has currently been found to satisfy the same level of security without adding that procedural step".[28]

The collection of intercept material is generally conducted without the target being aware that this is happening. This is a crucial factor for policymakers and customers of Intelligence to be aware of, as an inadvertent compromise can lead to the source of intercept being closed down as soon as the users are aware of a breach. In early 2020, for example, a multinational investigation by European agencies into a suspected terrorist's attack planning suddenly and unexpectedly lost the ability to intercept the suspect's WhatsApp messaging on his mobile phone, following a notification from the social media company to around 1,400 users, that their device may have been subjected to hacking.[29] In some cases, the target is aware of the collection efforts of an opponent, but will use a variety of transmission security (TRANSEC) measures (e.g. encryption, frequency-agile transmitters and the use of spread-spectrum technology) and emission security (EMSEC) measures such as the use of Telecommunications Electronics Materials Protected from Emanating Spurious Transmissions (TEMPEST) protection and shielding, to minimise the probability that its communications can be successfully intercepted at all, and if they are intercepted, to deny the opponent meaningful information from the analysis of them.

SIGINT has traditionally been a generous provider of "indicators and warnings" (I & W) that are used by Intelligence agencies to assess, for example, how close a target is to embarking on a course of action. As George states, "Warning is easiest when there are easily observable indicators......those indicators are more easily observed by US reconnaissance satellites and SIGINT systems".[30] When the target is a hostile regime, I & W might be collected into various sub-sets, such as preparations to move troops out of barracks and into deployment locations, or the dispersal of specialist elements such as those associated with chemical weapons. The I & W that are used to track the current threat of international terrorism are considerably more complex and often more vague and more difficult to manage. George's blunt assessment tells us that the track record in providing I & W for terrorism is "dismal".[31] This is especially the case with the increasing use of lone actors who may conduct little or no preparation before they move rapidly from a start-state of almost zero, through to the carrying out of an attack. While intercept may not always provide illumination into the thinking of a target, whether that constitutes a regime or an individual, it can provide detailed information about what the target is actually saying and doing. The mainly automated platforms that collect raw SIGINT data are constantly in operation and as long as they are sufficiently programmed, they will collect against their parameters around the clock unlike an individual HUMINT asset who might have only periodic access to the target and who also needs to sleep.

HUMINT relies on the collection of Intelligence from people, rather than from intercepted communications or imagery of areas. While most technical collection is automated to some degree, the collection of HUMINT remains largely non-automated. The people providing this information are classed as sources and they may be overt or covert. This landscape ranges from the overt debriefing of refugees or displaced persons, through to the discrete use of formal relationships, and on to fully covert sources, usually involving the employment of some kind of cover. The covert spectrum includes Covert Human Intelligence Sources (CHIS), the interception of communications, the covert surveillance of individuals and premises (both directed and intrusive, including lawful interference with property and vehicles). The targeting, recruitment, training, deployment and management of a covert source should ideally be subject to a very stringent set of legal controls, with robust oversight and accountability mechanisms.[32]

Some people become sources because they have voluntarily approached the Police, the Armed Forces, an Intelligence agency or similar. In conflicted and fragile states such as Iraq, Afghanistan and Somalia it is not uncommon for individuals from a wide variety of backgrounds to approach government agencies with information that may be useful for ensuring public safety, such as the location of weapons caches or explosives, or the identities of key figures in a terrorist group. Many sources are recruited for nothing more exciting than passively listening and watching when they are in the company of persons of interest, or in locations of interest. Their value lies in their ability to hoover up anything and everything of interest to the collectors, while remaining unobtrusive to the targeted audience. This type of source may be managed, and provide high-value information, without ever being tasked with more advanced requirements, such as penetrating deeper into the group, or covertly copying or removing items such as documents, USB drives or similar. The US Armed Forces identifies five sub-categories of HUMINT operation, although not all NATO countries follow this distinction. These sub-categories are:

1. "**Screening**—the process of evaluating and selecting human sources and documents for the prioritized collection of information based on the collection requirements and mission of the unit conducting the screening or its higher headquarters.
2. **Interrogation**—the systematic effort to procure information to answer specific collection requirements by direct and indirect questioning techniques of a person who is in the custody of the forces conducting the questioning.
3. **Debriefing**—the systematic questioning of cooperating human sources to satisfy intelligence requirements consistent with applicable law.
4. **HUMINT**—collection in military source operations (MSO)—directed toward the establishment of human sources who have agreed to meet and cooperate with HUMINT collectors for the purpose of providing information.
5. **Liaison**—with local military, government, or civilian agency officials provides an opportunity to collect information required by the commander…to conduct liaison, coordinate certain operations, collect information, and obtain leads to potential sources of information".[33]

The British Army describes GEOINT in its field manual on countering insurgency as the analysis and exploitation of "imagery and geospatial information to describe, assess and visually depict physical features and geographically referenced activities".[34] The range of raw products used in GEOINT is wide, including (but not limited to) "geographic, geodetic, geomagnetic, imagery, gravimetric, aeronautical, topographic, hydrographic, littoral, cultural, and toponymic" products.[35]

One of the most operationalised aspects of GEOINT is locational Intelligence or LOCINT, the ability to geolocate a device such as a mobile telephone, through the use of technological analysis of data such as the Time Difference of Arrival (TDOA). This technique has been used to successfully convict suspects in several high-profile murder cases such as the Soham murder case in the UK.[36] There are other methods used in LOCINT but it remains a sensitive area of Intelligence exploitation.

Within Intelligence communities, there are conflicting viewpoints on the importance, relevance and contribution of OSINT. Some, like Hulnick, view OSINT as providing the majority of the Intelligence database bedrock (more than 80% according to Hulnick).[37] Others, like Mercado, accept that OSINT has a valid role to play but do not consider it to be replacing covert Intelligence anytime soon.[38] In many ways, the arguments have become redundant in recent years as Intelligence agencies have embraced the OSINT sphere. Many now run dedicated OSINT courses for staff, as a compliment to the secret Intelligence disciplines more traditionally associated with such agencies (Nato School, 2020). The use of OSINT has increased from year to year as so much more information is placed online, with little consideration of what inferences may be drawn from it. This is one of the strengths of OSINT, in finding the linkages between seemingly unrelated items of information or events.

Analysis and Processing

The process of analysis is usually resource-intensive, due to the potential risks involved. At one level, it can be as short as manually scanning lists of identifiers such as email addresses or names. At the opposite level, teams can work against a target for years, such as the US team which was established to locate Osama bin Laden. The field of analysis has benefited from a vast array of literature but it was not always so widely studied. More than 25 years ago, Gentry was less than impressed with the available literature, dismissing it as "filled with judgments and assertions at variance with ...reality"[39] whereas just ten years later, Lowenthal described the literary landscape of Intelligence analysis as a rich one and it has continued to increase a pace since then.[40]

The process of analysis is often approached from a transformational perspective, wherein the raw output of the previous stages of the Intelligence process is converted into something understandable and, ideally, valuable. Lefebvre defines analysis as "the process of evaluating and transforming raw data acquired covertly into descriptions, explanations, and judgments for policy consumers".[41] The processing aspect to this stage has only increased over time, especially since the latter decades of the Cold War, as evidenced by a former Director of the NSA, when asked what were the three biggest problems facing his agency, he replied: "processing, processing and processing".[42]

Early processing involved considerable effort in "cleaning up" the collected raw material but modern communication methods have evolved exponentially, and processing is now an integral part of the Intelligence process. Processing generally covers the work needed to turn information into something that can be understood by humans and this can include stages such as decrypting, machine processing of text, the conversion of audio files, decompressing of files and many more similar techniques.

EVALUATION

After the US-led invasion of Iraq in 2003, various governments launched inquiries to examine areas such as the decision-making process which led to the invasion, the intelligence upon which such decisions were made, and similar questions.[43] Evaluation has been defined by Harfield as that which asks "to what extent can we believe each different piece of information before us?[44] The faith invested in each individual item of information determines the influence it exerts in the overall interpretation of all the information available". The Butler report, took a deeper approach to evaluation, explaining what was required of analysts working in the Intelligence community, when they were carrying out this function:

362   P. BURKE

The validation of a reporting chain requires both care and time, and can generally only be conducted by the agency responsible for collection. The process
is informed by the operational side of the agency, but must include a separate
auditing element, which can consider cases objectively and quite apart from
their apparent Intelligence value. Has the informant been properly quoted, all
the way along the chain? Does he have credible access to the facts he claims
to know? Does he have the right knowledge to understand what he claims to
be reporting? Could he be under opposition control, or be being fed information? Is he fabricating? Can the bona fides, activities, movements or locations
attributed to those involved in acquiring or transmitting a report be checked?
Do we understand the motivations of those involved, their private agenda, and
hence the way in which their reports may be influenced by a desire to please
or impress? How powerful is a wish for (in particular) financial reward? What,
if any, distorting effect might such factors exert? Is there – at any stage – a
deliberate intention to deceive? Generally speaking, the extent and depth of
validation required will depend on the Counter-Intelligence sophistication of
the target, although the complexity of the operational situation will affect the
possibility of confusion, misrepresentation or deception.[45]

Butler's list is certainly not an exhaustive one but provides an excellent view
of some of the processes that might take place during the evaluation of Intelligence or raw information. Omand agrees with this, adding that "every kind
of Intelligence needs validation".[46]

DISSEMINATION

At the end of the cycle or process, the desired output is some kind of report
or update which is of use to the end-user or customer. This can be as brief as
a one-line report that a target has been identified entering a building, which
may be the final piece necessary to allow an armed unit to conduct an armed
operation to detain the target. The output can also run to several thousand
pages and require regular updating, especially if the subject of the report is
a country or a large, well-organised terrorist group. Some reports will be a
single source, such as imagery of a new missile launch facility, against which
no other collection methods can be deployed. Other reports will be multi-
source or all-source, and will therefore be a synthesis of reports from different
agencies, possibly even from different partnering countries.

Formal reports, especially those which are destined for customers outside
of the producing agency, often include feedback mechanisms which solicit the
reader to assess the effectiveness, usefulness, accuracy, timeliness and other
similar criteria. Such mechanisms can be beneficial in helping an agency to
streamline its efforts along lines of customer requirements.[47] Reports are
usually subject to some kind of control mechanism to protect the sensitivity
of the Intelligence and this is particularly important in counter-terrorism. The
basic premise of this protection used to be the "need to know" principle but
this has been modified in various ways, so that in the UK, for example, the

currently expanded principle is now "need to know, need to hold, need to share".[48] A useful list of what government customers could ideally expect from an Intelligence report was provided by Australia's "Flood Report" (2004, p. 7) which provided the following points:

1. Warning, notably of terrorist plans, but also of potential conflicts, uprisings and coups
2. Understanding of the regional and international environment with which decision makers will need to grapple
3. Knowledge of the military capabilities and intentions of potential adversaries, a vital ingredient in defence procurement and preparedness
4. Support for military operations, minimising casualties and improving the environment for operational success
5. Support for an active and ambitious foreign, trade and defence policy
6. And beyond these vital roles of Intelligence in providing information, modern Intelligence can be a more active tool of government–disrupting the plans of adversaries, influencing the policies of key foreign actors and contributing to modern electronic warfare.[49]

The US Joint Chiefs of Staff has a list of eight "tenets of Intelligence" considered important for the dissemination of Intelligence reporting.[50] These factors state that an Intelligence report ought to be: timely; anticipatory; complete; usable; accurate; relevant; objective; available. All of these factors are especially relevant in counter-terrorism reporting, where operational decisions often need to be made with an incomplete picture, in order to preserve public safety.

Dissemination, especially of secret and top secret Intelligence, has suffered from a common problem across many, if not all, Intelligence agencies–the reluctance to release a report to end-users who need it, mainly because of worries about the material being too highly classified. Aid and Weibes provide a number of examples, such as US fighter pilots not being provided with "excruciatingly detailed and accurate" Intelligence reports on North Vietnamese fighter activity, because the US pilots did not have the necessary security clearance to read the reports.[51] There was a fundamental shift in policy just before the 1990–1991 allied invasion of Iraq, in which the concept of "support to the warfighter" was pushed from the top down. Initially beginning with the US and the UK, the practice is now far more commonplace.[52] This policy rejects the notion that highly classified Intelligence such as TOP SECRET material cannot be safely sanitised and passed to lower levels. While the sanitisation process had existed previously, the new policy forced Intelligence managers to consider their reporting from a new perspective, asking themselves what parts of the report could be released at the lowest possible classification.

Intelligence Gaps and Failures

The Intelligence process suffers from failures, like any other process. The discussion about Intelligence failures in the global media greatly increased in prominence, after the 2003 invasion of Iraq. Intelligence failures are sometimes confused with Intelligence gaps, but there is a clear distinction between the two. The CIA has defined an Intelligence failure as "systemic organizational surprise resulting from incorrect, missing, discarded, or inadequate hypotheses". The inclusion of "organizational surprise" is essential for the sense of a failure to be understood, as it highlights that the agency could have, or should have, been able to prevent such a surprise from happening. Marenic & Thornton describe some of the difficulties encountered by the Intelligence agencies, which can lead to an Intelligence failure, such as a high-value target (HVT) being located, but having moved locations by the time a capture-or-kill operation is launched.[53] The authors consider that a worse type of failure is one wherein "poor processes and avoidable oversight" result in the collected and available Intelligence not being passed on to the customers who require it. They link the need for timely and accurate reporting to the building and development of inter-agency trust, an essential concept for a truly joint Intelligence process.[54]

Intelligence failures can also occur within terrorist groups themselves. Ilardi cites a Volunteer in the Irish Republican Army (IRA) recounting that an Intelligence failure for the IRA would have included "an operation in which innocent bystanders were killed", as this would have resulted in isolation from, and condemnation by, the Nationalist community in Northern Ireland.[55] Aldrich describes the period following the end of the Cold War, in which US and European Intelligence agencies underwent seismic changes in areas such as the imposition of new legislative frameworks, a deeper embracing of human rights and the placing of several agencies on a statutory footing for the first time.[56] In the US in particular, HUMINT as a discipline was curtailed by a much more risk-averse culture in Washington and the ability to recruit, train and run human sources became much more difficult, something which Aldrich considers amounts to an Intelligence failure in itself.

Lowenthal analysed ten case studies often described as failures, examining factors such as the collection, evaluation/analysis, production and dissemination of the Intelligence relevant to the case, and finally assessing the impact on the national interest of the US.[57] The impact on US national security, from the Japanese attack on Pearl Harbor, he assesses to be high, as this failure made the difference between war and peace. Similarly, the Tet offensive by North Vietnamese and Viet Cong troops in 1968 resulted in insufficient warnings given to US troops, which in turn led to insufficient preparations made for an impending offensive against the US. The impact of this on US national security was a further reduction of domestic US support for the Vietnam war and reduced morale, for the US troops fighting the war and for the US public back home. Marrin tempers the point somewhat by noting that most instances of so-called failure "do not lead to direct negative consequences for the United States, simply because most daily foreign policy decisions to not reflect the use of—or defense against—an application of power".[58] Ultimately, however, as Richard K. Betts once said, intelligence failures are not just inevitable, they are also natural.[59]

POLITICISATION OF INTELLIGENCE

The realm of Intelligence failures leads us neatly into the topic of the politicisation of Intelligence. Mark Pythian takes a different approach to intelligence failures, examining the relationship between the Intelligence analyst and the policymaker, and considers some of the opposing arguments.[60] One position is that the Intelligence community exists to serve the interests of policymakers, and this requires a certain closeness between both parties. An opposing position is that distance is necessary between policymakers and Intelligence agencies, because such distance reduces the potential for the politicisation of Intelligence. When Intelligence becomes politicised, its impact upon national policy (and national security) can be adverse.

If we accept that the key function of Intelligence is to forewarn and forearm the policymaker, then it follows that the Intelligence community, and in particular the analytical and assessment cohort, must therefore be equally binded to the requirement for them to speak truth unto power. A number of authors, such as Ott and Hulnick,[61] agree upon this core principle that Intelligence should speak truth unto power, with Ott noting that the worth of Intelligence to high-level decision-makers lies largely in "the confidence that the process is not corrupt – that Intelligence collectors and analysts speak truth to power, however unpalatable that might be at any one time".[62] A key question is whether politicians and decision makers want Intelligence-led policy, or policy-led Intelligence. There are considerable risks associated with the second of these options. Gannon's definition of politicisation centres on the *deliberateness* of the Intelligence-shaping to achieve the desired outcome, as he considers it to be "the wilful distortion of analysis to satisfy the demands of Intelligence bosses or policymakers".[63] This deliberate shaping of Intelligence to fit a desired policy or outcome can result in an expansion of politicisation and have negative impacts on national security. Oversight, accountability, transparency and review all have a part to play in ensuring that this does not happen.[64] Apart from the risks of a policy being derailed due to it being based upon an altered Intelligence product, such a tactic also risks damaging the relationship of trust between the State and its organs on the one hand, and the body public on the other.

Marrin coins an interesting concept with regard to politicisiation, something he describes as "Intelligence to please", which he sees as happening either when truth is distorted as a result of political pressure, or where there is a desire to court favour with the powerbroking circle.[65] Hastedt[66] considers politicisation of Intelligence to have two strategies, soft and hard, which he derives largely from Nye's concepts of soft and hard power.[67] He analyses several historical US cases of politicisation, such as the "Bomber Gap" from 1954–1960, the "Missile Gap" (including the Soviet launch of the SPUTNIK satellite in 1957), the assessment of North Vietnamese and Viet Cong order of battle (1962–1967) during the Vietnam War, and the 2003 US invasion of Iraq. The types of politicisation varied, as did the impacts which ranged from pushing an agenda to increase budget spending on more aircraft (the "Bomber Gap") through to the problematic invasion of another country (the 2003 Iraq War).[68]

In 2007, Paul Pillar, a former Deputy Director of the CIA Counter-Terrorism Centre, wrote in an article in the *Washington Post* that:

> problems with the policy process (or rather, the lack of a process)…went beyond the (George W. Bush) administration's manipulation of intelligence on weapon programmes and terrorist relationships…the administration so successfully shaped the policy question around its chosen selling points involving these two issues that what passed for a national debate gave little attention to important questions about the likely nature and consequences of a war.[69]

Pillar's *ex post* assessment is lent additional credence by the *ex ante* "Downing Street memo", a record of the attendance of the Director of the UK's Secret Intelligence Service (SIS, also referred to as MI6) at a meeting with then US President George W. Bush and his advisers. The Director "…reported on his recent talks in Washington. There was a perceptible shift in attitude. Military action was now seen as inevitable. Bush wanted to remove Saddam, through military action, justified by the conjunction of terrorism and WMD. But the intelligence and facts were being fixed around the policy".[70]

Conclusion

Intelligence underpins a state's national security, regardless of how that state may definite its security. The validity and/or utility of an Intelligence model, in particular a cyclical one, may be subject to debate but without a process or model, the Intelligence process is unlikely to be successful. The stages of such a process and their cyclical order, as described in this chapter, are not meant to provide a fixed blueprint for an Intelligence process. Rather they are to give some flavour of the components of various models, and to explain how the parts work individually and collectively to produce an end-product of Intelligence for the consumer and/or policymaker. The operational costs (and potential benefits) of some of the sources and methods described here vary tremendously, from tens of dollars for the routine payment of a human source, to hundreds of millions for a space-based satellite. All of these sources and their sub-categories can contribute to the production of all-source Intelligence fusion.

Challenges such as Intelligence gaps, Intelligence failures and various forms of politicisation, both intended and unintended, will continue to throw spanners into the works and half the challenge is identifying them. The other half, of course, is fixing them. The uncertainty of the first two decades of the twenty-first century, coupled with the increased vista of threat vectors, means that it is now more important than ever that accurate, timely and actionable Intelligence is made available to policymakers. Such Intelligence should help to reduce the ambiguity and allow policymakers to at least be better informed, prior to making a decision.

Acknowledgements I would like to thank the following funders who provided the resources that made this work possible: European Research council (ERC) Advanced Grant Research Project: Global Terrorism and Collective Moral Responsibility—Redesigning Military, Police and Intelligence Institutions in Liberal Democracies, and an Australia Research Council Discovery grant, DP180103439 Intelligence And National Security: Ethics, Efficacy and Accountability.

NOTES

1. Burke, P. (2014). *The Double-Edged Sword: How Terrorists Collect and Use Intelligence in their Attack Planning.* Transport Security Conference, London, 25.
2. Davies, P. H. J. (2002). Ideas of Intelligence: Divergent National Concepts and Institutions. *Harvard International Review*, 24 (3), 4.
3. Burke, J. (2004). *Al Qaeda: The True Story of Radical Islam.* London: Penguin Books, 22.
4. Brown, H. (1983). *Thinking about U.S. National Security.* Boulder, CO: Westview, 4.
5. Omand, D. (2010) *Securing the State.* 1st edn. London: Hurst, 22. Emphasis in the original.
6. Omand, D. and Pythian, M. (2018). *Principled Spying: The Ethics of Secret Intelligence, Principled Spying: The Ethics of Secret Intelligence.* Oxford: Oxford University Press, 10.
7. CIA. (2020). *The Intelligence Cycle—Central Intelligence Agency, CIA Official Website.* Available at: https://www.cia.gov/the-intelligence-cycle.html. (Accessed: 30 June 2020).
8. Compare, for example, the US Army Intelligence cycle of 2010 (HQ Department of the Army, 2010) to the 2013 version (Joint Chiefs of Staff, 2013, secs I-1.3).
9. National Policing Improvement Agency. (2008). *Practice Advice on Analysis.* Wyboston, 11.
10. Sheptycki, J. (2004). Organisational Pathologies in Police Intelligence Systems: Some Contributions to the Lexicon of Intelligence-Led Policing. *European Journal of Criminology*, 1 (3), 319 and Burke, P. (2013). *Fit to Fight or Unfit for Purpose? A Review of the Effectiveness of the Intelligence Cycle in UK Counter-Terrorism, 2003–2013.* London Metropolitan University, 254.
11. See Schroeder, T. L. (1983). *Intelligence Specialist 3&2, Naval Education and Training Program Development Center.* University of Minnesota, 2–28.

12. See: Home Office. (2018). *CONTEST 2018: The United Kingdom's Strategy for Countering Terrorism*. London: HMSO; Home Office. (2018) *Covert Human Intelligence Sources: Revised Code of Practice (August 2018)*. London: HMSO, 50; and Harfield, K. and Harfield, C. (2012). *Covert Investigation*. 3rd edn. Oxford: Oxford University Press, 68–72.
13. Lowenthal, M. (2003). *Intelligence: From Secrets to Policy*. 3rd edn. Washington, D.C.: CQ Press, 91.
14. Burke. (2013). *Fit to Fight*, 203.
15. Lowenthal, M. M. (2016). *Intelligence: From Secrets to Policy*. Los Angeles: CQ Press, 143–144.
16. See: Department of the Army. (1994). *FM 34–2: Collection Management And Synchronization Planning*. Washington, D.C, Chapter 3.
17. See: Lowenthal. (2016). *Intelligence: From Secrets to Policy*; Treverton, G. F. (2001). *Reshaping National Intelligence for an Age of Information*. Cambridge: Cambridge University Press; and Frini, A. (2011). Intelligence Cycle Models–Canada. In *16th ICCRTS "Collective C2 in Multinational Civil-Military Operations"*, 6.
18. ACPO. (2006). *Major Incident Analysis Manual (Revised Edition 2006)*. Wyboston, 66.
19. Aid, M. M. (2009). All Glory is Fleeting: Sigint and the Fight Against International Terrorism. In Andrew, C., Aldrich, R. J., and Wark, W. K. (Eds.) *Secret Intelligence: A Reader* (pp. 40–77) 1st edn. Oxford: Routledge.
20. Richelson, J. T. (2008). *The US Intelligence Community*. Boulder, CO: Westview Press.
21. Dover, R. and Goodman, M. S. (Eds.) (2011). *Learning from the Secret Past: Cases in British Intelligence History*. Georgetown: Georgetown University Press.
22. Pfluke, C. (2019). A History of the Five Eyes Alliance: Possibility for Reform and Additions. *Comparative Strategy*, 38 (4), 302.
23. See for example: Solove, D. (2007). 'I've Got Nothing to Hide'and Other Misunderstandings of Privacy. *San Diego Law Review* (May), 745–772; and Anderson, D. (2015). *A Question of Trust: Report of the Investigatory Powers Review*. London.
24. Aid, M. M. (2000). The Time of Troubles: The US National Security Agency in the Twenty-First Century. *Intelligence and National Security*, 15 (3), 4.
25. Shane, S. (2015). Documents on 2012 Drone Strike Detail How Terrorists Are Targeted. *New York Times*, 25 June, https://www.nytimes.com/2015/06/25/world/middleeast/us-drone-strike-said-to-kill-doctor-trying-to-implant-bombs.html. (Accessed: 1 July 2020).
26. Joint Chiefs of Staff. (2014). *JP 1–02 Department of Defense Dictionary of Military and Associated Terms*, JP 1–02, 44.
27. Sterling, C. H. (2008). *Military Communications: From Ancient Times to the Twenty-First Century*. ABC-CLIO, 96–98.
28. Jacobs, F. (2015). *Some Bits from the NSA COMSEC Guide, Brain Overflow Website*. Available at: https://www.fredericjacobs.com/blog/2015/12/18/COMSEC/. (Accessed: 1 July 2020).
29. Lieber, D., Pop, V. and McMillan, Ro. (2020). Police Tracked a Terror Suspect—Until His Phone Went Dark After a Facebook Warning. *Wall Street Journal*, 2 January, https://www.wsj.com/articles/police-tracked-a-terror-suspectuntil-his-phone-went-dark-after-a-facebook-warning-11577996973.

30. George, R. Z. (2020) *Intelligence in the National Security Enterprise: an Introduction*. Washington D.C: Georgetown University Press, 150.
31. Ibid, 151.
32. See: Home Office. (2018). *Covert Human Intelligence Sources*; and Home Office. (2013). *Regulation of Investigatory Powers Act (RIPA) 2000 guidance*. London: HMSO.
33. Joint Chiefs of Staff. (2013). *JP 2–0 Joint Intelligence*. 22 October, 7–2 to 7–4, https://www.jcs.mil/Portals/36/Documents/Doctrine/pubs/jp2_0.pdf.
34. British Army (2009) *Army Field Manual Countering Insurgency. Volume 1—Part 10*, 5–9.http://news.bbc.co.uk/2/shared/bsp/hi/pdfs/16_11_09_army_manual.pdf.
35. US Joint Chiefs of Staff. (2012). *JP 2–03 Geospatial Intelligence in Joint Operations*. Washington D.C, I–2.
36. See: Coutts, R. and Selby, H. (2011). Safe and Unsafe Use of Mobile Phone Evidence. In *Public Defenders Criminal Law Conference 2009*, 1–10; O'Neill, S. (2003). Jessica's Mobile 'is Vital Clue to Murder'. *Daily Telegraph*, https://www.telegraph.co.uk/news/uknews/1446018/Jessicas-mobile-is-vital-clue-to-murder.html; and BBC. (2003). Soham Trial: 'Crucial' Phone Evidence. *BBC News*. Available at: http://news.bbc.co.uk/2/hi/uk_news/england/cambridgeshire/3246111.stm.
37. Hulnick, A. S. (1999). *Fixing the Spy Machine: Preparing American Intelligence for the Twenty-First Century*. Westport, CT: Praeger, 40–41.
38. Mercado, S. (2009). A Venerable Source in a New Era: Sailing the Sea of OSINT in the Information Age. In Aldrich, R. J., Andrew, C. M., and Wark, W. K. (Eds.) *Secret Intelligence: A Reader* (p. 90) 1st edn. Oxford: Routledge.
39. Gentry, J. A. (1993). *Lost Promise: How CIA Analysis Misserves the Nation* 1st edn. Washington, D.C.: University Press of America, 207.
40. Lowenthal. (2003). *Intelligence: From Secrets to Policy*, 96.
41. Lefebvre, S. (2004). A look at intelligence analysis. *International Journal of Intelligence and Counterintelligence*, 17 (2), 11.
42. Johnson, L. K. (2006). A Framework for Strengthening U.S. Intelligence. *Yale Journal of International Affairs* (Winter–Spring), 120.
43. See: Butler, R. (2004). *Review of Intelligence on Weapons of Mass Destruction*. 1st edn. London: The Stationery Office; Flood, P. (2004). *Report of the Inquiry into Australian Intelligence Agencies (Flood Report)*. Canberra: Government of Australia; and Kean, T. H. et al. (2004). *The 9/11 Comisssion Report*. Washington DC: US Government Printing Office, https://www.9-11commission.gov/report/911Report.pdf.
44. Harfield, C. and Harfield, K. (2008). *Intelligence: Investigation, Community and Partnership*. 1st edn. Oxford: Oxford University Press, 65.
45. Butler. (2004). *Review of Intelligence on Weapons of Mass Destruction*, Sect. 29.
46. Omand. (2010). Securing the State, 140.
47. CIA. (2007). *US Central Intelligence Agency (CIA) Handbook—Strategic Information, Activities and Regulations*. Washington DC: International Business Publications, 113.
48. Cabinet Office. (2011). *HMG Security Policy, Official Guidelines*.
49. Flood. (2004). *Report of the Inquiry into Australian Intelligence Agencies*, 7.
50. Joint Chiefs of Staff. (2013). *JP 2–0 Joint Intelligence*, chaps II-6 to II-8.
51. Aid, M. M. and Wiebes, C. (Eds.) (2013). *Secrets of Signals Intelligence During the Cold War: From Cold War to Globalization*. Oxford: Routledge, 12–13.

52. Burke. 2013. *Fit to Fight,* 67. For the earliest mention that the author has been able to trace however see: Ross, W. A. (1994). Space Support to the Warfighter. *Military Intelligence Professional Bulletin,* (January–March), 23–25.
53. Thornton, K. & Marenic, T. (2007). *Intelligence Dissemination to the Warfighter.* Monterrey, CA: Naval Postgraduate School, 19 http://citeseerx.ist.psu.edu/viewdoc/download?doi=10.1.1.902.2600&rep=rep1&type=pdf.
54. Ibid, 20.
55. Ilardi, G. J. (2010). IRA Operational Intelligence: The Heartbeat of the War. *Small Wars & Insurgencies,* 21 (2), 349.
56. Aldrich, R. J. (2009). Global Intelligence Co-Operation Versus Accountability: New Facets to an Old Problem. *Intelligence and National Security,* 24 (1), 32.
57. Lowenthal, M. M. (1985). The Burdensome Concept of Failure. *Intelligence: Policy and Process.* Boulder: Westview Press, 43–56.
58. Marrin, S. (2013). Revisiting Intelligence and Policy: Problems with Politicization and Receptivity. *Intelligence and National Security,* 28 (1), 657.
59. Betts, R. K. (1978). Analysis, War, and Decision: Why Intelligence Failures Are inevitable. *World Politics,* 31 (1), 54.
60. Phythian, M. (2009). Intelligence Analysis Today and Tomorrow. *Security Challenges,* 5 (1), 77.
61. See Hulnick, A. S. (2007). What's Wrong With the Intelligence Cycle? In Johnson, L. K. (Ed.) *Strategic Intelligence: Understanding the Hidden Side of Government.* Westport: Praeger; and Ott, M. (2003). Partisanship and the Decline of Intelligence Oversight. *International Journal of Intelligence and CounterIntelligence,* 16 (1), 69–94.
62. Ott. (2003). Partisanship and the Decline of Intelligence Oversight, 82.
63. Gannon, J. C. (2008). Managing Analysis in the Information Age. In George, R. Z. and Bruce, J. B. (Eds.) *Analyzing Intelligence: Origins, Obstacles and Innovations.* 1st edn. Washington DC: Georgetown University Press, 221–222.
64. Lester, G. (2015) *When Should State Secrets Stay Secret?* Cambridge: Cambridge University Press.
65. Marrin, S. (2013). Rethinking Analytic Politicization. *Intelligence and National Security,* 28 (1), 32.
66. Hastedt, G. (2013). The Politics of Intelligence and the Politicization of Intelligence: The American Experience. *Intelligence and National Security,* 28 (1), 10.
67. Nye, J. S. (2004). *Soft Power: The Means to Success in World Politics.* New York: Public Affairs, 5–6.
68. Hastedt. (2013). The Politics of Intelligence and the Politicization of Intelligence, 16–27.
69. Pillar, P. (2007). What to Ask Before the Next War. *Washington Post,* 4 February, https://www.washingtonpost.com/wpdyn/content/article/2007/02/02/AR2007020201551_pf.html.
70. Rycroft, M. (2002). *The Secret Downing Street Memo.* Washington D: National Security Arhive, George Washington University, 2, https://nsarchive2.gwu.edu/NSAEBB/NSAEBB328/II-Doc14.pdf.

CHAPTER 16

Machine Learning, Mass Surveillance, and National Security: Data, Efficacy, and Meaningful Human Control

Scott Robbins

INTRODUCTION

Machine learning (ML) is being promoted as a balm to fix nearly all of the world's problems. It purportedly will help us find love, find and cure diseases, flag fake news and propaganda, defeat hackers, and even prevent terrorism. In many domains (e.g., intelligence, policing, healthcare, etc.), the problem was having a lack of data. Now there is simply too much data—so much that it cannot reasonably be processed by human beings in a time frame that would be helpful. The speed and predictive power of ML are a natural fit for this problem.

The context of bulk data collection for national security presents us with serious concerns—both regarding its ethical acceptability as well as its efficacy. ML has been proposed to help with both of these. Regarding its acceptability in liberal democracies, advocates of ML hope to reduce violations of privacy by reducing the amount of data that actual humans will look at. The idea being that algorithms going through your data does not constitute a privacy violation. Regarding its efficacy, advocates of ML claim that these algorithms will enhance the intelligence community's ability to: collect relevant data, detect suspicious behavior, and predict terrorist attacks.

If true, this would indeed be a dramatic achievement. However, many pitfalls await national security practitioners if and when they adopt ML algorithms for the collection and analysis of bulk data. The first set of pitfalls

S. Robbins (✉)
Bonn University, Bonn, Germany
e-mail: sarobbins@protonmail.com

© The Author(s), under exclusive license to Springer Nature Switzerland AG 2022
M. Clarke et al. (eds.), *The Palgrave Handbook of National Security*,
https://doi.org/10.1007/978-3-030-53494-3_16

371

concerns the *data* that is used to train these algorithms. This data can come from the surveillance apparatus (including bulk data collection), governmental and public records, and third-party technology companies. As will be shown below, these sources face concerns of dual-use of the data, the legitimacy of the source itself, and how securely it holds the data. Moreover, we must ask why is it justified to use a particular dataset to train an algorithm for surveillance purposes? We will see that while it is possible to justify some bulk collection, this justification precludes the use of ML for such collection. Finally, for the data to be useful for ML, it must be labeled. This labeling can reinforce biases of the past and cause disparate impacts for different groups of people.

Once the ML algorithms are trained, another set of issues arise concerning its *efficacy*; namely, how can we be sure that these algorithms will be better than the processes that preceded them? Biased or unrepresentative training data can lead to ineffective algorithms. An algorithm that is biased toward labeling those with darker skin as suspicious could miss suspicious people with lighter skin—reducing its effectiveness by increasing false-positives and false-negatives. Further, depending upon what the ML algorithm is used to look for, there may not be enough data to train it. Algorithms looking for so-called lone wolf terrorists, for example, would be difficult to train because there are very few such attacks—and even fewer data with which to train an algorithm.

Even after we have an effective, well-trained algorithm using responsibly acquired training data there is the important issue of *meaningful human control*. That is, having some human who will be responsible and accountable for the algorithm's decisions. In morally salient contexts, like surveillance and policing clarity regarding responsibility and accountability are paramount. ML algorithms are opaque concerning the reasoning that led it to deliver a particular output. This makes it even more difficult for humans to meaningfully have control over them. The last section addresses the solutions currently on offer for this problem of human control.

Machine Learning for Mass Surveillance

Before we examine the many pitfalls awaiting those developing and implementing machine learning solutions for surveillance, we need a snapshot of what ML is already being used for in the national security context. Below is a non-exhaustive list of ML solutions for a variety of tasks. Many are already being used in the field as I write this.

Facial Recognition / Smart Surveillance Cameras

So-called smart surveillance, like CCTV cameras before it, is on its way to becoming ubiquitous. We hear about many of its applications in China; however, tools for smart surveillance are being marketed to police departments and intelligence agencies in the west as well as to general consumers.[1] These new ML enhanced cameras can, in real-time, detect suspicious behavior, the faces of criminals, license plates, falls, violence, etc. In a nutshell, these smart surveillance cameras can perform object recognition in real-time—tracking object movements and classify behavior.

Governments are turning to such technologies to fight crime, counterterrorism, and to facilitate 'public opinion guidance.' The latter phrase is used by the Chinese government to monitor dissent. A *New York Times* investigation revealed that 18 governments are using technology developed to conduct mass surveillance in China.[2] It is not merely institutions of the state using these cameras. Cameras like these are being used by private entities as well as individual consumers to monitor their businesses and homes.

Voice Recognition

Most of us are now able to command our smartphones via digital assistants like Siri and Google Assistant. Our smartphones (and other smart devices like Amazon's Alexa or Google Home) can take commands because ML algorithms are trained to understand speech. Now speech recognition is being taken a step further. Not only can it convert speech to text (which allows it to understand commands), but it can identify who is speaking. Amazon's Alexa, for example, can give personalized responses based on who is talking to it. Alexa can do this because ML can match audio input to a specific person.

The possibilities of using this for surveillance are huge. Searching on a database of recorded phone calls by a specific voice would be extremely helpful. When a known terrorist's voice is 'heard' by the ML algorithm, an alarm could alert the authorities. The European Union (EU) recently completed a project called the Speaker Identification Integrated Project (SIIP). The project hoped to identify criminals and terrorists from their voices. The project took audio from social media posts, internet websites, and lawfully[3] intercepted communications data. In addition to being able to identify people based on voice, the system 'identify gender, age, language and accent, and detect voice cloning.'[4] The United States' National Security Agency (NSA) also has a voice identification system that can identify terrorists, criminals, potential whistleblowers, etc. Analysts describe the system as 'Google for voice.' The NSA 'could use keywords and "selectors" to search, read, and index recordings that would have otherwise required an infinite number of human listeners to listen to them.'[5]

Attack Prediction

Using machine learning to predict the details of a terrorist attack before it occurs would help national and local officials divert resources, prepare, and hopefully prevent the attack. Using data from past terrorist attacks, or communications data leading up to such attacks, could allow algorithms to tell us something about a future attack. Police are using similar algorithms to predict crime hotspots and criminals with what is now called 'predictive policing.'

While there is much debate surrounding the ethics and efficacy regarding the use of such algorithms, adoption amongst police departments is increasing.[6] Examples include PredPol and Palantir. PredPol advertises their use of machine learning in the products directed toward police departments while Palantir is secretive about their specific techniques.

Others have used sentiment analysis on social networking sites like Twitter to predict who potential terrorists are. For example, Aizan and Aziz use the sentiments toward words associated with terrorism like 'bomb,' 'ISIS,' 'Muslim,' etc., to update an overall sentiment toward terrorism which is based on historical sentiments to those same keywords.[7] The hope is that those with a more positive overall sentiment toward terrorism (reduced to the keywords they chose as being associated with terrorism) are more likely to commit terrorist attacks.

Financial Fraud

When many banks receive a deposit above a particular threshold, say over $10,000 in cash, they are required to submit a Suspicious Activity Report (SAR). There is widespread agreement that an amount of $10,000 or above in cash is suspicious. It is hoped that these SARs will help combat the financing and profit of illegal activities. Of course, how to classify a transaction or a set of transactions as 'suspicious' is in many cases subjective. It differs from one institution to another and those trying to evade scrutiny change their behavior to evade detection. As criminal financial activity becomes more sophisticated, the ability of financial institutions to detect it decreases. The patterns may be simply too difficult for humans to detect.

Algorithms have long aided financial institutions with the identification of suspicious activity; however, until recently these algorithms used 'good old fashioned AI' (GOFAI) in the form of if–then statements (see above). GOFAI in its simplest form is a decision tree that automates previously decided upon human reasoning. A human could follow the same decision tree to reach the same output in a GOFAI application. ML, on the other hand, is being deployed to detect suspicious patterns that a human could not. The Israeli company ThetaRay, for example, is one of many companies now offering machine learning products to fight terrorists and organized crime financing and money laundering. They use unsupervised machine learning to identify behavior that was heretofore unknown to be associated with money laundering. This is significant as machine learning is generally used to detect patterns based on past known events. For example, there may be a specific set of transactions that are associated with money laundering. Machine learning might detect that pattern and then notify banks when similar patterns are detected in the future. ThetaRay goes beyond this to highlight previously unknown patterns of activity that deviate from the norm—which may detect new money laundering techniques before they are successful.

Propaganda on Social Media

The spread of propaganda on social media platforms is receiving a lot of attention from the media (see, e.g., Overly 2017). Terrorist organizations use it to spread misinformation and recruit new members. Mass shooters are posting live feeds of them killing people indiscriminately. Platforms like YouTube and Facebook are consistently criticized for not taking any actions for preventing the spread of these messages. They are now turning to ML to take down propaganda as soon as it is uploaded.

The British home office is using ML to detect ISIS propaganda videos. They claim that the algorithm detects 94% (recall) with 99.995% accuracy (precision). The algorithm was trained on over 1000 propaganda videos.[8] Facebook claims that 99% of Al Qaeda and ISIS posts are detected by machine learning before a user flags the post.[9] Google, in a blog post, says that it will use its 'most advanced machine learning research to train new "content classifiers" to help us more quickly identify and remove extremist and terrorism-related content.'[10]

Societal Implications of the Training Data

The first set of issues one faces concerning any machine learning application stems from the data that is used to train the algorithm. The use of machine learning in highly morally significant contexts—national security applications like policing, counter-terrorism, and intelligence—amplifies these issues. When a local police department purchases machine learning powered software enabling some form of 'smart' surveillance they should understand that there are significant concerns with that software.[11] The source of that data may be using the data for other purposes (e.g., targeted advertising), may be illegitimate when it comes to state surveillance, and may not have the security; citizens often expect when it comes to sensitive personal data.

The Source

If you were to find out that your local police department was using facial recognition to run smart surveillance in your neighborhood, you would be justifiably concerned. However, if you found out that the algorithm running facial recognition was trained on billions of images scraped from the internet—including social media, personal websites, and YouTube—you might be angry. And anger is what many felt when they heard about ClearView AI—a company that trained their ML algorithm on exactly that—and works with law enforcement around the world.[12] Three general issues can arise due to the source of training data for machine learning algorithms: legitimacy, dual-use, and data security. Legitimacy refers to the concern that it may be unjustified to receive and use data from a particular source. It would be unjustified, for example, if police officers went door to door and scanned your photo albums to collect data for their new machine learning algorithms because private citizens' homes are an illegitimate source for such data. Even if one were to commit a crime resulting in a search warrant for their home—it may be illegitimate to collect and use anything other than evidence relevant to the crime at hand.

How can we determine if a source is legitimate? There are a few variables that can help. The first variable is what exactly the collected data will be used for. If the data is connected to a specific algorithm with a specific function that we would (if asked) consent to, then the source may be legitimate. For example, if police had evidence that a serial killer worked in your office building, then work emails, browsing histories, and other network data may be collected justifiably. That is, your office's network activity is a legitimate source when it comes to the specific function of finding a specific serial killer. On this view, the purposes of the surveillance are necessary aspects of their justification.[13]

The problem with much of what was covered in the first section is that the algorithms that will be trained by the data collected have no such specific purpose. There is no specific person that is trying to be discovered. Furthermore, the uses of these algorithms are not tethered to a narrow set of 'serious' crimes. This makes it difficult to know in advance whether or not using data to build a specific algorithm is justified. Facial recognition algorithms, for example, may be used to ticket jaywalkers. This purpose is not serious enough to justify the collection and use of people's pictures.

The second variable that helps determine source legitimacy is who actually will be collecting the data from this source. It is one thing, for example, for government actors (e.g., police or intelligence agencies) to collect and use this data and quite another for a private company contracting with the government to do so. This is because government actors in liberal democratic countries have accountability mechanisms and oversight, whereby abuse of powers can be uncovered and perpetrators punished.

Dual Use

Dual-use technologies normally refer to technologies that have both military and civilian purposes. Think of a nuclear power plant. The energy it provides is a benefit to society (although there are downsides regarding the storage of nuclear waste). However, a nuclear power plant can also be used to create materials central to nuclear weapons. Data collection for ML algorithms is touted as providing safety (a benefit). However, that same data can be used by the state for harmful purposes. The widespread public acceptance of 'smart' technologies has given the state potential access to more, and new, data. Digital assistances like Alexa and Google Home provide them with voice data. Smart cameras like Amazon's Ring provide video. Online picture storage applications allow them to obtain a database of valuable image data. Smartwatches and smartphones provide location data (i.e., GPS). Social networks can obtain data on our social relations, political beliefs, and mood. While these devices may provide users some convenience in their daily lives, they open up the possibility for widespread surveillance by the state. There have been numerous cases of the state requesting or demanding data from these devices. For example, Amazon was ordered to turn over audio recordings collected by an Amazon Echo device for evidence in a double murder case.[14]

As I write this (May 2020), there is a raging debate regarding COVID-19 contact-tracing smartphone applications. While this technology has been touted as a solution to re-opening countries from their prolonged lockdown,[15] there are fears that the state could also use this technology to track dissident groups and political rivals. To many, the concern that state institutions are collecting and storing your personal data may seem to be rooted in paranoia and would only be a real concern for those who are criminals. However, in many places, such data is used to detect who dissidents and political opponents are. Furthermore, there is a concern that as people come to realize that the authorities could potentially access the data collected about them by technology companies, they will modify their behavior because they are embarrassed by some of the preferences they have or are scared of being put on watch lists by the government. This 'chilling effect' has been little studied; however, it has been shown to cause self-censorship.[16] Those fearful that the government is watching are less likely to express dissent—dissent which is crucial to a functioning democracy.

Legitimacy

Due to the widespread surveillance capitalism apparatus set up by technology companies, it is cause for little surprise that the state makes requests to use the data collected for criminal investigations. Amazon Alexa data has been used to investigate a murder, police are working with Ring to gain access to their doorbell cameras, and Edward Snowden revealed the degree to which intelligence agencies have access to the databases of Apple, Google, Facebook, Microsoft, and others. This creates a concern regarding the legitimacy of these companies to conduct activities normally reserved for the state. Citizens have not consented to a private company like Google to monitor them for criminal activity. In the surveillance and intelligence literature, there is generally a principle (or something like it) of 'legitimate authority' that must be met for an entity to conduct a surveillance or intelligence program.[17] Another approach looks at whether the use of surveillance products is legitimate, based on the justifications for that surveillance.[18]

On this approach, the police and intelligence agencies may be justified in requesting specific data from a technology company that may pertain to a specific investigation. For example, no one would object to the police requesting and obtaining call records from a telecommunications company regarding a suspect who is believed to have committed murder. Data collected by technology companies, therefore, should not be completely off-limits to the authorities. The line is crossed when technology companies are forced to collect and retain data that would not have been collected for purposes other than government surveillance. In other words, if a company does not need a dataset to operate their business (and would likely delete it) then they should be able to do that.

Security

Finally, as private technology companies are increasingly used as sources, collectors, and processors of data, there is an increasing risk of sensitive data being breached by malicious actors. It is one thing for the state to have this data with oversight regarding its safe storage and quite another for a technology company whose primary institutional aim is to maximize profits. For example, a third-party technology company was used to facilitate the monitoring of people and cars (using facial recognition and license plate recognition) passing through certain United States borders. This company was breached resulting in 100,000 records being stolen. The Customs and Border Patrol (CBP) agency is quoted as saying that 'none of their systems were compromised.' In effect, they have passed on the responsibility of safeguarding sensitive data used for the state to a technology company. Their quote makes it appear that the CPB does not see the breach as a failure for them.

This leaves the state in a dilemma. Either they are abnegating responsibility, thereby admitting that their use of a third-party company is illegitimate or they must accept responsibility and be blamed for breaches of security of the third-party technology companies they use. This is important because the state's agreements with third-party technology companies are increasing. Both the National Security Agency (NSA) and the Central Intelligence Agency (CIA) in the US have agreements to store and process data using Amazon Web Services (AWS). The US military, in its defense strategy document, says it will 'will enhance partnerships with U.S. industry to align civilian AI leadership with defense challenges.'[19] It is important that the security of the data involved in these partnerships is strong—and that the state accepts responsibility for said data.

Labeling

Once training data has been sourced and collected responsibly, there are still issues stemming from the labeling of that data. ML algorithms are taught what a cat looks like in a similar way children are taught. They are given many examples of pictures or live images of cats and told that the picture or video contains a cat. After many such examples, the algorithm can reliably classify an image or video as containing a cat or not.

Unfortunately, the labels applied are not always as benign as 'cat' and 'no cat'. Especially when discussing policing and surveillance these labels can be difficult to apply in an objective, fair manner. This then has significant ethical implications in a national security context.[20] If these labels are applied inappropriately, then the algorithm will result in inappropriate future classifications (i.e., 'garbage in garbage out'). A website called ImageNet Roulette 'is meant in part to demonstrate how various kinds of politics propagate through technical systems, often without the creators of those systems even being aware of them.'[21] When you upload a picture to ImageNet Roulette the algorithm detects faces and labels them. The labels are often racist, misogynist, and offensive. Young black males are identified as rapists and offenders, whilst white males are labeled managers and diplomats. What is disturbing is that this website used training data from the dataset which powers many of today's object recognition algorithms. Such applications in a national security context raise serious social, political, and ethical concerns.

Biases of the Past

Some of the biased data out there that can impact mass surveillance are historical criminal justice data. It is no secret that racism and racial profiling were, and still are, driving daily decisions by officers of many police departments. The data that we have regarding criminals, therefore, will be infected with these biases. For example, in criminal sentencing, it has been shown that 'inmates with more Afrocentric features received harsher sentences than those with less Afrocentric features.'[22] Were one to simply use the data from the past for an algorithm designed to make decisions regarding the sentencing of criminals, then the algorithms would simply reproduce the same bias. Indeed, this is what has happened. A report by ProPublica based upon the sentencing of 7000 people arrested in Broward County, Florida, US showed that black defendants were '77 percent more likely to be pegged as at higher risk of committing a future violent crime and 45 percent more likely to be predicted to commit a future crime of any kind.'[23]

Being pegged as higher risk means harsher and longer sentences. This is real-world harm caused by the underappreciated role of training data in ML algorithms. Data will also be needed to train ML algorithms used for mass surveillance. Detecting criminal activity will rely on what has previously been labeled as criminal activity. What data is chosen, and how it gets labeled has a high risk of reinforcing biases of the past—resulting in unjust outcomes for certain groups of people.

Disparate Impact

The above is one form of what is called 'disparate impact.' Disparate impact means that although something results in higher performance overall, the benefits from such performance are unequally distributed amongst different groups. It can also be that the negative side effects disproportionately affect specific groups—harms. With ML past biases in the data is just one of several causes that can result in disparate impact. In some cases, there probably is too little data from a specific group—resulting in the algorithm working poorly for that group. Facial recognition, for example, has been shown to misclassify darker-skinned females the most (up to 34.7 percent). For comparison, the same study showed that lighter-skinned males had a misclassification rate of 0.8 percent.[24] Similar issues with facial recognition have been shown for younger and darker-skinned people in general.[25]

When the United States Transportation Security Administration (TSA) claims that using facial recognition will speed up security lines at airports, it may indeed be true that overall the lines are moving faster. However, this benefit may not be felt by those whose facial recognition technology does not work well on (dark-skinned and female). These left out people will also face closer scrutiny by immigration officials. Facial recognition is just the most discussed and studied form of ML being used for surveillance that could result in a disparate impact. It will be important to make efforts to prevent this, and, most importantly, to check that algorithms being used are not resulting in such effects.

The Effectiveness of ML for Mass Surveillance

Any justification for the use of ML algorithms in mass surveillance will include something about the effectiveness of these algorithms. More specifically, it is a necessary condition for justification that these algorithms be effective. If they are faster and cheaper but are completely ineffective there isn't much to discuss. If facial recognition equipped smart CCTV cameras consistently deliver false positives and fail to provide true-positives, then we don't need to discuss privacy.[26] The case can be made not to use them based on efficacy alone.

This makes efficacy extremely important when it comes to any technology used in morally salient contexts like mass surveillance. ML comes with issues surrounding its efficacy. Any development and use of ML for mass surveillance will have to take such issues into account in order not to waste a lot of time and effort. Furthermore, the use of an ineffective algorithm for mass surveillance means that there is no counterbalance for its harms.

Not Enough Data

Inefficacy in ML can be caused when ML is used to detect something for which there is very little data. For example, there are many proposals to use ML for detecting terrorists. The amount of terrorists in the world is relatively small. Using the high end of the range given by a report by the US state department, we can estimate the total number of terrorists in the world to be about 100,000. That is 0.000014% of the world's population.[27] Detecting terrorists within a specific group is even more difficult if we are forced to break this out by type of terrorist group (e.g., Jihadist vs. Far right). For machine learning algorithms, this is important for the training data set's balance which will, in turn, have implications for the recall and precision of the resulting trained algorithm (see next section).

Trying to train ML algorithms to identify terrorists based on collected data would require that we have many examples that are associated with known terrorists. While there will indeed be some examples, the training data set will be highly imbalanced—meaning that the amount of non-terrorist related data far exceeds the amount of terrorist-related data. The algorithm could achieve a 99% accuracy rate simply by classifying all data as not terrorist-related (because so few data will be associated with terrorism). Imbalanced datasets are a subject of serious ongoing research, but the problem is far from solved.[28]

Precision vs Recall

The precision of an algorithm is measured by the total number of true-positives divided by the total number of true + false positives. If a smart CCTV camera was used to detect theft, for example, the precision rate would indicate the percentage of algorithm classified 'theft' incidents that were incidents of theft. A low precision rate means that many incidents labeled as theft were not theft. The recall rate of an algorithm indicates the total number of true positives divided by the total number of true positives + false negatives. Using the same example, the recall rate would indicate the percentage of actual thefts detected. A low recall rate means that many incidents of theft were not detected.

As can be seen from the description above, both recall and precision are desirable. However, they will always be in tension with one another. Social media platforms have long had to walk this tightrope. As they increase recall there arises an unacceptable list of examples of people's posts being flagged or taken down that should not have been. Journalists writing about terrorism find their posts taken down and their accounts suspended. However, when they turn up the precision to prevent taking down innocent posts, they inevitably miss taking down horrific posts.

Past vs. Future

Criminals are good at changing habits once they realize that the state is using those habits to catch them. When they figure out that cell phones are being monitored, they use 'burner' phones (pre-paid cell phones that are thrown away after a certain amount of use). Terrorists have taken to replacing and trading SIM cards to frustrate the ability to monitor cell phone activity. This cat and mouse game makes the use of ML incredibly difficult as ML is most effective at detecting fixed targets. This is why many headlines are describing the success of ML at games.[29] Games have a clear result in the end—win or lose (maybe draw)—and the rules of the game never change. ML is trained on past data. But in a national security context, the targets are not fixed. Cell-phone use patterns may give away criminal activity—but due to society changing the way communication occurs the patterns of the future will change. For example, many now use messaging apps like WhatsApp instead of text messaging. This drastically changes the patterns of cellphone use amongst not only the general public but of criminals as well. Furthermore, due to security concerns, criminals have further changed their behavior by using security-focused applications like Signal.[30]

An ML algorithm trained on old data will be useless. Now there are specific techniques for evading ML-based detection. For example, it was shown that wearing a sign on your body makes one algorithm not classify you as a person.[31] You can also put dots on your face and wearing specific makeup.[32] An over-reliance on ML can create a situation where criminals avoid detection whilst innocents are constantly surveilled. This is not only ineffective and unethical—as innocents are having their privacy violated without benefit to the state.

MEANINGFUL HUMAN CONTROL OVER ML FOR MASS SURVEILLANCE

When using ML algorithms in morally salient contexts, there is great concern over how to keep human beings accountable and responsible for the algorithm's decisions. For a human to be held accountable and responsible, they must have had some sort of meaningful control over the situation. The concept of meaningful human control gained in importance in the literature regarding autonomous weapons systems.[33] It is now of concern for whenever machines are deployed in morally salient contexts (contexts which could result in harm—broadly construed.[34]

For mass surveillance, we want to make sure that people are not being labeled 'criminals', 'terrorists', 'suspicious', etc., by an algorithm without meaningful human control. This is because being labeled one of those things could have harmful consequences, for example, being placed on a no-fly list. At the very least, it will result in increased surveillance toward such a person and this more targeted surveillance is caused by a process we do not understand. ML algorithms are opaque to their reasoning—that is, it is not clear why a particular decision was reached. Without ML, someone would have to give justification for more intrusive surveillance in the form of features or actions taken by the individual warranting such intrusive surveillance. With ML, one would only be able to point to the result of the algorithm. The issues of bias and efficacy highlighted earlier make such a situation unacceptable as ML may simply be using race, gender, or some other inappropriate correlation to deliver its output. To overcome this problem, there are a few proposals for ensuring that humans have meaningful human control over ML. Here we will highlight the major proposals and their problems.

Veto Power

The simplest and most naïve proposal for establishing meaningful human control over ML is to give a human 'veto' power. That is, to put a human 'on the loop' to allow them to stop or 'veto' the machine's decision. In the surveillance space, this could be a smart CCTV camera deciding that person A has committed theft. A human being could see that the decision had been made and could stop the process that starts as a result of that decision (e.g., authorities stopping and searching the individual). Another version of this (sometimes called human in the loop) requires that the human being consent to the decision made by the algorithm before the process continues.

At first glance, this keeps the human in control. However, as we take a closer look, veto power offers the appearance of human control without anything 'meaningful' about it. When an ML algorithm classifies a person as a terrorist, for example, there could indeed be a person in the loop or on the loop who can overrule that decision. However, on what basis would such an override be made? The algorithm had massive amounts of data at its disposal. Even if there is no evidence confirming the decision by the algorithm, could a human being reasonably say that the person was not a terrorist? ML is powerful in part because it will detect patterns and make associations that are impossible for a human to make. The default option is to confirm the algorithm's output. Without any information, then, the human will simply confirm the decision without any evidence to support their decision.

Furthermore, the person placed in or on the loop will be set up to fall victim to human cognitive biases.[35] The first being automation bias—in which humans fail to look for contradictory information when computers give solutions. When machines are widely used in a specific context to automate decisions, the human beings who previously made those decisions lose things like situational awareness which are necessary to have to make these decisions. This greatly reduces their ability to exercise their veto power.[36] This problem is also associated with confirmation bias—the tendency to look for information that will confirm something rather than contradict it.

Explainability

Another option to establish meaningful human control is to force algorithms to provide explanations for their 'decisions.' The opacity regarding the factors that contributed to a decision by ML makes it difficult to judge whether or not that decision is acceptable or not.[37] There are many research projects devoted to achieving explainable AI (XAI).[38] The idea is that with the decision by the algorithm there would be an accompanying explanation which humans could use to better understand why the algorithm resulted in a particular output. This could better enable someone in or on the loop to determine whether or not that decision was acceptable.

For example, if an algorithm decided that someone was a terrorist and listed the factors to include the height of the person and the color of their skin, a human could determine that this was an unacceptable justification for placing someone on a terrorist watch list and veto the decision. While interesting, XAI falls short in establishing meaningful human control. First, explainable AI is a theoretical idea for which there is no current solution—and is therefore not a real option so far.[39] Second, if we already know the factors which should contribute to morally salient decisions, then it seems we should simply be automating these decisions the old fashioned way.[40] Finally, the power of ML is driven by its opacity. The considerations used by ML to make a decision are incomprehensible to human beings—that is why they can do things we cannot. Restricting its power to only look at human articulable factors would greatly reduce its capability.[41]

Moral Machines

One idea gaining traction recently is to simply delegate moral responsibility to the machines themselves—making human control unnecessary. Research groups around the world have received significant funding to teach autonomous weapons systems ethics.[42] The hope is that ethical machines will not violate liberal democratic values—in this case, values of proportionality, necessity, discrimination, etc. Many others have been working on such endeavors for a long time.[43] There are a host of ethical issues that this idea raises as well as grave concerns over efficacy. If the whole point of machines is to help to achieve our goals and it is conceptually problematic to delegate moral responsibility or agency to them.[44] Machines cannot accept such responsibility even if we try to give it to them—they cannot be punished nor do they 'care' about anything. Their mistakes will be made without feelings necessary for moral responsibility.[45] Giving ethics to machines further complicates what we were trying to solve in the first place: gaining control over these machines. Ethics adds a complex layer to an already complex machine—making them less predictable and therefore more difficult to control.[46]

The most devastating critique is that ethics is not something for which we have a solution. There is widespread disagreement about the list of, and interpretation of, ethical values. Ethics is not like chess where we all agree about what checkmate is. Moral judgments will always be subject to disagreement. The methodology for incorporating ethics into machines, then, will be a highly moral choice. A moral choice without upside according to Van Wynsberghe and Robbins who argue that 'no critical or unique operational function appears to be gained through the endowment of ethical reasoning capabilities into robots' and therefore we should 'simply not do it.'[47]

Conclusion

This paper has highlighted the many ethical and efficacy pitfalls that await those who wish to use ML for national security applications like surveillance. A product powered by ML, when delivered to a state institution, may already have serious baggage due to the training of the algorithm used. The data used to train it could be contaminated with bias, come from a problematic source, and be labeled in ways that diminish its efficacy, and cause certain groups to be disproportionately impacted.

In the context of surveillance, in particular, there are problems with efficacy since there may simply not be enough data to make accurate predictions. Practices surrounding criminal activity change over time—causing ML trained on past data to be useless. Also, the precision/recall value hierarchy cannot be solved. Decisions about this in a surveillance context will always be subject to critical judgment. In light of these issues and the moral salience of the context, human control over these ML algorithms is of the utmost importance. However, the solutions on offer so far are woefully lacking. Veto power offers the veneer of control without anything meaningful. Explainable AI has yet to be developed and may significantly reduce ML's abilities. Moral machines face many ethical issues of their own and simply exacerbate the problem of human control.

This may all seem to be an insurmountable pile of problems for the use of ML for surveillance. However, by acknowledging these possible issues, one can focus on decisions that greatly reduce the possibility of these issues. A police department in Massachusetts, for example, uses speech recognition to allow its officers to write reports and take notes on patrol. This enables them to surveil the area instead of having to have their head down writing. Officers claim that this helps to prevent police ambushes and helps to increase their ability to do their job (Condon 2018).[48] While this solution is not as exciting as those offering to predict crimes, it is greatly beneficial and does not fall victim to the many issues highlighted in this paper. While the focus here has been primarily on surveillance, these problems are common in national security applications of ML. ML is no silver bullet for national security. Treating it like a silver bullet will lead the state into the many pitfalls highlighted in this paper.

Notes

1. See the advertisement for Gorilla's IVAR smart surveillance system for a look at some of the functionality being offered: https://www.gorilla-technology.com/IVAR.
2. Mozur, P. et al. (2019). Made in China, Exported to the World: The Surveillance State. *New York Times*, 24 April, https://www.nytimes.com/2019/04/24/technology/ecuador-surveillance-cameras-police-government.html. Accessed 21 June 2019.
3. Note that lawfully does not mean ethically.

4. Interpol. (2017 July). Speaker Identification Integrated Project (SIIP). https://www.interpol.int/en/Who-we-are/Legal-framework/Information-communications-and-technology-ICT-law-projects/Speaker-Identification-Integrated-Project-SIIP. Accessed 30 June 2019.
5. Kofman, A. (2018). Finding Your Voice: Forget About Siri and Alexa—When It Comes to Voice Identification, the 'NSA Reigns Supreme'. *The Intercept*, 19 January, https://theintercept.com/2018/01/19/voice-recognition-technology-nsa/. Accessed 30 June 2019.
6. Over 60 American police departments use predictive policing algorithms. See The Economist. (2018). How data-driven policing threatens human freedom, 4 June, https://www.economist.com/open-future/2018/06/04/how-data-driven-policing-threatens-human-freedom. Accessed 3 September 2018.
7. Azizan, S. A., & Aziz, I. A. A. (2017). Terrorism detection based on sentiment analysis using machine learning. *Journal of Engineering and Applied Sciences*, 12 (3), 691–698. https://doi.org/10.3923/jeasci.2017.691.698.
8. Home Office. (2018). New technology revealed to help fight terrorist content online. *GOV.UK*. 13 February, https://www.gov.uk/government/news/new-technology-revealed-to-help-fight-terrorist-content-online. Accessed 15 October 2018.
9. Horwitz, J. (2017). Facebook says it can stop the sharing of most terror-related posts within an hour of creation. *Quartz*, 29 November, https://qz.com/1140539/facebook-says-its-able-to-stop-the-sharing-of-most-isis-terror-posts-within-an-hour-of-creation/. Accessed 15 October 2018.
10. Google. (2017). Four steps we're taking today to fight terrorism online, 18 June, https://www.blog.google/around-the-globe/google-europe/four-steps-were-taking-today-fight-online-terror/. Accessed 27 August 2018.
11. See Henschke, A. (2017). *Ethics in an Age of Surveillance: Personal Information and Virtual Identities*. New York: Cambridge University Press.
12. Hill, K. (2020). The Secretive Company That Might End Privacy as We Know It. *New York Times*, 18 January, https://www.nytimes.com/2020/01/18/technology/clearview-privacy-facial-recognition.html. Accessed 26 May 2020.
13. Henschke, A. (2017). *Ethics in an Age of Surveillance*, 245–251.
14. Cuthbertson, A. (2018). Amazon ordered to give Alexa evidence in double murder case. *The Independent*, 14 November, https://www.independent.co.uk/life-style/gadgets-and-tech/news/amazon-echo-alexa-evidence-murder-case-a8633551.html. Accessed 27 June 2019.
15. Though there is little evidence that these contact tracing apps have any benefit. See Vogelstein, F., & Knight, W. (2020). Health Officials Say 'No Thanks' to Contact-Tracing Tech. *Wired*, 8 May, https://www.wired.com/story/health-officials-no-thanks-contact-tracing-tech/. Accessed 26 May 2020.
16. Gao, G. (2015). What Americans think about NSA surveillance, national security and privacy. *Pew Research Center*, 29 May, http://www.pewresearch.org/fact-tank/2015/05/29/what-americans-think-about-nsa-surveillance-national-security-and-privacy/. Accessed 24 April 2017.
17. See for example: Macnish, K. (2014). Just Surveillance? Towards a Normative Theory of Surveillance. *Surveillance & Society*, 12 (1), 142–153.
18. Henschke, A. (2017). *Ethics in an Age of Surveillance*, 253–254.
19. Department of Defense. (2018). SUMMARY OF THE 2018 DEPARTMENT OF DEFENSE ARTIFICIAL INTELLIGENCE STRATEGY. https://media.

defense.gov/2019/Feb/12/2002088963/-1/-1/1/SUMMARY-OF-DOD-AI-STRATEGY.PDF. Accessed 25 June 2019.

20. See Henschke, A. (2019). Information Technologies and Construction of Perpetrator Identities. In S. C. Knittel & Z. J. Goldberg (Eds.), *The Routledge International Handbook of Perpetrator Studies* (pp. 217–227). New York, NY: Routledge.

21. See: https://imagenet-roulette.paglen.com/.

22. See Blair, I. V., Judd, C. M., & Chapleau, K. M. (2004). The Influence of Afrocentric Facial Features in Criminal Sentencing. *Psychological Science*, 15 (10), 674–679. https://doi.org/10.1111/j.0956-7976.2004.00739.x.

23. Angwin, J., & Larson, J. (2016). Machine Bias. *ProPublica*, 23 May, text/html. https://www.propublica.org/article/machine-bias-risk-assessments-in-criminal-sentencing. Accessed 25 June 2019.

24. Buolamwini, J., & Gebru, T. (2018). Gender Shades: Intersectional Accuracy Disparities in Commercial Gender Classification. In *Conference on Fairness, Accountability and Transparency* (pp. 77–91). Presented at the Conference on Fairness, Accountability and Transparency. http://proceedings.mlr.press/v81/buolamwini18a.html. Accessed 25 June 2019.

25. Klare, B. F., Burge, M. J., Klontz, J. C., Bruegge, R. W. V., & Jain, A. K. (2012). Face Recognition Performance: Role of Demographic Information. *IEEE Transactions on Information Forensics and Security*, 7 (6), 1789–1801. https://doi.org/10.1109/TIFS.2012.2214212.

26. For more on false-positives and false-negatives see Henschke (2019). Information Technologies and Construction of Perpetrator Identities.

27. Department of Defense. (2018). SUMMARY OF THE 2018 DEPARTMENT OF DEFENSE ARTIFICIAL INTELLIGENCE STRATEGY.

28. Johnson, J. M., & Khoshgoftaar, T. M. (2019). Survey on deep learning with class imbalance. *Journal of Big Data*, 6 (1), 27. https://doi.org/10.1186/s40537-019-0192-5.

29. See for example, Thompson, A. (2019). Five AIs Just Worked Together To Beat a Top Human Video Game Team. *Popular Mechanics*, 16 April, https://www.popularmechanics.com/technology/robots/a27156719/openai-dota-2-victory/. Accessed 30 June 2019.

30. Detrixhe, J. (2018). Australia is a battleground for encrypted apps. *Quartz*. https://qz.com/1497092/the-signal-encrypted-app-service-wont-comply-with-australias-assistance-and-access-bill/. Accessed 26 May 2020.

31. Vincent, J. (2019). This colorful printed patch makes you pretty much invisible to AI. *The Verge*, 23 April, https://www.theverge.com/2019/4/23/18512472/fool-ai-surveillance-adversarial-example-yolov2-person-detection. Accessed 30 June 2019.

32. Thomas, E. (2019). How to hack your face to dodge the rise of facial recognition tech. *Wired UK*, 1 February, https://www.wired.co.uk/article/avoid-facial-recognition-software. Accessed 30 June 2019.

33. See Article 36. (2015). *Killing by Machine: Key Issues for Understanding Meaningful Human Control*, April, http://www.article36.org/autonomous-weapons/killing-by-machine-key-issues-for-understanding-meaningful-human-control/. Accessed 4 April 2019.

34. See for example: Robbins, S. (2019a). AI and the path to envelopment: knowledge as a first step towards the responsible regulation and use of AI-powered

machines. *AI & SOCIETY*. https://doi.org/10.1007/s00146-019-00891-1; and Santoni de Sio, F., & van den Hoven, J. (2018). Meaningful Human Control over Autonomous Systems: A Philosophical Account. *Frontiers in Robotics and AI*, 5. https://doi.org/10.3389/frobt.2018.00015.

35. Henschke, A. (2019). Information Technologies and Construction of Perpetrator Identities.

36. Cummings, M. (2012). Automation Bias in Intelligent Time Critical Decision Support Systems. In *AIAA 1st Intelligent Systems Technical Conference*. American Institute of Aeronautics and Astronautics. https://doi.org/10.2514/6.2004-6313.

37. Robbins, S., & Henschke, A. (2017). The Value of Transparency: Bulk Data and Authoritarianism. *Surveillance & Society*, 15 (3/4), 582–589. https://doi.org/10.24908/ss.v15i3/4.6606.

38. See for example: Adadi, A., & Berrada, M. (2018). Peeking Inside the Black-Box: A Survey on Explainable Artificial Intelligence (XAI). *IEEE Access*, 6, 52,138–52,160. https://doi.org/10.1109/ACCESS.2018.2870052.

39. Although promising progress has been made. See, for example: Wachter, S., Mittelstadt, B., & Russell, C. (2017). Counterfactual Explanations without Opening the Black Box: Automated Decisions and the GDPR. *Harvard Journal of Law & Technology*, *31*(2). http://arxiv.org/abs/1711.00399. Accessed 10 March 2019.

40. Robbins, S. (2019b). A Misdirected Principle with a Catch: Explicability for AI. *Minds and Machines*, *29*(4), 495–514. https://doi.org/10.1007/s11023-019-09509-3.

41. Robbins, S. (2019a). AI and the path to envelopment: knowledge as a first step towards the responsible regulation and use of AI-powered machines. *AI & SOCIETY*. https://doi.org/10.1007/s00146-019-00891-1.

42. Evans, J. (2019). Australian Defence Force invests $5 million in "killer robots" research. *ABC News*, 1 March, https://www.abc.net.au/news/2019-03-01/defence-force-invests-in-killer-artificial-intelligence/10859398. Accessed 30 June 2019.

43. See for example: Wallach, W. (2007). Implementing moral decision making faculties in computers and robots. *AI & SOCIETY*, *22*(4), 463–475. https://doi.org/10.1007/s00146-007-0093-6.

44. Bryson, J. (2010). Robots Should Be Slaves. In Y. Wilks (Ed.), *Close Engagements with Artificial Companions: Key Social, Psychological, Ethical and Design Issues* (pp. 63–74). Amsterdam: John Benjamins Publishing.

45. Johnson, D. G. (2006). Computer systems: Moral entities but not moral agents. *Ethics and Information Technology*, *8*(4), 195–204. https://doi.org/10.1007/s10676-006-9111-5.

46. Van Wynsberghe, A., & Robbins, S. (2019). Critiquing the Reasons for Making Artificial Moral Agents. *Science and Engineering Ethics*, *25*(3), 719–735. https://doi.org/10.1007/s11948-018-0030-8.

47. Ibid.

48. Condon, S. (2018). How police are using voice recognition to make their jobs safer. *ZDNet*, 20 July, https://www.zdnet.com/article/how-police-are-using-voice-recognition-to-make-their-jobs-safer/. Accessed 30 June 2019.

CHAPTER 17

Information as an Evolving National Security Concern

Adam Henschke

INTRODUCTION

This chapter is concerned with the issues that arise when malicious actors, agents or groups exploit information to further their ends in ways that pose a threat or challenge to national security. The chapter assumes that states have a responsibility to counter this: as part of its core functions, the state has a responsibility to protect its citizens against a range of threats. However, in order to maintain their legitimacy, liberal democratic states have constraints on how they discharge these duties, even where the provision of security is concerned.[1]

The specific focus for this chapter is the way that information is evolving as a national security concern. That is, that a range of information technologies are changing the role that information plays in our lives, and as part of this, the evolution of the uses of technologies mean that our understanding information as a national security concern also needs to evolve. I show this evolution by reference to three recent challenges to national security: the rise of international terrorism, the return of foreign influence operations and what we can call the *oligopolisation of epistemic power*.

Before beginning, I will not enter a discussion of what *information* or *national security* mean. For clarity, however, I will be using information to mean *a well ordered, meaningful data set that is judged to be true*.[2] On this account, information has moral importance,[3] and so ought to be treated with

---

A. Henschke (✉)
Department of Philosophy, University of Twente, Enschede, The Netherlands
e-mail: a.henschke@utwente.nl

© The Author(s), under exclusive license to Springer Nature Switzerland AG 2022
M. Clarke et al. (eds.), *The Palgrave Handbook of National Security*,
https://doi.org/10.1007/978-3-030-53494-3_17

389

a certain amount of care. In another chapter in this book I map out a range of ways that we can understand *national security*: as the duty of the state to protect its citizens (and perhaps others) from threats, when issues of the state's survival or persistence arise, and/or when institutions of force like the military, police or intelligence are being used (see Ethics And National Security: A Case For Reasons In Decision-Making in this volume). Given the moral and increasing political importance of information, this chapter will show information is evolving as a national security concern.

Terrorist Exploitation of Social Media

One of the defining features of modern international terrorism, as practised by groups like Al Qa'eda and so-called IS, is the way that they harnessed cyberspace to further their ends.[4] Given their somewhat decentralised structures, they exploited the non-geographic nature of the internet for recruitment, propaganda and command and control. This is not constrained to jihadi terrorism—a range of extremist groups are also making increasing use of cyberspace.[5] Despite the range of different extremist groups using information technologies in ways that pose national security challenges, the focus of this chapter will be on so-called Islamic state (IS).[6] This is in part because of the significant national security threat that they pose, but also because information played such a key role in their practices and strategy.

For this chapter, I will focus on the communicative elements of terrorism. "The success of a terrorist organisation depends almost entirely on the amount of publicity it receives…it is not the magnitude of the terrorist operation that counts but the publicity; and this rule applies not only to single operations but to whole campaigns".[7] One of the most important aspects of the current iteration of international terrorism is the modern terrorist's active and skilful use of social media as part of the communicative aspects of terrorism. That is, not only do we need to consider the communicative aspects of terrorism generally, but also that the threats posed by international terrorism are somewhat novel due to the evolution in information technologies and their impacts on society.

The evolution of so-called IS was due in part to their embrace of new media and social media (West Forthcoming). Following the shocking capture of Mosul in Iraq, in 2014, one of the key events in so-called IS's rise to prominence was their perceptive use of social media to distribute the shocking images and video footage of beheadings of western hostages. Analysis points to their three-tier media strategy, utilising "central media units, provincial information offices and its broader membership/supporter base".[8] On this analysis, the central media units "tend to produce [information operations] that are disseminated online and designed for transnational audiences", while the provincial information offices focus on presenting and discussing localised events, and the broader membership and base distribute and produce official and unofficial media for global consumption.[9] Information operations formed a great part of so-called IS's strategy, making use of shocking violence, provision of local security and community services and identity focussed elements for an international audience.[10] This has been tied to a general strategy wherein the information operations presented both pragmatic and perceptual factors, showing the military power of so-called IS (and the military failures of their enemies) and offering identity reifying elements, where so-called IS provides the core values and meaning to a person's life (coupled with the rejection of the other, non-IS values and meanings).[11]

In contrast to previous terrorist operations, information technologies like social media have played a key differentiating role as the modalities of communication are substantially increased, as is the ease in which the information operations can be rapidly spread around the globe. "IS often uses a combination of narrative, imagery and structure in communiqués that is designed to elicit mis-guided, but often predictable, [information operations] responses from its enemies. This, in turn, generates opportunities for IS to reinforce its core narrative in waves of secondary messaging generated by all levels of its media architecture".[12] Here, we can see the ways that so-called IS's information operations utilised western political leaders as part of their information operations—to have someone like the former Australian Prime Minister Tony Abbott to frequently discuss them, and the risk to Australia posed by "their tentacles" was surely a publicity coup—not only did it raise their profile, it legitimised them as powerful enough to pose a threat to a country geographically distant from the chief zone of conflict in Iraq and Syria.[13]

With regard to recruitment, so-called IS used social media to recruit foreign fighters from liberal democratic domestic constituencies.[14] This continues to poses a risk to those citizens being recruited in a legal sense, as a number of countries now have legislation criminalising those seeking to fight in particular foreign conflict zones.[15] It is risky in a physical sense, in that individuals with limited training or combat skills are in conflict zones, and so faced significant risk of physical injury or death.[16] Further, it is risky in a moral sense, in that participation with a group like so-called IS can result in extreme and morally prohibited behaviours which are likely to result in psychological trauma during or after the events.[17] Insofar as states have a duty to protect their citizens, then it follows that states ought to do what they can do to prevent their citizens from becoming foreign fighters.

Social media recruitment also poses physical and social risks to a state's domestic constituency from returning foreign fighter.[18] Capacity to cause large-scale harms is increased, following experience and practice accrued in combat zones. Returned foreign fighters pose a domestic security risk as they are more likely to have the means and motives to plan, prepare and carry out terrorist actions.[19] Further, one of the main determinants of whether domestic citizens will engage in violent extremism is exposure to extremists. That is, those returned foreign fighters pose a risk domestically as they can be a key causal factor in domestic terrorism. Finally, even if their extremism does not directly engage in violent actions, these extremists pose a threat to social cohesion in pluralistic liberal democratic polities.

Terrorists and other extremists also exploit information technologies as a means to broadcast propaganda. In addition to drawing people in for recruitment, the non-geographic nature of cyberspace means that a group located in one part of the world can produce, distribute and broadcast their content to people who have internet access. Further to this, the non-geographic nature of cyberspace makes policing such activities complicated—the consumers of the material might be in different parts of the world to the producers, who might be in different parts of the world to those putting the material online, and the means of communication might be in another part of the world. Information technologies allow for the ideas and ideals of violent extremism to spread beyond geographic and jurisdictional boundaries.

In addition, propaganda campaigns can be relatively anonymous, fitting with what Herb Lin and Jackie Kerr call *Information/Influence Warfare and Manipulation* (IIWAM):

> Because IIWAM operations can easily cross borders, IIWAM operators can take advantage of different laws in different geographic regions, engaging in IIWAM operations targeted against one national jurisdiction from the comparative safety of another jurisdiction that allows such behavior. In addition, IIWAM originators can operate from the territories of their target nation with minimal infrastructure and gain protective benefits that the target nation confers upon its residents.[20]

The digital nature of the materials, access and communications mean that there is a *whack-a-mole* problem—simply shutting down one user does not prevent the propaganda from existing and persisting online. "Attempts to remove information often (and arguably usually) leads to drawing more attention to that information, because it is impossible to destroy all copies of digitally stored information once a copy has become public".[21]

That said, though social media is involved in terrorism, typically it is only tangential to the command and control aspects of terrorist activity. This is because the *social*, open-facing nature of social media is clearly counterproductive to operations that require information security. Moreover, while the particular forms of information operations mark a novel feature of recent iterations of international terrorism, the effectiveness of this is heavily dependent upon many other factors including military success/failure and existing social and psychological factors.

To sum up, information technologies have played a key role in the evolution of current international terrorism in distribution of propaganda, recruitment and radicalisation. Though it is very hard to measure the *success* of propaganda and recruitment and radicalisation, there is definitely a strong correlation between modern international terrorism and social media (West Forthcoming). Given the strong connections between terrorist actions and communications, it seems reasonable to suggest that information, particularly the use of information technologies shapes the beliefs and actions of extremists including terrorists.

Foreign Influence Operations

Information presents another significant challenge to liberal democracies in the form of evolving foreign influence operations. While foreign influence operations are nothing new,[22] given the pervasiveness of cyberspace and certain of its attributes, the reach, impact and vulnerability to such operations are causes of novel perturbations that require careful responses.[23] This section of the chapter covers a range of different events in foreign influence operations and seeks to draw out the particular features of these operations as they relate to modern information technologies. This focus on new information technologies allows for analysis that is more than simply repeating that such foreign influence is nothing new. That is, it suggests that modern information technologies (and the opportunities offered by cyberspace more generally) create a context that is different from the Cold War era foreign influence operations.

Since around 2016, the political state of western liberal democracies has been one of uncertainty and insecurity. A series of unexpected political events—the vote for the UK to leave the EU, the election of Donald Trump in the 2016 US election, the collapse in support of certain traditional European political parties all signaled some significant shift in western liberal democracies. Parallel to this, the traditional political cleavage into *left* and *right* has evolved. While these existing cleavages certainly remain, there seems to be an important schism between what could be called internationalist or globalist politics on one side, and what could be called nationalistic or isolationist politics on the other. The Brexit vote, for instance, is easier to explain in terms of supporters of a British separatism versus a European/global integrationism, than in more traditional terms like left/right, Labour/Conservative etc. "[T]he anti-EU votes of those *left behind* by globalization, when combined with the more traditionally anti-EU Conservative and/or rural vote, seems to have played a major role in tipping the balance toward Brexit".[24]

As the fallout from these political upheavals were being picked through, a common factor was identified—the activity of foreign agencies with the potential aim of influencing social and democratic processes, Lin and Kerr's *Information/Influence Warfare and Manipulation* (IIWAM):

> (IIWAM) is the deliberate use of information by one party on an adversary to confuse, mislead, and ultimately to influence the choices and decisions that the adversary makes. IIWAM is a hostile non-kinetic activity, or at least an activity that is conducted between two parties whose interests are not well-aligned. At the same time, IIWAM is not warfare in the Clausewitzian sense (nor in any sense presently recognized under the laws of war or armed conflict),

which accounts for the "manipulation" part of the term. IIWAM has connotations of soft power: propaganda, persuasion, culture, social forces, confusion, deception.[25]

Russia is one state that is frequently associated with or accused of being behind these foreign influence operations.[26] The evidence for Russian activity is discussed below, but it is important to contextualise such actions by reference to a larger Russian strategy, the so-called Gerasimov Doctrine. This gives one explanation of how IIWAM might fit with a larger set of Russian objectives. A chief reason for interest in this Gerasimov Doctrine is its inclusion of informational tactics and their connection to psychological impacts.

> The doctrine stresses the importance of "cognitive-psychological forms of influence" in addition to "digital-technological" mechanisms... that is, information/influence war in addition to what we understand in the West as cyber war. These tools are likewise to be applied regardless of binary distinctions between wartime and peacetime, being used to shape perception, deter, delay, or compel opponent actions, and influence perception, combined with special operations, and diplomatic and economic forms of influence, as well as nuclear and conventional military deterrence, but preferably reducing the need for outright use of military force to achieve desired strategic goals... Gerasimov's view [is] that the appropriate ratio of non-military to military operations is 4 to 1 (i.e. the former is of greater importance than the latter).[27]

While following parts of this paper focus on suspected Russian activity,[28] it is important to note that Russia is not the only great power that seeks to use such informational and psychological levers as part of a grander military/political strategy. Further to this, these information operations are found in western strategies too. They are arguably, in the same set of strategies as what Joseph Nye termed *soft power*.[29] The point here is twofold. First, that information technologies are enabling the role of information in ideological, political and diplomatic conflict. Second, (insofar as this can be considered conflict) that western liberal democracies are deeply engaged in this conflict too.

The strategy of using information and misinformation for political ends is hardly novel. However, new information technologies like social media present new ways, impacts and vulnerabilities in which foreign influence operations can operate.[30] Importantly, countries like Russia have been publicly linked to, and accused of, deliberately exploiting social media for their purposes.[31] The distribution and maintenance of misinformation campaigns are a key part of these foreign influence campaigns. Historically, Russia was known to use factual information to compromise particular political targets, sometimes called *Kompromat*. "Leaks convey information to the target audience information that the adversary might wish to keep out of public view, and when disclosure occurs in the context of disclosing secret information, it gains notoriety and attracts attention disproportionately to its actual importance".[32] During the US 2016 election campaign, for instance, a key event was the hacking of the Democratic National Convention (DNC) Chair Jon Podesta's emails. These emails contained many controversial private conversations and were released to the public by WikiLeaks, and there is considerable evidence to believe that Russian agents were behind the hacks.[33] The emails were politically sensitive as they suggested that the DNC preferred Hillary Clinton to Bernie Sanders, and that they were willing to influence the selection of Clinton as the democratic presidential candidate.

These sorts of information operations have two means of achieving some national security impacts. First, by exposing some of the private conversations in which particular individual's motivations are at odds with the publicly stated values and beliefs of their political institution. This motivates and increases existing distrust of those political institutions. Second, by showing their vulnerability to hacking and exposure, the political institution's power and authority are undermined. The fact that these political institutions can be hacked suggests a weakness and fallibility, which undermines their legitimacy. In line with Lin and Kerr's observation that the hacking and leaking operations lever off existing social factors, such operations use information technologies like social media to exploit the existing social and political tensions and climate. Though the method is not new, the means—here, the exploitation of social media—are novel.

In this case, domestic actors were used to exploit US social media for propaganda purposes. In terms of propaganda, I'll draw from Lin and Kerr's observation that—

> contrasting definitions have in common an emphasis on conveying information to large audiences to influence opinion, attitudes, and emotion in ways that help the originator... propaganda should attract broad public attention, provide the most simple formulations of essential ideas, focus on appealing to the emotions of the public rather than their reasoning powers, and repeat the conveyed messages continually.[34]

Facebook, for instance, reported that there were significant, orchestrated and targeted efforts by Russian actors relating to the US 2016 Presidential election.[35] A key part of this was an organised operation to install foreign agents in the US, and to actively seek to be socially and legally recognised as Americans, organised, directed and funded through the St Petersburg located *Internet Research Agency* (IRA).[36] By *socially*, I mean that there were consistent efforts to align statements, tone and tenor of social media activity in such a way as to appear American.[37] These efforts were heavily orchestrated to have an effect on legitimate American citizens. The operations took heed of local times[38] and sought sophisticated feedback on the efficacy of these efforts.[39]

The operation also took significant efforts to appear as legal American citizens.[40] A key part of the US prosecutorial efforts against this operation focus on wire fraud and identity theft.[41] The operation included efforts to actively locate computer hardware—servers and the like—in the US.[42] This combination of social, legal and physical deception allowed the agents to not simply appear as if they were legitimate Americans, but to fund and direct funds towards a range of political activities that seemed to most legitimate participants as originating from real Americans.

Having established the fiction that they were Americans,[43] the agents were then engaged in running a range of *sock puppets* online. *Sock puppets* describes when a single person runs a series of fake identities on social media. This operation used Facebook and Instagram[44] and Twitter[45] in a range of ways. They utilised the advertising functions of social media to push out propaganda.[46] Given the appearance of the accounts as legitimate Americans, they were in contact with a range of legitimate American political actors, such as the real chair of the Trump Campaign in one Florida County,[47] and other Trump-affiliated campaigners in Florida.[48] They increasingly became engaged in levering their social media presence to influence[49] and orchestrate[50] actual political rallies. They coupled their social media presence with advertising to promote these political rallies.[51]

While these US located operations were in action, there were a series of Russian affiliated *troll farms* producing and distributing active misinformation as part of the overall propaganda campaign. A troll farm is a general descriptor for the orchestrated campaign that supplies and guides the agents, their sock puppets and social media presence. The Russian troll farms developed from 2011–2014, initially with a domestic Russian focus, seeking to discredit opponents and promote the Russian government's agenda and achievements (Sindelar 2014). This internal focus gradually evolved to include the US as a target of operations. According to one former employee in the St Petersburg offices of the IRA (formally named in the indictment against the Russian activists),

> the Internet Research Agency had industrialized the art of trolling. Management was obsessed with statistics — page views, number of posts, a blog's place on LiveJournal's traffic charts — and team leaders compelled hard work through a system of bonuses and fines. "It was a very strong corporate feeling," Savchuk says. Her schedule gave her two 12-hour days in a row, followed by two days off. Over those two shifts she had to meet a quota of five political posts, 10 non-political posts and 150 to 200 comments on other workers' posts (Chen 2015).

As early as 2015, these troll farms were known to be actively targeting sectors of the US population. One such troll account, *Spread Your Wings*,

> posted photos of American flags and memes about how great it was to be an American... The posts churned out every day by this network of pages were commented on and shared by the same group of trolls, a virtual Potemkin village of disaffected Americans (Chen 2015).

It seems that this strategy was tightened and improved through to 2016, with the identity theft and localisation of actors described above. The investigative journalist who identified these troll farms was saying in July 2016 that they thought the strategy had shifted from general pro-Russian and anti-Obama activities to a more concerted political effort, with a particular preference for Donald Trump. "I don't know what's going on, but they're all tweeting about Donald Trump and stuff... I feel like it's some kind of really opaque strategy of electing Donald Trump to undermine the US or something. Like false-flag kind of thing" (Bertrand 2016). This operation of hacking, running domestic agents and troll farms served a set of Russian purposes. A key outcome was the undermining of US democratic legitimacy through sowing of chaos. "Sowing chaos and confusion is thus essentially operational preparation of the information battlefield—shaping actions that make the information environment more favorable for actual operations should they become necessary. In addition, introducing sufficient chaos into the information environment may reveal targets of opportunity that can be exploited" (Lin and Kerr 2018). What lends support to this *chaos theory* is that the operation did not seem so much about installing Donald Trump. Instead, at least in the earlier parts of the 2016 US Presidential campaign, it was more about undermining the then favourite, Hillary Clinton. This was done by pushing the idea of substantial and systematic voter fraud.[52] Later, a series of pro-Trump and anti-Clinton rallies were organised.[53] These events were organised through social media.[54] Importantly, following the Trump victory, a series of pro-Trump and anti-Trump rallies were organised for similar locations and times.[55]

The deliberate efforts to sow chaos serve a range of strategic purposes for the foreign power:

> IIWAM perpetrators may also find that the sowing of chaos and confusion in an adversary for its own sake serves their interests. For example, an adversary whose government is in chaos and whose population is confused is unlikely to be able to take decisive action about anything, at least not without extended delay, thus affording the IIWAM user more freedom of action (Lin and Kerr 2018).

Second, a general sense of chaos undermines the democratic legitimacy of the political leadership, and potentially the sense of legitimacy in the democratic process more generally. Note here that it did not necessarily matter to Russian interests who won the 2016 Presidential election. If Clinton won, they could push the voter fraud angle and exploit disaffected Trump supporters. If Trump won, the same distrust of the President exists, only now it is anti-Trump Americans who question the integrity of the election. In fact, the publicity and exposure of potential Russian involvement, the very disclosure of the operation can ultimately meet the ends of the operation.

Third, this chaos can also serve domestic purposes. By flying a cloud of doubt over the democratic processes in paradigm examples of liberal democracies like the US, UK and the like, non-democratic leaders gain a comparative legitimacy. That is, they can say *look, the US calls itself the champion of democracy and their processes are suspect, their outcomes questionable and their overall relation to legitimacy is not to be trusted. By comparison, we don't seem so bad, in fact, we're the good guys.* That is, by bringing down the estimation of champions of western liberal democracies, those who are criticised by these western liberal democracies seem to gain legitimacy.

OLIGOPOLOGISATION OF EPISTEMIC POWER

The third relevant factor and frame of analysis are what I call the *oligopolisation of epistemic power*. In a traditional account of the state, the state is seen to have a monopoly of power, force or violence. "[C]ompulsory political association with continuous organization will be called a "state" if and in so far as its administrative staff successfully upholds a claim to the *monopoly* of the *legitimate* use of physical force in the enforcement of its order... The claim of the modern state to monopolize the use of force is as essential to it as its character of compulsory jurisdiction and of continuous organization" (Emphases Original Weber, 2012, pp. 154, 165). While information technologies do not directly disrupt the state's monopoly over physical force and violence, I suggest that, insofar as information is relevant to power, then new information technologies are disrupting the state's monopoly of *epistemic powers*, specifically when it comes to surveillance and information.[56]

What we are facing now is a diffusion of *epistemic* power. By epistemic power, I mean having control over information, including its distribution and the authority which that information confers. However, the generation and storage of information are now increasingly important in our information-dominated markets and societies (Zuboff 2019, 199–348). In this modern information age, those with control over information technologies gain power over people and institutions through the combination of the ability to generate information about people, to store and analyse this information, and to control the means of its distribution. "Surveillance capitalism is the puppet master that imposes its will through the medium of ubiquitous digital apparatus... [its] economic logic is directed through [its] vast capabilities to produce instrumentarian power, replacing the engineering of souls with the engineering of behaviour" (Zuboff 2019, 376). In addition to the power *over* information, those who control that information can also be seen as epistemic authorities. We grant them power due to their access to information that we do not have.

I would suggest that what are facing now is an *oligopolisation of epistemic power*, where an oligopoly is a "state of limited competition, in which a market is shared by a small number of producers or sellers" (Oxford Dictionaries Online No Date). Historically, states had a much tighter rein on information production and were often in positions of epistemic authority. However, as privately owned information companies gained power, that monopoly became diffused. In addition to the state and their massive informational bureaucracies, private information companies now play an increasingly central role in people's lives. Importantly for this chapter, individual citizens are as powerless as they were before this informational disruption. Rather than information technologies democratising societies, we now find oligopolies of informational power.

This points to what John Bellamy Foster and Robert W. McChesney dubbed *Surveillance Capitalism* (Foster and McChesney 2014). Shoshana Zuboff describes surveillance capitalism as "a novel economic mutation bred from the clandestine coupling of the vast powers of the digital with the radical indifference and intrinsic narcissism of the financial capitalism and its neoliberal vision that have dominated commerce for at least three decades... It was first discovered and consolidated at Google, then adopted by Facebook, and quickly diffused across the Internet" (Zuboff 2016). The key to understanding surveillance capitalism, Zuboff suggests, is the intention to use the data gathered on people to drive their behaviour. Zuboff quotes a Silicon Valley data scientist "The goal of everything we do is to change people's actual behavior at scale. When people use our app, we can capture their behaviors, identify good and bad behaviors, and develop ways to reward the good and punish the bad. We can test how actionable our cues are for them and how profitable for us" (Zuboff 2016).

To explain this point, let us examine the controversy surrounding social media's use in a political context—specifically, the events surrounding Cambridge Analytica, their relation to Facebook, and the larger political context in which these events occurred. The summary of the Cambridge Analytica saga is this—they were set up by the SCL Group (formerly *Strategic Communications Laboratories*). The SCL Group specialised in using behavioural and communications research for political purposes. They founded Cambridge Analytica in 2012 for the US market (Cadwalladr 2017). They were used by the Trump campaign for the 2016 US Presidential election. There a series of ties between the SCL Group and Cambridge Analytica to Russia. Finally, they engaged in a series of legally problematic activities around the access and exploitation of Facebook user data.

These events came to light in May 2018 with a series of newspaper articles following statements from former Cambridge Analytica employee Christopher Wylie.[57] Wylie claims that Cambridge Analytica worked with a developer Aleksandr Kogan to gather personal information from Facebook users. Steve Bannon, Trump's former advisor and a key actor in Trump's 2016 election campaign, was a Vice President of Cambridge Analytica. Further to this, the initial app designer, Kogan, is suspected of having ties to the Russian government, and Cambridge Analytica's parent company—SCL—is known to have communicated with Lukoil, a major Russian oil company on services that SCL could provide for election influencing (Cadwalladr and Graham-Harrison

2018). Following the very public criticisms of Cambridge Analytica's activities, Alexander Nix stood down as CEO, and the company itself closed down in May 2018 (Ballhaus and Gross 2018).

Cambridge Analytica did this through use of Kogan's test app *thisisyourdigitallife*. Despite the low numbers of those who actually used the thisisyourdigitallife app, it gathered data from user's Facebook friends. For instance, some estimates suggest that somewhere between 50–87 million Facebook users had their data scraped by the app. In Australia, 53 people used the app, which reportedly led to approximately 310,000 Facebook user's data being gathered. In New Zealand, 10 people used it, leading to approximately 64,000 people's data being gathered (Knaus 2018).

Cambridge Analytica provided services to people in the US during the 2016 Presidential campaign. There, they developed a series of different campaign advertisements that had a different tone, targeted to people that Cambridge Analytica decided had different personality types (Lewis 2018). Similar to IIWAM, the aim was to use/exploit particular information sets to advance a set of ends that are either contrary to the target's interests, or at least, secret or opaque to the target. This subterfuge occurs at two levels. First, there is the anonymity of the data user—those who are the targets of these influence operations are ignorant of who is seeking to influence them. Scraping tens of thousands of individual's data profiles off the back of a single person's use of thisisyourdigitallife is clearly a violation of any sense of informed consent. Importantly, none of the sources or targets of this information had any knowledge that this was occurring.

Second to this, the influence operation relies on microtargeting. Here, the data derived from the Facebook user profiles are used to create persuasion profiles from harvested information. This precision targeting means that Person A does not know that they are getting a different message to Person B. This makes it harder for the targets to recognise patterns, particularly patterns of deceit. "[T]hose who rely on social media and search engines to filter the information ocean are less likely to be exposed to information that contradicts their prior beliefs. These users are exposed preferentially (or almost exclusively) to information that conforms to their own individual predilections, and hence they reinforce their existing confirmation biases" (Lin and Kerr 2018). Note here that this does not necessarily rely on deceit qua deliberate telling of lies. The closer the message conforms to the truth, the more likely it is going to be believed and/or effective. What differentiates it is the selective targeting of particular flurries of facts and the framing effects around delivery of that information.

An important question to ask is how is this different from either state power or normal advertising? First, the rise of surveillance capitalism means that states have lost their position primary institutions able to conduct surveillance at population levels. That is, the states have lost their monopoly as an *epistemic power*. They are no longer the primary controller over citizen's personal data. While private companies have surely been gathering information on people for decades, the sheer quantity and concentration of this information by a few companies like Facebook and Google are unparalleled. Parallel to this, is a loss of jurisdictional exclusivity. These companies operate across the globe, and as such have a global power matching that of states. At the same time, the virtual nature of informational resources means that the companies can shift operations to jurisdictions more favourable to their informational purposes. Following tightening of privacy legislation in Europe with the General Data Protection Regulations (GDPR), Facebook shifted their base of operations as a legal entity to the US (Hern 2018).

This jurisdictional flexibility is compounded by a lack of accountability, or at least, different forms of accountability for non-state actors than state intelligence agencies. In most states, state intelligence agencies are subject to significant constraints, oversight and accountability (Lester 2016). Private information companies, however, are typically subject to far less scrutiny or control. The point here is that there are functional differences in the ways that non-state intelligence is conducted, different processes, different modes of accountability, different relations to the polis/citizens etc.

This is then tacked to corporate entities having a different set of ends, or different tele than state based intelligence and security agencies. A state telos is going to be something like *national security*, *protecting citizen's rights* or something like that. A private company's telos, however, is going to be something like *economic maximisation*, *shareholder interest* or even *owner's personal interests*. These private company tele may be morally justifiable; the point here is twofold. First, is simply that these ends are likely to be different from state tele. Second, that, as a result of the different tele, what is sought for, and the permissions and constraints around how they achieve those ends are likely to be different. A counterterrorism operation that causes terror, for instance, has failed by its own ends (Henschke and Legrand 2017)(Henschke and Legrand, 2017). Facebook's information gathering is for economic ends—if such an operation that makes money violates the privacy of individual, while it may wrong or harm those individuals, it has not necessarily failed by reference to the institutional telos.

In summary, this discussion has shown how information technologies are disrupting the *epistemic* landscape, suggesting that rather than states and obvious political institutions like political parties having monopolies of access and influence in these politically charged and relevant epistemic spaces, social media companies and their customers are becoming more active and increasingly powerful in these spaces. The overall point is that the access to personal information and the capacity for targeting individuals and small groups is being used for political influence. Though such efforts are hardly novel or surprising, what is new is that these private companies have the reach, and arguably exceed the reach, of a state's surveillance institutions. Coupling this with the recognition that social media companies have a different set of ends that they are aiming at, we see an *oligopolisation* of epistemic power.

NATIONAL SECURITY AND STATE RESPONSIBILITY: WHAT IS AT STAKE?

With all this said why are these issues matters of national security? The first and immediate concern draws directly from the recent experience with international terrorism. The physical safety of a state's citizens are at risk, and insofar as one holds that there are convincing arguments for international military action, perhaps a responsibility to protect individuals in conflict zones directly at risk from the remnants of so-called IS, AQ, Boko Haram, Al Shabab etc. Regarding state's responsibilities to domestic constituencies, this plays out in two ways. First is the use of existing security apparatus to protect their own civilians from domestic terrorist attacks. Second is active and passive measures to protect individuals in vulnerable populations from radicalisation. Though the means that these measures take are practically and ethically fraught, I assume that there should be no significant disagreement that a state has a responsibility to act here.[58] That is, it should be taking actions that both protect citizens from attack, and respond to the challenge of radicalised citizens. The main disagreements are what particular forms those actions should take, and what impacts the citizens of liberal democracies are willing to bear. On this threat, it seems like international terrorism poses the most significant risk here, rather than foreign states and private companies.

A second national security aspect is a state's democratic integrity. In contrast to physical safety and stopping people being killed or injured, protecting an amorphous concept like democratic integrity is a much harder thing to identify and secure. However, we can point to things public trust in electoral processes, and widespread public trust in political processes more generally (National Academies Of Sciences 2018). Even public engagement in electoral and political processes goes to issues of democratic integrity. Eric Uslaner's work on optimism and trust might be useful to think of here—In his account, an affective state of trust is more likely to occur as a result of optimism about the future (Uslaner 2002). That is, if someone has a more positive view of the future, they are more likely to trust in relevant social and political institutions. The threat posed by foreign influence operations via social media to democratic integrity then is operationalised through trust. If citizens feel like their votes and voices are not heard either because—they are told this as part of a propaganda campaign, or because they come to believe that the electoral and political processes are tainted—then are more likely to be pessimistic about the future, and lose trust in the relevant institutions as a result. I note that it is likely that *existing* distrust of political and social institutions is a background condition for a subset of a population that violent extremists like terrorists can and do make use of.

A third threat is to social cohesion. Rather than thinking of how individuals relate to and trust in their electoral and political processes, information operations can be detrimental to social cohesion. Like democratic integrity, this is a vague concept, but by social cohesion, I mean to refer to a recognised and supported collective identity and active interaction between different national subgroups. Here, the exploitation of information technologies can be equally threatening whether it is terrorists, foreign states or private companies. Terrorists like so-called IS utilised social media to exploit existing individual's frustrations with how they fit in or do not fit in with their given country and community. "IS leverages perceptual drivers in its IO campaign by producing narratives that link IS to the in-group identity (i.e. Sunni Muslims) and solutions (i.e. IS's politico-military agenda) whilst framing its enemies (i.e. anyone who is not Sunni and IS-aligned) as malevolent out-group identities (Others) responsible for Sunni perceptions of crisis" (Ingram 2015, 741). Foreign influence operations like that conducted by the Russian IRA sought to exploit and exaggerate existing political divisions in the US, and to sew chaos and frustration across a range of existing political and ideological schisms. Though social media companies frequently refer to their active pursuit of and support of shared community values, there does seem to be a significant body of research that correlates the rise of social media with echo chambers (Allcott and Gentzkow 2017)[59], informational/epistemic bubbles (Arfini and Magnani 2015, Selene, Tommaso, and Lorenzo 2018), increased extremist communications (Bright 2017). The point here is that, though social media companies and actors might have no particular agenda to negatively impact social cohesion, this seems to be an unintended side effect of social media. In addition, arguably, as long as the key social media companies continue to make massive profits and their institutional tele are tied to economics, then this is unlikely to change.

In summary, while national security is a contested term, at least for liberal democratic states, new information technologies pose *threats* by enabling terrorist activity, exposing domestic political processes to foreign operations and a loss of monopoly over intelligence and surveillance. I stress that these are *threats* only. That is, it is premature to suggest that the very survival of liberal democracies is at imminent threat of destruction because of social media. Though the conditions outlined above are significant and somewhat novel threats and liberal democracies are facing significant pressures, we are not at a point of existential risk. That said, these threats do need to be taken seriously; by showing the role of information as an evolving national security concern, this allows states to use their national security apparatus to anticipate and respond to those threats. In liberal democratic states, there are significant justified constraints on what the national security apparatus can do. However, those discussions are beyond the scope of this chapter.[60]

Acknowledgements I would like to thank the following funders who provided the resources that made this work possible: European Research council (ERC) Advanced Grant Research Project: Global Terrorism and Collective Moral Responsibility—Redesigning Military, Police and Intelligence Institutions in Liberal Democracies, Australia Research Council Discovery grant, DP180103439 Intelligence And National

Security: Ethics, Efficacy And Accountability and Australian Department of Defence Strategic Policy Grant, Countering Foreign Interference And Cyber War Challenges.

NOTES

1. As I have argued elsewhere, such duties to provide security need constraints: Henschke, A. & Legrand, T. (2017). Locating the Ethical Limits of National Security: Counter-Terrorism Policy in Liberal Democratic Societies. *Australian Journal of International Affairs* 71 (5), 554–561.
2. There are a range of different ways that people understand information, see: Zins, C. (2007). Conceptual Approaches for Defining Data, Information, and Knowledge. *Journal of The American Society for Information Science And Technology* 58 (4), 479–493. The description used here, however, is derived from Luciano Floridi's General Definition of Information, Floridi, L. (2011). *The Philosophy of Information*. Oxford: Oxford University Press. I talk in detail about different ways to conceptualise information in Henschke, A. (2017). *Ethics in an Age of Surveillance: Virtual Identities and Personal Information*. New York: Cambridge University Press, 126–151.
3. For instance, when used in a social context by semantic agents, information can impact individual's rights to privacy, property rights and basic recognition. Also, its use can lead to a range of harms and issues about justice see: Henschke. (2017). *Ethics in an Age of Surveillance*, 202–216, 222–236, and 236–242.
4. See for example: Droogan, J., & Waldek, L. (2016). Where Are All The Cyber Terrorists? From Waiting for Cyber Attack to Understanding Audiences. 2016 Cybersecurity and Cyberforensics Conference (CCC), 2–4 Aug; Albahar, M. (2017). Cyber Attacks and Terrorism: A Twenty-First Century Conundrum. *Science and Engineering Ethics* (Online First):1–14. https://doi.org/10.1007/s11948-016-9864-0; Al-Rawi, A. K. (2014). Cyber Warriors in the Middle East: The Case of the Syrian Electronic Army. *Public Relations Review* 40 (3), 420–428; Awan, I. & Imran, A. (2017). Cyber-Extremism: ISIS and the Power of Social Media. *Society* 54 (2), 138–149; Thomas, T. L. (2003). Al Qaeda and The Internet: The Danger Of 'Cyberplanning'. *Parameters* 33 (1), 112–123; and Shehabat, A. (2012). The Social Media Cyber-War: The Unfolding Events in the Syrian Revolution 2011. *Global Media Journal*: Australian Edition 6 (2).
5. See: Butt, S. & Byman, D. (2020). Right-Wing Extremism: The Russian Connection. *Survival* 62 (2), 137–152; Hardy, K. (2019). Countering Right-Wing Extremism: Lessons from Germany and Norway. *Journal of Policing, Intelligence and Counter Terrorism* 14 (3), 262–279; and Scrivens, R. Davies, G. & Frank, R. (2020). Measuring the Evolution of Radical Right-Wing Posting Behaviors Online. *Deviant Behavior* 41 (2), 216–232.
6. A 2016 Royal United Services Institute (RUSI) report, for instance, stresses the importance of right with and nationalist terrorist groups in liberal democracies. (Ellis et al., 2016).
7. Laqueur, W. (1977). *A History of Terrorism*. Boston: Little, Brown & Co., 109.
8. Ingram, H. (2015). The Strategic Logic of Islamic State Information Operations. *Australian Journal of International Affairs* 69 (6), 734.

9. Contrasting the view that their international communications were key to their information operations, these provincial information offices were, on one analysis, far more productive and important. "Despite the media attention given to communiqués released by IS's central media units, it is IS's *wilayat* information offices that produce the bulk of IS's official IO output". Ibid, 734–735.
10. Ibid, 739.
11. Ingram's account describes the identity reifying elements as "characterised by the interplay of in-group identity, out-group identity, crisis and solution constructs". Ibid, 736.
12. Ibid, 744.
13. Abbott, T. (2015). 'Submit Or Die': Tony Abbott Warns the Only Way to Approach Islamic State Threat is by fighting. *News.com*, 6 June, https://www.news.com.au/national/politics/submit-or-die-tony-abbott-warns-the-only-way-to-approach-islamic-state-threat-is-by-fighting/news-story/012397 69a4fa1d637d0400b90103dc00.
14. See: Cragin, R. K. (2017). The November 2015 Paris Attacks: The Impact of Foreign Fighter Returnees. *Orbis* 61 (2), 212–226; Cragin, R. K. (2017). The Challenge of Foreign Fighter Returnees. *Journal of Contemporary Criminal Justice* 33 (3), 292–312; Malet, D. & Hayes, R. (2018). Foreign Fighter Returnees: An Indefinite Threat? *Terrorism And Political Violence*, 1–19. https://doi.org/10.1080/09546553.2018.1497987; Wright, C. J. (2020). Sometimes They Come Back: Responding To American Foreign Fighter Returnees and Other Elusive Threats. *Behavioral Sciences of Terrorism and Political Aggression* 12 (1), 1–16; and Pokalova, E. (2020). *Returning Islamist Foreign Fighters: Threats and Challenges to the West*. Cham: Palgrave.
15. Pokalova. (2020). *Returning Islamist Foreign Fighters*, 137–164.
16. Rostami, A. et al. (2020). The Swedish Mujahideen: An Exploratory Study of 41 Swedish Foreign Fighters Deceased in Iraq and Syria. *Studies In Conflict & Terrorism* 43 (5), 382–395.
17. I'm drawing here on recent work in 'moral injury', in which an agent can suffer psychologically as a result of earlier actions that contain significant moral complexity. See: Frame, T. (Ed.). (2015). *Moral Injury: Unseen wounds in an Age of Barbarism*. Sydney: NewSouth Books.
18. See: Harris-Hogan, S. & Zammit, A. (2014). The Unseen Terrorist Connection: Exploring Jihadist Links between Lebanon and Australia. Terrorism and Political Violence 26 (3), 449–469; Harris-Hogan, S., Barrelle, K. & Zammit, A. (2016). What Is Countering Violent Extremism? Exploring CVE Policy and Practice in Australia. *Behavioral Sciences of Terrorism and Political Aggression* 8 (1), 6–24; and Zammit, A. (2013). Explaining a Turning Point in Australian Jihadism. *Studies in Conflict & Terrorism* 36 (9), 739–755.
19. Harris-Hogan, Barrelle & Zammit (2016). What Is Countering Violent Extremism?
20. Lin, H. & Kerr, J. (2018). On Cyber-Enabled Information/Influence Warfare and Manipulation. In *Oxford Handbook of Cybersecurity*. Oxford: Oxford University Press.
21. Ibid.
22. Jowett, G. & O 'Donnel, V. (1986). *Propaganda and Persuasion*. London: Sage, 118–152.
23. Singer, P. W. & Brooking, E. T. (2018). *Like War: The Weaponization of Social Media*. Boston: Mariner Books.

24. Hardy, J. & McCann, L. (2017). Brexit One Year On: Introducing The Special Issue. *Competition & Change* 21 (3), 165.
25. Lin & Kerr. (2018).
26. Noting here that Russia, and Russian President Vladimir Putin, has repeatedly denied being involved in these foreign influence operations.
27. Lin & Kerr. (2018).
28. Similarly, the detailed content focusses squarely on the US 2016 Presidential election. However, it should be noted that a similar set of operations may have been in operation in the UK, and likely elsewhere (Wintour, 2018), and have been considered an ongoing effort (Brattberg and Maurer 2018).
29. Nye, J. (2009). Get smart: Combining hard and soft power. *Foreign Affairs*, 160–163.
30. Sussex, M., Henschke, A. & O'Connor, C. J. (Forthcoming). Countering Foreign Interference: Election Integrity Lessons for Liberal Democracies. *Journal Of Cyber Policy.*
31. Mueller, R. S. (2018). *United States of America V. Internet Research Agency.* edited by United States Department Of Justice. District Of Columbia, 16 §42).
32. Lin & Kerr. (2018), 10–11.
33. Rid, T. (2016). All Signs Point to Russia Being Behind the DNC Hack. *Vice*, 25 July, https://www.vice.com/en_us/article/4xa5g9/all-signs-point-to-russia-being-behind-the-dnc-hack.
34. Lin & Kerr. (2018).
35. Mueller. (2018), 24 §58(b).
36. Howard, P. N. et al. (2019). *The IRA, Social Media and Political Polarization in the United States, 2012–2018.* edited by Congress Of The United States. Washington: US Senate Documents.
37. Mueller. (2018) 15 §38).
38. "The specialists were divided into day-shift and night-shift hours and instructed to make posts in accordance with the appropriate U.S. time zone… Specialists were directed to create "political intensity through supporting radical groups, users dissatisfied with [the] social and economic situation and oppositional social movements"…". Mueller. (2018). 14 §33).
39. Mueller. (2018). 15 §37).
40. "In or around 2016, Defendants and their co-conspirators also used, possessed, and transferred, without lawful authority, the social security numbers and dates of birth of real U.S. persons without those persons' knowledge or consent" (Mueller 2018, 16 §41).
41. Mueller (2018) 34 §94).
42. Ibid, 15–16 §39).
43. Ibid, 14 §32).
44. "Defendants and their co-conspirators also created thematic group pages on social media sites, particularly on the social media platforms Facebook and Instagram. ORGANIZATION- controlled pages addressed a range of issues, including: immigration (with group names including "Secured Borders"); the Black Lives Matter movement (with group names including "Blacktivist"); religion (with group names including "United Muslims of America" and "Army of Jesus"); and certain geographic regions within the United States (with group names including "South United" and "Heart of Texas"). By 2016, the size of many ORGANIZATION-controlled groups had grown to hundreds of thousands of online followers" (Mueller 2018, 14 §34).

45. "Defendants and their co-conspirators also created and controlled numerous Twitter accounts designed to appear as if U.S. persons or groups controlled them" (Mueller 2018, 16 §36).
46. (Mueller 2018, 14 §35).
47. "On or about August 15, 2016, Defendants and their co-conspirators received an email at one of their false U.S. persona accounts from a real U.S. person, a Florida-based political activist identified as the "Chair for the Trump Campaign" in a particular Florida county. The activist identified two additional sites in Florida for possible rallies. Defendants and their co-conspirators subsequently used their false U.S. persona accounts to communicate with the activist about logistics and an additional rally in Florida" (Mueller 2018, 27 §74).
48. "On or about August 18, 2016, the real "Florida for Trump" Facebook account responded to the false U.S. persona "Matt Skiber" account with instructions to contact a member of the Trump Campaign ("Campaign Official 1") involved in the campaign's Florida operations and provided... Campaign Official 1's email address at the campaign domain donaldtrump.com. On approximately the same day, Defendants and their co-conspirators used the email address of a false U.S. persona, joshmilton024@gmail.com, to send an email to Campaign Official 1 at that donaldtrump.com email account" (Mueller 2018, 27–28 §76).
49. "On or about August 19, 2016, Defendants and their co-conspirators used the false U.S. persona "Matt Skiber" account to write to the real U.S. person affiliated with a Texas-based grassroots organisation who previously had advised the false persona to focus on "purple states like Colorado, Virginia & Florida."... Defendants and their co-conspirators then sent a link to the Facebook event page for the Florida rallies and asked that person to send the information to Tea Party members in Florida. The real U.S. person stated that he/she would share among his/her own social media contacts, who would pass on the information" (Mueller 2018, 29 §80).
50. "To conceal the fact that they were based in Russia, Defendants and their co-conspirators promoted... rallies while pretending to be U.S. grassroots activists who were located in the United States but unable to meet or participate in person" (Mueller 2018, 20 §51).
51. (Mueller 2018, 21 §52).
52. (Mueller 2018, 18–19 §47).
53. (Mueller 2018, 21 §54).
54. "To assist their efforts, Defendants and their co-conspirators, through false U.S. personas, offered money to certain U.S. persons to cover rally expenses" (Mueller 2018, 21–22 §53).
55. "After the election of Donald Trump in or around November 2016, Defendants and their co- conspirators used false U.S. personas to organize and coordinate U.S. political rallies in support of then president-elect Trump, while simultaneously using other false U.S. personas to organize and coordinate U.S. political rallies protesting the results of the 2016 U.S. presidential election" (Mueller 2018, 23 §57).
56. In my *Ethics in an Age of Surveillance,* I present a case that surveillance is an epistemic action. It is a process that is "concerned with producing information as a product". See: Henschke. (2017). *Ethics in an Age of Surveillance,* 58.
57. See The Guardian's set of entries on Cambridge Analytica for a details on the whistleblowing and events that followed (The Guardian 2018).

58. As I argue elsewhere, there are a range of ethical issues around state use of, and responses, to the production and harvesting of personal information by new technologies (Henschke Forthcoming, Henschke and Reed Forthcoming).
59. Though I note that this view is contested (Dubois and Blank 2018).
60. I note here that I have a series of publications that are part of that ongoing discussion about the justifications and limits on state power (Henschke 2015, 2018, Forthcoming, Henschke and Ford 2016, Henschke and Legrand 2017, Henschke and Reed Forthcoming, Robbins and Henschke 2017, Sussex, Henschke, and O'Connor Forthcoming).

INDEX

A

Accountability, 5, 6, 18, 53, 58, 62, 66, 68, 77, 82–84, 88, 89, 359, 365, 367, 370, 372, 376, 387, 401
Advanced School of War (Brazil), 266
Ahmadinejad, Mahmoud, 247, 249
Air Defence Identification Zone (ADIZ), 123
Air-launched ballistic missile (ALBM), 310
Algorithms, 18, 253, 254, 371–376, 378–386
Al Qaeda (AQ), 16, 40, 51, 58, 59, 83–85, 98, 103, 110, 375, 402, 404
Amazon, 267, 269, 270, 274, 275, 278, 373, 376, 377, 386
Amazon Cooperation Treaty Organization (OTCA), 270
Amazon Cooperation Treaty (TCA), 267, 270
Anti-Ballistic Missile Treaty (ABM), 296, 300, 302, 303, 322
Artificial intelligence (AI), 8, 104, 374, 375, 378
Asia-Pacific, 19, 42, 119, 120, 178, 179, 346
Association of Southeast Asian Nations (ASEAN), 131, 193, 346
Attack prediction, 373
Authoritarianism, 35, 50, 66, 67, 71, 150

B

Balancing, 42, 48, 49, 100, 119, 155, 189, 197, 198, 272, 297
Ballistic Missile Defence (BMD), 302
Ballistic missile submarine (SSBN), 155, 307
Bandwagoning, 48, 153
Basic Principles of National Defense (1957), 172, 178, 184
Belt and Road Initiative (BRI), 15, 30, 42, 127, 154, 155, 158, 160, 161, 195, 196, 198, 300, 314
Bolshevik, 162
Bolsonaro, Jair, 14, 263, 274–277, 279
Brazil, 6, 13, 14, 105, 261–282, 299, 321
Brazil-Argentina Agency for Accounting and Control of Nuclear Materials (ABACC), 269
Brexit, 145, 157, 393, 406
Brezhnev, Leonid, 160, 188
BRICS (Brazil, Russia, India, China, South Africa), 131, 233, 263, 278
Brinkmanship, 15, 156, 166, 288, 289, 295, 308, 315
Burden sharing, 180, 344
Bush, George H.W., 142, 302
Bush, George W., 35, 39, 90, 102, 114, 124, 143, 148, 163, 178, 300, 302, 303, 307, 310, 366

© The Editor(s) (if applicable) and The Author(s), under exclusive license to Springer Nature Switzerland AG 2022
M. Clarke et al. (eds.), *The Palgrave Handbook of National Security*, https://doi.org/10.1007/978-3-030-53494-3

410 INDEX

C
Cambridge Analytica, 399, 400, 407
Cardoso, Fernando Henrique, 261, 269, 270, 275
Carter, Jimmy, 295, 298
Central Intelligence Agency (CIA), 56, 63, 69, 70, 244, 353, 364, 366, 367, 369, 378
Central Military Commission (CMC), 129
Chavez, Hugo, 272
China, 2, 6, 8, 9, 14, 30, 35, 42, 43, 71, 100, 103, 105, 110, 117–132, 135–137, 139, 140, 145, 152, 154, 158, 160, 188, 191, 192, 194–198, 203, 209–214, 228, 233, 247, 251, 262–264, 273, 276–278, 289, 295, 296, 300, 304, 308–314, 320, 321, 325, 326, 334, 337, 338, 344, 372, 373
China Dream, 128
China-Pakistan Economic Corridor (CPEC), 195, 214, 300, 314
Chinese Communist Party (CCP), 9, 43, 120, 128, 129, 132, 196, 309, 312
Clinton, Bill, 102, 125, 142, 147, 148, 247, 257, 302
Clinton, Hilary, 157, 395, 397
Cold War, 3, 7, 8, 10–12, 14, 15, 28, 32, 33, 35, 36, 38, 50, 55, 56, 79, 80, 98, 99, 102, 105–110, 118–122, 125, 134, 135, 141, 143, 148, 149, 152, 154, 164, 165, 169–173, 175, 176, 178, 184, 187–190, 192, 196, 212, 219, 225, 226, 230, 233, 245, 252, 264–266, 275, 276, 278, 287–290, 292, 293, 295–301, 306, 311, 316, 318, 319, 321, 336–338, 341–344, 352, 357, 361, 364, 393
Common Market of the South (MERCOSUR), 269, 271
Communications security (COMSEC), 358
Comprehensive Test Ban Treaty (CTBT), 299, 302, 309
Constructivism, 5, 24, 31, 37, 38, 44, 45, 153
Container Security Initiative (CSI), 340

Containment, 120, 292, 297, 301
Counter-force, 287, 294, 295, 311, 327
Counter-Intelligence (CI), 354, 362
Counterterrorism, 14, 16, 59, 60, 63, 65, 68, 102, 112, 355, 362, 363, 373, 375, 401
Counter-value, 293–295
Covert human Intelligence sources (CHIS), 355, 359
Critical infrastructure, 31, 43, 59, 195
Cuban Missile Crisis (1962), 288, 294
Cyber, 8, 9, 14, 25, 52, 64, 104, 126, 139, 144, 145, 152, 154, 156, 166, 249–254, 308, 311, 315, 316, 352, 354, 394
Cyberwarfare, 104, 251, 252

D
da Silva, Luiz Inácio Lula, 270, 272
Democratic National Convention (DNC), 157, 167, 395, 406
Democratic People's Republic of Korea (DPRK), 288, 299, 300, 303, 309, 312, 313
Deterrence, 15, 33, 59, 121, 173, 194, 287–290, 293, 295–298, 300–302, 304–308, 310, 311, 314, 316, 317, 324, 326, 394
Disinformation, 30, 259, 315
"Downing Street memo" (2002), 366

E
Engagement, 11, 42, 67, 97, 117, 120, 122, 124, 127, 177, 190, 210, 226, 231, 308, 334, 402
Entrapment, 9, 140, 161
Epistemic power, 18, 389, 398, 400, 401
Ethical reasoning, 75, 81, 384
Ethics, 4, 6, 17, 48, 73–77, 80–83, 85–87, 89, 90, 374, 384, 390
Eurasia, 30, 161, 164, 228
Eurasianism, 146, 220
Europe, 9, 12, 16, 37, 55, 96, 100, 119, 140, 143–145, 147, 154, 159, 163, 220, 224, 225, 233, 239, 262, 264, 266, 276, 288, 291, 292, 298, 306, 308, 321, 333, 335, 337, 339, 401

Evidence-based policy making, 57
Exceptionalism, 53, 60, 62, 69
Exclusive Economic Zones (EEZs), 123, 331, 339
Extended deterrence, 306, 316

F

Facebook, 157, 254, 375, 377, 386, 395, 396, 399–401, 406, 407
Facial recognition, 372, 375, 376, 378, 380, 387
Failed states, 8, 59, 103, 114, 302
Federal Bureau of Investigation (FBI), 84, 217, 353
First Gulf War, 10, 119, 170, 174–176
First strike, 15, 293, 295, 299, 308
Fissile Material Cut-off Treaty (FMCT), 299
Flag-of-convenience (FOC), 333, 335
Flood Report (2004), 363
Foreign fighters, 391, 405
Foreign influence operations, 18, 389, 393, 394, 402, 403, 406

G

Gandhi, Rajiv, 206, 207
General Agreement on Tariffs and Trade (GATT), 334
General Data Protection Regulations (GDPR), 401
Geospatial Intelligence (GEOINT), 354, 355, 360
Gerasimov Doctrine, 144, 163, 394
Global Financial Crisis (GFC), 29, 35, 127, 145
Google, 373, 375–377, 386, 399, 401
Gorbachev, Mikhail, 38, 147, 148, 163
Grand strategy, 95, 97, 109, 115–117, 122, 134, 136, 187–189, 301, 322, 344
Great powers, 8–10, 14, 29, 33, 36, 42, 47, 49, 52, 97, 100, 103, 108, 110, 113, 127, 132, 140, 143, 146, 147, 152, 154, 160, 161, 164, 165, 223–225, 245, 263, 267, 268, 276–279, 289, 313, 394
Green Movement (Iran), 247, 249, 253, 257

Gulf of Aden, 122, 131, 180, 339–341

H

Hedging, 48, 197, 198, 302
Hegemony, 30, 39, 46, 147, 151, 196, 264, 274
High-value target (HVT), 364
Human intelligence (HUMINT), 17, 251, 255, 354, 355, 359, 360, 364
Hussein, Saddam, 12, 13, 143, 145, 227, 241, 245–247, 255
Hybrid warfare, 154, 163, 327

I

Illegal Unregulated and Underreported (IUU), 338, 339
Illiberalism, 66
Imagery Intelligence (IMINT), 354
India, 6, 10, 11, 28, 105, 118, 119, 124, 131, 135, 156, 158, 179, 187–214, 216, 263, 264, 273, 278, 283, 288, 298–300, 303, 313, 314, 321
Indicators and warnings (I&W), 358, 359
Indo-Pacific, 8, 122, 124, 135, 170, 180, 197, 344, 348
Information/Influence Warfare and Manipulation (IIWAM), 392–394, 397, 400, 405
Information operation, 18, 154, 156, 157, 260, 390–392, 394, 395, 402, 404, 405
Intelligence cycle, 17, 352, 353, 356
Intelligence failures, 364, 365, 367
Intelligence requirements (IRs), 354, 355, 360
Inter-American Treaty of Reciprocal Assistance (TIAR), 270
Intercontinental ballistic missile (ICBM), 156, 292–294, 296, 297, 304, 307–312
Intermediate Nuclear Forces Treaty (INF), 300, 307
Intermediate range ballistic missile (IRBM), 310, 312
Internationally Recommended Transit Corridor (IRTC), 342

412 INDEX

International relations, 2–5, 13, 23, 24, 26, 31, 32, 34, 36–39, 43–48, 50–52, 69, 75, 80, 121, 127, 153, 241, 266, 289, 337
International relations theory, 4, 23, 24, 31, 42–44, 46, 146, 320
Internet Research Agency (IRA), 157, 395, 396
Iran, 6, 7, 12, 13, 96, 110, 116, 131, 224, 225, 228, 232, 233, 241–255, 289, 300–302, 309, 310
Iran-Iraq War (1980-1988), 245–247
Islamic Revolutionary Guards Corps (IRGC), 245, 250–253
Islamic State (IS), 83, 231, 238, 243, 246, 390, 404, 405
Islamic State of Iraq and al-Sham (ISIS), 7, 91, 96, 110, 145, 374, 375, 404

J

Japan, 2, 6, 9, 10, 29, 105, 119, 123–125, 131, 135, 158, 161, 169–185, 191, 195, 197, 214, 289, 298, 312, 313, 334
Japan Defense Agency, 172, 183
Japan Self-Defense Force (JSDF), 10, 124, 170–172, 174–184

K

Khatami, Mohammad, 247–249
Khomeini, Ruhollah, 243–245
Kissinger, Henry, 188, 317
Kompromat, 156, 394
Korean War, 118, 169, 225, 296
Kurdish Democratic Party of Iran (KDPI), 245

L

Labelling, 18, 372, 378
Latin American Association of Free Trade (ALALC), 266
Legitimacy, 5, 8, 29, 45, 53, 57, 58, 61–63, 66, 68, 78, 79, 91, 120, 128, 129, 132, 198, 351, 372, 375–377, 389, 395, 397, 398
Liberal democracy, 5, 6, 29, 35, 53–58, 60, 61, 68–70, 212

Liberal Democratic Party (LDP), 181, 183
Liberalism, 5, 24, 31, 36, 38, 44, 45, 49, 51, 148, 265
Libertarianism, 82
Limited Test Ban Treaty (LTBT), 296
Line of Actual Control (LAC), 313
Location intelligence (LOCINT), 360

M

Machine learning (ML), 17, 18, 199, 371–376, 378–386
Maduro, Nicholas, 276, 277
Major power relations, 126
Malacca Strait, 339, 340
Maritime security, 15, 16, 329–331, 333, 334, 337, 338, 342–344, 346–349
Mass surveillance, 17, 18, 371–373, 379, 380, 382
Meaningful human control, 371, 372, 382–384, 388
Microtargeting, 400
Middle East, 11–13, 29, 39, 101, 143, 183, 219, 224, 227, 228, 233, 234, 236, 241, 244, 258, 291, 339, 404
Military source operations (MSO), 360
Ministry of Finance (MOF), 172, 178, 184
Ministry of Foreign Affairs (MOFA), 172, 178, 264, 271, 273
Ministry of International Trade and Industry (MITI), 172
Missile Technology Control Regime (MTCR), 299, 310
Monroe Doctrine, 154, 166
Moral machines, 384, 385
Mosaddeq, Mohammad, 244
Mousavi, Mir Hossein, 247
Mujahideen al-Khalq (MeK), 207, 246
Multiple independent re-entry vehicles (MIRVs), 296, 307
Multipolarism, 9, 139, 142
Mutually assured destruction (MAD), 287, 294

N

National Defense Program Guidelines, 177

INDEX 413

National Missile Defence (NMD), 307

National security, 1–19, 23–28, 30–34, 36–40, 42–45, 47, 53–55, 58–69, 73–77, 79–87, 89, 90, 92, 99, 100, 102, 110, 118–124, 126, 128–130, 132, 137, 139–141, 146, 147, 151–155, 158, 160, 161, 166, 171, 172, 178–180, 182, 184, 188, 198, 210, 211, 218, 222, 223, 225, 241, 255, 261–263, 267, 268, 273, 275, 278, 290, 291, 299, 301, 302, 304, 305, 317, 318, 329–331, 334–344, 347, 351, 352, 355, 364–369, 371, 372, 375, 379, 381, 385, 386, 389, 390, 395, 401–403

National Security Agency (NSA), 85, 210, 211, 252, 357, 361, 373, 378, 386

National Security Council (NSC), 129, 130, 174, 178, 210, 211, 221, 317, 318

National security policy, 2–13, 17, 19, 23–25, 28–34, 36, 43–45, 53, 55, 59, 60, 62–64, 67–69, 85, 86, 96, 118, 122, 127–130, 139, 144–146, 150, 154, 155, 159, 161, 166, 169–174, 176, 178–181, 183, 184, 187, 188, 210, 262, 276, 288, 290, 291, 293, 301, 302, 317, 318, 324, 329

National Security Secretariat (NSS), 178

National security state, 7, 19

National Security Strategy (NSS), 11, 54, 56, 58, 65, 103, 106, 127, 129, 137, 178, 179, 187, 210, 211, 218, 301, 304

New Strategic Arms Reduction Treaty (New START), 299, 303

Nixon, Richard, 297, 298

No first use, 155, 304, 306, 310, 311

Non-Aligned Movement, 245

Non-alignment, 10, 11, 187–190, 197

Non-nuclear weapons states (NNWS), 290, 297, 298

Non Proliferation Treaty (NPT), 28, 46, 175, 269, 287, 290, 297, 299, 300, 304, 309, 310, 316, 320, 321, 325

Non-traditional security, 119, 122, 126, 128, 129, 131, 132, 337, 338, 341, 344

North Atlantic Treaty Organisation (NATO), 27, 46, 142, 147, 150, 151, 155, 157, 162, 165, 166, 223, 225–227, 231, 295, 306, 314, 315, 327, 336, 342, 352, 359

Nuclear Posture Review (NPR), 300, 301, 303–305, 323

Nuclear proliferation, 14, 104, 106, 131, 132, 252, 298, 302, 309, 321, 325

Nuclear strategy, 15, 295, 317, 319, 320, 322

Nuclear weapons, 10, 15, 19, 28, 30, 33, 37, 50, 105, 106, 124, 125, 141, 152, 155, 162, 170, 173, 191, 192, 225, 245, 287–293, 295–309, 311–313, 315–319, 321–326, 376

Nuclear weapons states (NWS), 105, 290, 297, 298, 301, 309, 321

O

Offshore balancing, 42

Oligopologisation, 398

One China Policy, 127

Open Source Intelligence (OSINT), 17, 354, 360, 369

Operation Olympic Games, 249

Organization of American States (OAS), 266, 271

P

Peaceful nuclear explosion (PNE), 298

Peer competitor, 15, 100, 109

People's Liberation Army (PLA), 118, 125, 129, 130, 133, 195, 306, 310, 311, 313

Piracy, 8, 102, 118, 127, 211, 277, 330, 338–341, 343, 347

PLA Air Force (PLAAF), 310

PLA Navy (PLAN), 155

PLA Rocket Force (PLARF), 311

Pluralism, 77, 81, 85, 91, 222, 249, 272

Post-Cold War, 8, 10, 101, 102, 106, 119–122, 126, 132, 134, 174, 176, 177, 190, 192, 196, 197, 226, 289, 299, 303, 316, 337

414 INDEX

Predictive policing, 373, 386
Primacy, 5–7, 126, 136, 154, 244, 288, 301, 302, 322
Private Military and Security Companies (PMSCs), 16, 330, 342–344
Proliferation Security Initiative (PSI), 300, 310, 340
Propaganda, 55, 103, 128, 157, 254, 312, 371, 375, 390, 392, 394–396, 402
Proscription, 37, 61–63, 66, 70
Public policy, 3–5, 13, 53–56, 58–63, 66, 68, 262
Putin, Vladimir, 7, 15, 96, 100, 143–146, 148–150, 154–156, 159–161, 163, 165, 276, 307, 324, 406

Q

Quadrennial Defense Review (QDR), 104, 107, 115, 301, 302
Quadrilateral, 124

R

Reagan, Ronald, 288, 295
Realism, 5, 24, 31–34, 36, 38, 40, 42, 44, 45, 48, 49, 51, 75, 151–153, 165, 166
Regional security complex (RSC), 2, 267, 268, 271, 276
Republic of Korea (ROK), 158, 179, 289, 312, 313
Restraint, 7, 96–98, 111, 193, 194, 296, 303
Revolution in Military Affairs (RMA), 307
Rogue states, 98, 101–103, 302, 313, 320
Rousseff, Dilma, 273, 274

S

Sea lines of Communication (SLOC), 340
Second nuclear age, 288, 299, 302, 320–322
Second strike, 296, 303, 310, 320
Securitization, 45, 60, 65, 70, 71, 80, 267, 275

Security, 2–17, 23–27, 29–34, 36–38, 42–45, 47, 48, 52, 54–56, 58–68, 70, 71, 77, 79–81, 84–86, 96, 98–101, 103, 104, 106–109, 118–132, 140, 142, 143, 147–149, 151, 152, 154–156, 161, 166, 170–184, 187–189, 191–193, 196–204, 206, 207, 209–211, 218–224, 226–228, 230–234, 241, 242, 244–248, 250, 252, 253, 255, 261–265, 267–274, 278–280, 288–292, 296, 299–302, 304, 309, 311, 315, 316, 330–332, 336–344, 347, 352, 354, 358, 363, 366, 375, 378, 380, 382, 389, 391, 392, 401, 402, 404, 406
Shanghai Cooperation Organization (SCO), 123, 131, 168, 233, 245
Shangri-La Dialogue, 131
Signals Intelligence (SIGINT), 17, 354–359
Smart surveillance cameras, 372
Social media, 13, 18, 167, 242, 247, 249, 253, 254, 351, 358, 373, 375, 381, 390–392, 394–397, 399–404, 406, 407
Soft power, 46, 47, 227, 228, 236, 250, 253, 255, 268, 270, 394
South American Community of Nations (CASA), 271, 272
South American Defense Council (SADC), 14, 262, 272
South Atlantic Zone of Peace and Cooperation (ZOPACAS), 270, 271
South China Sea (SCS), 10, 119, 123, 127, 131, 155, 170, 197, 198, 214, 338, 346
Southern Cone, 13
Speaker Identification Integrated Project (SIIP), 373, 386
Strategic Arms Limitations Talks (SALT), 290, 296, 297
Stuxnet, 249, 250
Submarine launched ballistic missile (SLBM), 292, 293, 296, 304, 305, 310, 311
Surveillance, 17, 18, 85, 253, 354, 355, 359, 372, 373, 375–378, 380, 382, 383, 385, 386, 398, 400, 401, 403, 407

Surveillance capitalism, 18, 377, 398–400
Suspicious Activity Report (SAR), 374

T
Terminal High Altitude Area Defence (THAAD), 307, 313
Terrorism, 8, 14, 16–18, 30, 38–40, 51, 59–61, 63, 65, 66, 68–70, 75, 84, 98, 99, 102, 110, 112, 123, 126, 132, 143, 156, 176, 177, 190, 193, 194, 206–208, 211, 275, 302, 338, 340, 341, 351, 352, 359, 366, 371, 374, 375, 381, 386, 389–392, 402
Time Difference of Arrival (TDOA), 360
Trilemma, 15, 288
Trip-wire, 292
Turkey, 6, 11, 12, 158, 219–236, 238–240, 288
Twitter, 249, 252, 254, 257, 275, 374, 396, 407

U
Union of South American Nations (UNASUR), 14, 262, 271, 272, 276
United National Peace Keeping Operations Cooperation Law (1992), 175, 183
United Nations Law of the Sea Conventions (UNCLOS), 331, 338, 339

United Nations Stabilization Mission in Haiti (MINUSTAH), 271, 275
United States (US), 6–11, 13–15, 17, 25, 27, 30, 35, 39, 41, 42, 51, 61, 63, 64, 66, 76, 83–85, 90, 91, 95–105, 107–110, 117, 119, 124, 126, 128, 131, 138, 140–143, 145–148, 150, 152, 154–157, 159, 166, 169–180, 182, 188, 190–192, 195–198, 212, 222, 225–228, 230–234, 239, 241, 243–245, 247, 249, 251–255, 263–268, 270, 272, 273, 275–278, 282, 287–317, 319, 321, 333, 334, 336, 337, 342, 353, 357, 358, 361, 363–366, 373, 378–380, 393–401, 403
Utilitarianism, 77, 82, 88

V
Vance, Cyrus, 244
Voice recognition, 373, 388

W
War on terrorism, 61
WhatsApp, 250, 358, 382

Y
Yoshida Doctrine, 171, 184